WHEN THE GODS ARE SILENT

WHEN THE GODS
ARE SILENT

Kornelis H. Miskotte

Translated with an
Introduction by
John W. Doberstein

Harper and Row, Publishers,
New York and Evanston

Original Dutch edition, 'Als de Goden Zwijgen', ©
1956 Uitgeversmaatschappij, Amsterdam, Holland

German edition, 'Wenn die Götter Schweigen', revised
and augmented by the author, © 1963 Christian Kaiser
Verlag, Munich

English translation incorporating author's revisions
and additions for German edition, © 1967 William
Collins Sons & Co. Ltd., London

Printed in Great Britain for Harper & Row,
Publishers, Incorporated
Library of Congress Catalog Card Number: 66-10229

Contents

CONTENTS

CONTENTS

CONTENTS

Translator's Introduction

When I picked up this book in the publisher's book store in Munich, I was immediately struck by its challenging content and sophisticated style, though I had read a number of the author's articles in German theological periodicals. Further reading in an hotel room and a train increased my enthusiasm, and a few weeks later, visiting my friend Professor Georg Eichholz in Wuppertal, I mentioned my 'discovery' to him. He immediately leaped up and went to his desk where it was lying open, and we shared the stimulation we both felt. In Germany the book has since been called the theological 'book of the decade.' It is, I believe, important for several reasons.

As far as I know, it is the first attempt in theological literature to use the Old Testament to provide an answer to the atheism and nihilism of our so-called 'post-Christian era.' It is interesting to see that Miskotte's frequent reference to Alfred Weber's 'fourth man' has its parallel in Dietrich Bonhoeffer's 'man come of age,' and that Bonhoeffer, too, in his letters from prison recognized this importance of the Old Testament and stressed its relevance for our time and modern man's experience of life, because in the Old Testament man is seen in his total 'this-worldliness' and his alienation from God. It is altogether possible that in the coming decades Old Testament theology with its emphasis on history will provide the corrective for the now somewhat tiresome preoccupation with New Testament hermeneutics.

Miskotte's purpose is not primarily to make a contribution to the present theological and hermeneutical discussion of the Old Testament, though I cannot see how Old Testament scholars can ignore this brilliant overview of its meaning, but rather to point the way to a dialogue with modern man. For the practical theologian, the preacher, teacher, and pastor, this is of ultimate importance. Never before have we read a book on the Old Testament like this one.

Another great value of the book is its opening up of the possibility of a long overdue dialogue with Judaism, which Christianity has so shamelessly and inexcusably ignored. Rabbi Dr. Robert R. Geis goes so far as to say: 'This book must have an epoch-making effect, for it is perhaps the first theological work in post-biblical times that concerns both Judaism and Christianity.' 'Without exaggeration it may be called "A Guide for the Perplexed," no less than Maimonides' work in his time. We know hardly one theologian who would have the courage, as Miskotte does, to break through the old gold of reverence, the dust of habit, to free us from the inner courts of melancholy.'

It is not a primary function of a translator to criticize a book which he has translated. I cannot conceal the fact, however, that I do not share one of its basic points of view, namely, its completely Barthian orientation. Though the author is certainly right in insisting that the Testaments must not be isolated from each other, he, following Barth, sees no real redemptive progress from the Old to the New Testament, but rather tends to regard them as two concentric circles which revolve around an identical centre. There would seem to be no qualitative difference between the Testaments, only a difference in manner of presentation. This results in the typically Barthian confusion of Law and Gospel. Since this is so, I include here portions of an evaluation of the book by Professor Helmut Gollwitzer, whose theological persuasions more nearly approach those of the author. This review appeared in *Evangelische Theologie* (October 1963), pp. 557ff., and is used with Professor Gollwitzer's kind permission.

'Who could forbear reaching out for this book? Surely not the philosopher, who is pursuing the potentialities of thought under the conditions imposed by the age of nihilism and is unwilling to ignore the presence of the biblical message. Surely not the scholar, who is struggling to understand antiquity and hears singing in his ears, and laments of Hölderlin and Walter E. Otto concerning the speechlessness of the gods. And certainly not the theologian, the systematician, the exegete, nor the pastor who has to deal with Old Testament texts in preaching and teaching. One would like to put it into the hands of cultivated contemporaries, Christian and non-Christian, as one of the most important books to appear in years, written for them no less than for theologians, for their orientation in an age of transition from the "third" man to the "fourth" man, in the barren drought of the "absence of God" and the temptation to flee from this desert back to the fleshpots of religion, which cannot feed them anyhow. For the silence of the gods in the time of nihilism reveals what they have always been, powers which never were alive and always dumb.

'The aim of Miskotte's book is to show our contemporaries that in the midst of the silence of the gods the living voice of God is raised and that therefore this time of silence is never really understood as long as this voice is ignored—and also to provide the ministers of this voice, those who are engaged in Christian preaching and Christian instruction, with the insights into the structure and meaning of the biblical witness for their task which has become so urgently necessary. This twofold audience enhances the difficulty of reading the book for the non-theologian perhaps more than for the theologian. Anybody who ascribes extraordinary importance to the book will regret this and at the same time hope that not many will be discouraged by it but rather that the attractiveness of this spacious, strongly sensitive, European mind which is unconstricted by any provincialism will invite many readers to overcome all the difficulties. There is also the difficulty of Miskotte's style, which is not always immediately perspicuous. The obscurity which has often been attributed to him is apparent in many parts of this book in so far as the logical sequence from sentence to sentence is often not immediately discernible and sentences are frequently loaded with all the associated ideas in the author's mind. But the very style itself also reconciles us to its difficulties—a style fructified by Claudel and Francis Thompson, animated with feeling, compelling attention through surprising adjectives, completely avoiding the aridity and cliché-ridden terminology which is often so strangely at odds with the subject matter of theological works, a style inspired with the breath of its subject and equally capable of amplitude, charm, and trenchancy.

'The result is a panegyric of the Old Testament which very little in Jewish or Christian literature can match. The magnificent meditations on some individual passage of the Old Testament which conclude the book are undergirded by an exposition of the inner structures of the Old Testament proclamation which is constantly related to preaching today, to the life-giving voice that would countervail our deadly resignation and should issue from our preaching. And here Miskotte draws upon the wealth of modern Old Testament scholarship, lifting it out of the remoteness of historical research into contemporaneity. In his unforgotten address at his retirement (*Evangelische Theologie*, 1960, p. 245) he described the systematic theologian as the dilettante and the director, or conductor of the theological faculty. And here he demonstrates this in a beautiful way. He is not afraid to come forward as a dilettante who utilizes the studies of others, nor to speak the language of the dilettante, that is, not the remote, dispassionate language of scholarship, but rather the personal speech of the man who selects from the results of research what has become meaningful to him in his struggle and encounter with life. And precisely in so doing, like a good conductor he brings into accord what various others have recognized in detail but without seeing the direct mutual relationships. He establishes relationships between scattered insights and questions and also relationship between history and life, our life today. The Old Testament specialists will not be able to ignore this as a mere subsequent utilization of their work and therefore of no more interest to them. After all, in so far as they are theologians, they study the Old Testament not merely as a bygone document, but rather as a text for preaching today. If they see, by a confrontation such as Miskotte achieves, that the problem of the God of Israel and the gods of the nations has tremendous relevance and importance for our intellectual and spiritual life today, they will be secured against the temptation to coordinate this problem with ancient theism and historicize it completely—as is done so blithely by present day theologians—or, as also happens frequently enough, to operate as Christian theologians and pit the New Testament against the Old as being the proclamation of a new faith, a new God, and a new gospel.

'Such formulations of the distinction between the Old and the New Testaments, which have a long tradition in the church's theology, Miskotte's book opposes emphatically and unmistakably. This gives it extraordinary importance for the newly begun conversation between Christians and Jews, which Miskotte rightly regards as one of the new things in our time, a determinative element in the history of the church, an application of grace after a long period of Christian injustice to Judaism. And there are few Christian theologians today who are as competent to speak in this dialogue as Miskotte. . . . The book has equal importance for the discussion going on between Old and New Testament exegesis, which, as the debates between the two disciplines show, is fundamentally determined by whatever view one holds concerning the unity of and the difference between the two parts of the Bible. For Miskotte the Old Testament is critical of both Judaism and the church in its history and its practice. Isolation of the New Testament leaves the church defenceless against the influx of paganism with its natural religion under a Christian guise and makes it impossible, in an age in which the gods are gone, to serve the God who seeks men, the God who through the acts of his Word and the Word of his acts long ago, even when religion flourished, exposed its delusiveness and baselessness and established the salvation of man on a new foundation. This isolation devitalizes the New Testament, since the New Testament constantly presupposes the Old Testament and its "surplus"; it is a false exaltation of the New Testament, which itself does not claim to be self-sufficient and has no wish to be exalted at the expense of the Old Testament. The old Calvinistic tradition secures this Dutch theologian against the danger of seeking the superiority of the New Testament over the old in the "idea of God," in new religious concepts, and therefore in the history and development of ideas and thus of regarding Judaism and Christianity as two different religions, instead of schismatic parts of the one community of God, the schism of which must constitute for both parts a continuing problem and a never-ceasing matter of distress.'

Kornelis Heiko Miskotte was born in Utrecht on September 23, 1894. He studied theology at the university of his native city. He turned to literature, especially to modern English and Dutch poetry, and then, under the influence of Hermann Kohlbrügge and Abraham Kuyper, found his way back to the history of dogma and theology, searching for a synthesis of dogmatics and philosophy after the model of J. H. Gunning (1829–1905). He was a minister in various churches from 1921 to 1942, lastly in Amsterdam, where in 1942 he was called by the church to a special ministry to intellectuals estranged from the church. In 1945 he was appointed professor of dogmatics, ethics, church law, and missions at the University of Leyden. Meanwhile, since 1938 he had been active in a large movement toward the renewal of the church, contributing to a draft of a new confession of faith, the new constitution of the church, and a new rhymed version of the psalter. He was the editor of *In de Waagschaal* (*In the Balance*), a weekly journal of culture and theology now in its twentieth year. He maintained contact with the world outside Holland through Günther Howe's group in Göttingen called *Glaube und Naturwissenschaft* ('Faith and Natural Science'), the European group of ten Reformed and ten Lutheran theologians who met in Arnoldshain to discuss interconfessional and ecumenical questions, and above all through his constant association with Karl Barth. In January 1960 he retired from his professorship because of illness and now lives in Voorst (Geldern), where he devotes himself to the study of hermeneutical questions. He received an honorary doctorate from the University of Glasgow in June 1964.

Miskotte's literary work is tremendous in scope and quantity. Among the most important theologically are the following:

Het wezen der joodsche religie (*The Nature of Jewish Religion*), 1932, comparative studies in Jewish philosophy of religion, which Rabbi Dr. Robert R. Geis calls 'one of the best books on Hermann Cohen, Franz Rosenzweig, and Leo Baeck, the reprinting of which is urgently called for.' This book received the Mallinckrodt Prize for the best dissertation presented to a Dutch university in the decade.

Edda en Thora (*Edda and Torah*), 1938, a comparison of Germanic and Israelitic religion, which reflects the intellectual and spiritual leadership Miskotte exercised in the years of resistance to National Socialism.

Bijbelsch ABC (*ABC of the Bible*), 1941, a published document which, along with his preaching in crowded churches in Amsterdam and his anonymous illegal pamphlets, constitute further evidence of his activity in the Resistance.

Feest in de Voorhof: Sermoenen voor Randbewoners (*Feast in the Forecourt: Sermons for People on the Fringe*), 1952, the precipitate of his preaching to intellectuals.

Hoofdsom der Historie (*The Sum of History*), 1945, lectures on the visions of the Apocalypse of John.

Als de goden zwijgen: over de zin van het Oude Testament, 1956, the Dutch title of the book here translated.

De weg van het gebed (*The Way of Prayer*), 1962, published in Germany as *Der Weg des Gebets*, 1964.

Two volumes of history and theological essays, *Grensgebied* (*Borderland*) and *In de Waagschaal* (*In the Balance*), exhibit Miskotte's lifelong fascination and association with writers and poets including Strindberg, Dostoevski, Rilke, Roland Holst, Der Mouw, Thomas Mann,

Bernanos, and others. Hendrik Berhof, his successor at Leyden, has spoken of the two poles of his life work, theological and cultural, and this bipolarity 'coupled with a mystical faith and a superior intellect,' he says, 'has made Miskotte a man of authority in all areas of the church and culture of the Netherlands.'

The present book is a largely expanded and revised version of the Dutch original, including some entirely new sections and omitting a number of chapters, so that the author now considers this and the German version to be the definitive form of this work. The present translator is, of course, deeply indebted to the German translator, Hinrich Stoevesandt, for making many things plain which might otherwise have been obscure and difficult, though where the text was identical he has invariably consulted the Dutch original, which is frequently closer to English idiom.

In his review Professor Gollwitzer also stated that the experts have said that it was impossible to translate Miskotte adequately into German. It would seem presumptuous therefore to attempt to translate him into English with its vastly different idiom. He is quite capable of a style sometimes so obscure as to be Stygian. Throughout it is dense, compact, and elliptical, full of qualifying phrases, alliterations, and many plays on words. I have tried to subdue some of the obscurity without in any way compromising the author's meaning. All translations of quotations are mine except where otherwise indicated. Instead of attempting metrical translations of Dutch and German verse, I have thought it better to give the original and append a literal line-for-line prose translation. Biblical citations are translated directly from the author's version, which often follows that of Martin Buber.

I am indebted to my friend and colleague Professor Robert E. Bornemann for his expert transliterations of Hebrew and Greek words. An index of Hebrew terms is provided and the meaning of each word is indicated in the text at its first occurrence.

I am grateful, as always, to my wife for the long hours she spent in checking and correcting the typescript.

JOHN W. DOBERSTEIN

Mount Airy, Philadelphia
January 1965

Foreword

The aim of this book is to offer some help in the lethargy into which we have fallen in our day, a help to all kinds of dwellers on the fringes of church and culture, both to those who still have something to give and also to those who are still willing to receive something.

Part one, 'A Mirror of Our Time,' presents rather tentatively and gropingly a sketch of a world in which a new type of man is in the slow process of being born. It deals with the hybrid character of nihilism, the root of which is found in the hybrid character of religion.

Part two, 'Witness and Interpretation,' deals with the meaning of the Old Testament for our time, and here I attempt to estimate the magnitude of the inner tensions to which the modern scholar and interpreter inevitably finds himself exposed. I have tried to bring the content and the various aspects of the sacred texts into convergence with the specifics of the 'doctrine of God' (to use our shallow Western term). To be able to bring out clearly this 'doctrine of God' in a time when 'the gods are silent' could be an act of humanity par excellence.

Part three presents a number of 'sketches.' They are not intended to be sermon sketches, but are, rather, nothing more than marginalia, glosses on the commentaries. They contain considerations which could lead over to the kerygmatic and above all the didactic work which is committed to the interpreter and witness in the present situation.

As is apparent, then, what I am after is a particular kind of applied scholarship, a contribution to 'practical theology.' Perhaps one might better say that it is an introduction to the practical significance that theology can have precisely by virtue of its scholarly content. In such an introduction various disciplines of theology recur more or less frequently and make their contributions. But they support and intensify one another, they assure and guarantee to one another their spiritual meaning, mutually illuminating the import of their views and

purposes. Without this 'dilettantism,' knowledge and scientific information remain strangers to each other or they touch each other at
certain points only by accident. It is well worth the trouble to diminish
the estrangement between scientific biblical study and general culture
and also little by little to bring about a *rapprochement* between theology
and the church.

K. H. Miskotte

Part I: Mirror of Our Times

THE FOURTH MAN

Wise men, wiser than we, have seen him (not deliberately, however) and given him this name (very deliberately, all too deliberately). The 'fourth man'[1] is the man who no longer believes, in the biblical sense of the term—yes, that too, but he is equally deaf to other gods and free from the binding power of godlike values. He is the man who no longer responds to any spiritual appeal. He lacks even the ability to do so. Are we to think that at least he is troubled by our times and the emptiness of life? This too we dare not assume, say the wise, who, being wiser than other wise men, have by means of incontrovertible statistics and analyses come to the firm conclusion that this 'fourth man' has been dehumanized. In France this 'fourth man' appears to have flourished with an unusual exuberance. Some do not believe that he exists, since, after all, man is religious by nature and man, they say, would have rebelled against himself, would have destroyed himself, if we assume that he is what has been suggested to us.[2]

But is it so certain that man is by nature and in the depth of his being religious? Is it so certain that he was ever completely in earnest about 'god'? Quite apart from the crisis to which religion is necessarily subjected by revelation, it always has its own immanent problems.[3] If the first statement, the crisis, points to a mystery and is to that extent a theological judgment, the second, man's religiousness, is a religious-historical fact which can be demonstrated in many ways.[4]

[1] Alfred Weber, *Der dritte oder der vierte Mensch: Vom Sinn des geschichtlichen Daseins* (1953). [In Weber's book the first man is the prehistoric Neanderthal man; the second man the plaything of the fluctuations of the ice age, the man of the magic cults; the third man the *homo faber*, the bearer of history who makes and shapes history. The fourth man, however, is no longer conscious of history, but is only the product of the technicizing of human existence—Tr.]

[2] Y. Daniel, *La France, pays de mission* (1943); G. Michonneau, *Revolution in a City Parish* (1946).

[3] Karl Barth, *Church Dogmatics*, Vol. I, pt. 1, p. 314.

[4] Cf. P. Radin, *Die religiöse Erfahrung der Naturvölker* (1951).

We face the fact of atheism. If mysticism is the ocean into which the streams of religion discharge, admixing in ecstatic negativism with the forms and tendencies of the concrete religions, sublimating, refining, and evaporating them, then atheism is the earthquake, the assault, which ruthlessly reveals how relative, how splintered and divided, how secretly mistrustful of itself human religion is in its very nature and foundation as it takes its place in the world. Self-criticism, however repressed it may be, is a structural element of religion itself. Even in an early stage of the development of religion one finds characteristics in which the self-understanding of the religious life betrays something of its playful character and suggests the comparison with the deeply serious ceremonial posturing and attitudinizing of children at play, the shaping of cult figures, the imitation of nature and world, the dances in which the figures are gods who are actually present, they themselves actually being gods. Secularized man no longer engages in this sacred play; he can no longer capture the earnestness of play—this is a part of his honesty. May it not be that in this phenomenon we are confronted not with man's self-estrangement but rather with his discovery of his real self? May not the 'fourth man' be ages old—finally disclosing himself to be man as he actually is or at least the constant man? This disclosure comes later, very late, in a period of advanced culture. Atheism is a late stage, not to say the last stage, of a culture. One has gone a long way by the time one clearly sees that 'god' is a projection, at least for the metaphysical type of man, and that ultimately all symbols can only point to the 'everlasting man' and that they do this even when the symbol includes a denial of the existence of that which is ultimately symbolized.[5] The 'everlasting man,' even though his nature may be just as undiscernible as the godhead,[6] is the constant, gives to the projections their duration and continuance. He can also be compared with the child who comes to know himself in his identifications with his environment.[7] And so it is necessary to recognize and assume the 'position of a metatheistic religiosity,' to

[5] S. Vestdijk, *De toekomst der religie* (1947), pp. 45, 73.

[[6] *Gottheit*, tr. throughout 'godhead,' meaning the impersonal deity in the sense of Meister Eckhart's *Urgrund*. Cf. Martin Buber's use of the term, in Maurice S. Friedman, *Martin Buber: The Life of Dialogue* (New York: Harper Torchbook, 1960), pp. 27, 225, 244—Tr.]

[7] G. van der Leeuw, *Der Mensch und die Religion* (1937), *passim*.

appraise Buddhism as 'the highest style of godless religion,' and to realize that 'superreligious' always contains within itself the urge to self-deification, even when the god, its specific product, is always meant to be merely temporal, so that man's religion is ultimately 'a round-about road to himself by way of the symbol of the god.'[8]

These analyses are now a part of common knowledge. Many find their own experience confirmed in it. It strikes them as being self-evident; they awaken from a beautiful dream. Then they feel that they have been deeply deceived and bitterness toward the flickering remains of the images of the godhead makes them react with a surge of disillusionment and humiliation.

So by this time it has also become a commonly accepted thing to say that we have transferred the beauty of the earth to heaven. 'What a fraud to pilfer these images of earthly rapture and sell them to heaven behind our backs!'[9] But in this stage man is still imbued with the re-flection of religious feelings which bathe heaven and earth in the after-glow of a poignant farewell. This becomes something different in the 'fourth man' in his last stage, the man who actually has no further need to idolize nature or humanity or the beloved, who actually can no longer be made subject to any substitute god in the form of an ideal.

The modern 'fourth man' is not so new as we thought, since the inner necessity of religion was never wholly wrought into the depths of human existence. On the other hand, there is in his emergence some-thing staggeringly new, though again not staggering because of the modernity of the phenomenon, but more in the way in which it stag-gers us, the abruptness, the radicalness, the definitiveness of the whole process.

Staggering—for whom? For the devout or for the pioneers and the victims, the free spirits? It would be strangely inhuman if the devout were not staggered; after all, here their own existence, their reason, their honour is at stake. Anyone who even merely leafs through the pages of Mauthner's history of atheism in the West[10] must conclude that theoretical denial and practical disavowal of God existed in every

---

[8] Leopold Ziegler, *Magna Charta* (1923), pp. 103, 121, 145f.
[9] R. M. Rilke, *über Gott, zwei Briefe* (an actual letter to L. H. in 1915 and a fictitious 'letter to a worker'; 1921), p. 32.
[10] Fritz Mauthner, *Der Atheismus und seine Geschichte im Abendlande*, 4 vols. (1921-3).

century. And anyone who studies the problem of estrangement from the church must realize that the church which is teeming with atheists *in spe* (i.e., atheists at heart) must already have its period of florescence behind it. This may well be called staggering.

But the 'fourth man'—who was begotten by the third man, as the third was begotten by the second, and the first had no son except the second—this 'fourth man' is staggering to himself—at least he has been for a long time, longer than we assume, and more profoundly than we see. Here is a point at which we believe we must differ from the commonly accepted image of our 'secularized' or 'nihilistic' contemporary. We do not accept without examination the assertion that it makes no difference to him to be 'without God in the world' (Eph. 2:12), that it is of no consequence to him whether others call him godless. We say rather that to be what he is has affected him and continues to affect him. For all along this has been the source of that paradoxical rebellion against a 'god' in whom he has long since ceased to believe.[11] It has even given rise to a concept of nomadic poetry, which, though full of splendid pride and all its verve and defiant pertinacity, is nevertheless 'nihilistic' and yet despite this (or perhaps just because of this) is warmly human. It is not long before atheism becomes a chilly companion and an inhuman despot. Kenneth Patchen put it this way:

'So it is the duty of the artist to discourage all traces of shame / to extend all boundaries / to fog them in right over the plate / to kill only what is ridiculous / to establish problems / to ignore solutions / to listen to no one / to omit nothing / to contradict everything / to generate the free brain / *to bear no cross* / *to take part in no crucifixion* / to tinkle a warning when mankind strays / to explode upon all parties / to wound deeper than the soldier / to heal this poor obstinate monkey once and for all / to have kids with pretty angels / to display his dancing seed / . . . to exaggerate all things / to inhabit everyone / . . . *to deviate at every point* / to offer no examples / to dismiss all support / to make one monster at least / to go underground immediately / . . . to multiply all opinions / . . . to extend all shapes / to acquire a sublime reputation / to consort forever with the runaway / . . . to masquerade as the author of every platitude / . . . to exclaim at the commonplace

---

[11] Recall such figures in Dostoevski's novels as Hippolyte (*The Idiot*), Ivan Karamazov, Kirillov, and Stavrogin (*The Possessed*).

alone / . . . *to admire only the absurd* / to be concerned with every profession save his own / . . . to lift the flesh above the suffering / *to
forgive the beautiful its disconsolate deceit.*'[12]

Another 'individualist,'[13] the hermit Theodore Powys,[14] interprets
'god' to mean the mystical fear which he has in common with all men
in so far as they have not wholly devoted themselves to the service of
Mammon. Those who have no fear, says Powys, are the misshapen
criminals, the monsters, who are condemned to eternal life; the people
who fear, however, receive the grace of a real death in the womb of
mother earth. We must be very much on guard against the judgment
that the post-Christian man is really a monster, a branded man, a dead
man. The assertion that these 'individualists'—remembering that all
literature consists of a multitude of these ambivalent, provocative,
hardened, and supersensitive 'individualists' whose disquietude can be
discerned from the face of the word itself—are not representative
would, in my opinion, be premature. The fact is that religion is man's
great venture and man's great, fatal failure. It would be very strange
if it had not taken centuries to overcome this failure by his own
strength of mind. It would therefore seem to be obviously improbable
that we shall find him in the foreseeable future enjoying a real, fatal
peace. On the contrary, how pathetic it is to see how until very recently
he has been extracting a new 'religiosity' from 'atheism,' as in Ziegler's
Mythos Atheos or in Mauthner's book (at the end of his fourth volume),
where such a 'religiosity' is allowed—albeit as a 'normal delusion, a
wholesome falsehood, an unavoidable, lifelong illusion'—and a 'concept of God' reduced to a 'comforting something' is introduced. The
same thing occurs among many of the expressionist poets who actually
use the word 'god' as a stock phrase for a scream. So even today—as
attested, for example, by the religious and Christian variants of existential philosophy—this business of religion has not yet been settled.
Naturally it takes a long time to arrive at a reintegration, for the individual as well as the whole—especially when, as lies in the very nature
of the case, men have the suspicion that this reintegration may possibly

---

[12] Kenneth Patchen, *The Journal of Albion Moonlight* (New York: The United Book
Guild, 1944), pp. 253f. [The italics are Miskotte's.—Tr.]
[[13] The term *'Einzelgänger'* means a person who goes his own way, a solitary, an individualist, an 'outsider,' a lone wolf, a maverick.—Tr.]
[14] Not to be confused with his brother, John Cowper Powys, the author of *A Glaston-
bury Romance* and other novels.

involve the restoration of a primitive belief which appears to be innate in man in countless, mutually contradictory variations.[15]

Thus in spite of themselves the 'individualists' are interpreters and representatives of this struggle to get rid of 'God' once and for all and at the same not to lose the love of life, its divine dreadfulness, its magnificent universality, its grand indifference. In his 'Great Hymn of Thanksgiving,' Bertolt Brecht is not deluding himself when he summons a whole congregation of votaries; he is their liturgist:

Lobet die Nacht und die Finsternis, die euch empfangen!
Kommet zuhauf,
Schaut in den Himmel hinauf:
Schon ist der Tag euch vergangen.

Lobet das Gras und die Tiere, die neben euch leben und sterben!
Sehet, wie ihr
Lebet das Gras, lebt das Tier,
Und es muss auch mit euch sterben.

Lobet den Baum, der aus Aas aufwächst jauchzend zum Himmel—
Lobet das Aas,
Lobet den Baum, der es frass,
Aber auch lobet den Himmel.

Lobet von Herzen das schlechte Gedächtnis des Himmels
Und das er nicht
Weiss euren Nam noch Gesicht;
Niemand weiss, dass ihr noch da seid.

Lobet die Kälte, die Finsternis und das Verderben!
Schauet hinan,
Es kommet nicht auf euch an,
Und ihr könnt unbesorgt sterben.

(Praise the night and the encompassing darkness!
Come, gather together,
look up to heaven:
already your day is past.

[15] Leopold Ziegler, *Der Gestaltwandel der Götter*, II, 5. *Betrachtung*; Mauthner, IV, 446.

6

Praise the grass and the beasts, living and dying beside you!
Behold, like you
the grass lives and the beast,
like you, they too must die.

Praise the tree, exultantly springing from carrion to heaven—
praise the carrion,
praise the tree that ate the carrion,
but also praise heaven.

Honestly praise the poor memory of heaven
and the fact that it neither
knows your name nor your face;
nobody knows that you're still here.

Praise the cold, the darkness, the corruption!
Look and see,
nothing depends on you;
you can die without a care).

WHEN THE GODS ARE SILENT

We are constantly showing a lack of understanding, appreciation, and admiration of *paganism*. Perhaps here and there even in our own time a voice will again be raised, to give expression to it as did Schiller in his poem, 'The Gods of Greece' and Hölderlin in his early poems and in *Hyperion*. So when we seek to suggest what is the feeling about life in our time by such words as 'The gods are silent; *hear* the silence of the gods,' we are respecting a limitation: we are not saying that the gods are dying or that the gods are dead. Practically this may at the present time come to the same thing; but the only people, the only genius (to use the parlance of social historians) which became aware of the silence of the gods, Israel, did not feel the need to deny the existence of the gods. And we have a fair idea of what the reason for this must be. It was the abiding consciousness that religion, despite its ungenuine-ness, its lack of reality, is invincible; it was Israel's constant confron-tation with the elemental powers and fundamental forces of existence

7

which found shape in the myths and culture of the peoples that surrounded Israel.

It was not too long ago that the great majority of German youth recalled the gods to life. With them it was a convulsive flight from a civilization that had become uncanny and unreal into a 'totality' of life and responsibility; it was a protest against the stifling atmosphere of a welfare state in which all sacral earnestness and holy play were smothered. The very same gods, from whose house of bondage Israel knew that it had been rescued, were conjured up, evoked, and contemporized in new myths and cults, and represented in modern heroes and modern exploits. And if they had not become the prey of cynical propaganda and if in this paganism there had not already been the glow of nihilism close beneath the surface of its words, we would have had a passing and virulent, but yet violent and in its way genuine, experience of what an East European had prophesied: 'The ancient gods will return, but with new faces. Only their power over men and their laughter over the sins of world history will be the same. They will come back; that is certain. The hour of this return will be the last hour of the Christian era.'[16]

In a sense the gods have returned. We can hardly think of a youth movement that has not been related to a kind of rediscovery of paganism. How could it be otherwise, at least if it is true that paganism and religion are virtually identical? Therefore to be contemptuous of paganism is simply to be contemptuous of man. Many years ago I wrote: 'We propose to honour paganism. We should learn to see it afresh. We should get to the bottom of the great simplification it imposes upon us and take it seriously. What is needed is a new seriousness and the realization that the (pagan-Jewish-Christian) syntheses fall apart as soon as paganism rediscovers itself. We must open our eyes and see the absurdity of the associations that have attached themselves to the word "paganism" as we have been using it. Paganism is not atheism; on the contrary, it is a very strong, vital faith. Paganism is not liberalism or libertinism; on the contrary, it has always had a strong bond with the state and with community life based upon veneration of the state. Paganism is not something antiquated; on the contrary, it is the everlasting ferment of human life. In the last analysis there are not many pagan religions [actually a pleonasm] and in so

[16] Janko Janeff, *Dämonie des Jahrhunderts* (1939), p. 349.

far as they do exist, they understand each other extraordinarily well, and when it comes down to it, they give an example of mutual tolerance. In short, paganism is the religion of human nature as such, always and everywhere.'[17]

This particular revival of the gods passed over, but not in such a way that we can say that the 'gods' or the 'godhead' are dead. We must say, rather, that the gods are silent. The idea is still in the air, but it is mute. The shape lingers on the horizon but is suffused in a silent fog. The words still resound, as in a strange, unknown language or like a song from childhood; but they no longer tell the mystery to us latecomers. We no longer feel secure in the bosom of nature; we know that all things far and near do not speak, neither the Milky Way nor the electron. The 'fourth man,' if one wishes to retain this figure, is bound by the spell of things; the facts have him in their grip. He still feels an occasional prickle of dread before a higher power, but that power is voiceless, it no longer shows any signs of life.

When the gods are silent, when existence all around us is not only filled but surrounded by a spectral stillness, this only makes apparent what has always been 'objectively' true. Whether there were always gods, we do not know; but that they never spoke is certain. In our situation (and this means the situation of every one of us) we are beginning to see how atheism has always been latent in religion and how presently it has actually gripped the heartstrings of the masses, yes, actually captured its heart as a stirring, that is, a terrible and exciting, emancipation, which man, for all his doctrinal and ritual conservatism, always surmised was there for him to have, for which he always secretly hoped.

This again does not mean that the tension between terror and emancipation will soon be resolved. Even the 'fourth man' (among the intellectuals and among the masses—and in this respect is there any essential difference between the two?)—is not wholly immune to suffering. He has not yet become a robot. He too has the desire to sing, and (to use Brecht's phrase) it turns into 'praise.' He too creates myths and figures (even though one should not be rash and dismiss all worship of prizefighters and racers as a surrogate for religion). He too feels a swelling in his heart when he hears the 'individualists' roll out the rumbling sound of dreadful things upon the earth. He too is afraid

[17] K. H. Miskotte, *Edda en Thora* (1939), pp. 28f.

of dull content and satiety. He too is not wholly without a vague sense of self-reproach when for a moment the emptiness that surrounds him makes his head swim. And along with this he declares (and quite rightly!) that he has no answer to the question whether there is 'a' god. But one thing he knows very definitely (and here he shares the bitter truth of this age and every age), and that is that the 'godhead,' if there is one, is silent and that it is experienced as a total silence.

When the gods were discovered to be mute, voiceless, abysses, Israel was born—or better, when Israel was born, when Israel's faith was awakened, the gods were unmasked as being nothing more than the utter silence, the total taciturnity which they had always been. Here for the first time in the human mind there emerged in a 'naïve' way what we today more learnedly assert as a thetical statement: the godhead is a projection of the human mind. At that time it was more than a thesis: it was a confession and a hymn. True, it is the negative reverse of a confession and a hymn, but the negative is such an essential part of the new recognition of YHWH that it borrows some of its passion from this negativity.

We are constantly being struck by this passion in the Old Testament; for example in Psalm 115 (for which the greatest Jewish theologian of our time, Franz Rosenzweig, cherished a special predilection):

'Not to us, YHWH, not to us, but to thy name give glory, for the sake of thy steadfast love and thy faithfulness! . . . Their idols are silver and gold, the work of men's hands. They have mouths, but do not speak; eyes, but do not see. They have ears, but do not hear; noses, but do not smell. They have hands, but do not feel; feet, but do not walk; and they do not make a sound in their throat. O Israel, trust in YHWH! He is their help and their shield. . . . YHWH has been mindful of us; he will bless us; he will bless the house of Israel; . . . he will bless those who fear YHWH, both small and great. May YHWH give you increase, you and your children! May you be blessed by YHWH, who made heaven and earth! The heavens are YHWH's heavens, but the earth he has given to the sons of men. The dead do not praise YHWH, nor do any that go down into silence. But we will bless YHWH from this time forth and for evermore.'[18]

Or the words addressed to Elijah in I Kings 19:11ff.: ' "Go forth,

[18 Text from Revised Standard Version with insertion of the tetragrammaton YHWH as in the author's text.—Tr.]

and stand upon the mount before the Lord." And behold, the Lord passed by, and a great and strong wind rent the mountains, and broke in pieces the rocks before the Lord, but the Lord was not in the wind; and after the wind an earthquake, but the Lord was not in the earthquake; and after the earthquake a fire, but the Lord was not in the fire; and after the fire a still small *voice*. And when Elijah heard it, he wrapped his face in his mantle and went out and stood at the entrance of the cave. And behold, there came a *voice* to him. . . .'[19]

When the gods are dumb, when the 'godhead' is silent, this is ultimately not so much because they have been put to silence, but rather because their eternal silence has been exposed as their most essential, their 'mystical' characteristic. In its first and purest form atheism is the reverse side of Israel's faith. It is a happy thing, a liberation for ever, for all the centuries to come. The 'hallowing of the Name' commanded to the People of God, always begins with a profession of this 'atheism.'

The presupposition of 'our' atheism is that for us YHWH had become, though not the whole, an element, the keystone in our universe. 'Our' nihilism declares that after the unmasking of this particular God no new revelation has occurred and that we are utterly convinced in every fibre of our being that no such thing can be expected to happen. In any case, our healthy—or decadent—scepticism includes the certainty that there is absolutely nothing in any new religion, however it may be cleaned up or stripped down. In so far as you and I are the 'fourth man' (for neither philosopher nor theologian, neither priest nor layman can wholly eliminate himself and stand off from this category), we ourselves are a corroboration of the fact that for us paganism, the splendid paean of praise to the primordium of all things, has become ambiguous, and that 'Christianity' as a religion presents to us a face marked with all the signs of an ultimately impenetrable silence. To the extent to which we are the fallen, the outcast, the rejected, or (what for the ambivalent attitude toward life that has laid hold of us is the same thing) the emancipated, those who have been brought to themselves, those who have been chosen to make an unprecedented venture of life, to that extent our sorrow over the fading and extinction of faith is also ambiguous. It appears to mean two things, a downfall and a

[19 The author here quotes the Buber-Rosenzweig German translation of the Old Testament. The italics are the author's.—Tr.]

birth, an excommunication and an initiation. In both forms it reveals to us the fact that the present power of theoretical and practical denial of God is the permanent environment in which we and all men have to live their lives, the ferment of our and all men's conception of life.

Because this is our situation, we are miles away from what is said about Zusya of Hanipol, the Hasidic rabbi: 'At the very start, when the maggid recited the verse from the Scriptures which he was going to expound, and began with the words of the Scriptures "And God said" or "and God spoke," Rabbi Zusya was overcome with *ecstasy*, and screamed and gesticulated so wildly that he disturbed the peace of the round table and had to be taken out. And then he stood in the hall or in the woodshed, beat his hands against the walls and cried aloud, "And God *said*!" '[20]

Not that no remedy has been found, for now we have a flourishing 'philosophical faith.'[21] Growing up tall, almost running wild, we are surrounded with a rank growth of existentialism, bearing fruits that contain a tonic to produce energy. There is also a great deal of deviation, hesitation, and resistance expressed in modern poetry, above all in the poetry which, as Guillaume van der Graft says, haunts the margins rather than the centre of life, and not to be forgotten, in humour, which is an outlet for indestructible freedom. It is characteristic of the 'post-Christian' situation that Christian Morgenstern, the author of the delightfully nonsensical *Galgenlieder*, (*Gallows Songs*), should define for his contemporaries the function of his work as follows: 'The Gallows Songs convey to the man of today above all a certain relaxation of tension. Enveloped in a time which in the main receives its watchwords from the savants and accordingly is doomed to dead-end streets on every side, he feels that as he reads such verse he can breathe again, as in an atmosphere in which the oppressive gravity and dullness of the so-called physical plan, which is being decreed with all the stern earnestness of an age gone godless and spiritless as the one saving reality, seems to be cheerfully banished, breached, and sometimes turned completely upside down. . . . Just to spread a little intellectual frivolity, cheerfulness, freedom, to liven up the imagination,

---

[20] Martin Buber, *Tales of the Hasidim: The Early Masters*, tr. Olga Marx (New York: Schocken Books, 1961), p. 236.
[21] The reference is to the title of Karl Jaspers's book *Der philosophische Glaube* (Eng. tr. *The Perennial Scope of Philosophy*). (Tr.)

just to thaw out a little of the soul's music frozen in the posthorn is enough.'

We understand and approve of such diversion; it takes a roundabout way to animate the soul and grazes the question of God only in passing. It is characteristic of our time that every direct witness to faith easily puts us off and challenges us to question its genuineness. Even utterances which only a relatively short time ago sounded natural and familiar, if they were transmitted through a Christian tradition, now sound strange to us. Often, of course, such religious utterances prove to be outworn and effete even in the life and work of those who still ventured to utter them in an unmistakably genuine way.

I am thinking, for example, of Rilke. When one looks back from his later work (the *Duino Elegies*, for example), the *Book of Hours* and above all the personal professions of faith with which his letters and journals are so thoroughly saturated sound like the voice of a different person, like the tone of a different age. It is the moving and 'sentimental' tone which has not yet been sicklied over with the immanental problems of religion. From many possible examples we cite one which is not included in any of the collections of his verse and which speaks for itself:

> Es gibt ein Väterliches, Fernes:
> in unbewegten Nächten war
> mir, wie vom Atem eines Sternes,
> die Seele klein und wieder klar.
> Allein im Leben bin ich hier,
> und ausser mir ist nur ein Zweiter,
> und mir ist bang, weil ich viel weiter
> von jenem bin, als er von mir.
> (There is something Fatherly, Far-away:
> in still nights,
> as by the breath of a star,
> my soul grew small and clear again.
> Here in life I am alone,
> and apart from me there is only one Other,
> and I am afraid, because I am farther
> away from him than he from me).[22]

[22] From *Bekenntnis eines Jünglings: Briefe und Tagebücher* (1899–1902), p. 244.

13

GENUINE NIHILISM

Let us attempt briefly to draw a number of conclusions from what we have said.

(a) We are no longer pagans because Being and its forms no longer call us to fellowship and union or no longer afford us such fellowship and union.

(b) We are nihilists because we can no longer go back into the past security of Being and because for us the Word of God points to no future—one can also say: because for us 'god' has become only a factor of the world, an aspect of Being; because the 'Word' has become a metaphor, a simile of the ultimate direction of our own reflection, in the last analysis our self-projection.

(c) But what is meant by the term 'we'? The question is a complicated one. Does it signify the subject of a mood, a solidarity, a way of thinking? Or is this something that has to do with Being? But then what about 'Christianity'? Can it be that its God too is one of the cosmic silent ones? This is a point that must be subjected to more rigorous analysis.

The subjectivism in which our modern thinking is caught seems to be unanswerable. Religion, the capstone of this subjectivism, is threatened by the consequence of this way of thinking and hovers on the level of intentionality. After all, it seems self-evident that faith in the 'Word' is a religion like any other religion; it seems even more self-evident that in order to arrive at certainty in this respect too, we must pursue the path of examining, ordering, and establishing relationships within that which we experience within ourselves and grasp in a divinatory way, and which we can account for according to the laws of reason. That God does not have a Being which is analogous to our being, that the Word is not a mystical experience, that faith is not an experience and not even something that man is capable of, that God cannot be thought of as substance, that God's work cannot be conceived as causality, that holy history cannot be thought of as a process—all these gravely passionate negations are simply inherent in the fundamental structure of the Bible. If we let them go—and how

14

can we hold on to them by our own ability?—then we lose the path on which we walk, and this is not only in the 'area of religion' (as the phrase goes), but also in our thinking and our life. And even if it be true that in all 'areas' we have to start with ourselves, where revelation and faith is concerned we cannot start with ourselves.

We need to go even further in our analysis. It is true that in a legitimate sense we can say that faith has its own autonomy, that it is personal and chosen in freedom, that the Word of God exercises an authority which not only engenders freedom but, being inherent in it, carries with it, creates, and preserves freedom. But 'somewhere' there must be a point where the criterion of truth does not lie with me; 'somewhere' (but this point is actually the qualitative 'all') there will be a point where it will not be a matter of agreement between my thinking and what has been thought. 'Somewhere' my thinking will be called upon to allow itself—in joy—to be brought into conformity with what God has thought about me. 'Somewhere,' when we ask ourselves whether the givenness of God satisfies our religious 'needs,' we shall come to the end of our tether. 'Somewhere'—unless we give up this *hubris* altogether—we shall have to see that if we follow the current method, we arrive at nothing more than a psychological fact, a thought or a feeling or a conjecture which pretends to be superpsychological. 'Somewhere' man must definitely submit; he must let himself be told that he is not autonomous, that he cannot be either a creator or a judge of the universe. 'Somewhere' he will have to grasp, not so much in ecstasy as in sober apprehension of truth, the privilege of understanding that he is understood and known and chosen.

These statements have the smack of edifying phrases. And the fact is that, philosophically speaking, they are based upon an unclarified bias, and religiously speaking, they are dubious because of their cool objectivity, because of the way in which they 'simply' start with the assertion that the living God is not a projection, indeed, that he cannot even be known, recognized, and ticketed by means of our conceptions. But the man who cannot make these edifying phrases his own is, in all innocence, a bellwether of nihilism, and what is more, of genuine nihilism. He is precisely the person who shows that the gods are silent, that they always were and always will be silent. And it is also in this light that we begin to see that the human mind cannot enter into any real relationship with the given, that the self-sufficient reason can find no point of contact in its reflection, that the objective intellect is bottomlessly subjective.[23]

It was the delusion of an all too easy-going, an all too bourgeois synagogue and church to imagine that an answer to these questions in accordance with the autonomy of reason leaves room for religious feeling, that this solution might perhaps present theological difficulties but was by no means fatal, and that practice would produce a spontaneous solution. That other 'areas' of life would also suffer damage, indeed, that this attitude must inevitably undermine the meaning of life itself, not only among the intellectuals but also among the people— this remained hidden from the thinking part of the nation, those who were at ease in Zion. In Turgenev's *Fathers and Sons* Bazarov gives the following definition of a nihilist: 'A nihilist is a man who does not bow down before any authority, and *does not take principle on faith*, whatever reverence that principle may be enshrined in.'[24] Compared with such bold utterances, philosophical autonomy looks innocent and solidly bourgeois. But why should one not go a step further with Nietzsche and reject even what is conceivable, what has by no means been untested? Why should not the right life really begin only when the whole concept of 'truth,' which is only an offshoot of the 'metaphysical' God, is eliminated? And why should one not be able to ground this 'elimination' in a 'faith'? Why should one not assert that nihilism is the 'faith' (i.e., let us say, the final insight), that behind all the statements of faith, but also behind all the statements of knowledge and 'values,' there is nothing that corresponds to them? And why then should we not methodically and consistently attribute whatever presents itself as faith or knowledge or divination or value-consciousness to the nonreal, the nonsubstantial, to an 'as-if' which is dangerous (or also necessary) to life? Nihilism can be understood as a reaction to 'Christianity,' which, after all, had increasingly put the stamp of the divine on worldly entities; and in this sense it was the Enlightenment

---

[23] Cf. A. J. de Sopper, *Dwaalwegen*, pp. 123ff.; idem, *Grenzen der Openbaring*, pp. 10f; idem, *Wat is philosophie?*, pp. 153f.; A. E. Loen, *Wijsbegeerte en Werkelijkheid*, pp. 214–220; J. A. Oosterbaan, *Hegels Phaenomenologie des Geistes en de theologische kenleer*, pp. 151f.

[24] Ivan S. Turgenev, *Fathers and Sons*, tr. by Constance Garnett (New York: Modern Library, 1950), p. 24.

that inaugurated the process of nihilism in Europe. Then the Enlightenment itself strengthened, by way of the disappointment it brought, 'the agonizing feeling of the nothingness of science'; for in a strange way understanding is an end, and it brings with it an emptying of life and initiative. But even more certainly, according to Nietzsche, nihilism comes as a reaction to the mind's habit of construing by means of a value judgment an increasing number of areas and goals of life as being desirable and meaningful. 'What is nihilism?' is the question asked in Aphorism 2 of *The Will to Power*: 'That the highest values disvalue themselves. The goal is lacking; the answer is lacking to our "Why?"' And in another section: 'The untenability of one interpretation of the world, upon which a tremendous amount of energy has been lavished, awakens the suspicion that all interpretations of the world are false.'[25]

But a judgment which takes pleasure and displeasure as its criterion [as does Nietzsche's] is soon exposed for what it is. It is itself a symptom of increasing despair because the hedonist and the utilitarian, if they are ever touched deeply enough by their failure, are necessarily driven to pessimism. 'It makes no difference whether the question of meaning was a proper question to which previously we have given a wrong answer or whether it was a wrong question which must always be followed by a wrong answer. Hitherto all for nothing!—this result remains and it drives the doubting and despairing one to the nihilistic assumption.' But the world's habit of judging by moral standards shuts the door for Nietzsche; for it shifts life, strength, health, vitality, and pleasure into a realm where they are treated with reserve, mistrust, and suspicion. Moreover, the victory of an ethical ideal is achieved with exactly the same immoral means as any other victory. This is the antinomy: in so far as we believe in morality, we condemn the existing state of things, and in so far as we believe in the existing state of things, we condemn morality—and thus inevitably we also condemn the existing state of things, for the sake of which we condemned morality. Deeply rooted as we are in the habit of thinking that an absolute good and an opposing absolute evil must guide us through the darkness and confusion of life, when these lights go out (because they turn out to be only a projection of tradition, race, and environment, bound to-

[25] Cf. *Toward a Genealogy of Morals*, §28; *Beyond Good and Evil*, §55; *The Will to Power*, §22ff., 418, 585, 846.

17

gether by our autonomous mind),[26] we cannot refrain from finding one last truth, from enunciating one final dictum, namely, that there is nothing behind morality either, except an individual or collective subjective *fixation* of an intrinsically worthless judgment, in which and by which we cannot live, unless we make Nothingness itself the content, the ultimate and emptiest, but actually again the formally 'absolute,' content of our faith. And Nietzsche unflinchingly held out in this steadfast persistence—becoming in the minds of many[27] a pioneer and martyr, who vicariously suffered and endured for us the ultimate consequences of honesty.

Then another began all over again to question faith from the bottom up. This was Heidegger. According to him the question that underlies all thinking is: 'Why is there any Being at all—why not far rather Nothing?'[28] And we understand that he calls this questioning piety.

We have no choice except in one way or another to become a victim or a conqueror of nihilism. But nihilism cannot be validly and effectively refuted any more than we can refute its inconspicuous and seemingly innocuous starting point, namely, the unconditional elevation of the subject (the self) to the position of being the centre and point of departure. When a person who has fallen into nihilism flees into the shelter of a world view, a tradition, a dogma, this, according to Jaspers, is for this doomed person a hopeless undertaking. But if he would dare to live 'by the whole of the infinite,' or better, if he put out of his head the desire to know the transcendent and, rather, transcending himself, stretched himself to touch it or be touched by it, he would break out of the state of mere situation and also out of the dogma of *nihil*, and in that instant would be himself, even if it were only in the shattering experience of the 'boundary situations.'

For Jaspers, however, on the broad level of reflection, where participation in the historically growing, always contemporaneous, and never outmoded truths of the great thinkers of the past as well as communication with our fellows in the present have their place, nothing remains so promising as a confrontation with the Bible, especially with the Old Testament. In the victory over nihilism which is in store for us

[26] Hermann Goldschmidt, *Der Nihilismus im Lichte einer kritischen Philosophie* (1941) p. 32.
[27] Karl Jaspers, *Nietzsche* (1936), pp. 200f., 385f.
[28] '*What is Metaphysics?*' tr. R. F. C. Hull and Alan Crick, in Martin Heidegger, *Existence and Being* (Chicago, Henry Regnery, 1949), p. 380.

the word of the prophets plays a great role.[29] But, we ask, has one heard the prophets if one has not heard that they are witnesses of the Word, which *a priori* and *a limine* breaks through the spell of nihilism, because 'somewhere' it cancels the autonomy of the human mind and in spite of its demoralization catches it up into the revelation, the presence, the love of him who intercedes for us eternally?

Genuine nihilism, which is threatening to many people because of its honesty, is nowhere rendered so radically superfluous as it is at the place where the Scriptures are allowed to speak in their own categories, in the strength of their own order and precedence. Here the Word proves its divinity, proves masterfully, sovereignly, and gloriously that it is wholly itself, that it presents itself as the particular and not as the universal, as saving power and not omnipotence, as the *melek* ('king') of an exodus and not as a 'shelter,' as 'one' and 'indivisible' and thus as the exact opposite of that which appears to us as a divisible and accessible being or event. Nothing makes the Scriptures and especially the Old Testament so acutely immediate and contemporaneous as the quiet and insistent, loving and mighty NAME; nothing can be such a liberation for the intellectually tormented as the death knell of religion sounded by the theophany of YHWH. When the gods and also the god whom we have constructed for ourselves by our autonomous thought go on exercising their depressive and destructive silence, it must become clear that they have always been silent gods who will always drive us to atheism, total alienation from meaning, the emptying of life, and the eclipse of 'God.' Nihilism is the necessary consequence of 'our Christianity.' And from that point of view, the word 'our' can be legitimate; indeed, it even forces itself upon us as a confession of solidarity.

UNGENUINE NIHILISM

In all likelihood many readers will have difficulty in admitting the force and relevance of what we have said above, because the nihilism of the masses, with which we are dealing and which has put its stamp

[29] Karl Jaspers, in *L'esprit européen* (*Rencontres internationales de Genève*, 1946), pp. 291 ff.; idem, *The Perennial Scope of Philosophy*, tr. Ralph Manheim (New York: Philosophical Library, 1949), pp. 170f.

upon the face of our time, does not look at all that important and serious. As a matter of fact, one can call this more widespread nihilism ungenuine, it can be characterized as 'rebelling conformism.'[30] Here again we meet the 'fourth man.' With reference to him C. Moeller[31] says that actually he never makes a real decision and never draws any consequence: 'If one declares oneself to be an "atheist," there immediately follows the sigh, "A pity God doesn't exist"; but this by no means prevents one from bringing God on the scene in a book or play, in order to go on quarrelling with him. If the word "nihilism" is used, one hastens to enumerate all the things to which one attributes some value and for which one would venture his life. If, on the other hand, something is said in praise of freedom, it is not without the sour refrain, "We are condemned to freedom." If one extols life, the reply is: "We are *thrown* into this life without any purpose whatsoever." If one can no longer hide his homesickness for God, the lament is heard: "Why hast thou forsaken me?" '

If we listen carefully, we see that here too, as so often, the differences disappear. After all, we are dealing with the 'fourth man,' of whom we have said that he no longer participates in classical and Christian culture, with the man who has not yet reached his full growth, but who is portrayed full grown, for example, in Orwell's *1984*. The allusions in the quotation above, however, refer to Sartre. Does this imply that Sartre is already the 'fourth man,' or does it mean that the 'fourth man' thinks or will think like Sartre and his followers? If we are to know the situation in which the church (but also art and philosophy) finds itself, it is not unimportant that we should gain a bit more clarity on this point. May not that which we have called 'genuine nihilism,' even though it grows out of inner struggle and though it does have practical consequences, turn out to be a purely intellectual affair, while this 'ungenuine nihilism' of the crowd, of the so-called 'mass man' (who, incidentally, can never be quite so empty as he is credited with being),[32] is far more strongly rooted in the totality of experience? And if this is the case, may there not be truth in the idea, which Moeller suggests, that even the optimistic spirits (who still

[30] J. C. Hoekendijk, 'Rondom het apostolaat' in *Wending* (Dec. 1952).
[31] C. Moeller, 'Le sens de Dieu dans la littérature contemporaine' in *Lumen vitae* (1952); quoted in Hoekendijk, op. cit.
[32] See the brilliant essay by Paul Tillich, *Masse und Geist: Studien zur Philosophie der Masse* (1922).

participate very considerably in classical and Christian culture) are by no means free of the inconsistencies implied in this word 'ungenuine'? Does this not finally lead to the paradoxical but obvious conclusion that 'ungenuine nihilism' is actually the genuine nihilism, that is to say, the true reflection of total human experience, whereas 'genuine' nihilism would prove to be merely an overstatement of a formal, intellectual analysis of the impasses into which the human mind can drive itself?

Thus a new feature enters into our picture of the situation in which the church stands. We have seen that religion turns out to be a non-necessary element of human life and self-consciousness. We saw that religiosity can glide off into atheism.[33] We have seen that atheism—which for a time still imagines that it can uphold ethical (Christian) ideals even though it denies their source—solidifies and darkens into nihilism. We have gained some impression of the heroic honesty that characterized Nietzsche and some of his followers and fellow sufferers. But now we see that nihilism too can never be perfectly serious; the nihilistic attitude toward life and the nihilistic verdict are ambivalent. In our connection it is not necessary to go through the mythical themes in Nietzsche's later years in order to ferret out the theoretical contradictions in them. Much more to the point would be to detect the really 'genuine' nihilism in the 'ungenuine' nihilism of the great impersonal 'they' [Heidegger's 'Man'].

And in actuality it is in this ambivalent form that it does appear: 'There is no God—too bad there is no God, but that's the way it is! Very well, then, let us take every alibi away from him and accuse him!' This kind of nonsense is genuine, warm, human, and understand-able.

Or it may take the form of saying: 'There is no reality behind any faith or any ideal. There is nothing but an abyss of absurd existence. But hail to the summer, the sun, laughter; blessed be life and strength and women! We roam the world with hungry eyes to see everything we can; we want to fly to the moon; there is not time enough to enjoy to the full this terrible life.' So in this cosmic contradiction the nihilism of the so-called 'fourth man' is precious in our eyes.

Or which of us does not feel a kinship with this much maligned monster (whom we call the 'fourth man') when we can find no practi-

[33] See O. Noordenbos, *Het atheisme in Nederland in de 19de eeuw* (1931).

cal way out of the inner antinomy of freedom (just as the philosopher has never found any theoretical way out)? In actuality we all seek the dignity of our humanity over against nature in our freedom, and in actuality we are all terrified of the curse (and it actually is a curse!) of this gift of freedom. Thus, for the present in the so-called 'post-Christian, postbourgeois, postpersonal century' the situation is no different from what it was in the recently vanished Christian, bourgeois, and personal century.

Exactly the same thing is true of the inconsistencies in our exaltation of 'life.' What religion can ever escape the hidden wavering between two extremes: that of highly exalting and glorifying life itself, without regard for its meaning and goal, life as it flourishes within self without any other thought of its purpose—and still groaning and complaining (when one's own life or that of one's family or community cracks up) over the sickening, revolting, cold indifference which is characteristic of happy, carefree life as such, the very indifference which previously, and almost in the same breath, could not be too highly exalted? This 'ungenuine' nihilism is simply the reverse side of 'ungenuine' religion. Neither of them as such possess any coercive necessity. But once a person has entered these ambiguous regions, he can no longer be in any way consistent. And this 'ungenuineness' is spreading in religion as well as nonreligion, irreligion, antireligion, and contrareligion. This 'ungenuineness,' this fractured thing, this not completely honest attitude that frustrates its own possibility of maturing, will always prove to be the genuine thing.

Because this analysis is undertaken in view of the ministry of the apostolate, it may be pertinent to deal right now with a question which can arise at this particular point. Will the witness be capable of understanding these things, and above all, will he be willing to recognize the situation? Will not this person, who unfortunately is only too often merely respectable and conventional, cause only harm, or at least create confusion, and perhaps evoke even greater obduracy? In Holland some leading people who speak out of a profound concern have expressed the opinion that the empirical church has so alienated itself from the real life of the world today that it ought to refrain altogether from discussion with the children of this world. We consider this overdrawn because it underestimates the beinglike quality (*Seinsmässige*) of the changes that have taken place and thus underrates what is common to all of us in the depths of our experience. This ambivalence runs through the hearts of Christian people, too.

When it is asserted that 'church' people do not understand this at all, that they tend to classify the nihilists as rarities, and that as professional 'church people' they are the worst possible ones to carry on a dialogue with the 'fourth man,' we listen attentively in order to give it due consideration, but many questions remain. When a person makes himself the spokesman of all the queer and rancorous and also the reasonable and natural reactions of those who are alienated from the church, this very attitude implies a concealed, aloof condescension which simply cannot coexist with a Christian's knowledge of what he is himself. To face the world in a relaxed, unstrained attitude must, in my opinion, necessarily mean that we simply cannot bring ourselves to assume this attitude of aloofness toward these others. Religion is never anything else but ambivalent; nihilism is always ambivalent. And it is precisely in this respect that these people are genuine; this is exactly what makes them our partners. This is what we ourselves are; this is the way we are what we still are, and this is the way we possess what we still possess. Even Christianity no longer manifests itself except in fatal hybrid forms; and the mighty 'Antichrist,' like the rest of us, is an old driveller who jumbles together ideas and feelings, judgments and wishful dreams for his own advantage, who ultimately does not himself know what is happening to him and is secretly unsure of what he really wants.

What is really wrong? Is it not that the end of religion simply refuses to take place? The end of religion—this would also put an end to nihilism. It actually would. The worst obstructionist, mischief-maker, and defeatist in this matter of leading an honest life is so-called 'natural theology.' The rejection and elimination of natural religion would open the way for a conclusive free decision. But religion does not die, even in the 'fourth man.' It still goes on living, even among Christians; and natural theology, no matter how often it is refuted, deposits its spawn on a secluded sandbank somewhere beyond the rapid streams of the times and proceeds to go merrily swimming upstream. And again religion seems to be the best choice.

Yet what has been said—the assertion that 'ungenuine' nihilism is actually the 'genuine' nihilism—would be impossible if it did not rest on the assumption that religion is ended and natural theology is nullified. This freedom could not be endured for a single moment unless the nameless Name, his matchless Self-witness, his glorious Presence were affirmed and accepted in faith. This is what the Bible is speaking of when it points to the Word, which completely unmasks the silence of the powers and the gods by cleaving the silence with his exclusive speech.

WITNESSES TO THE ABSENCE OF GOD

Reflected in literature we find insistent testimony to the experience of the absence of God. Anybody who reads the books by Françoise Sagan, *Bonjour tristesse* and *A Certain Smile*, may perhaps at first have the impression that this is a refined but unworthy frivolity. Love, which for a somewhat earlier generation was the last remaining sphere of decision whether life was meaningful or meaningless, has for this very young writer lost this quality of ambivalent hovering between bliss and despair in which romantic man found the presence of fulfilment, the parousia of sacred life. Here love has become a diversion, a distraction, not only from the discord of the world, but also from the normal and praiseworthy forms of life—a distraction achieved by blocking off feeling. In a disunited, split state of boredom the banishment of solitude is felt to be the only real presence. And passion is a way out to the extent that in passion a person can hang on to something and feel that for a moment at least he is real, experiencing these attachments to casual moods as a fulfilment of himself. Hence 'Bonjour tristesse,' 'Welcome, sadness'; it is the way high-spirited youth distinguishes its despair from that of the others.

Hence 'A Certain Smile'—it is the smile with which a heart has already given up and resigned itself even before the encounter of love takes place; for (shall we say 'Thank God' or 'Unfortunately'?) there can be no such thing as unhappy love. Where the happiness of the presence of 'I and thou' is impossible, there palpable unhappiness too is impossible. Is not the hidden meaning of this farewell to love, which seeks to rule out the infinite from every encounter and fulfilment, the one that (to use Ludwig Klages's words) declares that the cosmogonic Eros is dethroned, executed, and buried, because his existence and presence is illusory? *Bonjour tristesse!*—in this resignation, paradoxically enough, the absence of a presence is recognized and this realization is welcomed. This hopelessness is permeated with the conviction that any hope or consolation is impossible.

We completely deceive ourselves, I think, if we explain the fabulous success of 'Saganism' (as it is already being called) by attributing it to the continuing proliferation of corruption. What we are dealing with here is the absence of God from the point of view of the impossibility of man's being real in the here and now, of being real and of regarding himself as real.

No man can find a presence if he himself does not become present, and he does not have the freedom to give if he does not have the freedom to receive. Not only existence but also presence (if we may make this distinction) is the prerequisite of the authenticity of a 'being' in which we ourselves are present. It is our crude, confused, shackled mind that covers up its emptiness with a kind of irresponsible vivacity, an exaggerated mode of existence in the deliberately unreal. When affliction comes our emptiness will be revealed in the glare of the lightning flashes of the self that could have been present.

A second example, which takes us a step deeper into the field of our study, is found in Samuel Beckett, the Irishman who writes in French. *Waiting for Godot*—here the theme, utterly sober and very mysterious, is the waiting for somebody who is known but whose unreliability is just unknown enough to give the waiting a touch of foolishness. Here again this undramatic drama can be dismissed and decried as desperate, hopeless, affected, improbable, and, to sum it all up, 'existentialistic.' And yet it should be noted that the existential dialectic is expressed by clowns in a meaningless dialogue on an almost empty stage. But is it really on an empty stage? Could one not just as well say that it occurs at the point of intersection, the vanishing point of a fourth dimension, the dimension of the presence of 'Godot'? The complete vacuity of any relationship to the transcendent is portrayed by negating and derisive gestures, but at the same time the rules of life and thought are strictly observed by Vladimir and Estragon, these vagabonds with no standing or age. Nothing is further from the atmosphere of the play than rebellion or denial.

The producers of this play—which reminds us of Luigi Pirandello's masque dramas of the split consciousness, the clairvoyance of a Tennessee Williams with regard to avoided conflicts transposed to another sphere, and in its denouement is related to the appearance of the messenger in Kafka's *The Castle*—the producers are in disagreement about how it should be staged. Should the waiting flow along its course of empty monotony in an atmosphere of silent oppression, or should the monotony be accentuated by strong gestures and lighting effects which would function as a 'sadistic whipsawing of the nerves,' or should the preference be given to a pathetic charm of helplessness in the clownish movements of the characters?

I would choose the latter possibility, because this would make it clear that human life (however empty it may be for a certain kind of thinking) is not in fact conscious of such monotony, at least it does not particularly feel in this monotony the depths of its emptiness, and also because the experienced absence is of such a kind that it awakes a *hypomone*, a patient waiting and an expectation so 'positive' that we may well doubt whether the waiting could not just as well be a dreadful reality that has already materialized as a liberating way out. Be that as it may—what in a metaphysical, ontological, philosophical sense would be called the ground of the world or the meaning of life no longer comes into purview even as an abstract marginal possibility, and that is modern. Here the ambivalence of religion and nihilism has come to an end. These vagabonds are not overdrawn nihilists, a fact that is already suggested by the characters, Pozzo and Lucky, who represent amorphous types of unbounded vulgarity and absolute misery. The second act is an almost unvaried 'liturgical' repetition of the first act—the situation is unchanged, time has found its stop in the neutrality of space. And yet the one thing Vladimir and Estragon 'have' is time, motionless oceans of time. So they invent new actions and continue playing, celebrating their irrelevant rites as in a cultic play. 'Godot'—is it God, or is it death, or is it fate? In any case it points to a speaking presence in and above all the things of law and accident and their wordless presence. All that 'is' and all that may come in the prolongation of what 'is'—all of this cannot be what must come as a presence while 'waiting for Godot.'

The third example is Albert Camus's *The Fall*. Despite the experiences he went through in life which drive him to despair, the lawyer, Jean Baptiste Clamence, clings to actual life and his constantly recrudescing love of life. In the midst of absurdity he remains the chivalrous servant of those who are hurt at the point of their own selfhood by the processes of the law. But he is haunted by the incubus of memory, the gentle sound of a splash and bubbling of water into which a young woman has leaped, seeking death, while he looked on from the bridge over the Seine, only a stone's throw away, standing there incomprehensibly paralyzed without making any attempt to rescue her or to sound an alarm. After that experience he was never happy again. As he said, 'An overflowing stadium, and the theatre . . . are the only places in the world where I feel innocent.'[34] For where one does not participate in the action, one can feel innocent for a while. No forgetfulness can be found in dissipation and debauchery; once a person has become a little guilty, he is guilty all the way through. Clamence comes to a shabby, disreputable hotel in Amsterdam and, using this as his headquarters, throws himself into the task of representing criminal cases. Whereas before he took the official side and pleaded the cases of the 'insulted and injured,' the poor and the harmless, innocently caught in the toils of the law, he now defends definitely criminal types—and in so doing is hardly conscious that in all this zealous devotion of his intelligence he is really dealing with the trial of his own life, with his right to live, with the responsibility for his undesired presence. During this time the beautiful city of Amsterdam becomes for him an inferno, a dirty dive by the Zuider Zee. His loneliness is nowhere counterbalanced by a presence, for his given self, his being himself, his being unique and different from others is sufficient to wreck every form of community with others. This is the depressing seal of absence stamped upon his ultimate summons to existence. But in this absence there is a presence, standing watch like an alien sentry: the presence of guilt. And on this basis Clamence discovers a community with others, the community of all those who have a past. Nobody can be counted guiltless, nor can anybody plead extenuating circumstances. And then comes the denouement. In his room he finds in a cupboard the stolen panel of the famous Ghent altarpiece, 'The Adoration of the Lamb,' the panel on which van Eyck had portrayed 'The Just Judges.' Anybody who takes a hyperaesthetic delight in these figures has found the confirmation of the right to judge and remain innocent. All Camus's anger and indignation is directed against the denial of this first and last condition of community: 'When we are

[34 This and the following quotations from *The Fall*, tr. Justin O'Brien (New York: Alfred A. Knopf, 1957), pp. 88, 136, 113.—Tr.]

27

all guilty, that will be democracy.' Thus he becomes the *juge-pénitent* ('judge-penitent,' or better, the 'penitent judge'), for whom existing is in itself a crime, and he becomes this not metaphysically, as Schopenhauer would have it, but existentially in the full sense of the word. The one all-pervading and all-determining presence is guilt. 'Who would have believed,' said Clamence, 'that crime consists less in making others die than in not dying oneself?' Under the gloomy sky the vertical absence limns out its absence in leaded horizontals of self-knowledge and self-rejection. But is not that absence and this presence far more biblical than an ontological theology about the 'Omnipresent'? Has a godfearing man ever seen omnipresence as being able to cope with the presence of guilt? And what is to be said about the saints? One can say with Walter Nigg: 'The saint is the great counterpart of the nihilist.' And the fact is that one can see on the countenance of this criminal lawyer the lineaments of the saint.

The presence is always in the first instance a particular thing and only by way of legitimate extrapolation a general thing. The fact that the particular presence of guilt could be a reflex of the particular presence of Him who first cancelled guilt by bearing it Himself and in this way judged it—who proclaimed this to Clamence? Are not the two central problems which concern Camus—how a man can keep from committing suicide and how a man can become a saint without God —characteristic marks of an insight in which the subject of misery is dealt with twice? For the second question is no more tenable or palatable than the first, and thus both questions indicate man's titanic flight from the oppressive feeling of the absence of the accuser, who nevertheless confronts the continuing presence of guilt as the deputy of the Absent.

SHIFTS IN EMPHASIS

A part of the situation in which we find ourselves and in which the Word is spoken is also the deliberate shift, undertaken by a number of thinkers, to a new way of getting beyond the problem of being human or of being a modern human being. Humanism in its renovated and deepened form may be regarded as such a shift of emphasis. If the gods are silent, if the 'godhead' has faded into unreality, then man has a chance to lift his voice in serenity. We may doubt whether this voice actually comes out of that realm 'beyond' the problem and that the answers have really weathered the ambivalence of nihilism. Humanism may be regarded as a torso, a truncated Christianity, an indefensible ethos, and a short cut, but our attitude must be mainly one of gratitude. In any case, what we have here is a resistance to the rise of the 'fourth man.' It seems to me to be folly—indeed, I consider it a crime —to apply to the man for whom the 'godhead' is silent a kind of theory which must first reduce him to misery and wretchedness. It is a mistaken idea of methodology that before one can awaken the ability to hear the Word of God, one must first make a man poorer, more miserable, and more despairing than he is. Despair as a way to God, the demolition of man's self-confidence, the use of negations as a point of contact, the destruction of the 'fictions of world views'—these methods, in my opinion, not only hold no promise but also fail to recognize the truth that because of the way we are, our whole bent and attitude, we simply cannot refrain from clinging to these our inner faculties and potentialities. More than a quarter century ago Karl Barth said with very penetrating insight: 'That "loss of certainty" of the natural knowledge of God, that destruction of the "fictions of world views" which I can with my little piece of despair undertake and carry out, is bound to issue in the erection of the worst of all idols, namely, a so-called "truth," from the throne of which *I* consider myself able to see through all gods and unmask them as idols. The better I succeed in despairing, the more certainly this must be the end. The world which *I* have cleared of gods is truly neither the kingdom of the living God nor even a preparation for it, but probably the worst of all forms of diabolism, by which I can oppose that kingdom.'[35]

When I speak of shifts in emphasis which seek to get beyond the modern problems, however, I am thinking more of individuals, pioneers, spies, minds with a special kind of radar to discern what is coming.

Romano Guardini (who in his many writings has performed the great service of paving the way for a dialogue between the church and the world, between Christianity and culture on the highest level)

[35] Karl Barth, 'No! Answer to Emil Brunner' in *Natural Theology*, tr. Peter Fraenkel (London: Geoffrey Bles, 1946), pp. 119f; cf. his *Church Dogmatics*, Vol. III, pt. 2, pp. 325–344 (on the *humanum* as an ontological category).

cautiously begins to sketch out in his challenging book *The End of the Modern World* the outlines of a world in which nature, the individual, culture, and technology will function in a different way now that we have experienced the silence of the gods and discovered how wrong the modern view of man, the positivistic as well as the idealistic, has been. 'The wilderness in its first form has been subdued; external nature has been tamed to obedience. But now it is re-emerging within culture itself, and its proper element is the very thing which subdued the first wilderness, namely, power itself. In this *second wilderness* all the abysses of the primeval age have been opened up again.'[36] Since, in a cosmology which is hardly conceivable and can no longer be visualized at all, we have arrived at a 'non-natural nature,' we find ourselves in a 'noncultural culture,' and thus we suffer from a non-autonomous autonomy and a nonreligious religion. 'Everywhere within it he [i.e., the Christian in the modern world] found ideas and values whose Christian origin was obvious, but which were declared to be the common property of all. Everywhere he encountered what was peculiarly and specifically Christian, but which was turned around and used *against* him. . . . These obfuscations will be cleared up. When the coming age sets itself against Christianity, it will do so in real earnest. It will declare that the secularized "Christianisms" are sentimentalities, and this *will clear the air*. It will be full of hostility and danger, but the issue will be clear-cut and open.' The message of faith will come out of an ever deeper loneliness—this is inherent in the eschatological character of the age which is preparing to supplant and supersede the 'modern age.'

The fault that appears to me to lie in such a projection of the future is that it fails to see the shadow of the 'eclipse of God' that lies also upon one's own religion, and that here the clarity of a new hostility is not the reflection of that completely different clarity which the Word of God creates when it judges all religion, including our own, and rejects it for our good and for our liberation.

Another figure who represents a shift, a resistance, is Ernst Jünger— formerly an extreme representative of an aggressive nihilism, later the

[36 This and the following quotations are newly translated; they may be found in a looser version in Romano Guardini, *The End of the Modern World: A Search for Orientation*, tr. Joseph Theman and Herbert Burke (New York: Sheed and Ward, 1956), pp. 111, 107, 128f.—Tr.]

celebrator of a new type of humanity in *Der Arbeiter* (*The Worker*), and during the war, and after it, arriving at a new insight into the ambivalence of nihilism, both of what we have called the 'genuine' and the 'ungenuine' kind. In his book *Über die Linie* (*Over the Line*—what is meant is: beyond the boundary line, the realm of death, the zone where nihilism is impotent) he clearly believes that he can discern the signs of a new age. In his case one cannot easily have any doubt with regard to the depths of his experiences. In his entire work, for example, even in his war diary, *Strahlungen* (*Radiations*) we find a furious earnestness, which is similar to Camus's basic note primarily in that its central question is that of suicide, that is, the question of how a man can justify not destroying himself. But he is clearly aware of the 'presumptuousness' of radical despair. 'The difficulty of defining nihilism lies in the fact that it is impossible for the mind to form a conception of Nothingness. It approaches the zone in which perception and cognition, the two great means on which it depends, disappear. . . . Hence nihilism will relate *only to the outskirts, the suburbs of Nothingness* and never to Fundamental Power itself.'[37] He then refers to suicide—as a gesture on the outskirts—as it occurs in the characters of the works of Dostoevski, Malraux, and Bernanos. There, he says, the process of annihilation is not only described in literary form, but is also realized. The artist not only chooses dissolution as a theme, he identifies himself with this process. It comes out in his language, in the colour of his speech. This shift is not something which can be induced. The resistance to this haunting obsession, which so many endure behind the mask of a quiet unruffled life, bearing down upon the masses like a universal despondency, cannot be organized. And yet it is taking place, sparked by unknown regenerative forces. It is taking place visibly not only in the direction which theoretical physics is taking but above all in the fact that the modern novel and modern drama (in so far as they are important and thus are given a hearing) are to a large extent doing nothing but discussing theological questions. Compare, for example, the work of Mauriac, Graham Green, T. S. Eliot, Christopher Fry.

Jünger does not believe in the coming of the robot man; he is not willing to settle for a nonhuman man. This resistance movement has

[37] Ernst Jünger, *Über die Linie* (1950), p. 12; cf. Karl Barth, *Church Dogmatics*, Vol. III, pt. 3, pp. 334ff. (on the ultimate unseriousness of the concept of Nothingness in Heidegger and Sartre).

shown that there are other energies of simple faith, stubborn loyalty, and heroic sacrifice which have been repressed but not destroyed by modern civilization.[38] He is deeply concerned with the question whether there will be room for these hidden energies. A third world war would smother the last chance of this happening. War is the real exponent of nihilism, the demonic translation into action of the denial of God, though here and there moral or objective motivations are even now being put forward to camouflage the insane will to self-destruction. The prevention of war will therefore depend upon the churches, because the unmasking of nihilism is primarily their concern and their task. '*The true defeat of nihilism*, and thus peace, will be possible only with the help of the churches. Just as the reliability of a man in the new democratic state rests not upon his internationality but rather upon his nationality, his [spiritual] relationship must be directed not to indifference but rather to a confession of faith. He must know his native home, both in space as well as in infinity, in time as well as in eternity. And this education to the full life, to the whole man must be rooted in a *higher certainty* than that which can be provided by the state and its schools and universities.'

Jünger, then, cannot avoid going on to speak of preaching and theology. He is annoyed with the obtuseness with which we continue to follow the incorrigible liberal tradition of refusing to take theology seriously 'as a science.' It is true that theology needs renovation, because it must be able to approach in new forms the rational being that modern man is or thinks he is. 'To be sure, in order to do justice to this requirement, theology dare not continue to remain a second-class subject of study. On the contrary, not only the best hearts but also the *best minds, the finest spirits* must devote themselves to theology, the highest of the sciences—those who do not find their satisfaction in the individual disciplines or even in philosophy, but are rather coordinated with the whole, the *universum*.'[39] 'Since the atrophy manifests itself primarily as an illness, it is no wonder that physicians especially are addressing themselves to it, and doing so with very ingenious methods of taking depth soundings and basing therapies upon them. In one of the first places among the types of patients who consult them is the

[38] Ernst Jünger, *Der Waldgang* (1951), pp. 41f., 77f.
[39] Ernst Jünger, *Der Friede: Ein Wort an die Jugend Europas, ein Wort an die Jugend der Welt*.

person who has an urge to kill his father. One seeks in vain for the other kind who has lost his father and whose illness lies in the fact that he does not know what he has lost.'[40]

When we realize how many there are in the younger generation among whom Jünger finds a hearing, this is good news, because this too can be a sign that a 'conversion' is possible even among the groups and coteries with a past and even among the betrayed elite (who have been betrayed by their own attitude of betrayal). And we are inclined to attribute to this sign a certain symbolical regenerative power of far-ranging significance. And yet here too an objection must be raised, namely, that here again religion is rehabilitated, this time in the form of a refuge from chaos. Even though Jünger comes from another camp, from a less enclosed world than does Guardini, he too has failed to recognize that the ambivalence of religion is the breeding ground of nihilism. He too, in my opinion, tends to treat both of them with an 'absolute' seriousness. He too, it would appear, does not realize that the gods by their very nature are silent and that the 'eclipse of God' is only the terminal point of a self-overvaluation of man's capacity to believe. He too, despite the respect he pays to theology, lacks a proper perception of what is inherent in the specific category which we call 'the Word of God.'

In the third place our attention is drawn to the works of Eugen Rosenstock-Huessy which have appeared since the war, *Atem des Geistes* (*Breath of the Spirit*, 1951) and *Heilkraft und Wahrheit* (*Healing Power and Truth*, 1952). This great historian and sociologist [author of the standard work *Die europäischen Revolutionen* (*The European Revolution*), who was already writing works on the criticism of culture shortly after the First World War] never took nihilism very seriously. Why not? The answer tallies with the result of our reflections upon the silence of the gods, the 'godhead.' The answer is that he never took nihilism quite seriously because he never took religion quite seriously. He was a Jew—a member, participant, and a spokesman of a circle of Jewish intellectuals which also included Franz Rosenzweig, Hans Ehrenberg, and Rudolf Ehrenberg. He came to Christ (as did the others in the circle, with the striking and epoch-making exception of Rosenzweig, who, we may perhaps say, took the reverse direction and, though already on the threshold of the church, went back to the synagogue).

[40] Ernst Jünger, *Der Waldgang*, pp. 92f.

As a Christian, Rosenstock-Huessy remained Jewish in his whole habitude of mind. And from precisely this point of view he has been able to do much to make clear to us how radically differently the silence of the gods is experienced and interpreted when the Word becomes an event, takes on form, and makes history.

His latest works are insistently concerned with the miracle of language. He expresses the conviction that truth is dependent on language (and not vice versa), and that therefore it is defenceless against the violence done to speech, but that when God preserves it for us, it will reveal the healing powers which reside in it and, ultimately, in it alone. Rosenstock-Huessy's philosophy of language is far too complex to permit even a sketchy description of it here. Moreover, his own language is shot through with the flashes and gleams of discoveries which come from the mind of a genius. Thus he says, for example, in the preface to *Heilkraft und Wahrheit*: 'The sanctimonious have always complained that the world is transitory, and they have held up their truth as imperishable to the perishable world: this I understand quite well. But the living God has also made even the truth a creaturely thing. Instead of this blubbering over the transiency of the world, a counterfugue must also be heard, namely, the transiency of the truth. *The truth is more transitory than many other good creatures*, if no sacrifice comes to its aid. Within the compass of creation the truth is more mortal than a suckling child. Otherwise it would have been impossible for so many people to forget the truth! So it would be a great thing to make the truth at least as lasting as a creature. What am I saying? It *is* a great thing at a time when the peoples know that they have outlived their own truth. They are living in an unfavourable time. But God gave us the power to destroy the unfavourable time.'

Rosenstock-Huessy is aware that in all the sciences there is the beginning of a reversal parallel with that taking place in theoretical physics. That is to say, that (apart from the code of technical nomenclatures) it is not true that the concept exists before the word; and it is correct to say: 'Where concepts are lacking, a word presents itself at the right time,' that is, precisely where the words are lacking, the words from the 'wellsprings' of the mother tongue and the ancestral language of tradition. Just as Friso Melzer and Jean Gebser are illuminating the hierarchical structure of human consciousness by means of a careful analysis of the changes of meaning in the root words of the

Indo-Germanic languages, so Rosenstock-Huessy is examining the words of the 'fathers' tongue,' and this is concerned less with the precipitate than the root stock, less with the crown than the foundation of thought in communication.

'Language is the house of Being,' said Heidegger, and Jaspers says, 'Transcendence is the Being that never becomes the world, but that *speaks* as it were through the Being that is in the world.'[41] But to take this seriously means to break through the hierarchical structure of human consciousness to the specific logic of grammar without excluding from the field of experience the meanings with which words have been filled during the course of their history; and the field of experience is always essentially the realm of love, the 'I and thou.' Franz Rosenzweig said in a letter of July 9, 1917: 'From the beginning Rosenstock has mistrusted the "silent" God, because from the beginning he has believed in the Word.' And Rosenstock-Huessy wrote to his friend the following, which runs like a fundamental motif through his whole work: 'The Word became flesh—*on that statement, no doubt, everything depends.*' The only thinking that is worthwhile is that which 'has a standard *outside* of itself, in the *visible* life of God.' No wonder that to him many problems become pseudoproblems, engendered by an impaired and diseased language; and this includes all the rigid inferences of religion in the ongoing argumentation which its dogmatics carries on in a vacuum and also all the frenzied deductions of nihilism.

Even the great confusions in the life of the nations that lead to war and revolution grow out of diseased words which have conglomerated into ideological slogans for use in an 'it-world.' A universally valid judgment, which can be traced back to the transcendental unity of our consciousness, is possible only as long as a person remains a 'spectator'; *vis-à-vis* God and our fellow men such judgments are impossible, because neither God nor our neighbour is ever presented to us as an object. He, you, I—these constitute the basic form of language, because in them are reflected, nay, represented, the order of revelation. Moreover, the vocative and the imperative are more fundamental and more far-reaching than the indicative, and the form of cognition whose content is a command, an appeal, an outcry, an address of love is more

[41 Karl Jaspers, *The Perennial Scope of Philosophy*, tr. Ralph Manheim (New York: Philosophical Library, 1949), p. 12.—Tr.]

substantial than the form of cognition that relates to—describable—things and conditions. Language is a power that penetrates into the thing, the so-called 'given'—a life-changing, life-revolutionizing power. Prayer and command are the modes in which the living person meets the future. Outcries are the way in which he enters into the present, into the moment. Narratives are the mode in which he encounters the past. We cannot here reproduce what Rosenstock-Huessy has in mind when he speaks of a 'higher grammar.' We can only cite two theses: (a) substantives are also verbs; (b) names constitute the field of power.

If anybody should ask what all this has to do with the silence of the gods, with the intellectual hallucinations of subjectivism, with nihilism, he receives a straight answer: 'To give back to the vocative and the imperative their controlling character—this would do more to dispose of atheism and cynicism than all the pious tracts combined.' And that he is not only in dead earnest about this but also that he succeeds approximately (just as all 'speech about something' can only be an approximation) in making it true, this is borne in upon anyone who has learned from him (and from Franz Rosenzweig). Speech has been put in the world against death, against transiency, against the world's surrender to death, and against allowing the sinner to remain in death. And he who speaks in order to bear witness to the truth will cling to names—for names bear and convey the living action of communication in history—and he is himself transformed. The bringing of peace, the concluding of peace treaties, great and small, has 'healing power' only if such acts are done in sincerity while invoking names and proclaiming names.[42] Names always encompass our whole confession of faith. Therefore the time of 'mere antitheses' is past; and what we have left is nothing but the Name—or, if we betray it, the crushing weight of the silent gods, who provoke us to ever new abstractions and pitch us into the abyss of nihilism. Therefore creation in the healing, saving truth is not the first but the last creation. 'The pagan glorifies creation, Israel awaits it, the Christian experiences it.'

One of the most surprising consequences of this kind of thinking is that science itself emerges as a discipline for the care of souls, indeed, that by virtue of the very impulse of the methodical earnestness which it practises in human communication it is entirely and completely concerned with the care of souls. The individual as such is not the

[42] Eugen Rosenstock-Huessy, *Soziologie II* (1958), pp. 195ff., 624f.

receiver of knowledge, but rather the person in community: the teacher, the physician, the judge, the minister. And since the voiceless suffering of all creation erupts in every loving couple, the healing strength of knowledge is always in one way or another carried by a duality, by two persons together. For only he who speaks is a human being. And whatever he says aims at community, and only between two who trust and love each other is there anything to say. '*All know-ledge is deadly*; he who honestly cultivates science acquires the power to dissolve his object into nothingness. . . . Science always says: This is nothing more than. . . . By reducing everything to its elements, it deprives everything of its power over us. . . . But all love must prove itself in the face of death.'[43] Further: 'The higher intercourse of the couple who make use of science manifests itself in their undaunted listening to the truth, which thought intends that they should have. Yes, the truth is deadly. Therefore only the fidelity of him who really loves can triumph over it.' This philosophy then concludes with a question, an existential question, and sounds the note of encounter with God and our neighbour—the encounter that cuts straight through the silence of the gods and all the abstractions: '*Who is so faithful* that, thanks to his faithfulness, *all death*, which arises under the judgment of science, acquires meaning and leads to resurrection? Only the loved and loving person is capable of resurrection.'[44] Augustine said that as many periods and ages of life we must pass through, just so many times must we suffer death. On the way to hope!

Should not all this that we have heard be understood as a clue to how death amidst the silence of the gods may be transformed into a restoration? Through the Word! Through the truth which is healing and which brings life. The shift in thought which is here apparent carries the earnestness of existence into the innermost laboratory of science and releases the energy of the mind and spirit for the cure of souls.

[43] Ibid., p. 94.   [44] Ibid., p. 97.

37

THE CHRISTIAN-RELIGIOUS CONTINUITY [45]

We could mention other utterances aimed at the overcoming of nihilism.[46] We content ourselves with these few voices. It is conspicuous and characteristic of the situation in which the church (but also culture) finds itself that among the majority there are no voices of youth. Even the leaders of youth have only a changing and fluctuating picture of what 'modern' youth really is and wants.[47] Also noteworthy in the shift of attitude which is recommended and conjured up with words is the little account taken of the economic changes that still lie ahead of us. There still remains a basic Christian and religious stock, a continuity which is taken into account and by which one lives; and, as a matter of fact, there has never been a revolution which did not leave untouched, indeed, which did not save or even strengthen, a remainder, a basic stock or capital. Could nihilism be an exception to this? Could 'genuine' nihilism antiquate the essence of classical philosophy? Could it be that 'ungenuine' nihilism may completely lose sensibility to everything that comes from God or from the gods? This is improbable if only for the reason that the church and the synagogue still exist as very conspicuous phenomena. It is true that they have been declared to be mere survivals, but they simply cannot be dismissed in this way. Now the tide seems to be turning. The devout tradition is now going over to the offence, and we have a book entitled *Questions Christianity Addresses to the Modern World!*[48]

On the basis of the experience of this basic capital, however filtrated it may be, not a few are obliged to admit that many of our conceptions of life as well as our emotional reactions, our ideals and projects, are

[45 The term here used is *Bestand*, which can mean 'stock,' 'capital,' 'subsistence,' 'remainder,' and by the author's own extension, 'continuity,' 'continuum.'—Tr.]

[46] For example, Julien Benda, Georges Duhamel, Louis Lavelle, and naturally Gabriel Marcel, 'Remarks on Contemporary Irreligion,' in *Being and Having*, tr. Katharine Farrar (London: Dacre Press, 1950), and 'The Refusal of Salvation,' in *Homo Viator*, tr. Emma Crauford (New York: Harper Torchbook, 1962), pp. 185–212; and Georges Gusdorf, *Mythe et métaphysique*, pp. 241f.

[47] See, for example, the special number *Jeugd* ('Youth') of the periodical *Wending* (1954), which contains abundant material, giving evidence of a patient and ingenious attempt at interpretation, but with no unified conception which would give us an image of this generation.

[48 The title of a book by Helmut Thielicke.—Tr.]

by their very nature still 'Christian,' that they stem from the primitive mission and that they have their standard in the Bible. I am thinking of Spengler, Huizinga, Toynbee, Rauschning, Eliot, and others. Must we now accept that there is a contradiction between the discovery and recognition of a living, viable continuum and what we previously said about nihilism? No, for the question is whether the silence of the gods, the impotence of religion is not also having its effect upon this continuity, this remaining stock of piety. It was inevitable that the ambivalence of religion and the relativity of the 'absolute' projection should also manifest itself here. Here, too, Christianity, precisely as part of the religious stock, had to submit involuntarily to a continuing demonstration of the necessity of relativizing everything—a necessity which governs thought as well as life because we must escape the doom of the absolute even though a radical relativization cannot be carried out except by assuming that there is an absolute.

Once it is accepted that the 'exceptionality' of Israel is and continues to be an existing fact, that Israel is ruled by a god whose holiness in history is dependent upon his people,[49] is it not then evident that Israel, too, and Israel especially, is 'religious' and that in actual practice the historical form which this religiosity took in history is practically the opposite of what was intended? And does not the same apply to the church, because this reciprocal relation between God and man on which the continuity is based aspires far too high—or (to put it the other way around) because it puts too low an estimate upon the superiority of God in this relationship? I believe that both are true, and this invests the continuum with a heightened ambiguity of such fatality, of such vertiginous and, even in its finest achievements, revolting pretentiousness that even in modern times it can evoke prophetic wrath. The God who claimed to be superior to the existing gods is pretentiously betrayed in the pretensions of his confessors. The 'continuum' which comfortably evades the assault (*Anfechtung*) of nihilism may be superior in range and endurance to those tenuous 'shifts in emphasis' which are trying to get beyond nihilism, and yet on the other hand it is capable of producing an induration, intellectual and moral (which is not identical with what is considered to be outworn dogma and morality) but above all 'religious,' an introverted fanaticism which makes a mockery of any 'exceptionality' of a people that

[49] Fokke Sierksma, 'Volk zonder land,' in *Podium*, V. 319.

sanctifies itself before God and sanctifies the world to God! For he is its guarantor and dependent. He is the exponent of the continuum. He is bound to accept our petitions.

It was against this that the young Karl Barth turned.[50] And all the liberal lords and orthodox brethren mounted the barricades as one man against this kind of negativism and 'nihilism,' enraged by this emptying of life, this denial of culture and the process of culture, this affront to the faith (i.e., religion). For this wild iconoclast not only said that the gods were silent but that *this* God is a dead God and that he deserved to die. The silence of *this* God, he said, is the same thing as his being dead, because he and he alone has brought the glory of the Word into the world. But he has been made an object, reduced to merely the other party of a religious relationship, degraded to the role of a partner in a moral world plan, who when he lost the Word lost his essence, simply because from the very beginning the nature that was his nature could be found nowhere except in the Word. I know very well that *The Epistle to the Romans* was only a beginning, a prelude to a lifework quite different in range and depth; but what was uttered there and then as a prophetic protest remains valid as long as it is not recognized that the transition from religion to nihilism is structurally inevitable and as long as we do not realize that it was love that called forth all these negative statements of the young Barth. It may be apropos to quote here a few passages from the second edition of *The Epistle to the Romans* (1922), in which the 'nihilism' of the prophets resounds.

In protest against all romanticism we must be reminded again and again that our life on this side of the resurrection is an unending complex of the highest and the lowest, the noblest and the meanest, the most significant and the most unutterably banal possibilities. Man is characterized by art, science, and morality, and a fervent longing for communion with the infinite—yes, but also, God knows, by hunger and thirst, the sexual urge, somnolence, and the digestive process, and where is the line between the two to be drawn? . . . We *exist* in this ambiguity and nowhere else, and in broad areas this is completely clear. (pp. 311f.)[51]

[50] In his *Epistle to the Romans* and other early writings.
[51] This and the following passages have been freshly translated. The page references are to Karl Barth, *The Epistle to the Romans*, tr. Edwyn C. Hoskyns (Oxford: Oxford Univ. Press, 1933), a loose and frequently inaccurate translation.—Tr.

All the consolations, all the answers *we* try to give are inadequate and spurious, for *we* ourselves come from this questionable background. . . . The harmony which *we* postulate is relative to our disharmony, the Fata Morgana of our wandering in the desert. And the God whom we allow to exercise retribution and the balancing of accounts in a 'better' world to come is—if he were to be encountered, for example, by an Ivan Karamazov—a non-God, a God of this world, fashioned after the image of man and thus also not exempt from human criticism, indeed, from *human denials*. (p. 303)

The church is the place, on this side of the abyss that separates man from God, where revelation . . . has now become something given, commonplace, and taken for granted, where the lightning from heaven has become a dull, earthly, slow-burning fire, where the deprivation and discovery has become possession and enjoyment . . . and the 'Beyond' is transformed into a metaphysical 'something' over against 'this side' and thus into a mere prolongation of it, a place where we know and possess all kinds of things about God, and consequently do *not* know them and do *not* possess them. (p. 332)

There the ambivalence is revealed. And if anything can be said about the youth of today, it is that they suspect that something of this ambivalence exists.

Thus forty years ago a young pioneer attacked the continuum, unmasked the continuity as a danger, exposed religion in its impossible claim to fixate the Holy while it itself is fixated upon its incurable ambiguity. He did this not as an outsider but rather as an insider, not in hostility but rather in solidarity. And he did it on the strength of the call to point to the absolute boundary that lies in God, in his perfect sovereignty, which is at the same time the perfection of his nearness. He who takes his stand on the vantage ground of the 'continuum' and no longer sees this boundary turns the continuum into an idol and a hindrance. And he who recovers this view of the boundary sees the 'children of the world,' the 'third' (or 'fourth') 'man' of this and the coming ages, in a different light.

The church, no matter what its name, has all around it the heathen, the strangers, those who do not understand, the nonparticipating, those who do not seek after righteousness. This fact in itself is for those of finer sensibility a disturbing, perhaps in its quiet eloquence an intolerable, fact. . . . What is the state of a sanctuary if it goes on indefinitely being only the *peculiar* sanctuary of certain people here and there, but fails to command universal respect? What is the status of the 'Word of God' if we have to admit that when it is uttered by us nobody outside has much to say against it, but also that nobody has much to say for what we present? . . . *They have no religious interest, because God long ago interested himself in them.* . . . The children of the world, the unholy, the unbelieving in all their naked misery, and perhaps also in all their carefree gaiety are *not objects* of our preaching and pastoral care, our evangelism, missions, apologetics, and saving activity, for long before *we* appeared upon the scene to have mercy upon them, they had been sought and found by God's mercy, already they stood under the light of God's righteousness, already sharing in forgiveness, already participating in the power of the resurrection and the power of obedience, already appalled by Eternity and already hoping for it, already thrown existentially upon God. (p. 364)

What goes on *within man*, all the way from the spiritual exercises in a Benedictine monastery to the philosophical discussion groups in Social-Democratic meeting houses, these are all rungs on a *single* ladder. But that poverty in spirit, that absolutely nonchurchly attitude, which Jesus called blessed and which makes the Gentiles righteous before God, nobody has yet been able to boast of, because as such it has never existed. (p. 409)

Faith, unlike 'piety,' is not a thing which one can boast of, which one can weigh up before God and men and play off against them, something on which one can climb up. . . . *God* decides, and like his goodness, so also his severity (because it is *his* goodness, *his* severity) is new every morning. (p. 411)

Such statements must inevitably have consequences on the practical, political level. And thus we are shaken by the question he asks: 'What legality is there which is not at its root illegal? What authority is not tyranny precisely in that which makes it authority?' (p. 479)

No wonder that from the vantage point of the continuum, which walls us off from critical attack, such charges were scorned and repelled as negativism, rejected as a philosophy of despair! No wonder that the man who lived in the opinion that the gods are silent, but that 'his' God had spoken and put the truth into the hands of the religious people felt that this impugned his piety, that this was an assault upon his most precious possession! Nobody wanted to hear anything about the limits of religion, because here there was the presentiment that at these limits the ambivalence of the whole enterprise which is called religion would be exposed. And even more serious would be the consequences for order, the state, law, and society.

'It is, of course, true that there can be no more energetic *undermining* of the existing order than the sober, unceremonious, undeluded acceptance of it which is here recommended. The state, church, society, positive law, family, organized research, etc. really live on the credulity of man which must be constantly nourished by inspirational, morale-building *élan* and solemn humbug of all kinds. Take away their pathos and they would most certainly be starved out!' (p. 483)

Today we probably see more clearly the (nonhuman) heights and the (inconceivable) remoteness from which all these negative statements could and have to be made. These 'nihilistic' insights grow out of the recognition of the Word of God. Where 'nihilistic' insights come as the cause of a crisis, it becomes apparent that we have retreated into the religious stock and that we and our lives have not yet been brought, or have ceased to live, under the open heaven of the Word of God. Therefore it was possible for a great joy and a new freedom to come out of this kind of emptiness and disillusionment.

Human suffering, human guilt, human fate—as they are grimly and ceaselessly revealed in the highly dubious face and the highly *dubious life-story* of every individual, in the frenzy of our cities and the dullness of our villages, in the banal force of the primitive necessities of our life and in the estrangement of our knowledge and conscience from the world, in the terrors of birth and death, in the *riddle of nature* that cries out from every stone and the back of every tree, in the futility of the cycles of world history . . . —have in them, nevertheless a *voice* and a *light*. And the man who has *once* heard that voice and seen that light, and heard and seen them existentially, and therefore not psychologically, sociologically, historically, or scientifically, not in any sense exclusive, academic, superior, impartial, but also in no sense 'pious,' 'religiously detached,' and completely free of the surreptitious presupposition of a providence and harmony this whole, but rather existentially, which is to say, earnestly, set on fire, *himself thrown out of the saddle* . . . the man who has inescapably, irretrievably heard and seen with the eyes and ears of an Ivan Karamazov—that man no longer questions, but hears and sees. What does he see? Himself! As a believer . . .? No, a thousand times no. He rather sees himself confronted by the wholly impossible, the *absolute* contradiction, which ultimately cannot be justified, and can *never, never be reduced to a concept of God*. . . . Completely incapable of doing anything except cry out or remain silent . . . he nevertheless sees himself as God's child! For in, with, and under *this* hearing and seeing there is manifestly the cry, Abba! Father!—even though this man had never heard the name of God and even if *at the same time* he were to blaspheme it. In, with, and under this horror the man feels about himself, the new man, the man of a new world, is manifestly born; the theodicy, beside which all other theodicies are but mockery, has been effected and God has justified himself before us and thus justified us before himself. (p. 299)

As we have said, *The Epistle to the Romans* is only the first approach to a work whose range and stature was quite different; and since that time many statements in it have been withdrawn. But yet in principle, in the relativization of human religion, Barth has not yielded.

And yet we ask ourselves, after having received a brief shock, whether the continuum is not in process of re-establishing itself—in the church and the synagogue. Perhaps the tone of the protest was too strong, too prophetic, too 'one-sided.'

All in all, the question still remains whether these isolated, still, small voices, these breakthroughs which have occurred here and there —I am thinking of Guardini, Jünger, and Rosenstock-Huessy—are not making clearer what is implied in 'the end of the modern world' than church and synagogue appear to be aware of in their broadly established certainties.

UNSTABLE BALANCE

'God is dead'—this outcry or this assertion (or even this veiled invocatory appeal) is interpreted with great subtlety today. Sartre, for example, declares that it does not mean that there is no God, and that it also does not refer to His transiency; but rather that in times past He spoke to us and now He is silent; 'now we touch only His corpse.'[52] The strange thing about this is that, though 'Transcendence' is silent, the religious need persists, and that many thinkers (like Jaspers, for

[52] Jean-Paul Sartre, *Situations*, I (1947), pp. 153, 237.

example) continue to plague themselves with it. The answer that is given is that man must take upon himself the creative freedom attributed to God in order that in an unexpected way he may himself become creative, that is, in positing himself, designing his world, creating his future.

Why does this God remain silent? Is it not because, long before Sartre allowed him to vanish as an object in an object-subject relationship, Christianity and Judaism and Islam thought of him (and thereby rendered him innocuous) as a given, to which man could or could not stand in an I-thou relationship? Is it not because this divinity has become a stable element in our human mode of thinking, an element in the long run incapable of proving its usefulness? And now, according to Sartre, it is only a matter of humanism anyhow. The choice as to whether this humanism shall be with or without God, the decision for or against God, has become irrelevant, because it affects only a mental construct and, what is more, a mental construct which performs no function of any use and advantage to the *humanum*.

Heidegger also gives us a subtle interpretation of the death of God.[53] To be sure, he believes that Nietzsche in his cry 'God is dead' meant also to exclude metaphysics, even the classical concept of truth. This, however, does not decide the possibility of a Being of God or a 'Being towards God.' First one must know what 'Being' actually is; it requires a long preparation to elucidate the ontological significance of the words we use. In the first place, Heidegger assures us, we are not atheists and not nihilists. But at the same time he warns against religion and above all the prophetic principle in its Jewish-Christian signification. And so he too seeks to play off a 'god that is (perhaps) coming' against the 'gods that have fled'; he speaks of a future in which 'God and the gods' may possibly speak to us again,[54] though then both of them would present themselves only as forms of 'Being'—as forms of something which is still far from being adequately explained in conceptual terms, but of which this much can be tentatively said in connection with religion and nihilism, namely, that it is not God and not a world-ground.[55] 'Being is farther away than all entities and is nevertheless

[53] Martin Heidegger, *Holzwege* (1950), pp. 193ff.
[54] Martin Heidegger, 'Hölderlin and the Essence of Poetry,' in *Existence and Being*, tr. Douglas Scott (Chicago: Henry Regnery, 1949), p. 313.
[55] Martin Heidegger, *Platons Lehre von der Wahrheit* (1947), p. 76.

closer to man than any entity, whether this be . . . *an angel or God.* Being is the closest.' In this mirror of our times we need not quarrel over the ultimate meaning of such statements, if only the general tendency of the whole has become clear.

It is clear that in this way, pursuing a tortuous detour, thinking again issues in paganism, in the veneration of the fundamental forces and primitive forms of Being—a veneration which can in fact and in the full sense be called religious. This 'illumination of Being' means a 'rediscovery' of the truth, the essence of truth, the unhidden. Is it a *re*discovery?

Thus a way seems to be found by which it is possible to live in (or in proximity to) nihilism—a way based on assertions, to be sure, but, formally, everything that is alleged in the realm of these questions, no matter how much it may be approached, constructed, or dressed up with rational means, is assertion. Religious theses too are 'assertions.' It is this formal similarity which causes many to imagine that they can evade the real decisions in the question of God. This delusion is one of the factors that determines the realm in which preaching occurs today. An eloquent example of this is the humanist-minded scepticism of the *'honnête homme'* ('honest man') of the school of Menno ter Braak, in the work of H. A. Gomperts and Pierre H. Dubois.[56] Here a keen intelligence is applied—in essay style—to justify the decision to make no decisions and nevertheless to conceal the fact that a decision has been made in favour of humanity. The main point in this was to set up a doctrine which could serve as a prop for the political noncomformism of the kind which was painfully born of the illegality of the occupation period.

Dubois uses the word 'truth' in quotation marks in order to indicate that the 'posture (a posture) in time,' which he believes he must assume and can maintain in stable balance, is not a truth, but that it performs exactly the function which was formerly performed by the truth in religion and in culture.[57] This *'our truth'* coincides with the absurd (which in turn is identified with 'non-knowing'). It is *the* truth which (unlike the central problem of Camus's earlier works) does not compel him to commit suicide, because 'it does not compel us to any single act; but it also does not forbid us to commit any single act.' He wants not

[56] H. A. Gomperts, *Jagen om te leven*; Pierre H. Dubois, *Een houding in de tijd.*
[57] Dubois, op. cit., pp. 141f.

so much to rely on this 'truth' but rather to live with it, nay, to live *it*, to realize it. And what he wants to realize is that the conclusion of all that is implicit in this 'posture' (='truth') is to come to no conclusion at all. A doctrinaire, he says, would say that this is nothing but a 'euphemism for negativity.' The author replies: Perhaps! But the problem is not so simple; and for one thing it must be pointed out that the negativity in this absence of any conclusion means something entirely different from the absence of a posture. Then follow these words which are indicative of the unstable balance (in the inevitable realm of nihilism): 'The question mark we put after the "meaning of life" contains a large number of possibilities, because it does nothing more than to corroborate the conflict between the logic of the head and the logic of the heart.'

Thus, to that extent, we are back with Lessing and Jacobi or even with Pierre Bayle. But then follow these words: 'The absurd, viewed as a "wall," obstructs action, *all* action, or makes it meaningless; the absurd, viewed as non-knowing, leaves everything free.'

We have the impression that here we find the exact opposite of what existential philosophy has tried to teach us, namely, that this freedom is the consistent maintenance of the spectator's attitude. No wonder, then, that the author comes up against this question: 'But what then? On what do we base our morality?' And the answer, again very surprising, is that it is 'not upon this our "truth," not upon this conclusion-less conclusion.' He believes (despite the 'wall,' concerning which he has previously said some rather radical things with regard to actual practice) that with a 'calm heart' he can make a distinction 'between philosophy and practical life.' He asserts that he experiences a reality, which is not our deepest 'truth,' but is nevertheless real. 'Because our truth leaves so much room for *a* general concept of *man* [italics mine,] we can yield to the demands of the heart without coming into conflict with our "truth".' It is hardly possible to follow this argument, but the conclusion is completely unintelligible: 'The demands of the heart —but then one *would like to* call them the practical morality of our truth'—unintelligible, that is, if one puts all the emphasis upon this (arbitrary, absurd) 'would like to.'

In this way the author believes that he can also escape the necessity of choosing between faith and unbelief. He rejects Camus's decision in favour of unbelief—not because this choice would trouble him (would the opposite choice trouble him as little?), but rather, he says, because I challenge the necessity of choosing, 'at least I question that choosing should be a consequence of the logic of absurdity.' This form of unstable balance (in the realm of nihilism) achieves the most astonishing state of floating suspension when he says (and it is always a matter of his *saying* so): 'Our morality clings to *uncertainty* as our sole stay, the only one which has been able to hold its ground after all and in the midst of all the "absolute" truths which history has seen pass away.' He makes his own the words of Unamuno: 'If it is nothingness that awaits us, let us so act that it shall be an unjust fate,' and he believes that he has Pascal on his side when Pascal speaks of the Night (*la Nuit* here 'religiously' capitalized), in which lies the true wisdom for man.

We have discussed these reflections and assertions not because they are philosophically acceptable but because they are humanly respectable and also in many respects representative of the time in which the Word is proclaimed today. Here we also see how 'genuine' and 'ungenuine' nihilism overlap, how the intellectual elite is not very far away from the 'fourth man,' and how here again religion lingers on with its 'absolute' truths, its 'Beyond,' and its own peculiar ambiguity. Dubois, if he felt inclined to do so, could go on and say the same thing as Kenneth Patchen and Theodore Powys; he could in all earnestness —in a free-floating earnestness—join in Bertolt Brecht's 'Great Hymn of Thanksgiving.' He does not believe that Janko Janeff's prophecy of a return of the ancient gods will be fulfilled; he would laugh over a new religion. He sits in the cell of 'autonomy,' completely imprisoned by it; the gods are silent and God is dead; and yet he could (by cancelling out his absurd 'truth' with *a single* absurdity, since he has theoretically reserved room to do this) accept as his own what C. Moeller describes in *Le sens de Dieu dans la littérature contemporaine* as the shocking, or pathetic, inconsistency of the 'fourth man.' What is his motivation? The desire to salvage humanity as the reverse side of nonconformism!

It follows from this that we must be careful in the human judgments we make. As I expressed it above, it is precisely this ambivalence that is genuine, human, and warm. Humanism in its vacillation and inconstancy has the same basic structure of inconstancy which was peculiar to religion.

48

ECLIPSE OF GOD

Eclipse of God is the title of one of the later works of Martin Buber. This title provides a good opportunity to approach the point at which the sphere of nihilism and the voice of the Old Testament are tangent to each other.

1. That which we are experiencing today, the process in which all of us are involved, could be called an eclipse of God—in the sense that human thinking has dimmed and darkened God's light (or the light of the concept of God) for us and our fellows. It is possible to formulate the process in this way, provided that one is not so bold as to assert that it was genuine, lucid, consistent thinking that produced it, but rather confines oneself to the observation that in this period of the history of thought human thinking has in fact brought many people to this conclusion. If one starts with the assumption that man's reason is self-sufficient and is itself its own adequate foundation, if one regards the categories of Being as something which the subject brings into the chaos of experience, if one believes that the 'existence' of man means that man is a being of himself and toward himself—then this eclipse cannot fail to appear. But it is a *destructio* that deserves to be opposed with a *destructio destructionis*.[58] This is where a philosophical offensive could be launched!

2. What we are experiencing today can be called an 'eclipse of God' also in the sense that God has been 'stolen,' 'embezzled' from us, not only (or at least not conclusively) through thought but also through the totality of our experience (cf. Franz Werfel, *Embezzled Heaven*).[59] Inherent then in this totality of our experience, apart from our ultimately unfathomable fate, are especially those experiences to which we open ourselves by means of 'religious' experience. 'God' has been alienated from us through the inner contradictoriness, indeed, the impossibility, of the way in which we have accustomed ourselves to knowing, possessing, making him a mere partner, and passing off 'his' (as we imagined) world as a good world, the way in which we learned

[58] Cf. the conclusion of *Inleiding tot de Wijsbegeerte* by A. E. Loen, pp. 172ff.
[[59] The Dutch word for 'eclipse of God' is *Godsverduistering*. The verb *verduisteren* means, among other things, to 'steal,' 'purloin,' 'embezzle.'—Tr.]

to practise submission, and attempted to fulfil his commandment. Religion turns out to be that human undertaking which may be called not only the most comprehensive but also the most untenable. Here an experience is urged upon us which ends in the silence of the gods and the godhead and which has found its simplest definition in the outcry or assertion (however one may interpret it) that 'God is dead,' uttered by those who have become most conscious of the 'eclipse of God.'

3. Finally, what we are experiencing can in fact be called the 'eclipse of God' in order in this way to convey either that God is 'hidden' especially for us and our contemporaries or that he, when he is rightly seen, is in principle 'hidden.' And this too reflects an aspect of our situation. Buber himself, however, says in the book with this title—though more in the form of a question than a declaration—that that which has come over us could by its very nature be identical with the darkness that occurs when God hides himself. 'Let us ask ourselves whether it may not be literally true that God formerly spoke to us and is now silent, and whether this is not to be understood as the Hebrew Bible understands it, namely, that the living God is not only a self-revealing but also a "self-concealing" God.' Buber then refers to Isaiah 45 : 15, 'Truly, thou art a God who hidest thyself, O God of Israel, the Saviour.'[60]

THE WORD

The question that forces itself upon us when this possibility or this possible interpretation is considered brings us directly to that entity which is called God's 'Word.' In Isaiah 45 : 15 and in related passages in the whole of the Old Testament in which the fact itself is referred to, even though the words 'hidden' or 'hiddenness' are not used, it is everywhere evident that nobody knows about this self-concealment or hiddenness unless he has been told of it. It is true that the term 'hiddenness of God' (like the term 'the unknown God') includes a logical foreknowledge in which what is intended is an object of which we have a certain prescience, but 'hiddenness' also includes a dramatic biographical tension of possessing and not possessing. If, beyond this,

[60] Martin Buber, *Eclipse of God: Studies in the Relation Between Religion and Philosophy* (New York: Harper Torchbooks, 1957), p. 66.

a quality is ascribed to this 'hiddenness,' which naturally points at the same time to the quality of the Hidden itself, then we are confronted with a maximum of spiritual suffering, at least if this hiddenness is taken in full earnestness.

The complete negativity implied in this 'hiddenness' is charged with a remembrance, a presentiment of, a yearning for the revelation of a mystery, a revelation in which the mystery of our own existence would also be revealed. But as soon as 'hiddenness' is understood as an act of God, as one of the turnings of his sovereign freedom, as the withdrawal and closing up of his sovereign grace, then we have heard a dictum, a self-proclamation, then we find ourselves in the realm, the field of power, of the Word. This is especially clear in the text and context of Isaiah 45 : 15. Here there would be abundant opportunity to arrive at more conclusive, but also more happy, insights with respect to the intricacies of nihilism. That is to say, the thing is not so tragic as it is painted or even as it actually—and quite 'honestly'—presents itself to be. For to declare the hiddenness of God is in itself a confession of faith, and the discovery of the silence of the gods is only an accompanying, a secondary, acknowledgment.

It is valuable to note that, even according to our spontaneous perception, the 'incomprehensibility of the godhead' is a paltry, humourless, and sterile insight; whereas the hiddenness of God, pregnant with glad remembrance and full of happy promise, surrounds us, as it were, with the presence of an absence. The beginning of the knowledge of 'this' God, does not lie in the beginning we make with him. This beginning can come, and come again only in the beginning he makes with us.[61] In all our earnestness there is still a great deal of bad faith. We have angrily repressed God, precisely 'this' God, 'our' God.

A half childish, half demonic pride has driven us to try by every means to make ourselves inaccessible to 'him' and prefer to objectivize the *nihil* and become entangled in an 'absurd logic.'

We let the matter rest there; our purpose has been only to indicate how much easing of tension and happiness there can be when these insights dawn upon us. And what we mean by 'easing of tension and happiness' is the very thing that is meant by the 'Word.'

Here we can remain on another level, a level on which we are not

[61] Karl Barth, *Church Dogmatics*, Vol. II, pt. 1, pp. 204ff.

yet speaking theologically and exposing the secret misery and defection of the soul. We remind ourselves that, speaking purely historically, our whole thinking, the thinking of Western man, has developed in relationship and opposition to the 'Word' (or better, to the testimony about the Word). Western philosophy has always known that the 'faith' by which it lived and from which it distinguished itself, was not a 'direct' knowledge, not a communication with a divine being, but rather a hearing and a listening. Sometimes it has attempted on the basis of faith to develop this knowledge into a harmonious synoptic view, and sometimes on the basis of faith it has in the rebellion of existence shattered this very harmony into pieces.

If one surveys the whole development, as Karl Jaspers does, one comes to the conclusion that we in Europe have always known in our philosophizing that: 'A proved God is no God. Accordingly, only he who starts from God can seek him. A certainty of the existence of God, however rudimentary and intangible it may be, is a premise, not a result of philosophical activity.'[62] Elsewhere he says: 'The religious essence itself, inaccessible to the philosopher, must be present in advance.'[63] The elucidation of our human existence would really be impossible if society were areligious. Without the tradition, philosophy cannot illuminate the content of our existence. What the child has learned about God supports not only the philosopher but the philosophy itself. Indeed, Jaspers goes so far as to say that 'in order to participate in biblical faith one must grow up in the tradition of a definite denomination' and that 'a change of religion is difficult without a breach in the soul.'[64]

Even on this level of advancing reflection and historical communication (where in the nature of the case the essential difference between 'faith' and 'religion' cannot be made clear), the fundamental biblical concept of the 'Word' is regarded as the seal of the earnestness of thought, just as conversely (again in the nature of the case on this level) the exclusiveness of the Word is regarded as a stigma of intolerance.

However that may be, the Scriptures (as a witness of the Word) are recognized by the most thoughtful minds as an educative power. And it ought to disturb us that neither the church nor the synagogue (the latter in its orthodox form, however, more than the former) allows

[62] Karl Jaspers, *The Perennial Scope of Philosophy*, p. 32.   [63] Ibid., pp. 110f.
[64] Ibid., p. 114.

the Scriptures, especially the so-called Old Testament, to be fully heard, in order to preserve *their* people and the nations and bring them instruction. In a derivative, secondary sense, the derivative, secondary significance of the hiddenness of God (namely, that the Scriptures are not understood as the word about the Word) can bring to light an intellectual and a spiritual need which ought to spur us to fresh action in this respect. Here we are undoubtedly dealing with the repercussions of a deep, indeed, completely unfathomable, existential estrangement. Nevertheless this secondary nonunderstanding is in itself a negative phenomenon which, on the level of human society, we regard as catastrophic.

We would not use such a strong, menacing word if we were interested in the restoration of religiosity; but what we have said is aimed in exactly the opposite direction: the Old Testament will lead us out of the terror of nihilism to the degree that it leads us out of the dilemma of religion. Some will have only scorn for the idea, but it is our firm conviction that the Old Testament provides an aid that we need in order to free ourselves and our neighbours from the ambivalence of religion and of nihilism.

SPECTATOR OR PARTICIPANT

'The Old Testament has nothing to do with us; it's none of our business.' How natural it is for the 'fourth man,' and more or less for us all, who still represent the 'third man,' to react in this way! This reaction is not only natural, but, strictly speaking, perfectly true. The Old Testament is the book of God's covenant with Israel. 'God's' covenant —should we not rather say 'YHWH' and mean it as an idolatrous proper name? The fact is that it is really and essentially concerned with YHWH's covenant with this people and this land, with a future for this people and this land. But we are not Jews; and even if we were 'proselytes outside the gate,' the point of it would still be of no concern to us.[65] Nowhere are we addressed; nowhere can we be meant. And

[65] Well known is the animosity of Paul de Lagarde, the great orientalist and admirer of the human figure of Jesus, toward the Old Testament. It is no accident that it was a new educational law that prompted him to make his clearest (but at the same time most revealing) attack: 'But what are Adam and Eve to us, what are Abraham, Isaac, and Jacob, what are Moses and David to us? They are alien to us; they are of no

this is not to say that 'it says nothing to us,' but simply that YHWH does not speak with us; it is impossible that this God should want to say anything to us. The circle of duality and mutuality between YHWH and his people is a closed circle, and we are outside of it. We remain spectators, not because we have no desire to participate in these things, but simply because, since our background and the point of view of the Old Testament are given facts, we cannot be anything else but spectators.[66] And then, if further motivations are started, all kinds of typical differences will be found to be involved.[67]

If it is different for us, if this, which seems so obvious to us, nevertheless actually sounds forced and affected to other ears, then the reason is that the church has canonized the Old Testament. The Old Testament acquired a world significance, a universal applicability, the character of a universally human appeal only through the canon and the proclamation of the church. We do not wish here (any more than we did in the section on 'The Word') to say all that really must be said on this point, namely, that the specific quality 'Word of God' (=Christ) does not so much raise the Old Testament to the level of a fully valid voice of proclamation, but rather reveals it to be such. We do not want to discuss these things at this point. Here we wish only to say that even without existential participation the mode of our spectatorship vis-à-vis the Old Testament is radically altered (this is as much as we say here—for, after all, we are still in the intermediate area of purely intellectual facticity) through 'Christianity.'

The presupposition of biblical instruction—which, in our opinion, could be a remedy against the disease of our religious disruption and nihilistic ambivalence—is therefore (quite apart from the dimension

---

concern to us. They are worse than merely a matter of indifference.' So far this is understandable! But then comes an argument intended less to denounce the alienness of the Old Testament than to find fault with its great nearness to the New Testament: 'Original sin, the doctrine of the atonement depend *on Adam and Eve*, faith on Abraham, the Law on Moses, the Messiah and the system of fulfilment on David. . . . If you do not want the orthodox dogmas and views, you German fathers, then first get rid of the biblical stories of the Old Testament, but do it so thoroughly that your children in the present will never be allowed to mention their names.' 'Zum Unterrichtsgesetz' (1878), in *Deutsche Schriften*, last complete edn. (1903), p. 184; cf. A. M. A. Hospers-Jansen, *Tacitus en de Joden* (1949), pp. 35f.

[66] Cf. Hans Joachim Schoeps, *Philosemitismus im Barock*, pp. 45f., 114f., 131f.
[67] Cf. Constantin Brunner, *Die Juden und der Judenhass*, pp. 171f., 192f.

of the Word) that we accept this peculiar character of our spectatorship, this way in which we are drawn to the Bible, and allow it to stand. If need be, one may say that we must act as if the Old Testament does concern us; after all, there are attitudes and assumptions which must simply be assumed and made as a matter of course (even though they are by no means self-evident) in the interest of life, on the strength of ongoing history, for the sake of the highest necessity, the communication of minds, the human heart. This is why (we note incidentally) the critical historical study of the Old Testament has so often contributed, not because of its method or because of its results (this will be discussed elsewhere), but through its abstract attitude of spectatorship, to a progressive alienation of the 'third man' from the Old Testament, so that on this account too he very easily becomes a 'fourth man.'

We are therefore not talking about the fact that the Old Testament is the Word of God for the church (and what this means), but only of the fact that it was through the church that it came to the nations with at least the substance of a religion which *concerned* them. It will become apparent that ultimately this whole distinction between the qualification 'Word' and the qualification 'universal applicability' cannot be maintained.

Even at this point in our discussion the ambiguities are already appearing, the ambiguities of religion—and what else is Christianity as a public phenomenon but a historical demonstration of the unseriousness that characterizes human religion even in its best form?—the ambiguities, which inhere in religion, and thus the shadows of unbelief. Nevertheless, we can make provisional use of this distinction, precisely because we do not have control over the limits of its applicability. Precisely because of the fact that a verification of the qualification 'Word of God' is not found within the human realm, we can move in this middle area where, thanks to 'Christianity,' the Old Testament is put into our hands for our instruction. Now the question is: Instruction in what?

The structure of the Scriptures indicates to us that the answer to the question 'Instruction in what?' is not that of the Fathers: 'in divine truths'; nor that of the liberal theologians: 'in religious needs and their satisfaction'; nor that of the modern existential philosophers: 'in the limit situations of humanity'—although these three ways of approach need not be entirely fruitless and unrewarding. What then? Well precisely the fact that we are referred to the 'Word,' that is, the break-through of the God of freedom with his creative speech in the midst of the masks of divine power.

We conclude these paragraphs with the 'literary' judgment of the 'atheistic' Spinozist, Constantin Brunner: 'What literature is more national literature and universal literature than the Jewish? . . . Its purpose is to produce the life of mankind; it is itself a thing and life, and thus not only literature, and it has therefore produced life. . . . If one looks at the whole household and life of our culture, the earlier literatures including the Greek are nothing but memorials of antiquity, whereas none can deny that Jewish literature . . . is not only major literature, *universally readable*, as if written in the skies in huge letters for all peoples and times, but has itself become *life* in all our peoples and times.' It is 'the only literature which has been a living thing through all the generations of all times in all the ranks of the living, from kings down to the humblest farm hand. . . . To it and back again the noblest mind turns when Shakespeare no longer satisfies, and the saints with their wonderfully profound thoughts and unquenchable compassion read the Book as do those in the horrible cribs of prostitutes and murderers.' 'To the spirit, education or lack of education makes no difference; he who has gathered much has no surplus, and he who has gathered little has no lack.'[68] And it is the same writer who, in my opinion quite rightly, and just the opposite from de Lagarde, says that Abraham and David are closer to us than the heroes of our own country's history and that they are far more a part of our own bio-graphy than these others.[69]

THE TWOFOLD ACTION OF THE SCRIPTURES

In the situation here sketched in bold outline there is one fact, one accent, which has always proved itself to be true in history, namely, the fact that the Scriptures, especially the Old Testament, are both Word and teaching, voice and instruction, self-manifestation and direction. Though one in its form is never quite without the content of the other,

[68] Constantin Brunner, *Unser Christus, oder das Wesen des Genies* (1921), pp. 544f., 565.
[69] Cf. Herbert Schöffler, *Abendland und Altes Testament: Untersuchungen zur Kultur-morphologie Europas, insbesondere Englands*, 2 edn. (1941).

though, for example, there is no preaching which does not also contain instruction and explanatory elucidation and no instruction which does does not at least point (or intend to point) to the Word, we may nevertheless distinguish them for practical purposes. So when in view of this distinction we introduce the terms 'voice' and 'function,' our purpose is to reduce to a brief formula the fact that the 'voice' addresses itself more to genuine nihilism and the 'function' opposes itself more to ungenuine nihilism—that the 'voice' is a primary 'illumination,'[70] whereas the 'function' of the Old Testament is aimed more at a secondary explanation, elucidation, illumination. The ambivalence of nihilism can only be fully revealed in the theophany of the voice; the ambivalence of the surviving religion (the 'second religiousness,' as Spengler once called it)[71] can be unmasked by the lucidity of the fundamental biblical words.

Here again, with regard to the twofold effect of the Scriptures, there are parallel manifestations in the synagogue and the church, and since the synagogue in the new State of Israel is intent upon a theocratic structuring of life, also in the public life of Erets Yisra'el. Schalom Ben-Chorin[72] states that a new interest and understanding of the Bible has awakened there—new in comparison with the last century where in orthodox circles the study of the Talmud overshadowed the reading and learning of the *Tenak*[73] (i.e., the Old Testament), whereas liberal Judaism maintained vital contact with neither of them. Today the situation is different. Ben Gurion, the prime minister, has declared that the Bible is the foundation of Jewish culture; the army command distributes Bibles, the radio broadcasts the daily (Torah) readings as well as readings from the Prophets and the Writings. The newspaper *Chronicles* prints 'Latest News from the Past,' in which the Bible stories are told in the style of illustrated magazines. In the schools the Bible has the central place; it is the history book, the literature, the geography. Thus the influence of the Scriptures runs through the channels of the daily reading, regular presentations in the theatre, and the

[70] Cf. Friedrich Karl Schumann, *Der Gottesgedanke und der Zerfall der Moderne* (1929), p. 208.
[71] Oswald Spengler, *The Decline of the West*, tr. Charles Francis Atkinson (New York: Alfred A. Knopf, 1928), II, 310ff.
[72] Schalom Ben-Chorin, 'Die Bibel im heutigen Israel,' *Judaica*, X (1954), 170ff. [73] An artificial word for the Hebrew canon, formed from the initial letters of its three parts: *Torah*, *Nebi'im* (the Prophets), *Kethubim.*—Tr.]

revival of Hebrew vocal music. To what extent the *voice* sounds through this, is not for us to judge, although the fear is not unfounded that a new self-satisfied religion is coming into being and manifesting itself more and more confidently. But the function of instruction is to be distinguished from this, and it is of great importance.

But here too Ben-Chorin sees the beginning of a fatal development in the direction of a nationalizing of religion, 'the Baalizing of Jahweh.' This does not mean the rise of a paganism (apart from one extreme Jewish sect, this is no more acute in Israel than it is in Europe); it means rather that God and the Word of God are seen, understood, and treated as elements of this world. How far this goes is again beyond our judgment; but in so far as this falsification does occur, it goes back to a lack in that second factor of the 'twofold action' of Scriptures, namely, the explanation, elucidation, and illumination of the Old Testament. Judaism has produced many nihilists, though nihilists of a peculiar, fractured kind; but to the degree that it becomes a national religion, there is the subterranean threat of a new and peculiarly vulgar nihilism. For the historical as such cannot replace the immediacy of truth and is open to a doubt which undermines all values,[74] leaving behind a bitterness that turns against this God who has failed.

Among us in Christendom it may appear that the direction in which instruction must move is different: not from the collective to the personal, but the other way around, from the still surviving Pietism to community with the earth, history, and politics. However this may be, it remains that such intellectual correctives and directives will have to come out in the field of 'instruction' that they will have to be addressed to the intellect in order to cleanse it and give it wings. Thus in his time Franz Rosenzweig founded the modern version of the *beth-hammidrash*[75] in the Jüdisches Lehrhaus ('Jewish House of Instruction') in Frankfurt. Woodbrooke and Iona have also served as centres of

[74] 'All too many in Israel today have the Bible on their lips and not in their hearts. The nationalistic, historical, philological, and esthetic, indeed, also the romantic approach cannot take the place of living faith in the Word of the Bible. . . . The youth above all, with all their familiarity with the Bible, has not yet recognized it as the living Word of God to our time.' And Ben-Chorin goes on to recall the prophet's utterance concerning the hunger for the Word which the Lord will send on the land (Amos 8: 11), ibid., pp. 175f.

[[75] School, house of instruction; cf. Ecclus. 51 : 23.—Tr.]

strength in the intellectual awakening, and after the Second World War the Evangelical Academies came into being in Germany. So, in our opinion, we too must have a 'house of instruction' alongside the church, in which the work of the pastorate and apostolate can enter into encounter with the 'intellectual movements' (in so far as they still exist and are still moving), in which, however, it can devote itself above all to that 'second action' of the Scriptures, namely, the work of clarification and enlightenment. True, this can happen and does happen through literature, through conversations—and also, in a far more integrated way, in deeds and in the mystery of preaching. And yet there is room for a *beth-hammidrash* for incipient nihilists. I say incipient nihilists, conscripts, recruits for an army which is being enlisted among our 'own people.' And the recruiting is successful because Christians have very largely failed to learn to distinguish God from the gods and the godhead. These people are vulnerable in so far as they have fallen away from the God of the Word, the God of the breakthrough, the God of freedom.

When we are confronted with the church's loss of function, with a diminished church, we are not witnessing a defeat of the Word, but rather the unmasking of a religion which has wrongly imagined that it is secure in the Scriptures or covered by them. When we are told by those who know modern life and 'the Great Society' that the 'fourth man' lives and moves in a realm in which there is nothing left of civic, personal, and religious values, and we are given to understand that therefore the churchman must be regarded as utterly unsuited for the work of evangelization, then we are confronted not so much with a sign that the Word has failed but rather, as far as the 'church people' are concerned, with the consequences of a hundred years' lack of contact with the Scriptures and their concrete structures.

Naturally, this insight gains us nothing; it does not help us to find the bridge, the transition, the approach to the totally estranged. Nor does such an insight achieve a breakthrough in our epigonous nature, and the 'Constantinian' Christian is not thereby transformed into an 'apocalyptic' (to borrow J. C. Hoekendijk's term) witness, hero, or martyr. When we allow ourselves to be confronted with a sociological analysis, such as that given in various writings by Marcel de Corte, according to which anonymity has become the one thing held in common by men in the five continents, and the quantitive view has become the ultimate standard of human activity;[76] when we contemplate the picture of emptiness that Rauschning[77] draws of the progressive youth of Europe; if we look into the 'third or fourth day of spring' in Henry Miller's *Black Spring* where we meet with a courage of despair (a despair in the form of a hope for the annihilation of the world) and we hear an anabaptistically ecstatic Buddhist in a frenzied stutter: 'I am enchanted by the grand collapse of the world'—when we are faced with such facts and such statements, it is perfectly clear to us that preaching can no longer accomplish anything here and that the 'house of instruction' cannot play a part in any other types of evangelistic approach which may be invented or discovered.

Perhaps the situation will improve; perhaps there will be a turn for the better—or, after a short time, toward the worse; perhaps fate may be at work here, or may it not be a chastisement of God? It may be so; and yet do we not have reason to listen to Martin Buber when he says, 'It is a modern superstition that the character of an age acts as fate for the next'?[78] It may be so, but there have also been times in the past when there were frenzies of despair and pride, clothed with *esprit* or dressed up, armed, and masked with cool reasonableness. Nevertheless, though the judgment may be pronounced upon the 'lost groups,' though the disheartenment may have to be endured, though it may really be true that preaching and teaching have no more double, or even half, or even any effect at all, and that therefore a 'house of instruction' can accomplish nothing, we simply cannot stop asking where the 'fourth man' actually comes from. And even if it be true that a large part of these outsiders are the children and grandchildren of 'lost sons' who have long since left the church, may it not be that the church (and the synagogue) is a breeding place for this type of human being? I am certain that in the church there are whole pews filled with incipient nihilists; and just as surely as Europe has become a mission field, so surely the church (and the synagogue) has become a home base which it is still worthwhile to strengthen. And we believe that we must not push the dejection of our own hearts and the discouragement of others so far that we would deny this too.

The fact is, however, that a church which no longer receives the

---

[76] Cf. W. Banning, *Moderne maatschappij-problemen* (1953), pp. 43f.; Xaver von Horntein and Friedrich Dessauer, *Seele im Bannkreis der Technik* (1949), pp. 68f.
[77] *Die Zeit des Deliriums* (1947), pp. 259ff.   [78] *Eclipse of God*, p. 129.

'Word' and the 'instruction' of the Old Testament will continue to breed divided religious people, who, as it were, by a concatenation of circumstances just barely preserve what they call their 'faith,' but who, in another set of circumstances or if the trade wind of the time should shift, could just as well slip away, fall by the wayside, and apostatize. The truth is, however, that they are feeling the pressure of the silence of the gods, which combines with the pressure of the silence of 'this' God. If this trial of faith caused by the self-hiding and the hiddenness of the living God were only something that happened to the church when it is going through the depths! But if all the signs are not deceiving, what we are dealing with is the oft-repeated confirmation of the inner ambivalence of religion. A strip of no man's land has arisen, which runs like an undefended and indefensible corridor through the middle of the church; and if you want to see pariahs and nomads— well, despite the welfare state, you can see them springing up year after year from the soil of the church and leaving it. I therefore believe that a *beth-hammidrash* for those who dwell openly or secretly on the borders of the church would be a sensible undertaking, that it would have a preservative and enlightening effect, performing the function of clearing up wrong conceptions and ideas, that it could be a preparatory school for that *destructio destructionis*, which, if we are not completely deceiving ourselves, will ultimately prove to be a salutary contribution to the healing of the church and the people.

REMOVING THE RUBBISH

The fact is that the so-called Old Testament, even in its function as 'direction,'[79] teaching, and instruction, even from a purely intellectual point of view, is so dynamic that it is constantly surprising us. One can say that where it is allowed to act and speak for itself even a little, it sets up a happy carnage among the accumulated misunderstandings which are typical of 'religion' and therefore the typical lodging places of the 'ungenuine' nihilists. For what is the one thing that these (misguided) people are sure of? The Bible! Without it there would be nothing concrete to argue against; without it the ship of negation would simply run aground. Historically, we are so deeply determined and

[79 In the sense of *torah*, as direction and guidance.—Tr.]

impregnated by this entity that we are constantly bucking against something which—excepting all the variations and modulations which one naturally has not been able to follow—is supposedly hard and fast doctrine.

What, then, is hard and fast, and what is consequently denied? That which one knows for a certainty to be biblical teaching, even though one rejects it. And what are these things, as they suppose them to be? 'Providence' is a pious circumlocution for fate. The 'fear of God' is a gnawing feeling of guilt, a kind of permanent anxiety. 'Love' is an emotion and the 'neighbour' is simply everybody. 'God' is 'absolute,' and you can fill that with everything or nothing. 'Creation' is another word for the process of formation, or more precisely, its magical beginning. Further, the Bible says the world is 'good', but our experience has shown us that this is not true; the very opposite is the case. The goal of our life is happiness in the life to come, and the way to get there is by keeping the moral precepts, or, if there happens to be a touch of mysticism, by way of asceticism; for the Bible says (supposedly) that the essence of sin is sensuality, i.e., sexuality. Therefore original sin is rooted in procreation. And so the Old Testament has cast suspicion upon everything that is most natural, childlike, and important to us.

And it goes on in this vein: 'atonement' is a kind of fraud; the cross is 'a level bridge athwart the abyss of death for men who pay the bridge-toll' (Adwaita)[80]. Mortality is a punishment; self-denial is a revengeful self-mutilation (prompted by resentment, though these good people in the ignorant past did not see through this as we do); and the best attitude toward life is that of resignation. And all this is supposed to be in the Old Testament!

But the worst comes when the 'idea of God' is broached. Here there is such blatant certainty that not a flicker of doubt remains and almost nobody asks whether it is really true: God is omnipotence, i.e., he can do everything, he does everything, he wills everything. God is also 'holy,' i.e., ethically pure, flawless, and serene. And it follows from this that he must be either all-powerful or holy or neither. The simplest solution, however, is that he does not really exist but is rather a projection or a reflex of a wishful dream, or the aura of an archetype deep down in our subconscious. God's ruling will is to be deduced from what

[80 Pseudonym of the Dutch poet Johan Andreas dèr Mouw.—Tr.]

62

happens, and that is not exactly a cheerful thing. Is there not also such a thing as a moral will of God? Yes, of course, but this is to be understood as an ideal or principle, of which we ourselves, *nota bene*, must try to find the impossible application in a world which is what it is because God made it so. Moreover, God is very jealous of his own honour and thus manifests a colossal self-centredness and a certain embarrassing vanity. Further, God is present everywhere in the same degree, he is the 'all-seeing eye'; and he foreknows everything, and besides, he is unchangeable, eternally immutable.

No wonder that it is no small thing to believe in such a God, let alone live with him. A person has to do violence to his moral sense, make a sacrifice of the intellect, humiliate himself to the dust like a criminal, though he has done nothing but commit a few follies, which God surely ought to be too divine to bother about. So the upshot of all this must be that faith is a leap, a leap into the dark. The whole thing makes a man uneasy; and if the leap is successful—where else will one land except in the uncertainty whether the leap was worthwhile after all?

Of all of these cocksure religious statements the Old Testament says exactly the opposite. The Old Testament either says nothing whatsoever about this or, in so far as it comes within its purview, denies it all emphatically, vehemently, and passionately. If this is 'God,' if this is 'divine,' then the Old Testament could be used as a secret manual of atheism and serve as a very useful vade mecum of ungenuine nihilism, that is, for the purpose of forswearing the presence of this God and astutely undermining the truth of this God. We should not imagine that the 'fourth man' thinks in this way; absolutely not! But the 'third man' does, and therefore he grows daily riper for a quiet transition, a gentle dying away into the condition of the 'fourth man.'

These are the consequences of the religious interpretation of the Old Testament, this is the fruit of the obvious misunderstanding of its peculiar message and its specific teaching. Not until a person sees that the Old Testament actually says something different on all these points—even though this may not yet mean that he is hearing the Word—will he be at least open to its unparalleled significance and be willing, even though it be only on the level of rational discovery, to bow before the authentic form of a unique revelation.

When the gods grow silent, then sooner or later (and with a gradually increasing insistency) that unreliable, whimsical, omnipotent, immutable 'God' will also grow silent. Then he is no longer any good either as a stimulus to fear or as a comfort in fear. The instruction and the watchword of the Old Testament is brief and abrupt: This 'God' must disappear. Well, we say, hasn't he disappeared—in nihilism, in genuine nihilism? If only that were true! But always he comes back again, like a revenant; somehow he is in our blood. He is like us, he is our great congener in the ambiguity of Being and nonbeing. For do we not ask, 'Does he exist or not'—and in the same breath, 'Do we exist or not'? It seems as if we would never be rid of him; for what we have rejected on the word of the Old Testament itself has its ancient rights. It clearly betrays itself as an offshoot of paganism and a scion of philosophy, of metaphysics. It is even the burden of many Jewish and Christian sermons of the time when synagogues and church took its instruction more from the Stoics than from Moses and Paul, a kind of popular philosophy.

But we shall get rid of him and no longer have any need to seek shelter (*nota bene*, shelter!) in a 'genuine' or 'ungenuine' nihilism. And faith will again be the source of a joy, a peculiar joy which we do not have to whip up in ourselves by 'religious' means. It is characteristic of this miserable, shadowy, betwixt-and-between realm of a religion which ends in empty resignation and nihilism, this intermediate realm that wishes it could have back again the feeling of *being* and being meaningful that it once possessed—it is, I say, characteristic of this realm that for the most part men now find it so hard to laugh.

'Man laughs like a being who has not indulged in it very much. The terrible thing about laughing people, when for one reason or another we do not know why they are laughing and so cannot join in with them, is the depth of sickness and seriousness from which they seem to rise up like drowning men making despairing attempts to come to the surface, but over whose heads the waves will inevitably close again. A being whose features suddenly relax, a smile breaking out on the face of a "serious man"—it is difficult to imagine a clearer symptom of sickness. In this gasping and stamping search for a bit of happiness one discerns the sick animal, the burdened creature, dragging the sins and cares of the world about on his shoulders. There are other ways of laughing, explosions of euphoria and bliss: children can laugh like that, but it is rare among adults. You have to deal with them far more circumspectly than with children, who can laugh at any time. You have to prepare the adults, the serious ones; you must carefully indicate to them beforehand that perhaps there will be some laughing, that there is "something to laugh about".'[81]

When the Old Testament commits happy carnage upon traditional religion and smashes it to bits, then laughter will break out on the face of the 'serious people,' who find it so hard to grasp that in faith joy is understood and experienced as the essence of things, indeed, that in God there is an everlasting jubilation. For—more is the pity—along with many other notions, religious and irreligious people have this in common too, namely, that they are dead serious. When the NAME comes upon us, 'praise' goes out to meet it. This word 'praise' is a singular word: what it means includes thanksgiving and laughter and singing, but also sacrifice and devotion; and it also means to hear in trembling joy what is still to be hoped for, and—shamed into elation— to understand why it is that there is so much, so infinitely much, to hope for. And sometimes even the quieter paths of instruction lead us to those boundaries where we are left only with the breath to cry out: HE is good! 'This is the root article of redemption, the roof over the house of speech, the article which is true in itself, the article that remains true no matter how it is meant or who utters it.'[82]

THE NAME

All along we have been distinguishing between faith and religion. In doing so we have not been contrasting a false or erroneous religion with a true one, in order to reserve the honorific 'faith' for the latter. For example, Christianity too is said to be only a religion,[83] perhaps the 'highest,' the richest, or the purest. If one is misled by a currently accepted misuse of the word 'faith,' one can also speak, for example, of a Buddhist faith, which carries the confusion to the extreme and

[81] H. A. Gomperts, *Jagen om te leven*, pp. 270f.
[82] Franz Rosenzweig, *Der Stern der Erlösung*, II, p. 185.
[83] Though one must suspect that in the history of its use the word itself arose as a polemical term. De Lagarde expresses it frankly: 'The word "religion" was introduced in sharpest contrast to the word "faith," the accepted term in the church, and everywhere it presupposes the deistic criticism of the universally Christian concept of revelation' (*Deutsche Schriften*, p. 46).

obliges the prudent person to start from the ground up and secure clarity with regard to the structure of 'faith,' with the aid of phenomenology and, possibly, Jung's 'complex psychology.'[84]

In our view, faith is just as clearly and just as fluidly distinguished from religion as, on the other side, we are accustomed to distinguish between religion and magic. Religion signifies the experience and celebration of the cosmic equilibrium in a rite; faith relates to the *Word*.[85] Religion has a strengthening effect upon the movements of the intellectual life, whereas faith is more likely to be disturbing. In every crisis of society religion functions as an ordering force; faith adds to it a disturbance which goes deeper than a crisis, namely, the creating, establishing, and ordering of a relationship. Religion clings to the mutual relationship of 'God' and 'man'; faith clings to the free, spontaneous 'turning' of God to man. Religion issues in culture, is itself the foundation and pinnacle of culture; faith, cutting straight across the given existence, hears tidings of a breakthrough, an end, a fulfilment, which are beyond the grasp of all human action, which, in the full sense of the word, 'overcome' man.

In some such way we can describe the difference between faith and religion. But we must remember that such statements about structures touch only an external side of it. For one can go on from this level which has been uncovered 'phenomenologically' and proceed in two directions: either in the direction of psychological coordination (*Gleichschaltung*), which runs out into a new, introverted gnosis (as it does in Jung), or in the direction of a theological accommodation, which starts with the Name, the revelation of God, and then relativizes what we rationally discover about the nature of faith. 'Religion,' says Karl Barth, 'is a concern, indeed we must say, it is the one great concern of godless man.'[86] In making this colossally offensive statement, Barth is not passing a negative judgment upon human aspiration and experience; no prejudice against religion as such plays a part in this statement and consequently even less a prejudice against the biblical and Christian religion. The assertion expresses the insight, which by

[84] Cf. Rudolf Kassner, *Zahl und Gesicht*, p. 113; idem, *Grundlagen der Physiognomie*, pp. 83f; F. Sierksma, *Phaenomenologie der religie en complexe psychologie* (1950).
[85] Cf. Martin Buber, *De Godsdiensten der wereld*, I, 26, where he speaks of Jeremiah's attitude toward the temple. [Cf. Martin Buber, *The Prophetic Faith*, tr. Carlyle Witton-Davies (New York: Harper Torchbook, 1960), p. 164.—Tr.]
[[86] *Church Dogmatics*, Vol. I, pt. 2, pp. 299f.—Tr.]

its nature is unprovable, that the revelation means the crisis of all religion.

Therefore the believer will not say that he has come from faith to faith, that he has passed from an inferior to a better faith, or that he has risen from religion to faith. It is precisely the believer who will say that, with all that he is and possesses, he has come from unbelief to faith. No wonder, for what do we see when he, his people, and the community in its way become believers? Look at the Old Testament. What a confusing picture it presents: religion and faith, popular piety and cult, cult and prophetic opposition, prophecy and false prophecy. Idolatry and image-worship, hypocrisy, hankering for the gods, and human pride remain the order of the day. Where is the Law obeyed, gladly obeyed? Where does man remain in his place, in order to receive his divine portion and thus become himself? Where is the cult ever dealt with in real earnestness, where is there ever a really genuine prayer? Is not the whole concern the satisfaction of human needs, the gratification of the soul to the limit of religious persistence?

So it is also not surprising that religion becomes an element of custom, that it changes and grows out of date through changes of climate or the rise of technology or miscegenation. But, remarkably, religion never declines or dies because of the attacks made upon it by its youngest children, the atheists. It declines and dies by being supplanted by what is at first a small, new religion. As long as there are prophets like Amos and John the Baptist, it does not fall, because it learns to bow before the judgment of the 'Name' (Amos 4 : 4; 5 : 5; 9 : 7; Isa. 1 : 21f; Jer. 6 : 20f.; 8 : 8, etc.). But what shall we say of the history of the church as the history of the practice of faith—its demoralization and softening, its downright idolatry and, right alongside of this, its flight into all kinds of utopian dreamlands, its ignoble attacks and unworthy defences? What shall we think of the thousands who went along with all this because of fear and mere habit and demonstrated again and again that they could have done otherwise? Goethe called the history of the church a 'farrago of lies and violence,' and we cannot gainsay him. But the situation is even worse: here we are faced with the eruption of a concrete difficulty which is only a demonstration of a secret and permanent difficulty of the believing community, the believing man. How great this difficulty is can be estimated to some extent when before our eyes we see nihilism spring up, out of the former religion, out of a departed faith, a growth that flaunts itself in pure corruption, a rebellious gesture out of nothingness against no one.

The true measure of the difficulty, however, lies in the fact that through the Name faith too is judged as a human, all-too-human religion. True religion can come into being only in the same way that a justified sinner comes into being,[87] that is, in the sphere of the Name, which constantly makes it possible for the rebel to exist, to stand forth, and endure by virtue of the pardon, the valid pardon, which is contained in the revelation. It is God who says: *Écrasez l'infame!* On the other hand, 'strong human positions are only those which are fully abandoned to God, that is, positions which are seen to be quite untenable when measured by his will and judgment.'[88]

This is not the place to discuss how all of this is suggested and brought out in the Old Testament name of God, the tetragrammaton, in spite of the appearance of the denial of the Name. We refer the reader to two recent studies, one by Hellmut Rosin and the other by Frans Breukelman and Horst Dzubba.[89] At this point let us note only these two points:

1. The unutterable Name is the standard of that which deserves to be called godhead and not vice versa; so that YHWH, when he is called 'almighty,' 'just,' etc., is this in his way, with his purpose, and not according to the general, customary, religious conception.

2. The Name is encountered, the Name is perceived in the whole history in which he lives and reveals himself; he is the 'quintessence of its meaning,' which becomes a reality solely in his concrete presence.

Even this is enough to make it clear how it is possible to say: 'In every true service of worship the spirit of "nihilism" is exorcised. For in every service of worship the Name is named which is above every name, at which every knee shall bow in heaven and on earth and under the earth (Phil. 2 : 10). This was already known by ancient Christianity; we have learned it again in the last decade and a half [namely, the Nazi regime]: every genuine service of worship is an exorcism, a driving out of the devil. . . . Therefore every genuine service of worship

---

[87] Karl Barth, *Church Dogmatics*, Vol. I, pt. 2, pp. 325ff. [88] Ibid., p. 331.
[89] H. Rosin, *The Lord is God: The Translation of the Divine Names and the Missionary Calling of the Church* (1956); F. Breukelman und H. Dzubba, *Die biblische Sprache: Beginn einer Studie* (1955).

is . . . an act which far outweighs the carrying out of great projects.'[90]

The question may be asked whether the 'Name' itself, when it is thus detached from any known system of thought, from all religious categories, does not have a negative effect, does not awaken a distrust, a suspicion of everything that exists and is accepted as valid. Here we meet the ancient accusation which the Gentiles made against Israel and the Roman imperial age made against the Christians. They were branded as *atheoi* (atheists) and accused of 'hatred of the human race' (*odium generis humani*). They refused to bow to the powers, they would not bind themselves to the sacred symbols of the peoples, they would not accept old or new slogans whose purpose was to support the old order. This was also the accusation made by the culturally and philosophically conscious adherents of the Third Reich. Must it not be said that an accusation such as this is an absolute, a deadly, reproach— and that it obviously has some basis?

In any case, those who have sensed and rejected the 'atheism' and 'nihilism' in the Jewish-Christian revelation have a deeper perception of the new thing which the Name stands for than the others who try to incorporate the Name in a synthesis or to coordinate it with a synthesis of that which has been established as truth by tradition and the popular mind. For those who still have gods (even where this has reached the stage where the gods pass over into the state of invincible silence) there is every reason to speak of the 'de-divinization' of the world by the 'Name' and the proclamation of the 'Name.'[91] It appears that revelation degrades all the richness, drama, and beauty of the world to the level of signs, mere signs; it appears to reduce the substantial to mere functions. After all, there is an element of 'utilitarianism' in the Jewish-Christian attitude toward life: the cosmos is no longer reversed, it can be utilized; life is fragmented in moral earnestness, in the work of cultivation, and finally in the utterly prosaic necessities of the collective welfare of the anonymous crowd. Is not all of this inherent in the implications of the Old Testament? It is still a part of the picture of our times that such questions, such rhetorical questions are asked.

[90] Gerhard Gloege, *Das Evangelium und die Gegenwart.*

[91] Hermann Broch has inserted in the third part of his novel *The Sleepwalkers, A Trilogy,* tr. Willa and Edwin Muir (Pantheon Books, 1964), scattered fragments under the title 'Disintegration of Values,' alternating with another series of fragments called the 'Story of the Salvation Army Girl in Berlin'; cf., for example, ch. 73 ('Disintegration of Values') with ch. 83 (which is ch. 15 of this story).

We shall not now go into the question whether a misunderstanding plays a part in these value judgments and of what that misunderstanding is. One thing is certain: the 'Name' has brought 'de-divinization,' actually, radically, irrevocably. Therefore religion and nihilism are closely related, not only in their nature, but also in their destiny and their development. It is precisely the 'de-divinization' of the world that made it possible for nihilism to arise, since there is no longer anything to deny. But subconsciously religion goes on living. The negative effect of the Name is the very thing that is positive, since it frees men from the spell of the religions of Being. In so far as these religions are concerned with the glorification of the elemental powers and forces of the world, they continue to resist the undermining of the veneration of these powers. Religion and nihilism share a common destiny. I nothing which has eternal durability (even though it has entered into history) is to be found above and beyond the ambivalence of religion and nihilism, then the last act of Christian culture would in fact remain imprisoned in this at first strained, then stifling, and finally sterile vortex. But ever since the 'Name' itself became religious, it too has been one of the causes of the decay of values. And ever since the 'Name' has been written off, it has been necessary to protect 'human dignity' by means of arguments and an attitude of life in which this sterility is made to appear as intellectual 'integrity' and the protector himself as an *'honnête homme.'* [92]

But where there is a more intimate understanding of the 'Name' there are indications of negativity which (for the *participant*, at least, though less for the spectator) are far more disquieting. He whose being, 'significance,' and history is summed up in the 'Name,' is not accessible, does not render an account of himself, is not the mother god and not the father god. It is a hopeless undertaking to try to advance from the possibility of God to the reality of God. It is impossible to judge with our measures whether we now really believe in him or not. He is neither contingent nor necessary; he is not bound to the causality of the world, but also not to the good. And all in all the person who knows this—and not something he thinks is better—will feel that he is at the mercy of this power and will suffer and labour under his love, i.e., under his favour, his zeal, his election. This is a side of the matter

[92] Menno ter Braak, *Van Oude en nieuwe christenen,* p. 250; idem, *De nieuwe élite,* p. 30.

which we indicate in order to show that faith has something in common
with nihilism, in order to place an element of faith in close proximity
with a nihilistic reaction. But at the same time this already touches
upon something which is really essential.

OUT INTO LIFE

He who thus keeps moving around the 'Name' or the knowledge of the
Name will not immediately regard the whole thing as promising. When
we look at it and talk about it in this way from the outside, there is
hardly any room left for anything except temporizing and waiting—
in the manner, say, of one who says: 'I would rather be guileless, for I
know that when one is guileless, one can be cheated by others, but
when one is suspicious, one inevitably cheats oneself—but the suspicion has remained, a metaphysical distrust, which I feel obliged to
harbour toward Him whom I doubt, whom I must doubt. And yet
in this suspicious and active waiting the festal feeling has never wholly
left me, the hope of a final *démasqué*, when the masks will fall from our
faces and the scales from our eyes.'[93]

Nevertheless we already have a premonition that the power of the
Name will ineluctably send us *into life* that we may exist and act there
in immediacy, but above all allow things to come to us and happen to
us. We have perhaps already sensed that it is precisely the Name which
casts us out of the detached and scheming attitude of the spectator,
that it is the Name which is out to give us a place in ordinary life and
pave a way for us that seems strange and yet so obvious. Franz Rosenzweig once answered a doubting Thomas as follows: 'What are you
afraid of? For I do not take even unbelief too seriously. Do not think
that I want to tell you that faith will come. No, it does not come.
Perhaps it may even depart. It does not inhere like an attribute in a
person whom it has overcome. . . . After all, unbelief is the most
natural thing in the world. As long as we *are* mere creatures we have
no reason to know *that* we are creatures. But how can you deny what
has happened to you? Nothing whatsoever happens to the creature.
When something does happen to him, then—by that very fact—
revelation has happened to him.'[94]

[93] Evert Janssen in *Thomas en Trauma*.   [94] *Briefe* (1935), p. 383.

The superior power of the Name reveals itself in the fact that finally something comes upon us and we finally come to something. It does not take us out of the world, it does not pin us down to the world—it rather drives and pushes us out into life. We find that life is in some unimaginably deep way good and in some unimaginably majestic way real, and this experience, that comes over us while the gods are silent and we face the otherness of God, creates in this earthly life the ability to receive the good and do the good. So we venture to say with Paul Häberlin, even though it may sound somewhat 'dangerous'; 'True virtue is *that higher naïveté* which shares with original innocence the quality of being untroubled by the problems of life. It is a childlike affirmation of life, not out of blindness, but out of clear-eyed faith. . . . He who understands how to live, he and only he is virtuous. . . . True virtue consists in being happy.'[95]

These preliminary comments, with which we have interrupted our reflections upon the 'Name,' anticipate what we shall present in Part Two. What makes the knowledge of the Name so full of promise is not to be sought in a world view, not in a sound system of ethics, an inspiring ideal, a distant goal, which, to the satisfaction of our propensity to sadness (since, after all, the same weariness remains after both desire and privation), rises higher and higher to an unattainable zenith and recedes ever more certainly beyond the horizon. The Name, whatever else may be said about it, is immediately related to life—not so much to 'everyday' life as to elemental and immediate life, not so much to the moral life as to total and spontaneous life, not so much to what we have grasped at the moment as to what is surrounding us on all sides. Many have so accepted the breakdown of this age and this generation that they no longer know how despairing they are. For them the proclamation of a world view, a new ethos, a definite goal would in the first instance only drive life and the 'Name' farther apart. The 'death of God' is irrevocable. Nietzsche said that we have killed him. The death of God—what is meant by this is that the consciousness of God in men diminishes until it disappears altogether. The very proposition that God is dead reveals how modern man, completely imprisoned in his subjectivity, projects his loss into the objective. What is meant is always the Christian God (i.e., the God who is first attested

[95] *Das Gute* (1926), pp. 306f.; cf. idem, *Das Geheimnis der Wirklichkeit* (1927), pp. 163f., 198f.

in the Old Testament); everywhere men are secretly asking in their hearts how one can go on living. Even while the funeral is going on, we are reminded of immediate life. 'God is dead. This says all kinds of things, but it does not say: There is no God.' 'This is the death of the Absolute.'[96] It is not surprising that it is precisely the Name that points us to life, that sends us out into life. Heidegger speaks of 'security in faith as a specific way of standing in the truth.'[97] When he distinguishes and separates this 'way' from every kind of philosophical reflection, this is in accord with the call: Out into life![98] and it approaches the higher naïveté mentioned above: He who knows how to live, he and only he is virtuous. And finally, it is quite appropriate that the Name should confirm the 'metaphysical distrust' mentioned above (for 'godhead' is a metaphysical entity) and remove this distrust (for the witness of the Name manifests itself precisely in life).

PREACHING THE NAME

Because the Name of God—however 'other,' strange, repelling, destructive, objectionable, or conversely, however mysterious, fascinating, beckoning, and attractive to life, it may sound—in every case encompasses a definite time and takes a definite passage through the nations and the continents, we can here speak of a preaching of the Name, a witness, a history. We add at once that 'preaching' or 'proclaiming' of the Name is not the common way of expressing it in the Bible. The Name is invoked, or better, 'called on' (e.g., Gen. 21 : 33), it is known, told, feared, loved, acknowledged, and also sought and waited for. It is to be 'hallowed' and, by the very ones who have been called, it is 'profaned' and cursed, desecrated, misused, and associated with folly and futility (Deut. 28 : 58; I Kings 8 : 33; Pss. 5 : 11; 34 : 3; 52 : 11, footnote R.S.V.; 83 : 16; 122 : 4; Isa. 26 : 8; Matt. 6 : 9; John 12 : 28; Lev. 18 : 21; 19 : 12; 24 : 11; Exod. 20 : 7.)

Preaching is contained or intended in many of these phrases, and yet the fact that 'preaching' (as we commonly understand it) does not

[96] Martin Heidegger, *Holzwege*, p. 186.
[97] *Introduction to Metaphysics*, tr. Ralph Manheim (Yale Univ. Press and Oxford Univ. Press, 1959).
[[98] These are the last words in Franz Rosenzweig's *Stern der Erlösung.*—Tr.]

occupy a central place constitutes a warning in a number of ways. First, it reminds us that the Name came from afar to us as heathens; the European peoples are children of the mission. Second, it can make it clear to us that preaching in the sense of delivering a message is not such a self-evident thing that the chosen people particularly saw in it their first task. And finally, it impresses upon us the fact that proclamation, preaching, after it came to be such, especially from the time of First Isaiah on, did not become a regularly repeated phenomenon but rather remained, so far as its form was concerned, an incidental event. All this compels us to exercise a certain reserve and causes us to moderate our expectation (or possibly the offence we might take).

This reserve takes on form, it seems to me, when we comprehend that preaching cannot achieve full utterance and find complete understanding without the instruction. The Name lives out its nature in the Word; preaching (and the Scriptures as the precipitate of preaching) is a word about the Word. But this word of preaching has never been able to gain entrance and access, never has triumphed, as is its way, in purity and clarity unless it has gone hand in hand with direction and instruction. If we ask which takes precedence, the priority of preaching will have to be acknowledged, just as there can be no interpretation unless it is preceded by something given, an event which requires interpreting, explanation, elucidation, illumination. But this hierarchical precedence is not always identical with the didactic order, although the latter presupposes the presence and validity of the former.

So it is that quite ordinary conversation with those who are on the fringes of the church can be of such great importance, as has proved to be the case again and again. Sermons addressed to incipient nihilists must be translated into or replaced by words that listen and speak, venturously feeling their way toward the others and aimed at clarification and elucidation. It may then appear that the whole thing takes place far removed from the mystery of the Name, from the immediacy of testimony; it may seem that we are completely losing ourselves in little everyday affairs. But to those who have seen it happen it is amazing how the ultimate, most carefully hidden questions about the meaning and meaninglessness of life, about the ground and groundlessness of the world, about despair and resignation venture to show themselves in the quiet lamplight of this kind of tentative speech.

Not that I am unaware of the 'devaluation' of words and speech;

74

this is a vogue idea today. And I am not surprised that Honegger's *Le Roi David* is staged for those who are estranged from the church, that use is made of the puppet theatre, that readings of biblical stories are presented by actors, and that there is a widespread demand for plays in verse,[99] in which an event in which God is concerned with present-day life is acted out, i.e., presented with all the elemental force of physical gesture and expression.

We do not deny a priori that the Gospel can be 'presented' in this way. But here in the poem or play something is presented which is also intended to be understood, and understood in a more deliberate way. A verse play is a song that is sung, but Rosenzweig has quite rightly pointed out that the whole of Scriptures is prose in the strict sense of the word, that is, that in practice the Bible continues to live exclusively as a written document which is heard and read, as a written word whose power to send us out into life is dependent upon its also being understood.

It is quite possible that in a particular situation the silence of the gods may be 'outsung' by the song which has its source in the Name. But just because we go so far as to include this kind of presentation in the classification of proclamation, there is, in our view, all the more necessity that instruction, Torah have a place alongside of it, as with all other proclamation. And however improbable it may seem to us, the people who seem already doomed to sink into the tragedy of nothingness (which is always an ignorance, too) are, through their longing, giving us a sign that we should speak in order to give them clarification, insight, and certainty.[100] Where this instruction is a success, but also where the success appears to be weak, there often arises behind it a quietness, a peculiar kind of self-examination, a testing of words and the quietness that inheres in them, a pondering of the frailties of human speech. The arrest of the person's disoriented thinking lingers on, and sometimes, without his having sought for it, there arises from the unexpected clarity that remains a recovery of health. Preaching as the proclaiming of the Name, if done rightly, has the 'house of instruction' alongside of it. And this applies too where we are dealing with people on the fringe of the church. The Christian church is only a school, but it is that too.

[99] The finest I know is *Een ladder tegen de maan* by Guillaume van der Graft.
[100] Cf. A. F. L. van Dijk, *Nihilisme of Koninkrijk Gods*: idem, *Onder den vijgeboom*.

CHRISTIAN INSTRUCTION

The description of the situation in which preaching and instruction have or seek their place today would be incomplete and at one point quite unreal if, in our transition to the second part of this book, we did not say something about the presupposition, the nature, and the spirit of this instruction which accompanies preaching. If we really take seriously the silence of the gods and the godhead and also the possibility that God is hiding himself; if we take seriously the rise of the 'fourth man,' who is also recruited from the ranks of those who are on the fringes of the church; if the 'individualists' in their extreme outbursts are really voicing something that is alive in many people, and nihilism, even though it be in ambivalent form, is imposing itself upon our attitude toward life; if the 'genuineness,' the humanness of 'ungenuine' nihilism is even partially seen and we recognize that modern freedom is regarded as a burden and a curse; if there are individuals, pioneers, who prophesy the 'end of the modern world'; if the Word of God demands participants and not spectators—then it is impossible to meet the situation if we insist upon assuming a noncommittal attitude in the midst of these threatening dangers and open opportunities. We have seen how much depends upon a right distinction between faith and religion, how radically the Old Testament disposes of customary and seemingly ineradicable religious thought patterns, how in the 'Name' the secret of the Scriptures comes to us and sends us out into life.

With all this before our eyes, it is impossible for us to escape our origin, the place where we stand, the call we have received. It is impossible for preaching and instruction to be neutral, speculative, indecisive, and undemanding of decision. We will speak as Christians, because it is in this quality or destiny that we have entered into this general and at the same time this peculiar and particular situation. In so far as we have allowed these things to affect us, we have done so not as neutrals and also not nihilists (although we too have been affected by nihilism), not as pagans and not as Jews. We stand in the tradition, the dynamic line of the Christian confession, and this is where we intend to stand.

We know how much of 'Christianity' is apostasy from Christ; we do not know whether our faith is genuine and real; but we do know that from the beginning the church understood the Name of God and Jesus Christ to be one and the same. It has not merely experienced the 'infinite fascination' of combining by a process of thought the uniqueness of YHWH and the concrete 'once-for-all-ness' of Jesus;[101] it knows no other name under heaven given among men by which they may be saved (Acts 4 : 12) except Christ. In saying this, Christianity never intended to obscure the meaning of the Old Testament; on the contrary, it has always known that it was only in its preaching and instruction that the Scriptures were finally unseated. It reached out spontaneously for the testimony of the Name, it acted after the example of the Apostles, it walked the way of the kerygma which presented itself to it with power as the message of fulfilment, it read the Old Testament—'Christianly.'

We know how enraged Nietzsche was over this 'world-historical robbery' [of the Old Testament from the Jews]; we know that for century after century this has been an offence to the synagogue; we also know how much untenable allegorizing and typology has been read into the Old Testament. All this does not alter the fact that somewhere we have our place, where we are determined to stand, because we must stand there, where we are glad to stand, because we are allowed to stand there. The relativity and the wrong that hang upon us as a burden from the past cannot give us licence to approach the Scriptures as noncommital neutrals or nihilists, Jews or pagans when in fact we are not neutral, nihilistic, Jewish, or pagan.[102]

Nevertheless we cannot fail to see that in making this last statement we run the risk of establishing ourselves in the 'true religion,' despite the fact that we have just found that such a 'true religion' can come into being and have validity only if it comes into being in the same way that a justified sinner comes into being, namely, through justification.[103] And if we then also take into account what Karl Barth has so emphatically underscored, that synagogue and church together constitute a congregation of God,[104] we are in the midst of the question of how the 'Name' is heard, understood, attested, and carried into the

[101] Constantin Brunner.
[102] Franz Rosenzweig, 'Hic et ubique,' *Kleinere Schriften*, p. 475.
[[103] Cf. no. 83 above.—Tr.]   [104] *Church Dogmatics*, Vol. II, pt. 2, pp. 195ff

world by this congregation. Here again decisions are made, or better, they have already been made, for though one can believe in the one congregation of God, one cannot belong to the church and the synagogue at the same time.

'For what does the church have which the synagogue does not also have, and long before it (Rom. 9 : 4–5)—especially Jesus Christ himself, who is of the Jews, who is the Jewish Messiah, and only as such the Lord of the church? The decisive question is not what the Jewish synagogue can be without him, but what the church is as long as it confronts an alien and hostile Israel. "Jewish Missions" is not the right word for the call to remove this breach, a call which must go out unceasingly from the church to these brethren who do not yet know their unity with it—a unity which does not have to be established but is already there ontologically, who will not accept what they already are, and what they were long before us poor Gentiles. And what a dreadful thing when the church itself has so little understood its own nature that it has not only withheld this knowledge from its brethren but made it difficult, if not impossible, for them.'[105] On the other side, we listen to what Franz Rosenzweig says: 'What Christ and his church mean in the world, on that we are agreed: no one comes to the Father but by him. No one *comes* to the Father—but it is different if a person no longer needs to come to the Father, because he is *already* with him. And this is the case with the people of Israel (not the individual Jew).'[106]

This makes the question of the meaning of the Old Testament an urgent one, and it subjects the term 'Christian' instruction to a proper reduction.[107] When we are driven out of every 'noncommittal' position, this is done through the light of the one NAME, which has broken through the silence of the gods and thrust back the darkness that covers the peoples.[108]

---

[105] Ibid., Vol. IV, pt. 1, p. 671.   [106] *Briefe an Rudolf Ehrenberg*, p. 73.
[107] Cf. Martin Noth, 'Die Vergegenwärtigung des Alten Testaments in der Verkündigung,' *Evangelische Theologie*, XII (1952), pp. 6ff.
[108] Cf. H. J. Schoeps, *Jüdischer Glaube in dieser Zeit* (1932), pp. 74ff.

MAN COME OF AGE

Our point of departure in this study was the 'fourth man.' We have thought of the term as a kind of index, and for the most part we have relied upon the view of the sociologists. Without really believing (or disbelieving) this in the construction, it has been our desire to take the situation as seriously as possible. It is well known that Dietrich Bonhoeffer saw the modern man whom the church encounters (or no longer encounters) quite differently, namely, as the man who has come of age, as a part and a representative of a 'world come of age.'

By this he did not mean exactly the same thing that Kant had in mind in his characterization of the Enlightenment. But he certainly did not think of this man as being incapable of responding to any spiritual appeal. As he went deeper into the question of what the church must do, he thought it must approach this man with a 'religionless Christianity.'

The pages of *Prisoner for God*[109] that deals with this are especially moving because here a tormented man who came out of the German resistance, a man of integrity, under the pressure of loneliness, police interrogations, and later the sentence of death, is turning his thoughts completely away from his own life and in a penetrating way sees what the state of the world will be like in the immediate future.

It is not entirely clear to us how he visualized a 'religionless' translation of the Word of God. This much is clear, however: in his thinking he sought to get away from the 'religious a priori' upon which for centuries preaching had been tacitly based.[110] 'The foundation is removed from our whole previous conception of "Christianity" and there are only a few surviving old soldiers or a few intellectually dishonest people whom we can reach "religiously." Are these really the chosen few? Are we to go after this particular, dubious group of people with

[109] Dietrich Bonhoeffer, *Prisoner for God: Letters and Papers from Prison*, tr. Reginald H. Fuller (New York: Macmillan, 1954). The German title *Widerstand und Ergebung* ('Resistance and Surrender') is worth salvaging. The citations from this book are here translated afresh, though the page references are to this edition.—Tr.]

[110] *Prisoner for God*, p. 122; cf. the section 'Inheritance and Decay' in his *Ethics*, tr. Neville Horton Smith (New York: Macmillan, 1955), pp. 25ff.

zeal, pique, or fury, in order to sell our wares to them? Are we to fall upon a few unhappy people in their weak moments and, so to speak, commit religious rape upon them?' The question remains: 'How can Christ become the Lord even of the religionless?'[111]

We see that Bonhoeffer begins much less radically than did the young Barth around 1918. The latter discovered that religion is the principal obstacle to faith, whereas Bonhoeffer saw that this prop for faith was collapsing historically and factually. For Barth the question was: How can we make it evident that religion is the 'concern' of the godless man (i.e., the man who is separated or wants to separate himself from the 'Name')? For Bonhoeffer the question was: What meaning do church, preaching, liturgy still have in a religionless world? For him the question of truth is not under discussion; in his struggle he became more than ever convinced of the necessity of the 'arcane discipline,' of the unshakable continuum of ultimate mysteries which must express themselves in penultimate answers and should not be shown to just anyone at any time. What offends him is that 'religious people' only begin to talk about God when human knowledge and perception come to the end of their tether and human powers fail. For the 'religious,' God, if he is not nature, is always a mere *deus ex machina*.

What interests us most is the way in which Bonhoeffer, starting from the situation as he sees it, also turns to the Old Testament and points to it when he advocates a 'worldly Christianity': 'I should wish to speak of God not at the limits of life but at its centre, not in the weaknesses of life but in its strength, and therefore not at the point of man's death and guilt, but in his life and in his good. At the limits it seems to me to be better to keep silence and leave the insoluble unsolved. The resurrection—faith is *not* the "solution" of the problem of death. The "beyond" of God is not the beyond of our power of knowing. The epistemologically transcendent has nothing to do with the transcendence of God. God is beyond in the midst of our life. . . . This is the way the Old Testament sees it, and in this sense we still read the New Testament far too little on the basis of the Old.'[112]

Bonhoeffer goes on to give a penetrating description of religious speech as (a) metaphysical and (b) individualistic speech. He considers neither of them compatible with the biblical message. But here again he is not arguing from principle but on the basis of the fact that for most

[111] *Prisoner for God*, pp. 122f.   [112] Ibid., p. 124.

people today the question of personal salvation, for example, has completely disappeared. Concepts like repentance, faith, regeneration must be translated anew in a 'worldly' sense. 'Worldly' means: in the language of the 'world come of age.' Now, it is our opinion that Bonhoeffer has left this 'adulthood' (*Mündigkeit*) somewhat undefined and that in any case he very much overestimated it; otherwise the man 'come of age' would turn out to be the opposite of the 'fourth' man, although both epithets must ultimately refer to the same type of man. The term 'adulthood,' owing to Bonhoeffer's aversion to the prevailing apologetics of the Christian faith, is a bit optimistic.

True, he admits that liberal theology carried this 'adulthood' of the world to the point of absurdity, in that it gave to the world, for example, the right to decide what place—religious, logical, and practical—could be conceded to Christ. This naturally led to a swift defeat and a total capitulation.

But modern pietism forcibly drove man into a choice between Christ and despair and did so by constantly ferreting out weak spots in the heart and the anxious hours in life. Thus Christianity is put forward as a 'religion of redemption.' 'Is there not in this a cardinal mistake, by which Christ is separated from the Old Testament and interpreted in the light of the myths of redemption? . . . The emphasis then falls upon the far side of the boundary of death. . . . But is this really the essential thing in the proclamation of Christ in the Gospels and Paul? I dispute this. The Christian hope of resurrection differs from the mythological hope in this, that in a wholly new way and even more pointedly than the Old Testament, it refers man back to his life on earth. . . . This world must not be prematurely abandoned. *In this the New and the Old Testament are at one.* Myths of redemption arise from human experiences of the boundary situation. But Christ takes hold of a man at the centre of his life.'[113]

In the centre—this is where 'worldly' faith comes into being! By 'wordly' Bonhoeffer means (1) nonmetaphysical, i.e., existential; (2) nonindividualistic, i.e., collective and vicarious; and above all (3) not lordly and grand, i.e., in accordance with the powerlessness of Jesus Christ. For only the suffering God can help. 'To this extent we may say that process of the world's coming of age which we have described, by which a false conception of God was cleared out of the way, opens

[113] Ibid., pp. 153f.

up our view for the God of the Bible, who gains power and place through his powerlessness. This is doubtless where the "worldly interpretation" must begin.'[114]

If we ask what is the ultimate, common implication of these two images, the 'fourth man' and the 'man come of age,' for 'Christian instruction,' it is very clear that it lies in the fact that they both point us to the Old Testament. To stand in the dynamic line of Christian witness is something quite different from being an adherent of Christianity. Bonhoeffer too was very close to the insight that the structures particularly of the Old Testament point to that which is beyond human religiousness.

As far as we can discern, he did not see that the 'silence of the gods' evokes a nihilism which as such is difficult to conceive of as an ex-ponent of 'adulthood,' and, in our judgment, he did not take into account the ambivalent character of this nihilism. From very early in his life the all-important thing was the 'priceless presence of Christ.'[115] What was set in motion through him was not so much the question of finding other new, 'nonreligious' words about God as the question of another, nonreligious attitude toward life in the church.

Seldom or never does he use the word 'secularization.' May not this be because he sees that this word still betrays too clearly a romantic nostalgia for a sacral past? Despite his reference to the 'arcane discipline'—which would preserve the life of the truth as in an ark in rough, hostile times—he had little use for the liturgical revival, for example, as a counteraction to secularization. *'Only he who cries out for the Jews dare also sing in Gregorian.'*[116]

Such an attitude will be of critical importance for Christian instruction which deals with the 'directions' of the Old Testament. Here many Jews, humanists, and freethinkers are right when they (even if it were only a majority, or possibly all, who think in this way!) fight shy of 'religion' as a failure to recognize the times and a flight from difficulty.

[114] Ibid., p. 164.
[115] Eberhard Bethge, 'Dietrich Bonhoeffer, Person und Werk,' *Evangelische Theologie* (1955), p. 158.
[116] Bonhoeffer in Bethge, op. cit., p. 161; ibid., '. . . the concern that not every word is always appropriate in every mouth and for every ear.' Cf. Bonhoeffer, *Ethics*, pp. 326ff., 231.

'We have been behind the world (*hinterweltlerisch*) ever since we devised the vicious dodge of being religious, even "Christian" at the cost of the earth. It is possible to get along fine in this behind-the-world attitude. Whenever life begins to become painful and importunate, you simply leap up in the air and soar with ease and unconcern into the so-called Elysian fields.'[117]

Wilhelm Kamlah, the philosopher, also proclaimed the 'profaneness' of life, but he gives his criticism of culture, radical as it is, a turn toward a revival of religion,[118] in order to prevent so-called 'man come of age' from becoming a part of the masses and thus a prey of the tyrants of uttermost darkness. For in reality nobody is so much treated as one who is under age, and thus at the mercy of the prevailing immaturity, as is the so called 'man come of age.' To this extent he again comes very close to being the 'fourth man.'

In the last weeks of his life Bonhoeffer took instruction in Russian from a fellow prisoner (a nephew of Molotov), and he in turn instructed the Russian in the meaning of the Christian faith. One wonders what was the nature of this 'Christian instruction.' In this connection Bethge says: 'Did he also tell his Russian fellow prisoner about *his beloved Old Testament*? Because it is the book of those who cannot flee into any pious realm, but must live or are permitted to live on this earth either in blessing or in defiance with the derided Jahweh or under his glorious Name? Because he regarded this book as the greatest testimony of an *overcoming of the religious*?'[119]

We cannot live an integral and rational life if we do not face the fact that even we, children of the church and the synagogue, live in this present world 'as if there were no God.' This, precisely this, we have to confess before God and in the power of his Word. God as a hypothesis, as a comfort in boundary situations, as an asylum for our ignorance, as a 'stopgap,' God as a means to an end, God as an ornament—all this is a remnant of God as substance and foundation, as *ens realissimum* and as *summum bonum*, as the idolatrous godhead of our spirituality.

These remnants of the past all show the signs of ambivalence. The kind of instruction in the Scriptures we are thinking of cannot take seriously the contrariety of these remnants: worldly and spiritual, natural and supernatural, profane and sacred, rational and irrational

[117] Bonhoeffer, *Dein Reich komme* (1957), p. 5.
[118] *Der Mensch in den Profanität* (1949), p. 35.   [119] Op. cit., p. 160.

are not ultimate antitheses. Rather, impelled by the Old Testament, our journey goes in the direction of the profaneness of existence on the earth beneath the heaven of the dominion of creative grace.

THE COURAGE TO BE

We have found that the aim of the work which is committed to the interpreter and witness[120] is to send, to let loose, to thrust men out into life. For the nonreligious man especially this always remains a venture.

Ludwig Köhler once said that characteristic of 'Hebrew man' was his great uncertainty in the cosmos. He states that 'this vague awareness of cosmic insecurity forms the basis of the Hebrew's feeling about the world.'[121] He says that in the Genesis story it is the light that first brings security in the chaos (wrongly; in our opinion the security lies rather in the *raqia*, the firmament). However that may be, here in Israel we are confronted not with a biological, psychological characteristic but rather with a reaction of its unbelief in the gods and its dependence upon YHWH. It is denied that the powers have any independence, any autonomy, and thus trust in the cosmos is undermined. Israel lives by the wonder, the sign (*pele'*, *geburah*, *oth*, *mopeth*), which possesses the character of witness.

That is to say that in the Old Testament 'faith' very definitely has in it an element of the 'courage to be.' Anybody who moves out of the sheltering lap of the gods, anybody who stands up in unbelief against mere power and dumb existence, anybody who feels the soft breath of freedom blowing upon his brow and in his heart, must pay for it with insecurity at a point which the pagan would doubtless find to be the

[120 'Interpreter and witness' is an inadequate rendering of the original Dutch *tolk en getuige*. The phrase occurs frequently in the following pages and always describes the task of the person who performs this act of the church in the world. Normally it refers to the minister, but quite intentionally what is meant is not his office but rather his function, namely, the twofold function of 'teaching' and 'preaching' which he performs in accord with the 'two-fold action of the Scriptures.' In this original signification the word *tolk* and its verb form *vertolken* indicate the actual process of oral translation. Thus in English the term 'interpreter' is adequate only if we keep in mind its broadest meaning, such as that of an actor interpreting a role or a musician a piece of music. Here 'interpretation' is more than rational explanation or exposition. I owe the substance of this note to the German translator.—Tr.]

121 *Hebrew Man*, tr. Peter R. Ackroyd (Nashville: Abingdon Press, 1956), p. 109.

very last place where he would be insecure—that is, insecure about whether one really exists, whether one deserves to exist, whether one has the courage to accept one's being even when the gods grow more emphatically silent and even God, the free and almighty God, hides and withdraws himself. Thus there is in fact something of a 'vague awareness of cosmic insecurity' that is peculiar—not to a particular race of people, but rather—to faith. This is connected with the transition from 'space thinking' to 'time thinking,' from a static to a dynamic feeling about life, from the sense of being an element in the cosmos to the feeling of being the vis-à-vis, the partner, indeed, the superior and even the judge of the given; in essence, however, it is what Heidegger means by the 'held-out-ness of existence' (*Hinausgehaltenheit des Daseins*),[122] actually the opposite of faith in the Name.

It is around this problem that Tillich organizes the difficulty of modern nihilism. Starting from here he proposes a 'superfaith,' an 'absolute,' groundless faith as the ultimate answer to our present predominant insecurities.[123] Within this ultimate answer the Reformation proclamation of faith in 'justification' (=the courage to accept that one is accepted) is the penultimate answer; according to Tillich it is outstripped by absolute faith. Though the courage to trust God absorbs the anxiety of fate as well as the anxiety of guilt, modern man faces the extreme of temptation: the total meaninglessness of existence which cannot be resisted except by faith in the 'God above God.'

This hypermodern answer, it seems to us, comes very close to the insecurity that must have afflicted Israel in the midst of the oppressive silence of the gods, and 'God above God' could very well be a paraphrase of the 'Name,' if Tillich did not expressly deny that his 'absolute' faith has any definable content. 'The Lutheran courage returns but not supported by the faith in a judging and forgiving God. It returns in terms of the absolute faith which says yes although there is no special power that conquers guilt. The courage to take the anxiety of meaninglessness upon oneself is the boundary up to which the courage to be can go.'[124]

[122 In the sense of being held out or suspended over an abyss with no supporting foundation.—Tr.]
123 Paul Tillich, *The Courage to Be* (New Haven: Yale Univ. Press, 1952), pp. 171ff.
124 Ibid., pp. 189f.

These ideas of Tillich, in our opinion, far overshoot the mark. This does not empower us to send men out 'into life.' It is theory extorted from speculation on the concept of 'meaninglessness' and is radically, indeed, contradictorily, opposed to the structures of the Old Testament. It again leaves man to himself in the silent and threatening cosmos. It aids and abets a methodology of despair completely alien to the Scriptures and can provide no guidance for the interpreter and witness. Here we must carefully discriminate.

In Köhler's 'Hebrew insecurity' we may discern still another aspect of anthropology, even in the modern form of it which sharpens and reduces it to anxiety. This idea is certainly useful in instruction, if one sees insecurity as the consequence of the 'Name,' which begins to dethrone the cosmic powers and thus in this respect makes men insecure. It seems doubtful whether Köhler has seen this when he says, 'For the Hebrew the word of Christ is certainly apt: "In the world you have tribulation" '; but then the text in the New Testament goes on to say 'but be of good cheer, I have overcome the world' (John 16 : 33)! And what about cosmic insecurity in the Old Testament? Perhaps Köhler says something relatively true when he characterizes postexilic Judaism as a 'religion of anxiety';[125] but this cannot apply to the Old Testament. And to our surprise we hear Köhler himself saying, 'The divinely ordained content of human life is *joy*. There is hardly a word so characteristic of the Old Testament as the word joy.'[126] It can also be proved that this joy, even where it is confined to a narrow strip of boundary territory, does not allow any real sense of tragedy to arise in the Old Testament. The tragic sense of life is alien to the Old Testament, let alone that a dialectical 'tragicism' of accepted meaninglessness (like that of Tillich) could have its root in it.

The temptation to faith (which can in fact befall those who are sent out 'into life') and 'metaphysical suspicion' or 'distrustful temporizing'[127] are two different things. Doubt in all its forms and despair in all its deformities can also be ascribed to the insecurity that came into the world as soon as it was de-divinized by the 'Name.' But man wavers again and again in his faith. We have already heard Rosen-

[125] Op. cit., p. 117.
[126] *Old Testament Theology*, tr. A. S. Todd (London: Lutterworth Press, 1957), p. 151.
[127] Evert Janssen, *Thomas en Trauma*.

zweig's pastoral and sober comment on unbelief, which must by no means be regarded as tragic.[128] The demand that we affirm meaninglessness, the attempt to make total meaninglessness vanish into 'absolute faith' by a *salto mortale* of despair is not a demand which can be given consideration as background of 'Christian instruction,' if only because the very purpose of this instruction is to send a person 'into life.' And this does not occur apart from the creative and protective power of the 'Name,' which is anything but absolute and is very definitely, very deliberately related to faith—toward faith which again is anything but absolute and manifests itself in a very definite, very particular, very personal way. We may summarize as follows:

1. The faith we are talking about can, if one wishes, be described as the courage to be.

2. Under the dominion of the gods, of the godhead, Being was secure in the cosmic being.

3. When the gods are silent, this Being has become an enigma, but as such it is imposed upon us.

4. When the gods are dethroned, Being is impugned and called into question.

5. When the 'Name,' the God above God, commandeers life, then nothing is to be taken for granted, not even Being, not even the 'good purposelessness' which we so intensely enjoyed earlier as pagans.

The Lord speaks and summons us to respond to him with the courage to be, the courage that freely and necessarily emerges from the heart when it is filled with the echo and reflection of him who 'will be what he will be' (Exod. 3 : 14). The courage of trust is actually— necessarily and fundamentally—also the courage to be; and conversely, what appears to be a necessary clinging to Being is in fact an act of faith.

'It cannot be said that we are lacking in faith. Even the simple fact of our life is of a faith-value that can never be exhausted. "You suggest that there is some value in this? One cannot not-live, after all." It is precisely in this "Cannot, after all" that the mad strength of faith lies; it is in this negation that it takes on form.'[129]

---

[128] *Briefe*, p. 383.
[129] Franz Kafka, 'Reflections on Sin, Suffering, Hope, and the New Way' in *Dearest Father, Stories and Other Writings*, tr. Ernest Kaiser and Eithne Wilkins (New York: Schocken Books, 1954), p. 48.

In order to avoid one-sidedness we must mention here another tendency of the time, which simply starts with a philosophical consideration that circumscribes the 'madness' which Kafka ascribed to the act of faith and defines it so narrowly that the word 'mad' is nothing more than an expression for an emotional association. We have already mentioned in passing the work of de Sopper and Loen (and also of Oosterbaan). They are not willing to resign themselves to the dualism between autonomous thinking and faith in revelation and go over to a clear offensive against immanentist philosophy. We may doubt whether this is of any immediate help to the work of the interpreter and witness—although on the other hand a timid attitude toward philosophy as an alleged revelatory power in its own right is to be rejected. The available middle way will be for him to recognize that the specific realm of 'radical profaneness,' even in its most confused form, is the sphere in which human encounter takes place and then, immediately to let the 'desperate dissonance' between our dilemma and that of philosophy (including existentialism) be seen.[130]

That it is impossible to separate between the interpreting of the witness and the attempts of philosophy to fathom the truth of human speech is also the conviction of such a candid and rigorous thinker as Kamlah. He believes that, philosophically speaking, the adulthood of man consists in nothing else but the 'perceiving and acceptance of that more than human word (*Zusage*), the work of the "receptive reason" (*vernehmende Vernunft*) which is frustrated by the stubborn "obstinacy of profaneness." And the "courage to be," ' by which existentialism is both evoked and nullified, cannot be given a foundation apart from the mystery of history. For eighteen hundred years faith and philosophy have been so close together (up to Hegel and beyond him) that a return to a pre-Christian stage (as in the case of Heidegger) must be called an act of violence.

Kamlah arrives at the thesis that 'a beliefless thinking *within the closed horizon* of profaneness *does no justice* to the being of man and reality as a whole.' That may well be true! Nevertheless the interpreter and witness must be imbued with the conviction that a better philosophy, a broader reason, even reason infused with the powers of myth (such

---

[130] Wilhelm Kamlah, *Der Ruf des Steuermanns: Die religiöse Verlegenheit dieser Zeit und die Philosophie* (1954), pp. 30ff., 81ff.; cf. J. Defever, *La preuve de Dieu; étude crit. Museum Lessianum, sect. phil. XXXVII.*

as that proclaimed by Gusdorf)[131] still 'does no justice' to the Name of God. Thus our point of departure must still remain the text of Holy Scriptures.

THE GRAVITY OF EMPTINESS

In this little mirror of our times the background is dominated by the 'fourth man.' But on the level surface of this mirror there are also flashes of some extreme manifestations. They stand out in relief against a puzzling remnant of authority; they appear to be caused by the radioactivity that has been left in the air since the explosion, the holy catastrophe, of the Name. Therefore they are to be regarded at least partially, even from a rational point of view, as an unclarified attitude toward the meaning of the Old Testament, which testifies to this Name.

In the great and moving figure of Simone Weil various extreme experiences and ideas are combined, and the extremes themselves are combined in syntheses which are confusing to many.[132] A French critic has said that she seemed to him to be 'a Christian Buddhist who tried to realize a world view orientated upon Plato with Jewish pathos'— but one may doubt whether this hits the mark. In the context of our thinking and in view of our purpose it would be showing scant respect if we were to attempt to give even a brief survey of the whole range of her thought. Of greatest importance to us is her *experience vecue* ('lived experience'), to which she bears a truly germinal witness in ever different ways and in words that speak directly to our condition. It is above all the following emphases that move us, speak to us, and disturb us.

1. Simone Weil speaks of her encounter with Christ; she believes

[131] *Mythe et métaphysique: introduction à la philosophie* (1953), pp. 241f.
[132] Of the works of Simone Weil, published posthumously, we mention the most important: *La Pesanteur et la Grâce* (1947; tr. *Gravity and Grace*); *Attente de Dieu* (1950; tr. *Waiting for God*); *Les Cahiers de Simone Weil*, 3 vols. (1952–55; tr. *The Notebooks of Simon Weil*); *La source grecque* (1955); *Intuitions prechretiennes* (1956; tr. *Intimations of Christianity among the Ancient Greeks*, containing chapters from both of the latter two books). On her person and work: Herman Berger, *De gedachtenwerald van Simone Weil* (1955); Jacques Cabaud, *L'experience vecue de Simone Weil* (1957); M. M. Davy, *The Mysticism of Simone Weil* (London: Rockliff, 1951); Gustave Thibon and J. M. Perrin, *Simon Weil telle que nous l'avons connue* (1952; tr. *Simon Weil As We Knew Her*); Karl Epting, *Der geistliche Weg der Simone Weil* (1957).

that she was prepared for this through the suffering laid upon her. It was 'a real contact, person to person, here below, between a human being and God. . . . Moreover, in this sudden possession of me by Christ, neither my senses nor my imagination had any part; I only felt *in the midst of my suffering* the presence of a love, like that which one can read in the smile on a beloved face.'[133] She came to the conviction that the Christian faith contains an answer by virtue of which even 'the most dreadful and meaningless suffering could be accepted as meaningful.'[134] Here lay the reason why she sought anonymity, to be absorbed and to disappear in the suffering masses, but also to be absorbed in her own consciousness.[135]

2. As a Jew with an agnostic background she set out in search of the absolute, in radical opposition to the intellectual emptiness of our time. On the path she chose, which meant the sacrifice of traditional forms and judgments, she found no better way of describing her position—or better, her pilgrimage (and her temporary refuge)—than 'purifying atheism.' And we can say that in doing so she was drawing an important conclusion of the Old Testament message concerning the gods.

3. Nevertheless, it appears, Simone Weil herself made a different assessment; for she speaks of 'Yahweh' as an idol or at most a 'natural' God;[136] she names God the Father in the same breath with Allah and with—Hitler. These three 'earthly gods' are in all seriousness lumped together as being comparable in their madness and their cruelty. Yahweh is a despot, a tribal god, the self-consciousness of a collective, the projection of weak men's desire for power, a sociomorph, a fossil

[133] *Waiting for God*, tr. Emma Crauford (New York: G. P. Putnam's Sons, Capricorn Books ed. 1959), p. 69.

[134] J. M. Perrin, *Wir kannten Simone Weil*, Brief 4, pp. 50f.

[135] Ibid., pp. 66f. In Jacques Cabaud's book, *L'experience vecue de Simone Weil* (1957), we read of how in 1934 she, the daughter of well situated parents and a teacher of philosophy, took a job in a factory, not as an experiment but actually breaking the family bond (*Journal d'usine* and *La condition ouvrière*). She worked in Portugal and was a nurse in the Spanish Civil War. In 1940 she fled to Marseilles, where she worked as a farm labourer; in 1942 she fled to the United States by way of North Africa; wanted to return to London (*Ecrits de Londres*); championed de Gaulle; sought active service with the Maquis; lived on the equivalent of French rations and, severely ill, refused to accept any further assistance. On August 24, 1942, she died at the age of thirty-four in a sanatorium in Ashford, Kent.

[136] *Gravity and Grace*, tr. Anna Crauford (London: Routledge and Kegan Paul, 1952), p. 94.

entity. The question how this total misunderstanding is to be explained, we shall not pursue here; the second part of this book will, it is hoped, provide an answer which will show a way out of the labyrinth of this kind of thinking, which is 'Christian,' but ignorant of the God of Israel.

4. Even in her later years, after her encounter with Christ, Simone Weil remained outside the church. She stood outside the door, as she herself said; the liturgy and the life of the saints and the example of six or seven Catholics of 'authentic spirituality' might almost have been able to move her to enter. On the one hand all that was needed was the slightest push, and on the other reproaches against the church welled up within her. In large part these reproaches are the same which she levelled against Israel, for she saw in the Roman Catholic Church the continuation of the evil side of the Jewish attitude toward life, that is, the wicked consciousness of the presence of God, the belief in God's good Creation and wise providence, the clinging to this earthly life, the striving for happiness, the trust in vengeance, the sanctioning of holy (or unholy) war, the fact that it takes history seriously, as if any meaning could be found in it, and above all, the reluctance to suffer, the premature flight into paradox, the double standard of morality for the individual and the state. All this is just as much Roman as Jewish, indeed, it is to a large extent universally Christian and it makes the church, as she says in the language of the Apocalypse, the 'great beast' that corrupts the nations and causes them to forget the seriousness of man's hopeless situation and universal compassion.

As far as Israel itself is concerned, we find in this young Jewish woman statements that are clearly anti-Semitic, which confronts us with an even greater enigma. Many think, perhaps rightly, that what Simone Weil lacked was a valid confrontation with the Reformation (and this would prove to be true); but the deepest cause of the discrepancy between this profound insight and this exaggeration, this sincerity and this tormented stubbornness lies nevertheless in a lack of a real knowledge of the Old Testament and a well-grounded attitude toward it.

5. But we would be neglecting one of the chief reasons for her lingering on the threshold of the church and her decision to remain outside if we did not also refer to her sense of solidarity with the world, with the unbelievers, with the nihilists. 'In any case . . . nothing gives me more pain than the idea of separating myself from the immense and

unfortunate multitude of unbelievers. I have the essential need, and I think I can say the vocation, to move among men of every class and complexion, mixing with them and sharing their life and outlook, so far that is to say as conscience allows, merging into the crowd and disappearing among them, so that they show themselves as they are, putting off all disguises with me. It is because I long to know them so as to love them just as they are. . . . I do not speak of helping them, because as far as that goes I am unfortunately quite incapable of doing anything as yet.'[137]

But this solidarity we consider to be a self-evident presupposition of the apostolate of the church; and it is rather strange to see that things can have come to such a pass that noble spirits should think that they would be denying their apostolic vocation if they joined the apostolic (and Catholic) church. In view of the widespread alienation that actually exists, it is fortunate that people like Simone Weil remain in their place with the nihilists, with those who have cast religion behind them, however prettified and refined it may be.

6. It is curious to see Simone Weil immersing herself in the mysticism of John of the Cross, and also that of the Upanishads; but more typical, it appears to me, is that toward the end of her work she saw Buddhism looming up as a consequence and a way out of her thinking and became engrossed with Zen,[138] without wishing, however, to eliminate the mystery of the Cross.[139] However great the respect one may and must accord to this part of her pilgrimage, for our question of how the meaning of the Old Testament can make a breach in the solid front of (genuine or ungenuine) nihilism, these thoughts can only serve as an illustration of what is the opposite of the prophetic witness, the singular newness of which is here completely unrecognized. I have said elsewhere that there are only two religions which are not religious, prophetism and Buddhism, and that the one is the opposite of the other.[140] This is corroborated in Simone Weil's pilgrimage.

7. But how is such a mixture of Zen and the Cross possible rationally and existentially? Does Simon Weil's thinking evoke chaos? One could think so and yet there is certainly not the slightest indication

---

[137] *Waiting for God*, p. 48.
[138] *The Notebooks of Simone Weil*, tr. Arthur Wills (New York: G. P. Putnam's Sons 1956), Vol. II, pp. 395ff.
[139] Ibid., p. 415.   [140] Cf. Miskotte, *Edda en Thora* (1939), pp. 130, 353, 402.

that she had any desire to take delight in chaos. We believe that the basic impulse behind her searching and positive evaluation of all things lay in a new experience of pain and the effect of pain: 'The irreducible character of suffering, which makes it impossible for us not to have a horror of it at the moment when you are undergoing it, is ultimately designed to arrest the will, just as an absurdity arrests the intelligence, or absence, nonexistence, arrests love.'[141] Is not this a part of the picture of our time, does it not haunt the margins of the statements of the rejection of God—this absolutization of suffering above suffering? There is the stirring of rebellion against necessity, which is almost simultaneously suppressed by the realization of its absurdity. Suffering, because of which earlier generations shed tears, is a solidified segment of everyday misery, which hardly evokes a reaction any more, because the 'necessity' as well as the 'gravity' (*pesanteur*), the weight of human existence, are ultimate facts, are thought of ontologically. When our attitude toward life approaches the conclusion that existence itself is suffering, we have stepped out of the domain of the Name: then, to express it in dogmatic terms, Creation and Fall have been identified.

In what way is this the case with Simone Weil? As it came from God, Creation is not an act of expansion, but rather of withdrawal; he emptied a part of 'what-is' (*Seienden*) by withdrawing from it. This is why John says that the Lamb was slain from the foundation of the world (Rev. 13 : 8). The world weighs down upon us with the gravity of emptiness; and the providence which rules over it is nowhere relevant to the individual or to a people or to any finite goal. Therefore love of fate becomes the only genuine answer; for God has left the world to fate. Thus evil and wickedness reign more in the world than in men; and the author comes close to Manichaeism, in which an additional minus quantity comes into play in the sense that here God must be regarded as impersonal, to a large degree indifferent, and essentially absent.[142] What is left is a strange kind of *amor fati*.

But this does not preclude that room may be left for 'denial of self' (*rénoncement de soi*) and this transcending of self can be understood as an *imitatio Dei*. God does not create acceptation for himself; God turns himself into a 'negligible quantity,' without form, but also without

[141] *The Notebooks of Simone Weil*, Vol. II, p. 415; cf. p. 114.
[142] *L'Enracinement*; Eng. *The Need for Roots*, tr. by Arthur Wills (Boston, The Beacon Press, 1955), pp. 262f; *Gravity and Grace*, p. 99; *Intimations of Christianity*, p. 120.

being; seen from our point of view he exists only in the form of non-being. His presence takes on more reality the more it is experienced and recognized as absence. We find in Simone Weil many thoughts which are related to those of Bonhoeffer in the last period of his life when he speaks of the powerlessness of Christ and the cross as the fundamental form of reality. But in Simone Weil they are in various ways carried to the extreme, for example, in the direction of an *amor fati* analogous to the fact that the Powerless and Absent One reveals his will precisely in the harshness of fate; indeed, the presence of the love of God occurs in the downfall of a man. It is as if the emptiness of existence were transformed into meaningfulness through the harshness of fate. In connection with these ideas Philippians 2 is cited,[143] the proclamation of the *kenosis* as the prelude to the victory of Christ, indeed, more than this, as its reverse side. So it is with grace when it enters into suffering (which by its nature is suffering from the unreality of everything that surrounds us). Emptiness itself, then, seems to become the place of theophany, gravity itself becomes an illumination. Hence Simone Weil's predilection for the passage in Revelation concerning the Lamb which was slain from the foundation of the world.

8. This Jewish thinker's sharp aversion to the God of Israel is documented in her neglect of the text of the Old Testament. It is not only that it was not the subject of her study as were the New Testament, the Brahmanic texts, and the Greek tragedies; the Old Testament is hardly cited in all her writings, and then only incidentally and always the same passages, namely, those that refer to the Suffering Servant of the Lord (Isa. 53) and the 'tree of knowledge' (Gen. 3). Nothing about the doctrine of God, creation, election, history, and nothing at all about the history of salvation. So we are not too surprised to read that 'Plato is a Christian mystic, the *Iliad* flooded with Christian light, and Dionysus and Osiris are in a certain way Christ himself.'[144]

The meaning of the *Tenak* precisely for our modern age! Simone Weil seemed to be made to bring this to light; she appeared to be called to hallow the 'Name' (with the reason, too) because of her solidarity with the uprooted. In a certain sense, no one was so close to fulfilling that task—and no one so wilfully passed it by as did Simone Weil. J. M. Perrin's comment (meant to be paradoxical) that it was a false re-

---

[143] In detail in *The Notebooks of Simone Weil*, Vol. I, p. 208; cf. *Waiting for God*, p. 158.
[144] Lydia Schäppi, 'Simone Weil', *Judaica*, XIII (1957), p. 250.

jection of Israel that prevented Simone Weil from becoming a Christian, seems to us not to be ultimately paradoxical at all, but rather to exhibit an incontrovertible logic.

To equate obedience to God with acceptance of life as it is, in other words, to identify the will of God with moral law and things as they actually are—this is incompatible with biblical structures. Then the inevitable conclusion, which not only confuses but overturns these biblical structures, is that morality (which, according to Simone Weil, springs directly from mysticism) is everywhere identical and imperishable. 'This can be verified,' she says, 'by turning to Egypt, Greece, India, China, Buddhism, the Moslem tradition, Christianity, and the folklore of all countries.'[145] But in our countries this mystical morality eventuates in revolting man; and anyone who does not overlook this may be shocked to find that this doctrine of self-emptying, self-denial, and *amor fati* finally ends up in the discovery that the Lamb who was slain from the foundation of the world is really Prometheus.[146]

9. The profound mind, the great soul, and the brave life of Simone Weil have made her (quite unconsciously on her part) a real leader, a bearer of intellectual and moral authority in our time, a symbol of the new earnestness that flowers here and there in a nihilistic age. And the more or less isolated statements concerning the Prometheus-Christ appeal to the heart of the hardly conscious archetypal life that stirs in many younger people who still live in the Western cultural tradition. A balance between *rénoncement* ('renunciation') and *révolte* ('revolt') must be found; the dialectical unity of both must be placed as an axiom at the beginning of reflection or as a paradox at the end of it. The *pesanteur*, the gravity, the weight of emptiness in matter and substance, in the soul and the whole bent of our life must become a part of the description of what in the Old Testament is called sin and transgression. Suffering from life itself and suffering from guilt become identical, and likewise the sacrifice of the martyrs and the risks of the rebels. For an *avant-garde* of modern youth there is not only a magic splendour about *l'homme révolté* ('rebel man')[147] but also a mystical reason for his appearance on the scene. This experience can be met with even at the

[145] *Oppression and Liberty*, tr. Arthur Wills and John Petrie (London: Routledge and Kegan Paul, 1958), p. 161.
[146] *Intimations of Christianity*, p. 70; cf. Simone Weil, *Letter to a Priest*, tr. Arthur Wills (London: Routledge and Kegan Paul, 1953), p. 20.
[147] *The Rebel*, title of one of Albert Camus's books.

very threshold of the Catholic Church. Simone Weil is a tragic example of a failure to recognize practically all the principal and distinctive features of the Old Testament, which in our conviction contains the very healing and saving power the 'fourth man' needs. It is significant that at the end this great Jewish thinker (who wanted at the same time to be a whole and radical Christian) came to this conclusion: 'Our culture owes nothing to Israel and extremely little to Christianity; it owes almost everything to pre-Christian antiquity.'[148] And according to her opinion, what matters is that we should recognize the great extent to which our secular culture has arisen from 'a religious inspiration, which, even though chronologically it may be pre-Christian, can still be regarded as in essence Christian.' This completely explains her scorn for Yahweh; or better, her scorn for Yahweh was primary and this explains the necessity of such a distortion of the plain facts of the history of thought.

All this points to the great importance of turning away from all kinds of syncretism and even from all more or less justified and accepted syntheses. One can view the dismay or the relief that result from the silence of the gods with anything like calmness only if one has the courage to seek to 'hallow the Name' (with the mind and reason too). To hallow includes putting oneself aside, dedicating oneself to him who dedicated himself, revering the Singular One for the sake of his own majesty, isolating the signs which belong to the Name, in the expectation that its exclusiveness will result in inclusiveness. The confidence that neglect of the *Tenak* will prove to be the chief cause of our Christian inability to cope with genuine and ungenuine nihilism may help us to make progress. He who still believes that we have a mission to fulfil in our encounter with the 'fourth man' (which among other things includes both speech and reason) may discover that nothing provides such outstanding help in clearing up the confusion (which in many respects was caused and kept alive by the church) as the instruction of the Old Testament, if we listen to it with a fresh receptiveness. It would be an evidence of a complete unawareness of the vital problem which is here at issue to be surprised by voices, for example, from the church in East Germany beyond the Iron Curtain, which say: What we need above all is instruction of youth in the meaning of the Old Testament.

[148] *Lettre à un ouvrier*, p. 19.

10. When we do this, the central concern will be the hallowing of the NAME. This is what will clarify the confused situation. In Simone Weil's writings, however, the *shema' Yisra'el* is equated with an exhortation to preserve the Unutterable from defilement. One can say that this infiltration of alien ideas is common enough in Jewish thinking (contrary to the fundamental structure of the Old Testament). Philo and Maimonides, Mendelssohn and Constantin Brunner are evidence of this. But among Christian thinkers too it is something almost taken for granted, for they automatically, persistently, incorrigibly interpret *ehyeh asher ehyeh* as 'I am who I am.'[149] This profanes the Name rationalistically, turns it into the very thing that it was trying to break away from in order to safeguard our liberation from the chimera of the 'Absolute.' This passion for the abstract One is always seizing upon the tetragrammaton in order, if possible, to undermine its content.

Simone Weil thinks of the Absolute as an insistent presence; she calls it 'defenceless' and 'powerless'; often it is also called 'light.' When she declares: 'We know nothing of God's essence, but we do know what he does to us,' she is turning back to her paternal heritage. Here the intellectually sacrosanct concept of abstract being is breached. The dominant line of her thinking, however, derives from a contempt for the *shema'* ('Hear, Israel, YHWH our God is *echad*: one, unique, onefold, unexchangeable')—and from a disregard of the Name. She wants to understand and help modern man—and then proceeds to start again at the point where his godlessness has its origin and rehabilitates and reinstates its presuppositions.

Nihilism that is ungenuine, that is, when it is still mixed with remnants of a remembrance of the God of superbeing, who as such is the God of history, so that one can wait, however hopelessly, for a breakthrough of his presence and help ('waiting for Godot')—this kind of nihilism with its salutary ungenuineness, inconsistency, unrest, and expectation, has the ground pulled from under it. For one who is a fanatic for the absolute it smacks of 'superstition'; wherever there is existential thinking, he scents 'contamination.' And he 'thinks away' whatever can be thought away, until absolute being turns out to be absolute nothingness.

To try to verify this procedure by appealing to the Old Testament

[149] Exod. 3 : 14.

represents an infraction that makes any understanding impossible,[150] because this rips the given text from its root soil and renders the hermeneutical perspective unrecognizable. Lofty words!—and it seems quite impossible to bring them into relationship to the concrete distress (or the comfortable satisfaction) of the godless man. But *hic Rhodus, hic salta*! Just as it is one of the most urgent concerns of the work of missions to find a translation of the tetragrammaton,[151] so it is necessary for us in Europe in this time of great alienation to find a new approach to the understanding of names and the Name. Quite unreflectively, quite guilelessly, quite inescapably, this alienation is the universal obstacle. How pathetic, how dreadful to hear one of the finest critical minds of our time saying to himself: '. . . only in the tremendous and mysterious words of Jehova: I AM THAT I AM. . . . Not *cogito ergo sum* is the mark of the soul, but *sum ergo cogito*. . . . And what is God? . . . that greater I am to which my own I am acknowledges a binding relation. . . . The sense of this inward motion, the consciousness of this binding relation between the two I AM's, is what I understand by the word "religion".'[152]

---

[150] Cf. Simone Weil, *La connaissance surnaturelle*, p. 204; Constantin Brunner, *Unser Christus*, pp. 709–15; Herman Cohen, *Religion der Vernunft aus den Quellen des Judentums*, pp. 73, 386, 410f.; Paul Tillich, *Systematic Theology*, Vo. I, (Univ. of Chicago Press, 1951), pp. 133f., 141ff., 227ff. On the contrary view cf. Georges Gusdorf, *Traité de Métaphysique*; Leo Shestow, *Auf Hiobs Wage*, pp. 411f.; T. Goedewaagen, *Summa contra metaphysicos*, pp. 165f.

[151] Hellmut Rosin, *The Lord is God: The Translation of the Divine Names and the Missionary Calling of the Church* (1955).

[152] John Middleton Murry, *To The Unknown God: Essays Towards a Religion* (New York: P. Smith, 1930), pp. 159, 163.

Part II: Witness and Interpretation

1. Tensions

INNER TENSIONS

In the situation which has been described, in a certain sense the best course would be to start with our direct view of things and our first inspiration and begin at once to do whatever our hand finds to do and to speak what is given to us to speak. Our time demands plain, blunt answers; as a rule, people find it hard to concentrate. Whatever is to grip them must overwhelm them, and if this is to happen, then the doer, the speaker, the interpreter must live among them as one who is himself overwhelmed. The time is short and the truth is great and multi-dimensional. We understand those witnesses and evangelists who choose the direct method, who in their way feel responsible for the task that has been laid upon them and are accused, in our opinion wrongly, of a lust for sensationalism. They are gripped by the mystery of the NAME and the dark enigma of their godforsaken and godforgotten fellow men. They want to get down to business quickly. They feel that too much time has already been wasted in reflections that are theoretical and remote from the world.

Nevertheless, this cannot be our approach. Even though we do not have the office of the ministry and perhaps are rather far removed from the centres of church leadership, in our opinion the preacher and interpreter, precisely in order that he may thereby draw a fresh breath as a witness, must subject himself to a deliberate and progressive accounting. And this will mean that for the time being there will have to be some stopping on the way, because the inner tensions affect the outwardly directed energies.

We call them 'inner' tensions not primarily because we have in mind those that are personal and ministerial, that have to do with the scientific difficulties of faith (though naturally these too are involved),

99

but rather primarily with respect to the object of faith—the realm in which it stands, the atmosphere which surrounds it. After all, when we examine the matter, it is anything but a self-evident thing that we should at the same time (and in the same sense?) connect such great expectations as those we attach to a concept like the 'Word of God' with a collection of writings, which, shaped and consecrated into a canon, are supposed to be the humanly verbalized medium of the witness as well as the interpretation, of the message as well as the instruction. And it must always appear somewhat forced and unnatural that, despite this multitude of inner difficulties, the power of the evidence that this is the Word of God nevertheless tends to assert itself, even though it be only with a secondary immediacy, in the midst of the silence of the gods.

It is necessary to deal with these inner tensions in more detail.

1. When we preach or teach 'from the Old Testament,' we must always be thoroughly conscious of a number of simple historical facts which, even before we engage in further theological reflection, may evoke in us reverence and expectation and a peculiar receptiveness for this strange and alien thing. But despite its strangeness, this in itself seems to have within it a promise of future intellectual affinity and community, since for centuries it has already been reaching the nations with its intellectual substance and must be regarded as a decisive factor in the unification of Europe. Why is it, then, that this Old Testament repels so many people who regard it as primitive, vengeful, inhumane, or, compared with the sacred books of other peoples, colourless, estranged from nature, and moralistic? This may be the reaction of our original pagan blood—there is something in this, and so it evokes a certain tension in all of us, even in the convinced interpreter.

2. The attacks to which the Old Testament is exposed are not of such great consequence that they do not vanish from our minds as soon as we remember that this book was the Holy Scriptures for Jesus,[1] that the Apostles in carrying out their mission always appealed to the Word of God as they found it in the Old Testament, that the New

---

[1] J. Hänel, in *Der Schriftbegriff Jesu* (1919), attempts, in my opinion wrongly, to interpret the phrase *'en pneumati* in Matt. 22 : 43 and Mark 12 : 36, as well as the word *kalōs* in Matt. 15 : 7 and Mark 7 : 6, as expressing Jesus' preference for the pasages here cited and as a critical reservation with regard to other Old Testament passages.

Testament nowhere claims to set forth a new idea of God, that the ancient church held the Scriptures to which the Apostles appealed as the Scripture. The very fact that the apostolic fathers applied the otherwise untenable method of allegorization to the Old Testament is an evidence that for them it was the highest authority and the deepest source of the knowledge of God.[2] But this confronts us with spiritual facts, that is, events which must be re-enacted in our spirit until they have at least the value of a 're-enacted decision.' And who would really have arrived at the point where it would have become for him a guide for his life and spirit?

3. We call attention further to the strong difference in feeling and attitude toward life that appears among peoples according as they have no, or some, or a deep sympathy with the Old Testament, say the Spanish, the German, and the English people. We may also point out how the anti-Semitism, which is natural to all of us, decreases or increases in proportion as this collection of writings is recognized in a particular circle of people as the Bible of Jesus, as the intellectual and spiritual world from which the apostles emerged with an old yet new commandment. And we may note further how the whole problem of church and state has always been solved either secularly or Baptistically except where the covenant of God with Israel has been proclaimed as a present reality and thus where the Old Testament has been recognized as holy, authoritative, and life-regulative Scripture. These, too, are historical and psychological facts of world-wide dimensions. Perhaps we are already getting too far ahead of our discussion in making these suggestions, but he who understands them also knows that in themselves facts have no normative power and that facts which are qualified (by God?) to be able to guide our spirit must be constantly reappropriated—in this case, it seems to us, not without a secret or admitted feeling of shame over the fact that anti-Semitism actually exists among us and that it derives partly from our non-genuine appropriation of the Old Testament.

4. Consider further that the hegemony of *ratio* (reason), the consistent application of an autonomous scientific scholarship in the theological disciplines, has been concentrated first of all and with an acute and incisive force precisely upon this human, all too human book

[2] J. L. Koole, *De overname van het Oude Testament door de christelijke Kerk* (1936); H. J. Schoeps, *Theologie und Geschichte des Judenchristentums* (1949), pp. 145f.

which is so full of irregularities and contradictions—and that nevertheless even today not a single central passage of the Old Testament can be translated in any but the accustomed way without its having an effect upon Christian preaching and more or less perceptibly influencing the subsequent course of the church's history in a country or even in the world. But in this connection it must also be remembered that this concept of science (though it can perhaps be relativized) is in fact our own—not merely something that has been forced upon us, but mind of our mind, pride of our pride, burden of our burden, and the really precarious thing in our precarious intellectual life.

5. Finally, we must constantly remind ourselves that the great schism between the church and the synagogue is (and remains) something grand, shocking—and fruitful, only if both recognize the Old Testament in the full sense as God's Word and both interpret and apply it on the basis of this confession. But the stubbornness and equal earnestness with which something completely divergent grows out of the same soil must shock us—and it should bind and compel us to work at it continually. This work cannot be 'unengaged' and neutral in the sense that what we discover in detail is simply regarded as established in advance (or must we say, settled for us in advance?) and then accepted as being scientifically defensible and responsible so far as our faith is concerned. When we are dealing with the church and synagogue, we are not dealing with a dogmatic apriorism, but rather with an a priori *existentiale*,[3] which determines what must be thought of as the holy in each of these realms.

The Proclamation

The fact that this is holy ground and chosen ground that we tread naturally increases our reverence and responsibility, but also considerably magnifies the tension. Preaching is never merely telling how things were nor testifying how we see the truth that is 'revealed' to us, nor does essential preaching occur when one explains the world and man's fate or holds up ideals for the individual and the community 'on the basis' of biblical facts. In short, preaching has no religious purpose, as the 'second' and the 'third man' (and the majority of our contem-

[3 Heidegger's term; cf. *Being and Time*, tr. John Macquarrie and Edward Robinson (New York: Harper & Brothers, 1962), pp. 70, 79.—Tr.]

poraries) understand it. Preaching means proclaiming that life, the whole of life as we know it, is visited, justified, and destined for a new future by God, and that through this it has been completely changed, objectively, gathered up into a different God-relationship, receiving a new value. Right preaching will at least in its intention be in accord with that *propheteuein* which relativizes all human considerations, rules out all pretension by virtue of the seriousness of God, and thaws all seriousness with a warmth that comes from other latitudes. Preaching and instruction, that twofold action of which we spoke above, are a happening, of which one does not know how it happens—although on the other hand one knows very well that when certain things are denied or neglected, it is not to be expected that anything of consequence will happen. Though we cannot make a final judgment, we may nevertheless assume with good reason that the proclamatory character of preaching gives the response to it the character of acclamation, and that instruction, when it really eschews all search for a point of contact, produces evidence of having a validity and power of its own. Therefore everything depends on whether we talk *about* the Scripture (or even about a passage of Scripture)—or whether we preach *the* Scripture and instruct *from* the Scripture. This latter dilemma perhaps pushes the tension to its extreme, but at the same time it also reduces to relative unimportance all those tensions of which we spoke above; those tensions which have swollen to such importance are almost insignificant in comparison with the question of how we, whether Jew or Christian, stand in this realm.

For no heart can give something from a treasure which that heart does not value and treat as a treasure, even though it has it at its disposal. But it is also true that no one can give something as long as his valuation of the treasure has not become a positive, existential valuation rather than a formal, cultural, and religious one, as long as he has not made the treasure his own.

In other words, how can one preach from the 'Old Testament' if one really regards it as an *old* testament, if it is actually old in the sense of being passé or outworn, half-valid, provisional, about ready to disappear? Then there is nothing to preach *from* the Old Testament! In this case how could this book be anything but illustrative material, a reservoir of examples and spiritual anecdotes, and naturally also, for us Christians, an explanation of historical causes and psychological connections? But this would be to move on an entirely different level from that marvellous act which is called preaching. And on this level it would be impossible to expect the response of acclamation to proclamation. 'For the true life of the Spirit knows no "tendencies" [schools of thought]. . . . There is nothing more homogeneous than the "intellectual," simply because it moves a person only intellectually and is not created by the Spirit,' says Rosenzweig[4] in connection with his thesis that only three 'are physically and spiritually begotten,' the pagan, the Jew, and the Christian. Therefore one can preach as a Jew or as a Christian, but not as an idealist, a moralist, or a scientific expert. All 'religious' valuation of the Old Testament, except when it remains within the bounds of its object, cuts off the preaching *of* the Old Testament at its root.

Many think they have conceded a great deal when they accept that we cannot possibly 'understand' the New Testament without the Old; and whether this is intended in the archaeological sense (just as it is useful, for example, to show children in a confirmation class a model of a caravanserai) or whether one is directing one's attention in a highly cultured and religiously interested way to the Semitic thought-world, the Israelite attitude toward life, the specific character of its piety— it still falls just as short of the view which in its simple and unreduced form is the necessary prerequisite if a proclamation is to arise out of such a book.[5]

Nor will it do actually to talk about something else, for example, about persons and sayings in the New Testament, and merely bring in the Old Testament in a secondary way in order to use it as an example of an antiquated point of view.[6] One may think that one may allow oneself to do this at one's own risk, but how can it deserve to be called preaching of the Old Testament and instruction from the

[4] 'Hic et ubique,' *Kleinere Schriften* (1937), p. 471.
[5] Cf. on the concept of the authority of Scripture in the ancient synagogue: Strack-Billerbeck, *Kommentar zum Neuen Testament aus Talmud und Midrasch*, IV, pp. 419–51.
[6] Emmanuel Hirsch, *Das Alte Testament und die Predigt des Evangeliums* (1936): 'The point is to use the Old Testament in the proper Christian way as a book which has been nullified and cancelled out by the New Testament.' And in another passage: 'It [the Old Testament] is parabolic of the New Testament not according to what it is, but rather in that it is shattered by the New' (p. 63). Cf. also Bultmann's view of the Old Testament as a documentation of 'miscarriage' (*des Scheiterns*). [See Bultmann, 'Prophecy and Fulfilment,' in *Essays Philosophical and Theological*, tr. James C. G. Grieg (New York: Macmillan, 1955), pp. 205ff.—Tr.]

Old Testament? Is not the whole meaning and purpose of the word 'preaching' devaluated when it becomes synonymous with assertion plus illustration, edification plus refreshing our knowledge, consolation and admonition on the basis of words which have affected us? And what is more, does not this annul the purpose for which the canon was formed? When we do this, are we not departing from the church of all the centuries, and also from the living Israel? Is it not true that the canon of the Old Testament has been 'closed' (and thus given permanence) precisely through the kerygma of the Messiah—and that this closure of the canon contains within it the disclosure, in so far as the apostolic preaching contains nothing new except that the promise has been fulfilled? At that moment the function of prophecy as pure witness to the expectation was completed and the prophecy itself was turned by the Apostles into a witness to the Messiah who entered into this present time. This is the paradox from which Christian preaching proceeds: when the time has come that the Old Testament is closed, then the time has come to let it speak 'for itself' as a fully valid witness of Him who has come.[7]

COMPROMISES

The whole complex of questions raised by the Old Testament shows us how strange it is that we should have this book in the pulpit, in the midst of the service of worship, as a source and norm of liberating truth and on a table or lectern when we are giving instruction for the purpose of making this truth better understood. But the problem becomes even more pressing when we remember that the Reformers and our Reformed fathers started out from the concept of the unity of the Scriptures. And on no account did they mean by this a historical continuity that would be visible to any secular eye nor even an agreement in the kind of piety and attitude toward life that could be divined or detected in it. This unity, nay, this similarity they confessed; they declared their faith in the Scriptures. They *confessed* the unity, indeed, the likeness (*similitudo*) of the Scriptures. They would not have understood or

[7] H. H. Rowley, *The Unity of the Bible* (1953); Martin Noth, 'Die Vergegenwärtigung des Alten Testaments in der Verkündigung,' *Evangelische Theologie*, XII (1952–53), pp. 6ff.

would have emphatically rejected a statement like this one made by Hermann Gunkel: 'When we call Jesus the Christ, we do so in the sense that we consider him the one who fulfilled but at the same time the one who *surpassed* the religious and ethical *ideas* of the prophecy.'[8] But what is our position? Here one may hesitate, perhaps for a long time; but hesitation does not get us anywhere, here even less than elsewhere.

What is at stake here is something other than the tension or controversy between a historical-critical and a theological judgment, between an academic and an ecclesiastical outlook, between a theoretical and a practical treatment. We should be gravely underestimating the question which has been and still is at issue if in endeavouring to bring the two points of view closer together we conclude that we have found a solution as soon as we have arrived at a certain synthesis (which need by no means be considered impossible). However laudable a preliminary synthesis may be, there is no way out of the difficulty in which we find ourselves as long as we operate with a concept of revelation, with tendencies either toward the right or the left, which remain rationalistic, no matter how much we spiritualize it and, historicizing, no matter how much we deepen it. We must break with this view. But it cannot be done with one blow; it obviously requires a long process and painstaking labour.

Apparently ineradicably ingrained in Western man is the shallow, distorted interpretation of 'revelation' as the communication of supernatural knowledge or knowledge about the supernatural. Even those who are wont to protest violently against the Roman Catholic view, who want to rule out Aristotle in order to make room for Moses and Paul, even they often remain under the influence of this concept. Then it takes this form: Moses 'teaches' something different from Aristotle, Paul 'thinks' differently from Philo or Plotinus; in the New Testament something different or something greater is 'revealed,' told, explained, recommended, made acceptable to us.

In the biblical area, this is the source of the talk about a 'higher' revelation, a 'development' of revelation, a 'continuing' revelation— terms intelligible only if it is assumed that a more primitive concept is gradually being superseded. And those who assail the reality of history

---

[8] Hermann Gunkel, in *Die Religion in Geschichte und Gegenwart*, 1st. edn., V, 1877; cf. the article on the same subject, 'Weissagung und Erfüllung,' by Heinrich Schlier in *RGG*, 2nd. edn., V, 1813.

as irrational nevertheless are always finding in this history that which makes it important, namely, that it follows a path which leads to new insights, that it brings with it a growth in knowledge—even though this may be a more existential knowledge than that which the orthodoxists and modern rationalists have in mind. It remains a point of view which, we suspect, can easily miss the real secret of the Scriptures. Then, quite unintentionally, one will go on confusing 'Covenant' and 'testament,' and this finds expression in statements like the following: 'The break with the Old *Covenant* became complete only when Israel rejected its Messiah'; for 'the New *Testament* comes into being, as Jesus himself expressly states, in his blood.'

The Apostles know a great deal about a new covenant, but nothing about a new testament; the new covenant can be read in the Scriptures, i.e., in the Old Testament, if the veil is taken away from Israel's and our eyes.[9] But even this would not bring about a 'historical, scientific, incontrovertible, clear, and certain position with regard to the Old Testament.'[10] As long as we start out with the idea that at least the New Testament is revelation—and everybody, fundamentalists and speculative theologians, rationalists and moralists, begins there, even though they have different concepts of revelation—that somewhere or everywhere in the New Testament revelation is to be found as it were in pure culture, so long will the uncertainty with regard to the Old Testament in the church and the world remain. Now, it is precisely the Old Testament which can free us from such a shallow, Westernized concept of 'revelation,' because it shows us that no human word as such is revelation, whether it be profane or sacred, New Testament or Old Testament, the language of the priests or of the great writing prophets. Neither a report about God or what God says can express, represent, much less take the place of the NAME.

Schemata

Nevertheless there is a difference between what we call the 'Old' and the 'New' Testament. Even the preacher and interpreter cannot do without an approximately correct formulation of this difference.

[9] Cf. H. F. Kohlbrügge, *Wozu das Alte Testament?*, pp. 41ff.
[10] W. J. de Wilde, *Het probleem van het Oude Testament* (1938), a summary of an article by H. Strathmann in *Theologische Blätter* (1936), cols. 257f.

Formulas like 'provisional' and 'definitive,' 'typological' and 'keryg-matic' are not adequate.[11] A rejection, in itself justified, of the false ingenuity which sets itself up as master of the holy Book by allegorizing everything will do us no good unless we have in another way seen, recognized, and faced the difficulty out of which the allegorical method grew. For allegorization presupposes the unity of the Scriptures in the religious sense, and its aim is to make this clear in the rational sense. But the Scripture is not a unity in the religious sense, and the rational content of theology does not grow out of a process of religious con-sciousness but rather from the response to the Word.

Then such schemata as 'law and gospel,' 'prophecy and fulfilment,' etc. might still be of some help to us, at least if they were more clearly understood than is generally the case. And as a matter of fact, we are now in process of correcting all kinds of distortions. Today almost nobody would deny that there is no sense in talking about a vengeful God of the Old Testament over against a loving God of the New Testa-ment, and that the distinction between collective (Old Testament) and individual (New Testament) piety is untenable.[12] We could doubt-less list more advances of this kind, but perhaps we shall also have to learn to admit (if only for the sake of an honest attitude toward the synagogue) that the schema 'law and gospel,' even though it exhibits several elements and accents which we dare not neglect, ultimately misunderstands and distorts the Old as well as the New Testament.[13]

[11] Experience in listening to sermons and instruction teaches that often many a person, because of an honest but short-sighted feeling about the intellectual local colour of the texts, cannot adopt as his own even this inadequate view of the relationship between the Old and the New Testament. Examples: (a) One places oneself in a New Testa-ment atmosphere and illustrates this with images and events from the Old Testament stories. (b) One confines oneself strictly to the Old Testament and proceeds to eluci-date the religious ideas (thus the purely subjective expression of the revelation) in order at an arbitrarily chosen moment to leap over to 'Jesus,' which in most cases means to Jesus' preaching. (c) One tries to let the Old Testament speak for itself, without mentioning the New Testament, thinking that in this way one is speaking of the 'Father' and not (not yet) of the Son—as if the 'Name' were essentially identical with 'Father,' as if the word 'Father' were really a central word in the Old Testament, as if the 'Son'—in the figure of *Ebed Yahweh*—were not present everywhere in the Old Testament (and not only in the songs of Deutero-Isaiah), not in words but in deeds and sacrifice!

[12] J. Hempel. *Das Ethos des Alten Testaments* (1938), pp. 32ff.; Albrecht Alt, *Die Ursprünge des israelitischen Rechts* (1934), pp. 42ff.

[13] Luther, sermon on John 1 : 1–14 (*Kirchenpostille*, in *WA*, X, I, 1, 181f.): 'The first

This requires that we see that the 'Old Testament' *berith* ('Covenant') is a bequest, a gift, an accompaniment of grace, a realization of the election, the sovereign love of God.

It is really on this basis that the great decision must be made for or against the identity of the God who is attested in Israel and in the church. Often it seems almost taken for granted that the church has prior possession of a concept of God which is then subsequently filled out in detail with conceptions of the God of Israel. Such a prior possession and such a procedure not only lead to a 'predecision,' which robs the great decision of its earnestness, but they also introduce into our attitude toward the saving truth which is proclaimed to us a division with respect to the Word. And they keep the church of the Gentiles in a *secessio judaica* ('Jewish secession') and falsely convert the Gentiles' consciousness of election into a usurpation.

The difference between the two parts of the Scripture can also be only partially comprehended in the framework of the schema 'promise and fulfilment.' Apart from the fact that, more often than not, 'promise' is understood to mean words of promise, whereas 'fulfilment' is interpreted as an actual event, so that the schema which is a distinction between two associations of words, is thrown away, since, after all, in the 'testament' the fulfilment is the word of fulfilment, there is too much in the prophecy that goes beyond what is said in the New Testament concerning the fulfilment, and conversely, the fulfilment itself is too much of a mystery (which is why hope so necessarily keeps its place beside faith) even to permit us to be quite satisfied with the scheme of 'promise and fulfilment.' On the one hand the Old Testament is more than mere preparation, and on the other hand it has no independent validity; if this is the case, what sense does it make to say that it stands alongside the Gospel? It certainly is not such a superfluous supernumerary, but even less is it a doubleganger which neither undermines the existence of the other nor cancels itself out.

We have attempted herewith to bring out the inner tensions which

---

thing to know is that everything the apostles taught and wrote they drew from the Old Testament . . . as St. Paul says in Romans 1. . . . For the New Testament is nothing more than a revelation of the Old, just as if somebody at first had a sealed letter and then opened it. So the Old Testament is a testamental letter of Christ, which he caused to be opened after his death and read and proclaimed everywhere through the Gospel.'

are characteristic of the place and the atmosphere in which the preacher and the interpreter stand. These tensions cannot, in my opinion, be eliminated by means of distinctions on the religious-rational level. Thus we can hardly be content with a statement like this: 'Considered from the point of view of this avowal [i.e., reconciliation with God] many things in the Old Testament are no longer of current interest—they have passed into history: but even so they can teach us an infinity of lessons.'[14] We note with regard to such a statement: (a) that the Old Testament provides lessons, (b) that (strangely) even though much falls to the ground, 'an infinity of lessons' still remains, (c) that the ancient church, which, after all, lived primarily 'from the point of view of this avowal,' did not speak in terms of such a divided religious evaluation. But even from this point of view it is not convincing to speak rationally of a 'history of revelation' when one means 'history of the Israelite religion,' or to state as a religious judgment that in Israel the concept of chaos is a 'survival, not yet [unfortunately!] abandoned' (p. 181) because it was such an 'extremely difficult task' to arrive at a new philosophy of life (p. 185)—or, on the other hand, to consider it an advantage that the prophets arrived at 'the exclusiveness of Yahweh as such' (p. 23). That is to say, it is highly important (theologically) and of immediate practical concern (for the ministry of the apostolate) that the reality of that chaos should not disappear from the preaching of the Name and that the exclusiveness of YHWH can never be upheld unless the mystery of the power of the Name becomes a reality.

However that may be, we cannot in this way secure any help in meeting the inner tensions of which we have here been speaking.

THE ONENESS OF THE TIMES

God's Time and Our Time

As in the case of other difficulties with which ordinary orthodox teaching has troubled us, the so-called 'dialectical' theology has also brought us a good bit farther on the way to understanding this knotty problem of time. What is not at all unusual in exegesis, the historical

---

[14] Th. C. Vriezen, *An Outline of Old Testament Theology*, tr. S. Neuijen (Oxford, Basil Blackwell, 1958), p. 38; in many respects we value this book very highly.

disciplines, and practical theology is a great exception in dogmatics, namely, that the science is 'advanced' by a discovery, a view, a new grouping, which can be tested by more and more facts in the relevant area and gradually confirmed as correct. This is not the place to expatiate on what Karl Barth has brought to light in this matter, at first alone and under attack and later with the increasing authority he gained as a teacher of the church.[15] The insights which are of most importance for the preaching of the Old Testament and which are of immediate relevance in connection with our task today are concerned with the doctrine of 'theological time' (Noordmans). Briefly summarized, they are the following:

1. In God's revelation we are dealing with God himself, as he unrepeatably and irrevocably unites himself with human life in Jesus Christ at one point in time. This time is at once God's own time and the time in which we find ourselves. As such it is distinguished, despite its participation in human time, from all time in which our human experience and knowledge takes place. It is equally different from everything that has taken place since and previously in the world, and by its nature as God's time it is equally near to everything that has happened and will happen in the course of time to men in their alienation. Only such a strict, exclusive concept of revelation, which transcends the categories of accepted thinking and falls outside the scheme of prevalent conceptions, can leave room for the data of the Bible and, as we then say, do justice to it. To use New Testament terms, only when the Father is recognized in the Son through the Spirit, or in Old Testament terms, only when the Name of God is recognized as the essence of God (instead of a 'secondary centre alongside of Jahweh') as it is present for his people in the sanctuary,[16] is the difference between the times relativized and the times related to God.[17]

[15] See among others Karl Barth, *Church Dogmatics*, Vol. I, pt. 2, pp. 70-121; Vol. III, pt. 1, pp. 45-103; cf. Hermann Diem, *Theologie als kirchliche Wissenschaft* (1951), pp. 57-91.

[16] Cf. O. Procksch's article 'hagios' in *TWNT*, I, 90ff. Also Karl Barth, *Church Dogmatics*, Vol. I, pt. 1, p. 365: '. . . the revealed Name itself (which in content is the refusal of any name) by its wording is to recall also and precisely the hiddenness of the revealed God. But still under this *Name*, which itself and as such expresses his mystery, God *does* reveal himself to his people, i.e., he begins . . . to *deal with* Israel.'

[17] Herein also lies the profound intent of the classical statements: *Vetere testamento*

2. We have no direct knowledge of the revelation of God, but rather receive it indirectly through the testimony of its happening and the saving power contained within it. The relation of the Scripture, the Old as well as the New Testament, to this testimony is that of being its deposit, its repository, its codification, and explication. Accordingly, the Scripture is the word about the Word of the *WORD*. The prophet says, 'The word of the Lord *came* to me';[18] that is to say, the content and purpose, the truth, and the salvation of this event are this. These three, this saying of the word, this event of the Word, and this salvation which is the *WORD* belong together, lie in the same perspective. Nevertheless, the distinction between them and the order must be observed, if on the one hand preaching is to be more than a mere report and on the other hand the word of the prophets and Apostles is to remain distinguished from the Word of the Lord.[19] For any direct iden-

---

novum latet et in novo vetus patet (Augustine, *Quaest. in Ex.* 73, in Migne, *Pati. Lat.* XXXIV, p. 623); *Hē diaphora ouk estin pata tēn ousian alla kata ton chronon enallagēn* (Suicerus, *Thes. Eccl.*); cf. also the formulations in Zwingli's *Elenchus contra Anabaptistas*, Op. III, pp. 412, 418, 421.

[18] Cf. Jer. 1 : 4, Ezek. 1 : 3, et al., where Luther's translation reads *Das Wort geschah zu mir*, in which the verb *geschehen* means 'happen,' 'occur,' 'become an event.' —Tr.]

[19] Augustine, commenting on Ps. 121, 'I have lifted up mine eyes to the mountains, from whence shall come my help,' says: 'Consider, then, brethren, if perchance John is not one of those mountains . . . . Therefore, my brethren, if you would understand, lift up your eyes to this mountain, that is, raise yourselves up to the evangelist, rise to his meaning. But, because though these mountains receive peace he cannot be in peace who places his hope in man, do not so raise your eyes to the mountain as to think that your hope should be placed in man; and so say, "I have lifted up mine eyes to the mountains, from whence shall come my help," that you immediately add, "my help is from the Lord, who made heaven and earth." . . . For the mountains receive what they may minister to us; therefore, from whence the mountains also receive, there should also our hope be placed. . . . Since they were men who wrote the Scriptures, they did not shine of themselves, but "He was the true light, who lighteth every man that cometh into the world" A mountain also was that John the Baptist, who said, "I am not the Christ," lest any one, placing his hope in the mountain, should fall from Him who illuminates the mountain.' In *Joannis Evangelium*, Tract. 1 n. 6 (Migne, *Patr. Lat.* XXXV, 1381f.; also *Lectures or Tractates on the Gospel According to St. John*, tr. John Gibb (Edinburgh: T. & T. Clark, 1873), pp. 4f. — Therefore the form of introduction to the reading of the Scriptures which is still used here and there among us, 'Hear the Word of *God* as it is *recorded* in. . . .,' must be repudiated as untenable and confusing.

tification of the Bible with the revelation itself introduces a confusion of all categories and value judgments, which first produces religion and then breeds denial.

3. The testimony of the Old Testament goes out into the time of expectation, that of the New Testament into the time of recollection. Both are relative to the time of revelation itself. What they have in common is their relationship to, their orientation toward one and the same Object, one and the same Name, one and the same Event, one and the same Salvation. The words of the New Testament do not contain this Salvation any more than do the words of the Old Testament; they attest and proclaim it, they point to it and present it. Their purpose is to be serviceable and nothing but serviceable. They are not self-sufficient like a philosophical truth; in themselves they do not constitute an ethical ideal, but rather point away from themselves to the thing itself. Where these words are heard and understood, they resolve themselves into the presence, the speech, the speaking presence of God. 'Today this scripture has been fulfilled in your hearing' (Luke 4 : 21), that is to say, on this day of Jesus' presence there began the year of jubilee to which the years past had looked forward and which, now that it had come, had entered into the world's years to judge and to bless them.

4. If we fail to be realistic, if we refuse to admit that all the words of the Old Testament and the New Testament are in themselves only words, if we attempt to give these words as such an order of precedence (in accord with our spontaneous evaluation), then we shall land in religion all over again. When we insist that the whole of Scripture is the object of doctrine and instruction, this is not because we are more 'conservative,' but rather just because we are more critical. We do not make the biblical data somewhat more 'absolute,' but actually somewhat more 'relative.' And in order to arrive at this unity of the Bible, we are by no means thrown back upon allegorical devices and typological ingenuities. We take our stand and remain within the contingent event of preaching and instruction. We bring nothing with us but faith in the 'self-evidence of Holy Scripture in the act of its being proclaimed.'[20] We reject the strange charge of 'dogmatic apriorism,'

[20] Hermann Diem, 'Die Einheit der Schrift,' *Evangelische Theologie*, XIII (1953), 388, in reference to the fact that the Reformation, unlike Rome, dealt quite freely with the problem of the canon.

and here we can concur with Bultmann when, in reference to the New Testament, he says: 'Unity of doctrine was assured by the canon and not by some normative system of dogmatics.'[21]

The One Object

The question whether other words have this same power cannot arise for the preacher and interpreter, at least it cannot become a serious question as long as nobody has any knowledge of any other words that point to this same thing. Either they are the 'same' words, i.e., they are a development and application of the biblical testimony, or they are other words, which come from the climate of another world, from the regions of human religion, other words which therefore also have another function. If what has been said above is true, we certainly cannot ascribe the function of revelation to the human word, which in form and content and the substance of its piety, wisdom, or ethos comes closest to the prophetic and apostolic witness (in so far it does not in fact have this underivable and irreplaceable Object), any more than we can ascribe it to human words which may have a very different sound or may actually appear to contradict the witness.

The vocabulary (*Wortwelt*) of the Old and the New Testament have the same Object (where can we find an equivalent substitute for the splendid word *Gegenstand?*). In this respect and to this extent they are at one with each other. To be sure, we have here a very considerable multiplicity of voices, mythical, legendary, cultic, and ethical—'religiously' speaking, of varying levels, rationally speaking, no longer, or scarcely, acceptable. The unity, therefore, does not lie in the form, not even in the content, of the texts, but rather in that which the content (along with this form) attests. Undoubtedly there is also a similarity in conception, cosmology, and feeling about life, an agreement in piety, wisdom, and ethics. Nevertheless the unity is not to be sought here, and naturally much less in the continuity of the same terms, metaphors, and phrases. God himself, this God who is different from all gods, before whom the godhead vanishes as a dream, is himself the power that brings into a unity all the love and devotion, all the living and the striving of man which is directed through Him to Him.

[21] *Theology of the New Testament*, tr. Kendrick Grobel (New York: Charles Scribner's Sons, 1955), II, p. 141.

In a word, is not this the meaningful unity which is actually pre-supposed when the great Book lies on the pulpit, the lectern, or the table and can be opened everywhere with equal trust? Trust—in what? That everything happened just as it says? That this is the acme of everything we can know about the gods and the godhead? That herein is contained the true ethics which we as men of good will can practise? That here at last the riddles of life will find their solution? No, rather the trust that, while the gods are silent, the 'Name' rises above us, as it once rose above Abraham and Moses and David and countless persons unnamed, who, if they had been left to themselves, would have remained caught in the ambivalence of religion. But in the presence of that Name they found fulfilment and expectation in the Voice that cleaves the spectral silence between heaven and earth to find its mark in the heart of man.

The time of expectation belongs to the revelation; for this phrase cannot mean simply the centuries before Christ in the sense of an undifferen-tiated, neutral something, an empty lapse, a lengthened extension of time. It is a time of expectation, of awaiting, in the sense of being the dimension in which the waiting ones stand and wait. They wait, mark you, not just for something, not for a possibility, but for a very definitely promised coming stage in which God will be for them what—by his revealed nature and what has already been fulfilled in their present life —he has always wanted to be for them from all eternity. It must there-fore be remembered that 'expectation,' in contrast to 'longing,' expresses an attitude with a definite content. 'Expectation' presupposes not merely the possibility but also the actuality of revelation. Genuine expectation is not limited by the words 'not yet' any more than genuine remembrance is limited by the word 'nevermore.'

This character of fulfilment and expectation as well as fulfilment and remembrance points to the great riddle of time itself, which con-fronts us with the universal, insoluble aporias. The riddle of time can only be thought of as a mystery; it can be borne only if it is the re-flection of that completely different mystery, the saving mystery of revelation, the time of God. If we regard the revelation merely as a special case in the general category of revelation, if we naïvely say that all religion 'rests upon revelation' or at least claims to rest upon it, then we give up the meaning of the time of expectation as partici-pation in God's peculiar, particular, unique self-revelation, and hence the Old Testament, as a book in which one can, indirectly, hear the Word of God, is lost. This would be to establish a gulf, Lessing's 'broad foul ditch' of historical distance, which compels men to build their house in religion and take upon themselves the fate of religiosity. Then the *oikonomia* of God can no longer be understood as an ordinance of *God* into which he himself has entered with us, in which he erects the sign of the *assumptio carnis* as a sign which is inseparable from the sign of the saving event itself. But if this is the way it is with God's 'economy,' then it follows that these signs erected in the time of expectation, even though as signs they belong to the expectation, are, as signs of God, of far more concern to us—yes, to us who, even though I do not say we are living in the time of remembrance, have heard at least from afar the testimony of the time of remembrance, i.e., the New Testament. When a person reads one part of the Scripture, he is certainly reading *the* Scripture, and just as certainly when he reads the Old Testament, he is reading the witness to the God of whose revelation the expectation speaks no less than does the remembrance. We shall never succeed in isolating a part of the Scripture without its thereby ceasing to be Holy Scripture. 'Holy,' after all, means set apart with all its faults by *this* God, related to this God, dependent on this God. On which God? On the one who from the beginning ordained and prepared himself to be with men.

All this loses its force if YHWH is only a 'special case' among the gods or of the godhead. But it also loses its force if we do not take seriously the words 'with all its faults.' Among these 'faults' are not only the inadequate religious conceptions but above all the fact that the whole of the Bible has something of religion about it, indeed, consists in large part of religion. Anybody who knows how profound pagan mythology is and how close it comes to our philosophical ideas about the totality of the world and the identity of God and man will also want to track down the special contributions in these Israelite conceptions and will not be easily persuaded to include religion itself among the necessary faults of this form of revelation. The doctrine of 'theological time' evaporates if both sides of the structure of the Old Testament are not accepted as real, namely, (1) that YHWH is the Other over against the gods and the godhead, and (2) that a large part of the testimony concerning him comes to us in a garment of language which was originally cut to fit the gods and the godhead.

The One Covenant

If it sometimes appears as if the one object to which the testimony of the Old and New Testament is related is equivalent to what the pagans and the philosophers call 'God,' and thus there is the danger that Jesus Christ will be viewed Docetically, then the only way in which preaching and instruction can be radically freed from this danger will be through a right understanding of the covenant in the Old Testament. In preaching, the idea of the covenant must become a witness to the covenant itself as it remains in force in all its unity and plenitude. Not as if the covenant were a locus by itself or a theme for particular occasions. When we speak of the covenant, we are speaking of God, his character, his attitude, his action. What we see and understand of this—in God's relationship to Noah, to Abraham, to Moses, to Israel, to David—shows a glory that points back to the glory of God's nature. But none of these covenant gifts satisfies and none of these relationships is perfect in itself. True, the covenant is called *le 'olam* ('everlasting'), but this applies to another covenant. No, this is exactly what we dare not say; if the covenant points to the future, it does only in order to point upwards to the depths of the elective grace of YHWH. It is said of him that he is *shomer habberith wehachesed*: he who 'keeps covenant and steadfast love' (Dan. 9 : 4). But the actual covenant, which is kept and preserved, is a torso, which evokes before our eyes the lineaments of a better covenant. No, even this is not correct; we must rather say that it directs our attention to the *shomer* ('keeper') himself, in order that we may see that he is different from all other divinity, that we may see that he is what Jesus the Messiah is, and that Jesus, the 'one who was sent' and the 'coming one,' is the 'very stamp of his nature' (Heb. 1 : 3).

The reverse side of this concentration upon the founder and preserver himself, is, then, inevitably the fact that the violation of a particular covenant through distrust, wilfulness, or apostasy does affect not the covenant—not even the one Covenant which is the background of all the ways in which salvation is realized among the chosen people, tribes, peoples, and worlds—but rather that such a violation is direct rebellion against the heart of God, this heart of God, the heart of this God. In the very violence of wrath with which God reacts to this violation and what is, to our mind, the disproportionateness of the retribution, one begins to see how tremendously God himself is committed to this covenant and how astonishing it is that he should have lowered himself to be a partner and party to it. So in First Isaiah the 'covenant' is almost identical with the act of election, and yet here the note of divine sadness is sounded: 'What more was there to do for my vineyard, that I have not done in it?' (Isa. 5 : 4). So in the priestly code the *berith* with the patriarchs, of which the other covenants are only extensions, has almost the colour of a gift of revelation. So in Ezekiel after the devastation of the city and the temple only the jealous God remains. So in Second Isaiah it is precisely the heathen who wait for the righteousness of the God of the Covenant (Isa. 51 : 5, 60 : 3).

So in both the accounts the Creation, the foundation of the world and the creation of man are viewed retrospectively as having the characteristics of a free entrance into a covenant. Therefore the postbiblical Jewish Haggadah says profoundly that before the Creation there were seven pre-existent things: the Torah, the throne of God, the patriarchs, the people of God, the tabernacle, the name of the Messiah, and *teshubah* ('repentance'). This is nomistic, arbitrary, and incoherent, but it does point to the fact that the covenant, entered into in time, is also the intent of the Creation, that the Creation is already a part of God's redemptive history, that the existence of salvation is superior and antecedent to that of Being (*Dasein*).

In preaching, the covenant, which is wholly a covenant of grace (even the so-called 'work covenant' is a part of the covenant of grace), despite the historicity of its forms, must be elevated beyond all contingency. Its foundation is eternal, its content is God's everlasting good pleasure toward men. God himself, that is, this God who is so minded, takes the initiative and is himself his absolute initiative. The Scripture is one by virtue of the oneness of God; it is 'holy' because of its fundamental theme, because it bears witness to nothing else but this one covenant. It needs to be repeated, interpreted, preached as a whole, and ultimately it has only this one theme: YHWH is the Godhead. As interpreters of the Old Testament how could we ever speak of anything else but this? But by virtue of the same Scripture we hold fast to the very definite meaning which is here associated with the word 'God.' He is so far from being a variant of a general concept of God that, if we want to understand him, we must listen afresh to various concrete things in the testimony—and then it becomes evident that this God is in every way distinct, unique, and different from the religious conceptions which we bring with us, which automatically and constantly suggest themselves to us. YHWH is the Godhead! No, he is not 'absolute,' he does not wear his omnipotence on his sleeve, he is not as the world is, but rather more what man is. He is not God in that he is the God of the gods, but rather in that he wills to be the God of men, and in precisely this way manifests himself to be the God of the gods. If he is 'great,' greater than all powers, he is so not by reason of his omnipotence but rather because of his perfections. YHWH is sublime, more than for any other reason, because in the covenant he gives himself to the uttermost, even to humiliation, without obscuring his majesty. The 'Covenant' declares that the Lord becomes man with men, not in spite of his deity, but because of his deity.

THE UNUTTERABLE NAME

The Old Testament has many names for that which we call God, and also for him whom Israel calls God. Some of them are alike and some of them are different. But beyond these the God of Israel has a special name, and this is the name that is always meant when the intention is to speak of the Other, of the 'Name' in the sense of revelation, disclosure, the sphere of power, the order of blessing, guidance. Actually, the possibility of our understanding the meaning of the Old Testament as a whole depends on whether we understand what is at issue here. But not only this, for the relevance of the Old Testament (in particular) in our situation is also dependent on this. Our discussion in the last section took us to some extent away from the world which was sketched in the first part. We were concerned with a theoretical and technical summary of the Old Testament data, presented, as it were, more in the form of an instruction or briefing of the troops; the interpreter and witness received, as it were, some intellectual instruction. Thus for the moment it may appear that we are nevertheless out to establish what is the timeless, usable content of the Old Testament and forget the current questions.

Now that we come back to the 'Name,' we may recall from the first part how much critical power we there ascribed to this concept, namely, the critical power it has over against religion, but also over against nihilism. The latter is in part implicit in the critique of religion and in part it goes beyond it in an important effect which is peculiar to it. We found that what is meant by the 'Name' actually takes us to a realm beyond all religion and apparently makes even the 'Name' itself a cipher of nihilism. Constantin Brunner declared that when Jesus said 'Father,' this was a veiled rejection of the religion of the disciples and a hidden profession of 'atheistic' salvation.[22] Naturally this raised a storm of indignation among the religious liberals. We too believe that Brunner's assertion is untenable, but that it comes closer to the mystery of this giving of a new name to God than does the interpretation which regards the name 'Father' as the apex of general religious experience.

But in our opinion it is much more true to say of YHWH that he constitutes a radical crisis for all religion, or, to put it in another way, that his self-disclosure includes the abolition of religion. Where religion has never flourished, there we also do not find any of the flaming autumn colours of atheistic defiance. And conversely, where this defiant pride appears, whether it be demonic or calm, aggressive or sad, there we stand on the soil of a religion. YHWH cuts the ground from under the one as well as the other; but today it is as if the human spirit must first be tortured, keelhauled, as it were, by nihilism if it is to take seriously the Name of the unknown God.

1. YHWH is not an originally Israelite name.[23] Only a few scholars adhere to an Israelite origin. In a certain sense, the question of the provenance (as well as the pronunciation) of the Name is intellectually irrelevant. But in our connection of thought the non-Israelite (Kenite or Ugaritic) origin is more welcome. This God wills to be the only God, because *in* the world he distinguishes himself *from* the world. This would be in accord with a general religious origin of the Name. Also the 'newness' of the Name (according to Exod. 3 : 13ff.) and, on the other hand, the effort of the Yahwist to project the Name back to the beginning of mankind may point to this paradox: *in* the world as one Name that is distinguished from the world through a new meaning which was

[22] Constantin Brunner, *Unser Christus oder das Wesen des Genies* (1921), pp. 17, 98f., 389; Friedrich Gogarten, *Glaube und Wirklichkeit* (1928), pp. 21, 65f.; Ernst Wolf, 'Martin Luther, Das Evangelium und die Religion' in *Peregrinatio* (1954), pp. 16, 24f.
[23] J. de Groot and A. R. Hulst, *Macht en Wil*, pp. 74f.; Th. C. Vriezen, *An Outline of Old Testament Theology*, p. 194.

supposed to have been its original meaning; for the Yahwist is concerned about the continuity of meaning, not the identity of the sound.[24]

2. YHWH is an anonymous name. When the people of Israel ask, 'What is his name?' (Exod. 3 : 13) or what is his nature? the answer is given in the form of a verb: 'I am,' or 'I will be,' or 'I will be present [with you],' or more precisely, 'I will be what I will be' (cf. Exod. 33 : 19). The primary meaning is that the God of Israel withdraws himself from all conjuration;[25] he cannot be conjured up with this nameless name and be made subservient to an ulterior purpose. But more specifically (and this concerns us directly), Israel is referred to the *action* that proceeds from YHWH, to what he undertakes to do, the long journey he takes with Israel from Egypt to the Promised Land and from there into the exile and the Diaspora, the 'days' and the 'deeds' which are the days and the deeds of God.

Hence the translation 'the Eternal' is internally impossible (even though it too could be called an anonymous name); in the struggle with religion and nihilism everything depends upon our freeing ourselves from ontological misunderstandings. We can only allude to this here, but anybody who reads the Old Testament knows that no antecedent concept of 'being' and no subsequent reflection upon the 'being' of God plays any part in it. When in everyday life and even in the cult the full Name was not uttered, this was probably, if one prefers to say so, because of a 'magical' fear. But fear of what? Not of the being of God, but of the presence of God, and not of the presence in itself and as such, but rather of his presence in his activity, in which he reserves the freedom to act as he wills, the freedom of election and rejection, of judgment and grace, which can sometimes mean glory for others and misery for oneself. This is the sense in which he is nameless: I will be what I will be. Therefore the translation of the Name as 'the Eternal' is altogether misleading. But, says Rosenzweig, this idea of ' "the Eternal" can also be informed with genuine forces of the human soul. After all, for us mortals the word of longing, the last word in our "Song of the Earth" [Mahler], is eternal. Our hearts know no desire beyond this. . . . The God of the Bible also stills this longing, but not by fulfilling it or promising it fulfilment, but rather by actually stilling

[24] G. Kittel, *TWNT*, III, article on *kyrios*; O. Eissfeldt, 'Jahwe-Name und Zauberwesen,' *Zeitschrift für Missionskunde* (1927); W. Vischer, *Jahwe, der Gott Kains* (1929).
[25] Martin Buber in *De Godsdiensten der Wereld*, I, p. 184.

it, by silencing it. For the man who experiences and hopes for God's presence in this aeon the yearning for his own eternity in this aeon passes away.'[26]

3. YHWH is nevertheless a proper name—not only because it stands in correlation with a people which also bears a proper name, but rather because everything depends upon his concretely distinguishing himself from all others in the world of gods and proving himself to be the 'one' God. If the 'Name' has taken on the full significance of 'revelation,' the principal reason for this is that this Name YHWH is *more* than the godhead, because it has become *less* than the godhead. The whole conception of 'revelation' simply cannot be maintained if 'one' God is not acknowledged and recognized as the Godhead. If we 'start with' a primary experience of the 'godhead,' and then within the realm of this general experience proceed to bring out the particular, secondary features of 'our' God by putting in our own shadings, this results in a denial of all 'revelation.' In dealing with the Old Testament the procedure will have to move in precisely the opposite direction—for many different reasons, but also on account of the fatality of nihilism which is latent in the development of the 'idea of God,' a development we must constantly keep in view.

Just as we never come to an encounter with Jesus by starting with the 'Christ-spirit,' so we never find a determinative, central, monarchic place for YHWH as long as we start with a general concept of the 'godhead.' The Name, the revelation, is concentrated in a proper name. It is also the bolt that bars the way to the theoretical kind of 'mono-theism.'

The proper name presents us with, or offers us, the decision whether we shall recognize this One as 'our' God and thus as the God of the beginning, the cosmos, and the consummation. 'Know that YHWH is the Godhead' (Ps. 100 : 3).

4. YHWH is an untranslatable name and an incomprehensible concept. But it must be 'translated' by means of a risky identification, and it is comprehended through a risky self-estrangement or self-depreciation. On its way to the nations, to the heathen, Israel appropriated their words (e.g., Elohim or El Elyon). By this appropriation, heathenism was on the one hand honoured and on the other degraded,

---

[26] Franz Rosenzweig, 'Der Ewige' in *Die Schrift und ihre Verdeutschung* (1936), pp. 208f.. and in *Kleinere Schriften* (1937), p. 197.

in so far as all names for God perform a service but none is adequate. The meaning of these names of God is taken entirely from the open secret of the Name, YHWH. In missionary activity, especially the translation of the Bible, a perennially immediate and urgent problem is how to employ the divine names in the 'primitive' or the 'higher' religions in order to use them as accompanying expressions of the Name.

In Helmut Rosin's book[27] we find a very clear discussion of this subject, and we regard these insights as important, indeed, we attach decisive significance to them. Though it may appear that all this is of little concern to us in Europe and to those on the fringes of church and synagogue, nevertheless closer examination will show that it affects in a very essential way the work of proclamation in the church and in the world. On the other hand, we are not much helped by the acceptance of the 'irrational,' the thought that God (in the general sense) is perhaps not dead after all, or by the call for reintegration, by the 'Christianity' that will bring about improvement, by the myth of Europe or the ethos of humanity, by the Christian man who sets out to think in terms of positive social welfare and to overcome his individualism (or even his middle-class mental attitudes). All this seems to have more relevance to human need; it seems to be more easily understood and more practicable. Talk about whether 'YHWH is God' seems so remote from our real situation, so alien to our urgent concerns. It therefore requires some courage to maintain the thesis that the problem of nihilism will only be taken with full seriousness in the church when these questions again become central and are brought into contact with, for example, the questioning thought of Heidegger.

This comes strongly to the fore in Rosin's study. He maintains that the identifying copula in the phrase 'YHWH is God' is 'irreversible.' It is not as if God bears the name YHWH along with other names. And the fact is that such a transposition occurs nowhere in the Old Testament. The identification 'YHWH is God,' however, is a self-translating statement that empowers us to paraphrase the Name with general religious concepts. Not that these can take the place of the Name; the danger is that they do this nevertheless; and we may say

[27] *The Lord is God: The Translation of the Divine Names and the Missionary Calling of the Church* (Geneva, 1955). [The author quotes from the French résumé of this dissertation.—Tr.].

that when this does happen, faith degenerates into religion, religion becomes idealism, and idealism becomes an insight into our self-projection, and from then on nihilism is practically inescapable.

The right accent, 'The *Lord* is God,' although it actually includes (by means of the copula) an element of self-estrangement and self-depreciation, safeguards the 'translation' from having this destructive effect. 'The name Yahweh determines the content of the word *elohim*. It fills this word with its truth and its light. The general name *elohim* can then finally play an independent role, as we see in the second part of the Book of Jonah; the general name then acts as a proper name and can even fulfil all the functions of the Name.' But the prerequisite of this is the content which is expressed in the name YHWH, both as an anonymous name and as a proper name (as the expression of the fact that he can be known only in his acts), so that the whole of the testimony gives shape and substance to the Name and imparts the character of faith to the response to the testimony, to the calling upon the Name, the worship, the obedience. But faith, groundless, incidental, and fragmentary in its nature, is awakened not only by the accent 'the *Lord* is God' but also by the risky identification with the projections of religion.

Therefore, says Rosin, the name of God itself must remain untranslated in all languages;[28] but this missionary equation of the Name with the godhead contributes its part to the awakening of faith. In translating one should not search for different words for the godhead, with which YHWH is equated, and for the gods of the nations. This would deprive the hearer, the religious thinker, of the necessity of freely recognizing YHWH, of making a decision and believing. 'A translation which employs different terms according to whether the term *elohim* designates God, gods, or idols prevents the necessary confrontation between these ideas; such a translation, having already made the choice between YHWH and the other gods, deprives the reader of the possibility of making this choice himself in the faith which the text imposes upon him.'

[28] Or—another possibility—it can be rendered, following the example of the Masoretes and the Septuagint, by the term *Adonay-Kyrios*. 'This substitution for the sacred tetragrammaton is a surrogate, which means that the title "Lord" is simply put in the place of the Name, without giving it a new content. The title indicates a personal relationship (=my Lord) . . . uses it as a title, prevents it from appearing as an autonomous concept or even from wishing to express the content of the NAME.'

Here we have come in our thinking to the heart of the matter. The meaning and purpose of the Old Testament is this: to verify with all the means of language the confession 'YHWH is the Godhead' is 'irreversible.' From the time of the Apologists the church, and from the time of Philo and later of Maimonides the synagogue, have been pursuing the path of reversibility. The idea of God, we have heard modern theologians (of all stripes) saying, is the dominant idea of religion. Reflection upon it is philosophical in character; it may take various courses depending upon the controlling philosophy, but the conclusion is always that belief in a primal mystery 'is born of the temper of mind and the thought-content of the present.'[29] It was thought that the question of essence must precede the question of truth, and the next step is to steep oneself in the question of the 'development of the idea of God.' One then encounters the numinous and the effort is made to give it an ethical content besides its demonic content, a rational orientation along with its irrational element. It then becomes necessary to delve into the symbols of language and to discriminate among them; one disputes over the question whether an 'absolute personality' is conceivable. Then, indeed, it becomes clear that a theology or philosophy of religion which is based upon our needs will in the course of its development always encounter Feuerbach, who will promptly brand it as disguised anthropology.[30] The appeal to the age and influence of Christianity as a proof of the superior value of the gospel soon became a sword that cut both ways. Christianity as the true religion of conscience or of love or as the source of the purest kind of prayer—how arbitrary all such assertions sound within a historical or philosophical framework!

Then at a certain point something had to be said about the 'real,' the 'highest'; something had to be said very straightforwardly, about God, Christ, the Holy Spirit, the church—either by way of a gradual transition, in the sense that this 'real' is to be regarded as the stage of final maturity in the human development of religion, the sum and substance which had always been the goal of religious thinking—or by making a 'leap,' more or less abrupt, and speaking boldly about the one faith, the one truth, the one salvation.

This is a path which not only does not lead us to the goal but actually leads us farther away from it. That is to say, it is intended to lead us to

[29] M. C. Mourik Broekman, *De vrijzinnige Godsidee*, pp. 160, 183.
[30] Werner Schilling, *Feuerbach und die Religion* (1957), pp. 132ff.

'religious' certainty, and it actually lands us in the midst of the ambivalence which is peculiar to all religion. If we ask where the difficulty is, various answers are possible. The most essential and fundamental one, as I believe, is that the interpreter and witness in preaching and instruction has failed to recognize the structure of the Scripture (and especially of the Old Testament) for what it is, namely, the pointer to a totally different kind of thinking about a totally Other, an indication of that which goes on resounding in this world when the gods and the godhead are silent. It is regrettable that many theologians have persisted so long in the attempt to start with an 'idea of God' or a 'concept of God,' especially when it was their concern to restore order and direction in the chaotic intellectual life of their contemporaries. Nobleness of purpose must not make us forget how futile—and how dangerous—this way of approaching these things must be in our situation.

The Name is 'intolerant' in that he turns to us freely and creatively and desires, in free, creative wills to be our apriori and thus the disclosure of the life and the truth—or if he is not this, then he can be nothing except a fresh, and perhaps the most searing, confirmation of the silence of the gods. Therefore, when in our reflection upon the proclamation the question constantly arises, 'Instruction—but in what?' it can be a liberation for us to know, as we have heard above, that it is not in divine truths or in religious needs or in the boundary experiences of humanity, but rather in the deeds of Him whose anonymous proper name calls, forms, breaks into, and fulfils human life in history. It is this revelation and presence which the Scriptures bring into a unity. Where this becomes a reality, 'all these things shall be yours as well': the splendour of divine truth, the assuagement of the heart's dismay, the justification of man beyond the boundary experiences of humanity, freedom, and prayer.

We conclude this section with a quotation from Karl Jaspers. We present it with respect and hesitation, but nevertheless as a contrast to the Name (and of the response to the Name, which is prayer). With all his scepticism and reserve, all his refusal to acknowledge that 'transcendence' has being and effect, he is nevertheless one of the few philosophers who have seriously concerned themselves with prayer, and this is what he says: 'Prayer is an importunity which irrupts in secret, which man may dare in the depth of solitude and distress.'[31] I

[31] Karl Jaspers, *Philosophie*, III (1932), p. 126.

do not know whether the prayer of Asaph or Job can be described in this way—but even if prayer may sometimes have been this for them, they could not possibly have assented to Jasper's thesis: 'The one God exists only as I think him.' Alas, no 'importunity' can help where the silence of the gods prevails anyhow.

The Anthropomorphous Name

The unity of the Scriptures is audible rather than visible. It may be of advantage if the interpreter—and above all one who feels that he possesses little imagination—can visualize the world of the past; after all, the Bible records history and aims to present history, even where we would speak of myth or saga. But what the mind's eye can see will hardly represent an essential contribution to an insight into the unity of the Scriptures. There are connections and continuities in landscapes and physiognomies, gestures and ceremonies; nevertheless, the unity undoubtedly lies beyond these imaginable worlds. It must be sought for in a word, a voice, an answering, a testifying, an accusing, an intercession; it is a breaking in of the creative utterance of the God of freedom into the midst of the masks of divine power, into the midst of things as they are.

And yet we would still go wrong and would ourselves thwart what we think we have understood if the audible did not clearly grow out of something which is clearly visible. That is to say, without the stamp of visibility, that which is heard could again be construed as a religious idea, instead of being heard as a voice. And since in preaching the practical concern is always with the possibility of an actualization of the unity of the Scriptures, there would be all the greater temptation to wish to find this unity in an idea, in some objective content, in a substratum of wisdom, a selection of divine names which are common to both the Old and the New Testament. No, the unity which is heard will not be received as Word, i.e., as *dabar*, i.e., as creative and normative utterance, if it has not been permeated with historical visibility, or better, if the content of the Name has not taken on concrete form in it.

In so far as the unity becomes visible, it leaps to the eye by way of anthropomorphism. The one Object, the one Life, the sublime, sovereign God cannot possibly become manifest except through revelation, i.e., through incarnation, through becoming man, entering into the existence of human life, acting in the dimension of human history, making himself known in actual events—whereby man then meets a greater fellow man, a greater hand, a greater face. This 'mythical' manner of speaking must be distinguished from the mythology of religion; indeed, it is the very opposite of it, because it actually forced itself upon the biblical writers by reason of the tremendous impact of the historicality of the existence in which God is implicated. It can also be expressed in this way (though because of its abstractness it does alter a little the Old Testament idiom): the 'transcendence of God' prevents any natural relationship whatsoever; nevertheless a perfect communion between God and man is possible.[32] And if we understand the word 'communion' in its full sense and the word 'perfect' in a genuine and limited sense, we will be thrust out of our theological abstractions and thrown back upon the covenant and the intercourse which exists between God and man in the manner of men.

In all our experience we have no 'Thou,' no object over against us which can be of help to us, except in our fellow man. Anybody who simply cannot 'put up with' the incarnation will also not know what to do with YHWH, who speaks and hears, who wounds and heals, who comes down and visits us, who walks in the garden and confuses the language of the tower builders, who accompanies his people in pillars of cloud and fire, who sits enthroned on the cherubim and precisely as such is the God of heaven and earth, of whom it is said that heaven and the highest heaven cannot contain him and that in the face of this God the nations are like a drop from a bucket and accounted as the dust on the scales. But he who hears the witness of the time of remembrance will not wonder at the witness of the time of expectation —or rather he will stand before it in utmost wonder, but in such a way that both will equally arouse his wonder. He will marvel at both as signs that the Lord God has truly taken on human nature. This is not a dogma, but rather a fact of salvation.[33] It is not a statement which is 'prepared for in the Old Testament,' it is rather assumed in the Old Testament. It is there assumed not merely as something which is to come, but rather as something settled, as something grounded in the

---

[32] Th. C. Vriezen, *An Outline of Old Testament Theology*, p. 130.
[33] Cf. 'Anthropomorphismus,' in *Encyclopaedia Judaica*, II, and also Franz Rosenzweig's criticism in *Kleinere Schriften*, pp. 525ff.

very nature, character, and intent of this God. We get on the wrong track if we proceed to clarify this form by means of a doctrine of religious symbolism. We are free to speak of symbols, primary and secondary symbols, and also of saga and legend, and even of myth. But if these are understood as projections of human experience and not as the concrete form of the Name, not as the precipitate of the meeting with YHWH which is initiated, established by Him, then the qualification of this event as a history of God with men again goes to ruin.

As long as this anthropomorphism is for the most part only an embarrassment to us, we cannot preach from the Old Testament. But then can we preach even from the New Testament? As long as the strangeness, the 'event' character of God's manifestation strikes us as not being universal enough, we feel inclined in our preaching to give to the Old Testament (and then necessarily to the New Testament too) a universal basis of principles and insights. But this only leads to the point where the given data which strike us as 'undivine' are emptied of meaning.

We must see that the 'national limitation' is the form in which election takes place, here and everywhere, down to the present day; the fact that the revelation is 'earth-bound' is the reverse side of the real coming of God to the earth, today and always. Are we not missing the essence of the mystery and belittling our preaching every time that we disparage this anthropomorphism, instead of falling on our faces before this evidence of God's love? We must ask ourselves whether our preaching and instruction do not still have clinging to them the eggshells of a stubborn natural theology, which in tragic misunderstanding and despite all our 'orthodoxy' still secretly persists in the opinion that a 'general revelation' would be more basic, comprehensive, intelligible, more convincing. Real candour will be lacking as long as the preacher is not imbued (and he will never be completely that, because by nature we are all pagans like the others) with the knowledge that omnipresence, which is the omnipresence of the one true God, cannot be known in any other way except on the basis of his special presence, that his universal love is perceived only in a very special election, his omnipotence in a very special redemptive power, his nature in the Name and his Name in the Messiah, his divinity in his humanity and his divine act in his human act. He who hears the special and particular encounters the centre and core.

On the other hand, when we start with the general ideas, we can never be witnesses and interpreters of the Name. Then the names, the qualities, the acts of God lose that which is engraved upon them by a concrete occurrence, and automatically they become dark symbols or pale allegories, which in principle we can get along without and ought to abandon. And in pursuing this path on which anthropomorphism, which is precisely the way in which this God demonstrates his divinity, is allowed to evaporate, the whole manifestation of Christ becomes merely an illustration of a truth which we already knew from somewhere else, and 'God's blood'(!) (Acts 20 : 28) becomes only a seal of our own natural, innate religion.

With such notions in our minds we can hardly maintain resistance to the nihilism within ourselves and the world. We have no authority if we are not ourselves in the service of an ultimate authority. And authority is grounded in a particular superiority and in a particular, concrete communion. If for us the Old Testament does not have the sound of a direct witness of God, then perhaps we may look for some central religious idea, which we think may be predominant in it, such as God's righteousness or God's guidance. But it is impossible in this way even remotely to do justice to the whole of the actual facts, and even if this were to succeed, we would only be reconstructing the 'Israelite religion,' not spelling out the Name; we would not be seeing the pre-eminence of the 'Word' of God, we would not be in communion with him.

But the many-coloured, tension-filled, contradictory composition of the Old Testament canon certainly does not leave us even the possibility of setting forth one theme, whether it be the power of its ethos, the holiness of God, the progressive spiritualization of the concept of God, the course of the kingdom of God, or the formal characteristic that God's speech is regarded as continuing on through time. There is no sense in praising the Old Testament religion—no matter whether it be the one that was actually practised among the people or the normative one, the one that was upheld by the men of God—and judging it according to the standard of its power or perdurability in the history of religion, its religious profundity or purity. Even though such a laudatory judgment may be true, even though it may even be a generally accepted truth, it hardly contributes to what a preacher needs in order to justify himself when he begins and continues his work, clothed with authority and therefore with the joy of earnestness and the earnestness of joy that accords with the 'Name.'

The revelation to which the time of expectation relates cannot first be regarded as a religion in order that afterwards it may possibly be elevated to the status of the sole valid religion. By what standard are we to defend the assertion that Israel's legitimate religion was superior to the pagan religions? In the end we might be more right in saying that in many respects it is 'lower,' because it is more primitive than the speculations of the Egyptian priests (not to speak of the Indian systems). The best, no, the only possible, attitude for the interpreter and witness will be for him to seek to understand more and more deeply that this 'lower' is part of the condescendence of God.

It is noteworthy that the very features which seem most offensive to enlightened thinking appear to be implicit in the proclamation of the fullness of time, the incarnation of the Word, the *assumptio carnis*. The real, the childlike, the offensive thing is the way in which what happens here enters into the event that took place in the stable in Bethlehem. Just as in the Nativity, so here in these anthropomorphic concepts—no, not concepts, but facts—the whole Godhead is hidden, the eternal glory and power, the mercy and the righteousness, the immeasurable way of Being, compared with which heaven and earth dwindle away, the unfathomable faithfulness in which a thousand years are as a day. God's 'being-one-with' and God's 'being-with' human life are revealed simultaneously in the theophany. And this not as if something happened to God that is alien to him; it is inherent in his nature to be allied with man, to be intelligible to man, to have communion with man, indeed, to be a man among men. And again this condescension is so far from detracting from his absolute majesty that actually the sovereign power of his being is nowhere so strongly evident as it is precisely in these theophanies, in all that happens when a face shines, a hand moves, and a voice speaks out of the midst of the fire. He who rejects the phrase 'witness to Christ' for the Old Testament, but rather prefers to speak of it as 'witness to God' has not yet dealt seriously with the revelation. For it is precisely as witness that these two—witness to God and witness to Christ—are identical, and this is precisely the mystery of the Name. There is no other God! This fanatical (if you want to call it that) cry 'No other God' is the unity of the Testaments. Nevertheless, when we so interpret the Old Testament, we are not making it a Christian book, for even the New Testament is not a 'Christian book.' As a whole it is not a book at all, but rather a series of fragments which testify concerning the One who came and is to come, just as in other ways the fragments we call the Old Testament do. But together these two series of fragments actually constitute a book, that is, precisely in so far as together they are a unity by virtue of their function of testifying to Christ, that is, to this God, who takes on human nature in order to unite it with himself.

It is a matter of him who is present as God-with-us, as he wills to be present. It has to do with him whose deepest singular self is at the same time his revealed manifestation. It has to do with him who is nowhere more Spirit than he is in his earthly being, who deals with us humanly —humanly, not despite his divinity, but by virtue of his divinity!

Therefore we miss the mystery altogether if in our explanation of this anthropomorphic language we speak in terms of the inadequacy of human speech, the limitations of human thought, the unavoidability of metaphorical language, the relativity of theophanies. All this may be epistemologically correct; and to this extent it applies to all science, even to exact science as long as all words are not resolved into a series of numbers. But the Name creates relationships; the Scripture is the testimony of 'meeting with God.'

'God is never described—which, after all, is what we implicitly assume when we speak of something being "ascribed" to him. That is to say, never are two or more "attributes" placed in relationship to one another, which is, after all, the basic principle in every description. . . . There are no biblical statements, even the most scurrilous and offensive, which cannot become realized facts, today as always, in encounter with creation or the creature. . . . When a man stretches out his hand for help, God's *hand* can grasp it; when he would approach Him in yearning or withdraw from Him in defiance, God will *come down to him*.' Yet we cannot say that God 'has' a face, eyes, hands; this is prevented by the Name—not because seeing, hearing, and touching would be beneath his dignity, but rather because this 'having' (as well as 'being') is an assertion that conflicts with the Second Commandment, 'You shall not make yourself a graven image, or any likeness. . . .' We are cut off from knowledge of the 'being' and 'having' of YHWH in order that instead we may have unlimited trust in his unlimited power 'to meet at every moment our and all creation's

132

momentary corporeality and spirituality corporeally and spiritually, in body and spirit.'[34]

It is a striking thing how evident these things usually are in poetry and how superfluous all explanations seem to be for the poet and the poetic mind. But poetry could not live in an atmosphere of epistemological reflections, and therefore it would in my opinion be dangerous to look for a special affinity with the poet in connection with the particular anthropomorphism we are speaking of here.

[34] Franz Rosenzweig, *Kleinere Schriften*, pp. 528ff.; cf. Rudolf Otto, *The Idea of the Holy*, tr. John W. Harvey, (Oxford: Oxford Univ. Press, 1923), pp. 77ff.; G. Ernest Wright, *The Challenge of Israel's Faith* (Univ. of Chicago Press, 1944), pp. 36ff.; M. A. Beek, 'De vraag naar de mens in de godsdienst van Israel,' in *Vox Theologica* (1952), pp. 69ff., 75f.

2. The Facts

It will be well to call attention to a number of formal characteristics which in themselves contain a specific reference to the peculiar character of the Scriptures as a whole, with which the interpreter and witness is concerned apostolically and prophetically, pastorally and politically.

The unity of the Scriptures is to a large extent determined by the demarcation of bounds over against heathenism. He who is of the opinion that 'heathenism' is only a religious-historical concept will necessarily find that there are many chapters in the Old Testament which he cannot accept as relevant, as a message, much less as a proclamation of God, i.e., God's Presence in the 'flesh.' But he who sees that heathenism is identical with the religion which is by nature peculiar to us men, the religion which in a thousand forms is out to justify existence as it is and to achieve union with the ground of the universe, will understand that the unmasking and rejection of heathenism in the Old Testament still proclaims to us today that God's thoughts for us are 'thoughts of peace' (Jer. 29 : 11). The God does not cut himself off from the flesh, but debars the flesh from the gods. And this is all one and the same Love. The same elective love dwells in his leading of the people out of Egypt and the giving of the Law on Sinai. And who is it that is led out, who is commanded to be faithful to the Liberator? We are the ones who are addressed, we who no longer need to be heathens, though that is what we are in every fibre of our being.[1] Where the anthropomorphism of God is understood, the apotheosis of man is cut off at its root. And the judgment that is pro-

---

[1] G. K. Chesterton, *The Everlasting Man* (New York: George H. Doran Co., 1925); Leopold Ziegler, *Gestaltwandel der Götter* (1922); K. H. Miskotte, *Edda en Thora* (1939), pp. 29, 81, 129f., 395ff.; Walter F. Otto, *Die Götter Griechenlands*, 4th edn. (1956), pp. 127f., 171, 179; G. van der Leeuw, *Religion in Essence and Manifestation*, tr. J. E. Turner (New York: Harper & Row, 1963), II, pp. 543f.

nounced in this cutting off of the deification of man is in the highest degree an act of grace. If we wish to characterize in more detail this demarcation from heathenism, we can do so here only in a very sketchy and apodictic way. We cannot devote much space to this question, because nihilism concerns us far more today than does heathenism. Putting aside nuances and varieties, and stated in thetical form, we may set down the following structural differences in which this salutary demarcation from heathenism may be seen.

1. In the Old Testament, Creation is opposed to eternal becoming, history is opposed to the cycle of existence, Providence to fate, the virtues of God to the dark ways of the gods. Election is opposed to the whim of fortune, obedience to tragic heroism, the future of the Lord to the world's collapse. The Messiah is opposed to the god-king, being-with-god to the 'hereafter,' the sacredness of ordinary human life to the demonization of the powers, prophecy to divination. The command from above is opposed to self-sufficient custom. The individual (Ps. 22 : 20, variant) is opposed both to the vulgar and the elite, the *qahal*, the congregation, to the total state, the 'servant of the Lord' to the men of Nimrod, the seer to the astrologer, the *chokmah* (wisdom) to philosophy, the Speech of God to natural or supernatural Being. And all this, even though it is tremendously critical of the world as it is, signifies and has as its purpose one incomparable liberation, which in part has already made itself felt and had its effect in the culture of Europe.[2]

2. It has gradually become the common and accepted thing to contrast the Israelite way of thinking with the Greek (at least the Hellenistic).[3] This is right, but the question remains whether the proper profit has been drawn from this in preaching and instruction. Greek thought is rarefied classical humanism; we are saturated with it and we regard this, in a certain sense rightly, as our European advantage. In comparison with the fantastic metaphysics of a vegetative and vitalistic naturalism and its endless varieties, the classical attitude toward life has an ordering and purifying strength for which we may be forever grateful. In preaching and instruction, however, we must take

[2] Cf. Hanns Lilje, 'Kirche und Politik: Die Krise des europäischen Freiheitsgedankens,' in *Kirche und Welt* (1956).

[3] Ph. Kohnstamm, *De Heilige, Proeve van een Christelijke geloofsleer* (1931), §1 and§7; Thorleif Boman, *Hebrew Thought Compared with Greek*, tr. J. L. Moreau (1960).

a different direction and be fully aware that this gratitude has limits which are set by the limitations of humanism itself. Here we merely refer to the matter as it relates to the problem.[4]

3. In large part the preaching of the church ceases to be biblical when and to the degree that it has not yet taken seriously the Israelite idiom of the Scriptures, of the Old Testament as well as the New. The fact that frequently it still remains diatribe, penitential sermonizing, parsonical or papal fatherly exhortation is a mere externality compared with the prevailing assumptions that faith is essentially assent, that truth is a doctrine, that man is superior to the animal because he thinks, that we have to free ourselves from the material in spirit, that grace is an infused power, that justification is a process in the soul, that the Command of God lies on the same level with the commands of the church and that these in turn are on the same level of mutual encounter and in the same comprehensive framework with Christian morality. Rome (like modern Protestantism) proceeds on the cultural assumption that what is catholic (that is, universal) is narrowed and constricted by the Israelite way of thinking, in which the prophets and apostles move[5]—and also that this essential characteristic of the Scriptures must be translated, broadened, eliminated, or retouched in order that it may reach intellectual people, indeed, in order to be intelligible. But from the heart 'flow the springs of life' (Prov. 4 : 23), and this language is the peculiar speech of the heart; only on the basis of this kind of speech can the general phenomenon of languages and their dispersion be rightly understood. Into this idiom the Bibles of all peoples can and must be faithfully translated.[6] Here it turns out that teaching and language condition each other.

Where is the source and the end of this dogmatic encystment by which we cut ourselves off from Israel and thus from the critical power of the Scriptures? Here again we can only give an indication, but for

[4] All that is essential to the problem has, in our opinion, been said by Karl Barth, *Church Dogmatics*, Vol. III, pt. 2, pp. 333–44; cf. also Vol. IV, pt. 2, pp. 483ff.
[5] J. H. Gunning, *Blikken in de Openbaring*, I (1866), 158: 'If we really want to understand Christ as completely universal, as the head of mankind, we must understand him and the New Testament completely Israelitically.' Cf. ibid., p. 157: 'Actually, the whole hierarchy is to be understood as an extremely remarkable anticipation of that which is impending in Israel.
[6] Cf. Constantin Brunner, *Unser Christus*, p. 544; Martin Buber, 'Die Sprache der Botschaft,' in Buber and Rosenzweig, *Die Schrift und ihre Verdeutschung* (1936), pp. 55ff.

the interpreter and witness it is undoubtedly of importance that he should see how different and also how 'modern' this old Bible is. We think of many basic words in our catechism and how far they depart from the basic words of the Old Testament. *Chesed* ('grace,' 'favour'), for example, can never mean *gratia infusa* ('infused grace'); *tsedaqah* ('righteousness') is never a growing possession; *qadosh* ('holy') is never the equivalent of ethical excellence, and YHWH must never be equated with *ens realissimum* ('most real Being'). In preaching, however, the recognition or nonrecognition of the hegemony of these classical thought structures becomes an acute question. What can the Word of preaching be, if we learn to know God better and more originally elsewhere and if he is present in a different way from that in which he is present in his Word? The 'truth' is the spoken word, it is speech and must be responded to in speech; nowhere in the Bible is the message merely appended to the story like a moral—it is the power by which every member of the sentence structure lives. Nowhere can the truth be isolated as 'content.' The text is its own commentary in that it contains in spoken form everything that needs to be known. The story retains its epic conciseness and so by its own power raises itself to the level of a message that speaks. Repetitions of the same word, shifts of emphasis, recollection of similar sounding narratives which have a different inner rhythm—these are the quiet ways in which the proclamation in the sacred texts give emphasis to this or that promise, commandment, consolation, or admonition. In our secondary way we shall have to follow this example, in the sense that we must never again let go of the insight that the truth is not true and never attests itself as true except in an exposition which is already application in itself, which combines the holy earnestness of deliberative reflection with the holy act of joyful testimony, a song of liberation.

4. It will also be well to pay attention to the discrepancy between form and content, the frail, defenceless witness to that which is true, valid, and commanded. This kind of attention must cure us of the habit of supposing that here and there we shall find some 'direct' proclamation which preaching simply needs to repeat. This will not do! We mention a few examples.

We read the ancient genealogical tables, and the seemingly purposeless juxtaposition of names show that in selection and grouping they are envoys of the message. At the time in which this Scripture was written the substance of the sermon was hidden in this indirect form.[7] We do not make a sermon of it—it was already a sermon, and we recognize it as an ancient psalmody that goes on humming through time.

We read narratives which, like that of Abimelech, the son of Gideon, appear to be completely concerned with profane history, until we realize that here we have an antitype of 'naïve theocracy'[8] which is one of the elements of the message and has a political relevance which is quite as great as that of Romans 13 and Revelation 13. This must be utilized and, as far as possible, turned to account for the church and those on its outskirts.

We read the laws and ritual regulations, prosaic, precise, and disturbingly casuistical—and the Epistle to the Hebrews teaches us to interpret these things as being but a 'shadow.' Nevertheless there is in the outline of them a restrained passion for the holiness of everyday life and a reflection of the faith that all things, even the bells of the horses, are inscribed as being holy to YHWH (Zech. 14 : 20). This prevents us from too quickly assuming that there is no connection between the ethical and ceremonial parts of the law.

We read psalms which seem to be no more than the cry of a tormented man for help, but we need only to listen more carefully to see that this is not the crying of just any man, but rather of one who cries out because he is permitted to call upon the Name, and his crying is itself a way of testifying to the revelation. Such a psalm is not a revelation in the strict sense, but the way in which it transmits a word of God to us becomes clear when we see this permission to cry out to God, this privilege, this acceptance of man's complaint. This God is our God, throughout all the ages and for ever!

We read the *chokmah*, the wisdom literature, parts of which strike us as being sceptical, and we see in the midst of their melancholy the great affirmations of God's faithfulness to man and the earth, outshining our despondency.[9] Therefore the wavering and irresolution: many sayings seem too profound, others too superficial; many ideas seem to revolve in circles of contradictory truthfulness around the truth that has been grasped, and then are forgotten again because they have lost sight of

---

[7] Cf. A. van Selms, 'I Kronieken,' in *Tekst en Uitleg*, pp. 24f., 80–112.

[8] Martin Buber, *Königtum Gottes*, pp. 27f.

[9] Martin Buber and Franz Rosenzweig, *Die Schrift und ihre Verdeutschung*, pp. 55f.; Fritz Horn, *Der Prediger Salomo*, passim.

the ultimate truth. This is precisely the way that man is revealed. It is precisely in this discrepancy between the form and content of the saying that it becomes clear what the fear of God means. Do not fear the bogey which every man creates in his imagination and then calls God. Fear God, and not the emptiness of life. Don't be afraid that your righteousness may turn out to be futile; don't fear your own wickedness.[10]

We read in the so-called 'historical' books of the prophetic struggle to turn a judgment about the kings of the past into a message for one's own time. To prepare people in the church to make such judgments is one of the goals of preaching today. Who is the person who is independent in his political judgment without being a crank? Perhaps only one who has learned in this school.[11]

We read the songs of lamentation, which never degenerate into a flight from history because of the hopelessness of disappointed expectation; we read of the failure of the Judges, the anarchy against which they launched their active intervention, but which nevertheless came flowing back again—and we hear the message that nothing is lost as long as this God, whom none of this can touch and who in comparison with what is still to come has done nothing, is the Living One.

In all these diverse, confused, and obscure parts of the Old Testament one single history is reflected. The history of God's 'revelation'? No! The history of the 'kingdom of God'? No! The history of the recognition of the revelation? Certainly, but it is difficult to trace. The history of the proclamation of God's Name? Yes! It is there to be perceived and it can be traced! But just as Leopold von Ranke said of world history, 'Every epoch stands in a direct relation to God' (we should like to know where he learned this!), so we can in fact say of the proclamation that it does stand in a direct, living relation to the Name, to the heart of the matter, to that one concern of God's heart, the holy process in which he calls and gathers his own into a fellowship in light.

[10] Fritz Horn, ibid., p. 37.
[11] Wilhelm Vischer, *Das Christuszeugnis des Alten Testaments*, II, 8: 'It is the nature of this history, which takes place in the dialogue of the eternal and living God with man on earth and in time, that it cannot be understood as a past fact. It remains for all times God's Word, the command and promise of the Lord for all generations of his people. It is recorded in the Old Testament as prophecy and this also means as prophetic history, as advent history, moving and straining towards its goal, namely, the revelation of the royal sovereignty of God over the earth.'

5. The structure of the ancient canon also deserves attention, precisely in connection with preaching and instruction. The arrangement of the books of the Bible, as we have it now, taken over from the Septuagint, appears to be based upon a literary principle: historical, poetic, and prophetic books. This disturbs the inner structure of the canon.

The Torah is the real basis, because it contains the testimony of God's direct intervention. The Prophets (which include the historical books, e.g., Samuel and Kings) call Israel back to recognition of the Covenant and the command. The Writings (including books as different as Psalms and Lamentations, Ruth and Esther) describe how the community reacts to God's intervention and testimony, whether this be in lyrical and liturgical song, didactic exposition and defence, or in the more remote areas of biographical occurrences, where there is no theophany and no prophecy and where in an atmosphere of idyllic (Ruth) or heroic (Esther) secularity and despite the absence of prophecy and 'wisdom,' a relationship to the Name is maintained, even though the way in which this takes place remains hidden.

This hierarchy or, if you will, this formation of the testimony in concentric circles establishes the unity as one that is extremely different from the unity of a codex. It makes preaching richer, because in this way the Torah, as the witness to the primal acts of the Lord, with its strong anthropomorphism, acquires a fundamental importance and gives to the congregation a sense of the coming action of God. It cuts the ground from under the procedure of making an anthology of fine passages and prevents our undertaking to put the Prophets in first place because we approve of their ethics and our preferring the Psalms because they accord with our piety. The most direct testimony of the time of expectation lies in the theophanies and in the *toledoth* (genealogical table) of the Torah. What God really is, what he will prove himself to be in the coming day of the Messiah, is here proclaimed—not specially, be it noted, in the so-called 'protevangelium' (i.e., the establishment of enmity against the Evil One, Gen. 3 : 15), but rather in the broad dramatic whole, in the historical peaks and in the quiet presence. The Torah speaks to us in the Creation as well as the Covenant, it sees God in his manifestations as well as in his veiled hiddenness, in the Garden of Eden as well as in the flaming sword, in the saga of the rivers in paradise and in the tree of life, in the *dibre* YHWH (the words and acts of Yahweh) interposed between the *mishpatim* (laws) in the tabernacle which suffers itself to stand among the tents, in the sacrificial cult, and in the power of intercession in which God himself carries out his purpose, in the choosing of the patriarchs, and in Balaam's unwilling blessing of Israel. All this is testimony of God and his Name—and these two are one—all this is history in the style of the 'One History.'

But not losing sight of this order of Torah-Prophets-Writings in preaching and instruction presents still other advantages. The relation of priest and prophet is removed from the purely polemical, into which it is usually so quickly drawn, and set into the dialectical-irenic Whole. The prophet cannot be regarded as being in opposition to the cult as such. Often priest and prophet exist together in one and the same cultic life; the prophet, however, battles against the spiritual emptying of worship, through Baal worship as well as through formalism, and therefore drives men's hearts back to the covenant in which the meaning and purpose of the cult is anchored.[12]

The praise of the Psalms, the complaints of Job, the scepticism of Koheleth, it becomes apparent in the context of this structure of the *Tenak*, the ancient canon, are not just any kind of praise, not the complaints to which we are all too prone, not the scepticism with which we are all too familiar. It is the praise of him who believes and is privileged to follow the Torah, the complaint of him who no longer sees its promise, the scepticism of the man who has seen its light fade and go out. It is wonderful to know that this bewildering totality of rebellion and doubt, of groping, blundering, and failing to grasp—that all this is incorporated as human reaction, *nota bene*, in 'God's Word,' i.e., that it belongs to the testimony of God's Word. But this knowledge would again be derailed if we forgot that this does not sanctify all praise, all complaint or scepticism, and that they spring from an Adamite heart, a human brain, or a human conscience; though on the other hand we must cling to the conviction that there is no praise, no complaint or scepticism which, if it please God, cannot be devoted to a pure witness of these same things. Thus something of the splendour of the Name is caught (1) through the medium of the Scripture's demarcation of

[12] P. A. H. de Boer, *De boodschap van het Oude Testament* (1940), p. 62: 'Ezekiel, himself a priest, outlines detailed regulations for the temple services; Haggai and Zechariah encourage the people to rebuild the temple; Jeremiah is also a priest; Isaiah receives his call in the temple. Elijah's zeal against the priests of Baal on Mount Carmel is at the same time a zeal for the cult of the God of the Covenant.'

itself from heathenism; (2) in its differentiation from the Greek way of thinking; (3) in its departure from customary preaching and teaching; (4) in the discrepancy between form and content in biblical teaching; (5) in the concentric circles of the arrangement of the writings, through which room is left, indeed, created, for the antinomies of human reactions.

EXEGESIS

In this study of the content and structure of the Old Testament, the purpose of which is to help the interpreter—the interpreter who seeks clarity for himself before he faces the people who still represent the 'third man'—it cannot be our purpose to enter into the discussion of so-called 'theological exegesis,' which has been and still continues to be carried on.[13]

It would be better so speak of exegesis *tout court*, if on the one hand it were not that exegesis is still usually understood to mean historical and philological study, which deliberately disregards the unity of the Holy Scriptures, and if on the other hand there were not the danger that the broadening or deepening of the task by conceiving of it as 'pneumatic' exposition would lead to fanciful and cerebral whimsicality. Just as a 'faithful husband,' a 'provident father,' an 'accurate notary' should be pleonasms, so 'theological exegesis' is in fact a

---

[13] Rudolf Kittel, 'Die Zukunft der alttestamentlichen Wissenschaft,' *ZAW* (1921), pp. 84ff.; H. Gressmann, 'Die Aufgabe der alttestamentlichen Forschung,' *ZAW* (1924), pp. 1ff.; H. Frick, *Wissenschaftliches und pneumatisches Verständnis der Bibel* (1927). Also O. Noordmans, 'Licht en donker in de exegese,' in *Geestelijke Perspectieven* (1930), pp. 68ff.; K. H. Miskotte, *Opmerkingen over theologische exegese* (1934); idem 'Das Problem der theologischen Exegese,' in *Theologische Aufsätze* (Barth Festschrift) (1935), pp. 51ff.; W. Vischer, *Das Christuszeugnis des Alten Testaments*, 2 vols. (1934–1941); J. de Groot, *Exegese* (1936); A. H. Edelkoort, 'Het homiletisch gebruik van het Oude Testament,' *Nieuwe Theol. Studien* (1937), pp. 194ff.; H. W. Obbink, *Theologische bezinning op het Oude Testament* (1938); W. J. de Wilde, *Het probleem van het Oude Testament in verband met de verkondiging van den Christus* (1938); H. Hellbardt, *Das Alte Testament und das Evangelium* (1938); A. R. Hulst, *Hoe moeten wij het Oude Testament uitleggen?* (1941); L. K. H. Bleeker, *Hermeneutiek* (1947); R. Bultmann, 'Ursprung und Sinn der Typologie als hermeneutische Methode,' *Festschrift für G. van der Leeuw* (1950), pp. 89ff.; M. Noth, 'Von der Knechtsgestalt des Alten Testaments,' *Evang. Theol.* (1946), pp. 302ff.; C. H. Dodd, *According to the Scriptures* (1953), pp. 61ff.; J. Coppens, *Les Harmonies des deux Testaments* (1949); H. Diem, *Grundfragen der biblischen Hermeneutik* (1950.)

pleonasm, unless the man erroneously seeks his spiritual freedom in his autonomy. 'And what the heart refuses the head will not let in' (Fichte).

We may sum up the difference between theological and pneumatic exegesis in the following statements:

1. Theological exegesis of the Old Testament is that endeavour to understand and explain the Scriptures which starts with the faith that the Old Testament in its totality is the testimony of the time of expectation, which, though it is fulfilled through the time of Revelation, is by no means rendered obsolete by the time of recollection. It begins with a view of unity which has its basis in the relation of the Word to the one NAME.

2. It follows from this that we cannot make a selection, an anthology (of the Messianic prophecies, for example) as a witness to Christ—if only because we cannot set limits to the freedom of God's own message. 'We certainly do not listen to the Old Testament because there are so many passages in it which seem plausible to us, but rather because we believe the word of the apostles and Jesus Christ that the God of whom the Old Testament speaks is the Father of Jesus Christ.'[14]

3. It must surely be regarded as a mistake to relate the testimony of the Old Testament to the *Logos asarkos*. This would assume that the time of expectation *in* its expectation looked forward to a definitive repetition of 'revelations' but not to a definite Revelation which is unrepeatable. Here it seems to be forgotten that the Scriptures as scriptures point to the revelation which is one, historically unrepeatable revelation, and as such points at the same time to the time of God, the history of the unrepeatable mystery, the Word made flesh, which before as well as afterwards is justified in the Spirit.

4. The multiplicity of 'revelations' (a perverse word used in the wrong place and a relic of a rationalistic or historistic point of view), the stages, the evolution are nevertheless to be taken as real. Historical criticism rightly emphasizes that we must resist any reduction of the given data to one level. Allegorizing is admissible only when the texts themselves contain a reference or a demand in this direction. Otherwise *krinein*, discrimination, examination, arrangement, and critical evalu-

---

[14] Gerhard von Rad, *Fragen der Schriftauslegung im = Alten Testament* (1938), p. 7; cf. idem, 'Typologische Auslegung des Alten Testaments,' *Evang. Theol.*, XII (1952–53), 17–33.

ation must be given their full validity. It must be understood, however, that the synthesis of this multiplicity of revelations which must be given some order cannot be based upon a high appraisal of the 'great religious ideas' or a judgment that the prophets and psalmists were men 'filled with the Spirit of God.' This they perhaps never or only seldom were. The synthesis must lie in the inspiration of the Scriptures. What we are given is the juxtaposition, the fact that the texts stand together, and this is their intended synthesis. The determinative factor here is not something that can be seen.

5. A Christological 'interpretation' in the sense of pious 'reinterpretation' is inadmissible. An exegesis that begins with the fact that everything in the Old Testament speaks indirectly of Christ, of the Revelation, the Kingdom, the Messiah, the supreme Prophet, the one Priest and eternal King and his adversaries, of the cult to be performed and the commandment to be fulfilled, this is simply required of Christian faith, and in many respects it can also reveal the essence of the matter for any scholarly investigator.[15] The ark 'is' not the church, the *Ebed YHWH* 'is' not Jesus, circumcision 'is' not baptism, and so on; but they do speak of these things in the form of testimony and its relation to a content which is not 'given' in the words.

6. Such an exegesis is not a 'reading principle' (*Leseprinzip*), as Helmuth Schreiner charged it with being[16]—in so far as one does not degrade faith itself and the Spirit himself into such an intellectual principle; it is rather a 'fruit of reading' (*Lesefrucht*).[17] It is not an 'exposition that is bound to the confession of the church,'[18] unless one here understands 'confession' to mean the faith that Jesus is the Messiah and that God is none other than his Name (i.e., his Revelation) and that faith by its criticism relativizes religion.

7. It would be a failure to recognize the 'new thing' by which we now live conclusively and predominantly in the time of recollection, if we were to understand 'fulfilment' (to use an older and incidental term of Barth, namely, *Erfüllung*) to mean that only through it has the promise become 'full,' unambiguous, and thus effective. Recollection

[15] 'We face the undeniable fact that very often the "theological" exegesis has also resulted in the best "historical" exegesis.' G. von Rad, *Evang. Theol.*, XII, 32.
[16] Helmuth Schreiner, *Das Alte Testament und die Verkündigung* (1937).
[17] A. A. van Ruler, 'De waarde van het Oude Testament,' in *Religie en Politiek*, p. 149.
[18] Hans Hellbardt, 'Die Auslegung des Alten Testaments als theologische Disziplin,' *Theol. Blätter*, XVI (1937), 129ff.

cannot possibly be thought of in any way except as recollection of an event in which the expectation is wholly or partially eliminated. One-sided eschatological thinking overstrains the unity of the Testaments and unduly neglects the real difference between them which is plain to be seen.

8. In the exposition of the Old Testament as well as the New it is an unpromising undertaking to try to discover or reconstruct a true text, a conception of what probably happened, the 'true' history behind the text. The traditional form of the text (in the broadest sense) is from first to last the material of exegesis. This is also of importance for a right insight into the unity of the Scriptures, for it is not in the con-tinuity of the history but rather in the spiritual continuity of the words that this unity is located and becomes apparent.

9. The fact that the vicious circle (*circulus vitiosus*) in which faith in the unity of the Scriptures seems to move is actually a circle of truth (*circulus veritatis*)[19] is something that cannot be proved—at best it can be supported by the insight that theology has its own logic, namely, the logic of grammar,[20] which in every use of conjugation or syntax already presupposes and has in view the total continuity of the lan-guage.

10. Theological exegesis becomes bad gnosis when it is not oriented toward the actual practice of preaching and instruction, in which, in poor human words, all the mysteries of the cosmos and all the saving mysteries of the heart may be made articulate,[21] in order that they too may contribute to the overcoming of the ambivalence inherent in human religion.

[19] On this term see Karl Barth, *Church Dogmatics*, Vol. 11, pt. 1, pp. 243ff.

[20] Cf. Franz Rosenzweig, *Der Stern der Erlösung*, II, pp. 49ff.

[21] The following passage from Al-Ghazali on the interpretation of the Koran (quoted in A. J. Wensinck, *The Muslim Creed* (1932), pp. 100f.) will serve for comparison and differentiation: 'The true middle path between a complete allegorism and rigid Hanbalism is narrow and obscure. It is found only by those who enjoy divine help and who reach the heart of things by divine light, not by hearsay. Then, when the mysteries of things are revealed to them, so that they see them as they are, then return to Scripture and tradition and their working; whatever accords with what they have witnessed by the light of certainty they affirm and whatever does not accord with it they interpret allegorically. . . . But a closer definition of the middle way in these things would belong to the vast subject of esoteric knowledge, which we must leave aside. Our aim was only to make clear that the literal and the allegorical conceptions may be in harmony with one another.' (Hanbalism was a school which interpreted the anthropomorphisms in the Koran literally; it was opposed by the Mutazilites.)

General Hermeneutics

So-called 'historical exegesis' has burdened our intellectual conscience with problems which, however orthodox our solution of them may be, rob our preaching of inner freedom. In order to be relieved of them we must cease claiming an exceptional position for the Scriptures even in the formal rules of exegesis. To read the Bible historically is not a procedure which we accept (more or less reluctantly) because we have to admit its usefulness; on the contrary, we demand it as necessary, and for strictly theological reasons. God's Word has become completely man's word; therefore it cannot be advisable to seek an a priori place for a special biblical hermeneutics. Every spoken human word is misunderstood or has violence done to it if one does not respect its property of being filled with the intention of saying something to us, of communicating something to us about a matter (Sache). It is never a question of the word, but always of the matter. It is an inhuman way of treating a man's word to direct one's attention to the word itself and as such, or to direct it to the character of the speaker or his past or his authorities and then make this a matter of great importance. What does he want to say, to what matter which deserves all our attention does his word refer? Only when I see this matter do I really get back to the speaker himself and what he is saying. Thus the sequence is as follows: first comes the word as a sign, a summons to pay attention, a pointing to something; then follows the matter which is intended; and finally comes the word again, but now to be understood on the basis of the intention of the speech.

There is no special hermeneutical method which is reserved for the Holy Scriptures. Actually we must describe the method of liberal biblical criticism as being 'special' in a fatal way; its inhuman refusal to understand the biblical writers on the basis of the matter that motivates them is a breach of ordinary humanity.[22] We misunderstand the Scriptures if in our preaching or teaching we start with a closed

[22] Karl Barth, *Church Dogmatics*, Vol. I, pt. 2, p. 466: 'Far from it being true that the word of man in the Bible has an abnormal significance and function, it is precisely in the Bible that it manifests itself in its normal significance and function. It is precisely in the word of man in the Bible that we must learn what has to be learned concerning the word of man in general.' [Translation altered.] The entire argument here follows closely the statements of Barth.

world-picture to which the Transcendent or the Mystery is added as a supplement, or also if we start with an autonomy to which a heteronymous margin is attached, or from a method of understanding which happens to meet a strange object, which we then suddenly must deal with in a different way. Then perhaps we make a bit of a concession; we want to 'leave room' for something different which we cannot 'dispose of' in any other way. The interpreter and witness must at least know that even such a 'religious' circumvention cancels out the unbiasedness of theology and destroys the genuine guilelessness, which would otherwise have a certain latitude if we did not surrender ourselves to our world-picture, our autonomy, our methodology. What is briefly indicated here has its analogy in other areas, and it becomes apparent that here too even the formal considerations affect the heart of the matter. We mean this not in the dogmatic but purely phenomenological sense.

Just as we must understand God's omnipresence from the viewpoint of his special presence, just as we can conceive of God's omnipotence only as we start with the special saving power of the Name, just as we can use the term 'kingdom' in a nondemonic way only on condition that we think of God's kingdom as the rule of this particular, self-determining God—so we can learn the general methods for real understanding of our neighbour only by hearing the Word, only through openness to this divine Neighbour, to the Majesty who has become our neighbour in his revelation, in his incarnation.

These appear to be radical ideas and yet they are simple, they seem to be exaggerated and yet they are pertinent and evident to anyone who has to preach, at least if he knows what preaching—and what instruction—is. And like all methodological principles, when they are considered theoretically, they appear to present us with a hard choice, but in their actual application they quite spontaneously become singularly obvious.

On the horizon of our thinking we sense that there is a permanent mystery; but more than this, the light of the horizon is here, near at hand; and what is even more, this mystery is present and manifest when I confess and proclaim the Name as it is written, as it 'took place.' Then wherever I may stand (perhaps, for example, crammed into the 'wooden breeches'),[23] there I am practising historical exegesis

[23 *de houten broek*: jocular appellation for the pulpit.—Tr.]

in so far as I myself stand in the stream of the holy history, which secretly contains and carries with it the meaning of universal history.

This engagement with historical reality, so understood, so defined, and so oriented, leaves room for all really verified historical-critical findings. That is to say, the biblical texts must be investigated for their own sake, because the Name, to which they bear witness, is to be sought and found, not behind or beyond them, but in them, because the thing which they declare to be a very special reality claims to be the ground of all reality. And here again, if we will not or cannot recognize this—and who can really do this willingly as a religious person?—we shall slip back into the diversity and the chaos, but above all, the ambivalence of religion. The theological deepening of exegetical freedom which has taken place in recent years brings with it a change in our evaluation of exegetical methods—a change that must inevitably create confusion if one has not taken this deepening into account. After all, it must be remembered that up to this time it was taken for granted—for example, by Schleiermacher as well as his opponents—that rejection of a special hermeneutics was tantamount to the denial of special revelation. In dialectical theology it is just the reverse: on the basis of a denial of 'general revelation'—or rather, actually providing the basis for this denial—God's own revelation is seen to be so divine, but also so human, that it can contain and reveal the rule of life and thought for the whole of life. God is too great merely to be an exception; God has made himself so small that he cannot fail to be seen in his small form, in which 'the whole fullness of deity dwells bodily.' And also in the small Bible the whole object is to witness to Him who took upon himself the nature and the judgment, the trial and the justification of the whole of human life in all its dimensions. In doing this we have not read anything into the Bible; we have taken the intention and the structure of the whole seriously in order that we may also take it seriously in this its positiveness when we engage in discussion with modern man.

One may find Goethe more beautiful and Luther more edifying, but the matter which is at stake is here attested in a unique way, namely, in such a way that, though it is divine, we meet it humanly, that, though it is eternal, it confronts us with God's actual historical dealings with men, and, though it is inconceivable, it is experienced as elementary truth. There must be an end to the controversies between a Docetic exegesis (which takes flight into mystical essence) and an Ebionitic reduction (which retreats to atomistic *concreta*); they have been burdening and oppressing preaching on the Old Testament for almost a century. We must try to free the preacher from this unnecessary burden. It is of greatest importance for the church and the people that the Old Testament should be interpreted, explained, and applied with frankness and enthusiasm, without bad conscience, without sectarian sentiment, without jealous side glances at the riches of general intellectual life. The brief discussion in this chapter has no other purpose but that of making us free. If you ask, free for what? the answer is, free in order, with the support thus gained, to tackle the work of interpreter and witness without losing too much time.

The Humanity of the Scriptures

In one's preparation for the task of preaching and instruction one can never get along without a sober look at the humanity of the Scriptures. Just as the church in the past had to take issue with Docetism and Ebionitism and its consequences in the field of Christology, so it must go through a similar development in the matter of the Scriptures— although here we cannot say, any more than it could be said at that time, that it is necessarily Docetism that must first be combated and overcome. The sequence is determined by historical and psychological factors. But however that may be, allegorizing as a method must be called Docetism.

Allegorizing was first born in the minds of men who were embarrassed by the Scriptures. And why were they embarrassed? Because they brought with them a philosophy or at least were preoccupied with philosophical principles; holding their conception of 'Spirit,' they did not know what to do with the anthropomorphisms in the Bible; with their conception of 'truth,' they could not come to terms with a concrete given of ultimate validity. History gave them trouble because they were obsessed with the idea of the eternal. Form could only be an emblem for them because they had a disparaging view of *hyle* ('matter'); and because of their concept of the Logos in the cosmos, the event-character of the Word, remained inaccessible to them. It is not only a philological adherence to the text, but even before this a theological view of the actual matter with which the Old Testament is concerned that makes the allegorical method impossible. Even before the allegorical method brings its Docetism to the text-form, it has already been thinking Docetically about the Name of God taking on form in this world.

In general our 'religious' thinking seems inclined to mix or to identify 'God' and 'man.' Our reason (*ratio*) and its emotionality (for *ratio* brings with it its own emotionality of will and purpose) seems, however, to be more inclined to make the entities 'god' and 'man' limit each other. In the light of the Name, justice can be done to the truth intended in both of these tendencies, but before this happens both the concept 'god' and the concept 'man' must come under the crisis, the judgment, of the Name. This crisis does not mean the dissolution or annulment of our concepts, but rather an emancipation of our minds. Even the form of the Scriptures reflects this. The rejection of allegorizing as a method is therefore an act of faith, an applied confession of the *assumptio carnis*. It would be a fruitless undertaking, and also one that was based on a misunderstanding of the Name, if we were to attempt to separate a divine 'factor' from a human 'factor' in the Scriptures. For, after all, the unfathomable mystery is that a completely human work is in the service of a completely divine work and that both works exist together unseparate and yet different.

Preaching on the Old Testament and instruction from the Old Testament presuppose that we keep in view the ancient Oriental background, the historical contours of the context, and also that the Oriental conception of soul and body, life and death, intercession and dependence, the power to sacrifice which rises up to God and is given by God, in short, the whole anthropology and psychology (if one can apply such weighty words to such unreflected expressions) is different from ours, that it looks in another direction and expresses a feeling about life that is different from ours. Here is where the expert knowledge of the scholars becomes useful; in every form of instruction (even of so-called 'simple people' and even of the 'fourth man') it is necessary to make use of this knowledge. And here we have an abundance of guidance and information in popular, intelligible form.[24]

[24] We mention the following: H. W. Obbink and A. M. Brouwer, *Inleiding tot den Bijbel* (1927); Martin Noth, *The History of Israel*, rev. edn. (1960); O. Weber, *Bibelkunde des Alten Testaments*, 2 vols.; J. de Groot and A. R. Hulst, *Macht en Wil*; W. Zimmerli, 'I Mose 1–11,' in *Prophezei*; Th. C. Vriezen, *Oud-Israelitische Geschriften* (1948); M. A. Beek, *Wegen en voetsporen van het Oude Testament* (1953; German tr., *Auf den Wegen und Spuren des Alten Testaments*, 1961); H. H. Rowley, *The Biblical Doctrine*

EXEGESIS

We may be troubled by the objection that in this way the text becomes more and more strange and more and more remote from us; and yet we must go through this trouble; and the experience that in precisely this way the significatory content (*Hinweisgehalt*), the divine sign, the witness of the Spirit comes out more fully and clearly is in accord with what we alluded to above as the combination of a completely human and a completely divine work. The interpreter and witness fears the same danger of strangeness and remoteness from life today when his studies reveal to him the spiritually conflicting tendencies that prevail in various writers or sources of the Old Testament. These varying tendencies are to be understood—if not entirely, then in large part—as owing to the historical situation, to a definite one-sidedness or deteriorization of popular religion, etc. One need only to read Ezra alongside of Ruth, Proverbs alongside of Job, First Isaiah alongside of Jeremiah and it becomes clear that from any abstract point of view their varying attitudes and tendencies remain irreconcilable. One who sees these things will perhaps regret these shifts in point of view mostly because they weaken the appeal of the Old Testament for the present day. Nevertheless these 'facts' must be faced and we must find a practical way to deal with them, as we seek the meaning of the polyvalent unity of the Name in history and place the polyinterpretability of the words at the service of this unity.[25]

Opposition to or coolness toward these ideas are a consequence of the habit (among the more philologically as well as the more theologically inclined scholars) of regarding the Revelation of God as being

---

of Election (1950); B. Duhm, *Israels Propheten* (1916; still important); P. Volz, *Prophetengestalten* (1938); W. Eichrodt, *Das Menschenverständnis des Alten Testaments* (1952); Norman H. Snaith, *The Distinctive Ideas of the Old Testament* (1944); Ph. Kohnstamm, *Staat dan in de vrijheid*, I (1947); F. J. Pop, *Bijbelse woorden en hun geheim* (1952).

[25] Th. C. Vriezen, *An Outline of Old Testament Theology*, pp. 76f.; 'Indeed, the truth of faith can only be expressed fully in antinomies. Divine reality is so full of life that not only a rational but even a paradoxical judgment cannot exhaust it. A religious truth, even a truth revealed by the Spirit is per se a one-sided truth, and therefore a misrepresentation of the truth if it is represented rationally. When considered only by itself it is, therefore, an untruth. For instance, the truth of Israel's election is an untruth if it is rationally understood to mean that *for that reason* God has rejected the nations of the world. . . . When Israel thinks it possesses in its sacrificial cult the divine means of grace, the prophets must reject this means of grace and remind the people that God's mercy applies only to those who obey God. From the cult the people is thrown back on the mercy of the living God.'

scattered here and there in more or less pure form, and thus again as a series of thoughts and events. They are also a consequence of lack of familiarity with the insight that in the strict sense nowhere in the Old or New Testament is Revelation 'given,' since Revelation is the same thing as the Name of God, the presence of God, the time of God, which simultaneously embraces human time, the one superhistorical history, the year of jubilee, the fullness of time. The fatal idea that the New Testament as such is revelation, but that the Old Testament must be regarded as preparation for it, helps keep alive a number of problems which would long since have been buried or at least would look quite different if it were not for this foreshortened perspective.

But the humanness of the Scriptures goes even further. The character of the patriarchs and judges is a part of it. The coarseness of certain rites (which are not expressly disapproved by God or men), the institutions and customs which not only bear the stamp of Near Eastern forms of culture but also hint at an inner attitude toward life which can become easy prey for the probing psychoanalist; and further, the ideas which Israel took over from an alien tradition or brought with it from a tradition it had in common with other peoples and which, however transformed, still retain the stamp of a definitely mythological or folkloristic origin—all these things are further corroborations of the complete humanness of the Scriptures. And in this connection it is especially noticeable that literally nowhere in the Old Testament is any attempt made, by means of abstractions or new 'universal' ideas or the creation of new myths, to reach a stage at which (as, for example in the Upanishads or the Bhagavad Gita) this complete humanness is given supertemporal form.

Here the humanness remains an earthly, definite, concrete, confined humanity, one that is born of a race and nation and circumscribed by tradition and cultic custom. Nowhere else, at least for our Western minds, is this more insistently apparent than in the Old Testament. And if we take this as a witness to the Word of God and present it as such to the congregation, then, not only as *goyim* ('gentiles'), children of the Western world, or modern intellectual men, we shall inevitably encounter a mass of difficulties, but also, as sensitive, artistic, ethical, religious, or even consciously Christian men, we shall run into a whole swarm of things that are offensive. We cannot get around them and we dare not jump over them. And on the whole, even an attempt to evade them is a reliable sign that, despite a better theoretical insight, we nevertheless regard the anthropomorphism of the testimony of the Name as well as the anthropomorphism of the Name itself as something to be ashamed of, or at least that we have not considered whether this secondary, disturbing humanness of the testimony may not perhaps be a reflection of the primary, saving humanness of the theophany and its testimony. For the Word not only became man—it became flesh, and the witness not only occurs in humanly pure forms but also bears the marks of all kinds of impurity, a fact that, instead of detracting from the perspicuity of Holy Scriptures as far as salvation is concerned, can actually lend it a new and rich corroboration.

THE WORD AND THE HUMANITY OF THE SCRIPTURES

This humanity of the Scriptures in all its breadth is the instrument of the Word, the temple in which it is present, in which it dwells and appears. That this particular humanity should be fit for such a purpose can only be understood as an act of election. The humanity of the Scriptures is also the reason for the fact that, though the one Word is the same in the Old Testament as in the New, it is nevertheless very decidedly different. This differentness gives to the Word a special breadth in its applicability to all times. It is not to be understood as meaning that this 'differentness' may be only one of the possible aspects of the truth, but rather that it is always this potentially, particularly as a corrective of Western dogmatic thinking. Here too certain preliminary lines of demarcation must be laid down in the thinking of the interpreter and witness which will teach him how to distinguish the ways in which the light of the Name differentiates and intensifies itself. Anticipating the third section of this part of our book, we here present the following for consideration now.

1. The Old Testament teaches us more emphatically and fully than does the New that we do not know the Creation except through the Word—in so far as the Creation appears in the Old Testament only as the foundation and beginning of the history of God's covenant and intercourse with men.[26] Therefore the Creation account is a story which

[26] Cf. Gerhard von Rad, *Old Testament Theology*, Vol. I, tr. D. M. G. Stalker (New York: Harper & Row, 1962), pp. 136ff.

is connected with the historical accounts which follow it. The late dating of the Creation story is not a question of mere chronology; it rather helps us to discern this spiritual structure. The terms of Genesis I are a part of a coherent whole in the priestly theology; they presuppose Israel and the temple, the Law and the knowledge of God, the Sabbath and the expectation of salvation.

The consequence which is to be drawn from this in connection with atheism is surprising. The negations of atheism assume that Creation can be known from nature. Its most passionate bitterness is levelled against the cold or hot or indifferent state of things in which no 'God of love' is to be found. For the Old Testament, witness to Creation is a secondary affirmation concerning the Name of God; in itself it is not a foundation, not a starting point, nor is it anywhere ever a problem. For he who took Israel by the hand in history and established the covenant also made room for history. The fact is that it is impossible to know YHWH from 'nature'! This is not the way it happened then in his revelation, and it never does happen in this way. When Creation is called 'good,' this is an affirmation of faith concerning the meaning of history, which in its essence and purpose is saving history.

2. The Old Testament teaches us that the *Law* is encountered nowhere else except in the purposeful Word which accompanies history.[27] So far it is from being possible for us to discern a Law in the 'Orders of creation' that the attempt to do so in spite of this has continued to lead to new forms of paganism; the attempt can produce as many 'Christian' interpretations as there are groups, positions, persuasions, and interests. The Word uses human limitations in order to limit all human ethos. The stress which is laid upon the Law as a saving guide is nowhere retracted.[28] The Word has allied itself with the Law in this its form and function *be 'olam* ('forever') that is, for the other times which are to come. The consequence of this for atheism is that it is futile to think of 'God' as the ground and guarantor of a 'moral world-order.' In the Old Testament there is no universal morality; the varieties of human morality come from the difference in their 'religion.' What the will of YHWH is must be heard, perceived with the 'per-

[27] Cf. Martin Noth, 'Die Gesetze im Pentateuch,' *Gesammelte Studien zum Alten Testament* (1957), pp. 9ff.
[28] Cf. W. Eichrodt, *Theology of the Old Testament*, Vol. I, tr. J. A. Baker (1961), pp. 242ff.

ceiving understanding.' What the commandments aim at is the concrete task and obligation, and this has its source in the intervening grace of God, who releases his people from all bondage to general principles with which they usually torment themselves. The Commandment is an instruction in how one is led to freedom and how one can oneself stand in freedom. The meaning of the Commandment can be summed up as follows: Abide with him who frees you, realize your own election, do not shun his care, be willing to overcome your natural striving to become a good man and live a good life. ' "There is" no command of God. . . . What "there is" is not as such the command of God. . . . But the core of the matter is that God gives his command . . .'[29]—this is a rule which we accept and hold on the strength of what we have learned of the testimony of the Old Testament.

3. The Old Testament testifies that grace is not received as a spiritual power, but rather that it is an enunciation of the Word, a merciful decision, a pardon, a bestowal of grace. The connection between gracious election and sanctification in the Old Testament, one of the high moments in the history of the People and also in the history of the Davidic dynasty, is made by the Word into 'an everlasting sign which shall not be cut off' (Isa. 55 : 13). The opposition of the religious man in flight from this grace often expresses itself in the following logical speculation: Either there is such a thing as election (this may be offensive, but one sees such marked, unexplainable differences in the lot and talents of people) and then it makes no difference how one lives; or some kind of ordering and hallowing of life is one of the requirements of human dignity, but the idea of election cuts at the very root of human dignity. That election and sanctification are two sides of the same thing, that pardon becomes effective in free guidance and free guidance leads to freedom, to the act of obedience—this is characteristic of the Old Testament because it discloses one of the mysteries of the Name. The Name reveals religion and its morality to be an attempt at self-liberation, but once and for all it prevents the life of the elect from breaking down, and henceforth there can be no despair concerning the goal of their life.

4. The Old Testament recognizes man's essential difference from the other creatures as being founded solely upon the Word that came and

[29] Karl Barth, *Church Dogmatics*, Vol. II, pt. 2, p. 548.

shall come to him. The fact that the human mind, the existence of man as a 'personality,' does not in itself involve any close relationship with God is an insight which we can easily lose sight of in our reading of the New Testament writings. The witness of the Old Testament elevates and hallows this ancient confession and makes it a critical testimony of enduring validity.

Biologically and cosmologically, we are not compelled to think of man as a unity; whether this is right or wrong, manhood as such does not begin when reason awakens, but rather when the heart (together with understanding, will, feeling, and imagination) is kindled by hearing the address of God[30], by 'knowing' God. (*Da'ath elohim*, 'knowledge of God,' and *chesed*, 'favour which creates fellowship,' are the two sides of one and the same event of becoming a man; Hos. 4 : 1, 6 : 6.) Wellhausen once put it quite bluntly: 'Even the born Jew must make himself a Jew,' meaning by this that no biological fact can be a guarantee. One could say it even more explicitly: even the born man must still be made a man by being called. Then he comes to that *aheb* ('love') that 'cleaving to YHWH,' to that bridal time (Hosea and Jeremiah), that 'love' (through which the Deuteronomist gave an inner unity to the multiplicity of laws), which makes it possible in the postexilic Psalms (Pss. 4, 16, 40, 90, 119) to celebrate the inward festival of rejoicing in the Law. To be a man means to be known, to be loved; what the material which we think we know from nature of from the 'Creation' looks like is according to the Old Testament testimony an altogether secondary question. And only as we begin here, namely, with this concept of how one becomes a man, do we understand the utterly amazing fact that this man, just this man, can have a quarrel, a lawsuit with God, without falling out of the Covenant.[31]

5. The cult can only be understood according to the hidden order expressed in the words: 'We give it to thee [as] from thy hand' (I Chron. 29 : 14; cf. Lev. 17 : 11; Deut. 21 : 8). The prophecy does not set up any demands which are sufficient in themselves and at most sanctioned by the Lord. The Word itself insists upon making the so-called 'moral demands' into personal contacts, into elements of the

[30] W. Eichrodt, *Das Menschenverständnis des Alten Testaments*, II (1947); *Oud-Testamentische Studien*, II (Leiden, 1943), pp. 87ff.

[31] M. A. Beek, *Het twistgesprek van de mens met zijn God* (1946); B. J. Oosterhoff, *De vreze des Heren in het Oude Testament* (1949); Wilhelm Vischer, 'Hiob, ein Zeuge Jesu Christi,' *Zwischen den Zeiten* (1933), pp. 386ff.

covenant fellowship. It is the Word that preserves the order, and this applies in the cultic as well as the ethical service of God. Always it is a matter of an ability which comes from the Word, and this ability, which is a minus quantity in all religion, is a plus quantity which the Name adds to all human, cultic action, for then it has 'received power' to give with a free will, as is said in the passages cited above.[32]

6. Every culture sees a correspondence between the order of the cosmos and that of human society; indeed, every culture has its own image of nature and in consequence a corresponding feeling about life. The Word does not cast off the primitive Semitic culture in which it occurred; the Word cannot be heard except through the medium of cultural elements which are not our own. All cultures are relative, but God chose the least brilliant, the least cohesive, the poor and despised culture, in order to transmit to us something which, for example, cannot be conveyed through our Western conceptions; even the Ptolemaic cosmology (which, of course, is not 'correct') serves to say something which cannot be said with the Copernican cosmology. When one respects this functional unity of the testimony and these human conceptions, one may, of course, try to translate; but if one really wants to translate this, it is impossible to 'substitute' the new cosmology for the old.

We could add many other examples; but these are sufficient, if some light has been cast upon the factual relationship between the Word and poor human words—light in which the way that atheism's negation of religion is on the one hand substantiated and on the other hand shown to be missing the point in the given facts of the Old Testament.

Anybody who wants to speak on the Old Testament must, if he is to be obedient to its lineaments, constantly keep these things in mind. For here he meets Creation expressed in the humanness of the saga, the law made concrete in the humanness of ritual regulations, the proclamation of grace in the spiritual destinies of human figures whose stories are told (those who are chosen and rejected and chosen again). Here we find man, a peculiar, different, grateful being, placed in the

[32] 'While the Old Testament is very full of allusions to the divine activity . . . and full too of the most intensive address and of "revelation," there is a realm of silence and secrecy in respect to what God works in sacrifice' (Gerhad von Rad, *Old Testament Theology*, Vol. I, p. 260). 'Only in virtue of the declaratory word of the priest did the sacral event become a *gracious act of God*' (ibid., p. 262).

same order with all other creatures who of themselves have no God-relationship. Here we find the strange sign of the cult set up and maintained in the centre of life as a gift of the 'presence' of the Name. Here we find the relativity of cultural conditions being put at the service of an absolutely authoritative speech, the speech of YHWH, our God and Judge and Preserver. If this were not so, we could find no meaning in the Old Testament, we could not preach its message, we could not draw any instruction from the Scriptures. We cannot set aside the humanness of the *Tenak* (which is primarily and fundamentally the Pentateuch) in order to retain the kernel. Form and content, however severely we must distinguish between them up to the point of sundering them, are not to be separated from each other. What we need to do is to understand how the content takes on and uses the form, respects it and alters it, preserves and fills it.

The much abused statement of Luther that we must seek in the Old Testament that 'which promotes Christ' ('*was Christum treibt*') cannot, even if it were so intended, be used in such a way that we can set up a criterion according to our conception of what is 'Christian' and use it to distinguish between what is vital and what is sterile, what is enduring and what is outworn.[33] In this way the secret of the Old Testament is subjectified, and we are left only with what we knew before.

Above all, in giving instruction it is of great importance that we should feel imprisoned (and thus liberated) by the formative power of the Word, that power which is busy here and today, animating, possessing, and sanctifying to its service this human figment. Here too the creature, in this case the word of man, is subject to the Creator of all community; it is lifted out of its own sphere and given a superreligious value which no man can bestow upon it and which it does not 'have' of itself.[34]

Therefore in our preparation for our work, our experience cannot be any different from that which Origen described in his commentary

---

[33] Johann Georg Hamann, *Erster hellenistischer Brief*, Roth edn., II, 207; 'If therefore the divine style chooses the foolish, the shallow, the ignoble, to put to shame the strength and ingenuity of all profane writers, there certainly is need of the illuminated, enthused and eager eyes of a friend, an intimate, a lover, in order to discern through such a disguise the beams of heavenly glory.' [Tr. from Ronald Gregor Smith, *J. G. Hammann: A Study in Christian Experience* (New York: Harper Row, 1960), p. 186.—Tr.]

[34] Jan Baptist Huysman, *Het geheim van het oude boek* (1941), p. 14.

on Matthew: 'Time and again we perceive about ourselves that, before we find the true insight into a particular truth of Scripture, we experience a certain impoverishment of insight—until this impoverishment is done away and those who merit it are given their food in due season.[35]

PROMISE AND FULFILMENT

'Rummage about and choose; everything is in it'—this comment made about the Talmud can also be applied to the Old Testament, with this difference, that in the first case the word 'everything' points to an encyclopedia (though a completely unsystematic one) and in the second case to religion. In a certain sense, the whole of ancient Asian religion, as it is expressed in cult and myth, flowed into the Old Testament; and at the present time the signs are increasing that it profoundly influenced Israel's knowledge.[36]

When we say that 'everything' is in the Old Testament, then as Christians we also mean that the New Testament is in it. It may be that we have to make a number of exceptions as far as details are concerned, in so far as there are in the New Testament possible influences of the mystery religions and certainly of apocalyptic which affect even the fundamental words which are the vehicles of the message. But where it is a matter of God and his Name, where the related evaluations of history, the Law, man, the priest, the prophet, the king are compared, where atonement, forgiveness, faith, sanctification, temptation, and the future are mentioned, we must say that everything essential has been said in the *Tenak*.

Hence it certainly cannot be the purpose of well-advised Christian instruction to interpret backwards and read the message of Christ into the Old Testament. The process is rather the reverse; we need constantly to be learning from the Old Testament what is the content, the meaning, and the intent of that which we call 'Christ.' To know who he is, is the ground of the church. What he is—which Messianic

[35] For once we let the term 'truth' and the heretical phrase 'those who merit it' pass.
[36] Cf. Martin Noth, 'Geschichte und Gotteswort im Alten Testament,' *Gesammelte Studien zum Alten Testament*, pp. 239f. (on the messengers of God in the Mari texts).

revelation and determination, which qualities of value and effect, which course, and which future can and must be connected with the Christophany—these things we must constantly learn from the Torah and the Prophets.

Here the Old Testament must speak for itself. I do not think that there is anybody, either on the right or the left, who would deny that there is a connection between the Testaments, even a certain unity of content. On the contrary, in my opinion, this was found all too readily by many liberal theologians of the last century and asserted with too much confidence. The reason for this was that in general they were inclined to reduce the meaning of texts to an idea, a truth, a doctrine. And in this, in exactly the same way as High Orthodoxy, they were faithful pupils of Western (i.e., rational, moral, classical) humanism. But the strange thing is that, with us, real encounter with the living phenomenon of elemental humanity must always come by way of the aesthetic, of the imaginative faculty. Without Hamann and Herder, Boeckh and Dilthey, von Hügel and Rudolf Otto—men whose work pointed the way long before phenomenology as a scientific method prevailed—we would still be measuring the consonance and divergence of literary documents according to the ideas, truths, and doctrines expressed in them. But now this is out of the question.[37]

It does not lie within the purpose of this book to sum up the phenomenological and systematic conclusions drawn from the apparent similarities in structure between the Old and the New Testament. Still less does it lie within its scope—though this would be more tempting—to pursue the traces of this similarity in philosophy, particularly contemporary philosophy—for example, the whole complex of ideas about subjectivity, 'I and Thou,' existence, freedom and guilt, man's being bound to time, 'decision,' mankind, world peace, work, sacrifice, are in their delineation and intention basically biblical.

[37] Joachim Wach, *Das Verstehen*; Eduard Spranger, *Lebensformen*; W. B. Kristensen, *Het leven uit de dood*; G. van der Leeuw, *Religion in Essence and Manifestation*, tr. J. E. Turner (especially the Epilegomena); K. A. H. Hidding, *Geestesstructur en cultuur*, e.g., pp. 46f.; Erich Auerbach, *Mimesis*, tr. W. R. Trask (1953). When Gerhard von Rad, *Werden und Wesen des Alten Testaments* (1936), p. 141, says that we are struck by 'the ease with which statements of faith (*Glaubensinhalte*), which to our way of thinking are very dissimilar in character, are placed side by side,' his intention seems to us to be clear and correct, but even the words themselves are too Western. What are 'statements' and what is 'side by side'? And does not 'ease' describe an impression that we have, we who find or would find it hard to discover a synthesis here?

To go into this at length would take us away from our theme, which is the meaning of the Old Testament for the 'religionless' man in the midst of the silence of the Gods.

1. The unutterable Name can be known only in an event of a peculiar quality. Hence there is a relationship between the revealed-hidden character of the Name and the narrative character of the Old Testament. But even the Torah itself is a part of the event, an accompanying and regulative standard for what is narrated; the Prophets also relates itself to the story (or history), though this is not thought of as a continuum, but history seen in a context of 'signs.' Even the Kethubim always stick close to the side of the road travelled by the Name. The Psalms contain no independent poetry, and in Ecclesiastes there is no independent philosophy or doctrine of life. Everything is dependent on the presence and the real creative action of YHWH. Therefore one can if need be, and not wholly without irony, speak of a 'narrative philosophy,' as does Rosenzweig.

2. This combination of Name and event produces a unique anthropomorphism, which is the result of 'event,' of 'encounter.' YHWH alone is God, a definite event (not everything that happens) occurs as pre-eminently his act; thus this anthropomorphism is the actual seal of the truth, the faithfulness, the Covenant, which 'happen' in the event. And only in this perspective are we really confronted with the question whether we are willing and prepared to affirm that God is with us without at the same time cherishing the strange notion that when we do this, we are really departing from the high, universal truth of the 'Godhead.' Here, in the contingency of life, the somatic, the human, we are not dealing with something inferior to speculation about God, but rather with something that surpasses it, namely, the earthly Presence among us and with us, the Figure in whom this relationship becomes a reality.

3. This threefold uniqueness, Name, Event, Figure, cannot be derived from reality as we would derive a truth; what the encounter is, where and how it takes place, must be spoken, shown, called to remembrance. No figure reveals its own peculiar content except through the revealing word. What do we have in the Old Testament? As literature it contains *toledoth* ('genealogies'), *mishpatim* ('laws'), *meshalim* ('proverbs'), *tehillim* ('praises'), ancient genres, parallels of which can be found everywhere; or to put it in commoner terms, epic and

poetic parts, chronicles and short stories, cult legends, sagas of origin, aetiological fantasies—indeed, what has not the 'poetizing memory' (Buber) brought forth! What holds it all together? The Word in its role of serving, in its function of exhibiting the coincidence of Name and event.

4. The Name is exclusive, and only so is it universal. 'You shall have no other gods before me' (first commandment of the Decalogue); love is the love of *El qana'* ('the jealous God'; see, among others, the second commandment). Therefore there is no such thing as Nature *per se*, no prince or potentate, no human creation, no value which would be sufficient in itself. There is also no image of YHWH himself, as if he were like any other existing reality. Nor does he have any real house (see, e.g., II Sam. 7 : 4ff.). Dreadful as it is for the Ugaritic gods not to have a house, this is simply natural and self-evident for this (for this once we let the word pass!) 'wilderness God.' There is no room for him. And for his people too, despite the fact that there is a Covenant giving them the land, there is no place where they can lay their head. Zion is a temporal entity and Canaan too is temporal. And yet as a sign of the Name, Zion is 'eternal'; and as a sign of the Covenant, the land is bound up, from primeval time to the end of time, with this event, this 'holy' history ('Holy' because it is completely different, and its ultimate meaning is sealed until the end-time comes). Therefore YHWH loves the *ger*, the sojourner; therefore the little treatise on statecraft in Psalm 72 declares that his representative in the realm of the state brings justice to the poor and oppressed. Therefore from Him there goes out the sound of promise, of new life, of a future, for everybody and everything that exists.

5. This 'nomadic' God is himself the God who is repeatedly reviled, often despised, constantly misunderstood. He is derided, abused, exploited. He is a forsaken God; his Word appears to be no match for paganism; the ark, the place of his 'presence,' is 'captured' by the Philistines. His priests deceive and are deceived, defencelessly his holy Name is uttered by the false prophets, defenceless are his own prophets, the messengers, in whose hearts the message was as a burning fire. He is a rover, mighty and unpredictable; he is like a consuming fire. He is described as a man of war and a bowman, a lion who roars from the forest, a bear lying in wait, a moth in men's clothing (Exod. 15 : 13; Amos 1 : 2; Hos. 11 : 10; Lam. 3 : 10; Hos. 5 : 12). Or it is said

of him that he is a rock (Pss. 18 : 2; 62 : 2; 89 : 26) or like a house
(Deut. 33 : 27), a fortress (Ps. 91: 2). But, lo, he is also like a farmer
who learns that his own cattle do not know how to find their way to the
master's crib (Isa. 1 : 3), like a husband who is betrayed by his wife
and despite everything remains with her, but all in vain (Hos. 3 : 1).
He must look on while Israel, which acts as if it were the defender of
God and his sanctuary, does not 'know' him and has nothing more
to do with him, no longer takes his aims and purposes into account
(Hos. 4 : 1; 5 : 4; 13 : 6). This Mighty One is not only a nomad, he
is an outcast. Therefore he is surrounded by a rising storm of
reckoning upon all men and all things. His anger has been long
restrained.

6. And yet this neglected, rejected God remains the Lord; the power,
the 'omnipotence' of this Lord lies mostly hidden in his patience, his
suffering. But this lowliness of a nomad, of one who has been cast out
of his rightful place, does not detract from his omnipotence, because
for him power is always the power to judge, that is, to decide, to set
things right in his way, according to the way of his nature, which no
religion ever dreamed of. His lordship, the power which is peculiarly
his, is the breath that hovers about the 'revelations,' the Spirit who
establishes the many mediating figures, the many holy laws, the
various forms of *berith* ('covenant') and then proceeds to go beyond
them; the will which bears the End within itself in the form of expectation, the end of all revelation, of all figures, of all law, all covenants. Israel's history 'signifies the proclamation of world judgment
in fulfilled time.'[38] This is the way in which YHWH is the Mighty
One.

7. And what about the partner, Israel? The elected man suffers in
two ways because of his election: through the reaction of the heathen
and their gods—in so far it is a suffering for God; but he also suffers
through his own self-estrangement and the denial of his own vocation
and election—in so far it is suffering from God, at the hand of God. As
an anointed one he is the servant of God, and as an anointed one he is
also the betrayer and reviler of the Name.

These are a few elements—perhaps already too sharply isolated and
generalized—in this 'narrative philosophy.'

Wherein does the plus of the *New* Testament lie, what does it have

---

[38] Karl Barth, *Church Dogmatics*, Vol. I, pt. 2, p. 86.

that goes beyond the Old Testament? I hardly know how to state this; but what is new in the new *covenant* lies in the fact that the Word became flesh. The time of God has come. The promise is fulfilled. The shadows have fled.

Whether that is true, nobody can prove; but since it went out into the word as truth, the Old Testament was brought to the *goyim*, the Gentiles, in order that, speaking for itself, it might bear witness to the fulfilled time. But why did not the great majority of Israel recognize this? Because in the Old Testament it is not apparent to unenlightened eyes.

The Schism

Why does the Old Testament have another sequel besides the New Testament, namely, the Talmud? Because the old covenant can be interpreted as being realized in the flesh of the people of God, which is biologically and spiritually different and separate from the blood of the rest of mankind—this flesh of the people of God which through circumcision acquires a special quality and, in contrast with all other peoples, has within itself a psychophysical ability constantly to repent and renew itself.[39] This is the fundamental reason why we are so 'definitively' confronted with this schism, this unfathomably unnatural schism within the community of God. Other reasons, which are very important but secondary, are that during the exile the Scriptures were more and more interpreted as Law; that this whole view forced the history, the events, but also the cult, the sacrifice, into a yoke of legalistic thinking, so that they seemed to be serviceable at most as illustrations of God's will; that such 'absolutizing' of the Law was the result of the want of nearness to the Name and a lack of prophetic appeals. All this is quite true. And yet it would appear to us that, after all, this is

[39] H. J. Schoeps, *Judischer Glaube in dieser Zeit*, p. 76: 'Through the accomplished consecration of the *blood*, the people of Israel—down to the last generation—is given the *supernatural* ability to decide freely without any mediator ... in favour of direct allegiance to God.' Cf. O. H. Schmitz on the attitude in Pharisaism: 'True, it is the bearer of Messianic hope, but at the same time it is *the watchman who sees to it that no Messiah should arise.*' Quoted in *Der Jude*, (Sonderheft 1925), p. 31. Cf. this expression of Titanic self-consciousness: 'In ourselves we struck root; therefore we are rootless on earth, everlasting wanderers, and yet deeply *rooted in ourselves*, in our own body and blood. And this rootage in ourselves and in ourselves alone assures us our *eternity*' (Franz Rosenzweig, *Der Stern der Erlösung*, III, p. 57).

owing at bottom to the way in which the Jews understood themselves
(*Selbstverständnis*), as we attempted to describe this in an earlier
book.[40]

The rejection of Christ comes out of this self-understanding; expressions of it accompany the course of the Gospel from the beginning.
The schism constitutes a tremendous gulf. But added to this is the
attitude of the church. The church declares itself to be the successor of
Israel in God's plan of salvation; it installs itself in all the rights of the
ancient covenant people, as if that people were dead and buried and
the inheritance were ours—Except that at that time these rights meant
the burden of bearing the enigmas of God's providence, and election
brought with it its own peculiar afflictions. This has largely changed.
. . . But, hopefully, even these unguarded, naïve words may make us
realize why it is that Israel and Christianity depart from each other
and yet accompany each other; both have largely become religions;
the one poor, the other rich,[41] the one defiantly lifting its head, the
other striding on like a lucky prince who has inherited what he never
dreamed of getting.

The desire to compensate for this may well be one of the ways by
which Christianity dissociates itself from the nomadic life of the poor in
spirit in order to reconstitute itself as—a religion. But this is to dispose too quickly of the meaning of the promises and the content of the
fulfilment; then the prerogatives of Israel simply pass over to the
church; then the church simply proceeds down the centuries to
Christianize the world; then Ahasuerus, the wandering Jew, the
'eternal Jew,' becomes a projection of the offence we take at Israel's
stubbornness and hardness of heart. But the fact is that the Old Testament is not 'Jewish,' and the Apostle holds open the prospect of Israel's
return to its heritage (Rom. 9–11).

Though a number of other things might be said with regard to the
question of guilt in the matter of the schism, we shall refrain from this
in order to dwell for a few moments upon the most recent, and in our
opinion too simple, judgment concerning the schism or (what actually
amounts to the same thing) the value which we must attribute to the

[40] *Het Wezen der joodsche religie* (1932), pp. 368f., 466f, 531f.
[41] Cf. Martin Buber, *Die Stunde und die Erkenntnis* (1936), discussion of religion with
K. L. Schmidt—at the close of the parable of the cathedral and the church-
yard.

Old Testament. I refer to Rudolf Bultmann's thoughtful idea of 'miscarriage' (*Scheitern*) as being the perspective and focus of the Old Testament witness.[42]

Bultmann declares that the popular view of prophecy and fulfilment has been made impossible by the philological method of interpretation. Nevertheless, the view which was developed by Joh. Chr. K. Hofmann in his great work *Prophecy and Fulfilment* (1841–44) contains an element of truth. Hofmann says that it is not the words of the Old Testament but rather the history of Israel itself which is to be understood as prophecy. Bultmann makes the concept of the Covenant central. 'God's Covenant with a people whose individuals suffice for the moral demands of God as members of the people, is an eschatological concept, because such a people is *not a real*, empirical and historical, but an eschatological dimension.'[43] It was an error to regard a real, empirical people as the partner in God's Covenant and to believe that such an obedience would prove to be possible within this world. A real, empirical, historical people must necessarily fail to meet this expectation. And to show this is the ultimate meaning and purpose of the Old Testament. All the prophets, Jeremiah and Ezekiel especially, were caught in this delusion of a possible realization of God's command within this world. Only the New Testament drew the right conclusion, namely, that the new covenant is no longer to be understood as a 'structure of history within this world.' Nor is the community a real, empirical people. It is true that in his concept of the 'kingdom of God' Bultmann appears to admit that in this new aeon (which was inaugurated by Christ) the community must be thought of as an entity 'at one and the same time within and beyond the world.' But this again becomes vague when Bultmann says that the people of God in the New Testament does not have the character of an empirical historical entity; it requires no institutional ordinances; it is not interested in the state; and from this there arises the peculiar dual existence of the believer and the man, of the Christian and the citizen, which, however, has fortunately 'not become a subject for reflection as yet in the New Testament.'

The question is, then, in what sense has the history of Israel itself

[42] Rudolf Bultmann, 'Prophecy and Fulfilment,' in *Essays Philosophical and Theological*, tr. James C. G. Greig (New York: Macmillan, 1955), pp. 205ff. See *Glaube und Verstehen*, II, (1952), pp. 162ff.
[43] Ibid., p. 193.

become 'prophecy'? How can one say that it has become 'fulfilment'? Bultmann's answer is: 'It is fulfilled in its inner contradiction, its miscarriage.'[44] It looks as if the first question, what makes Israel's history prophecy, is passed over. But the astounding disclosure follows immediately: 'The miscarriage demonstrates the impossibility [of an empirical people of God] and *therefore* the *miscarriage* is the *promise*.'[45] But this miscarriage, this failure, this frustration, is to be understood as a promise only a posteriori, 'on the basis of its fulfilment, that is, on the basis of the encounter with God's grace, which makes itself available to those who understand their situation as one of impossibility.'[46]

The consequences of this conception are enormous and disastrous. For this means that not only is the meaning of the Old Testament history found solely in profound meaninglessness, but also that no meaningful history can be ascribed to the New Testament community; the new beginning, inaugurated by Christ, is in no sense the beginning of a real historical development; except that man has learned that the conflict of Israel is the universally human conflict in which it is not two views but rather God and man that collide. For man is called by God, but yet it is his doom to be 'imprisoned in secular history.'[47] What are we to do with this? Bultmann's answer is that Christian faith constantly needs to look back to Israel's 'miscarriage' and thus (!) to the 'promise,' 'in order to know that the situation of the justified man arises only on the basis of this miscarriage.'[48]

The inevitable result of this is a failure to appreciate the Law, a withdrawal from history, a depreciation of the world, a negation of creation, a deafness to the typical Old Testament affirmation of god-given life. And 'desecularization' (*Entweltlichung*) becomes the key word, the deepest mystery, the fulfilment of human existence.

Many other questions could be raised here, since this construction presupposes an anthropology which, whether it is right or wrong, can be found just as well elsewhere than in the Old Testament, and which, applied methodologically, simply leads back to a bad kind of Pietism. But enough—enough to understand that when we are unable or unwilling to face up to the great schism between Israel and the church

---

[44] Ibid., p. 205.   [45] Ibid., p. 206. [Translation mine.—Tr.]   [46] Loc. cit.
[47] Ibid., p. 207.   [48] Ibid., p. 208.

and then proceed to look for a radical solution, we suddenly find ourselves on the point of twisting or denying the structures of the Old
Testament all along the line. No, it is far better—and for our purpose
simply mandatory—to let the schism stand as it is without explanation.
Meanwhile, at the beginning of this second part, 'Witness and Interpretation,' under the heading 'Inner Tensions,' we have already arrived
at the conclusion that the various schemata are not sufficient. They are
necessary and useful as attempts to set forth the unity within the
differences and the difference in unity between the two 'Testaments.'
But even the best schema, namely, that of promise and fulfilment,
can only apply to the words, to word relationships, and to associations
of 'ideas.' It fails, however, when it proceeds to subject the 'Name' of
God to an inner distinction and to subject the revelation itself, by
historicizing it and subjecting it to our value judgment, to a hierarchical order of 'more' and 'less,' 'higher' and 'lower,' 'limited' and
'universal.' On the level of words the distinction between promise and
fulfilment can be used; but if we allow it to apply to the subject to
which the words refer, then through this distinction the mystery would
be lost, namely, the mystery that the Name of God is eternal truth,
divine presence, love, and loving act, coming down from outside of
human time into time.[49] To do this would be to hypostatize and elevate
human time (whether it be regarded as cyclic or linear) to the status
of time itself, and the good 'naïveté' of the Old Testament, which seeks
and finds the Name in the 'event,' would become an affected naïveté,
which is unaware of how this causes the revelation to lose its origin in
God, its superior meaning. Even if one ascribes to God the ability to
'conceive' and 'measure' endless Time, or even if one asserts that
'eternity' is the Lordship over immeasurable periods of time, this is
still not to have shown that this unendingness (*Unendlichkeit*)—which
is to be distinguished from the endlessness (*Endlosigkeit*) of a linear time
line—that this unendingness, which is inherent in the Name even in its
finite form, is qualitatively different from human time.[50] The 'Name'
includes not only Lordship over the times and seasons (*kairoi*), but
also the ground of all time and the root of the redemptive history. It is

---

[49] Therein lies the chief objection to the otherwise important and in many respects
illuminating conception of Oscar Cullmann, *Christ and Time: The Primitive Christian
Conception of Time and History*, tr. Floyd Filson (Philadelphia: Westminster Press, 1950).
[50] Cullmann, pp. 69f.

not only philosophically absurd but also theologically naïve to describe the eternity of God as 'the linking of an unlimited series of limited world periods' or to assert that 'eternity is the endless succession of the ages (*aiones*).'[51]

The essence of the mystery of the Name is to be sought precisely in the fact that that which is divinely free and sublime joins itself to and enters into that which is human and near, that the unending a priori enters into the ongoing course of the centuries, that the eternally valid content of salvation enters into human beings, wonders, and signs. It is still legitimate and salutary to ward off a fresh intrusion of Idealism and its dialectic of 'the infinite' and 'the finite.' If only we remember that here the unending is His unendingness, that the apriority and sublimity are His, and further that eternity does not mean the negation or abrogation of time—then we can without danger set both the time of promise and the time of fulfilment into relation with 'God's time,' that is, into relation with the presence of His eternal salvation in time, in our time, in the manifestation of the Messiah.

Surplus and Deficit

Thus we arrive at a slightly altered view of the abiding significance of the Old Testament.

1. We regard the Scriptures, and thus its fundamental first part, as the testimony concerning the voice of God, as the reverberation and reproduction of the Word. We cannot speak of the 'Word' if we think of the primal data (*Urgegebenheiten*) of the world as factors in the 'totality' (or the experience of totality). Nor can we speak of the 'Word' if we interpret the primal data of the world as necessary stages in the self-unfolding of the Idea. One can say that 'Word' is also an image; actually, however, it is an irreplaceable image for that which lays hold upon us, comes to us, out of the combination of 'Name' and 'history.' From this point of view the Old and the New Testament are subsumed under the same category, seen in one and the same category of reality. From this point of view and measured by this standard, we may and we must regard the silence of the gods as the stigma of human religion.

2. We find in the Old Testament a deficit. The multiplicity of things

[51] Ibid., pp. 46, 62. Cf. the article by R. Bijlsma in *Chronos en Kairos*.

in it are organized more for the spiritual ear than for the eye that looks for coherence and continuity. There are many prophets, many ceremonies, many symbols; their allusive power is restrained, their light is obscured. The various forms of *berith* do not clearly exhibit their unity and the basis of their unity. Tensions between cult and ethos, between nationalism and universalism, exist not only in the popular religion but also in the Scriptures as testimony. And as far as the doctrine of God is concerned, his holiness, it is true, is an aspect of his nearness to men, but this nearness seems often to withdraw itself arbitrarily.

The love of God is abundantly proclaimed, though seldom with this particular word; but in many respects it is overshadowed by God's sovereign power. And no prophet could call himself 'the word,' no 'servant of God' carried within himself the ultimate secret of God. We say all this so that it may not remain unsaid; but it applies solely to the realm of words (*Wort-Welt*); and in this book we shall concern ourselves not with the 'deficit' but rather with the 'surplus.'

3. We find in the Old Testament a surplus. If as testimony to the Name it is essentially identical with the New Testament, we are nevertheless also struck by the fact that the outlook on the future which the Old Testament presents is in many respects not fulfilled in the New. An important point in the controversy between church and synagogue! But this hardly affects us at all as we now proceed to look for the meaning of the Old Testament as such and to do this in connection with its independent testimony, its own voice in the world of today. Therefore in using the word 'surplus' we are much more concerned with those elements in the Old Testament which are especially relevant and topical today. These elements are not surpassed in the New Testament, nor are they denied; but there they have receded into the background. We observe that when the essential substance and tendency of the Old and the New Testament are balanced there remains a margin of ideas; we see that precisely these utterances are of special importance for the work of the interpreter and witness, because, intellectually, they are an indication of the conflict with the religion of the nations, didactically, they provide us with rich practical material, and have proved themselves to be indispensable in the apostolate of the church, in the education and guidance of the nations.

If we assume that the 'fourth man' arises to a larger or smaller extent from the 'third man,' and if we admit that—even though 'instruction' is only one aspect of our intercourse with people—there is no reasonable expectation that we shall find anything that has more convincing power than communication through the human word, then we may confidently conclude that this 'margin of ideas'—which includes scepticism, rebellion, erotics, politics (themes which are hardly mentioned in the New Testament)—will prove to be an excellent help in our encounter with the 'ungenuine nihilism' of which we spoke above and which we found, for all its ungenuineness, to be so genuine, warm, and human. Or do we really believe that all past cultures and civilizations were at least partially willing to listen to augurs or druids, Brahmans or mandarins, gurus or mullahs, rabbis or preachers—and that it is only this postbourgeois, postpersonal, postcultural civilization that is automatically less willing to accept reason? Do we think that the destroying angel of technology is dragging us into the Gehenna of the void in which the witness to the covenant of God is struck dumb? What we call 'the masses' may finally slip into total deafness. But are we not forgetting that it was the aristocrats of the mind who took the lead in dismissing the importance of the Word, speech, address, and that already in an early phase of the nineteenth century people had become somewhat weary of the multiplicity of words about the Word. The church cannot of its own strength, initiative, and originality very deeply change this constellation. This does not mean, however, that we are not critical of much rejection of the Word, that we have not at least some appreciation of the reasons for it, and that we have not, with a certain horror, seen the consequences of it descending upon everybody.

> Dein allererstes Wort war: Licht:
> da ward die Zeit. Dann schwiegst du lange.
> Dein zweites Wort ward Mensch und bange
> (wir dunkeln noch in seinem Klange),
> und wieder sinnt dein Angesicht.

> Ich aber will dein drittes nicht.
> Ich bete nachts oft: Sei der Stumme.
> der wachsend in Gebärden bleibt
> und den der Geist im Traume treibt,
> dass er des Schweigens schwere Summe
> in Stirnen und Gebirge schreibt.

(Your first word was 'Light'
and Time came into being. Then you were silent for a long
time.
Your second word became Man and afraid
(and still we gloom in the sound of it),
and then again your brow returned to brooding.

But I do not want your third word.
Often I pray at night: Be the Silent One,
who confines himself for ever to signs and gestures
and moves the mind in dreams to write
the heavy sum of silence
upon the brows of men and mountains).[52]

Thus the young Rilke in the first part of the *Stundenbuch* (*The Book of Hours*, 1905). According to this view, God was silent between the creation and the incarnation. And now the times need a different kind of word, but the religious-aesthetic man shies away from Him; He again comes out of his cave to meet a world that does not even ask for him. Whatever 'word' there is to be, let it be 'written' in the over-whelming sum of silent things, in the irrational existence of the world. Away with the Word; let the burden of existence rest upon us! Here—quite revealingly—the silence of the gods is evoked—against the possi-bility that the 'Voice' may speak.

But is is precisely this abysmal silence that has led our generation to '*la nausée*' (Sartre) and brought us to the point where in long, re-peated litanies we call mere existence—'absurd.'

[52] A metrical tr. can be found in *Poems from the Book of Hours*, '*Das Stundenbuch*' by Rainer Maria Rilke, tr. Babette Deutsch (Norfolk, Conn.: New Directions, 1941), p. 31.—Tr.]

3. The Surplus

THE PRIMITIVE MENTALITY

Formerly the Old Testament was placed lower than the New because it spoke of God in such anthropomorphic terms; but now we are rather inclined to regard this as a spiritual necessity, indeed, a spiritual enrichment.

We shall not discuss here the question why the New Testament is different in this respect (the answer being that in the kerygma the Man who came from God, the one who was sent, the Son himself, absorbed the human form) and avoid repeating what we have said concerning the meaning and purpose of anthropomorphism in the Old Testament. What we have in view here is the primitive mentality in general; and we see in it, in principle and didactically, a possibility of getting away from the spell of religion, to which it has again and again been thought that the New Testament testimony could be subjected. God is spirit, light, love—these profound and sublime metaphors (for these, too, are only metaphors!) tend to get away from the concrete substance of what is actually meant by these spacious words; at the same time the powerful glitter they have and their pretension to universality—after their original meaning has been inverted and changed to 'the spirit is God' and 'love is God'—makes them especially vulnerable to the nullification and negation of their message-character. Nihilism then sets itself up to be the demasking of these phrases (in their inverted form).

The Old Testament speaks of 'one' God, and what it says refers to acts. Indeed, thinking itself is regarded as an act; it is extremely motory, and practical;[1] it can also be called 'naïve,' and here this would be equivalent to 'unconditional.' Where is there any starting point or basis for logic? Where is there ever any 'coercive' argumentation? (How are we to translate the word *lema'an* in Ps. 130 : 4; Exod.

---

[1] J. Pedersen, *Israel: Its Life and Culture*, I–II, tr. Mrs. Auslang Möller, (London: Oxford Univ. Press, 1926), pp. 125f.; Martin Buber, *Reden über das Judentum* (1921), p. 151.

4 : 21; Isa. 6 : 9f., 'that,' 'in order that,' 'because'—that the truth may become evident, in order that the reality may be manifest, because there is a reason, a sin, etc?)

We can never be too conscious of the fact that what we Westerners (even though we may not philosophize) always tacitly assume, everything that we mean by terms like causality, determination, and evolution simply has no function in the Old Testament. There are hardly any conjunctions in the Old Testament, and those that do occur (like ki=for) are imprecise and vague in their meaning. The verb is always and everywhere the prince of the sentence, it is the tree of the language in general and the green shoot in every flowering garland of cognate words. Even the verbs of inaction have dynamic character; and the 'logical' conception of 'being' is implicit in the designation of action or attitude or becoming. Thus even on the basis of the language itself the hermeneutical horizon is a very definite one.[2]

Now, we can say: Yes, like all Semites, and more strongly, for example, than the Babylonians, Israel was dynamic, voluntaristic, realistic. It is, of course, possible to describe it in a very vague way; but the testimony was given in such a way that God, his Name, his deeds were situated not in a generalized 'world,' not in the world as conceived in our cosmology, but rather in the milieu of an Eastern conception of life which brings out much better what is unique in YHWH. Religion has tried to 'translate' it in order to make it fit our categories. Atheism, when its hour comes, furiously attacks the logical and quasi-logical arguments, whereas atheism itself operates with the causal nexus, glories in determinism, and protests against predestination. Apologetics, with its spindly shanks and slow pulse, defends a logic afflicted with lacunae, a causality suffering from hiatuses, etc. In the vanguard and the rearguard, on the right or the left, this is the wretchedness of a

---

[2] Cf. Martin Buber and Franz Rosenzweig, *Die Schrift und ihre Verdeutschung*; Thorlief Boman, *Hebrew Thought Compared With Greek* (1960), passim; J. Pedersen, op. cit., p. 114: 'The Israelite does not know the logical progress which leads us from one idea to another. That which stirs his mind-images is the action, the event. Therefore Hebrew descriptions are dominated by the verbal phrases. The vividness of the description is created by the verbs, which constantly succeed each other and form the stages of the progressive narrative. First and foremost the verb expresses the *occurrence* of the action; then from whom it issues and against whom it is directed. . . . The time of the action, which for us is the principal thing, is of no importance to the Hebrew—when an action is born, then it takes effect, but it has been prepared by other actions, and new actions group around it, and it is this cohesion of actions which interests him.'

rationalism that prevents us from really coming into contact with the primitive message, prevents us from understanding the voice in the dynamics of this language.[3]

I do not deny that dogmatics is a rational endeavour to deal with the mystery; but here we are not writing a dogmatics. If this is what we were doing, we should also have to point out here that the 'mystery' has come to us in *this* primitive form; and it could turn out that in our searching for the spiritual meaning of this primitivity some corrections of our logical presuppositions would quite spontaneously occur. But however that may be, the Old Testament can help us to break through the closed religio-logical circle; compared with the New Testament it possesses a formal priority, because it does not employ the great words with their spiritual and universal pretentiousness. The interpreter and witness will have to be concerned above all with the preservation and application of the primitive idea of God (it would be better immediately to put it in quotation marks: 'idea of God'). This is in my opinion one of our great tasks in the late stage of a culture in which the silence of the gods is oppressive and then ceases to be oppressive—a culture in which the highly intellectual offshoots of the New Testament which appeared in Idealism are declared to be mere ideas and idols that no longer speak to anyone—not because, but in spite of, the fact that they represent a return to sublimated heathenism.[4]

When we preach, we proclaim nothing else but God, nothing above him, nothing beside him, nothing with greater emphasis and nothing with less self-certainty, nothing so rich and overpowering—although the truth of God can shine through our words in simplicity and still-ness, like a new springtime light that is meant for men. No other word can be so intimate and cordial and yet so filled with objective power, so completely 'other,' so holy.

But we have already discovered that this cannot happen without taking into account the concepts and ideas that men have about God. And so in practice the old question of monotheism (with all its logical and causal implications) comes back into preaching. But if it is stripped of the overformal content of the term 'monotheism,' another possibility

---

[3] On the prelogical, see Georges Gusdorf, *Mythe et Métaphysique* (1953), pp. 185f.; Lucien Lévy-Bruhl, *La mythologie primitive* (1935), p. 166; idem, *Les carnets* (1949), pp. 197f.

[4] Cf. S. L. Steinheim, *Die Glaubenslehre der Synagoge als exacte Wissenschaft* (1856).

opens up, namely, that we may begin to understand from Hebrew psychology the indefinite definiteness of God. Then the metaphorical use of words for parts of the body will neither be nullified in an enlightened way nor taken literally in vulgar Western fashion, but rather understood in the light of the changing views of man himself; the *nephesh* ('soul') for example, 'is the complete personality as a unified manifestation of vital power,'[5] dwelling anywhere, but manifesting itself outside of its dwelling place in magical exertions of power in curse and in blessing. The Old Testament can speak of the extension of a presence in a word of blessing (Gen. 27 : 33ff.); in the survival of a man, of his 'soul,' in his descendants, his 'name' (II Sam. 18 : 18; Job 18 : 17; cf. the institution of Levirate marriage, Deut. 25 : 5ff.); in the work of the servant of the house (the *mal'ak* 'messenger,' is an extension of the *adon* 'master,' the servant is the master, the representative is the presence of the principal; Gen. 24 : 9f.), in negotiations having to do with one's property (II Kings 4 : 29). The giver himself is present in the gift (Judg. 1 : 14f.; Gen. 23 : 11; I Sam. 30 : 26); a man is present in the temple by means of a consecrated object he has placed there with the intention of its being venerated.[6] More or less closed groups of people (II Kings 1 : 13; Isa. 66 : 3) are viewed as 'forming a single *nephesh* or corporate personality'; a city like Abel of Bethmaacah can be called a 'mother in Israel' (II Sam. 20 : 19).

Why should not the figures of the patriarchs be understood as such superpersonal, undefined figures,[7] and, looked at from this point of view, would not the familiar 'community-self' (*Gemeinde-Ich*) in the Psalms appear in a new light? Singular and plural are used alternately for the same city, group, or body. Everywhere in the Old Testament there is a 'fluidity of reference from the One to the Many and from the Many to the One';[8] this underlies the figure of the priest as well as the king in Israel. And Jeremiah too regards himself as a member of the community of those upon whom he pronounces judgment and for whom at the same time he makes intercession (cf. also Dan. 9 : 3ff.; Ezra 9 : 5ff).

If we carry this over to the 'idea of God,' we find that God cannot be

[5] Aubrey R. Johnson, *The One and the Many in the Israelite Conception of God* (Cardiff: Univ. of Wales Press, 1942), p. 6.

[6] B. D. Eerdmans, 'Sojourn in the Tent of Jahu,' *Oudtestimentische Studien*, I, (1941).

[7] Cf. Thomas Mann, *The Tales of Jacob*, prelude, 'Descent into Hell.'

[8] Aubrey R. Johnson, p. 20.

confined within the monotheistic concept of a god of heaven or god of the world, to whom the feeling of an immeasurable remoteness, an infinite horizon, and the idea of a prelogical monism are attached. YHWH reveals himself in Gideon's and Samson's strength. YHWH extends himself, creates room for himself in the 'world' (which is not a biblical concept—it would be better to say, in the environment, the surroundings which are dependent upon him, permeated by him, the field of his activity). His *ruach* ('breath,' 'spirit') goes out and girds itself with the vigour of the judges (Judg. 6 : 34), and the hosts of angels come in and with this *ruach* (cf. also the words of Jesus in Mark 13 : 27). His word is creative. His blessing and his curse are effectual from afar as well as in his immediate presence.

Thus his Name is a power with which the community is charged (Num. 6 : 22–27); thus the ark is a form of extension of the personality of YHWH, his being (Num. 10 : 35f.; I Sam. 4 : 5ff.); the rod of God (Exod. 17 : 9) and the staff of Elisha (II Kings 4 : 29, 31) are extensions, expansions, bearers of the realization of his saving power. We fail to see the very structure of the Old Testament if we simply ignore a conception like this as being ancient Semitic or interpret it symbolically as a philosophical omnipotence or omnipresence. YHWH is the great magician.[9]

This 'idea of God' is the vehicle for the proclamation of the living God; even the 'mythical' element in it has its definite function and contributes to the opening of men's hearts to the sovereign presence of God. Nor do we read the prophets and the *chokmah* aright if God suddenly pales, even though it be in the most sublime way, into a spiritual being, a universal godhead, a guarantor of a moral world order. The living intervention, this inclination to let go of himself and come down, to enter into and involve himself in human doings— none of this detracts from God's sublimity; on the contrary, this is the manifestation of his own peculiar sublimity. In his humiliation his glory shines, in his nearness his remoteness casts its beams upon us, in his definite, circumscribed existence in particular places his perfect freedom is revealed and, as in anticipation, the full counsel of peace becomes effective.

Wherever the naïveté of the Old Testament is lacking, the exposition

[9] Cf. G. van der Leeuw, *Religion in Essence and Manifestation*, II (New York: Harper & Row Torchbook, 1963), p. 580.

and application of the New Testament always runs into the danger of evaporating into 'spirit,' 'light,' and 'love'—the supreme expressions of a universality which is tenderly cherished by natural theology as the most elegant form of flight from the reality of God.[10] Wherever in church and synagogue the congregation is gathered, it will be 'edified,' i.e., built up and strengthened, only if the growth of its initial knowledge and the broadening of its progressive (but always eventlike fragmentary) knowledge is accompanied by an elemental amazement at God's condescension and self-giving. In any case, the description of God as 'a single *nephesh* or corporate personality,' 'a fluidity from the One to the Many and from the Many to the One,' is closer to the mark which preaching and instruction are striving to attain than terms like *ens realissimum* and *summum bonum*.

'The New Testament has three statements which look like definitions of God's nature: "God is a Spirit," John 4 : 24; "God is light", I John 1 : 5; and "God is love," I John 4 : 8. The Old Testament has no statement to compare with these.'[11] This is a well-known Old Testament scholar's assertion of the supremacy of the New Testament concept of God. Here one must be very careful. Apart from the anthropomorphous revelation, how does one receive any impression whatsoever of the Subject to which the predicates spirit, light, love, are attached? These New Testament statements are not reversible.[12] They

[10] Cf. Franz Rosenzweig, *Der Stern der Erlösung*, III, 199; idem, 'Jehuda Halevi, 99 Hymnen und Gedichte, Anmerkungen,' p. 185.

[11] Ludwig Koehler, *Old Testament Theology*, tr. A. S. Todd (London: Lutterworth Press, 1957), p. 22. It is correct for Koehler to say: 'He is spoken of as a man so that we should understand Him not as a thing, power, or impersonal Being, but as one set over against us in a personal relationship'; but it is nominalism when he goes on to say: 'Again, however, this manner of speaking is only a concession to our human insufficiency of understanding . . .' and it is a latent denial of the incarnation, which is attested in the Old Testament, when he says: 'God is no man. God is simply God'; for it is not given to us to know God except as we know this 'man' and understand him precisely as 'simply God' (p. 23).

[12] This is often forgotten precisely in the more recent anthropological hermeneutics. We give only one example: 'As long as faith is not plausible, we *cannot* believe . . . . But then what are we to do? The answer is: First you should live! And in your life you should note the experiences you have with love. . . . But always in that language-context which is connected with this history of love in everyday life! Now, what is it that motivates people, for example, in their dealings with little children? . . . Does not love challenge me to believe in the continuation of the history of love? . . . Now, if man is not able to be the guarantor of love, who does guarantee it? Is it not love itself that does this? . . . He who has this experience believes. . . . Now replace the

presuppose that the word 'God' is already filled with content; he is a definitely circumscribed god (in scholarly jargon: 'member of a pantheon'). Everything that is said of his oneness and manyness, of the oneness and manyness of his *mal'ak* (Gen. 16 : 7ff., 32 : 22–32; Hos. 12 : 5f.; Judg. 6 : 11ff.), of his identity, his distinctiveness, of his coming and his presence (Gen. 28 : 12; Ps. 34 : 8; Judg. 13 : 3, 6, 8), of his heavenly origin and his earthly manifestation, for example, in the man of God, the prophet, or more precisely, in his message—everything that is said about these things can only be a disturbance to a scholastic-rational doctrine of God, and for that matter something which one can do little with in preaching (and, rightly seen, also in instruction). On the other hand, these and similar insights can only be welcome to those who see the ambivalence of religion and nihilism. For all of these identifications and distinctions of God and his Name, of God and his angel, God and his messenger, can be helpful to us and preserve us from trampling under foot the mysteries of the true knowledge of God and obscuring the offence that is inherent in them. This is what God is; in his image man was created. This is the way he remains himself—by becoming something other than himself. This is the way—that is, through his care—he delivers himself into the life and into the hands of men (Deut. 29 : 5; Isa. 63 : 9; Jer. 9 : 1f.; Ps. 31 : 8). This is what God is like, the God who commands us not to make any image of him besides that which he himself sets before us as his own image, in his deeds, in the living act of his revelation. Through this richly varied presence we are presented with a full, living mode of being which, even though it is constantly intersected and corrected by the cry of the Shema', *YHWH elohenu YHWH echad*, nevertheless vindicates itself as an incomparable (let us say it without hesitation) 'trinitarian'[13] comfort.

The *melek* ('king') too, is neither bound to one place nor is he 'omnipresent.' YHWH as the *adon* ('master') or even as the *ba'al* ('possessor of the land') is in heaven as well as on earth. The *El qana'* is 'jealous' of

---

word love with the word God. Then we understand that faith in God is the most natural thing there can be. And then it immediately becomes self-evident to the practical reason.' Ernst Fuchs, 'Das Neue Testament und das hermeneutische Problem,' *Zeitschrift für Theologie und Kirche*, LVIII (1961), pp. 224f.

[13] Cf. J. Rottenberg, *De Triniteit in Israels Godsbegrip*, pp. 62, 85f., 131; Franz Rosenzweig, *Der Stern der Erlösung*, II, p. 145.

being himself and of having his own as his possession, but not in such a way that his *shem* ('name') would not dwell in the *mal'ak* ('messenger'), that he would not dwell, as it were, outside of himself, on Zion and wherever it pleased him to 'cause his name to be remembered' (Exod. 20 : 24). Even the Holy One, the Self-sufficient One fights for the love of his chosen ones, suffers from their rejection of him, remains in their midst. Nowhere in the Old Testament is the absolute sovereignty of God reduced to static tranquillity; nowhere is his intervention anything but human and precisely in this way divine, i.e., in accord with the nature of this God who is to be praised for ever and ever.

Where God grants to him who speaks and prays power over Himself —for this is what He does, so that one can say that prayer contains its answer in so far as it accomplishes this—then even while he yields himself and condescends to the sphere of creatures, he still remains the absolute sovereign Power who, just as he directs all things on earth (cf. Rom. 9 : 28), can also turn the answer to the prayer into a calamity, i.e., into a disaster which will bring salvation to his people.

Thus the Old Testament serves us as a testimony of the one revelation, the one covenant, the one incarnation, the one presence of God on earth—a treasure to be preserved for the stricken people, for *Shear-jashub* Isa. 7 : 3), the remnant, which remains because it returns, which returns because it is allowed to remain.

GROUNDLESS—AND YET IN THE MIDST OF THINGS

The New Testament too does not proclaim its message from a standpoint in the Beginning or in eternity. When God (or also Christ, as, for example, in Revelation 1 : 4, 8), is called the One 'who is and who was and who is to come,' the sequence indicates an inner order. And the first clause, the 'is,' quite certainly does not mean God's eternal being, but rather His being in time, in the midst of time, in his present revelation. And yet it is not accidental that in other transmissions of the text the sequence can be altered to allow the logical to prevail over the given, over the chronological order and history. Nor is it accidental that Origen and even Augustine interpreted the fact that 'is' stands at the beginning in these passages as meaning eternal being. And here again the Old Testament has an advantage and presents a 'surplus.'

According to the structure of the Old Testament it is impossible to speak of YHWH in any way except from the midst of things, from the present, from his action in history.

But this connotes that the revelation, the presence, the covenant, the election—are groundless. Or must we say: appear to be groundless? When we adopt the interpretation 'appear' to be groundless, we are again making an arbitrary leap into a reality that would lie behind the Name and would contain the explanation of what 'appears' in time. Now there can be no doubt that when in our preaching and teaching we conform to the order according to which 'in the midst' is identical with 'groundless,' we are in danger of remaining caught in the adventitious and arbitrary. In order rightly to understand the 'surplus,' which the Old Testament here presents, it may be helpful to go somewhat deeper into this question.

There has been a great deal of toying and juggling with the term 'revelation.' In order to prevent this we ought to reserve the term 'revelation' for *phanerōsis*, the disclosing of what is hidden in the definitive sense given in the New Testament; and, historically and grammatically, we also have a certain right to regard as invalid the application of this term to other religions (which themselves do not make this claim) or to the experience of the genius. But the Word is always more defenceless than we think, and the protection we would like to give it by means of our distinction has little effect in a time when words are universally subject to deterioration. Then we ought simply to leave such a word to others and concentrate upon the special meaning which it has for us. One can even go as far as Karl Barth did in an article which is too little known[14] and interpret the word so broadly that even all the arbitrary conceptions find their place in it. Barth leaves room for the useful, life-enriching, but not indispensable revelations, even for those 'whose desirability may be doubted' (e.g., that of occultism); he speaks of 'revelations,' which may be superseded tomorrow and (esoteric) 'revelations' which apply only to individuals. He distinguishes between 'disclosures of matters of fact' in the cosmos and the 'actualization of existing possibilities' in the human soul, and

---

[14] Karl Barth, 'The Christian Understanding of Revelation,' in *Against the Stream: Shorter Post-War Writings*)1946–52), tr. Ronald Gregor Smith (New York: Philosophical Library, 1954), pp. 205–240. [The translations of quotations from this work do not always coincide literally with the English version.—Tr.]

he also assumes that there are genuine revelations which can be 'capitalized,' which man can use after he has received them. He calls 'approximate revelation' those phenomena of human religion which 'in the process of increasing knowledge approach a certain optimum of man.' There are also 'revelations' which enable man to take up the spectator's attitude toward them, spectaculatory or speculative revelations. And common to all these revelations is that they contain and set forth a 'self-revelation of what is (*des Seienden*).'

Now the Scriptures are concerned with the revelation of a 'relationship *to* what is' (*zum Seienden*)—a nonfacultative, nonoccult, nonesoteric, nonsubjective-latent, nonobservable, nonpossessable revelation. The Scriptures are concerned with an existential revelation of which it is really true (according to our way of knowing) that existence precedes essence, a knowledge which 'was completely new to man yesterday and the day before yesterday, a thousand and two thousand years ago, which is completely new to him today and will be new again tomorrow.' (This is what we mean by the term 'absolute,' which, however, it is better not to use.) This revelation is at every moment and from every point of view the fulfilment of past, present, and future, the fulfilment of time itself. 'Revelation . . . is the self-revelation of the what-is-not (*Nicht-Seienden*) in relation to what is, in relation to man and the cosmos.[15] God 'is' not 'there' as the cosmos and man 'are there.' We cannot place him in a general world picture, he does not fit into a general mode of thinking. 'If this general world picture is the measure of all things, then there is neither a revelation nor a God in the Christian sense. Then we would indeed have been speaking of "nothing".'[16]

But if we have been speaking of something that is a reality, then it is clear why no word or image in itself possesses the clarity and power to express it; then it is clear why it is that when we say 'YHWH is Elohim,' this very confession (or, seen from the outside, this assertion) includes the affirmation that what appears 'in the midst of things' is not the Almighty but rather his way of exercising power over the All, that it is not a *ruach* (or the *ruach*) that is sent out, but rather his *ruach*, i.e., the way in which he carries out his purposive work in men, in his people. No word as such has validity; for the event, seen from the point

[15] Ibid., p. 6, in the German version, 'Das christliche Verständnis der Offenbarung,' *Theologische Existenz Heute*, n. s., XII (1948).
[16] Ibid., p. 9, German version; p. 211, Eng. tr.

of view of our world, is groundless; but everything that is word is sanctified and renewed out of the midst of things in order to declare that YHWH is holy, i.e., that he is different, that in his way he is himself, though not far away, but rather near at hand, in the sphere of his present, inflaming and assuaging intervention.

It is precisely this 'groundlessness' which manifests itself so disturbingly and fascinatingly in the Old Testament. Where does YHWH suddenly come from? Where does Israel come from? Where does its faith come from? What grounds do the prophets have for speaking, as they do, as men who are called? In what context of meaning do the wonders and signs appear? Why this 'exclusiveness,' this 'intolerance'? But at the same time one must say that this 'groundlessness' is a secondary manifestation, an accompanying phenomenon compared with that which occurs—without any ground or basis in man or the cosmos —here, in the midst of things. The terms 'groundless' and 'here, in the midst of things' are correlative. If this correlation is left out of account, it is possible to say that faith in YHWH is nihilism. And Rosenzweig says that 'all revelation begins with a great No. The conversion which all concepts of the former world undergo when they enter into the light of the real world is none other than this No.'[17] Whether the 'negativity' of groundlessness and the 'accidentality' of the 'midst' contain, besides aspects of the Name of God and his deeds, a wisdom which not only judges but also supersedes and reintegrates all philosophy and anthropology—this is another matter (ultimately the great concern of systematic theology); faith does not have a ready answer to this question but only the trust that it is so and will prove to be so. 'Once it is incorporated in the reality of revelation, everything gains the freedom which it lost under the domination of ideas.'[18] Through the structure and the basic words of the Old Testament it becomes far clearer than in the New Testament that God strides right through the negation of all that is given in order to rescue life from the futility of our 'interpretations' of it, and that in the same way his servants must go through God's negation of the gods and the powers in order to find a meaningful way in this world. So it was with Abraham, Moses, Elijah, Jeremiah, and Baruch, and—John the Baptist.

For the interpreter and witness it is of primary importance to keep firmly in mind that one can look back to the beginning only from the

[17] Franz Rosenzweig, *Der Stern der Erlösung*, II, 110.   [18] Ibid., pp. 130f.

midst of things in order to call it 'creation,' and only from that vantage point can one look forward to the time of the end in order to call it the 'kingdom.' The beginning of Genesis is not the beginning of revelation, but rather a retrospective application of faith in the Name, which has entered into the present. The silence of the gods is broken by the Voice; the Word can never be inferred and derived from the world. That which resounds in the midst of things puts its stamp upon extended time, it accompanies and fills it.

And now I ask myself, is not this 'groundlessness in the midst of things' the driving power behind that spiritual mode of existence which we have characterized as 'nomadic'? If this is so, then what a young poet has said concerning Abraham's exodus from the religious culture of Ur of the Chaldeans may well be listened to, especially for the spiritual insight it contains. I quote a few lines of the poem, taking the liberty to italicize a number of passages for emphasis.[19]

> Een *stem* doorbrak de stomme ring
> van het bestaan, waarin hij was
> besloten; hij wordt waterpas
> geschoven op de lange baan
> waarlangs hij voortaan voort zal gaan.
>
> .   .   .   .
>
> Het is als een *abortus*, dit
> afdrijven uit het oergelid.
>
> .   .   .   .
>
> . . . hij vraagt niet meer
> naar de geheimen van het weer:
> de *neerslag van het lot*, de schijn
> van het aurora-rode *zijn*,
> de nachtvorst van de dood, de kou
> van ouderdom, geboortedauw
> en alles wat daartussen ligt
> in de spiralen van het licht.
> *De transen vallen in elkaar*
> en hij laat het evenwicht daar.

[19] Guillaume van der Graft, 'Aangaande Abraham,' in *Vogels en Vissen* (1953). [A prose translation follows the Dutch text.—Tr.]

Er is geen heen en weer, er is
alleen maar de geschiedenis,
de inbreuk op het eigene,
de zege op het zwijgen . . .

. . . .

Dan wreekt zich het bestaan met licht
het *wreckt want* het *rechtvaardigt* zich.
De loofhut van den dageraad
doet zich voor als een toeverlaat,
een prieel van de *mogelijkheid*
zich in te leven in te tijd.

. . . .

Dit is het eerste einde. 's Nachts
begint de reis weer onverwachts
opnieuw, de hemel weet wanneer.
De hemel weet het ook niet meer
sedert de ban brak als een ei.
De stilstand is voorgoed voorbij
de scherven van de eierschaal
liggen verspreid over de taal
en Abraham treedt aan het licht
als een *los woord* uit een gedicht.

. . . .

Nog klam van het geboortezweet,
blind als een vogel die niet weet
hoe hij zich eenzaam redden moet
buiten de banen van het bloed,
ademt hij diep de *vrijheid* in.—
De wereld staat aan haar begin.

(A *voice* broke through the silent circle in
which existence was enclosed; then it was
thrust out upon the long road on which
henceforth it should go.

It is like an *abortion*, this expulsion from
the primeval prison . . . he no longer
seeks the secrets of the weather, the *rains
of fate*, the rosy dawn of *existence*, the
night-frost of death, the grey sky of age,
the dew of birth and all that lies between
in the spirals of light. *The heavenly bodies
go askew*; all equilibrium ceases to exist.

.   .   .   .

There is no going out and coming back,
only events remain, only the inbreaking [of
God] into your own [life], only *the victory
over the silence.*

.   .   .   .

Then existence avenges itself on life; it
avenges itself for it *wants to justify itself.*
Dawn's feast of booths passes itself off as
a refuge, a bower of *possibility that one may
be able to live one's life in time.*

.   .   .   .

This is the first act. Come night and
the journey unexpectedly begins anew,
heaven knows where. Even heaven does
not know *since the spell broke like an egg.*
Resting is gone for good, the eggshells
scattered   among   the   nations;   and
Abraham steps out into the light, like
one *separate word* from a poem.

.   .   .   .

Still damp with the sweat of parturition,
blind as a bird that does not know how
one must shift for oneself, all alone and
without the protection of kindred blood,
he breathes deeply of *freedom: the world
is at its beginning.*)

186

HEAVEN AND EARTH

There is a refuge of defence against the nihilistic feeling about life, a religious, a Christian refuge of defence which is imagined to be storm-proof because of the unassailable mystery of nature. Who can resist the charm of being at home in the world, as we find it, say, in the work of Ernst Wiechert?[20] Despite the fact that we have been impregnated by the Bible, we still imagine that we are meeting this same at-home-ness in the world in what the Scriptures mean by the phrase 'heaven and earth.' But even though it be true that this term stands for the realm in which God does his work and that hence potentially 'every-thing' can be hallowed and 'everything' can be counted as acceptable, the structural difference between this term and terms like 'cosmos' and 'universe' is striking, and to neglect it will lead only to misinterpre-tations. Immediately significant is the addition to 'heaven and earth' of 'the sea, and all that is in them' (Ps. 146 : 6), the 'naïve enumeration of the incidental phenomena' as in Psalm 104, but also statements such as that 'heaven and earth' are rolled up together (Isa. 34 : 4), that 'in their duality they are nevertheless one in their transiency,' that they 'flee' (Ps. 114 : 3), that they are summoned to listen and to be wit-nesses of that which happens between God and man. The earth quakes, the heavens drip, even the foundations of the heavens tremble (Judg. 5 : 4; Deut. 32 : 1; II Sam. 22 : 8; Ps. 68 : 8; Isa. 51 : 6; Rev. 20 : 11). And, to conclude this sketch of the structural difference of the Old Testament, it speaks of a new heaven and a new earth (Isa. 65 : 17, 66 : 22).

We, who are by nature pagans, look for the reality of God in that which is the first and the ultimate ground of experience, in the world, in the unshakable durability of things, the inexhaustible coherence of cosmic forces. Therefore the witness and the interpretation will have no power if they do not follow the direction given by the sacred texts and begin to get away from this way of thinking—not in order to sur-pass it with a higher, broader conception of the world, but rather to fit oneself into what looks like the far narrower framework of the relationship between YHWH and his people, his help for the wretched,

[20] For example in *Missa sine nomine*; Eng. *Tidings*, tr. Marie Heynemann and Margery B. Ledward (New York: Macmillan, 1959).

his signs, which, erected on this earth, are in every respect—intellectual, moral and material—poor.

In the New Testament precisely this line is continued: 'nature' is a
hardly noted background of the saving events; the night is rent by the
light of the proclaiming angel and the singing of the multitude of the
heavenly host; the sun is darkened when the Son of man yields his
spirit into the Father's hands; the lilies of the field and the birds of
heaven are not celebrated for their beauty, but rather function as
emblems, as examples of God's care for his own; the stars stand above
us to perform the service of shining upon the doings of men and are
destined to fall from the heavens; the clouds pass across the face of the
sky, called in due time to encompass the coming in glory like a dazzl-
ing escort that will strike terror into the hearts of men. Nature as such
is speechless. Thus one of the main lines of the Old Testament is carried
through and maintained in the New, namely, that faith in the Creator
is a conclusion from the acts of God which have been manifested on
the basis of the covenant. It can also be called an extrapolation, but
in this case it is a valid and necessary one. In the last analysis the New
Testament persists on this main line, which is the complete opposite
of the ancient mythological conception, according to which even towns
and temples and other sacral things are represented as 'created'[21]—
precisely where the cosmos itself is seldom thought of as being created.

Now, when we ask what is the function of the Old Testament in
preaching and direct our attention to those points which the New
Testament passes over, we discover still other lines of testimony, a remainder of wider experience, an approach to a broader praise of God,
a torso of different knowledge, a reference to creation, its depth and
breadth, its peculiar beauty and terror, its more independent speech,
and its hidden intimation of the last things. All this should still have its
place in the church's preaching and instruction. That which was in
the first instance necessarily ignored comes back into the picture, is
rediscovered as being a surplus, a hidden spring of wider ranging
promises. But everything goes awry again the moment we forget how
greatly dependent the power of all this is upon the Name; even heaven
and earth have only a flashing and flickering career as an accompaniment to the history of salvation which is enacted in and upon the
nomadic life of those who are called. When we keep a secure hold on

[21] Cf. Th. C. Vriezen, *An Outline of Old Testament Theology*, p. 217.

this, the 'naïve' world picture of the Old Testament begins to show its peculiar superiority.

In so-called 'nature Psalms' (8, 19, 24, 104), in the testimony of the prophets concerning the creation, that primal act which was the ground of all the later acts of God in history (Amos 4 : 13, 5 : 8; Isa. 17 : 12ff., 51 : 9ff.; Jer. 5 : 22, 31 : 35; Hab. 3 : 10), there lives a future that is full of peace, and what the *chokmah* contains takes on a new radiance from the revelation, the time, the presence of Immanuel, the God who is with us.

Retrospectively, the preaching of the church appropriates all of these words, and particularly the creation accounts in Genesis 1 and 2. And when we do this, we are not only testifying that this is not a theogony, that God is not the demiurge, etc., but rather we understand that *holid* ('begetting') and *qana* ('creating') and *'asah* ('doing,' 'bringing forth') and *vatsar* ('forming') are very closely connected and that they support and accompany the basic word *bara'* (creation exclusively by God), in order to describe the miracle,[22] the incomparably new thing, which in a certain sense looked at from the point of view of the time of revelation, assures us beforehand of the consummation of all of God's works in proleptic perfection. This is now plain to be seen; therefore it must be newly understood.

Notwithstanding the prophecy which has set the stamp of judgment and alienation from God upon the world (Amos 7 : 4; Jer. 4 : 23ff.; Zeph. 1 : 2ff.; Isa. 51 : 6) and in spite of the inescapable apocalyptic destruction which is to come, the gaze of the Old Testament remains fixed upon a new universe (a new 'heaven and earth'), a new reality in which righteousness will dwell even though it too will remain the dwelling place of men (Isa. 11 : 1–9, 9 : 6, 25 : 6f., 65 : 25).

If we remember, however, that this new reality burst forth in the resurrection of Christ as the hidden glory of YHWH's definitive redemptive action, then here too the enclosure of the Old Testament leaves room for its disclosure; in other words, then there is room in preaching and instruction for the creation, for the joy of light and

[22 The term used here, *das Entrückte*, is from Martin Buber's translation of the Old Testament, 'Miracle' may be misleading, but I despair of finding an English equivalent. The term means that which is 'removed from understanding,' incomprehensible, strange, paradoxical, On Buber's concept of 'miracle,' see Maurice Freedman, *Martin Buber: The Life of Dialogue* (New York: Harper Torchbook, 1960), pp. 234f., 243ff.—Tr.]

harvest, for the song of the furrows, ridges, and meadows settling and softening, shouting and singing beneath the showers from 'the river of God' (Ps. 65). Then there must be room in preaching and instruction for the resounding or the whispered proclamation of the fact that the creation is good, that it is very good, that this 'beginning' is the beginning of an End but also the beginning of the Beginning, the prelude to the inbreaking of the Messianic time[23] and the eternal destination of all things.

It is a strange thing how the doubt of some Old Testament scholars whether the Old Testament writings ever speak of a creation at all, whether their prevailing conception is not that of an endless, continuing passing of time, with no *creatio ex nihilo* and no 'new heaven and new earth,' can, in all its soberness, be of service to preaching. Not if we flatter and reduce eternity to endless time,[24] but rather when we see time as being gathered up into the purpose and work of YHWH, so that we cannot for a moment think of a 'beginning' of the world (which, after all, is humanly inconceivable) apart from him who is the Originator of the world as well as his people, who is the voluntary partner of general history as well as redemptive history, from him who by his nature is eternally the Creator, who calls into being the things that do not yet exist, just as he called into being the things that did not exist.

This preaching of the depth and breadth of creation is an effective preventive of a kind of spiritualism and dualism which could, with some reason, be read out of some (isolated) New Testament, especially Pauline, testimony. Correction on the basis of the 'surplus' of the Old Testament often proves to be an urgently necessary operation in order to get away from the compulsive temptation of falling back into a religion, a biblical, pneumatic religion. The soteriological cannot be derived from the cosmic, but even less dare it be isolated. Salvation embraces the creation; it is inclusive, not exclusive; but in order to arrive at this perception one must travel the right road.

The voice of the Old Testament, however, also prevents us from thinking of the presence of God in the world as being evident and

[23] 'Perhaps in his first word *bere' shith* [Gen. 1 : 1] there was already in the author's mind a far distant goal of the course of the world, the *acharith hayyamim*, the end of days.' W. Eichrodt, *Theologie des Alten Testaments*, II, 53. Cf. O. Procksch, *Die Genesis* (1924), p. 441.
[24] Oscar Cullmann, *Christ and Time*, pp. 62ff., 92f.

demonstrable. Creation, no less than redemption, is a work of eternal love; but as such it is also no less hidden than the redemption. Only in the Word is it perceivably present to faith through the working of the Holy Spirit. Therefore preaching is concerned to bear witness to the Word, which, as Guido Gezelle said, 'plunged so deep' and is 'so sweet'—sweet, because it radiates God's good pleasure (Pss. 145 : 9, 15f.; 147 : 7ff.; 148 : 3ff.)

The depth dimension to which the New Testament points ('All things were created through him and for him. He is before all things and in him all things hold together,' Col. 1 : 16–17), the depth dimension that reveals itself only as we understand the creation in the light of that other affirmation (which according to Genesis antedates our perception), namely, that 'he is the head of the body, the church' (v. 18)—this depth dimension dare be preached and testified on the basis of the whole breadth of the created world as the Old Testament does. The creation, the created world is good; it sings a song of praise out of the pure creation (we should not speak of a 'fallen creation'!) in the midst of our present time. This work of God, like the work of atonement, knows no past. And precisely in our age of epidemic melancholy, preaching must bear witness to the healing and salvation that lies in 'mere existence' itself, because and in so far as the Lord our God is and was and will be the Creator of it. 'Joy is indeed the first word and the last word of the whole gospel. . . . Joy and truth are the same thing, and where there is the most joy there also is the most truth. What this joy is I will not tell you; you have only to follow the counsel of the psalm and open your mouth: "Open your mouth wide and I will fill it" [Ps. 81 : 10].[25]

THE DEEDS OF YAHWEH

Teaching, sacred instruction, is never so much obscured as it is by the insistent endeavour to reason everything out to the end, to be logically consistent. It hardly needs to be said that in itself this inherent tendency of the human mind constitutes a great gift, though even on the level of the natural and immediate it is threatened at once because of its lack of a binding rule and a meaningful purpose, and therefore often turns out to be sterile. However this may be, in trying to understand

[25] Paul Claudel, *Positions et Propositions*, II.

the Word we must not be unrestrictedly logical, attempting to be absolutely consistent. Nor can we do this with impunity. Translated into the language of exegesis and philosophy, this simply expressed precept means that every word, every concept stands within a 'hermeneutical horizon,' in its own characteristic milieu, in the context of the whole from which it receives its signification, its formative power, its tone. For example, anybody who uses the word 'omnipotence' cannot reason out the content of this word to its conclusion without ending up with the idea of an empty, monstrous tyranny. And so it is with all the 'attributes' of God in the Old Testament. The 'layman' is now having to bear the consequences of a rationalistic theology which has estranged itself from the mystery of language in general and the language of the Message in particular. What the spokesmen and self-acknowledged leaders of intellectual life have permitted themselves to perpetrate in the way of asserted logical 'conclusions' and caricatures of the Message is often enough to be traced back to a fault of theology itself. Theology has largely ignored what Johann Georg Hamann had to say to it; later on, phenomenology passed it by, and the modern Jewish philosophy of language has as yet hardly caught up with it. Here the thinking of Eugen Rosenstock can be instructive to us. All this must be incorporated into the practice of preaching and teaching. We need to know the function of the basic words of the Old Testament. The basic words are the core of the Message. The structure of the whole, which is not directly given as such, continues to be determined by these basic words.

One of the most important of these basic words is the word *ma'aseh*. It is in most cases translated as 'work' (in thirty-seven of the thirty-nine places in which it appears in the Psalms, the Septuagint renders it as *erga* and the Vulgate translates it in all thirty-nine instances as *opera*).[26] This makes it clear that the being of God is assumed to be a *nunc stans*[27] to which the 'attributes' are attached as appendages; this reduces the 'works' of creation and the 'deeds' of history to the same level and defines them throughout in terms of the former. In the use of the word *opus* the emphasis is upon the constant performance of a particular

[26] Fr. Breukelman, 'Die Kirchliche Dogmatik Karl Barths als Hermeneutik' (unpubl.).
[[27] The One who is 'standing now,' in the traditional conception of the eternity of God.—Tr.]

work and thus the word signifies what is to be done, what has been done, what has been performed. But in the Vulgate the word *mela'kah* ('work') and also in many places the word *'abodah* ('service') are translated as *opus*. Nothing but 'works'! The differences and nuances must be more sharply defined. Here it is sufficient to state that in no case dare we reduce the *ma'asim* of God to a common denominator. What we are dealing with here is a—albeit 'primitive'—perception of the God who always manifests himself in a completely concrete situation in an act which has a definite purpose (with respect to man) and in which his 'virtues' are made known. Anticipatively, we may say here that the 'deeds' must not be interpreted on the basis of the 'works,' but rather the 'works' must be seen in the light of the 'deeds.' This is highly important for preaching and instruction today.

It is precisely the act-character of God's being that determines the fact that God distinguishes himself *in* the world *from* the world. It is the reverse side of the fact that he elevates himself above Being. The fact that God's revelation can be called the revelation of 'what is not' in the sense we attempted to set forth above, has its counterpart in this act-character of revelation. The presupposition of the witness which we owe to the world can be summarized in the phrase 'the Being of God in act,' namely, the act of his love, which we find in Karl Barth.[28] This is not a 'dogmatic statement' but simply a transcription of the hermeneutical horizon which we must take into account if we are to understand the Old Testament and the whole of the Scriptures. It constitutes a great illumination that comes out of the essence of the Bible and a great outreach for the essential thing in the Bible. From God's deeds there grows the knowledge of his 'virtues'[29] and in the knowledge of his virtues his nature. 'The Lord, the Lord, *a God merciful and gracious, slow to anger, and abounding in steadfast love and faithfulness*, keeping steadfast love for thousands, forgiving iniquity and transgression and sin.' This is at once the standing formula and the liturgical doxology which holds together the Old Testament at its core (Exod. 34 : 6f.; Num. 14 : 18; Pss. 103 : 8, 86 : 15, 145 : 8; Neh. 9 : 17; Jonah 4 : 2). Here we must think through to the end and be thoroughly consistent, but always within the given horizon, which is Being in act.

[28] *Church Dogmatics*, Vol. II, pt. I, pp. 257ff.
[29] K. H. Miskotte, *Bijbelsch ABC* (1941), pp. 83f., 95ff.

This opens up still another side of the act-character of revelation, namely, the unity between the 'inward' and the 'outward.' This is true in the Old Testament even with respect to men; we find there no experiences, feelings, or attitudes which can be separated from conduct, performance, action. 'Hearing' is 'doing,' not-doing is not-hearing (cf. Gen. 39 : 10, 22 : 16–18; Exod. 18 : 24, 24 : 7). Likewise God's *chesed* is not limited to an attitude; rather *chesed* burst forth of itself as soon as he proceeds to act. He performs mercy (Exod. 20 : 6; Deut. 5 : 10). The whole sphere of human existence, the whole of man's life, the whole history of the people is conditioned by the fact that God is 'rich in mercy.' And this is to be perceived precisely in his acts, not behind them in his 'essence', not apart from them in the world, not in the everyday experience of events. The deeds are revelation of his being, which lies beyond what we call existence (*Dasein*) and which distinguishes itself *from* the world *in* the world. His revelation could never be distinguished from the facticity of the world if it coincided with the universe or were mingled with the totality of history. On the other hand, his revelation would not be open to men, it could not be grasped by man, if it did not actually and actively establish real encounters, going beyond the experiences of 'nature' and sometimes running contrary to them. In such meetings there is no sense in distinguishing between attitude and act; actually such a distinction would again nullify the only kind of knowledge that is appropriate when we are dealing with 'Being in act.'

This can also be demonstrated in the remarkable fact that the language of the Old Testament has no word for our term 'thinking'; *chasaab* and *machashabah* signify 'purposing to do something.' It has to do with the plans and imaginations of the heart, which are already the inception and beginning of the act and are discernible in the 'work of the hands.' A striking example—as it were, at the end of our conception of the sequence of attitude–act–result—is the use of the word 'fruit' (*peri*). It is the result of an action—as in the case of man, so also in that of God—in which 'Being in act' is already contained (Isa. 3 : 10; Jer. 6 : 19, 21 : 14; Mic. 7 : 13; Amos 6 : 12). In Jer. 32 : 19 'great in counsel' is parallel with 'mighty in realization' (Buber's translation), thus the inward goes into action in the outward —in an instant, one would say, if we think of their unity as being simultaneity in *time*. This is not the case, however. Rather the complete unity of attitude–act–result insists upon maintaining itself on the horizontal level of experience; it insists upon being felt, recognized, feared, and praised in history. 'The Lord said, "I will blot out man whom I have created from the face of the ground" ' (Gen. 6 : 7), and when he says this, it is already accomplished, it is already *ma'aseh*; the act begins already in the declaration of the intention. And this action is to be understood as God's response to the imagination of the thoughts of the heart of the creatures who do not respond to him. Of them it is said, 'The wickedness of man was great in the earth and . . . every imagination of the thoughts of his heart was only wicked continually' (v. 5). This does not mean that they merely had wicked intentions, but rather that they were out for nothing else but evil and accordingly did nothing else but evil.

We see how this kind of thinking attacks and shakes our customary doctrine of God. But this is the very thing that can be a liberation for modern man, a liberation from his ordinary conceptions, say, of providence, which is still foremost in his mind (even though it be in the form of denial of it) and block the way of the Word to his mind and heart. The point of reference for his thinking is still the creation, the universe, nature, the great power of natural law, which he admires and almost worships, and the great demonic monster, which he fears and almost curses. If the Message is carried into this province of ancient ontology which has now lost its lustre, it becomes distorted beyond recognition, though less where it is radically rejected than where the attempt is made to take it seriously with the help of the apparatus which is customary in that ontology. Modern man has basically forgotten how to orientate himself upon history, how to think of himself as a recipient and doer of history. How then can he understand a special history in which God gives himself up to be his master and companion, his guide and partner? He cannot think in any terms except that of the triangle relationship of God-nature-man and he feels that God is in league with nature against him, instead of being his ally over against nature. And where he still has some notion of what history means, he also charges all the blows of fate, all the powers and dominions, to the account of this hostile or indifferent entity. All that remains for him is to resign himself to the world as it is or rebel against it (the divination .of a new creation of the world by man is—as yet—almost completely ruled out for the European mind).

It is clear that rebellion is a last attempt to stand firm in history; it lives by the fact that in the hotchpotch of paganism and Christianity the latter at least contains an element of reminiscence of the acts of God and the corresponding acts of men. Resignation, however, is the actionless answer, a late offshoot of paganisn. It means to 'answer silence with silence'[30]—utterly, dumbly, hopelessly.

But for the teaching of those who are on the brink of atheism in the church, for protection of their spiritual health (or even for the healing of their schizophrenia, which derives from the amalgamation of paganism and Christianity) the thinking of the Old Testament is indispensable.

We give another example of this: the references to the strife, the controversy of YHWH. True, the idea of judgment should really come into consideration first. The fact that YHWH is also the Judge, and is so in all his acts by reason of his nature, his virtues, would in itself include the fact that he is not on the side of the world; his 'wrath' is the majestic example of his rebellion against the powers and dominions, against the chaos, against unrighteousness. But this can all too easily be understood as a figurative expression for a 'principle.' Now, 'Being in act' is also 'being in fellowship,' and this is what kindles the strife, the battle of God. In the cosmic drama of his judgment God the helper fights the battle, the *rib*, the case of the downtrodden *tsaddiq* ('righteous'), the oppressed people. But this means that he is fighting his own *rib* against those who 'rise up against him' in order to topple him from his throne; but in doing this he is fighting against the persecutors of the afflicted. In this battle it becomes apparent that these oppressors are destroying the peace of his covenant, that they are actually his oppressors (cf. Matt. 25 : 40, 'As you did it to one of the least of these my brethren, you did it to me; Acts 9 : 4, '. . . why do you persecute *me*?').

One could almost think that the controversy of YHWH embraces the whole life of the world, so that one would be dealing with an Israelite parallel of the ancient Greek wisdom that 'war is the father of all things.' The opposite is true, however; for the necessity and the passion with which the *rib* is constantly being fought among men originate in an all-controlling motive: it is fought for the sake of the

[30] Alfred de Vigny, quoted in Albert Camus's *The Rebel*, tr. Anthony Bower (London: Hamish Hamilton, 1953), p. 51.

covenant in which life as 'being in fellowship' is preserved from extermination. And it is primarily his faithfulness that makes God such a doer, such a warrior; he acts and strives in order to create a new peace in righteousness and constantly to launch the freedom of the *'aniyim* ('afflicted') against their enemies (*tsarim*; cf. Gen. 13 : 7f.; I Sam. 2 : 1–10, 24 : 9–23; Isa. 50 : 1–9; Ps. 74; Ps. 98).

Thus in this matter of controversy it must be remembered that Being in act includes a Being in fellowship, that the life of God, like the life of man, is designed for relationship, meeting, and encounter. Therefore there is no partiality in God's action; therefore the controversy is waged equally, if not even more vigorously, against the people, (*'am*), because of the privilege of election—and it is waged in deeds, in the history in which nature merely participates as a spectator. Listen to the language of the prophet Micah (6 : 1–3):

> Hear what HE says,
> 'Arise, declare the controversy before the mountains,
> that the hills may hear your voice.'
> Hear, you mountains, HIS *controversy*,
> and you primal ones, foundations of the earth;
> for HE has a controversy with his people,
> he contends with Israel.
> —My people, what have I *done* to you?
> And what have I refused you?[31]
> Answer me!

In his deeds God distinguishes himself *in* the world *from* the world. In his deeds his perfections are manifest, in them his nature shines forth as it is. But how shall we distinguish the deeds of God from other events? By listening to the Word! What we mean is the Word that contains power, if you will, the magical, evocative Word, at least the dynamic, effectual Word, the Word that does not return empty (Isa. 55 : 11).[32] True, this Word is the prerogative of YHWH, as when he 'calls the stars by name,' makes decisions with his 'deed-word' and

---

[31] Luther's translation: '. . . *und womit habe ich dich beleidigt*' ('in what have I injured you?'). [Here as throughout, I have followed the Revised Standard Version as far as practicable, but have translated the author's version literally, including capitalization and italics for emphasis. The author most frequently cites Buber's translation, but he does not always indicate this.—Tr.]

[32] Cf. Gerhard von Rad, *Theologie des Alten Testaments*, II (1960), pp. 98ff.; Thorleif Boman, *Hebrew Thought Compared With Greek*, p. 58.

'word-deed,' establishes covenants, creates anew; but the prophetic word is joined to it as is a satellite to its planet. And just as every Word of God is independent and unique and cannot be placed in one category or relegated to one sphere, so the word of his servants always stands by itself. And it is precisely in this independence (in which at the outset we must leave it and not immediately look to see whether it has any cross-connections with other utterances and whether it discloses a general meaning-content) that the prophetic word shares the momentousness of the Word of God.

If we were to say that the prophetic word accompanies and illuminates the history, this would be to jump to a hasty conclusion; the continuity of history is hidden, the contingency is manifest—or better, there is no history at all in the ordinary sense in which we use the term. But then how are the acts of God to be remembered? In a uniquely appropriate kind of narration in which a special way of remembering is actualized. The narration is again Word, but in a derivative sense, a completely human word, not the 'act-word' of God himself, not prophetic utterance, which is raised to the level of functional identification with the Word of God, but rather the *Torah*, the instruction, which receives its light from the original acts of YHWH in order to present the contingent events in the continuum of the tradition, the memory, in the permanency of the teaching.

It must be understood that the narrative, just as it is, is implicitly teaching. We are not to seek for something behind it, we are not to hang a moral on it. We need not look for the original experiences of the persons involved in the story. What pity it is that we have been so long accustomed and are still inclined to think of the narrative as a mere vestment of some higher content! And what a pity that later Judaism thought of it as an illustration of the Law and extended this conception to the whole of the Scriptures! But Psalm 78, for example, announces that it will present parables and dark sayings—and then presents no Law or *chokmah* at all, but rather enumerates the glorious deeds, the wonders of God's guidance:

> Listen, my people, to my teaching,
> incline your ear to the words of my mouth.
> I will open my mouth in a parable,
> Dark sayings gush forth from of old.

What we have heard, that we may know,
and our fathers told,
we do not hide from their sons
in a late generation,
telling HIS praises,
his victorious power and his wonders
which he performed.

THE NARRATIVE

Israel thought of the creation as being the first act of holy history.[33]
He who lives in it must tell about it. He must pass over from the naïveté
of merely observing to the still deeper childlikeness of telling a story.
For later generations than ours it will be almost incomprehensible that
academic scholarship was capable of reducing the sacral narrative (not
to speak of the preaching of the narrative and to say nothing of the
Christian preaching of the narrative) to little stories which mean
nothing whatsoever to us in our existence, which affect us less than the
Greek or Teutonic myths and contain less wisdom than the Grimms'
fairy tales. And even stranger will it be to those of a later generation
(in so far as they again become conscious of their task as interpreters
and witnesses) that the preachers allowed themselves to be cowed by
this attitude. But already we are in the midst of a general awakening
from this hypnosis and lethargy, which was a consequence of the habit of
reducing the word-structure to its elements and tracing these back to
their origin.[34] We have now discovered that the narrative as such is
teaching and that the teaching comes *anōthen* ('from above') from the
order of divine truth. We are gradually being freed from the delusion,
inherited from the nineteenth century, that (a) the narrative is 'only

---

[33] Cf. O. Procksch, *Die Genesis*; W. Zimmerli, *1 Mose 1–11*.
[34] Cf. S. F. H. J. Berkelbach van der Sprenkel in *Handboek voor de Prediking*, I (1948),
p. 37: 'What has happened with the Old Testament is like what happens when a man
obsessed by historical interest tears an old building apart piece by piece until he is able
to visualize each stone back in the quarry and the timbers as trees in the forest. Such
knowledge may have increased our knowledge of wood and stones; what we are
concerned with is the building, its style and its purpose.' This is, of course, somewhat
sharply expressed, but it does convey rather strikingly what preaching and instruction
have missed in the scientific treatment of the Old Testament data.

a story' and (b) that the teaching can be summed up in a few main ideas. It has dawned upon us that both orthodoxy and liberalism have strangulated the dimension of the Word in order to understand the words pseudohistorically, pseudologically, and pseudoethically. The 'historical,' measured by the standard of the Word, does not get at the history (*Geschichte*); the 'logical,' measured by the standard of the Word, does not extend to the truth; the 'ethical,' measured by the standard of the Word, remains beneath the level of the Commandment; and the 'religious' obscures the Word, as what has been said about 'Being in act' has demonstrated to us. It is the acts of God that count. They need to be narrated.

This other dimension is indicated by the form of the narrative. We are thrown off the track when we interpret the narrative as a myth which has formed around a 'historical' kernel, the livery of a universal truth, an illustration of an admonition.[35] The event, the truth, the Commandment are not to be enucleated from the time process in such a way that we recover rational or superrational data while the narratives remain as empty shells. The time pattern of the narrative always asserts itself in the quality and direction of the divine action and Commandment. We all have in our blood the religious notion of an eternal content in an accidental form; and it also seems to relieve us of many intellectual difficulties and emotional impediments. Nevertheless, such a reduction from the concrete to the abstract, from the accidental to the general, dare not be applied here. How are the Name and the acts of God related to each other (we have met this question before)? And how can the concrete be an enduring element of the true reality that surrounds us, that 'happens' to us? And how can man preserve and interpret the encounter with these acts of God? Bergson's well-known distinction between *memoire* and *souvenir*, between the image of past facts consciously and intentionally recalled to consciousness and the spontaneous encounter with the atmosphere, the purport, indeed, the 'essence' of past events, which cannot be achieved by any exertion of effort, can probably be helpful to us here. Buber's concept of a 'poetizing memory'[36] certainly contains an important indication. But in the last analysis there are no 'analogies' which would be adequate

---

[35] Cf. Eduard Buess, *Die Geschichte des mythischen Erkennens* (1953), pp. 192ff.
[36] *Dichtende Gedächtnis*, cf. Maurice S. Freedman, *Martin Buber: The Life of Dialogue*, p. 234, where this is spoken of as 'mythicizing memory.'—Tr.]

to make clear what happens when God's action becomes manifest as *ma'aseh*, as his acting in history, when in all history he distinguishes himself from history through what he does, when he is mighty in his 'virtues,' in his love, when he moves the world and thereby and therein and beyond this *is himself*, when his Name rises high like the face of the sun—which shines for all men—and when he makes his dwelling place with the lowly.

When we preach from the Old Testament we must speak of the acts of the Lord. From the very beginning the world was really created as the realm of a real covenant. The quickening *ruach* descended upon the places which he had separated, upon the men whom he had chosen. Should we ever forget what lies in the phrase 'acts of the Lord,' we shall completely forget how to 'preach from the Old Testament'; for there can be no preaching from the Old Testament if we abandon the sphere of the story of God. It is true, of course, that preaching cannot be reduced merely to the telling of how things were, but it is certainly a telling of how things were in such a way that the hearer can understand how things are, how things stand now between God and man in 'ongoing history.' Hence, there is already something dubious about speaking of the righteous*ness*, the mercifulness of God; for actually the 'attributes' of God are really attributes of his action.[37] He causes to be told to us from mouth to mouth and from generation to generation what he has *done* (to this extent it is 'past') and what *he* has done (to this extent it is present). In both cases, however, the act-event is bound up with the narrative, because YHWH precedes us and is still ahead of us. This statement is inalienable; it rules out the kind of false subjectivism which would interpose an anthropology before the acts (which is wrong even philosophically), as is done in the following: 'The being of things depends upon our attitude toward them; things give themselves to us in the way in which we comport ourselves toward them. This also applies with respect to God. God gives himself to us according to our attitude toward him. The way in which we believe we know him is the way in which he is toward us, the way in which we too have him.'[38] No! Fortunately, honestly, in conformity with the

[37] Cf. H. Cohen, *Religion der Vernunft*, pp. 109ff.; K. H. Miskotte, *Bijbelsch ABC* (1941), ch. VII, 'De Daden.'

[38] Heinz Zahrnt, *Es begann mit Jesus von Nazareth* (1960), p. 160. [This passage is omitted from its context on p. 142 of the Eng. tr., *The Historical Jesus* (New York: Harper & Row, 1963).—Tr.]

narrative of his deeds, this is simply ruled out by the Word. And better things are provided for us. Never can our attitude be more than a response; anything that would be more would be less. Response is the only appropriate thing, for the narrative becomes an address which speaks to us here and now.

What we say about God, whatever of praise and prayer is laid upon our lips, is an answer to his glorious and fearful acts. Therefore the preacher is charged with the task of understanding and retelling the story. If there is any chance of getting away from the paltry talk, the dogmatic assertion, and the moral tyrannizing in preaching, it lies in the endeavour to discharge this task with a new reverence and joy. Even those on the fringes of the church will be served by this; and in a world of things, of overconscious reportage and talk, it will be felt as a blessing if the unconscious, the imagination is touched and awakened. This happens through the naming of real things (as opposed to emptying them of content)—the thing that happens, for example, in terse, lapidary, moving poetry. But along with the moving power of poetry there goes a kind of personal address, which modern man hardly knows except in the form of propaganda. This address speaks to him, appeals to his freedom, not to his needs and wants, and he begins to breathe again, for he is hearing that he is really a part of the story. But the narrator and witness is glad that he simply has the privilege of telling it without guile and without any other motive.

If we take up the task in this way, we shall discover that we must be clothed with a new childlikeness. With us Western intellectuals this cannot happen except by way of reflection. But, thank God, it is not true that it is impossible to become more childlike through reflection and thinking things through to the end; the child, the artist, the people live in a direct, plastic, imaginative comprehension of life as having promise, in an unsophisticated acceptance of the wonders in which existence moves. Just as Christ was not a 'smasher' of things (*Kaputtmacher*), as Blumhardt said, so theology dare not carry to extremes the Western tendency to murder the child in us.

Telling the Story

The storyteller—and the preacher is also a storyteller, one might even say, essentially a storyteller—is not concerned to say how things 'actually were,' but rather how they actually took place.[39] For the philosopher this popular conception resolves itself into something else, but this 'something else' is in the last analysis his own existence, that is, his own spontaneously conceived attitude toward reality; indeed, one can say that this 'something else' is his own self-realization in the un-

[39] There are three tested means of convincing ourselves how thoroughly the older Biblical criticism—with its brilliance and quite apart from the unmistakable truth (or better, accuracy) of its content—was a prosy, Philistine affair, determined in every respect by a civilization which had cut itself off from any sense of culture as a totality: (a) the reading of a literary work which, though based upon nothing but 'scientific' data, probes the depths of pagan values themselves to discover their deep human core—I am thinking of Thomas Mann's *Joseph and His Brothers*, with its four parts, (1) The Tales of Jacob, (2) Young Joseph, (3) Joseph in Egypt, (4) Joseph the Provider; (b) an examination of the phenomenology of religion, in so far as it is presented by sympathetic minds—I am thinking of Rohde, Dilthey, Scheler, Otto, Kristensen, van der Leeuw; (c) an encounter with a self-interpretation of Judaism carried out with the assistance of a well-grounded hermeneutics of the Old Testament, such as that of B. Jacob, Martin Buber, and above all Franz Rosenzweig. In these three ways the disintegration to which the Eastern texts have in many respects been subjected by the Western, formalistic intellect (which, indeed, has exercised only a temporary dominion) can be ended and replaced by a better and more congenial kind of understanding, in which the gains won by scientific analyses and deductions dare not be lost. On this general subject see Joachim Wach, *Das Verstehen*, 3 vols. (1926, 1929, 1933). Treasures of wisdom which make all vapid reduction look ridiculous are found in the works of Johann Georg Hamann. In another way they are to be found in a man like G. K. Chesterton, in his *Heretics* (1905), especially the chapter 'Science and the Savages,' and also *The New Jerusalem* (1920) and *The Everlasting Man* (1925). Paul Claudel should also be mentioned in this connection (*Figures et Paraboles*, etc.). We are thinking also of Stefan Zweig's drama *Jeremias*, Franz Werfel's Jeremiah-epic *Hearken Unto the Voice*, and Richard Beer-Hofmann's *Jacob's Dream* and *Der junge David*. The purpose of these references to literature is, naturally, not to advocate an esthetic approach to exegesis; we are talking about preparation for and initiation in the art of narration. And naturally, it is also not our purpose to say that this is to be learned preferably from literary works with biblical themes; the fact is, however, that we become more readily aware of the plasticity and graphic quality of the narration when art is devoted to these materials with which the interpreter and witness is dealing every day. It is urgently necessary to seek for an antidote to the modern reappearance of dryness in the orthodox as well as the 'dialectic' style of preaching (after all kinds of rank growth had been, quite rightly, pruned out). Even a few drops of imagination can work like a tonic. The fact that in many respects the nineteenth-century academic mind, even in the field of the social sciences, failed to recognize the legitimate place of intuition, of the vision and anticipation of a synthesis, has resulted, especially among such sober-minded people as the Dutch, in a dangerous impoverishment. Dry soberness without the counterweight of 'imagination'—which is to be distinguished from any kind of mere caprice—leads to a vulgarity which can hardly be compensated for by later instruction.

moving timelessness of his mind. He is afraid of the *verbum scriptum*, the written Word, and the *ecclesia visibilia*, the visible church, because they are a threat to the 'pure presence and immediacy of experience.' So here we stand in the pulpit, facing people who come from a life which is more and more determined by the concrete and material, and as likely as not our heads are full of terms and concepts which come from an intellectual life that is increasingly split by controversy. The people and the concepts do not meet. Only a few have the gift of giving blood and life to abstract ideas; but we shall not escape the danger by—even formally—striking the attitude that now one is going to talk about God with real power and liveliness, that is, present a really convincing argument.[40]

In our conviction the Bible is essentially a narrative, a story, which we must pass on by retelling it. And in this way it can come about that the story may 'happen'—so to speak, in an 'unbloody repetition'— to those who listen to us. Look!—this is the way God dealt with men back there; but because it is he, will he not also deal with you in the same way? Yes, as soon as you discover who this He is, your telling of the story will begin to run; if you are united with that other life outside and beyond your own, then your own drama of salvation will begin to unfold and show that it is already moving toward its solution—how, you yourself do not know.[41]

To tell a story well means to tell it in such a way that the centre, the

---

[40] Cf. Martin Buber, 'Die Sprache der Botschaft,' in *Die Schrift und ihre Verdeutschung*. p. 56: 'For it would be a fundamental failure to understand the nature of the Bible if one were to assume that it always attaches to the message, in the way that bad parables have a "moral" attached to them.'

[41] Franz Rosenzweig, 'Die Schrift und das Wort,' *Kleinere Schriften*, (1937), pp. 134ff., reminds us that the Scriptures were intended to be read aloud in a narrative prose rhythm and states that the oral word (e.g., in the form of commentary) must not stand alongside of the written word, but rather that the Scripture itself must again be heard as spoken word, not as spoken poetry (which even as spoken word remains self-sufficient within itself) but rather as declarative, 'addressive' prose, nonlyrical, non-magical. Rosenzweig closes with these words: 'Before and beyond it [i.e., poetry] there was prose, and it was nonpoetry; it was non rhythmical, unbound but not disengaged speech, unmeasured but not extravagantly fulsome (*masslos übermässiges*) word. All poetry which has since come into being within the circle of its light is inspired by its prose spirit. *Since that time* in the dark silence that surrounded the beginnings of mankind the door which separates each from every other and all from the Outside and the Beyond *has been broken* and never again will it be altogether closed: the door of the Word.'

beginning, and the end of all things becomes visible; every human life and human endeavour is related to Christ, to this particular Presence of God—and related to him, they are related to the beginning and the end. If among us men no story is worth the trouble of telling if it does not have love at its centre, from which we see at the beginning the mystery of birth and at the end the mystery of death, bleeding, shining, threatening on the horizon, then far less is the Bible story told biblically if the Centre, the Beginning, the End do not clearly appear as parts of the one Presence. For the Presence is act, *actus purus*, which is directed to the future;[42] and we go to church or the church school or to a religious drama to listen to the telling of it, and we keep on going until it speaks to our own life here and now, and again and again—as the story of how life itself, and therefore our life, is judged and saved. 'God is present, and if he acts through messengers, they are not mere letter carriers who bring news of something that happened the day before yesterday and may perhaps already have been rendered obsolete by events; rather God is acting and speaking directly through them in this moment of *their* lives.'[43]

Thereon depends the power of *aletheia*; for truth is not located anywhere, truth happens, it comes to us, involves us in its process. Truth in its Old Testament meaning is neither a pure object of 'knowledge' nor a pure encounter with 'being'; truth is the act of God through which unfathomable human existence is drawn into the history which is at once his history and ours. Our past is his, his future is ours. His hand was in our past, our future is participation in his ultimate and penultimate acts.

Thence comes the rich colour of Sunday, of the way to church, of the light that lightens our 'going up,' and the eager expectation that says: This is the day of salvation, of understanding, of coming back to the truth.

[42] O. Noordmans, *Herschepping* (1934), pp. 83f.: 'The creation has cosmic proportions; but we do not in pagan fashion carry the cosmic in the direction of the colossal, but rather toward the human dimension, toward the side of history. We do not fight shy of history; the Christian concept of God is not afraid of confinement; Jesus' ministry on earth is counted as extending over three years. Compared with the incarnations of the Buddha this is nothing at all. . . . Augustine rejected the idea of cosmic periods and opposed to it the "once-for-allness" of history. If we think of creation too much as a system of orders, this suggests repetition. Creation can be thought of in good critical terms only as we keep our eye on history. Thus "history with God" goes with history.'
[43] Franz Rosenzweig, 'Die Schrift und das Wort,' p. 136.

Warum ist Wahrheit fern und weit,
Birgt sich hinab in tiefste Gründe?
Niemand versteht zur rechten Zeit!
Wenn man zur rechten Zeit verstünde,
So wäre Wahrheit nah und breit
Und wäre lieblich und gelinde.

(Why is truth so far away,
hiding itself in the deepest depths?
Nobody understands at the right time!
If we understood at the right time,
then truth would be near
and kind and gentle).[44]

At the right time! Now is the acceptable time, now is the day of salvation. No religion can be transmitted by narration; but faith lives, today as always, by the telling of that which the Lord did then and in such and such a way on earth. And he himself, he who now speaks to me, is with us on earth. His Name is in the sanctuary, and it is glorious above the whole world.

The telling carries the truth on. Even the Law, even the revelation that came there and then, is a factor in the story of God which is now unfolding. 'Narrative philosophy' therefore often bewilders the systematician; sometimes the storyteller seems to him to be an artist, an actor, a lively juggler, an enthusiast, sometimes a one-sided bigot, then again a refined bungler, often a muddlehead and alarmist. All this is inaccessible to dogmatics, unless it is itself transposed into a way of thinking which is open to the acts of God, to the open arena of his benefactions and judgments. It then becomes apparent that right here is where objectivity and order prevail, the objectivity and order which lie in the course of the divine narrative itself.

We may believe that narrative preaching remains the most appropriate vehicle for the witnessing of the Name in our day. Much that generally annoys the systematician remains indispensable if one is to do even partial justice to the suprareligious character of preaching. So again and again it depends—humanly, instrumentally speaking—on the depth, the contours, the perspective, the transparency which are caught and evoked by the so much despised 'artist.'

[44] Goethe, *West-östlicher Divan, Hikmet Nameh (Buch der Sprüche)*.

I am thinking of the great example of the eminently graphic sermons of John Donne (preached between 1619 and 1629). In Holland, H. W. Creutzberg and H. J. de Groot in an earlier generation, and A. van Selms and M. A. Beek in more recent times have given us magnificent, refreshing examples of what 'ordinary' storytelling can do—though I must admit that such storytelling if it is to remain pure, as it does in the case of the men mentioned above, (quite properly) presupposes some unspoken theological insights, which are often sadly lacking in popular tellers of the Bible story.

Moreover, doctrine is already inherent in the form of the Biblical narrative itself. This becomes evident in the point of the story, the key words, the trend of the events, the accents and idioms, and above all in a 'dialogical element which stretches the narrative upon a framework of question and answer, dictum and counterdictum, statement and added statement.'[45]

It requires no further demonstration that what has been said applies especially to the preaching of and instruction from the Old Testament. It would require too much space at this point to show that narration can in itself be pure exegesis in the full sense and thus can help us to perceive that we are being introduced into the uninterpreted world of living, ongoing time.

THE OPEN FUTURE

The narrative form as an internal law which encompasses the other forms of proclamation presupposes a definite understanding of time, which is characterized by a sense of the pulsating rhythm of phenomena in all the wealth of their present manifestation. The Old Testament conceives of time with its points, extensions, and intervals, as a qualitative magnitude; one can even say that time is identical with its content. It does not speak of time in general as a quantitative space and framework of events. It has no word for this at all. We hear only of 'days' and special festival seasons, of the 'day of Yahweh' and 'those days.' Everything has its time and fills it with something—light and darkness, joy and sorrow. Especially the days which 'Yahweh has made' (Ps. 118 : 24), the feasts in which his saving acts are represented,

[45] Franz Rosenzweig, 'Das Formgeheimnis der biblischen Erzählungen,' *Kleinere Schriften* (1937), p. 139.

as it were, in a contraction of the times, and the congregation celebrates the days of the deeds of YHWH as if it were living in contemporaneity with those deeds.[46] But now if we see that the Creation is
retrospectively understood as being the prelude to the acts of God,
then we must immediately see that it contains the sign and pledge of an
open future. We cannot go into a detailed characterization of the com-
plexity of this understanding of time, but from what has been said it
should already be clear that it furnishes a rich yield for the practice of
preaching.

The goal of the sacral narrative, this spoken prose, this contemporiz-
ing of the acts of God, is to point to the consummation. All time,
everything that happens, keeps reaching out for that goal. It is the
newborn child, rather than the dead man who is gathered to his
fathers, that bears witness to what Israel may still expect. Defeat and
victory, crop failure and harvest are signs of the time that moves on to
its appointed end. The utterances of prophecy, whether they come from
the mouth of Moses or Balaam, point the way to the horizon. The
feasts of enthronement, New Year, royal marriage, the celebrations of
royal victories and the dividing of the spoils proclaim the theocratic
order for the land and promise that righteousness will reign on earth.
Everything strains toward this goal.[47]

In this respect the royal psalms (e.g., Pss. 2, 21, 45, 72, 110) occupy
a central place in the Old Testament. The ancient Oriental style of
court ceremonial which plays a part in these psalms cannot conceal
their real intent. Signs which elsewhere accompany only the manifestation of God appear sooner or later in the context of Messianic
events (Isa. 10 : 16f., 29 : 6, 30 : 27ff.) and the Messianic figure (Pss.
72 : 9, 110 : 1, 72 : 3, 16f.). The goal is far off and yet very near. The
signs all point to the future—no, into the future.

A people, a country, a dynasty, a man are, as it were, appointed to be
the bridge of continuity over which the contingent acts of God advance
toward the consummation. Therefore they are sanctified, therefore they
are 'visited'—punished but not cast off, humbled but not destroyed
(Amos, Hosea). They are already caught up in a great, high sequence

[46] Thorleif Boman, *Hebrew Thought Compared With Greek*, pp. 193ff.; J. Hempel, *Altes
Testament und Geschichte*, pp. 29f.; Gerhard von Rad, *Theologie des Alten Testaments*,
II, pp. 117ff.
[47] W. Eichrodt, *Theology of the Old Testament*, I, tr. J. A. Baker (Philadelphia: Westminster Press, 1961), pp. 476ff.

of events, living in hope. Is this sequence of events 'within history' or 'outside of history'? It is eschatological (*endgeschichtlich*), it is the act which is heralded in all the acts of God.

Then there are the passages that speak of a marriage, a breach of faith and a new betrothal; and the later, new beginning of life is 'better' than the original beginning of life, because its newness is that of a new time, the time of the intervention of the Prince of salvation and Helper (Isa. 50 : 4ff.; Zech. 11 : 4f., 13 : 7ff.). The stereotyped apocalyptic images of the future, which flourished in the popular piety and arose under the influence of alien conceptions, did not play so large a role that they could not be purged and toned down, as they are in the post-exilic hymns (Pss. 93, 96, 97, 99), until they were restored to the level of the 'spoken prose' of the narrative. The Parsistic dualism is incorporated and integrated into the affirmation of an open future.

God, as *God*, is essentially manifest in his coming. His coming is already present in his action upon the whole earth and upon all peoples. In the course of history (and in reflection upon history) we do not see a process of spiritualization taking place; the concrete places, times, figures become paradigms, signs, pledges, and seals of the reality of the last things, which will cover the earth in judgment and blessing. The consummation of the kingdom of God is not to be understood as a 'fundamental idea' which must be divested of temporal, ethnic, national, cultic conceptions; these are rather abiding enigmas and stigmas, riddles and pledges, which assure the faith of the community of the earthly reality of the consummation. Therefore the expectation starts out with historical life. Therefore the fulfilment is guaranteed in the ancient exodus, in the exile and the ending of the exile. As Hempel says, 'In the midst of threat, promise, fear and yearning, Israel faces the last time as a future time.' The sovereignty of YHWH will impress itself more and more upon life that has grown perverse, will set its stamp upon the flesh. The expectation of the Last Things does not rob the course of history of its content and importance, but rather gives it eternal weight—not, of course, so far as its inherent worth is concerned, but rather with respect to the quality which is bestowed upon it by God's action in time and brought to light for the people today.

'*YHWH beqirbenu*,' the Lord in our midst! It is no wonder that we cannot find a satisfactory formula for the relationship between God and the Messiah, the people and the 'remnant,' between God's kingdom and the kingdom of the Messiah (cf. above all Dan. 7),[48] the 'apocalyptic' and the 'eschatological.' Does the reason for this lie in our faculty of perception or in the discordancy of earthly things? Is it not rather the obverse side of this present time in which the Story and our life story are enacted? What is the height of this present time, this 'today'—the immeasurable remoteness of transcendence? What is the depth of our present time, our 'today'—the staggering encounter with our unknown self and the ensuing entrance of silence? The heights and the depths of our 'today' lie in this *beqirbenu*! In it the time of the end is prefigured, heralded, and (in faith) received.

When we preach from the Old Testament, we shall have to remember—otherwise there will not be the right kind of elevation and strict objectivity which must go hand in hand in the pulpit and our sermon preparation—that the 'telling of the story' must be steeped in the streams of light which flow over the earth from the Beyond, from the Distant which keeps coming closer to us and pressing in upon us, remembering at the same time that the Beyond cannot be known if it is not 'Here.'

And who will know it? Who will be touched by it? Will it not be the poor in spirit, the oppressed, the despairing, those who are appalled by the chaos within them and around them? Will it not be those who are utterly disappointed with the evil fruits of the times? Will it not be those 'ungenuine' nihilists who are so genuine? Will it not be the people for whom, as Kafka says, 'the music has broken off at the root of things'? '*YHWH beqirbenu*'! May this never remain a mere spiritual concept, a pious feeling! Let it be lifted above the ambivalent notion which we call our profoundest experience and become concrete for faith! Before it can be said to us 'You are not far from the kingdom of God,' we must be told that 'the kingdom of God is at hand.' Never has there been faith on earth without 'near-expectation,' and never has 'near-expectation' affected men's hearts unless our life today has spoken of the good that is near, the already imparted salvation, the time of God that prevails here and now.

The kingdom of God will one day reveal that life is good now, that it is very good, that it has always worn the hidden glory of the divine *chokmah*. What one day will be manifest to all is now present for the con-

[48] Gerhard von Rad. *Theologisches Wörterbuch zum Neuen Testament*, I, p. 569, on the term *malkuth*.

gregation in him whom it calls its Lord and its God. The knowledge of
God will one day be so deep and full that it can be compared with
seeing him 'face to face.' But now, in our town, in the hearts of the
simple, and in the simple unfolding of the story of God which sounds
forth from the pulpit, the Holy Spirit is creating a foretaste of that
perfect knowledge, in so far as our limited knowledge is already inwardly understood to be a knowledge of that which 'surpasses knowledge' (cf. Eph. 3 : 18f.).

One day it will be said, 'It is done!'—but our knowing that this is
so, sets us and the history of our own time under the light of the promise. And the contours of that promise are to be found in the foretokens of fulfilment which surround men as the people of God on every
side. And we unriddle the meaning of those signs by listening anew to
the speech of the original promises in the so-called Old Testament.
We refresh ourselves with the good that we are allowed to see in the
'lifting up of his countenance upon us' as we sing of it in the church
and in the world, singing songs that imitate the Psalms and doing
works that imitate the deeds and the ordinances of the Torah. We
discern something of the meaning of today and we are refreshed by the
good as we grow in the knowledge that not one jot or tittle of the
'primitiveness' of the Old Testament has been invalidated. Here the
pagan becomes a 'man of God'; here, through the revelation, the
endless cycle of things becomes the history of God; the emptiness of the
infinite (or closed) universe becomes the space of time into which the
Kingdom enters; the chaos is de-demonized; the struggle of all against
all ceases even now to be the mark of human life; the earth becomes for
us an Eden, even though we labour for our bread in the sweat of our
brow. 'Salvation is at hand,' says Psalm 85:

Surely his salvation is at hand for those who fear him,
    that the light of glory may dwell in our land.
Mercy and faithfulness meet each other;
    righteousness and peace kiss each other.
Faithfulness springs up from the earth,
    and righteousness looks down from heaven.
The Lord will also give us the good,
    and our land will yield its increase.
Righteousness will go before him,
    and guide his footsteps on the way.

The fulfilment of the law, i.e., the whole testimony of the Old Testament, is not given its full right in witness and interpretation until it is understood as the realization (both of the promise and the command) which occurred in the coming of Christ. Without this there is no horizon, but only a vanishing-point. By looking at the 'body' which has appeared, we learn to understand the direction in which the 'shadow' (to use the imagery of the Epistle to the Hebrews) points. By looking at the completed work of the Messiah, we see the meaning of the prototypes. And yet it is not the New Testament which is the realization (how could it be, in words?); it is rather the revelation itself which is the realization, the Word that became flesh, the eternal act, the eternal time of grace, through which God in his eternal counsel reconciled us to himself.

As Word, as witness, as summons, as consolation and promise, the Old Testament is not farther away from revelation than the New; they both have the same function as bearers of authority and as helpers. But as 'narrative philosophy' the Old Testament possesses a peculiar power of making things concrete as it sets forth the movement of time toward the open future. And yet the power and validity of the appearance of the Messiah is not 'unambiguously' and 'incontrovertibly' discernible.

So too it must now be said concerning the terms *malkuth* and *basileia* that the first is not farther away from the Last Things than the second. Proclamation learns from both, and in the copious detail, the richer articulation, of the Old Testament, preaching has an immediate inducement to place God's action in closer, more concrete and living relationship to the events of the day and to direct attention to the way of the people of God, to the saving Presence of God in the great forms of the common life in nation, state, and society, in marriage and friendship, in labour, and culture, in morals and law, in dream and tragedy, in visions of hope and their futility.

As the narrative proceeds, we note that everything in it occurs and is carried along within designated time; for the primal given facts of life, if they are touched by God, will never fall into the total decay which the nihilist smells everywhere and tries to impose on others. What has been broken asunder by man's thinking is therefore not yet broken; what seems empty to man's feeling remains a living impulse in the ongoing course of the Anointed.

Het wil niet, als geheel een vorige eeuw
puinhopen zien en zingen van mooi weer.

.   .   .   .

want nimmer is, wat ook, ooit puin geweest,
Een eerste steen ligt nauwelijks terneer.
Een woord vernieuwt de stilte, die het breekt,
Al wat geschiedt, geschiedt nog voor het eerst.
Geprezen! Noach bouwt, maar geen ark meer,
En Jona preekt, maar niet te Nineve.

(It[49] does not propose, as a whole past century did,
to look at ruins and sing about fine weather. . . .
For whatever existed, it was never a ruin,
The first stone had hardly been laid.
Every word renews the silence which it breaks;
everything that happens still happens for the first time.
Praise God! Noah is still building, but no longer an ark.
And Jonah is still preaching, but not in Nineveh).

We are exasperated by the endless round of torments and the vain dreams of life; we are the antireligious ones when we turn away from humility and patience. These things are serious, of course; but there is a patience of God that grows out of the unshakable firmness of his Kingdom. And it is precisely in this patience, through which human life is spared, ordered, and judged, that the God of Israel shows his mighty power. Let anybody who wants to proclaim the Kingdom of God point to the signs of this patience, which is the seal of true omnipotence![50] How long is the church going to go on being bowed down

[49] That is, this song. From the beginning of the poem 'Awater' by Martinus Nijhoff.
[50] Karl Barth, *Church Dogmatics*, Vol. II, pt. 1, pp. 410f: 'It is to be noted that God is not more powerful in his action than in his forbearance from action. Indeed, there is no antithesis here: God's forbearance is only a specific form of his always powerful doing and being. God is therefore no less effective in his patience than in his grace and mercy, than in his holy and just wrath which includes his grace and mercy. God does not repent when he forbears to act, but it is also—and properly understood, precisely—the unrepentant outbreaking of his whole divine glory that he is patient in his grace and mercy and therefore *patient* also in his holy and righteous wrath.' *Makrothumia* must not be connected with the idea of hesitation, weakness, indulgence; rather 'the term implies that God's will is great and strong and relentless and victorious. . . . This waiting, by which God grants us liberty, is itself and as such to be understood as a plus, not a minus of God's freedom, power, and activity. It too is to be understood as a specific form of the divine majesty—exactly like his mercy.'

with the burden of a fundamentally mistaken conception of the power, the sovereignty, the omnipotence of God? Here in the unfolding of the Old Testament story as the proclamation of God's times and the open future, as signs of the past history of the Kingdom of God (and of the Kingdom itself in the sense of the creative dominion of Patience) is an opportunity to proclaim, as 'in new tongues,' the goodness of God, the real depth of every livelong day, the perspective in which we see every estate in which man is placed in order to act, as husband or wife, father or mother, servant of the church or servant of the public, worker or thinker, pioneer or follower. Just as Israel in the subsequent course of the story did not regard what it was then allowed by God to possess as being primarily a hindrance to the coming of the *malkuth* (the kingdom), but rather as an earnest, a pledge of its coming, so the real and still remaining gifts of today, if we see them in the light of the coming of the Lord, can be the foretokens of a victory over the world through the God who is the beginning and the end of time, the God who has entered into our midst. Into our midst—but here again *pars pro toto* applies.

'Say among the nations, "The Lord reigns! *The world too will be established*, it shall never be moved.". . . For he comes, for he comes to judge the earth. He will judge the world with righteousness, and the peoples with his truth.' (Ps. 96 : 10, 13).

THE NAMES OF GOD

The narrative reflects the ways of God, the meeting of God and man, the turnings of God and Israel to and away from each other within the covenant. The author of the covenant is also the author of the singular history which is contained in the simple story, in the metatragical narrative. It would not be correct, however, to go on automatically and monotonously calling this author 'God.' The fact is that it is always a matter of the acts of YHWH, who is in the midst of his people, protecting, guiding, and ruling them. To this extent the unutterable Name is sufficient to indicate the Subject of this nameless saving action.

The Name expresses everything; just as surely as the Name is not an empty thing, so surely the naming, the pleading, the praising of that

Name and the calling upon it will not be in vain (Exod. 20 : 24, 20 : 7; Prov. 18 : 10; Zech. 14 : 9; Ps. 86 : 11; Isa. 26 : 8, 13). But just as it is dangerous in Christian preaching always to speak about God without any qualifications, about God *tout court*, without conveying the full charge of power and light that stream from the Name, so Israel too was in danger of using the Name without nuance and without distinction. The Old Testament itself, replete as it is with great spiritual figures of speech derived from its historical origin, can be a great help in avoiding such an isolation of the term God; after all, the Old Testament itself, by virtue of its provenance, quite artlessly uses various names by which the One and Only is legitimately called in the congregation and in the world.

The relationship of these various names to 'the Name,' the development of the Name also indicates that the Name has been enriched and intensified.[51]

Apart from the name YHWH itself there is hardly anything which is of such great importance for interpretation as the explication and application of the appellations used for God. It ought not to be possible that all the names and words for God should amount to about the same thing in the ear of the congregation. If only we keep in mind that these appellations, *Elohim, El Shaddai, Yahweh Tseba'oth*, and the others, are a salutary preventive against seemingly recognizing the revelation and then taking this once-given revelation and making it reversible, so that one could say, for example, 'love is God,' just as well as one says 'God is love.' That this is impossible, that this completely destroys the light and the power of the proclamation—this is precisely what is stated in the (rightly understood) phrase, *ehyeh asher ehyeh*, 'I will be (with you), as I shall be (with you).' But this is again very distinctly confirmed by the addition of these accompanying names, this added garland of names which crown the Name.

1. We have already referred to the key saying: YHWH is *Elohim*! This is not reversible. The proper name YHWH defines the (seemingly) more general name, which actually is rather to be regarded as an epithet ('Know that the Lord is the Godhead,' Ps. 100 : 3). The name-

---

[51] Here reference should be made to A. Dillmann, *Theologie des Alten Testaments*, p. 210; W. Eichrodt, *Theology of the Old Testament*, I, 178ff.; M. Buber, *Königtum Gottes* 2nd edn. (1962), pp. 89ff., but also to A. Kuyper, *Dictaten Dogmatiek*, I, 224ff., and Johann Tobias Beck, *Vorlesungen über christliche Glaubenslehre*, II, pp. 14ff.

less Name is understood through the acts which occur and will continue to occur in the carrying and fulfilling of the covenant. Thus 'the Almighty' is an epithet which is to be understood on the basis of the proper name YHWH. The 'primitiveness' bars the way to any ontologizing.

'Omnipotence' is not something that can be experienced or thought, conjectured or revered—it can be known and confessed as the power of this God, this particular God who becomes man, who unites himself with humanity. The *melek*, the one who leads the way, the leader of the procession, the king, is the author of a covenant for the realization of the theocracy. Not every authority that relies on the general idea of 'God' as a guarantor of order is to be recognized as the authority of the royal covenant; 'God Almighty' is usually an idol. But what are we talking about! The term 'the Almighty' never appears in the whole of the Old Testament as a name; it occurs only as an attribute! But even this is to be qualified, for in the liturgical formulas which laud the virtues of God (Exod. 34 : 6f.; Num. 14 : 18; Ps. 103 : 8, etc.) the word 'almighty' is not mentioned.

2. *Yahweh Tseba'oth*, 'the Lord of hosts.' This name, whether it be called upon or proclaimed, conveys the meaning that this special, exceptional revelation is cosmic in scope; angels, stars, and contending armies are all embraced in this name in order to show that God, when he makes history through his awe-inspiring presence, is turning the universe upon its axis. In the performance of his acts he is never alone, but always surrounded by seraphim and cherubim, thrones and powers, or in lower spheres by messengers and judges, warriors and anointed ones. They are all in the service of a world-historical purpose in which the meaning of the silent world is being manifested (Judg. 6 : 34; Isa. 45 : 1; Ps. 24; Ps. 46).

3. *El Shaddai*, God of the mountain, the mountain of the gods, the mountain of the universe. This is usually translated as 'God Almighty.' But this name certainly does not signify an abstract power, nor the ruling power of the universe (a 'monotheistic' godhead). It refers to a particular power, the power, for example, which brings forth from dead loins and a barren womb the wonderful birth of Isaac. And so through this appellative, one side of the one Name is disclosed, namely, that he exercises power over death, foils fatality, marches toward the future, performs wonders, calls the miracle (*das Entrückte*, Buber) into being.

It is he 'who gives life to the dead and calls into existence the things that do not exist' (Rom. 4 : 17).

It should be noted that *El Shadday* appears as a code-word for power only in the discussions of the despairing Job with his religious friends. *El Shadday*, far from dwelling in sublime inviolability, was very near to the heart. Even when the Name is buried under the gold of veneration or the dust of custom, a beam of light upon our human experience still shimmers through the (probably) less accurate ordinary translation, because and in so far as this light streams from the whole of the biblical concept of God. We think of the Septuagint translations of *El Shadday*; sometimes it was read as *shedi*, 'my protector-God,' and sometimes the word was divided into *she* and *day* and translated as *theos hikanos*. The Midrashim sometimes appear expressly to concur in this view; then, exceptionally for them, they are practising theological exegesis of the best kind—the kind that breaks through the grammar in order to make it possible to preach more practically and comfort more pastorally. On Genesis 17 : 1, for example, we read: 'I am he who said to my world, "Enough"; if I had not said "Enough" to heaven and earth, they would still today be developing into the unbounded. . . . I am he before whose divinity the world and its fullness are not sufficient; but for you it is enough that I am your protector, and not for you alone, but it is enough for the world that I am its protector.' The fact is that this is actually in the Old Testament, not in a particular passage, but it is implicit everywhere. It is not exclusively owing to a name that this outreaching consolation and peace is imparted to Israel and the seventy nations whenever the sabbath—the seal that is stamped upon time, the sign that creation has been completed and brought to its bounds and its rest—comes to meet us with a smile, from every being in heaven and on earth. This is the meaning of *El Shadday*, and it is quite the opposite of that Medusa-stare that emanates from abstract 'omnipotence.'

4. The 'attributes' are charged in a way that almost makes them names, appellations. And actually, in order to get away from the deadly atmosphere of so much speculative assertion and equally speculative defence, it may be well to remember that liturgically all these 'attributes' can be used vocatively. The terms that are used in the theophany in Exodus 34 : 6f. as typical characteristics of Yahweh's perfection are to be understood as marks of his love, i.e., his free good pleasure in that

which has its being from him, to him, and through him in creaturely freedom: grace and faithfulness, righteousness and mercy, retribution and forgiveness. They take precedence over and completely determine the seemingly more perfect, more 'divine' attributes, such as omnipotence, omnipresence, and omniscience. Isolated and hypostatized, these attributes would make Yahweh too a silent God among the silent gods. Here everything depends on the order and the sequence, on the right kind of separation and connection, and also on the exclusion of the pagan elements which are always creeping in. Any instruction that reverses this order is doomed to failure and, if the Spirit does not prevent it, merely causes harm. Here is an arcanum of holy doctrine that must be guarded, just because at the present time it seeks to be as exoteric as possible.

When we start from the infinity of God, we destroy the knowledge of God's special Name, for then right from the start we destroy the decisive character of the encounters of God and end up in a polyinterpretability that is precisely characteristic of that which is silent.

When we start from the omnipotence of God, we destroy the knowledge of God's Name, for then we can find no place for the deeds, the special acts from which alone the true knowledge of God can come. He who says 'The Almighty is merciful' is merely stating a theory; he who proclaims 'The Lord, the Merciful, *he* is Almighty' is imparting super-religious consolation and excellent wisdom.

When we start with the equivalence of the so-called 'communicable' attributes, e.g., righteousness and mercy, we empty of content the manifestation of the Messiah and his saving work, in which mercy is given precedence over judgment and in which grace has proved itself to be far mightier (Rom. 5 : 15, 20).

This kind of misrepresentation of the Message is still a burden upon the man of our time. He is simply bewildered by the unreliability and characterlessness of God, for it is right here that the feeling of God's absence has its origin. And what about those in the church? How many there are who never learn to love God, who never get beyond a cool respect; how many there are who never learn to praise God and never give him more than a loyal salute! Is it not, among other things, a wrong kind of preaching that causes so much religiosity to run wild and then capsize into nihilism? The true infinity is the infinity of this

God with these attributes, virtues, perfections (Pss. 86 : 5f., 103 : 8ff., 145 : 8ff.). The true omnipotence is the power that brings forth the Messianic kingdom despite the 'unending' opposition of the separated world. The true omnipresence is the way in which the Lord knows his own, is near to them, saves, judges, uplifts, honours, crowns them (Pss. 1 : 6, 139 : 14ff., 7 : 10; Jer. 17 : 9f.; I Kings 8 : 39; Deut. 32 : 11; Jer. 20 : 12; Isa. 61 : 10).

5. Finally, we dare not forget the frequent use of the name *Yahweh Elohim*. What shall we call it, a double name or a proper *cum* functional name? This name appears for the first time in the redaction of the Old Testament handed down to us in Genesis 2, the middle part of the creation account. It implies that the creation of the world is ascribed to YHWH retrospectively, although he is really primarily and in the truest sense the creator and liberator of the holy people and the giver and protector of a particular land. The concept is colossal, and if we should ever lose it, we would lose a characteristic mark of faith as lives and moves in its boldest form. 'What is here recorded as creation history is in the last resort incomprehensible if we do not see that the form of this *covenant* is already prepared and outlined here, characterizing both the totality and the individual constituents of the "pre-historical" origination described. Of course the writer fabulizes, yet not accidentally, arbitrarily, or at random. He does so with a definite intention and according to the definite law of a divination and imagination *stimulated, but also regulated* by the revelation given to Israel. Hence he has neither the time nor the desire to be occupied with the origination of the world and man in general, but with that of the world and man whose existence will receive its meaning in the execution of God's covenant. Already, then, in this origination as God's creation he can seek and find not merely the intention of a future covenant but its *foundation* and *lineaments*.'[52]

It is probable that this combination of the special Name with a general name in the liturgy found its way into individual prophets and then, afterwards through the redactor, into important parts of the traditional material. Whatever we think of the psychic and cultic origin of it, we are here confronted face to face with the meaning of the

[52] Karl Barth, *Church Dogmatics*, Vol. III, pt. 1, p. 267 (italics are Miskotte's). Cf. H. Rosin, *The Translation of the Divine Names and the Missionary Calling of the Church*; A. Bertholet, *Götterspaltung und Göttervereinigung*, pp. 16ff.

Old Testament; here, as it were, the 'cosmic' meaning of the strange phenomena of God's being 'groundless—and yet in the midst of things' becomes manifest.

THE POWERS

In the Old Testament the 'powers' have the function which we refer to when we use such words as the Absurd, Chaos, Nothingness. Unlike the gods, they have no clear outlines. They achieve nothing but their own exhaustion, but their exhaustion never kills them. The grave, death, and desire never say, 'Enough' (cf. Prov. 30 : 16). Perhaps at no other point does the testimony of the Old Testament come so close to us as it does here. And right here even the rationalist in us will have retained some feeling for the significance of primitive speech. It is actuated by the most elemental experience of life. But it should be noted that when we speak of the powers in the sense of the Old Testament we are not speaking of the essence of life. No, the gripping thing is precisely the fact that what is referred to here is a margin, a remainder, and that this is taken so seriously. The Old Testament writers did not conceive of death, chaos, and decay metaphorically, even when it is clearly a matter of death in the much broader sense which includes sickness, madness, infirmity, age, and decay. On the other hand, recuperation, health, strength, youth, flowering are equally characteristic aspects of the one land of life or land of the living. But the Name of God, in which life is grounded, spiritually and materially, in its duration and depth, is constantly finding a limit being put upon its purposes. Then the Old Testament raises its laments over death in this or that form and utters its prayers to be saved from this or that way of being dead or of dying. And the same is true of what we would call chaos and the absurd: the power and the experiencing of the power are always so fused together in one experience that the dread and the aversion themselves are a part of that in which the power of the 'power' consists. It is still an ocean that surrounds our life like a girdle of dark experience, and which is illuminated in the Messiah. What this illumination really can mean can be understood only by one who knows this darkness. Such knowledge can be gained from the Old Testament.

1. On the margin of creation dwell the powers, who seem to be more than creatures and yet are not gods; in the midst of creation, in the human heart, whatever creaturely peace we still have left is threatened by these powers.

'The most common indication of this disturbance of creation is anxiety, an undefined uneasiness which youth knows even better than adults. The anxieties of the child have often been described, but they are not really imaginary at all. It is a feeling about the void, a terror of the great dark, associated with, but preceded by, the feeling of guilt. One might call it a *cosmic dizziness*, a fear of existing without God. Existence itself seems to be a fault that has to be paid for with non-existence.'[53]

The Old Testament speaks of this, and we must be familiar with this environment of the testimony of expectation in order to be able to preach nonreligiously (in line with Bonhoeffer's concern) instead of merely asserting what everybody likes to hear asserted. Whenever we speak about the powers without the Word, we are in peril. The depth psychology of Freud leads us into the power sphere of the erotic, Heidegger's philosophy of existence leads us to death; they are related to each other. Cain and Achan, Saul and Ahab move within and fight against the spell of anxiety—fear of something which does not come out of themselves and also is not from God. We are equally familiar with it.

But, measured by the purpose of the Old Testament, this is expressed in too individualistic terms. It is no accident that in precisely these areas it speaks in mythological terms, even though it may be in an indistinct way. In the Old Testament we hear of the *tanninim*, the sea monsters (Ps. 74 : 13; Gen. 1 : 21; Ps. 148 : 7). It is clear that they are given only a side-glance, because, though they are to be regarded as real, they are to be seen only in confrontation with God's opposition to them. God, we thought, had to do with human beings, and this is the kind of world in which we have to live our days. But here we are disconcerted by the fact that 'demythologization' is so completely disregarded that the text of Genesis can say that God *created* the *tanninim*! Between the swarm of living things and the birds that fly above the good earth, 'across the face of the sky,' there is the creation of the

[53] O. Noordmans, 'Binnen den Pinkstercirkel,' in *Jeugd en Kampwerk* (N.C.S.V., 1925) p. 78.

Monstrous, the Terrible. The monstrous and the terrible cannot be excluded from the circle of creation and preservation, and therefore, for this very reason, there cannot be any opposition and struggle of God against them. And yet in Psalm 74 : vv. 13–14 we are told that their 'heads are broken.' Are two different dimensions meant here, one belonging to the cosmos and the other to chaos? But so close is the threat to the existence of the good world that our vision shifts and becomes confused. The same is true of the concept of the sea (Ps. 146 : 6; Exod. 20 : 11 and then a quite different view in Ps. 74 : 13; Job. 7 : 12; Rev. 21 : 1). What is the position with regard to the chaos? The saga itself has already advanced to the simple assurance that these are merely created sea-animals which populate the created sea; if the hostile and monstrous did threaten to frustrate the beginning of the acts of God, then it was in no case a part or a side of creation, but something else whose head is 'broken' by YHWH.[54]

And now the external enigma simply cannot be separated from the internal one. Hence, the anxiety, which we spoke of above, and which we provisionally relegated to the background as being 'individualistic,' is in some way related to this threat to the good creation. We search for words to express these hybrid powers, to banish the twilight that lingers on the margin of things. We speak of demonic powers without and demonic urges within and in so doing go completely wrong. So, using other words, the Old Testament too seeks to cope with it; it stands on the same level with us and is not ashamed to share our perplexity. 'Rahab' (Pss. 87 : 4, 89 : 11; Isa. 51 : 9) and 'Leviathan' (Pss. 74 : 14; 104 : 26; Job 40 : 20; Isa. 27 : 1) haunted the minds of prophets and poets; but no less were they haunted by the unfathomable anguish of the self-estrangement in which a man knows not what he is doing, in which he turns his back, his heart changes and turns into Nothingness (I Sam. 10 : 9). The 'beasts' rise up from the primeval sea, the chaos, the nether world (Dan. 7)[55] At its margins the earth, the world that was made habitable by God, though not abandoned, is constantly threatened. The creation is not simply 'given'; it must be defended and protected.

[54] Cf. Karl Barth, *Church Dogmatics*, Vol. III, pt. 1, pp. 172f.
[55] 'The nameless powers of Nothingness are, in our world whence the gods have been driven forth, the analogy of the demons. . . .' Karl Jaspers, *Man in the Modern Age*, tr. Eden and Cedar Paul (Garden City: Doubleday & Co., 1957), p. 191.

2. Death and *She'ol*, the decay and the unending silence ('In the grave who will praise thee?') have too often taken possession of the 'personality' with all its accretions of insight and knowledge, of sin and desire, that anyone who has never encountered these powers could ever understand the depth of joy there is in the Name.[56] In the time of expectation, the time of God (the active presence of God) is proclaimed in spite of this terrible pressure; in the time of remembrance, on the basis of fulfilment, the Word is again proclaimed in spite of this pressure. The difference lies in the fact that the first 'in spite of' brings a strange dispeace even into the possession of salvation and the second brings a strange peace even into our doubts and despairs. The fact that the Old Testament, with its dread of the powers, is included in the canon is significant, because this strange dispeace as well as the strange peace are a part of the faith which is fixed upon the Messiah, Immanuel, *YHWH tsidqenu*, the God who sets things right for us and sets us right ourselves.

3. Congregation and preacher can never be too conscious of the fact, which is so often repressed, that we live in the real world, the world of death, the world of the powers, the world which is open and vulnerable to Nothingness.[57] This remains true even if we mean by 'real world' not the world of general experience, but very emphatically the world which we encounter through faith. Much Christian preaching hangs in the air because it refuses to admit that there are dark experiences even for faith and precisely for faith. When we no longer face the powers that walk without shape or form within and around us, the liberating power of the gospel tends to turn from a miracle of God and become an axiom of religiosity. Either we ignore them or we live together with them in a world that corrupts us and nevertheless, as our world, gives us a certain perverse pleasure.[58]

[56] Cf. Christoph Barth, *Die Errettung vom Tode in den individuellen Klage- und Dankliedern des Alten Testaments* (1947), passim.
[57] Cf. Ludwig Köhler, *Hebrew Man*, p. 109; Paul Tillich, *The Courage to Be*, pp. 36ff.
[58] 'And if the good man asserts that we must sacrifice the best to the gods, the wicked man knows that the gods are hungry. We set the table and the gods sit down to eat. You do not hear him, O good old man, yet to me, who am not good and not bad, his voice comes through as well as yours, and therefore I say to you: Life is absurd, and further, life is mixed up, and finally, life is trivial. . . . One must either stay in this triviality altogether or flee from it, flee anywhere, into a palace or a hovel, into the house of the gods or a tavern, to a woman or to the graves.' Rudolf Kassner, *Melancholia*, p. 260.

The immediate de-demonization of life through the New Testament is just as impossible as it is through the Old Testament alone. It is in fulfilled time itself that, through the nearness of the Son, in the Spirit, we escape the outermost darkness. But the testimony of this Time is and remains twofold; we cannot possibly understand the time of remembrance apart from the time of expectation, any more than vice versa. The 'nevertheless' that triumphs over the powers is not given into our hands; it remains a sovereign act with the realm of the Name. And the words 'in spite of,' spoken by the prophets as well as the Apostles, is a reflection of this 'nevertheless' (Gen. 3 : 1–5; 6 : 1f; the enthronement Psalms 24, 27, 93, 96, 99; Job 26 : 12; Ps. 89 : 10; Job 3 : 8; Ps. 104 : 26; Ezek. 29 : 3; 32 : 2).

The fact that the Name itself must do it does not mean either a higher appeal to a higher divine will or a constant trust in an ever-present help.' "I will call out the Name YHWH before your face, *that I will favour whom I favour*, that I will have mercy on whom I have mercy" (Exod. 33 : 19)—this is a saying in which the meaning of the Name YHWH is stated to be not "unvarying faithfulness," nor even "grace and mercy," but rather the perfect autocracy of the divine Presence; and therefore *charis*, as it stands above all magic, also stands above all law.'[59] The dominion of God over the powers does not have the character of a public trial of strength; it is hidden, but it is not arbitrary, just as it is impossible to find in the text Exodus 33 : 19 any further explication of the Name which would say: I forsake what I forsake and I will destroy what I will destroy.

The Gods

The emphases of exegesis are influenced and determined by the time in which it is given to us to live. Not so long ago the hard crust of the generally held rational idea of God was threatened by an eruption from the depths of beings which had risen again, half fluid and half congealed in form, in the minds of many people as 'gods.' This renascence of paganism appears now to have died away. But a sense of threat and fascination has remained, not unlike the feeling of Israel, which no longer believed in the gods and yet found traces of them in

[59] Martin Buber, *Königtum Gottes*, 2 edn. (1936), pp. 145f.; cf. idem, in *De Godsdiensten der Wereld*, I, pp. 189f., 213ff.

life. Perhaps it is healthier to see the gods still walking on the horizon than to hear them haunting us behind our backs. It is part of the suffering of our time that we are subject to certain influences which cannot be attributed to 'God' and which go far beyond 'nature' (as the object of science), that we are subject to the impact of certain 'images' which give form to a vague but yet powerful experience.

It is a liberating thing to discover in the Old Testament how much the gods are there regarded as being real. There the Lord, the Name rises up in the midst of the gods, in order to take the part of his people and thus of confused mankind. The God of Israel is more like the figures that inspire fear and peace in the soul of primitive man than a deity postulated by the reason. For the preaching of the gospel it will always, but especially in a historical boundary situation like that in which we find ourselves, be of great importance that we declare with authority: Your lack of peace with God as well as your fascinated dread of the gods, the Scriptures show us, is deeply understood by the Highest.

God is great, but not 'absolute'—God is revealed, but not comprehensible. God, the eternal and true God, humbles himself to become 'a' god in the assembly of gods and to appear within the sphere of influence of the powers. It must be said to us that he says: 'I am the Lord, and there is no other, besides me there is no God' (Isa. 45 : 5). This is not to be understood as an hypostatizing of a monotheistic avowal of the existence of God, but rather as an appeal for a qualitatively new trust in the nature and quality of this one Governance which reveals itself in the history of Israel.

The Old Testament can even go so far as to say: 'Besides me there is nothing' (Isa. 45 : 6). This 'nothing' is anything but a metaphysical negation. It is rather a theological negation: besides me there is nothing that has being and value, nothing that can help and give hope. In the midst of the silence, but even in the face of the figures that seem almost to speak, no voice and no answer can be expected: 'They have mouths, but do not speak; eyes but do not see. They have ears, but do not hear' (Ps. 115 : 5f.). That even 'God' is the object of natural knowledge of God, that he is such a 'figure,' a god—this knowledge is part of the gospel, though we shall not hear this strong note that is sounded in the New Testament if we do not first and always allow the Old Testament to speak for itself. Let us never forget that the power of the gods can remain very real to the primitive recollection of man, even under the sway of nihilism! How much needs to be done to bring to light and sweep away the buried impulses of our pagan nature! May not this be the reason why in the Torah the animals which were regarded as holy among the nations are declared to be unclean (Lev. 11)? Is not this the reason why the rites for the dead and soothsaying were rejected? Did not the 'sacred' deities have to be cursed with scathing, devastating prophetic scorn, even to the extent of coining such an epithet as 'dung-god?' Is not the mockery on Mount Carmel the fire with which bewitched souls must be 'salted' (cf. Mark 9 : 49), even among us, in the time of the new covenant? And is not this the reason why in Israel the cult is removed as far as possible from the sphere of human atonement, from any suggestion of self-redemption? Was not this the reason why the abundant and extravagant sacrifices had to be rejected by the prophets as signs of degeneration (Micah 6 : 7)? Paganism with its numinous figures is always present; it is constantly coming to the surface as an 'archetype' from the unconscious. And its aim is to reintegrate the divided life of the epigoni. And in one way or another we affirm it, and we do not know what we are doing.

How else are we to distinguish the 'affirmation of life,' which is indeed a part of Christianity, from the pagan attitude without constantly listening to the prophets, whose criticism of religion is anything but rationalistic and didactic—who want to teach us, not so much that there are no other gods, but rather that we must constantly choose the Lord in the midst of the gods, and that this choice loses its earnestness if this Lord is simply taken for granted like any other god, if for us his existence becomes as certain as that of nature, if his will becomes as plain as our religious longings, if his actions become as clear as the seasons or as dark as the catastrophes in which the gods are at work? The reality of God is not a 'given' like the gods; therefore, our present situation and condition being what they are, we must know about the gods in order to test whether we have really been admitted into the knowledge of the true God (Deut. 3 : 24, 4 : 7, 29 : 26, 32 : 12; Pss. 82 : 1, 97 : 9; I Cor. 8 : 4–6).

One may ask whether this aspect of the Old Testament has not lost much of its actuality in consequence of nihilism, which has broken down religiosity (but also philosophy and trust in reason). We recall that nihilism took over and retained something of the structural ambivalence of religion. Therefore the 'godhead' is doomed to be betrayed and mistaken for another, and the gods are such that faithfulness to them would be a virtue, which they themselves as nature gods in the broadest sense, do not evidence. The 'godhead' is the world, including the godless world, seen as a sacral presence. As long as it merely exists, one cannot actually choose it; a god among other gods, a god who can be chosen, does not appear in the Old Testament. But one does not really choose YHWH in the sense of giving him preference over another god. To this extent, then, we must define more precisely what we said above about choosing YHWH. When Joshua says, 'Choose this day whom you will serve' (Josh. 24 : 15), it is clear from the context that this becomes a wide choice as soon as the covenant is no longer kept. If Israel forsakes YHWH, there are all kinds of choices. 'But as for me and my house, we will serve YHWH.' We can speak of choice only in the sense of a liturgical affirmation or confirmation in whatever (sometimes improvised) form this may take (as, for example, on Mount Carmel). It is precisely this choice or decision which, to the degree to which it is freely and consciously made, would render the religion more ambivalent.[60] But here the choice is the confirmation of God's choice, God's election. The choice is made by virtue of a freedom which responds to God's liberating act. Thus this choice of YHWH does indeed take place 'in the midst of the gods,' but it is not a choice among the gods, between one and another godhead. And in the world of religions Israel

[60] Karl Barth, *Church Dogmatics*, Vol. III, pt. 1, pp. 7f.: 'Therefore between the constraint of God's Word (or of God attested by his Word) and the certainty of our knowledge of God there exists the same necessary relationship as between our *free choice* of this or that "God" and the *uncertainty* which will then afflict our knowledge of God. . . . Questions as to its reality and possibility which may be addressed to the true knowledge of God from without can *never* carry any weight. Addressed to a false knowledge of God they are *always* weighty.' — This does not mean that no explanation can be given, but it will be 'supplementary,' 'incidental,' 'implicit.' Conversely, it means that it will not do to deny the reality of the gods. Therefore, faith, 'in its polemic against them, will have to show, not that they are false gods, but only *to what extent* they are false gods.' Moreover, a *desire* to bind oneself to God can only prove that a person is not yet bound. 'And any supposed certainty [for example, through a *sacrificium intellectus*, which God has never demanded] built on a desire for this self-binding, will only show his actual uncertainty to himself and others. Binding by the Word of God must take place at the beginning. That is, where there is no sort of intention of creating a position for ourselves, but where we find ourselves in a position without self-willing or choosing.'

can only be regarded as atheistic. It makes no choice and its election is hidden beneath its own insignificant appearance. Even if all gods are understood as being manifestations of the one supreme principle, such as Ishvara or Brahman, choice is part of the character of all serious worship of God. Thus the Hindu is wont to call his Ishvara his *ishta*, i.e., his 'desired one,' his 'chosen one.'

THE TORAH

In the New Testament much is said about the Law and mostly against it. Paul, especially, pitted the Gospel, not always, but preponderantly, against the Law. It is certain, however, that the translation *nomos* ('law') stands in the way of our understanding. 'Torah' must not be translated as 'law,' not even in the sense of a court that makes juridical decisions with respect to salvation.[61] 'Torah' is rather 'holy teaching,' instruction for the chosen people. And here 'teaching' must be understood as the act of teaching and instruction, as the precipitate of the teaching, but in such a way that the act is still perceived in it.[62] For God speaks in the midst of the silence of the gods. He speaks through his acts, his Word becomes audible in the prophets, he bears witness to himself in the cultures, he also speaks in the commandments, which are many, and all of them are concrete.

1. The character of bindingness which inheres in the instruction cannot be rightly considered and honestly accepted if one sees in it something other than the continuing action of the gracious presence of the Teacher from on high in the present hour. And this Teacher is the same one who performed the acts, who effected salvation for his people and honour for his Name. What does the 'Torah' do in the pulpit? It teaches us to consider the gift and the tasks of the covenant and also to do this above all in the areas that lie beyond our personal existence. It presents variations on the theme of human life by applying it to the concrete situations of changing life; it intensifies the seriousness of the individual act by putting it into the context of our life with

[61] Martin Buber, 'Über die Wortwahl in einer Verdeutschung der Schrift,' in *Die Schrift und ihre Verdeutschung*, p. 158.

[62] The substantives with a t-prefix serve more as designations of actions than as results or objects of actions. Cf., for example, *tocheleth* ('expectation'), *tokachath*, ('reprimand'), *todah* ('praise'), etc. See A. van Selms in *Onder Eigen Vaandel* (1938), p. 92.

others; it refines things to the point of casuistry. This is true, of course, only of the lawgiving parts of the Torah. But it also contains narratives, poems, genealogies, proverbs. All these elements together contain 'direction' and instruction; they can give guidance. By its very nature, faith is action; there is no realm of spirituality behind the act into which one can retreat, before or afterwards. Therefore the 'direction' is a factor in the narrative and the response of the person is a factor in the same narrative.[63] It is a matter of knowing God through his acts. They point man to his freedom, they bring him expectation so that he will grasp his freedom.

2. The instruction is an anticipatory event that comes from an age-old event. Abraham is set forth as a New Adam, Canaan is the new garden of Eden, and the shadow of the Messiah takes on form in many human lives. The narrative moves, and to the degree that God's act continues to speak through it, the narrative reaches down into the hearts of those who are given this instruction. It reaches right down into a man's actual deeds. 'Here as there, we are hedged about with the form handed down; here as there, we are surrounded with the flowers of adult freedom.'[64] From hour to hour the act is required and demanded of us. The Christian church (wrongly following the footsteps of postexilic Judaism which was afraid of history) was always inclined to stop the movement of the narrative, at any rate with respect to the ethical element. It either wished to present a code of laws plus models in order to furnish life with an order (Charlemagne, Cromwell, and the whole idea of a *corpus christianum*), or it regarded the Old Testament legislation as an outmoded, irrelevant phenomenon from which nothing is to be learned except a bit of sociology of religion, a mere survival of ancient Israelite ethical feeling and conduct. And between these two attitudes there is still a whole gamut of borrowings and rejections. The one attitude as well as the other leads to an undermining of the act-character of our life. The one as well as the other evokes nihilistic reactions. The preaching of an ethical 'attitude,' a 'principle' of love—particularly when these, so understood, are bound up with the preaching of Christian 'freedom'—inevitably leads to a decline of the spiritual life. Therefore it is necessary to listen to the Torah as an event (some-

[63] Martin Buber, 'The Man of Today and the Jewish Bible,' in *Israel and the World: Essays in a Time of Crisis* (New York: Schocken Books, 1948), pp. 89ff.
[64] Franz Rosenzweig, 'Die Bauleute,' in *Zweistromland* (1926), p. 58.

thing that happens) which comes from an event (something that happened), and which is directed toward an event (something that is meant to happen). It gives directions and instruction only to the sons of this hour, the people of the living historical present. This instruction incorporates itself into forward-pointing history—according to definite objective presuppositions, just as they must also be kept in mind when we are dealing with the tradition.

3. He who thinks that this implies a reversion to a 'legalistic' standpoint, who takes the Torah to be identical with the Law, who regards the Law as a burden, is forgetting that it was the rabbinical interpretation that first brought about the isolation of the *Halachah*. Moreover, he himself is not keeping in view how much the Torah in its present redacted form has already borrowed from the spirit of the prophets and also how much it owes to the *chokmah* (Deuteronomy).

But even if this is taken into account, there is still sufficient reason to approach the understanding and application of the Torah with restraint. It should provide a background for the New Testament commandments, counsels, admonitions, and encouragements, and at the same time furnish an approach to greater concreteness. But yet the Torah itself looks rather chaotic, at least at first sight. The material we are presented with is very heterogeneous: historical and prehistorical narratives, sagas, anecdotes, hymns, prophetic lore, the fortunes of individuals and peoples, laws, regulations, descriptions of journeys, inventories—in short, life itself, as it resists the ordering power of the mind and evades the experimental power of feeling, and which is still not ordained or intended to rule us, but is rather, as Fichte said, 'nothing but the material for our duty.' This life lies spread out before us in the Old Testament in almost wild profusion. But with all its historical potency, life cannot be the norm or give us guidance.

4. Within this life, on its borders, there rises the sign of the presence, through which God, by entering into our condition, actively differentiates himself in the world from the world as 'the Lord our God.' This life is judged and saved, and thus its meaning and appointed purpose is preserved; people and individuals are called away from bondage to the world in order to find a new relationship to the world in a new destiny. Go—out of the land; come—to your inheritance! You shall be to me a crown domain (Exod. 19 : 5); you shall have no

other gods before me. Break camp, fight, halt, choose, divide, settle down, and live! And do all this in order to serve in freedom the God who creates liberation on earth.

These too, mark you, are commandments. It is wrong to isolate the 'Ten Commandments' and elevate them into timeless principles over against these other commands, as if these were irrelevant. On the contrary, if we do not regard the 'Ten Commandments' as the crown of what happens between God and man, as part of a sacral order, then they are less binding than the concrete instructions and commands, whose application to our personal life we are quite able to, if need be, visualize. YHWH is good in that he is the great liberator; to be with him is not an attitude, a mood, a frame of mind, but rather walking with him, rising up from the sunken state of nature or custom in order to be really with him, the Liberator, day after day and in act after act. Thus Israel accepted the whole of the Pentateuch as 'instruction' and perceived in it God's own voice. Such an attitude is altogether new and strange to modern man's 'morality' (as he calls it). And yet his hostility to God certainly has grown out of the soil of this morality.

All this is your story, your history with Me; no, rather, My story, my history with you! 'He has not dealt thus with any other nation; they do not know his ordinances,' they stand outside (Ps. 147 : 20). Thus in the Torah we see the 'law' passing over into 'gospel' and the 'gospel' passing over into 'law'; so the promise unfolds into commandments and so the commandments are bound up into the promise. You will not be, you need not be the sport of fate and the dupe of your own lusts. You people!—here are the statutes and laws, the forefathers and exemplars, the wonders and the ceremonies, here come the burdens and the feasts. Behold, a people with their own book of law, Mosaic and Hammurabic, ceremonial and casuistic; but it is a covenant book, wherein God is more than nature and the Sabbath more than all striving, wherein singing is more than fasting and the living soul more than all goods and property (e.g., Exod. 21 : 16f.; Gen. 9 : 5f.).

5. This covenant had hardly been made when it was already broken; and though it was really broken, it was again really restored. For a decisive ferment in the statutes is the cultic legislation.

A nation is the place of the habitation of the Lord in the tabernacle; a congregation presents *qorban*, oblation, offering (a correlative concept), *'olah*, burnt-offering, *minchah*, the meal-offering of veneration, the *shelamim*, the peace offering of the congregation; a people sets out as a holy army to occupy a part of the earth (*pars pro toto*) and to preserve it as the place of the manifestation of another law than the naturalistic or idealistic law which the heathen have in mind.

We dare not isolate the meaning and purpose of the cult from the meaning and purpose of the narrative, the history of God which is also the history of man. It is certainly not true that only in the later parts of the Old Testament was the cult given a central place. It is also certain that the procultic and anticultic statements cannot be understood without taking into account the historical shift that took place and the 'instruction' or 'direction' that necessarily pertains to it. In the Old Testament the unchanging which is characteristic of all cult does not remove it from the changing course of history. Moreover, its relative constancy is based upon a spiritual component, namely, the fact that YHWH is not nourished and supported by means of the cult, like the godhead which must be nourished and supported as a cosmic force of order by means of sacrifices. And finally, the integration of the relationship between God and his people, which is in fact the meaning and purpose of the cult, must not be thought of apart from the *lust ratio*, the purification, and the renewed passing beyond the cult to daily acts, to the holy war, to actual encounter with the earth.

6. The Torah lays hold upon the earth in that it instructs the people in the knowledge of him who does not forsake the works of his hands, who comes to judge the earth, and for whose nature there is no fitting response except that of action. Personal action? Yes, personal action within the congregation—the act which in a particular way performs that which is expected of the covenant people. Here the prophets are the great interpreters.

One often hears it said that only in the New Testament does the personal relationship with God come into its own and the community recede into the background. In so far as this is correct (and it is by no means altogether true), we must say that, thanks to the Torah, *after* seeing the personal element we *again* see the community! The same is true of personal guilt, personal vocation, personal experience. After concentration upon the new element it needs expansion; it must enter into a broader context. The Spirit turns back to the earth, and the human spirit, which has found the heavenly things, seeks a goal to be striven for on earth. The way to that goal is pointed out by the Torah. Without seeking the counsel of the Torah, no Christian man can arrive at wisdom concerning the questions of cult and culture, of people and state, of collective misery and deliverance, concerning nature, which spurs us to the praise of God, concerning fate, which oppresses us as does all flesh, concerning eros, war, the social order, and the administration of justice. True, all this must pass beneath the Cross, but the suffering of the Messiah-Prince does not do away with the *Word-in-the-words*, it does not nullify the Torah. On the contrary, it confirms it— so much so that through the centuries we must learn from the Torah how we, as a people and as individuals, should live on this earth which once was cursed and now is blessed.

7. A blessed earth! This is not so much the goal as the presupposition of the Torah. The Noachic covenant (Gen. 9) is a covenant with the earth and all living beings. It includes the regular course of the seasons and the course of nature. Here the concept of 'covenant' is projected back from the covenant with Israel. Here too, the sacred writer is saying that there is a reciprocal relationship, a living exchange, which has its constant source in the pre-eminence of YHWH. It is never true, he is saying, that man is really too good for the earth; he can rejoice that he shares in the blessing of the earth.

Who YHWH is—this is what the Torah aims to hold before us, not so much as a threat from on high but rather as a comfort and consolation from nearby, a consolation which is meant for all creatures. Who we are, as men on the earth and with the earth, is shown us, not so much to make us conscious of our nothingness but rather to deepen the consciousness of our security—the security that includes both us and the earth together.

8. The content of the history of salvation is infinitely more than the enduring constancy of existence; and yet we can learn from this enduring constancy what a covenant really is (cf. Jer. 31 : 35f.).

So, if by virtue of the covenant a series of special rules and regulations remains in force in the Torah, we dare not forget that the same Torah speaks of another, 'older' covenant. 'The law came in beside,' says Paul (Rom. 5 : 20). And the one covenant as well as the other is only a prefiguration of the fulfilment of the Name. To this extent the commandments too must be a part of both covenants, commandments which must be understood as signs of the grace of God, as seals of a meaningful and disciplined existence. It is in the fact that God's earth and God's people are spoken of together, in the fact that the blessing of the creatures and the blessing of those who are called go together, that we hear the summons to listen anew to God's Commandment and act according to it. Thus arose the Festival of 'Rejoicing in the Law,' to which the whole of Psalm 119 is a prelude, the psalm from which the festival constantly renews its certainty and cheerfulness. For even though this festival did not arise until the ninth century, in connection with the yearly cycle of Torah readings, in spirit it is not based only on the Talmud but rather has its origin in the deepest springs of piety in the Exile. Processions with the Torah scrolls are organized, the children speak the blessing, as many persons as possible are called upon to read, and the last of them is called the *chathan Torah*, 'the bridegroom of the Torah.' Always the children are involved. In the festival prayers the 'Law' is by no means thought of as 'legalistically' as we probably think—not because the acts of God are represented and visualized but rather because there is a fervency and exaltation that arises from the knowledge of the law: 'With everlasting love thou hast loved the house of Israel, thy people; a Torah and commandments, statutes and judgments hast thou taught us. . . . Blessed be thou, O Lord our God, King of the universe who at thy word bringest on the evening twilight, with wisdom openest the gates of the heavens . . . and arrangest the stars in their watches in the sky, according to thy will.'[65]

So much for this festival which shines with light, even though it be through a mist, and holds up even to the people of our time the message that the ultimate and decisive reason for God's demands and human obedience is God's original gracious purpose to lead men into freedom. Deuteronomy is a veritable mine of testimony for this relationship of claim and obedience, mercy and freedom (Deut. 6 : 20ff., 10 : 12ff., 26 : 17ff., Deut. 6 : 4).

9. It is therefore of great importance that the movement which runs in the direction of rabbinism should be reversed and for the following reasons: (a) the Pentateuch is not the whole; it does not really speak without the prophetic interpretation; (b) in the Pentateuch itself we dare not isolate the lawgiving parts from the theophany, the wonders and the signs; (c) in the lawgiving parts we dare not balance the 'cultic'

[[65] Tr. from *The Authorised Daily Prayer Book*, rev. edn. by Joseph H. Hertz (New York: Bloch Publ. Co., 1948), pp. 305, 307.—Tr.]

against the 'ethical' nor screen off the 'ethical' from the 'cultic'; (d) the special covenant is reflected in the more universal Noachic covenant with the earth; the unity of the two lies in the 'Name,' which calls the creation and consecrates it as a place for the community—thanks to the limitations and despite the estrangements of history; (e) in general, a distinction must be made between performance (or nonperformance) and existential commitment (or refusal of commitment).

Because here nothing can be carried out literally and also because nothing concrete follows automatically from a principle, the function of the holy teaching remains unfulfilled, if the Commandment does not come forth afresh and confront the slave of the letter or the idealistic visionary in narrative and law, in the Noachic covenant, in theophany and the journey through the wilderness, in the Ten Commandments, and in the summoning and commanding of the individual. But this happens when the heart and mind are lifted from the law to the Lawgiver. Then the command is full of promise. But one cannot lift one's heart to the Lawgiver without being directed by him to the earth, the blessed earth. And even the judgment must serve to bring to light the blessing of the earth, which obediently moves of itself in the covenant. Thus it becomes a lofty promise: 'The sinners will disappear from the earth and the wicked will be no more. O my soul, praise YHWH!' Thus the conclusion of a 'nature psalm' (Ps. 104)!

The Commandment

We have every reason not to carry the mutual relationship of promise and command so far that both are halved or identified. In preaching we cannot bring the Commandment as command to men in such a way that it is at the same time promise. In our reflection upon our sermon we dare not forget the situation of autonomy in which the religious as well as the irreligious man often finds himself, and all too often finds himself quite comfortable.

1. In the time of remembrance, from which the testimony of the New Testament arises, man seldom escapes the danger of thinking of the gospel as if it were a mystical truth and forgetting that there is no Word without a command, no reconciliation without sanctification. And even this linking of the two may easily seem slightly theoretical;

but it affects the practice of godliness, the essence of the holy interaction between God and man. This interaction forms the heart and extends over life in all its dimensions: the use and the enjoyment of our time, our concrete tasks in family, state, and society, the ordering of marriage and work, the burden of man's struggle with the earth and the pain of childbirth for woman. The commandment, which can be a life-giving commandment for us, was included, elevated, limited, and made unshakable in the tidings of salvation, in the message of God's covenant-faithfulness (Deut. 6 : 4–9, 10 : 12–18; Lev. 19 : 11–18).

From the Old Testament we must learn to understand—without legalistically reproducing it, but nevertheless in spiritually concrete application—what the purpose of the congregation is in the whole breadth of life, how the 'face of life' should be formed (beginning with the so-called 'externalities') if it is actually true that the commandment is included, elevated, limited, and made unshakable in the gospel. What about the 'justice due to the poor,' for example, the precise regulations for the protection of the socially insecure (Exod. 23 : 3ff.; Isa. 1 : 17b.); the precepts for the administration of justice (Deut. 16 : 18ff.; Ezra 22 : 12, 18 : 8b.); the precautions against all forms of bribery (Deut. 16 : 19f.; Zeph. 3 : 3)? Thus those who are responsible are called upon, not merely to maintain a status quo, but rather to take the lead in the ways which are fitting to the holy land and accordingly to exhort the people to observe the cancellation of debts in the sabbatical year, the year of jubilee. Such appointed times point beyond the times and beyond the practical to the will of YHWH, which prevails in cosmic time. The land and the earth are his—but this does not mean primarily that he is to be recognized as the sole owner, but rather that he is to be acknowledged in fact as the friend and avenger of the oppressed, the underprivileged. This is also to be understood as the purpose behind the rule of the 'sabbath of rest for the land' (cf. Lev. 25 : 2–7 with Exod. 23 : 10f.). Are we to dismiss as a trifle what is said in the legislative parts of the Torah about the limitation of the right of ownership, the tithes (Deut. 14 : 28), the firstlings (Deut. 26 : 1ff.), the gleanings, the forgotten sheaves, the fruit that grows after the harvest (Deut. 24 : 19ff.), the years of release, the return of a pledge before sundown (Deut. 24 : 10ff.), the freedom of the city, the protection of the *ger*, the stranger and sojourner—which is almost the keystone of a tremendous concept of humanity (Lev. 24 : 22; Num. 15

: 15f.; Deut. 1 : 16, 24 : 17)? Not to speak of the sabbath, which is the quintessence of all the commandments, both in its 'religious' (as we are accustomed to say) and its 'social' meaning.

Let him who dismisses the Mishna and Talmud as the monstrous children of legalistic thinking see to it that in the process he does not lose the concreteness of the Commandment as instruction in right living.

2. What then is the superreligious meaning and purpose of the concrete commandments? In the first place this, that if the concrete itself does not build across the centuries the air bridge of evidence (i.e., the evidence that it is the commandment of this God), then the reduction of the commandments to a 'principle' will inevitably turn out to be an air castle, a mirage. On the positive side, their meaning is that there is a living bond between this God and the highly 'accidental' element in the situation of this or that man, so that of itself the Name enters into the 'little' day, the 'little' struggles, the 'little' decisions. Religion —the necessary reverse side of atheism—has got itself mired in two dogmas, both of which the Old Testament had long since cast aside, namely, (a) the dogma of the general providence of God and (b) the dogma of a universal morality for men. These two illegitimate, ungenuine, degenerate children have corrupted the whole generation of biblical ideas. Just as a man can start with the 'providence' of the ancient Stoics and end up with the most modern kind of rebellion or resignation, without any notion of what he is doing when he rejects God, so he can start with the 'morality' of conventionalized conduct (and fixation upon some particular polis, city, state, or estate), go on to Philistine respectability, and finally end up in inhuman libertinage or even more inhuman dictatorship, The only thing that can be said of these two monsters is: *Écrasez l'infame*!

3. The *Shema' Yisra'el* in the centre of Deuteronomy is surrounded with ordinances and regulations from which we can read, as in a mirror, which areas of life are especially intended to become places of sanctification: the cult, the exercise of authority, marriage, the harvest, poverty, and the animal. These are important because of the admonition that all these things must be dealt with earnestly, not in the sense of a general feeling or attitude, but rather in openness and receptivity to the commandment, as the congregation has been given to know it through the Spirit, who breathes in and pervades these ordinances

and regulations. The commandments and laws and statutes are *theopneustos* ('divinely inspired'), breathed by God and breathing the breath of God, that is, this God. Everything depends on the word 'this'; for the creation is the sphere in which his covenant is established, and his covenant is the foundation of the existence of the creation. Who is the Creator? He who led us out of the house of bondage! Who led us out of the house of bondage? He who chose our life and ordained it for sanctification. How is life sanctified? Through concrete restrictions and extensions given to us by our Liberator, who is also protecting us from ourselves.

4. The *telos* of the 'Law' (i.e., the Old Testament) is Christ, because he is the ultimate ground of the creation. The power of the Commandment proceeds from the Spirit who brooded over the waters at the beginning, who girded the Judges, who was given to the Messiah 'not by measure' (John 3 : 34), and who speaks to every man wherever he may be. The 'abolition of the ceremonial law' can also be properly extended to the 'ethical' commandments without losing anything of that which the Name has to say to us at all times and in the whole breadth and depth of life—precisely by means of what was then and there regarded as commandment.

'Israel regarded the will of Yahweh as extremely flexible, ever and again adapting itself to each situation where there had been religious, political, or economic change. Leaving the ossification of the postexilic period out of the picture, Yahweh's will for justice positively never stood absolutely above time for Israel.'[66]

The striking verbal agreement (to which Buber has called attention) between the *ruach* of the creation and the *ruach* which animated the Judges, between the ordering of the world and the building of the Tent of the Presence, between the Sabbath which the Creator himself observes and the Sabbath commandments of the Torah is to be understood as an emphatic declaration of the oneness of creation and covenant, of Torah and history, of the one course of God's activity, which out of pure love draws others into its life (Gen. 1 : 2b and Deut. 32 : 11; Exod. 24 : 16 and 25 : 9; Exod. 23 : 12, 31 : 17, 35 : 2).

In not a single respect can there be a commandment for the 'external' ordering of man's life unless it has its root in God's own action, in God's building and God's resting. To this extent it is possible to

[66] Gerhard von Rad. *Old Testament Theology*, I, p. 199.

speak of conformity with the Commandment as an *imitatio Dei*, which is performed 'typically before and after the Messiah to a greater or lesser degree and which is hiddenly and royally accomplished in the Messiah Jesus.'[67]

The Ethos

The connection between the two Testaments is so far from being uniform that as far as possible we should not neglect any of the very dissimilar aspects, variants, and accents in both. When we say that the Old Testament as such must be allowed to speak for itself especially and specifically with respect to moral life, this means in practice that in many respects—not only with regard to actual conduct but also the conduct which is commanded—it presents a different picture from that of the New Testament, without causing the one common Object, namely, God as he commands, to fall into different images of God. If we also interpret the New Testament legalistically, these many variegations can only lead us astray. For then the Commandment of the one Testament conflicts with that of the other, and then we proceed to introduce a theory of development, a theory of accommodation, in order to be able to arrive at Jesus. But then, are not the Sermon on the Mount or the apostolic ethical exhortations determined by the time in which they were uttered? Then we also begin to look at the exceptional conduct of the men of God to see whether this might not serve us as a direct standard of conduct.

The questions whether Abraham's sacrifice or Elijah's sacral destruction of the priests of Baal are given to us as an example to follow is typically Western, rationalistic, moralistic in character. Here again we have a departure from the *Deus praesens*, the God who speaks here and now, the God who speaks first in the indicative and then on that basis in the imperative, and always differently, though never saying anything but that which he pleases.

Certainly never for a moment did the sacred writer intend that his readers were to imitate these men in this conduct; but in his 'narrative philosophy' he did want to show how God, this God, can be under-

[67] Martin Buber, 'Imitatio Dei,' in *Israel and the World: Essays in a Time of Crisis* (New York: Schocken Books, 1948), pp. 66–77; M. A. Beek, 'De imitatio Dei als motief van zedelijk handelen bij de profeten,' in *Vox Theologica* (1949), pp. 101ff.

stood or misunderstood. As long as we start with the assumption that the Old Testament, but not the New, is human and relative, determined by time, circumstances, character, and situation, as long as we do not also recognize that the ethos was commanded at a particular time and place, addressed to particular persons in a particular way, and that we need to listen to it until it addresses us here and now as command, counsel, or admonition, we shall always remain in difficulty.

In the face of every commandment which is recorded as being spoken to Moses, Israel, David, the disciples, the rich young ruler, the congregation at Corinth, etc., we must look up to God who is such that he has also spoken in this way in the time of expectation and in the time of remembrance. Therefore it is especially profitable not only to see all of the motifs of the Torah, of which the legal is only one, and not only to regard the Law as being carried to its highest pitch or broken through by the Commandment, but to realize that the ethos, as a binding sphere must also be discerned in the *chokmah*.[68]

It would be unrealistic to leave out of account the half-conscious ties and obligations which are expressed in a saying like 'Such a thing is not done in Israel' (II Sam. 13 : 12). Even though such a custom is not 'absolute' (any more than the code of commandments is absolute), yet as a tie and obligation they have a no less liberating effect, that is to say, the effect of liberating us from arbitrariness, perversity, wilful independence, stubbornness, individualistic concepts of life (religious or moralistic in pretension). We know very well, not in the abstract, but within the intellectual history in which we participate, what is the meaning and purpose of certain services, favours, gestures, abstentions, and reticences which are prescribed or recommended by tradition, gentlemanliness, courtesy. Much wisdom is stored up in all this. And yet precisely in the Old Testament the hallowed custom is at the same time subjected to criticism, not the criticism of the 'free personality' but to that of the free, sovereign God who speaks in his liberating acts —speaks in such a way that we know with whom we have to do in all our actions. From the point of view of ethics and custom it would appear that the wisdom literature, e.g., the Proverbs, has the last word. But we would very badly misunderstand it, if we did not hear in these practical counsels the voice of the Liberator.

[68] Th. C. Vriezen, *An Outline of Old Testament Theology*, pp. 315f.

Especially when we face dilemmas in our conduct, the gods are beings who wrap themselves in very emphatic silence. Often because of a fear that this deafening silence will recur, the Word of YHWH has been thought of in terms that are all too massive, global, and undeviating. And the 'third man,' because he is a narrow-minded moralist who follows the straight and narrow under the leadership of a robot-god barking out commands, is well disposed to turn into the 'fourth man.' But those are rather more right who say that, ethically speaking, one can appeal to the 'Old Testament' for practically anything, for polygamy and nationalistic hate, for racial pride and *Realpolitik*, but also for monogamy, love of enemies, cosmopolitanism, and disarmament (and all this not in such a way that one is to be found in the 'Law' and the other in the 'Prophets'). We must keep side by side the Torah (=Pentateuch), the Commandment which is heard, and the ethos, which is largely identical with the *chokmah*, and bring them into relationship to each other.[69] And we must understand that the whole is less a system of morality with illustrations than one of the mysteries of God's intercourse with men, through which they learn to know him, through which they learn to hear the questions he is asking them, through which they learn to understand how far beyond human religion and human morality we are when we are with him. In sketching out the great key words we may well find it hard to keep a steady hand because of the vibrations from the Torah's magnetic field, but it should be clear to us that ultimately there is no unity except in the Name, no consciousness of unity except through the Word. The Law has not only its ordained ministers; it also comes to a man charismatically and generates a symmetry, an order, a moral decency which is governed by 'wisdom.' Perhaps it is here that we see most clearly how the deed is related to the Name, how it is the reverse side of a living relationship to the Name, the 'fear of God.'

In contrast with Islam, the real religion of law, Rosenzweig emphasizes the binding character of the biblical ethos. 'For faith the individual ethical act is really worthless and at most it can be evaluated as an indication of a man's whole attitude of humble fear of God. Here the soul itself, the genuineness of its faith, the strength of its hope is weighed, not the individual act.' In Islam, on the contrary, 'the innermost heart, the piety itself (that by which all acts would have to

[69] W. Eichrodt, *Theologie des Alten Testaments*, III, pp. 18ff., 'Die Gottesfurcht.'

be judged, if this were possible to men) is seen from the point of view of actual performance and judged by the obstacles which have been overcome.'[70]

The fear of God is a matter of knowing God, of 'proving what is the good and acceptable and perfect will of God' (Rom. 12 : 2). And in this testing and proving, this tripartite distinction of Torah, Command, and ethos will undoubtedly again become a threefold connection.

We include this aspect of the Torah in the 'surplus,' which the Old Testament very definitely transmits to us as an extra. But this 'surplus' might again appear to us to be only a survival, a rudiment if it should in any way take on a fixed form, like silt from a river, and separate itself from the stream of God's acts. Therein lies the great danger, which was fought by the prophetic spirit and to a lesser degree exorcised (though always only temporarily) by the practical vigilance of the 'chokmatic' attitude of mind. Here again the 'surplus' of the Old Testament is an effective preventive of the kind of inversions we have mentioned: God is good, therefore the good is God; God demands the good, therefore the ideal is divine; the goal of the Commandment is freedom, therefore freedom should be the goal of our attitude, and so on. Just as the doctrine of God is completely corrupted by inverting statements like 'God is Spirit' and 'God is Love,' the same thing happens to the doctrine of the Commandment of God if the fear of God is not one that is very concretely defined and does not occur in the context of knowledge of precisely this God and the human freedom which is analogous to his freedom.

The doctrine of God is crucial and decisive; the Revelation is the answer to the ethical problem. In and through the Name the Commandment is binding for those who hear it. In order that we may understand what this includes for us, we are given the 'summaries,' as Barth calls them, contained in the Decalogue and the Sermon on the Mount. In the framework of these summaries the Commandment is intended to come over to us here and now; it expects of us the confirmation of the fact that 'he has shown you, O man, what is good' (Mic. 6 : 8). What obedience is, what discipleship is, namely, an abiding with our Liberator, a 'standing' in freedom (which seems to be an exceptional, a boundary-line area, but rather represents and is in fact the centre)—this can assume very different forms. And here we also

[70] Franz Rosenzweig, *Der Stern der Erlösung*, II, p. 109.

see those boundary-line figures, those boundary-line acts, which very emphatically occupy the foreground in parts of the Old Testament (Rebecca, Tamar, Rahab, Ruth, Hosea, Jeremiah). The question is not 'What must be done?' nor 'What must I do?' but rather 'What shall we do, and therefore what should I do as a member of the people with whom the Lord has made his Covenant?' Many have the idea that the Old Testament leaves less room for the concrete exception. The opposite is the case, and it is here that we can find new inspiration to allow the Old Testament to speak for itself. Then it will become apparent that the 'respectable rogue' (to use Vestijk's term 'fatsoensrakker') will not find much here that suits his taste.

Then, too, in the Old Testament our bewilderment, our predicament is stated more clearly: 'I am a sojourner on earth; hide not thy Commandments from me!' (Ps. 119 : 19). The Ten Commandments represent the marking off of a space within which we ourselves are to listen for God's command in this particular hour. The 'more excellent righteousness' (Matt. 5 : 20) is certainly not to be interpreted as a higher morality but rather as acting on the basis of 'rejoicing in the Law.' When it is stated that Psalm 119 is a sign of a 'withdrawal from the immediacy of the God-relationship in the direction of obedience to the revelatory testimony,'[71] does not this mean that one has either overvalued the immediacy and understood it wrongly (i.e., as separated from faith), or that one has thought of the testimonies, ordinances, and laws apart from the One who commands? It is above all Deuteronomy and Proverbs which have lost all charm for the religious mind and are neglected in our preaching and teaching, because we have not sufficiently freed ourselves from a self-sufficient, autonomous morality (Gen. 17 : 1; Deut. 6 : 4–9; Lev. 19 : 18, 34; Prov. 9 : 12; 3 : 10ff., 2 : 7–9; 3 : 5–7; 8 : 32–36; Job 28 : 28; Ps. 111 : 10; Mal. 2 : 14f.; Prov. 6 : 16ff.; Deut. 8 : 2f., 11ff., 17f.; Ps. 40 : 8).

What is the purpose of distinguishing and relating Torah, Commandment, and ethos? The answer is that what is called for in the face of the silence of the gods is that we must not think of the voice of God as being so absolutely clear that we listen to it as if we were listening to a god giving us instructions. What is called for is to allow the Law too to remain in the history and the narrative in which it is embedded.

[71] J. Hempel, *Das Ethos des Alten Testaments* (1938), pp. 189ff.

This reservation is not specifically Christian. It is also to be found in modern Judaism:[72] 'We mean a Book, we mean the Voice'—'all *wholeness* is the image of God'—'but it is not true that wisdom comes of itself; it begins in true learning and ends in true teaching,' says Buber. Or as Schoeps says, 'God's Word is his demand which we encounter in the Torah; it is not eternal moral law, but rather the Word by word of mouth [and thus] the *address* of God in the tradition always spoken for the present human moment.' If the interpreter and witness is to set into proper relief the distinctive element, the 'surplus' in the Old Testament it is highly important that he should not fall back into the habit of operating with closed religious and moral concepts.

Only people who are facing ethical perplexity are receptive to what lies in the distinction and connection between Torah, Commandment, and ethos. And it is a great thing that there is still room in this world for this concern about the moral life. Perhaps it may not be long even in our latitudes before this ethical concern will be thrown, along with other expressions of the spirit, on the trash-heap of sentimentalities.[73] This is one of the symptoms of nihilism.

No remedy for this is to be found in hypostatizing the Law, as if it were actually to be understood as a Mediator between 'God and man,' as some Targums and Talmud passages would have it,[74] or as if it had to be viewed as one with the Kingdom or the Spirit or culture or even with the eternal Counsel of God.[75] This kind of hypostatizing is dic-

---

[72] Cf. Martin Buber, *Daniel: Gespräche von der Verwirklichung* (1913), p. 82 [Eng. *Daniel, Dialogues on Realization*, tr. Maurice Friedman (New York: Holt, Rinehart and Winston, 1964], idem, *Cheruth: Reden über das Judentum* (1919), pp. 217, 228; idem, *Mein Weg Zum Chassidismus* (1918), passim. Cf. Franz Rosenzweig, 'Die Bauleute' (on the Law) in *Zweistromland* (1926; see a portion of this tr. in Nahum N. Glatzer, *Franz Rosenzweig: His Life and Thought*, pp. 234ff.), in part directed against Buber's earlier vague idealism and his arbitrary isolation of important points. Cf. further Jacob Rosenheim, *Ausgewählte Aufsätze und Ansprachen*, I, 21.

[73] As, for example, in Nietzsche, who said in a passage of his literary remains which is to be dated fairly late in his life: 'It happened late that I discovered what actually I still lack altogether, namely, righteousness (*Gerechtigkeit*). What is righteousness? And is it possible? And if it should turn out to be impossible, how could life be endured? This is what I kept asking myself continually. I was deeply distressed to find wherever I delved down into myself only passions, only obscure perspectives, only the irresolution which lacks even the preconditions of righteousness.'

[74] Cf. W. Gutbrod, article on *Nomos, Theologisches Wörterbuch zum Neuen Testament*, IV, pp. 1048f.

[75] A. A. van Ruler, *De vervulling der wet* (1947), pp. 403f., 471, 486f., 508f.

tated by the fear that we may not understand that the Commandment in every respect concerns our salvation and the salvation of the world. But the mystery that the Commandment leads us 'to life' is a mystery of faith, or in other words, it rests in the Name of God and his nearness to us in every day and hour, in the flowering and the crisis, the rise and the fall of history.

Nihilism not only issues in ethical perplexity but also in the denial of any meaning in the choice between good and evil. It cannot be appealed to either on the basis of a precept or a principle of order. And behind its best earnestness is the 'simple' conviction that the injustice and misery of the world simply cannot be changed. The Jewish thinker, Leo Shestov, however, speaks in typically un-Jewish fashion when he says, 'Man only begins to think effectively when he is convinced that he can do nothing, that his hands are tied. It is probably for this reason that all profound thought must begin with despair.'[76] Rather it is Jewish and biblical to focus upon the call and the possibility of 'thinking with the hands' (*penser avec les mains*, Denis de Rougemont). And it is a good thing that Barth's foundation of ethics has aroused so much offence among religious people and so much attention among those who have separated from the church: ' "There is" no command of God. . . . What "there is" is not as such the command of God. . . . But the core of the matter is that God gives his command.' And the form of the divine claim is the allowing, 'the granting of a very definite freedom.'[77]

We have been able only to indicate the outlines of the structures of the Torah, but their historical verification will be found in the findings brought to light in the studies of the history of the tradition by Martin Noth, Gerhard von Rad, and others. There is no homogeneous, continuous history of salvation, and thus there are various confessions of faith. On the other hand, the acts of God receive their peculiar contour from the peculiar character of the freedom which he effected; and thus the concrete commandments are enveloped by one command (*Weisung*), the aim of which is to elicit a response in action from man, a response which springs from the freedom offered to him. Within the sphere of life thus circumscribed by the Ten Commandments 'there lies a wide field of moral action which remains completely unregu-

[76] Leo Shestov, *Sur les Confins de la vie*, p. 86.
[77] *Church Dogmatics*, Vol. II, pt 2, pp. 548, 585.

lated.'[78] This is the situation in which we also find ourselves. It under-scores the admonition at the beginning of the Decalogue: Abide with your Liberator—in deeds!

Not to make use of this freedom is a typical mark of the stupidity of the 'heathen,' who think they know 'religiously' what is in principle good and salutary, and equally typical of the 'Christian' presumption which thinks that it has once and for all been 'religiously' enlightened concerning the ethical principles of the Scriptures. If there is any power which can take hardened material and make it formable, which can crack open what is narrow and hidebound and give it malleability and new wisdom, which can dampen delusion and bring it to a new humility, then it comes to us from the Torah, in which nothing is literally applicable and yet in which every letter contains a reference to an intimate contact, which constantly exists between the Name and every area of life, between the Word and every moment of life, between the Commandment and every decision of life, between Wisdom and every perplexity in life.

But without 'the gracious presence of the Teacher from on high,' everything hangs in the air—for 'everything has its time,' and God 'has made everything beautiful in its time,' and he beautifully gives his Commandment in its time (cf. Eccles. 3 : 1, 11). Was not Eugen Rosenstock also referring to this when he said of the nations: 'They live at the wrong time (*zur Unzeit*). But God gave us the power to destroy the wrong time'? And is not this also part of what Goethe's sentence is referring to: 'If we understood at the right time, then truth would be near and kind and gentle'?

DARK DESTINY

Suffering

Another reason why the so-called Old Testament is in the one book of the Scriptures is that we may learn to confess and speak out our pain before the face of God. When we say, as does Barth, that in the New Testament the 'nevertheless of faith' is replaced by the 'therefore of faith,' this can be true only in so far as we understand that this 'there-fore' does not belong in the psychologically conceived order of belief.

[78] Gerhard von Rad, *Old Testament Theology*, I, p. 195.

We know our sorrows, and they know us and they know how to find us. 'Dark is life, dark is death,' says a voice in Mahler's *Lied von der Erde* ['The Song of the Earth']. This mood and experience of life is no stranger to those who have been called; to those who stand far off it seems to be the alpha and omega of all experience. We must think of the 'fourth man,' in so far as he has not given it up, as living (involuntarily—cf. Rom. 8 : 20) in such darkness.

In the church and in the house of studies (*Lehrhaus*) sit Asaph and Job and the Preacher and a young Jeremiah, breaking down under the weight of his task and crying out to his mother: Why? (Jer. 15 : 10). And what answer are they given? The strange fact is that for centuries among Christians Job has been regarded as an exemplar of submission, contrary to the express purpose of the whole book. And the terrible fact is that modern man has lost confidence in preaching precisely because of this apriorism of submission. Here again we have reaped the bitter fruit of ignoring the Old Testament or of degrading it to the level of a document of inferior quality. If one keeps firmly in mind that revelation does not lie on the same level with our world-time, it is clear as day that Asaph's lament, Job's protest, and the Preacher's scepticism make sense even 'after Christ'—not, to be sure, as revelation of the piteous misery of humanity but rather as evidence of the spirit and the power, the genuineness and sincerity of faith. We must not be confused by indications to the contrary.

How can we do our spiritual work if we do not help the congregation and every one of our neighbours to realize that the suffering to which they cannot resign themselves is understood, that we can lament and protest in the Spirit that allowed the ancients to lament? What the Old Testament says in this matter is not merely a part of the documents of the 'Israelite religion' but rather is one of the reactions to the revelation itself which is authorized by the Holy Spirit and faithfully caught and preserved for the centuries in the *Kethubim*. Here the Spirit causes men to speak to men in the congregation about terrible things and about the salvation which is prepared for us. Perhaps we may say that we men have need of a twofold 'revelation,' first in order to learn to question and then to hear the answer. The Old Testament belongs in the canon also because it says to us today in the name of God that in order to complain, protest, and doubt in this way, a man must first have been touched by the Name and participated in the blessings of the

Covenant. Would it not be the part of that inner compassion which we should have for the 'crowd,' the *ochlos* (which also belongs to the Covenant), not only to speak of the great sufferings which they bear, not only to interpret them but also to recognize them as the sufferings of faith, the suffering that comes with seeking (for seeking is also an act of faith), as a sign not that they are far away from God but rather that they are near to him? (Cf. Job, Eccles., Pss. 49 and 73; Jer. 5 : 23–28; 15 : 10; 20 : 14–18; Lam. 3 : 1–32).

The author of Lamentations is not indulging in purely personal statements with no reference to the fate of the people; he was able to enter into the invisible company of those who have had similar or the same sufferings and have been exalted. Who speaks of exaltation? In their laments the men who prayed 'represent themselves as the paradigmatic sufferers, upon whom has come not merely this or that suffering, but the ultimate elemental suffering of abandonment by God.'[79]

There is a silent speech of tears which nobody, not even the angels, can hear and understand except God. 'Tears are the deepest depth of the heart, the most intimate sign of human intimacy. But tears are precisely the language which some superb souls speak when they speak to God. A language magnificent and universal, victorious over Babel and confusion of tongues! O marvellous unity of the language of the soul, which among all peoples . . . and in all latitudes speaks through and understands tears. Tears come when words fail; they express the ineffable . . . and St. Rose of Lima, who perhaps did not know how philosophically lofty her remark was, said that tears belong to God and must be reserved for him alone.'[80] (Cf. Pss. 39 : 12; 42 : 3; 56 : 8; 126 : 5; Isa. 25 : 8; Lam. 2 : 18).

But such speech, it would seem to us, has about it a beauty and fervour which we are wanting. Closer to the suffering of our time is another tone, another need, one might say, a naked need. 'In these days the question is to be asked over and over again: After Auschwitz how is a Jewish life possible? I would like to frame this question more correctly: How in a time in which Auschwitz existed is any life with God possible? The strangeness has become too cruel, the hiddenness too deep. One can still "believe" in the God who permitted to happen

---

[79] Gerhard von Rad, *Old Testament Theology*, I, p. 400. [Translation altered.—Tr.]
[80] Ernest Hello, *Paroles de Dieu*, p. 56.

what did happen, but can one still speak to him? Can one still call upon him? Do we dare to recommend the Job of the gas-chambers to the survivors of Auschwitz: "Call upon him, for he is good and his mercy endureth forever"?'[81]

Poverty

The prophets were always championing the cause of the poor. In the Psalms we hear their laments and in Proverbs the admonitions are often directed specifically to the rich. In the New Testament, apart from several passages in Luke and the Epistle of James, we find little attention devoted to the mystery and the promise which are hidden in poverty and little light is shed upon the naked suffering of poverty. It will be necessary for the preacher of the Gospel to understand and actualize afresh the peculiar accents of the Law and the Prophets. Perhaps one can go so far as to say that in areas stricken by war, where ordinary life is depressed by deprivation, this could be neglected only at the price of a fresh alienation of the people from the church. For here it would appear that the logical justice of a socialistic order is overtaken by the far more primitive exigencies of immediate naked life and its elementary needs. Here it would appear that it is no longer a question of lifting the poor to middle-class status but rather of bringing everybody in the future to endure or to experience poverty as a severe trial of the heart and a threat to personal life. Beside the distinctions of gifted and ungifted, good and bad, religious and irreligious, there arises anew the most humiliating distinction of all, that of poor and rich.[82] It is a typical Old Testament question how this difference can be reconciled with the oneness and justice of God. In the Prophets, however, there is no concluding from God's sovereign power, as this is revealed in his apportioning of the varying lot of men, that man may deal with man according to this (supposed) divine example. The poor man is the real neighbour; the way in which he stands, or rather lies, in his life has something to do with the nature of the fear of God itself! Often the term 'poor man' is used as a synonym for the devout,

[81] Martin Buber, *An der Wende* (1952), pp. 105f.; cf. *Gog und Magog* (1957), p. 227 and the Epilogue. [See *At the Turning: Three Addresses on Judaism* (New York: Farrar, Straus and Young, 1952); *For the Sake of Heaven*, tr. Ludwig Lewisohn (New York: Harper & Brothers, 1953).—Tr.]
[82] Hermann Cohen, *Religion der Vernunft aus den Quellen des Judentums* (1929), pp. 155ff.

the humble, the righteous, the *tsaddiq*.[83] The poor man is above all the figure in whom the neighbour meets me, as it were, in classical form, as a test case. The book of Proverbs bears witness to this. According to the instruction of the acts of God, to make of poverty a mystical virtue, as is done in Georges Bernanos's novels about priests, does not accord with the purpose of the Spirit.

In the Old Testament, Yahweh 'dwells' in and 'roams about' the earth in order to free his human children in many different ways from 'oppression,' from their oppressed and threatened existence, from the narrow straits of their 'lot.' The root word for liberate, deliver, rescue, lead out, *yasha'* (and cognate terms), means in its positive sense 'to give room or space' (Gen. 1 : 28; Ps. 27 : 13, 'land of the living'; Ps. 74 : 12; Ps. 4 : 1; Ps. 18 : 17), to cause to 'inherit' or 'possess' the land (Judg. 2 : 16, 18; 3 : 15; Ps. 37 : 9, 11, 18, 22, 29, 34). Actually it is always a matter of a *rechoboth* (Gen. 26 : 22), undisputed space, free dwelling place. Because the world is the way it is, this deliverance becomes a form of God's entering into all kinds of suffering and helplessness, and also a form of 'putting things to rights' (*shaphat*). And in not a single one of these kinds of suffering, oppression, affliction can the person or the people say, 'My own hand has delivered me' (Judg. 7 : 2). YHWH is the Deliverer, and as such he is the 'King.' He throws back the powers of oppression. He is also concerned with the special affliction caused by poverty; indeed, even the earthly king, the specially anointed, Messianic king finds here his highest glory:

> For he delivers the needy one who groans,
> the afflicted one who has no helper.
> He pities the poor and needy,
> the soul of the needy he delivers,
> redeems their soul from oppression and injustice;
> precious is their blood in his sight. (Ps. 72 : 12ff.)

Just because he is this kind of a king and rules in this way, 'all kings will do homage to him and all nations will serve him' (v. 11).

And here again—and this is not only the teaching of the *chokmah*—there is an *imitatio Dei*; compare Ps. 146 : 7ff. with Ps. 112 : 5, 9 and II Cor. 9 : 8f. Nowhere is there any mention here of a purely material poverty which accompanies spiritual well-being. The whole man is laid low, thrown into and bound by this suffering. We recall what we

---

[83] W. Eichrodt, *Das Menschenverständnis des Alten Testaments* (1944), pp. 47ff.

said above concerning the unity of the external and the internal which is grounded in 'Being in act.' The same thing applies to the forms of suffering.

Seldom or never in the Old Testament is genuine suffering simply spiritual suffering; in genuine suffering the real sting is usually poverty, because it brings with it material and moral degradation that ends in a feeling of being an outcast. On the other hand there is in poverty a glory which seems to point rather to being specially chosen. The greater is to serve the lesser; there is a 'justice due to the poor' which is not so much a matter of ending the poverty of the poor as it is of subjecting the careless existence of the others to the yoke of the Command-ments.[84] Israel itself is a poor man among the nations, the gods, and the powers; and this too goes with the fact that it has been specially chosen. But the consciousness of being chosen must include the knowledge that Israel (or the remnant of Israel) must not accept poverty as fate but must do all in its power to prevent distress (Zeph. 2 : 1–3; Jer. 20 : 13; 49 : 11).

Although the value which God bestows upon a human being, the value he is wont to conceal in a life of want and deprivation, although the poor experience a nearness to God which is not given to others, this provides no justification for those who would make the poor poorer or leave them in their poverty. The poor man is the representative of the God who humbles himself in order to dwell with us on earth. A Messianic overplus of value lies in the very existence of the poor; and to see this or call attention to it can open up a whole treasure of wisdom (Deut. 15 : 7ff.; 24 : 12ff.; Pss. 10 : 14; 37 : 16–19; Prov. 17 : 5; 14 : 20; 19 : 7; 28 : 8; 29 : 13). The rich man and the poor man 'meet together' (as does the poor man and the 'defrauder'). And this is a great test; we are being tested as to whether we believe that the Lord has made them both as human beings and as children of the congregation (Prov. 22 : 2; Isa. 61 : 1). The Messiah appears 'humble and riding on an ass' (Zech. 9 : 9). There is a straight line that runs from the whole of the Old Testament to the radical dialectic in the parable of the Rich Man and Dives in the Gospel of Luke (16 : 19ff.)[85] 'They have Moses and the prophets; let them hear them'—that is, in order to learn how the people of God deal with the poor. Here salvation

[84] Cf. C. van Leeuwen, *Le développement du sens social* (1955).
[85] Cf. O. Noordmans, *Zondaar en bedelaar* (1946), pp. 9–26.

is at stake. He who does nothing has hardened his heart against YHWH our Lord, just as he who has nothing but his (outward and inward) poverty has almost necessarily opened himself to the Lord. Is any further demonstration required to show that, like almost all the indurations and derailments of the empirical church, its reduction to a middle-class institution is also related to its having cut itself off from the Old Testament testimony, an attitude which acts as if the New Testament really bears witness to another God, another justice, another obedience?[86] Is it not plain that we too must see in poverty more than an economic misfortune, a social catastrophe? Especially when it is a question of whole peoples who for centuries have been marked with the brand of humiliation, and here we are, facing them with our welfare-state! Is this not an area in which we need to hear 'Moses'? And will it not also be true of our churches that if they will not hear Moses and the prophets, they will not listen even though Christ has risen from the dead and come to them in the Spirit? Is this really only a matter of the 'social question' (even though this is important and pressing enough)? Is this not perhaps also a question of the very preservation of the world and the saving preservation of souls for other times in which the glory of the welfare-state will fade away and the 'underdeveloped areas' will come to lie somewhere in our own latitudes, when it will be up to us to preserve ourselves in altogether new humiliating circumstances, in a lot which will come hard for us, the spoiled children of life?

Weariness

The Preacher says, 'All things are full of weariness' (Eccl. 1 : 8), that is, they make one so weary that they look as if they would succumb to their own weariness. In so far as the preacher in the pulpit also regards himself as a pastor of souls (not tomorrow in people's houses but here in this hour), he cannot overlook this insoluble mystery which is shared by Valéry, the washerwoman, Sartre, and the factory-worker alike, and he finds himself facing hearts which are almost collapsing under the burden of their weariness. For weariness is not merely a manifestation of the exhaustion of creaturely life but also of a deterioration of the power of

[86] Georges Bernanos, *The Diary of a Country Priest*, tr. Pamela Morris (Garden City: Image Books, 1954), pp. 91f.; 124f.

faith to affirm life. What am I saying—do not the priest and the prophet and the disciple also become weary, weary of life's dull round and (as their experience shows) the futility of their soul's labour? The Old Testament is full of sighings and groanings over the inexplicable amalgamation of the good and its frustration, of wickedness and success, full of amazement at the malice and deceit of the human heart. And it is especially the rebelliousness of the elect that remains an unfathomable enigma. This rebelliousness manifests itself in the form of an inert laziness beneath the show of activity. The more one learns to see that sin is rebellion against grace, the more one thinks about it, the more unfathomable it becomes. And yet the cult continued, and prophecy had to struggle for a place in the market of life to gain at least an outward hearing among the rebels. Then a different, one might almost say, a 'holy' weariness ensued. The prophets have been called 'tragic' figures. With all our reservations with regard to the term 'tragic' (for strictly speaking the Old Testament is devoid of the tragic view of life)[87] one may well say that the enduring of spiritual weariness was the lot of the best, a trial almost beyond human strength, a pain which is comparable to the pain of YHWH.

But strangely enough, this weariness can also be called foolishness and in the case of the upright man, the *tsaddiq*, this goes along with an acknowledgment of his solidarity with the godless. The proverbs of Agur begin: 'I have wearied myself over God, I have wearied myself over God and am at the end of my wits. I am too stupid to be a man and I have not the understanding of a man. I have not learned wisdom, so that I am unable to know the Holy One' (Prov. 30 : 1–3). And the proverbs of Ecclesiastes reveal the heart of a man who has lost his trust in history. He has lost his faith in God; how could He have become so pale and remote? Precisely because God has always spoken in his deeds, and when his deeds are long in coming he is left with only cyclical thinking, but this has been robbed of the greatness and mythical foundation which it had in paganism. Now this is very modern; for our turning away from the dark, unfathomable sway of history has also driven us to nature and the silence of 'infinite' space and sealed the ancient silence of the gods. And just as Agur in his wisdom and honesty confessed his solidarity with the godless and forged his proverbs out of a

---

[87] Cf. Th. C. Vriezen, 'De overwinning van het tragisch levensgevoel Israel,' in *Kernmomenten der antieke beschaving, Ex Oriente Lux* (1947).

bitterness that was a distant echo of Hellenistic popular philosophy, so the witness should not scorn to give utterance to modern weariness. We should not think of this as being merely accommodation to the times; it is in itself a dialogical attitude, and the believer in his weariness is immediately seized upon by a higher court, so that he knows that he too is involved and in this very involvement is in solidarity with the rest of mankind.

We still have not mentioned the final appalling thing. We hesitate to go into it because it is better to say ten words too few about it than one word too many. Moreover, it would appear to be quite exceptional, and this too may be a reason for only touching briefly upon this specific kind of weariness. Baruch, the helper and scribe of the prophet Jeremiah (Jer. 45), is weary with his groaning over the complete fruitlessness of their critical and prophetic work—and he is told that God himself is breaking down what He built and plucking up what He planted. In the face of this he is asked, 'And do you seek great things for yourself?' It is therefore more than men dare to expect if they begin (and it is precisely the believer who does so begin on the strength of the promise) with the idea that—even if they themselves will see no results— the fruits of their labour will one day be visible to others.

'Even youths shall faint and be weary' (Isa. 40 : 30); a new age lacks the necessary power and endurance. Must this be censured, or shall we gloss it over by saying, 'But *we* are always of good courage'? If we forget that it is the Lord who gives strength of his strength to the weary *as* weary ones, then we simply contribute to the camouflage of weariness with which all of life in our time is characterized and we turn men who are close to (salutary) despair into men who give it up.

It seems to me that the church, by underestimating, despising, denying, and brushing aside the weariness which is the mark of our time, has greatly contributed to the unleashing of an aggressive pessimism, which can also be called 'nihilism,' and that it has given its blessing to the religiosity which secretly resides in resignation like a deposed king, opposed to faith. It appears that it has frightened away poor souls with its all too confident show of assured faith; a curse lies upon its unhesitating asseverations. The promise that this God will be God for all ages can liberate us from the spell of this pessimism before it hardens into the state in which whole nations have calmly and despairingly, dully and comfortably settled themselves. But this is a mystery that reveals itself in another dialogue.

True, the Old Testament says that he who will not allow himself to be liberated from this pessimism makes God weary. 'Is it too little for you to weary man, that you weary my God also?' says King Ahaz. True! But then you will be dealing with this God—and in this the Old Testament is true gospel—which means the God who knows that weariness is also the portion of the elect and accepts it as the trial which he allows to befall them too. The Old Testament is good news, it is testimony concerning him who bears with the poor and afflicted, who does not demand too much of them and understands their constantly repeated cry: How long? True, they are reproached for wearying God, but this reproach is taken up into God's condescendence, which in this case is precisely his entering into and accepting human weariness.

'Let God be God!'—this is easily said and it is exposed to every kind of pagan misunderstanding (all the way from black *amor fati* to rose-coloured resignation), unless when we say 'God' we do mean this God, namely, Immanuel, who in the form of man actually makes the time of fulfilment a present reality. Then a light falls upon the time of remembrance, which is acquainted with weariness just as the time of expectation was, and this light awakens the children of the congregation and calls them not to be wearied by their weariness but rather to cast their desolation upon God, as I Peter 5 : 7, quoting the Old Testament, admonishes the church. As long as we fail to give the Old Testament its full value, we shall be burdening hearts and overstraining their strength. It is a peculiar misunderstanding that the 'Old Testament God' (but there is no other!) should be thought of primarily as the God of judgment. But the fact is that, when the New Testament is isolated, it is experienced by deeper natures as a devastating judgment, because they are not yet able to hold on to the joy and preserve their buoyancy. Those who wait for the Lord receive new strength, not those who 'possess' the Lord (Gen. 47 : 9; Pss. 55 : 6; 74 : 9–11; Hab. 1 : 2f., 12f.). For actually we do not 'possess' the strength and resilience to hold fast to God's word. Here we should remember Kohlbrügge's warm, patient, pastoral sermons.

How does the 'third man' become the 'fourth man?' Does it not happen, among other ways, by way of repressed weariness? It may be objected that not all weariness is spiritual in character; not all doubt is the testing of an antecedent faith, not all rebellion has the dignity of those who have struggled long and are now, by the standards of their experience, quite rightly disappointed in God. But the answer, put in the form of a question, will have to be: Do we know with such certainty that modern weariness, at least in many cases, is not a consequence of what were originally difficulties of faith, impasses encountered on the road of prayer and dilemmas in ethical conduct? If (and in so far as) it is true that, as Keyserling said, Europe has, psychologically speaking, remained Christian, does not fairness require that we view all this negation which we see before our eyes in the context of this origin and this tradition? Ought we not perhaps in this respect, too, to regard 'ungenuine' nihilism, the nihilism which is still basically ambivalent, as being actually the 'genuine' nihilism? In other words, should we not, despite its disastrous breaches and the obvious fissures, regard it as still moving on the dynamic line of the European tradition, the line of questioning which at the beginning was still willing to make a clean distinction between God and fate and still clung to God in his acts as the God of freedom and the God of miracle? In this question of the spiritual character of modern weariness we are really meeting again with the view of Eugen Rosenstock, who believes that the problems of Europe arise from a language that has grown sick. If it is not clear what this God has promised and what he has not promised, what is and what is not required of man, if the way in which God is hidden and the way in which he is revealed are not distinguished according to the direction of the Old Testament, will not this inevitably produce a confusion which is spiritual in form if only because it is the tragic result of a misrepresented and simplified Word of God? 'The Names constitute the field of power,' says Rosenstock, and this means that the disturbance of this field is related to the extrapolation of the Names beyond the order of its validity; and no one has the right to deny that this disturbance does not have the quality of a negative reference to the genuine Names or that it is a true trial of faith (*Anfechtung*), an honest weariness. And Ecclesiastes is a preacher of righteousness. 'It was in this way that the Spirit of God lighted his way into the confused darkness of human endeavour and human life. He had to endure with pain everything he saw. Men search and seek out of curiosity; but he who is obliged to see, as did this king of Israel, loses the desire.'[88]

[88] Fritz Horn, *Der Prediger Salomo* (1922), p. 20.

Und da erlahmt auch die Ernennung, die stiftende Macht des Wortes.
Dem Unfassbaren hascht das träge Wort
Vergeblich nach, das nur in dunklem Schweigen
An unsres Geistes letzte Grenzen rührt.

(And there the naming [of things], the creative power of words flags
    and fails.
Laggard words strive in vain to catch the incomprehensible,
which only in dark silence
touches the utmost bounds of our spirit).

—Georg Trakl

THE HIDDENNESS OF GOD

The assertion that God is more hidden 'in the Old Testament,' i.e.,
in the words of the books in question, than 'in the New Testament,'
i.e., in the words of the Gospels and Epistles, is untenable. To put the
accent here is to fail to see the Revelation as a historical, once-for-all,
and eternal act of God and constitutes a fresh attempt to identify this
act with the words which testify to it.

Revelation is in itself a presence of the hidden in an unveiling which
necessarily includes a veiling precisely because it is a fulfilment of God's
promise. When these acts of YHWH by which he distinguishes himself in the world from the world intervene, they appear in a form in
which they are veiled by being-in-the-world. In the same dialectic,
faith too is distinguished from human mental powers.

In the Old Testament as well as the New the hiddenness of God is
proclaimed and confessed as the obverse side of his free sovereign
choice of men and his relationship to them. 'After Christ,' Gospels and
Epistles speak of the joy of God's presence in the knowledge that this
presence is grace and remains grace, an irrevocable grace. And yet
the church cannot grow up in the adoration of this grace without remembering the free sovereignty, the inexplicability, or if you will, even
the 'capriciousness' with which grace and the gifts of grace are bestowed. That is to say, it cannot thus grow unless the Old Testament witness
is given its full voice, unless that witness in which the groundlessness
of the ground on which God's election of and relationship to men is

based is forcefully, even 'one-sidely' presented. God is incomprehensible, the only begotten Son has declared him to us; but this is incredible, it cannot be believed according to the terms of our thinking because it cannot be reduced to any universally accepted category. In the sense that there is no more fundamental truth than the fundamental Word (which is identical with the facticity of God's election of and relationship to men), one can say that God's hiddenness actually increases in the New Testament. As far as the world's experience is concerned, God became even more radically hidden in the cross of Christ than he was 'before Christ.' When we see our salvation in him, this can only be for us ourselves a matter of utter amazement. As we see him distinguishing himself in the world from the world, we become aware that this vision comes to us by virtue of the miracle that occurs in faith. Having become an element of the history of salvation, faith shares in the hiddenness of salvation. We have already seen that YHWH must also be the one who is misunderstood and scorned, the unsuccessful wooer and lover, the rejected and despised. This applies to the delay in the fulfilment as well as to the lowly form which it takes. This affirmation of the testimony binds the preacher and teacher; but it also unbinds him, that is to say, from the cheap way of wanting to make God's action sensible and credible. 'Truly, thou art a God who hidest thyself, O God of Israel, the Saviour (the Deliverer)' (Isa. 45 : 15).

Not to allow the Gospel to become banal for man to any degree or in any way will be the concern of everybody who has the task of bringing the kerygmatic content of Gospels and Epistles to men. Therefore he can never cease drawing from the testimony of the patriarchs, psalmists, and the wise men concerning the hiddenness of God. The hiddenness of God rises to a special peak where people are undergoing and trying to understand a hard lot. One must, in my opinion, be careful not to make too much of a principle of regarding this peak as secondary to the hiddenness which is inherent in the revelation itself. The Name is a unity, the Word encompasses spirit and body; man is one and he experiences his lot as a unity. It is correct to say that what is visible as a peak is only an upthrust of a greater submarine realm of suffering because of God and the need for God, but this must not mislead us into putting this theologically indispensable distinction into the foreground of our work as interpreters and witnesses. It is quite true that the answer to the existential trial of faith as well as this peak in the suffering of one's lot is to be found in him who 'nomadically' walks the ways of life with us, who was himself scorned and rejected and in all our 'affliction was afflicted' (Isa. 63 : 9). But if the New Testament is isolated from the Old, these features of the veiled presence of God are always exposed to a generalizing symbolization that reduces them to the 'idea' of the Godhead, of mystery, of love.

Our congregations, in so far as they are living congregations, are always facing the 'questions of life,' which arise in life itself and torment some people year in and year out. For them the 'godhead' becomes a mockery.

Without the Old Testament, the God who submits himself to our lot of life and death becomes a mere transparency, a symbol of the mystery of cosmic 'love,' of the reconciliation and neutralization of darkness and light. In this matter the testimony of the time of remembrance can have no greater clarity than the testimony of the time of expectation. In both the hiddenness of God arouses questions, because the Lord has revealed himself as this God, the God who is righteous and patient, great in mercy and great in wrath—and things do not turn out as they should, and we cannot accept this! But Israel learns to live with it. But to live with it means to believe.[89]

In order to live with it, faith lives by the remembrance of the deeds of the Lord, but most decidedly it lives by the gift of a new grace, a newly given ability to listen to a new Word. Here we should not try to render a theoretical account of the various degrees of hiddenness in all its various respects. When we undertake to differentiate the hiddenness of God in revelation, election, history, suffering, and trials of faith, classifying it as slight or severe, comprehensive or personal, open or closed, we are encroaching upon the mystery of God and men's hearts. Faith is always having to deal with all of these things—and in doing so man is always confronted with a question of life, with an aspect of theodicy.

Theodicy is a crude, brutal, almost blasphemous word; but in Israel it can be ventured on better grounds than anywhere else in the religions and the philosophies and prognoses of history. It has a past that will not be blotted out; it has a future that will not lie.

[89] Hans Ehrenberg, *Hiob—der Existentialist* (1952).

I will again perform a miracle[90] with this people,
miracle upon miracle,
so that the wisdom of their wise men will be lost
and the wit of their clever men will be hid.

—Isa. 29 : 14

In Israel, as in Babylon, there was no theoretical theodicy. The Babylonian texts counsel men to hold fast to the tested religious experience of the generations; in Israel man waits, cast back again and again upon his own nothingness. Here man waits, as if he had not been chosen from of old for *da'ath 'Elohim* ('communion with God and knowledge of God'), as if he had not been elected for the Word which shines upon the created world and illuminates ongoing history.[91] Nor are we exempt from this waiting. We do not know what we are doing to the souls of those in the church and outside of it when we relieve them of the necessity for waiting by urging upon them an optimistic view of God and the world,[92] always with the suggestion that nature is a good creation, that history as such is the sum of God's saving acts, and that true belief is an unshakable foundation.

Anybody who goes through the prospectus and minutes of the organizational meeting of the Dutch Union of Freethinkers, *De Dageraad* ('The Dawn'), will find to his surprise that faith in the God of nature, trust in God's guidance in the education of mankind through the course of history, and the recognition of the goodness of the universe

---

[[90] *Entrücktes*; see note 22, p. 189.—Tr.]

[91] Cf. J. J. Stamm, 'Die Theodizee in Babylon und Israel,' *Ex Oriente Lux* (1944), pp. 99f.

[92] 'Obviously the reason for this change is not that a more harmonious, more optimistic, more joyous attitude to life holds the field, or that the Evangelists and apostles have ceased to be aware of the depths of forsakenness, even God-forsakenness, out of which man must cry to God. Job, the Preacher, and the Psalmists are in place in the midst of the New Testament with their bitter, nay embittered questions, but not now as independent figures, not as those who still have to discuss a problem, and not in such a way that their bitterness or embitterment must have a further outlet. . . . We must know their problem, the problem of man's suffering at the hand of God, in order to understand the New Testament. But with the New Testament we must know it as a problem solved, if our knowledge of it is to be real. All those who are led by so strange a way find here their journey's end. And how strange the way was, the fact that it was a way through complete and trackless darkness, that on this way they really had no comfort save God alone and Him only as the hard master, to whom they had to cling in a hope against hope—it is only there that all this becomes unambiguously clear.' Karl Barth, *Church Dogmatics*, Vol. II, pt. 1, p. 108.

are stated as the starting-point of all action on the part of the Union. It is easy to see that, beginning with this starting-point of a semi-Christian, deistic, natural theology, this dawn had to end up with the 'dawn' of the atheistic movement.[93] It is a great document of the denial of the hidden, the mysterious, of the refusal to look at reality—on the basis of a faith! This was the beginning of fervent atheism.

The Presence

The Lord, the God of Israel, 'dwells' in Zion, dwells in heaven, and inhabits the praises of Israel. Hiddenness is the dark aura that surrounds this dwelling, this presence. The hiddenness always remains. Over against the hiddenness stands—momentarily—not the Revelation but rather the presence in the 'tent of the presence.' The Lord 'desired Zion for his habitation' in order in some way to dwell on earth. In the hands of the Old Testament writers the holy places, Shechem, Hebron, Beersheba, Bethel, and Penuel, which originally were permanent dwelling places of God, became places of temporary manifestations. Nevertheless, Sinai is the mountain of God (Exod. 3 : 1; I Kings 19 : 8) where he entered into the Covenant; and the writers (including the oldest sources) also speak of God's dwelling in heaven. Thus the holy places are transposed from space into time; they constitute a sequence which expresses the historicity of the intervening action of God who is present in his real acts. We have to pursue this sequence in order to understand what is meant by the presence of God in the midst of his people. Here Zion is the 'dwelling place' that towers over the other places, which are regarded merely as lodging places, caravanserais, stopping places. For it is in Zion that the public cult and the feasts of remembrance and meeting are celebrated.

The 'omnipresence' of God as such is a specimen of mongrel philosophy which is an embarrassment to epistemology and hardly convincing to faith. Preaching must begin with the particular presence, just as it begins with the particular revelation and consequently with a particular kind of hiddenness. But this truth fades, this way from the

[93] O. Noordenbos, *Het atheisme in Nederland in de 19de eeuw* (1931), pp. 31ff.; cf. F. A. Lange, *Geschichte des Materialismus*, (Reclam edn.), II, 201f., 604f., 683f.; cf. also J. G. Fichte, '*Über den Grund unseres Glaubens an eine göttliche Weltregierung* (1812), and the whole 'atheistic' controversy which it stirred up (documents edited by H. Lindau, Munich, 1912).

particular to the general is abandoned, this presence evaporates when we no longer maintain communion with the witness of the 'house of God.' It is my opinion that the religion of Tom, Dick, and Harry and their way of spending Sunday are also a consequence of the neglect of the Old Testament; for the fellowship, the cult, the liturgy, hymns, common prayer are robbed of their living substance when the link with the Old Testament witness as the proclamation of the real and variable presence of God is severed. At the time when 'New Testaments' were put on the market, there was also brought into being a way of life in which there was no longer any real place for churchgoing. 'Tom, better go to church in nature—and smoke cigars.' Special closeness to the place 'where the people are assembled' can also be a help which we need as we experience the suffering caused by the hiddenness of God. To impress this upon the hearts of people is also a part of the office, the teaching and the instruction of the interpreter and witness (Exod. 25 : 8; 29 : 45f.; Num. 5 : 3; 35 : 34; I Kings 6 : 13; Ezek. 43 : 7, 9; Isa. 37 : 16; Pss. 9 : 11; 22 : 3; 132 : 13; 135 : 21; Joel 3 : 17; Zech. 2 : 10f.).

The Hidden Communion

There is a series of themes which are common to both the Old and the New Testament, but which occupy a broader place in the Old Testament, so that in order to do justice to the unity of the Testaments in preaching and instruction we must at these points go back to the Old Testament, which as it gives its independent witness, demands that it be allowed to speak 'for itself' (if and in so far as we know and trust that 'speaking for itself' it does proclaim in a unique way the fullness, the multitudinous oneness, the trinity of God). Among these themes is what, to use an incautious term, we might call the mysticism of faith. The encounter with God in the theophanies, the hearing and understanding of the Word that comes in the guidance of life, participation in the prophesied salvation, the submission, the humbleness, and the quietness which rise up in the heart and encompass all things—all these things which are so clearly and fervently recorded in the stories of the patriarchs and in many Psalms belong to the substance of preaching as well as instruction. We would misunderstand the matter if we took this knowing of God among the patriarchs and psalmists merely as 'illustration' for the inner experience which is connected with faith in Christ.

Here we are dealing with a genuine knowledge of God, with an experience of faith in the day of Christ, with a proleptic encounter with his presence.

By faith the patriarchs lived and acted, suffered and struggled (Heb. 11). Abraham saw the day of Christ and rejoiced in it (John 8 : 56). They all 'had witness.' Faith is not without experience, which surrounds like an aura the act of entrusting oneself. Or are we to say that they did not really find reconciliation and receive forgiveness? Or is the *yir'ath YHWH* ('fear of Yahweh') nothing but a variant of the *mysterium tremendum*? Is the Old Testament only a primitive prefiguration of Kierkegaard's dialectical analysis of dread? Is the fear expressed here completely stripped of love? And what is the basis of this love? Is not the *he'emin*, the trusting and venturing, an affirmation of the 'miracle' (*des Entrückten*), a response to the revelation of this God, who as God becomes man in all the acts of his progress over the earth? Is not certainty an accompanying experience, an outflow of their experience of the steadfastness of the *berith*, the Covenant? Are not 'those who wait for the Lord' (the *qoweh YHWH*) themselves Messianic figures; did they not bear the Messianic suffering as the necessary accompaniment of the experience of expectation? Is not *dabaq* ('clinging,' 'cleaving to') a description of a mystical surrender and devotion, which is to be found presented with more detail and nuances in the Old Testament than in the New? 'O taste and see that the Lord is good!'—to proclaim this and offer its comfort is a part of the peculiar task of expounding the Old Testament witness (Gen. 16 : 13; 24 : 12ff.; I Sam. 6 : 19ff.; II Sam. 6 : 9; Exod. 19 : 21; 33 : 20; 24 : 11; 33 : 18; Isa. 30 : 15; Pss. 34 : 8; 25 : 14; Isa. 12 : 1ff.; Pss. 4 : 8; 16 : 6f.; Deut. 30 : 6; Ps. 73 : 25). There is a hidden communion, a spiritual intercourse that runs through the whole of the Old Testament. It would only be a misplaced and excessive zeal for correct doctrine that would leave no room for such 'mysticism.' The Psalms and the stories of the patriarchs are often very close to each other. There the personal, the individual experience surrounds the mystery of faith, accompanies, seals, reveals it.

This inner experience of faith also embraces encounter with the other creatures, contact with the mystery of creation. The fact that in the depth of its origin the creation is a blessing cannot be demonstrated within the framework of a world view, but in the experience of faith we do learn that in view of the Coming Day the Lord did not create the days in vain, that as the work of his hands the world is good (Gen. 1; Ps. 8; Ps. 104) and that, seen from the point of view of the Name, it was always turned toward the good. And this judgment of faith will not be without an element of comfort and of confidence, of presumption and hope, of anticipation and joy. If preaching has blundered when it has ignored the world's darkness and the terrors of life or even glossed over the fact that in themselves they are completely incomprehensible, it has on the other hand been mired down in a dualism of light and darkness in its concern to reserve a place for the streaks of light that come from Revelation. But the fact is that by nature every man has a dim idea not only of the logical consistency but also of the religious wealth which is inherent in the alternation of light and darkness in our lot and the way in which we experience it. Nevertheless, this is not the starting-point in the Old Testament; it is concerned with the superiority of light and the praise of the light. This praise develops out of what we call the 'inner experience' and therefore presupposes not only the trial of faith that comes from the unexpected hiddenness of God but also the comfort that comes from the presence of God, even though it be intermittent and momentary. Here again a shift of emphasis would break down the very nature of faith and open the way to religion, which projects its own ambivalence into the unstable balance of a correlation of light and darkness. Here again deviation has impeded true nearness to Him who stands above light and darkness, but stands above them as light.

EROS

In the New Testament marriage and family are held up to the light of the Coming Day and the church is given the admonition that 'those who have wives live as though they had none' (I Cor. 7 : 29). Thus says Paul as he characterizes the expectant, paradoxical situation between the Resurrection and the Parousia. And in the tradition of the Synoptics we are told that in the new order of the Kingdom there will be no more marrying, but those who are called will be 'like angels of God' (Matt. 22 : 30). This proclamation is Christian proclamation, and the sound of it must not disappear in the church. And yet if it is isolated, this proclamation leads to anxiety and confusion.

It is not so much because the Parousia fails to take place and the church has to enter upon a centuries-long road, but more because the presuppositions which were still a part of this proclamation have long since disappeared. By its very nature the New Testament is not ascetic, because, even after the fulfilment, its thinking remains Israelitic. It presupposes the order and the value of marriage and the family. It therefore also presupposes the value of eros. For without making much fuss about it, married love was for Israel simply taken as a matter of course to be a part of the good gifts of this earth. And to understand this rightly it is necessary again to turn to the Old Testament, listen to its peculiar note, and to scan once more its specific accents.

It is correct to say that for the most part in the Old Testament the meaning and purpose of marriage is definitely sought in propagation with a view to the preservation of the 'holy seed.' We need not discuss here the extent to which this has its roots in general Near Eastern concepts or whether it was intended to be just the opposite, a defence against the cult of Astarte, or to what extent this evaluation of marriage is connected with the Messianic expectation of the 'everlasting people,' or whether the accomplished fulfilment modified this latter motif in the eyes of the Apostles and evangelists.

Be that as it may, it is really only in Genesis 2 and the Song of Songs that the man-wife relationship is regarded, if not as self-sufficient, yet as peculiarly self-fulfilling. Added to this are many metaphors in the prophets Hosea, Jeremiah (ch. 2), Ezekiel (ch. 16), which compare the covenanant relationship between YHWH and Israel much more with marriage itself, with married love, rather than with the order and the fruit of marriage. We have every reason to keep these passages and these metaphors close together.[94] This is a part of the 'surplus' of the Old Testament, and perhaps it will enable us happily to clear up many persistent misunderstandings which beset this point in the Scriptures. It is a shameful thing that those on the fringes of the church should be astonished by such a statement and think at first that it is impossible that 'such a thing' should be in the Bible.

With regard to the Song of Songs, even shortly before its canonization it was disputed because of a false dilemma which still casts its spell upon our exegesis to this day. We are asked to choose between a

[94] See also Isa. 54 : 4; 1 : 21; Deut. 31 : 16f.; Exod. 34: 15.

mystical interpretation and the literal meaning of a collection of wedding songs. The text favours the second possibility, but the pure fact of its reception into the canon of Holy Scripture favours the first possibility. The fact must have been that the mystical interpretation was already to a large degree universally accepted. But is it absolutely necessary to make the choice? Was the 'mystical interpretation' necessarily an allegorical interpretation? Is it not conceivable that the mysticism was sensed and found in love itself? Is it inconceivable that eros in and of itself became for an enlightened mind a sign of God's love and faithfulness to Israel? There were no traces of such early allegorization in Palestine, and where the Targum goes in this direction it points (quite in accord with the structure of the Old Testament) to the metaphor or image of history, to the narrative of the event of the meeting between YHWH and his people. On the other hand, there can be no question that the Song of Solomon was 'spiritualized' a posteriori, after its canonization. The controversy for and against it was of long duration and lasted from the middle of the fifth century before Christ until the Jewish synod of Jamnia (A.D. 90), since which time the book 'defiles the hands' (that is, is 'holy'). The settlement of the controversy is, we think, to be approved, indeed, celebrated as a triumph of genuine Israelitic thought, which apparently was able to assert itself even in those times when rabbinical thinking on the one hand and Gnosticism on the other had gained the upper hand. This is how we received the Song of Songs.

What happened there appears to us so strange or so bold only because we ourselves are still caught in the Hellenistic antitheses of earthly and heavenly love, of natural and supernatural, of flesh and spirit.[95] But is there in the Scriptures any expression for what is meant

---

[95] Cf. the respectful, revealing, and critical book by Fritz Tanner, *Die Ehe im Pietismus* (1952), pp. 58ff., on the 'warrior's marriage'; Zinzendorf's 'clerical marriage,' pp. 115ff.; the passages which indicate and give the reasons why all desire, even within marriage, is to be condemned, pp. 123f.; why among the followers of Gichtel the regenerate did not marry, pp. 27f.; why, according to Labadie, only the regenerate are called to marriage, pp. 71ff. Cf. the spiritually high-flown and turgid verses of Gottfried Arnold: 'O feverish desire, O chaste bed, wherein my love [*Sophia*, wisdom] finds me, and there, vying with me, strongly binds my spirit in her embrace, until thy body of light completely surrounds and swallows me up like an ocean, until false love vanishes away' (*Poetische Lob- und Liebessprüche*, p. 77). All this in complete contrast to the structures of the Old Testament! Cf. Leo Baeck, 'Marriage as Mystery and Commandment,' in Keyserling, *The Book of Marriage* (1926).

by spiritual life other than just this penetration of reality and this spontaneous impulse of the 'sensual'? Can anything be total which refuses to become flesh? Is it really surprising that, following the precedent of the above-mentioned Targum, the Song of Songs became the prescribed reading in the Passover celebration? Can God's Revelation and Presence be understood in any other way except precisely in his action, his election, his guidance, his peace- (*shalom*) giving, rest- (*menucha*) giving nearness, his life-engendering closeness? The saying of Rabbi Akiba has been handed down to us: 'Far be it that anyone in Israel should ever have had a different opinion about the *Shir hashshirim* (Song of Songs), as if it were not canonical; for all the world is not as worthy as the day on which the *Shir hashshirim* was given to Israel, for all the *Kethubim* ('Writings') are holy, but the Song of Songs is the Holy of Holies.'

On this assumption then, we are given large freedom in the exposition of the love songs themselves.[96]

Following Ewald, one can interpret the book as a drama, a musical play, or following Herder and Budde, as a cycle of lyrics, or one can accept Wetzstein's folkloristic findings and G. Dalman's descriptions of the wedding customs among the shepherd folk in which the bridegroom is addressed and celebrated on his day as 'king' (so that the distinction between the figure of the king and the figure of the shepherd would be rendered unnecessary). We are free to make use of all of this, as long as the one theme is kept in view. What is to be regarded as impossible, however, is the mythological interpretation following the analogy of the Babylonian Istar-Tammuz cult—and perhaps the even more impossible completely 'mystical interpretation' which is set forth in Bertus van Lier's ingenious composition *The Holy Song* (the yearning of the soul, which is held captive on earth by the 'king,' for the heavenly home, the land of the 'shepherd'). We are shocked, however, by the fact that such a great Jewish scholar as J. L. Seeligmann (Jerusalem) appears to be very sympathetic to this 'happy solution,' that is, to a Hellenistic interpretation. If these anti-Israelitic structures really hold together the Song of Songs, this garland of love songs, then the oppo-

---

[96] The limits of this freedom are so evident that they hardly need to be mentioned: for example, it excludes the perverse love, which is glorified by, among others, H. Blüher, *Die Rolle der Erotik in der männlichen Gesellschaft*, II, pp. 156ff. Cf. the profoundly Israelitic protest in Isaac Breuer, *Elijahu*, passim.

sition to the canonization of the book was legitimate and Jamnia is to be regretted; then the book must be excluded and opposed, not because it is so 'sensual' but rather because it is so 'mystical'!

The corrective implications of this for the conventional dualism of popular Christianity are tremendous. Love is celebrated, love as the gift and the power that seeks, establishes, and fulfils marriage. It is a total, personal, mutual relationship. The bond, the primal relation, the I and Thou, the mystery of the other person, who is so different and yet so akin,[97] the attraction and estrangement, the passion, the rage, the ardour, the jealousy—all of these factors in the psychophysical love life of man and woman are a reflection of the love of God (and not the other way round).

In the Old Testament the love of God is not understood as a universal truth, nor is it limited to a divine sentiment or attitude. Love is not at all a fixed religious concept; it is not a central word, it is sharply distinguished from the idea of 'universal love'; it is an 'event,' something that happens, a choosing, outreaching, intolerant, gladdening nearness in our actual life in the course of our days.

'I will betroth you to me for ever; I will betroth you to me in righteousness and in justice, in steadfast love, and in mercy. I will betroth you to me in faithfulness' (Hos. 2 : 19f.). And the response to that love? Existence itself, responding with one's whole existence, springs from the deepest humility of the elect and the passionate pride of now being justified, secure, and pleasing to YHWH. Here is where that which Hasidism calls *hithhalawuth* ('ecstasy,' 'exalted joy,' 'fervour') has its source, and here is where the *'abodah* ('service'), the quiet, simple practice of it begins.

Concerning the arrangement and disposition of the songs, there is a great variety of opinion, ranging from Herder's *Vom Geist der hebräischen Poesie* and Goethe's *Noten zum West-östlichen Divan* to Budde, Max Brod, van Andel, and Gemser. The greatest attempt to translate them into the Dutch language that we know of is that of Jacobus Revius (1586–1658).

The most profound and comprehensive, genuinely Israelitic interpretation is that of Franz Rosenzweig in the second part of his *Stern der Erlösung*. He undertakes to illustrate the whole theological distinction

[97] Max Brod, *Heidentum, Judentum, Christentum*, II, pp. 3ff., the section entitled 'Liebe als Diesseitswunder.'

between 'creation' and 'revelation,' between man's creaturehood and his being addressed, with the figures, songs, and images of the Song of Songs. Here we need only to point out that this interpretation of Rosenzweig's also has another side, namely that human eros is subject to the inspiration, the patience, the forgiveness, and the exhortation of God, and the reader will understand what a 'surplus' we have received in the Song of Songs in this respect too. One cannot in every age admonish 'those who have wives to live as though they had none' (I Cor. 7 : 29), but surely it is true in every age that psychophysical love is (not should be, but is) an image of the divine Covenant; and Ephesians 5 also bears witness to this.

The Song of Songs celebrates love as an amoral and supermoral event; it is full of the fragrance of spring, of anticipation and promise. It is sensual in the guileless and perfect sense of *The Thousand and One Nights*;[98] passion is celebrated like a 'flame of the Lord' (Song of Sol. 8 : 6). Amoral? Yes, except for the fidelity; for this is the kind of love for which Jacob served seven years in the house of Laban, 'and they seemed to him but a few days because of the love he had for her' (Gen. 29 : 20). Must we correct this, then, and say: Therefore it was not amoral? But for what lover has the exclusiveness, the 'monogamy' of his love ever been anything but constant and faithful? Who would think of praising faithfulness as an additional quality or attitude of love? 'Set me as a seal upon your heart, as a seal upon your arm; for passion is strong as death, jealousy as cruel as the grave. Its blaze is fiery and a flame of the Lord. Many waters cannot quench love, neither can floods drown it. If a man offered for love all the wealth of his house, it would be utterly scorned' (Song of Sol. 8 : 6f.). Here there is no place for some additional, extra moral value, no place for the praise of a special virtue of fidelity. But this also puts an end to all talk of 'existence without security' (*Entsicherung*)—the latest vogue

[98] 'If we see the limitless sensuality from the inside, illuminated by its own light, then the whole of it is at the same time shot through with a poetic spirituality. . . . And the eternal, simple, holy feelings—hospitality, piety, faithful love—blow like a soft, pure, strong wind through the whole of it. . . . But what might not be said of the wise speech of the birds . . . the dying fathers, and the ancient wise kings . . . and the inexhaustible dialogues in which the lovers withdraw themselves, as it were, from their bliss and the burden of their ecstasy, lift themselves above it, and return to their existence. . . . Because the pure words of the poet are in every mouth like the air which everyone shares, the baseness is removed from all things.' Hugo von Hofmannsthal, *Gesammelte Werke*, III (1924), pp. 105f.

word of an anthropotheology grown rigid in its tortuous one-sidedness
—especially if this 'existence without security' as such is to mean man's
salvation. What kind of bond would that be in which the lover did not
by his nearness assure us of the unending future?

When we seek, then, to review in our minds the canonization of the
Song of Songs, we note that no allegorization or spiritualization played
any part in it. According to Israel's faith, this is just what God is,
'amoral' in his choice, giving all and demanding much, jealous (*El
qana*, 'the jealous God'), burning in his nearness, formidable in his
faithfulness, free in his call, passionate in his espousal, fearful in his
rejection. But this is not only attested by a series of poetic metaphors;
love itself, love as it flowers in actual life, is the real metaphor, the
resplendence of the nature of the world which is godly. And the godly
'world' is always in movement, it is a contingent event, a seeking of the
beloved, a carrying along and a blessing of the partner, a fulfilling,
crowning, and adorning of the people which, ready and willing to
serve him, has entered with him upon the tormenting and victorious
march of history. This has nothing to do with the religion of experiencing the All, the religion of universal love; and therefore nihilism can
find here nothing to take hold of in order to show how different it is.
Here it is a matter of a 'groundless' choice. Here faith trembles in expectation of the Coming One. 'It is the love in which all the demands
that are made upon the concept of the Revealer come true, the love
of the Lover, not that of the beloved.' And to this extent here one cannot even speak of religious mutuality, and all the talk about 'God is
love and love is God' can cease.

'Only the love of the lover is this constantly repeated self-giving; only
he gives himself in love. The beloved receives the gift; it is this, the fact
that she *receives* it, that is her gift in return, but in receiving she remains
with herself, and becomes a completely passive and blessed soul.'[99]

He who reads the Song of Songs in this way begins to surmise why
it is that for centuries faith has recognized itself in this monogamous,
polyvalent eros. The fact is that there is no balanced reciprocation.
God is the author of the covenant forevermore. And the preservation
of it depends upon him to the end of the age. 'Every day love loves the
beloved a little more. This steady increasing is the form that constancy
takes on in love, because love in itself is highly inconstant; it is faith-

[99] Franz Rosenzweig, *Der Stern der Erlösung*, II, p. 96.

fulness devoted only to the single, present moment. It can become constant faithfulness only by the deepest unfaithfulness [to the world]; for only the inconstancy of the moment enables it to re-experience every moment afresh and thus to carry the torch of love through the whole realm of night and twilight which is this created life. It goes on increasing because it wants to be ever new; it wants to be ever new in order to be able to be constant; it can be constant only as it lives in the inconstant, in the moment, and it must be constant in order that the lovers may not be the empty vehicles of a fleeting excitement, but rather living souls.'[100] Franz Rosenzweig's interpretation and application of the Song of Songs goes much further and deeper than this; we can only refer the reader to it. But following this quotation (and this is the important point) there comes this statement: 'This is how God loves!'

It is therefore completely wrong to say that 'faith condemns us where every man finds his most natural source of life and delight,' as Rilke and many half-informed people who were born and grew up in Roman Catholic countries never weary of asserting in a puerilely injured tone. Truly, the mystery is 'great' (Eph. 5 : 32), incalculable, very near in order that we may touch it, too far for us to be able to embrace it, since it rather embraces us in our innermost being.

POLITICS

In the New Testament, politics stand quite on the periphery of its field of vision. The eschatological expectation overarched the chiliastic tension and *hypomoné* (patient endurance, steadfast resistance to everything that opposes the expectation) had subdued the impatience of the heart. What is really the function of God's commandment in questions of human social and political life, which arise as soon as a church is appointed to live in a particular historical context, this we learn from the Old Testament, unless we are willing simply to be content with the formal position and attitude stated in Romans 13 and I Timothy 2.[101]

[100] Ibid., p. 97.
[101] 'It is, however, a perennial problem upon which, paradoxically enough, the Old Testament has more guidance to give us than the New. Wherever and whenever Christians have found themselves in a situation where they were obliged to exercise political responsibility, the Old Testament, with its theocratic idea centring in the Covenant between God and Israel, has taken a contemporary form.' John A. Mackay,

He who regards the Torah as 'the Jewish Sachsenspiegel,'[102] as Luther did, and with Thomas Münzer keeps in reserve the great words of the Sermon on the Mount as maxims of a permanent revolution, relieves himself all too easily of concern for social life and responsibility for the interests of people, society, and the state. And how could such a person give any concrete help in ethical questions, which in a time like ours are less than ever susceptible of being dealt with in isolation from public policy and the social order?[103] How can the mechanisms of the world market and the murderous processes of mutual preventive espionage, how can the really perverse and stone-hard minds of those who must lead and rule the masses be expected to subject themselves to such a remote, strange authority as God and his Word?

If one proposes to withdraw into the church and confine oneself to making it easier for the complaisant to form a judgment about political events—even then, in this very reduced situation, we shall come out only with abstract demands if we operate with the New Testament alone and only with a confusingly untimely and outworn concretion if we use only the Old Testament by itself. Historically, the latter is no less dangerous than the first.

How are we going to preach if we do not admit that the questions of the common good are constantly disturbing and sometimes utterly depressing us? But also, how shall we escape being the mouthpieces of petty, particular, and partisan views and advice, which would make the church's witness speak ambiguously and with a thousand different tongues? The answer is: only by our understanding that the field and domain of the proper state is a sign and pledge of the Messianic dignity of Christ.

How are we to gauge and form life, serve it and judge it, if the Torah is not able to give us guidance? Guidance, not by means of rules and not by means of 'principles' which we have 'derived' from it by the use of our ability to produce abstractions, but rather by listening to and

---

Heritage and Destiny (New York: Macmillan, 1948), p. 83. Cf. A. A. van Ruler, *Religie en Politiek* (1945); idem, *Heb moed voor de wereld* (1953), meditations on Zechariah. [[102] Thirteenth-century 'Saxon code of law.'—Tr.]

[103] Cf. T. Haecker, *Der Christ und die Geschichte*, p. 56: 'The spirit, Catholic or heretical, with which a Christian statesman gets wisdom from the Old Testament determines the destinies of the nations.' Pascal, *Pensées*, No. 171: 'Since justice cannot be fortified, we justify force.'

hearing what the concrete word is saying there and here and now, if we really desire in our hearts to be obedient to the will of God as it ranges over the whole domain of the common good.

We dare not abandon men to the catchwords of the day and the slogans of their party. In a world where the whole of life is held in tension by political speech and dominated by political action we dare not, as preachers with a priestly calling, evade the task of expounding and applying the Scriptures in relationship to this need. And I would not know what we would have to say if we were not allowed to listen to the Old Testament as a fully accredited witness of the salvation which is prepared for the earth—for the ordering of human society and the sanctifying of our life together (Gen. 6 : 12f.; Isa. 5 : 16; Ps. 119 : 137, 142; Isa. 11 : 1–9, 51 : 1–5; Mic. 4 : 1–4; Ps. 37 : 11, 29, 37).

The danger that is conjured up by a general preaching of salvation will be better eliminated by starting with the Old Testament rather than the New. I mean the danger that it will be taken over by the 'idealists.'[104] In the Old Testament it is more clear that the basis of the expectation lies in the concrete reality of the covenant[105] and that the fulfilment must make its way by means of a struggle which is political; here in the Old Testament one never steps outside the framework of history. And just as an idealism is a secularized form of the religion of the wise, so this political faith is a childlike waiting and watching for God's action. Therefore it is inevitable that faith will always find itself on the margin of apocalypticism and sectarian enthusiasm. In the political concern the 'eschatological' and the 'apocalyptical' cannot be as neatly (if at all) kept apart as they are in the phenomenology of religion. Even though apocalypticism may necessarily go astray as a

---

[104] A great deal of Biblical wisdom may be hidden in a sharply denunciatory rejection of 'idealism' in politics. Thus J. de Kadt says at the beginning of his *Verdediging van het Westen* (p. 5): 'Naturally, among the moon calves, who call themselves idealists, and the hypocrites, who do the same, "cynicism" is not only allowed but is unavoidable and desirable. And as long as rhetoric appears where realism and common sense are so urgently necessary it is still permissible to laugh at the noble, eloquent jackasses and the treatment of things under discussion with humour, even gallows humour, is still better than the omission of any effort to break the spell of sublime stupidity.'
[105] F. M. Böhl, 'Genesis,' in the series *Tekst en Uitleg*, on Gen. 17:1f.; S. R. Hirsch, *Peutateuch-Kommentar*, I (1920), pp. 246f.; B. Jacob, *Das erste Buch der Tora* (1934), pp. 210f.

273

primitive philosophy of history obsessed with numbers and dates, the 'apocalyptical' is a genuine mark of real life in real history. Among the apocalypticists, even though the foretokens of the end may often have been little regarded, quietism has no basis because 'the promises and the law were indissolubly bound together.'[106]

But however that may be, where the Old Testament is preached and instruction given from the Old Testament we can no longer remain slaves of accident and our emotional inclinations. And however strange it may seem, it is very logical that it is precisely faith in God's hidden and ultimate action that makes men sober and realistic, so that actually we are constantly on the way to scientific politics.[107] When nature is 'de-deified,' then there is room for natural science; to the extent that history is 'de-demonized' a political ideology becomes a superfluity and a hindrance. In the sources of the Old Testament *politeia* (the books of Samuel and Kings) the kingship is by turns rejected and approved, the theocracy is regarded as absolute or charismatic or placed in the Davidic dynasty, and in the setting of the ancient East it presents an almost complete relativization of the possible forms a state may take.

The writing prophets do not in every situation read the same message from the world political power shifts of their time. Here we must exercise experimental thinking rather than thinking in terms of principles; it is more a matter of the hidden continuity in the contingent choosing of positions than of contingency as the accidental variant of an obvious continuity that results from principles.

Certain established facts appear to remain even apart from the Name of God and without the Word, namely, that soul and body are not separated, that the spirit cannot withdraw itself from politics, that individualism is a flight from and a betrayal of humanity, that under all circumstances it is justice that is at stake. This appears to be self-evident, it appears to be the a priori of the art of living together. But is this really so? Not only in their historical genesis but also in their actual appeal these incontrovertible ideas are dependent upon revelation, upon the special revelation. The alarm which the assertion of

---

[106] M. A. Beek, *Inleiding in de joodse apocalyptiek van het Oud-en Nieuw-Testamentische Tijdvak*, pp. 3f.

[107] Ernst Bloch, *Geist der Utopie* (1918), pp. 345ff.; cf. Beek, p. 125; H. van Praag, *De boodschap van Israel*, pp. 96f., 125f.

this dependence used to arouse can only stem from a misunderstanding of the Name which thinks of it as a source of dogmatic convictions and religious practices. The truth is that it is rather a matter of being freed from all these more or less sacral bonds, these more or less dogmatic conceptions.[108] Whether one lives and thinks on the basis of a pure eschatology or on the basis of a utopian expectation mixed with apocalyptic images, it is the Scriptures which have set in motion the secularization of what is customarily regarded as sacral, and despite the countermovements (such as l'Action Française, Fascism,[109] etc.), this movement will never again be reversed. We cannot be exclusively negative toward secularization, and the pious laments about it are mostly beside the point.

When we attempt in such a very uncongenial way to reduce this to essentials, what remains in tangible form is ultimately two things: (1) God rules; (2) he demands righteousness. Though expressed in a very formal way, this does sum up the twofold mystery. And this summary may be allowed to pass on condition that in the words 'God,' 'rule,' 'righteousness,' 'demand' everything that is distinctive in the Old Testament meaning of these words is respected.[110] If one insists upon speaking of 'thinking in terms of principles,' then 'principles' would have to mean here obedience in every detail and nuance, and here the nuances are for the most part incidental applications of responsible action in the service of the mystery of the Name: I will be (with you) as I will be (with you). There 'is' no command of God, but rather God gives his command, as Barth says,[111] and therefore, says Buber, 'the only thing that can become a fatality for man is to believe in fatality.' Therefore the ethical character of politics depends on right

---

[108] Cf. Hermann Herrigel, *Das neue Denken*, pp. 67f.; Eugen Rosenstock, *Die europäischen Revolutionen* (1931), pp. 534f.

[109] Cf. Julius Evola, *Erhebung gegen die moderne Welt*, esp. pp. 20ff., 'Raum, Zeit, Boden'; also pp. 136ff.

[110] If we want to look for a comparison, we shall do better to turn to the exact sciences rather than to philosophy: 'The pivotal points . . . are not to be sought in particular given things which are singled out from all others as favoured systems of reference [e.g., fixed stars in the case of Galileo; in our case, e.g., theocracy, human rights, social democracy, etc.]. . . . Not just any thing or concept is truly invariable, but only certain fundamental relationships and functional dependences, which in the symbolical language of our mathematics and physics we register in definite equations.' Ernst Cassirer, *Die Relativitätstheorie*, p. 56.

[111] *Church Dogmatics*, Vol. II, pt. 2, p. 548.

dealing with that which lies at hand and what our hands find to do.[112] And this is what is to be done next because it has to do with the one who is next to us, our neighbour. How does God rule? The Old Testament rejects—very 'primitively'—any notion of world-determination or omnipotence, and the prophets tear us away from the fatal definition of power which equates history with politics and the acts of princely rule with the will of God. The dominion and rule of God can never be general religious truth; it is to be found only in Israel, and it is recognized and known as a 'dialogical mystery' in the holy history. Only in translating and applying this special knowledge to the universal development of things does faith speak of a divine rule over all things.

But what does the word 'rule' mean when we apply it to God? The 'third man' thinks that 'to rule' means either 'to do everything' or to have a programme, an ideal, a plan. Religious philosophy inclines more to the first and religious idealism more to the second. Not one of the basic Old Testament words which signify thinking, desiring, willing, striving, refers to an intellectual preoccupation or projection; they are all without exception descriptions of acts. Neither in the case of God nor of man is there any being which does not consist of an act. When YHWH hears, he does something, he causes something to come into being, he fulfils his Word. And so too when he 'remembers' or 'forgets' (casts the sin behind his back, Isa. 38 : 17).

He 'does mercy,' he 'does righteousness,' with YHWH there are no merely inward feelings, thoughts, purposes. He is 'great in counsel and mighty in deed' (Jer. 32 : 19). He gives himself in his *asah* ('his doing'), we encounter him in his *ma'aseh* ('his deed'). Ruling is acting, but a special action through which God distinguishes himself in the world from the world; and ruling, far from 'doing everything' that happens, is mastering and using, instituting and judging, creating and erasing what happens in actual deed. If it were otherwise, then world-history would be identical with holy history, and the de facto grouping of political power would be the dwelling place of the Most High. All the acts of God are his 'mighty acts' (*geduloth*, Acts 2 : 11; *magnalia Dei*), deliverances (*yeshu'oth*), acts of justice (*tsiedaqoth*), acts of favour (*chasadim*). As long as the religious idea of 'omnipotence' continues to live,

---

[112] 'The goal of an action is confined to the nearest thing not because of resignation or because our strength does not reach any farther, but rather because the nearest thing is more important than the faraway thing.' Hermann Herrigel, op. cit., p. 214.

it will be very difficult really to hear the note of deliverance that lies in the proclamation of the *magnalia Dei*. God's power is not an abstract faculty, not a potential acting, but the actual exercise of power which occurs in his way, in accord with his nature, and in pursuance of his goal. And this power is inherent in the 'Name.'

So he also requires of his people, not thoughts, feelings, principles, ideals, but acts. Politics is the doing of deeds which are the creaturely reflection of that which YHWH does in the holy, the special, history. Politics lives by the urge of the *chokmah*, the urge to move into deeds, to concretize, but into special acts of righteousness. And where this is not possible, the result is a disillusionment in which the one positive thing that endures is the determination not to put up with such conditions. One can find this attitude expressed in the sober and yet impassioned words of Bertolt Brecht:

> Wir bitten euch ausdrücklich, findet
> Das immerfort Vorkommende nicht natürlich!
> Denn nichts werde natürlich genannt
> In solchen Zeiten blutiger Verwirrung,
> Verordneter Unordnung, planmässiger Wiilkur,
> Entmenschter Menschlichkeit, damit nichts
> Unveränderlich gelte.
> (We beg you emphatically, do not accept
> as natural what is constantly happening!
> For nothing should be called natural
> in such times of bloody confusion,
> ordered disorder, planned caprice,
> dehumanized humanity, in order that nothing
> unalterable may prevail.)

How does YHWH demand righteousness? Again and again the Old Testament says that righteousness is not an idea of law and justice, but rather a quality of God himself. Righteousness is the drive to bring to realization the relationships between God and man and man and man according to the basic model of the covenant. This means that by its very nature, by its origin in God, it actually has to do with 'politics,' for there are no relationships which do not concern being and the well-being, the *esse* and the *bene esse*, of the community and the common-wealth. That God 'demands' righteousness will only be rightly under-stood if we see that the demand is permeated with the liberty to refuse or consent. After all, the enduring liberation lies in the fact that in the midst of the silence of the gods, God speaks. 'God speaks, and it comes to be; he commands, and it stands forth' (Ps. 33 : 9)—but also, 'The Lord YHWH does nothing without revealing his counsel to the prophets, his servants' (Amos 3 : 7). 'Only through the living God's speaking to men does the dark fatefulness of their existence cease. His Word calls them into the responsibility to give answer to him through what they do and do not do in the obedience of faith.'[113]

If we do not clearly see that the privilege and liberty of righteousness has precedence over the command, or better, as long as we do not realize that the command is surrounded and sustained by liberty, politics will be for us a matter of 'principles' supplemented by practices. As soon as we arrive at that other view of this holy matter, politics will be believingly experimental and *chokmatic* (which in practical terms also means realistic in the highest possible degree and, in its tendency, 'scientific.)'[114]

Politics, as the concern that this freedom from fate which has been granted to us be used to the honour of our Deliverer and the welfare of the commonwealth, runs very clearly through the whole Old Testament. This is why the so-called 'historical' books are called the 'former Prophets,' this is why sometimes even the whole of the *Tenak* is called Torah. A sociological explanation is superfluous here because, however unreflected it may be, it is implicit in the whole. More important than a special investigation of this point is that we be alert to the Messianic suffering which gives depth and dedication to this political concern. Then at the same time an ethicizing conception of the matter discussed here is kept within its proper limitations; the suffering is so oppressive

---

[113] Wilhelm Vischer, *Das Christuszeugnis des Alten Testaments*, II, p. 7, 'Die früheren Propheten;' cf. Charles West, *Communism and the Theologians*, (Philadelphia: Westminster Press, 1958), pp. 120ff.; Reinhold Niebuhr, *Moral Man and Immoral Society* (New York: Charles Scribner's Sons, 1933), pp. 19f.

[114] Among the best that has been written on these questions in the Netherlands and what can be used directly in the work of the interpreter and witness are, in my opinion, the brief (if you will, popular) writings of the great jurist Paul Scholten: 'Recht en liefde', 'Gedachten over macht en recht,' 'Gerechtigheid en recht,' 'Recht en billijkheid,' 'Recht en moraal,' 'Recht en gerech ;heid,' 'Beginselen van samenleving,' 'Over de rechtsstaat,' all now in *Verzamelde Geschriften*, I, pp. 162ff., 188ff., 216ff., 225ff., 282ff., 296ff., 330ff., 382ff. Very important 'political' insights (in the Old Testament sense) will also be found in F. Kuiper, *Israel en de gojim*, especially chs. 8, 10, 13, 21.

because it is nonhuman norms which are being administered and applied, betrayed and violated. What is at stake is a day by day response to the great 'way of the Anointed.' It is a matter of faith to hold fast to the fact that God, this God, rules in his way; it is a matter of faith to understand the righteousness that is peculiar to him and to fulfil the demand of righteousness that he makes. Always it is a question of YHWH.

The fact that here nothing is to be taken for granted, that nothing is a matter of course, is confirmed by the use of varied, polyvalent alternation of charismatic leadership and royal dynasty, the acceptance and rejection of foreign aid, defence of the holy city and pacifism. One could not call the political concern and activity in the Old Testament a 'sacramental transfiguration of life,' as Noordmans does. Nor does the structure of the Old Testament permit us to say, as van Ruler does, that marriage is 'completely the work of God' and that the state, even Israel's ecclesiastical state is a 'creation' of God. Man and unrighteousness, the approximate and the broken are far too interwoven and the whole remains too fragmentary to permit us to venture such asssertions. The kingdom, the present rule of YHWH does not lead in a straight line to the ultimate Kingdom of God. The ever present theme is freedom, the freedom which in the silence of the gods is choked, destroyed, or shattered in the giddiness of autonomy, but is born and constantly renewed through the prophetic word. In the Old Testament there is no unbroken anticipation any more than a continuing uncertainty that could lead to a 'take it easy' attitude.[115] Politics remains a work in the midst of uncertainty, but not an uncertainty about the last things and not about the thing nearest to hand.

Here arises the question which has long been waiting in the background of our biblical reflections, namely, the question of history and the history of salvation (*Heilsgeschichte*) and their relation to each other. Dogmatics has made this question complex, partly through its presupposed concepts which in most cases have not been critically purged by contact with the Old Testament idiom. The testimony of the Old Testament shows that: (1) the acts of the Lord (in contrast with his work) exhibit no continuous line for our experience and knowledge; (2) if one wants to use the term 'history,' the word refers to the history

---

[115] O. Procksch, *Theologie des Alten Testaments*, p. 591; cf. H. J. Kraus, *Prophetie und Politik*.

of the covenant; (3) there is, however, no profane history which does not as such also belong to this history of the covenant; (4) the Old Testament starts with the inclusive meaning and intent of the re- demptive events (*Heilsgeschehen*); the tradition is oriented upon this and, starting from here, the teachers, prophets, psalmists, and wise men immediately turn their eyes to world events as a whole; (5) the special and particular is not an end in itself, but rather the prototype and pattern of the universal; (6) the special and particular is the prototype and pattern especially of a divine action that implicitly determines universal events; (7) one must therefore not say that history is the history of salvation or that the history of salvation is world history; rather the redemptive events attested in the Old Testament relate to the whole of universal events; (8) what is manifest in the history of salvation is hidden in universal history, but both in the history of salvation and in universal history the same character of YHWH is expressing itself, in both his qualities are at work in his deeds; (9) the ethos of such statements is described in the teaching of the Old Testament; the human response is to consist in an active life, including an active political life, in the service of these qualities of God. This is knowledge of God. 'What is unchanged and unchangeable is that the beginning of all things with God is itself history, encounter, and decision.'[116]

Certainly a great deal of insecurity was removed and many pious anticipations were realized for Israel through the figure of Solomon. In him Israel saw the glow of a wisdom and the radiance of a glory which assure an ideal order of society. 'The order of the earthly king- dom in the time of Solomon corresponded fully with the order that prevails in the heavenly kingdom.'[117] It is a time of peace, expansion does not occur through force of arms; Solomon builds the temple, and his throne is described as the throne of the Prince Messiah. He renders justice and speaks wisdom; from Ophir comes the gold and from Hiram come the artists and craftsmen. Solomon is *le Roi Soleil*; to him was ascribed a knowledge of the art of living which David never knew. His glory was thought of as the objective reflection of the glory of YHWH; for his transgressions against the Torah, his extensive harem, the pantheon he built for the religious needs of his 'thousand' wives,

[116] Karl Barth, *Church Dogmatics*, Vol. II, pt. 2, p. 282.
[117] J. M. ben Gorion, *Die Sagen der Juden*, I, p. 167.

all this casts no serious shadow upon his splendour. That the prosperity already concealed much corruption and apostasy simply does not count. It appears that 'everything is forgiven' him because he exercises the rule of peace and thus in one small sector of reality bears witness to the goal of God's deeds, to the unity of history and redemptive history.

He is supposed to have written the Song of Songs, most of the Proverbs were fashioned by him, and the sceptical plaints of Ecclesiastes are ascribed ultimately to him. But even this, with all the importance it deserves, cannot compare with the political figure, the righteousness of which Solomon was the bearer in the mind of his people, the herald of the time of the end, the prince of peace. It is this hallowing of the face of life which not only banished the insecurity but confirmed the fulfilment of all their good and audacious expectations. It is true that one cannot see this sign either without hearing. But in this case the hearing is a matter of the meaning of what one sees. God's nearness (Ps. 85 : 9) is known by the fact that 'glory' dwells 'in our land.' And immediately following this the Psalm, on the strength of this nearness, passes over into the future tense, but in the end, thanks to this nearness, clings to the sign which it has in the present.

> Yea, he speaks peace to his people, to his beloved,
> and [says], 'That they may never turn back to folly!'
> Surely, his freedom is near to those who fear him,
> that glory may dwell in our land,
> that steadfast love and faithfulness may meet,
> truthfulness and peace kiss each other.
> Faithfulness springs up from the ground,
> Truthfulness looks down from heaven.

Part of the message which we have to deliver is that it is directed to the structure of human society and life, in so far as that society serves that which is politically good and partakes of something of that peace, that *shalom*, which is the quintessence of prosperous, undisturbed, salutary work. Men should be revived and refreshed, meeting God's *chesed* ('steadfast love') and '*emeth* ('faithfulness'); they should hear the message that these are God's 'qualities' and conduct themselves accordingly. A ray of hope and encouragement should comfort and encourage them, and they should also take courage in the face of reality as it is. What we read about this in the Old Testament are not 'Jewish dreams.' It reveals a pledge in the given world, it discloses in the 'dwelling' of God's glory on earth a command to respond in deed to this God. It proclaims as irrevocable truth what Psalm 72 affirms in song—the blessing, the promise, and the guidance that accompany us on our way.

Hans Henny Jahnn, the poet, uttered this phrase: 'My thoughts—the steeds which swiftly move to every place and do not set their hooves in time, but in the moss of dreams—fly away.' We may reverse this image. The steeds of faith cannot set their hooves everywhere in space, but they can do so somewhere in time. There is such a thing as life becoming whole and healthy in the midst of time as truly as YHWH lives and his saints with him, and fights with deeds the world as it is. Here is the sound of a call to the church not to renounce the world and the outward things, not to betray politics and political ethos, but to stand firmly in the midst of history and establish peace.

And so it must also be in our interpretation of the Old Testament today. 'Peace' means that prosperity of earth and people, of mind, soul, and all the senses, through which the fundamental purpose of life gains form and permanence. *Shalom* is neither an inner feeling nor an external projection, but ultimately a political reality for which YHWH is the surety. There every man dwelt 'under his vine and under his fig tree' (I Kings 4 : 25). And everyone was happy, and multitude upon multitude found room to celebrate and rejoice (4 : 20). 'The source, however, was the Garden of Eden, in order to give to the children of Israel a foretaste of the world to come. . . . But one day the least in Israel will be greater than King Solomon in his time,' says an ancient commentary.[118] The clearest expression of what the people saw in this vague, inviolable, symbolic figure of Solomon is found in Psalm 72. The superscription of the Psalm states that it is 'by (or for) Solomon'; this means that because of its symbolical character the reign of Solomon is the model of the right order. The broken heathenism of our political decisions should at least be constantly readjusted to this model.

[118] Midrash Esther Rabbah, I, 2.

THE EXPECTATION

In addition to the powers and the gods, the suffering and the weariness, eros and politics, there is another factor, which, though it is presupposed and included in the New Testament witness, does not occupy
a key position and is not set forth in full detail. If in this matter we
ignore the Old Testament or merely recite it but do not expound and
proclaim it, we shall miss the proper 'point of contact' for the kerygma.
That is to say, listening to the Old Testament is the one point of contact upon which the hearing of the New Testament depends; and here,
without losing sight of the unity of the Testaments, we must allow it to
speak for itself. This applies especially to the factor of expectation.
Among the ideas which trouble the mind of modern man, in so far as
he is still a seeker, is the fact that Christians consider themselves
'saved,' that they remain in the world but are not faithful to their
mission, that they write off the world and give it up as lost. That
expectation should really come alive and be strong after the fulfilment
that came with the first appearance of Christ—it is the fault of professional believers if this is news to thousands within and without the
church.[119]

We need to realize how many people consciously or unconsciously
suffer because of this world if we are to have any conception of their
feeling that we have left them in the lurch. These people have been far
removed from any sense of celestial harmony, and they can never be at
home in a house without windows toward the 'last things,' as, for
example, the Catholic Church. And among us have not these windows
become quite opaque? And can we not understand why it is that when
we make all our solemn affirmations about peace and happiness or
about individual misery, there rises up in these 'Jewish' spirits (as
they are called) a feeling of constriction, though we can consider
ourselves lucky that this feeling has only turned into a distrust of all
such 'fine words' and has not yet changed into black hatred?

[119] 'The moral tragedy of human life comes almost wholly from the fact that the link
is ruptured, which normally should hold between vision of the truth and action and
that this pungent sense of reality will not attach to certain ideas.' William James,
Principles of Psychology, III, p. 541. One might call this the first relatively harmless germ of
the later despair which has now become epidemic.

The forces of destruction are immense, and more than ever before man meets them more victoriously and at the same time more often falls victim to them. He hangs above a frightful void; and who is there to lead and save him, who is there to hold him back from plunging into collective madness? Is it not a wicked thing to sing him a song about better times which (for Christians) have already come or about the beautiful isles of the blessed (for many? for Everyman in the next century?)? Both are recognized and unmasked as frauds, as 'escapism,' as *mauvaise foi*. The pictures which Karl Kraus painted after the First World War in an enormous fresco entitled 'The Last Days of Mankind' have been outstripped by the horrors that have since occurred. In earlier times men broke through the ring of demonry and sought a way out by turning inward or upward. 'For us the outlook above is closed,' and the inward too; and it turns out that there never were two ways but only one double road. Where is there a beginning of understanding on one side or the other? In his book *Monsieur Ouine* we hear Bernanos's lament: 'Christianity is dead. Europe is perishing.' It is a sad thing that neither Christians nor anti-Christians seem to have discovered that it was the expectation that died. One could say that sometimes it is the hour of the 'holy war' against despair, that is, it is the hour in which faith learns from the holy war the source of its attitude, learning, precisely in this impossible position between two fronts, to expect and to accomplish the impossible, almost defenceless, no, completely defenceless and utterly dependent upon God. But this attitude seems to be alien especially to the Christian person today.

And what is even worse, because the church itself seems to be lacking not only in expectation in history, but also in the mysticism of spiritual life, many people, filled with disappointment, have walled themselves in, as once they did with Maeterlinck or Anker Larsen, in a self-constructed mystical sphere, and today with Heidegger and Sartre, in existential reticence. But very often the marks of this flight, the evidences of self-narcosis, can still be detected. This world is no longer accepted as rational; and one cannot really see oneself except as an unacceptable being somehow misplaced in the universe, overrated and overburdened. What may be genuine in genuine nihilism is precisely the fact that even the supergod of mysticism is rejected as an escape. 'God is dead,' and man becomes a stranger to himself; he no longer finds his way to his own fate, because there is no consciousness of guilt but also no more courage in him. What must this mean for politics, now that (apart from occasional exceptions like Aldous Huxley) the suprapolitical sphere of mysticism no longer fulfils its function! What an accumulation of impotences this would bring about—under the guise of the potency of the welfare-state! How can we muster up any other faith with regard to the world's future except that which techno-cracy urges upon us? It is significant that despair is already taking on epidemic forms in the society of the 'third man.' Why is it that Sartre's *No Exit* and Arthur Miller's *Death of a Salesman* could become best-sellers?

The silence of the gods and the ambivalence of nihilism do not pre-clude the fact that the 'third man' is able to stupefy himself with despair. Despair is an opium for the dizzied brain of reason; it is a delight in the spectacle of the living structures of existence being butchered and boned, the ultimate experience of an ever-expanding universe which is recognized with increasing certainty to be a closed universe. This is then supposed to be 'intellectual honesty.' Inevitably it must cut off any expectation whatsoever.

This is also the case when eschatology is interpreted as a matter of personal decision and it is taught that in Paul 'history is swallowed up by eschatology' in the sense that the 'last things' are shifted into the present, the 'now,' the inner consciousness. 'The decisive history is neither world history, nor the history of Israel or other peoples, but the history experienced by every man himself;' 'the "now" receives eschatological character through the encounter with Christ or with the Word which proclaims him, because in the encounter with him the world and its history come to their end and the believer as a new creature is "*desecularized*" (*entweltlicht*).'[120] Some may find such Doce-tism plausible as a way out of the difficulties in which we are caught. But man is not helped by eliminating 'heaven and earth' from his field of vision and wiping out the 'acts of God' from his horizon.[121]

This world, the 'third man' must learn afresh from the Old Testa-

---

[120] Rudolf Bultmann, 'Geschichte und Eschatologie im Neuen Testament' (1954), in *Glauben und Verstehen*, III (1960), pp. 102, 105. [See *New Testament Studies*, I, tr. E. Kraft (1954), pp. 5–16. The word *entweltlicht* means that for the believer the world and history have lost their reality.—Tr.]

[121] Cf. J. M. de Jong, *Kerugma, een oderzoek naar de vooronderstellingen de theologie van Rudolf Bultmann* (1958), pp. 268f., 275f., 292f., 346.

ment, was created as an open-ended world; the last has not yet happened and the total renewal has not yet appeared. Even in the first germinal Messianic conceptions in the Old Testament the coming of YHWH is understood as being a return of paradise. The holy land already stands for the lost Eden (Exod. 3 : 8, 17; 13 : 5; 33 : 3; Num. 23 : 21f.; 24 : 7). The myth becomes the garment of an expectation which arose out of the holy history itself, not only in the sense that the Messiah will consummate the world but also in the sense that the Spirit renews the hearts of men (Isa. 9 : 6; Jer. 23 : 6; Zech. 9 : 10; Ezek. 37 : 24; Isa. 2 : 2ff.; Jer. 31 : 33; Ezek. 36 : 25ff.; Isa. 30 : 20ff.). The 'spiritual understanding of God's Word,' the clear opposite of 'spiritualization,' leads to realism,[122] and the theological exposition of the texts, which is easy to distinguish sharply from 'pneumatic' exegesis, subjects the human spirit to the objective event of the promise, on which our spirit (*pneuma*) does not reckon and for which our spirit in its despondency no longer seems to have any need, since we have been imprisoned in our subjective religious or nonreligious world, which is no longer a world at all.

This despondency must always be reckoned with. It appears to be the atmosphere and precipitate of repressed dread of the meaninglessness of existence. And it seems to be possible to remain immersed in this despair even when one has heard the Word of God with the spiritual ear. It appears that there are many, or at least some, who confirm Tillich's thesis that the acceptance of meaninglessness is in itself a meaningful act.[123] No wonder that it is in fact necessary that the utterance of the promise always be an event which transcends despondency, introspection, and evaluation of the facts. So it was also with the prophets, especially Jeremiah.

The expectation of a creative act of God which makes all things new is so necessary in preaching and instruction because the man of valour who refuses to sink into being-unto-death, into spectral Nirvana of his soul, is capable of saying 'nevertheless.' In the consciousness of an obligation that comes down vertically from above he can choose to do the good, despite the hopelessness on the horizontal level, and thus he celebrates his creativity. Let us not think that the root of such ideas lies

---

[122] J. H. Gunning, *Blikken in de Openbarung*, I (1868), pp. 165ff.; cf. Daniel Chantepie de la Saussaye, *De Toekomst* (1868), pp. 96ff.
[123] *The Courage to Be*, p. 140.

only in the intellectual activity of certain highly developed individuals who are defiant of things as they are. Often very simple people live quite soberly and realistically, without any hope, in a half-conscious tragic heroism, or in an attitude of moral earnestness that seeks to assert itself against the pervasive feeling of the meaninglessness of existence, hoping against hope and seeming to be well aware of what is right.

When the latter course is taken, one encounters the fatal idea (or escapes it only by a hair's breadth) that man is nobler than God or what is called God. God has no open-ended world to offer, these people say, though he is rich enough; but we hold fast with our poor helpless hands and keep on digging 'as if' it were an open-ended world. What does the church have to say? It should sustain this expectation which is directed toward today and tomorrow in the world by its very presence, by its exemplary existence as a bride who is waiting in disappointment but still clings to the promise of her betrothal. Here the fulfilment of the expectation is presupposed as in a betrothal. But the church should not think in spatial terms of 'above' and 'below' but rather in terms of time, of 'now' and 'then.' It must accept the fact that it is forbidden to locate this 'then' in the unimaginable future. It cannot allow itself, after having in the past stirred up trouble in a closed world, now to accept this world as it is because it is weary and then merely devote itself to the care of souls, as if the expectation that the superpersonal powers are facing its judgment, its deliverance, and its new ministry had been wiped out of its horizon. There is no good in a care of souls which does not seek out man in his world (which more and more coincides with the one world in its historical movement) and feed him with the daily bread of expectation. The church dare not carry moral unrest into the world without proclaiming that there is rest in God; but rest in God cannot be conceived in purely personal terms, for man lives within the community, the church, which itself—by its very origin is characterized by its estrangement from the given world as it is, its breaking away from the grip of the elemental powers, and its bond with the coming glory of an unknown world. The church in cult and politics, as a community of worship and a host of nonconformists, is never disquieted without at the same time knowing that there is rest in God, God's own rest. It is the rest of Him who does not forsake the work of his hands, that work of which we are at most a small part. It is the rest of the Messianic expectation.[124] The Brahmanic saying, 'In motionless eternity rests fleeting time,' is reversed by the Name; in the stress of events rests the blessing of eternal faithfulness.

When we speak of this expectation, it must be remembered that the Old Testament is 'existentialistic' (to use the current term) and not 'essentialistic.' In our connection this means that the decline of expectation goes hand in hand with a blurring and a volatilizing of the creation (as we see, for example, in the function of the word 'vanity' in Ecclesiastes). In the Old Testament there is no place for a logical development of the being of creation into the more perfect being of a new world, but there is also no place for a courage of despair which would spring from the conclusion that no ground can be found for the meaning of things in their origin; the ground lies in the midst of things. And this is precisely what justifies the paradox: the rest of the Messianic expectation. The figures of the ongoing narrative (among whom we ourselves belong) do not live in expectation because the story goes on and must have a happy ending, nor because they held themselves open to a kind 'resolution' to face death and decline, recurrence and recovery. They live in expectation because they take their refuge in the Name, which has broken into the midst of time and become form and word and sign. 'My King is from of old, who works deliverances in the midst of the earth' (Ps. 74 : 12).

PROPHETISM

In the New Testament, in the kerygma, the eyewitness and apostle is the medium of the message of God concerning the fullness of time, the consummation of the aeons, which has broken into the midst of time. Here again there is the danger that in the light of an isolated New Testament we shall no longer see what the character of the multiplicity of aeons is and how the times that have gone before and the times that followed are always sought out and addressed in a distinctive way by God.

It is true that on the margin of the New Testament there are

[124] Cf. the lack of this 'rest' in Hans Kohn, *Martin Buber, Sein Werk und seine Zeit: Ein Versuch über Religion und Politik* (1930), pp. 233, 245, 275f.

'prophets' among the charismatics in the church; but they are rather accompanists and interpreters of the apostolic Word; and one can assume that with the waning of the imminent expectation these figures receded completely into the background. Hence the prophet figure of the Old Testament rather came to its full flowering in the Christ himself. Therefore it behoves us—if we are not to remain on the level of vague generalities—to turn afresh to the Old Testament in order to see what prophet and prophetism really mean in the *Heilsgeschichte*.

The prophet, though at the beginning he may have been regarded as an ecstatic, is essentially a spokesman of the concrete Word of God, and he speaks to the whole people in a time which on the one hand is being hard pressed by the powers and on the other is (vainly) seeking to find new strength to resist in a formally administered legal and cultic tradition.

In the prophet, far more than in the priest, the 'nomadic' character, the sovereign freedom of YHWH expresses itself. In the prophet, even when he is the son of a priest, the tradition has taken on an intimate, creative relation to the questions of his time. We may say that we can hardly speak of a definite teaching of the prophets, since the common element recedes almost completely behind the specific application of the Word to the events of the time. In this the power and authority of the earlier magical utterance is at once excelled and overcome: excelled in so far as God himself is, so to speak, the 'Magnus,' and overcome in so far as the human spokesman is relegated to the sphere of an office, a ministry. 'At bottom—paradoxical as it may seem—the prophet says the same thing to everybody; he only varies it according to the differing situations of those who receive his message. Here is the root of the great difficulty which stands in the way of setting forth the message of a prophet, a task which on the one hand is impossible for us to evade and yet which we cannot solve in such a way that we are able to set forth an ideal summary of the great number of prophetic logia.'[125]

We consider that we are excused from this task because it would go beyond the scope of our essay and especially because in Gerhard von Rad's theology of the prophetic tradition of Israel we have an excellent presentation which is so solidly and carefully done that there is little danger that it will soon be put in the shade by another.

[125] Gerhard von Rad, *Theologie des Alten Testaments*, II, p. 101.

For our purpose, and in line with the special concern of this book, it is sufficient, even though a total summary of the prophetic utterances is impossible, to present a cross section which can be a help to the interpreter and witness in his task of giving better instruction to the 'third man' in matters of the biblical doctrine of God. And the first emphasis that must be pointed out is this: 'This Word is your life' (Deut. 32 : 47; cf. Isa. 55 : 10f.); that is, since your life stands within the stream of time, of events, you must hear in this present moment that there is a power of life, nourishment, and endurance which is with you and accompanies you just as it did in the exodus and just as it was promised in the covenant (Deut. 5 : 2f.; cf. 29 : 9ff.). What is impending is a 'resumption of the historical drama' (Vriezen) in accord with the promise which is implicit in the Name: 'I will be as I will be' (Exod. 3 : 14). The eschatological is not something that hangs in the air; it is in every repetition and renewal of the message of the promise which was hidden in all the acts of God. Even the enigma of God's hardening of men's hearts is hidden within them, surrounded and saturated by the virtues, the 'qualities' of God. And the same is true of the failure of the work of God's messengers (Isa. 53; Jer. 20 : 7f.). In this way the figure of the prophet rises to tremendous proportions, overflows its bounds, as if he were no longer an individual standing among men in the midst of his people. He experiences God's horror and judgment as the subject of it, though he still remains its object. And yet we cannot think of him as having a divided mind. With all his rebelling against an apparently fruitless office and a seemingly wasted life, we cannot fail to catch the secret of his self-estrangement, which is rooted in his surrender to God.

He is like God in the suddenness, the surprisingness of the encounter he initiates. He speaks in the name of God, and he utters grace and judgment with an authority that goes as far as functional self-identification with God.

He suffers with God, who is despised and rejected; he suffers because of the violation of the covenant.

He suffers because of God and his incomprehensible decrees, and yet he shares and accepts the knowledge of God's future. He shares the impartiality of YHWH, who addressed himself both to Israel and the nations, rises up both against them and for them; he reflects the freedom of the Word, he stands watch over the secret of the

Name,[126] and he proclaims a new covenant, a new man, a new age with all the authority of the original Founder.

And, remarkably, in all this he is only the exponent of that which the people, or at least the community (as 'edah, 'assembly of the people,' and qahal, 'congregation,') could or must be and will be. In his extreme position, paradoxically, he becomes the type, the prelude, the forerunner of a community that never existed before. If the priest is very clearly a man who vicariously performs his service in a work and an ordinance (the cult) which YHWH himself instituted as a way of preserving and renewing the covenant,[127] if the function of the priest is limited by the sovereign freedom of God, who offered and still offers this cultic way of renewal and absolution, and if the priest therefore never becomes a mediator who stands over against the people in a superhuman position—then the prophet, though he far more definitely puts himself on the side of God and the people, is nevertheless not in any sense an exception among his fellows in the covenant. In his special calling he carries out vicariously what is a latent, God-given possibility within the people itself, in so far as it would be obedient to God. Moses says, 'Would that all among the people of YHWH were prophets and that YHWH would put his spirit upon them' (Num. 11 : 29), and figures like Eldad and Medad, who were outside the order of the prophets because they did not come to the sanctuary but remained in the midst of the camp, are examples of this possibility.

The prophecy of Joel 2 : 28 proclaims the promise of the outpouring of the ruach ('spirit') on all flesh, that outpouring which will cause even menservants and maidservants to speak direct words of God in the days to come, in a 'miraculous' (entrückten) and yet not impossible time.

Whether the prophets in later times had a place in the cult, as they became counsellors to princes, whether they themselves played a part at least in domestic politics—these are questions which are of only incidental importance to the work of the interpreter and witness today. On the other hand, however, the protest of the prophets against self-sufficient religion, the withering of the ethos, the institutionalizing of

[126] Cf. Pedersen, Israel, III–IV, pp. 112f.; W. Eichrodt, Theology of the Old Testament, I, pp. 345f.; W. von Soden, 'Verkündigung des Gotteswillens durch prophetisches Wort in den altbabylonischen Briefen aus Mari,' in Die Welt des Orients (1950).
[127] Cf. A. C. Welch, Prophet and Priest in Old Israel (London: S.C.M. Press, 1936), pp. 86f.

religious life so that it became merely automatic custom—this is still of the greatest importance for us today.

Added to this is the fact that the Torah itself is certainly influenced by the spirit of the prophets and that the core of the book of Deuteronomy, for example, reflects the essence of their spirit. We must also remember that the critical historical accounts of the acts and negligences of the kings of Israel and Judah (in the books of Samuel and Kings) are to be regarded throughout as an application of the prophetic word to the past. And finally, it must not be overlooked that many Psalms are permeated with the spirit of the prophets, not only those in which outward sacrifice is rejected as inadequate or the poor are honoured as God's elect (who will inherit the earth), but above all those which, like the 'royal Psalms,' rise to a view in which the future of YHWH and the future of the world are one and inseparable.

Formerly much was said about 'prophetism' as being the proclamation of the ethical triumph of the Kingdom of God. This view (in part rightly) neglected the predictive character of prophecy and (completely wrongly) left out of account its character as the concrete speech of God spoken in its situation at that time. The tendency was strongly spiritualizing, and the effect of it was to encourage all kinds of 'fanaticism' and chiliasm, and yet, in my opinion, there is a truth in this reduced view of 'prophetism' which puts in the right light a part of the 'surplus' which is peculiar to the Old Testament. For prophetism is actually an imperial spiritual power, a ferment, which in any attempt to define it more precisely cannot be described as anything but vague, but which nevertheless penetrates to the 'distant isles.'

Or is it not true that prophetism so understood brought the Torah into direct relationship with world history, with the salvation of the nations?[128] Is it not true that the prophets, far from being jurists and philosophers, were in faith intent upon subjecting 'politics' to 'ethics' (if it is permissible to use this Western vocabulary in this case)? Is it not true that our conception of the one humanity, its course and its destiny, its opposition and its honour, its shame and its glory, has its source in Messianism? Is it not true that the universal mystery of the Name was brought to light by the prophets? Did they not bring to men in a new way the idea of 'social justice'? Were they not the ones

[128] H. Cohen, *Ethik des reinen Willens*, pp. 214, 407f., 597.

who saw and proclaimed the day of YHWH and in the face of it scorned all the problems of the world to come, all belief in immortality and rising from the dead?[129] Were they not driven, contrary to all natural instinct and political wisdom, to declare their disbelief in power and not only to advocate but even more to announce World peace? Was it not in their hearts that the cry was born: 'O that thou wouldst rend the heavens and come down, that the mountains might flow down at thy presence' (Isa. 64 : 1)?

We can also express it this way: prophetism showed how the very 'narrowness' of Israel, the 'particularity' of election, the 'singularity' of the Name, the limited course of the story of YHWH and his people, opens up a legitimate way to the universal message. That is to say, here the deliverance, the redemption and fulfilment, is viewed and proclaimed by looking to and appealing to, not the Creator, but the Deliverer, the Redeemer, who had long since appeared in history as the Deliverer from Egypt, the Leader and Guide in the wilderness journey, the *Go'el*, the Redeemer and Guarantor in the distress of the day, each different and each darker day. Here there was no timidity about anticipating the Kingdom, without becoming apocalyptists in the process. 'Without this anticipation and the inner compulsion toward it, without "the desire to bring in the Messiah before his time" and the temptation to "take the kingdom of heaven by violence," the future is not a future, but only a past infinitely drawn out and projected forward.'[130] In order rightly to wake up out of a bad kind of quietism one must perhaps go a step further to the verge of apocalypticism (or somewhat beyond the verge) and with Ernst Bloch connect the primacy of the practical reason[131] directly with the call of the time, the appeal of the moment, the category of danger, the a priori of the *eschaton*,[132] with the yearning to find in the Omega the Alpha finally made good, in the faith that 'never would the world have been so dark for us if the absolute Storm, the central Light were not immediately imminent.'[133]

[129] H. Cohen, *Religion der Vernunft aus den Quellen des Judentums*, pp. 286f., 289, 364.
[130] Franz Rosenzweig, *Der Stern der Erlösung*, II, p. 180.
[131] Ernst Bloch, *Geist der Utopie*, pp. 349f.; cf. the article by G. Scholem in *Almanach des Schocken-Verlags auf das Jahr 5699*.
[132] Ignaz Maybaum, *Der Messianismus der Propheten und der Geist der Utopie*.
[133] Ernst Bloch, *Thomas Münzer*, p. 296; cf. Ignaz Maybaum, 'Die Nachfolge der Makkabäer—das Wesen der unpolitischen Aktivität,' in *Jüdische Rundschau*, Dec. 4, 1931.

Christian conservatism (whatever practical truth there may be in it) turns indignantly away from this voice—partly on the ground that the prophetic message is bound to its own time, partly by pointing to the basically tragic structure of life, and partly with reference to the sinfulness of man. But where is the actualization of the Word with which men are so busily occupied in other areas? Where are the signs that should be erected, the signs of the Kingdom in a world in which there is no way out? We appear to be straining ourselves to the limit—while neglecting the obedience that must be rendered in witnessing precisely at the point where the world seems so sadly to have lost its way. We talk in many different keys about a 'fallen creation' (an entirely unwarrantable concept according to the standard of the Torah) and precisely in doing so we let mankind fall. Mankind drops out of the picture and this accounts in large part for people's estrangement from preaching, their turning away from our gospel.

But it is also a fatal flaw of the dogmatic system in its classical form that it hardly leaves room for prophetism, because, exactly the opposite from the prophets, it begins with the absoluteness of God and his 'incommunicable attributes,' always traces history back to the bed of nature or creation, and interprets redemption as a kind of restoration and elevation of the perfected creation. The prophets, however, spoke of creation only incidentally, suggesting it as a background, a theatre, a springboard; they saw no direct path from creation to fulfilment, but rather followed the wonderful road from the little deliverance of the little people of Israel through YHWH (who also appears only as 'one' of the gods, cf. Ps. 82) to the final redemption and (now indeed!) the 'creation' of a new heaven and a new earth. But what is new in this new thing? The answer is that 'heaven and earth' may enter into a new time. This is the strain that recurs in many Psalms; it is this perspective which is presented to enraptured view (or better, to enraptured ears), for example, in Psalm 149:

> Praise the Lord!
> Sing to the Lord a new song,
> his praise in the assembly of the faithful!
> Let Israel be glad in his Maker,
> let the sons of Zion rejoice in their King!
> Let them praise his name with dancing,
> making melody to him with timbrel and lyre!

For the Lord takes pleasure in his people;
he adorns the humble with victory.
Let the faithful exult in glory;
let them sing for joy on their couches.
Let the high praises of God be in their throats
and two-edged swords in their hands,
to wreck vengeance on the nations
and chastisement on the peoples,
to bind their kings with chains
and their nobles with fetters of iron,
to execute on them the judgment written!
This is glory for all his faithful ones.
Praise the Lord![134]

THE PRINCIPLE OF HOPE

I have forbidden myself every time it seemed desirable, to touch upon the great schism and to ventilate the controversy over the Old Testament that is the basis of it, not only because I have already discussed this in detail in an earlier book,[135] but also because experience shows that at this point the church stubbornly dodges the question and constantly relegates the Old Testament as testimony of the God of Israel to the realm of things Jewish, nationalistic, and legalistic—and thus elevates itself as the seeing church above the blind synagogue and is always on the point of boasting that it has another God.

Nevertheless, here at the close of my discussion of what I have called the 'surplus' of the Old Testament, I shall select one point of the controversy and comment on a contrast to the prophetism just described, namely 'Jewish' Apocalyptic. Not that it is lacking in the New Testament—on the contrary, it is if anything stronger and more vigorous there; and the hermeneutics which is applicable to such passages in the New Testament[136] is also to be applied to those in the Old

[134 In the original Dutch of this book this Psalm is given in a modern Dutch metrical version. There seemed to be no point in attempting an English translation through the Dutch and German versions, and it is therefore given in the translation of R.S.V. —Tr.]

135 *Het wezen der joodsche religie* (1932).

136 Cf. Karl Rahner, 'Theologische Prinzipien der Hermeneutik eschatologischer Aussagen,' in *Schriften zur Theologie*, IV (1960), pp. 401ff.

Testament. And yet Judaism (not to be simply equated with the synagogue), has, for reasons which would take us too far afield here, a tendency to emphasize strongly—sometimes over against the synagogue and the rabbinate—the apocalyptic view. Witnesses rise up in almost every time of crisis in world history who ring out with penetrating enthusiasm a call to stand up in faith and lay hold upon a concrete future, a perspective of fulfilment. Such a call goes out today from the work of Ernst Bloch. And not just today, for his *Geist der Utopie (Spirit of Utopia)* appeared in 1918 and encountered rejection on the part of his fellow Jews, orthodox, liberal, and Zionist. After many disillusionments and apparent false starts—*Durch die Wüste (Through the Desert)*, *Erbschaft dieser Zeit (Heritage of this Age)*, *Spuren (Tracks)*—Bloch has launched a new assault upon stubborn conformism in his book *Prinzip Hoffnung (The Principle of Hope)*.[137]

It is curious to note how frequently the concrete expectation of the apocalyptic alternates with, or is dialectically connected with, a spiritualization of the great future. Yet this is not a path that departs from that of the synagogue; nor has the church, when it has been well advised, ever held otherwise. A certain chiliasm has always accompanied it, and it was natural that it should have been interpreted in a symbolic sense, as pointing to something penultimate, as merely heralding the last things. Therefore at bottom there need be no difference between the church and the synagogue as long as they both listen to the voice of the Old Testament. It would be a (regrettable) relapse into the procedure of the ancient church if we were not to stand essentially with Israel in this matter.

If chiliasm nevertheless seems delusive, dangerous, and misleading to us, we dare not become obdurate again and evade the truth of God's history of salvation (*Heilsgeschichte*). On the contrary, when Israel goes astray, we should step into the breach and be a better Israel. It is of great importance that we should not step in with our ontology, mysticism, and philosophy of history, our pessimism, or worse, our closed bourgeois minds, our silly, simple 'welfare' notions, and our warped idea of sin at precisely the point where the 'spirit of utopia' is in the right and where to raise a hue and cry against the 'fanatics' is a sin against the Spirit. And when, added to this, there is the fact that Bloch is an admirer of Jesus, that he regards Isaiah 53 as relating

[137] Suhrkamp-Verlag, 2 vols. (1959).

to him, and that he finds the *tertium Testamentum* ('third Testament') proclaimed in Romans 9–11[138] ('His shed blood burns not outwardly, but inwardly'), we need to stop and reflect.

In the first place, we must here keep clearly in mind the structures and accents of the Old Testament. In an entirely new sense Bloch relates the unity of the Old Testament to the figure of Moses; even the prophets live by his Messianism, even though this was still completely veiled in the man Moses. But 'the *impulse of Moses* holds the whole Old Testament together, including Messianism which appeared later, or rather was late in enunciation.' How is this to be understood? On the basis of the actual findings which appear within the horizon of hermeneutics. The name 'Yahweh,' which Moses formulated 'I will be there as I will be there,' already has as its essential content the setting free of the utopian consciousness: 'Already at the threshold of the manifestation of Yahweh the name *'Ehyeh 'asher 'ehyeh* sets forth a God of the end of days, with *futurum* as the quality and nature of his being.'[139] Moses therefore has the rank of a founder, is even to be called an 'archetype.' And since, according to Bloch, Messianism must be understood as being the secret of the whole history of religion, this concerns the meaning of world history. Through Moses Yahweh became the 'spirit of exodus.'[140] 'In order to judge the uniqueness of this passage (Exod. 3 : 14, compare it with another interpretation . . . with another divine name, Apollo. Plutarch ('De EI apud Delphos,' *Moralia*, III) records the tradition that the sign 'EI' was carved over the portal of the Delphian temple of Apollo. He sought for a numerical-mystical interpretation of the two letters, but finally came to the conclusion that EI means the same thing grammatically and metaphysically, namely, "You are," in the sense of a timeless, immutable divine existence. . . . This end-and-omega-god would have been foolishness in Delphi, as in any religion in which the god is not one of the exodus.'[141] Bloch is therefore concerned to keep open the future for the acts of God. He wants to break away from the 'encrusted ritardando,' the state of the world in so far as it is bound to unalterable, fixed decrees and thus sealed by men into the inhuman rigidity of the 'historical.' In *Prinzip Hoffnung*, more emphatically than in the earlier book, *Geist der Utopie*, the name of God is a name for a goal. Bloch speaks of a *Deus Spes*

---

[138] *Geist der Utopie*, pp. 323ff.   [139] *Prinzip Hoffnung*, pp. 1456, 1457f.
[140] Ibid., p. 1453.   [141] Ibid., pp. 1457f.

('God of hope') in contrast to a *Deus Creator*. The Exile gave the most grievous glory to the *Deus Spes* in that YHWH himself was carried into exile with his people. This modern thinker appears long since to have concurred with the mysticism of the Kabbala, especially that of Isaak Luria in his doctrine of the exile of the *Shekinah*.[142] In the beginning, *bere 'shith*, the world originated as a contraction (*tsimtsum*) of God. Instead of the glory of the alpha and morning of creation, the emphasis is upon the prospect of the day of freedom, when God's homeless presence in Light will join itself everywhere to the sparks of that light which dwells in every creature. 'The real Creation is not at the beginning but at the end.'

The apocalyptic spirit stands alongside the Talmudic spirit, and for the most part opposes it, and it must be revived again in a time and in a country of which it may be fairly said: 'He for whom the belly is not his God the state is his God; all else has become a joke, an amusement.'[143] Hence the thesis that utopia is the a priori of all culture and politics. The Kingdom of God, justice, the fulfilment must remain established as axiomatic, must be thought of as the prerequisite of the possibility, if we are ever to pick up courage and set to work at some point to realize a church and a community. Actually this is the fundamental axiom! From here Bloch's thinking reaches out and embraces all human endeavour, and the contribution he makes in his interpretive, illuminative, profoundly fundamental work (for example, his theory of music) is tremendously rich in insights and outlook. His is an incomparably potent intellect. We cannot pursue any of this here, but as an opposite view of one factor of the structure of the Old Testament it is extremely important, though it is also important as a new orientation with respect to the ambivalence of religion and atheism. We select several points.

1. One important result of Old Testament study is undoubtedly the insight that belief in the Creation was not the first credo of Israel;[144] that it was precisely the God of deliverance who was worshipped from the 'midst' of history as the one who is also the Creator; that the appeal to creation in the prophets as a theme of consolation does not occupy

---

[142] Gershom G. Scholem, *Die jüdische Mystik in ihren Hauptströmungen* (1957), pp. 271ff., 370; Eng. tr., *Major Trends in Jewish Mysticism* (New York: Schocken Books, 1946).
[143] *Geist der Utopie*, p. 9.
[144] Cf. Gerhard von Rad, *Old Testament Theology*, I, pp. 136ff.

anywhere near such a dominant position as does the remembrance of the exodus; that for the prophets the concept of creation concerned them more as an act, while as a resultant it remains somewhat suspended and incomplete, as if the real essence of the mystery of creation were sealed within this suspension in hope of fulfilment and would not be unveiled until the end of days. And we have seen what a liberating significance these insights have for the modern world, what an effective defence this gives us against speculative ontology, against the grounding of the conscious and the unconscious mind in 'nature,' against the binding of the individual and the collective to the past. This does away with the dream of yesterday, with the fundamental disappointment and disillusionment. There is hardly any more salutary antidote to the self-satisfied and melancholy attitude of bourgeois comfortableness precisely in the church than the clear speech of the Old Testament. This, of course, cannot mean that God the Creator must disappear; such an idea would appear to us to be completely alien; it would never even occur to us. And yet here the idea is put forward.

2. In Bloch's thinking the idea of a Creator ultimately drops out altogether. This makes it clear to us why this also totally changes the teaching of the prophets concerning the End and also the genuinely biblical apocalyptic. It is precisely in the teaching of the open future that the majesty of God and the *contingentia mundi* is presupposed according to the biblical witness. When this is systematically juggled away, then man is made the ruler of history, then he is left alone in all his ways, then the 'exodus impulse,' the 'new category,' becomes a grasping after the power to dispose all things, and then it is inevitable that, since there is no standard for the fulfilment of the world, man will want to persevere in the impulse to grasp power as such (or is compelled to persevere in it). And the only effective inspiration for this perseverance will be the serpent's suggestion, *Eritus sicut Deus* ('You will be like God'), and Bloch makes no bones about this. The earlier Bloch still exhibits the ambivalence of the lived, objective moment: 'Even God—as the problem of the radically new, the absolute deliverer, as the phenomenal element of our freedom, our true content—has his existence in us only as something that happens in a shadowy way but objectively does not happen, only as a meeting of the darkness of the experienced moment and the self-symbol of the absolute question. . . . He "weeps," as several rabbis said in answer to the question of what

the Messiah does when he cannot "appear" and redeem'—and then comes the groping statement: 'He haunts the deepest depths in all of us as "I am what I will be," as the "darkness of the experienced God," as the darkness . . . before his ultimately-to-be-discovered face.'[145]

In *Prinzip Hoffnung*, however, this wavering, this ambivalence is overcome. Now the '*regnum humanum* in nature' is definitely linked up with atheism. God 'dies,' because in the beginning he was not recognized in his divinity, in his aseity, and did not as Creator signify that which is eternally pre-existent. He 'dies,' because man takes over his role in history. He also 'dies' for the mystic and the seer who bids the moment to tarry. 'God dies because he is born in the *nunc aeternum* ('the eternal now').' But 'the real, the actual is that which is not yet, which presses toward itself, which awaits its genesis in the tendency and latency of the process.'[146]

Here is where the 'Jewish,' apocalyptic interpretation of the acts of YHWH really exacts its toll. It is true that these acts create history in progressive faithfulness. It is also true that man is dialogically included in this progress and is able in his own obedience to erect a sign of what is to come. But everything is rendered precarious and unsteady if the acts are not joined to the beginning of the ways of God. In this kind of 'act-mysticism' prophetism must inevitably lead to unrest as a principle, to a state of permanent revolution. The partners of the covenant lose each other; the (in this case) uncreated Adam Kadmon holds the field alone.

3. This can make it clear to us how important the Creation is precisely for faith in the future. Hope itself has no ultimate basis, no standard, and in the last analysis no content if the certainty and the glory of that which is to come are not grounded in God's sovereign majesty and power. Hope cannot be a 'principle' if events (*das Geschehen*) do not hold good in principle and do not actively take part in the *Heilsgeschichte*.

> Thus says HE
> who gives the sun for light by day
> and the fixed order of the moon and stars for light by night;

[145] *Geist der Utopie*, 2nd. edn. (1923), p. 246.
[146] *Prinzip Hoffnung*, pp. 1527, 1537, 1625.

who beckons up the sea
so that its waves roar—
his Name, HE the Lord of hosts. (Jer. 31 : 35)

Or listen to what Amos says (5 : 18):

Woe to those who yearn for HIS day!
What would HIS day be for you after all?

What will the power of such a threat and (hidden) promise be? Who
is speaking here?

He who makes the Pleiades and Orion,
turns the shadows of death into morning light
and darkens the day into night. (5 : 8)

He who builds his high chamber in the heavens,
founds his vault upon the earth,
who calls for the waters of the sea
and pours them out upon the face of the earth,
his Name: HE IS THERE. (9 : 6)

4. Though sometimes everything falls apart (in Bloch's presentation
even the Ophites have their say), though the *homo absconditus* becomes
the substitute for the *Deus absconditus* and finally atheism becomes the
religious presupposition for apocalyptic earnestness, we must not forget what is here seeking *sub contrario* to manifest itself and raise its
voice or at least to suggest itself (and this again is Israel's voice—no,
it is the Word of God in the midst of the silent powers); and the Word
creates an assurance of the Kingdom which does not annul the 'penultimate' and cancel out the small and the great fulfilments (by rele-
gating them to the universal futility). To remind us of this would
perhaps be the abiding task even of a modern Apocalyptic, which
otherwise would be condemned—even though and because it stakes
everything upon concrete history—to find its home in a despair which
says, ' "Home" has never yet been occupied or possessed by any
man.'[147] The concern of the witness today would be to say plainly and
bluntly, over against a false two-world theory of the kind to which
Christianity is generally addicted, that hope, as hope in the 'ultimate,' is not really taken seriously if it insists upon regarding the

[147] H. L. Goldschmidt, *Die Botschaft des Judentums* (1960), p. 132.

'penultimate' as nothing but an illusion. 'He who thinks—where he is, that is, *before* the goal and end has come, and thus at his next step from the present into the future—that he should and can hope only in the "ultimate" and not at all in the "penultimate," let him see to it that he does not grossly deceive himself, that he does not become a fervent lover of the Eternal and a cool despiser of the temporal, that he does not finally arrive at the painful conclusion that the ultimate, which he supposed to be his exclusive hope, really means nothing to him, but that the penultimate, which presumably he did not hope for at all, turns out at bottom to mean everything. That is to say, in the realm of the penultimate, which has been emptied of meaning and turned into a realm of hopelessness, because all hope is put into the ultimate, there will be the exultation, triumphing, and dancing of the demons of the vilest—because now in a kingdom on the left—uncontrolled, and undisciplined worldliness which has always proved to be the outcome of a too rigidly eschatological Christianity.'[148]

But the deepest reason for this distinction and connection between the penultimate and the ultimate is the proclamation of the continuance of Creation, as is actually done in the doxologies of the Apocalypse of John: 'Worthy art thou, our Lord and God, to receive glory and honour and power, for thou didst create all things, and by thy will they existed and were created' (Rev. 4 : 11; cf. 5 : 12ff.). The 'four beasts' stand 'round the throne, on each side of the throne' (4 : 6); they sing, and their song goes out as a song of hope through the world, the innocent world.[159] The beings exist along with the white throne, the radiant sovereignty, which is the foundation of all grace—and all created things.

[148] Karl Barth, *Church Dogmatics*, Vol. IV, pt. 3, sect. 2, p. 936. [My translation.—Tr.]
[149] Cf. K. H. Miskotte, *Hoofdsom der Historie, voordrachten over de visioenen van den apostel Johannes* (1945), pp. 117ff., 406ff., 446ff.

4. Authority and Outgoing of the Word

PROPHECY AND HISTORY

'In the Bible God tells us what he has experienced with man. God's history with man would be a good subtitle for it. But God does this in his own way. He knows that he can reach us only if he tells us our own story, man's story with God. And so the Bible immediately shows us the nature of God's work in us. He steps into our place. He comes to us and puts himself on our side. He tells us his history as our history.'[1]

But we have been saying that history as event (*Geschehen*) is qualified history, and that history as narrative is interpreted history, or to put it another way, the events are 'holy' events and the narrative is 'prophetic' narrative. And as we have already seen, even the 'law' is an element of the narrative, much more than the other way round. This differentiates Israel and the church from all religion and drives them out into the world. They carry the Word to distant coasts. This work, called mission, has its own dynamic. The events (*Geschehen*) go on, because the Name remains: 'I will be what I will be' (Exod. 3 : 14). In the events we meet the Name; and prophecy, which is an out-reaching light, a revealing and blessing power of the Spirit, a reconciling and quietly triumphing presence, is an essential part of the events. The narrative too goes on, because the Word keeps watch over the interpretation of events. Whenever it has pleased God, the essence, the act, the virtue of the Name has entered into the speech of his messengers, so that we meet the event in the narrative just as we meet the event in the Name.

And in this potentiated form prophecy keeps creating new history. The Word is current and contemporary, not, as we say, because it is 'eternal' but because it actualizes itself today, reveals itself as light and

---

[1] G. van der Leeuw, *De Bijbel als boek*, p. 6—although here this is thought of in terms of 'continuity' with religious myth. Cf. Edward Buess, *Die Geschichte des mythischen Erkennens* (1953), pp. 84, 197, 209ff.

guidance, consolation and power. These things must be kept in mind in the carrying out of the ministry, in the work of the interpreter and witness. Without this we shall not rightly understand the authority of preaching. That is to say, preaching is neither rationalistic, nor ethical, nor mystical in orientation; it is prophecy, that is, an envisaging, a making-present of the holy events, repetition of the great narrative which never passes away, application of the history, the story of God, which has gathered up into itself the history of men, and for their good assures its days and its meaning.

Exegetically, hermeneutically, one can properly say that the content of the Bible dare not be subjectivized and that the form dare not be objectivized; but in actual fact both occur by and large in history, namely, where the story of God is told and the prophetic narration happens, becomes an event. A formal similarity to the relationship of cult and myth cannot be denied. Here too it is a matter of an envisaging, a making-present. The telling of the story of the Name is well suited for this; and the myth of the presence of God—'groundless —in the midst of things,' surrounded by his acts—evokes other than religious reactions, it provokes to repentance.

'We must not be surprised that this dreadful virus, Christianity, has produced reaction when it has been introduced under the skin and even into the heart of pagan society. It is not merely a novelty but an enigma, something at once consuming and insatiable. Nor is it something for the calm musings of the philosophers. It is a question of saying yes or no. Say no at the risk of eternal death. Say yes and it means a sure transformation of the flesh and the soul, which is a terrible thing for both.' So says Paul Claudel, using a physical metaphor.[2] But even though this statement emphatically stresses the authority and the power of the new thing that happens, there is nevertheless no real understanding of the word-character of the Word. And thus the creative, intermittent, free, autonomous element of prophecy falls away; one may even say that the Israelitic understanding has almost completely disappeared and along with it the secret of the special Presence which is promised in the special language of the message. Over against this we must point out the 'mythical' character of the message, even though the use of this term may be misunderstood.

[2] Paul Claudel, *Pages de prose*, ed. Blanchot (1949), p. 394. [Quoted in French in the original.—Tr.]

In any case, it at least suggests that the history referred to here has altogether different dimensions.

We may confidently assert that the language of the Bible is to a large extent 'mythical'—if only one adheres strictly to the fact that this myth, unlike the pagan myth, recognizes no figures which stand outside of time and no events which are not within the course of nature. However, this term 'myth' actually has no importance except when it is used as a defence, that is to say, if it is used to say that when the literal as well as the spiritualizing exposition of prophecy is employed, then the prophetic preaching is lost. A genuinely naïve listening is not a listening to the sound and the letter, nor does it enter into an *immanental* process of appropriation—it is rather a participation in the drama of 'prophecy and history,' the drama of the authority and the outgoing of the Word.

Radius of Action

The authority works itself out in the outgoing of the Word. The Word has a broad radius of action. The history of the church is essentially the history of the prophetic-apostolic Word. Everywhere in it we can sense something of the 'exodus impulse' (Bloch). The openness of the Christian existence is directed toward an end. Where the Lord's Supper is celebrated as remembrance of and participation in the sacrificial act of the Lord, in the accomplished act, the future opens up (I Cor. 11 : 26), for the supper is at the same time a food of hope, a drinking of promise. The apostolic Word shares in the authority of the prophecy, which since time immemorial has always shattered the foundations, the shelters of human religion and society. The inertia of the fundamental forces of existence is assailed by the mission. He who moves to other countries need fear no exile. And as Israel in the Diaspora could call the Torah the 'portable sanctuary,' so the church of Christ could go out with the kerygma—and in its estimation it was not bidding farewell to indispensable wisdom when it went on its outward journey, leaving other lands and culture behind. 'Christianity *must* missionize. It is as necessary to it as the seclusion of the pure spring of blood from alien admixture is necessary to the self-preservation of the eternal people. Indeed, missionizing is nothing short of being *the* form of its self-preservation.'[3]

[3] Franz Rosenzweig, *Der Stern der Erlösung*, III, p. 104.

Beyond the 'holy city,' beyond the Roman empire, beyond the frontiers of Europe, the first area to be fully blessed, the Word went out. We cannot measure or set limits to the proclamation's radius of action. Nor do we possess any standard by which we can separate what is ecclesiastical and what is cultural, much less what is divine and what is human in the ongoing and outgoing of the Word. It is true that we may take it as certain that the image of God's rule is not to be sought in the form of an empire, in the likeness of a state, for here too the authority remains above all power; but at the same time it is only in the outgoing that the operation of the authority develops. The Word of God celebrates its sovereignty in its service and ministry, its constancy in its crusading, its enthronement in the winning of new domains. It is a brief occupation which serves to curb the pagan blood and its idle dreams. It is true that 'the prince's hand is as large as the land,' and (in the church!) the 'sovereignty of the people' would in fact lead to a kind of mob rule, but God's sovereign rule takes place more in a free governance of continuing decisions than in ruling a conquered territory. We see this in the history of the church's mission: the church must remain apostolically organized, or it falls victim to the old powers, or it hardens into a new institution of religion. God is concerned with the procession, the ongoing and outgoing passage. In the liberated area he leaves behind a few free cities and installs plenipotentiaries, each with his own mandate. Even his orders and instructions prove to be just so many liberations because they are intended to enable men to launch out into the open future. Where he has passed by in his procession, a shining track is left behind, a culture or a broken culture, a sphere of power, large as a fruitful border march or small as a hidden, 'useless' work of art. Where his authority concentrates and intensifies itself and makes its way through, there the horizons in which men have been imprisoned, suffering the silence of the gods until the hour of their liberation, are always lifted.

It was in the month of spring, the ancient rabbis said, that Israel went out from Egypt, and 'the desert received this people like a welcome guest'; after the years of confinement they could again breathe the air of freedom. According to Hosea (11 : 1), the time of wandering in the desert was a time of real honeymoon, though even then there were frequent murmurings.

The desert! This would be the opposite of the cultivated land

(*Kulturland*)—if it were not that freedom is more, always more than its outward form. But freedom—freedom in dependence—is the very signum of the desert, if the 'face of the Lord' accompanies us (Exod. 33) and the stiff-neckedness of God's partners is transformed into a resolute turning away from the gods (Josh. 24). Then spring comes again and full young life on earth. Preaching comes along in the train of this new springtime with its new note and breaks open the soil of the earth. The mission, the apostolate, renews the face of the earth. Thus the church 'makes' history. To be sure, it did not take Israel's place in the plan of salvation in an ultimate way, but vicariously it has to fulfil Israel's missionary call and mission to the nations. Therefore there is good sense, born of a deep intuition, in the practice, especially in Calvinistic countries, of calling preaching 'prophecy' precisely when it is done in Christianized areas. This presupposes an analogy with the prophetic office of the Messiah, it retains a continuity with the witnesses of the Old Testament, it avoids a soteriological contraction of the Message. It assumes that the Word in the preaching finds its own concrete application with respect to government and people, in all areas of life. And it declares that 'profane' life should be sanctified, without being elevated to something sacral, because authority levies its claim upon it and the passage of the Word leaves its tracks upon it, so that actually there can be no such thing as a 'post-Christian' time, even though whole nations, by denying their election and predestination, can exhibit a pre-Christian attitude.

Apostasy

In the preceding section we spoke in ideal terms, or better, from the standpoint of God, in a way that corresponds to the destiny which he gave to the Church in the authority of his Word. How could it happen that whole areas through which the prophecy has passed have fallen away again, sometimes so completely that hardly a trace of it has remained? We are thinking primarily of the conquests of Islam, a whirlwind in which Asia Minor, Egypt, North Africa, and Spain saw their Christian communities swept away, but also of the 'Babylonian captivity' of the church, and finally of the modern alienation of the nations in open apostasy. It is possible to discern a few clear lines in the confusion of attraction and repulsion, synthesis and diastasis, but we must abstain from deciding on which side the greater fault lies. We certainly cannot say what happened because of human confusion and what was God's providence, but we can certainly assume that the apostasy of the nations is always connected with unfaithfulness on the part of Christendom.

This unfaithfulness of Christendom, we may say, was unfaithfulness in life and doctrine, in the superpersonal forms of living, and with respect to God's intention and purpose. In the course of the argument of this book we have had to speak above all of the blurring and obscuring of the idea of God itself. And we ask, how long did the church proclaim the God of Israel, how long did it hold to the act-character of his Word, how long did it continue the telling of his acts? How long did it resist the powers, the astral myth of the existence of the world? How long did it regard the gods as nonentities? How quickly the Christians abandoned the exodus, how soon they grew ashamed of overstepping the bounds and crossing frontiers, how quickly many exchanged their expectation for the pleasure of a settled intellectualism! But all the manifestations which prompt these critical questions and demand our judgment are actually never to be found in pure culture. At the risk of seeming to trivialize apostasy by reflecting upon it, we must first look at theology, preaching, and instruction in the light of the standard of the Old Testament.

The **God** of Israel! Had not Christendom already in the second century largely lost the knowledge that its God was the God of Israel; did it ever enter its mind that Israel's election was the root of its salvation? And across the centuries—was this knowledge a living, vital element in the *corpus christianum*; had it not rather died out completely? And finally today—in the Protestant churches is it an unshakable part of our knowledge that we are 'incorporated' in Israel; is it not rather an enormous affront to remind people of it? Still today the God of Israel is an outcast for his newly won people. 'This is a hard saying,' we say. But then it must follow that the whole Scripture becomes distorted; and this is also the very reason for our helplessness over against modern man. He sees or expects to see among us the godhead of the heathen, a metaphysical construct, the giver and guarantor of laws, the protector of institutions whose origin and aims modern man has seen through. And not without reason he cries out his angry reproach: 'God, or the church, or Christian morality [for to him they

308

all mean the same thing] is guilty of witch trials, slavery, class injustice, and so on; in order to justify these things He has inspired these hypocritical ideologies.' Modern man throws himself against this with his weapons, forged in the fire of his honest regard for truth, and this fire he identifies with the fervency of his unbelief, with the vehemence of his nihilism. This is the end of the road that began by putting in first place the metaphysical God, the ontological cosmos, natural law, providence, *amor fati*, and thereby dimmed the light of the God of Israel. This mixing or duplication of the idea of God in our witness encourages the growth and flourishing of that denial of God which manifests itself in experience both as a liberation and an emptying of life.

Thus we have come deep into autumn, far away from the springtime, the honeymoon, the desert. But we have already noted that there are signs of conversion here and there. Conversion never results from the changing seasons; it cannot be dealt with in natural categories and hardly in historical categories. It belongs to the holy events, the holy history, to the authority and the outgoing of the Word, which itself has always made history. The purpose of our discussion here has only been to point out the shadows that accompany the course of prophecy and make the history of the church a field of struggle, the struggle not only of the Word against the *goyim* but also the struggle of prophecy against the churches of the Messiah Jesus.

THE QUESTION OF JUDAISM

Within this struggle of the Word belong the questions Judaism has to put to the church. In the content and character of these questions we see not an overshadowing but rather a help toward the clarification of the Message which will be useful to preaching today as it comes to grips with the ultimate apostasy, that of the 'godless' man. Israel always asked questions where others did not question. Paganism is an unquestioning celebration of the given world. Israel searched for a meaning in life, or rather, it received that meaning. Where meaning was obscured by fate, where God hid himself in events which were in contradiction to his promise, Israel searched and persistently struggled for a new answer. But in the dispersion (*galuth*) this questioning attitude touches above all the right of the Christian church to enter upon the inheritance of Israel.

The difference between synagogue and church breaks out perhaps most sharply in the question of prayer. And here the quiet reproach of Judaism is this: is your prayer a mere wish or is it the reverse side of the action of your life? If you regard the creatureliness of man merely as a dependence and not as a call to participate in God's purpose, if you say that God does not need man and his service in the healing of the world, what is left of the peculiar earnestness of human life which the prophets were constantly proclaiming in rebuke and challenge? Does not such a self-sufficient God degrade the life, the striving, and the suffering of his children to a game of self-exaltation? Is he not an idol, an object for man's contemplation, a mere construct to help safeguard man? 'Eternity must be hastened, it must be able to come constantly, to come "today"; only so is it eternity. If there is no such power, no such prayer, which can hasten the coming of the Kingdom, then it will never come—not even in eternity.'[4]

Then the questioning of the synagogue and Judaism broadens out into a series of pointed questions. They dare not be brushed aside, either simply or learnedly, for the sake of a certain overstrained polemical attitude. We mention a few of these questions, especially those which have a direct or indirect relation to the witness which the church must give to the modern world.

What else can 'faith' mean, asks our Jewish interlocutor, except to trust in God, in his presence as well as in his absence? But Christianity appears to make this trust and confidence in God dependent upon a 'belief,' that is, the recognition of and assent to supernatural but nevertheless historical facts. What else can 'conversion' mean except to 'turn away?' Is *metanoia* an adequate translation of *teshubah*? What is the meaning of a 'mediator' between God and man, when after all, God himself intervenes for man? Is not the figure of a mediator possible only in the framework of a concept of a passive divine substance (*cohen*)? And what are the Christians, at least those who hold on to the unity of the Testaments, to think of a God who cannot forgive by himself and, contrary to his promise, does not accept penitence, but demands the sacrifice of the mediator, without which the repentance is invalid or not even possible?

[4] Franz Rosenzweig, *Der Stern der Erlösung*, III, p. 37.

It is true that these questions are full of misunderstandings, but for the most part they are based upon what is actually an erroneous interpretation on the part of theology, as the history of doctrine shows. And yet even in the misunderstanding evidenced by Judaism there is expressed a concern which concerns us: it is a question of honouring the nature of the God of Israel and hallowing his Name.

Much freer of misinterpretation is the Jewish protest against the church's proclamation where it touches upon chronological time and the centre of time and the meaning of time after Christ. According to the synagogue, the Christian reckoning of time has a profound purpose, namely, to proclaim the redemption as having happened, as completed. And the synagogue asks: in what sense is the world redeemed? And is this, so to speak, magical miracle the fulfilment of what the prophets envisioned? Listen to the echo of the 'third man's' uneasiness in this question—and that of the 'fourth man' in so far as he should happen to listen to this profoundly moving message. Surely the distinction between reconciliation and redemption should be brought to bear here as the conclusive answer; and it is not very difficult for theology to show the divergent import of both. But through the centuries it has simply failed to do this. And so it is also with the 'nearness of God,' with 'rejoicing in the Law,' the 'honouring of the Noachites,' the 'humanity of God,' and the 'expectation of the coming day'—Jewish teachings which in principle should also be heard in evangelical preaching but which in fact are still hardly ever heard.

All this is set out here in order that we may take some account of the reality of the confusions which overshadow the course of the Word, especially with regard to the man of the present crisis, who until recently, when he heard the word 'God,' intuitively and rightly understood this to mean the saving power which both synagogue and church desire to worship in obedience.[5]

---

[5] For more detailed accounts of what is presented here only in sketch form see: H. J. Schoeps, *Jüdisch-christliches Religionsgespräch in 19 Jahrhunderten* (1937); H. L. Goldschmidt, *Die Botschaft des Judentums* (1960); E. L. Dietrich, 'Das jüdisch-christliche Religionsgespräch am Ausgang des 16. Jahrhunderts nach dem Handbuch des R. Isaak Troki,' *Judaica*, XIV (1958), especially pp. 18ff.; Ernst Müller, 'Wandlung des jüdischen Bewusstseins in den letzten zwei Jahrhunderten,' *Judaica*, X (1954), pp. 129ff. Among the older literature the following should be mentioned: Max Brod, *Heidentum, Christentum, Judentum* (1921); Leo Baeck, *Das Wesen des Judentums* (1905).

Opponent and Partner

In order to discern the open secret of the outgoing of the Word, the synagogue must be seen to be a real partner accompanying us along the way. In this relationship the synagogue is negative when it rejects the Messiah, and positive in so far as it does not meet the church merely as a hostile brother on the way, but also brings to it a definite openness in its evaluations. 'Christianity' is recognized as 'the way of the Gentiles'—and it was so recognized not only in the striking statements of Franz Rosenberg but from ancient times and even in the times of persecution, expulsion, oppression, and extermination. Thus even Judah ha-Levi said in his book *The Kuzari*: 'Those nations are a readying and preparation for the Messiah for whom we wait, who will be the fruit, and all will acknowledge his fruit and him, and the tree will be one. Then they will praise and honour the root, which they once despised, as Isaiah says.'

This recognition looks not only to a solution at the end of history; it is often reinforced with a doctrine of historical decline from which Israel itself will not be exempt. 'In the generation when the son of David comes, the house of assembly will be for harlots . . . the wisdom of scribes in disfavour, God-fearing men despised, people be dog-faced, and truth entirely lacking. . . . He who departs from evil will be dubbed a fool by his fellow-men' (so R. Judah); and in the same context[6] R. Nehemiah says, 'In the generation of Messiah's coming impudence will increase, esteem be perverted'; and R. Isaac says, 'The son of David will not come until the whole world is converted to the belief of the heretics'; and another says that 'the son of David will not come until . . . the redemption is despaired of' by the Israelites.

This doctrine of gradual decline was countered by the way of the Gospel among the Gentiles, until even this way was broken off by frequent eruptions of hatred against the Jews. This would mean the end of the way of the Gospel in irrevocable apostasy, if in this apocalyptic threat the Word of God to the Gentiles did not reveal itself to be the Word of the Covenant, the Word which was specifically entrusted to Israel. A new meeting of minds is beginning to take place today, and

---

[6] *Sanhedrin*, fol. 96–98; translation from *Sanhedrin*, II (*The Babylonian Talmud*, ed. I. Epstein [London, The Soncino Press, 1935], pp. 655, 656).

the church has even begun to stand up for Israel, however dividedly and haltingly this espousal of its cause may be. 'Exterminate it!' screamed the demonic barbarians, and this was affirmed almost without shame or inhibition in the collective unconscious of the German people. Then the church, the way of the Gentiles, took a turn which had already been prepared for in the preceding decades, but this time a turn not only toward humanity but toward spiritual brotherhood. In the world of the 'fourth man' this has not been forgotten, and it dare not be allowed to come to nothing because of any reaction on the part of the church.

As in our entry into modern times the historical potency of Israel was more and more discovered to be the decisive event, so now the most horrible victimization of the people of God has stimulated a long overdue rethinking of Israel's election. And on the other hand, the awakening (however hesitant) gave to the Jewish remnant a new trust that the way of the Gentiles was nevertheless intended by Israel's God for the best welfare of Israel itself. The ancient doctrine of two ways, the 'two types of faith' (Buber), is again in evidence at least in the form of 'the recognition of Christianity as a religiosity on an equal footing with its own piety and teaching.' As evidence of this we point to the breakthroughs to Jesus (and also to Paul) as found in Leo Baeck, *Das Evangelium als Urkunde der jüdischen Glaubensgeschichte* ['The Gospel as a Document in the History of the Jewish Faith'] (1938!) and in the books by Joseph Klausner on Jesus and Paul. The literary endeavours indicate the same intent: *Jesus as Others Saw Him, A Retrospect A.D. 54* by Joseph Jacobs, *The Nazarene* by Sholem Asch (1939), *Der Meister* by Max Brod, *Paulus unter den Juden* by Franz Werfel. The way is opening up toward an 'affirmation of Christianity not because it is rooted in Judaism but because and in spite of the fact that it has taken root and is blooming and maturing outside of Judaism.'[7]

We are not of the opinion that these endeavours really deal with the ultimate question; the Messiahship of Jesus is denied with the same old passion and rejected with all the powers of mind and spirit. But we do see in this movement a gain for our work of enlightening modern man. Bonhoeffer anticipated and called for a 'nonreligious' interpretation of the Gospel. Though we do not altogether understand what he meant by this, in our connection we may say in a preliminary way that

---

[7] H. L. Goldschmidt, *Die Botschaft des Judentums* (1960), p. 153.

the result of a closer approach between synagogue and church could be that of reminding 'ungenuine' nihilism of the great fact (which was never completely hidden in the previous stages of the 'way of the Gentiles') that in the midst of the swarm and confusion of religions these two, Israel and the church, are not religions. Israel and the church live their life under the Word. The argument that there are so many religions among which one must choose, if the confusion were not too great, is untenable.

Religion as a magical or mystical relationship to Being; religion as an elevation and deepening of human self-understanding, all the way to the experience of oneness with the All; religion as deeply serious worship of the manifestations of God wherever he makes himself known; religion as a ritual for the restoration of cosmic balance; religion as the ethos of willing accommodation of oneself to the laws of life as these are so cogently set forth in the myths of ever-recurring cycles—this is religion as such, and it is impossible for Israel and the church (and in part also for Islam) to assimilate it or to welcome it as a variant of themselves, unless it were to disavow its most peculiar characteristic.

This has always been sharply discerned by the Gentiles, whose eye was guileless at first but soon becomes profoundly distrustful. But where does this disavowal of the peculiar character of religion begin? Is not the touchstone for this the Old Testament, which is common to both Israel and the church? We do not need to repeat the arguments set forth in the third section of part two of this book ('The Surplus'). Through the Torah, the whole *Tenack*, the religion of man is nullified, that is, even rebellion against its impressive power is rendered superfluous. The Old Testament is not only our actual ally in this struggle, it is the source of it. And this last is so important because the struggle is also one against our own house, in so far as religion may have regained entrance to it.

This twofold faith is a trust in and a giving of oneself to history (an entity which religion has not even seen in the qualified sense which it has in the Scriptures)—no, not a trust in history but rather in the acts of the Lord, or more precisely, in the Name. The 'world'—one can say, religion, heathenism—however rich and profound and splendid (but above all, human) it may be, does not know the divine freedom, the mystery of time, the open future, elective love, and therefore it also does not know the hiddenness of God, the continuing questioning of existence, the cry from the depths; and therefore it knows no hope, does not need to know it. But in the eyes of men Israel and the church are characterized by this knowledge, this kind of need, and therefore by this hope.

The Glory and the Shame of Christendom

The way of the Word is the way of the Gentiles. But the word 'is' denotes a mystery, and it cannot be lightly passed over. For the unprejudiced eye, is it not the most obvious thing to interpret the history of the church as profane history? Today, when people even less than in earlier times experience the phenomenon of the church from the inside as a determinative element of their own history, it has already become simply a matter of course to regard this phenomenon—'the miracle of the church'—in this way.

Thus the spectacular claim of the church must inevitably be interpreted as invincible intolerance. Its progressive extension must inevitably be regarded as a series of happy accidents promoted by favourable sociological circumstances. Its power to recover from many defeats and humiliations must necessarily be interpreted as the virulent power of certain survivals which possess a peculiar tenacity through 'metaphysical projection.' Seen from the inside, it is the Word itself which is the cause of the continued existence of the church. On the way of the Gentiles there are no infallible courts of appeal; the outgoing of the Word does not move forward tidily and triumphantly. On the contrary, this way has been distorted because Israel was not in it and it has been disgraced by antisemitism. Israel's rejection of the Messiah accompanies the church like a continuing shadow. It is always present, even today, even in the mouth of those who have devoted much thought to and evidenced much understanding of the Gospel. Listen once more to a voice from this group, that of Franz Rosenzweig who says: '. . . we do not go along with the world-conquering fiction of Christian dogma, because (though a reality) it is a fiction (and *fiat veritas, pereat realitas*, for "Thou God art the truth") and learnedly declares that we deny the foundation of modern culture (and *fiat regnum Dei, pereat mundus*, for "you shall be to me a kingdom of priests and a holy nation") and rudely declares that we crucified Christ and, believe me, *would do it again at any time*, we alone in all the wide world (and *fiat nomen Dei Unius, pereat homo*, for "to whom will you liken me and make me equal?").'[8]

It is true that we can see suddenly illuminated in such a candid statement how far Judaism too departs from the Old Testament and lives in a pride which draws its strength from a 'religious' misinterpretation of the election, a 'correlative' understanding of the covenant. But what has the church on the 'way of the Gentiles' set over against this and, except for some intervals of patience, conversation, and peace, continued to pit against it with a shocking persistence? It has proclaimed that it has taken the place of the people of God; it has tutored the Gentiles in an almost unbounded contempt for the Jews and not infrequently incited them to pogroms. The *corpus christianum*, from the extreme west (Spain) to the extreme east (Poland), was the field for one great hunt. On the Rhine and the Rhone practice drills for the Crusades were carried out in the burning of the Ghettos and horrible butchery—in the name of Christ.

Let us not forget—for this is the point of the matter—that all this has been in part brought about by our preaching. It would take us too far afield to pursue in detail the features of its content which have produced such fruits. Certainly among them would be such impossible teachings as our doctrines about God's power and dominion, about righteousness and merit, about imputation and retribution, about human nature and its (falsely localized) corruption, about the power of the sword and obedience, about the honour of God and the glory of Christ—in short, almost all of it has been infected by the blood and the spirit of the *goyim*. The most impossible doctrines!—yes, impossible, measured by the Gospel witness to Christ. Right here is where we find asserting itself what has been 'added to' the doctrine from the 'world of the three rings' (Friedrich Heer). And right here emerges large as life the danger of an isolated New Testament. For the abiding presupposition of the New Testament is the Old Testament; but it is likewise the genuine supplementation of the New Testament in matters of applying the Gospel to the questions of a pagan environment and a broadly established secular society—entities which were not foreseen in the New Testament, because it was mercifully hidden from the Apostles that the church had before it a long road of pilgrimage and struggle in history among the nations.

[8] *Briefe* (1935), pp. 670f.

That the hope of the world becomes darkened without a reconciliation between Israel and the Gentiles, how remote this thought (or
even an inkling of it) was from the church in earlier and later times!
We cannot get it into our head or our heart that by grace we are grafted
into the ancient tree of the Covenant people. How far beyond our
understanding are the words of the Apostle: 'Now if their trespass
means riches for the world, and if their failure means *riches for the
Gentiles*, how much more will their full inclusion mean! . . . For if their
rejection means the reconciliation of the world, what will their acceptance mean but life from the dead? . . . If you do boast, remember
it is not you that support the root, but *the root that supports you*' (Rom.
11 : 12ff.)! Also remote from the thinking of the church was the insight
that the 'body of Christ' (in Paul's thought) is to be related first of all
to the given unity of Jews and Gentiles and that thus both are called to
preserve and confirm the Messianic gift, namely, their reconciliation
and mutual relationship—in hope; the *goyim* are 'fellow citizens with
the saints' (i.e., of the elect) and 'partakers of the promise' (Eph.
2 : 19; 3 : 6). In the 'body of Christ' is fulfilled what is said in Zech.
14 : 6 and Isa. 25 : 6f.[9]

What are all the confusions in the history of doctrine and all the
crimes of the Christian powers compared with this twofold burden
which has been put upon the progress of the Word of God: the absence
and deviation of Israel on the one hand and the usurpatory presence
and unreceptiveness of the church on the other? If we were to discuss
'Judaism' and 'Christianity,' there would be much that is essential
which would have to be said, much that would accentuate the contrast
between them and much that would be conciliatory. But here we are
concerned with the Word and the world, the way of the Word in the
way of the Gentiles. What we need to see and acknowledge is that
God himself must be in the fight to preserve the church in its crisis,
to renew it to a life of reconciliation and lead it out of the prison of its
offences.

And this is just what he has done. And so the 'miracle of the church'
is the miracle of the workings of the Word against the accumulation
of opposition from within and without. Then the realization of this
usurpation and confusion on the part of the church would prompt us
right here to praise the providential guidance and the victorious

[9] Cf. J. J. Meuzelaar, *Der Leib des Messias* (1961).

governance of God. The God of Israel has given to the church character and continuance, conversion and rebirth. We see that the church of the Messiah Jesus has repeatedly withstood corruption, 'that again and again it has been plucked out of its fears and preserved at the last from completely succumbing to its temptations, that suddenly or after a seasonable time its wounds have been healed, that its Babylonian captivities have come to an end, that its foes and oppressors have one day disappeared from the scene, that again and again it has been raised from the dead to newness of life.'[10] But we never see this, it seems, without again failing to see it. This seeing is the seeing of faith—faith in the God of Israel. But this faith is not without signs, without experience, without knowledge. And the (negative) signs may be especially eloquent. Among these signs we would count above all the fact that the church has lost its authority and respect in the world and finds itself sharing a *de facto* fate with Israel, which here and there has also led to a sense of spiritual solidarity—though it will not do to interpret this as being quite so wholly balanced as H. L. Goldschmidt has recently attempted to do.[11] But we should not fumble about with the enigma too long, for the mystery of God that presents itself in this experience touches us too deeply and will sink into our hearts in a salutary way only if we do not talk it to pieces in our theological furore.

INTO A STRANGE LAND

In part one of this book we attempted to describe a number of features of the so-called 'fourth man' in the light of some literary witnesses. We found that he has lost paganism, the feeling of being secure in existence, without there being any hope that the gods or the godhead will return with a new face. We spoke of 'genuine' and 'ungenuine' nihilism, the former characterized as rejection of security in divine existence, the latter broken by a memory of the God of Israel and because of this still retaining a minimum of irrational expectation of one who is to come ('Waiting for Godot'). Before the complete emptying of existence becomes finally fixed, it is pierced for a moment by a tiny shaft of

---

[10] Karl Barth, *Church Dogmatics*, Vol. III, pt. 3, p. 208. [Translation altered.—Tr.]
[11] H. L. Goldschmidt, *Die Botschaft des Judentums* (1960).

light, a dim sense of a presence. The 'eclipse of God' has come upon us, and for many it wears the mask of fate, but for others it still bears the face of the God whom they knew before (though it may be heavily veiled). A certain ambivalence, carried over from a religion which has not yet been entirely abandoned, expresses itself in reproaches against God that contradict the previously asserted denial of him, and in denials of God that contradict the reproaches which still continue to be launched against him. Here and there a bit of humour breaks out, 'just to thaw out a little of the frozen music of the soul in the post horn.'[12]

One can say—with reservations, because we cannot fathom the depths of unbelief in the soul of other times and places—that such an experience of the absence of God as that which we see today in the way of the Gentiles never existed before. In any case, the way of the Word presents itself more than ever before as a journey into a strange land, precisely because the Word is the only thing that launches out against the distress which has been brought about by the fact that the world has been stripped of its gods. The attestation, the interpretation, and the application of the Word in human words are in themselves subject to great weakness, and now their weakness becomes especially apparent as they enter into a strange land.

One may be tempted to reply that the depth dimensions of human existence always recrudesce in the questions man cannot help asking about the origin, the meaning, and the goal of life. It may be asserted that man's newly acquired 'maturity' (*Mundigkeit*) has not stopped this questioning. It least of all can indulge in the bliss of an unquestioning immediacy. The man who has 'come of age' cannot fend off the question of death; he simply cannot be indifferent to this radical reversal of existence into nothingness, this annihilation of his existence. Thus in a time when the gods are silent, the question would be intensified tenfold.

Often we find in the church a preconceived notion, born of love and perplexity, to the effect that 'the fields are white for harvest' (Jn. 4 : 35), because, after all, the people who no longer find any answer in science, philosophy, new religion, and pseudoreligion and have been largely left in the lurch by literature must surely find it impossible to close their minds to the Word. Hitherto the real need for decision has

[12] Christian Morgenstern.

repeatedly been covered up and repressed in the face of the glamour and power of worldly wisdom, but now men who are in flight from this hellish emptiness must surely run straight into the arms of salvation. Godless men, we are told, are easier to reach than religious men! We suspect that here the strength of this questioning on the part of modern man is being overestimated. The truth is that men's disillusionment and weariness have burrowed into and established themselves in the depths of the soul in the form of an infinite sadness.

But the most important thing has not yet been mentioned. The real and original questioner is God. God questions man, and man has to answer him, even if for the time being the answer is veiled in questioning words. In the precedence of his eternal priority God takes the initiative. He rules in freedom over the indeterminability of the liberating answer. Therefore a man, thus called into question by God, should stand up and face the question, even though he has shut himself up in ultimate sadness. But despite the fact that he has shut himself up, something has touched him, and the despair that is thus churned up in his life leads to the projection of fresh questions—questions which he has already dismissed and put behind him as hopeless. Then he begins again to set up a barrage of problems. And he does so because for him this is more tolerable than to be the one who is himself being questioned. In these questions he moves in the opposite direction from that he previously took. Once he sought God by way of religion; now he flees from him by way of claiming that he has 'come of age' in order to shake him off once and for all—and all because this God, this misunderstood, rejected, and by this very token sovereign, God has come too close to him.

When we say that because of this situation, the way of the witness takes on the character of a journey into a strange land, it may be objected that though it may be true that modern man's compulsive resort to his independent 'adulthood' is occurring in a gradually more serious form, it must nevertheless be regarded fundamentally as a process which has existed in the way of the Gentiles at all times. Then the strange land into which the witness must go today would have to be regarded only as a relatively greater, more radical, more closed and sinister strange land. But today the strangeness of the strange land has been intensified by its appearance in our common intellectual life, and as far as I can see, no parallel for this can be found in earlier times.

320

But this fact is a threatening one only in so far as we start with the assumption of the necessity and the salutariness of words, thinking, speaking, preaching. This brings us up against something exceedingly practical. What we are referring to is the depreciation, the devaluation of human words. It is not necessary here to attempt an analysis of our time with special reference to this statement. We shall rather examine what the church has done and is doing in the 'mission territory of Europe' in order to face this phenomenon or to evade it and conclude from this examination the extent of its embarrassment. We shall do this, of course, always keeping in mind that we too share responsibility for the church's plans, endeavours, and experiments.

It should be noted that we barely mention the criticism of the 'preaching church' which is going on within the church, the insiders who are tired of preaching, the approaches toward liturgical renewal, the use of plays and drama to proclaim the message, etc., and concentrate upon those endeavours which proceed on the assumption and assertion that preaching can be dispensed with. We concentrate our attention at this point because here the attempt is made to show how universal is the ineffectiveness of words and how greatly preponderant among the disciples are the negative reactions to it—the utter boredom, the irritation, the reproach of *mauvaise foi*. How can this be remedied? We really cannot believe that here a fundamentally new procedure has to be introduced when up to this time speech as the creator of interhuman relationship has been a part of fundamental anthropology and when even a few decades ago the church was able to accommodate itself to a new armament by recognizing a philosophy of language as a universal basis of the knowledge of human existence. In the context of our consideration of the authority and the outgoing of the Word it is impossible to avoid dealing with this amazing position which is being put forward by certain pioneers and is meeting with a remarkable, hardly audible, but far-reaching response.

1. We encounter one line of thought in a rejection of preaching, based upon a depreciation of human speech, fostered by a group of ministers and young laymen who have discovered the epigonous character of our communication and oppose the 'eschatological' Christian to the 'Constantinian' Christian. They believe that we have lost the presuppositions of the Scriptures, and since it would be uncharitable and fruitless to initiate the multitude or even an elite into

the procedures, the only way left is that of direct testimony, if indeed even this is not doomed to futility because preaching, the press, and propaganda have juggled away the substance and meaning of words. Somewhat after the fashion and the venture of the French worker-priests, but in this case with the intellectuals and the younger generation in view, the idea is to submerge oneself, to make oneself unrecognizable, to dispense with verbal testimony and operate only through example, through one's existence (though even this way of putting it still sounds too deliberate). Fellow humanity, identification with one's fellow men should be left to speak for itself. In their judgment, words, clear, purposive, definite statements, indicative as well as imperative, are merely destructive of communication. Everything is 'talked to pieces'; only the ordinary, everyday speech that is used in our work and our leisure still has any function. Oddly enough, in these circles there is a new approach to the understanding of the Lord's Supper, which becomes an uninterpreted celebration where friends gather together for a daily meal, where warm inwardness irradiates the materiality of things. They would allow the church to go on its way, not without some amazement at its somnolence, doing what it has always done according to tradition and what in this post-bourgeois, 'post-Christian' age may for a time continue to be a help to an older, dying generation. For their part, however, it is time to keep silent. And this means that there is not even any place for the 'non-religious' proclamation of the Gospel. It is not religion as such, they would say, that produces alienation and ambiguity, but rather words, empty, divisive human words, which can be twisted and interpreted in a thousand different ways. This petrefact is regarded almost as a mythical enemy who blocks our way to the man who has been touched by nihilism or has already been brought back into line as a conformist, but is completely lonely. Speech, conversation remains, but it moves on the level of the profane; it has special, unexpected accents, it is a brotherly kind of pointing to an existence in brotherliness in the midst of the spiritual suffering of this age.

2. Still more radical is the sound of other voices that tell us that we still do not know what it means to live in an industrialized age. Not that they deplore industrialization or that they would wish to obstruct its sweeping power. On the contrary, they welcome it, if not with undivided joy, nevertheless calmly, in solidarity not only with the in-

dividuals who are threatened but also the world in its tremendous new advance. They say quite objectively, not laying down a norm but simply stating a fact: in the past man resorted to prayer in time of famine, but modern man proceeds (more or less adequately) to act. Men in past centuries regarded heaven as the place which would give ultimate meaning to life; the new man believes in the earth, the heritage which has been assigned to him. Former man was oriented toward God, modern man is oriented toward his neighbour, his fellow man. Why?—because the man of the European centuries lived in the church, whereas the new man lives in society. In the process that led up to this and its present conclusion, the gods have fallen. The way of the Messiah was not in vain. Now the Name ('I am present as I will be present,' Exod. 3 : 14) has revealed itself as the guarantor of the real unity of mankind. Then it would be translated 'I happen' (*Ich geschehe*). Here there is nothing to explain or interpret. Even ethics becomes more and more self-evident. Readiness to serve, self-sacrifice, perseverance, confidence, courtesy are the virtues needed to endure the scrupulous exactitude of life together in a technical society. Word and prayer may be regarded as a luxury, but work and service are indispensable. Thus the simple, factual recognition that sociological changes have taken place becomes an impulse compared with which a special ethics is superfluous.

The horizon of the industrial age with its work and its 'spontaneous' ethics is the osmosis, the mutual inclusiveness, of all nations. This is our heaven, which came down as the kingdom of heaven when the heavens were rent—first in ancient Israel and conclusively in the Messiah Jesus—and which since then has accompanied the way of the Gentiles and, so to speak, absorbed its plans. Now we are with the Father when we are in the world with all our heart and strength. No other people in antiquity regarded the earth as the dwelling place of one united humanity. Israel in its prophecy and its songs (and its genealogical tables) extolled the land promised to it as a pledge of the future; one earth for the one mankind under the one heaven. This is the great love story which is called life. Long before Abraham lived, love had already driven men out of their ties to mother earth, their veneration of their many progenitors, their many fatherlands, each of which had its own ideological heaven. Christianity discovered these heavens and also the heaven that is revealed to faith and merged them all in the heaven of the universe, the heaven that belongs to the earth.

But wherever discoveries take place one must expect reactions from the object discovered. Our modern society is built upon a false idea of creation. 'Nature' must be subdued, and our work lacks effectiveness because it scorns the Sabbath which points beyond 'nature' as the object of science to the original Creation: No one can live without visions, and there are narrow visions, of which Communism is one. We men of the age of discoveries are compelled by our own discoveries to become believers, believers in what we have discovered, and to make this faith visible in what we do, which today means in our actual work in the world—in an age in which heaven has become objectively identified with the earth, but which still largely fails to give a modern response to the grace of such a common gift.

What further purpose can preaching, teaching, ethical guidance serve in such a situation? The salutary event of the industrial age is, so to speak, completely forensic. We have only the freedom to accept it, and the burden of the admonition is nothing but a warning not to allow ourselves to be diverted by what no longer obtains. The Christian has abandoned the church as a temporary makeshift in favour of society, in which, by God's will, the really important thing is happening, in which the one mankind is in process of being born and new virtues are ineluctably springing up from the cursed and blessed earth. We must learn to see that church and society have merely represented transitory spheres existing side by side, but which in principle and now in fact represent events in time, so that now 'society' has become the successor and takes the place of the church.

If the watchword of the first group was existence, simple, unobtrusive 'being there,' then here the marching order (given without emphasis) is presence, the kind of presence which wipes out its own tracks and loses itself in service. The striking thing about this is that the Old Testament is made to serve as a basis for this attitude. But more important than expressing our surprise at this is that we ponder the profound earnestness of this interpretation and beyond this our real situation. It is not difficult to recognize in what is here set forth certain lines which remind us of Rosenstock's *Soziologie*.

'In hard tasks God's daily preservation; we need no other revelation.' Today in the technical age this should read: 'In happy tasks practical preservation, by virtue of the ancient revelation'.

You shall know ME.
It will happen on that day—
His utterance it is—
I grant the heavens,
And they grant the earth,
And the earth grants the grain, the wine, the olive oil,
And they grant to him-whom-God-sows. (Hos. 2 : 20–22)

To put such vistas into words or even to think of them is highly exceptional, a gift and inspiration of the moment. Our proper and customary speech is our presence in the world; we ourselves must become wholly worldly, not merely under the guise of an incognito but in a genuine, unreserved sharing of the lot and fate of the world.

3. A third—seemingly less radical—group is concerned to regain human wholeness. To this end they endeavour to establish educational centres where people, who are more or less active in evangelistic and apostolic ministry in specialized social areas, can study and practise methods by which the wholeness of man can be renewed and in some measure be given exemplary embodiment. But here too the central problem is the derogation of verbal communication—in two respects: first, because the world around us is conditioned to this derogation, and second, because it is believed that it also constitutes a definite obstacle to new initiative and enterprise. We look abroad—the people of Asia and Africa come into our purview, and near at hand the rootless rebels, juveniles and adults, demand our attention.

The *saeculum* in which we live is tremendous, and the secularization which has already occurred is accepted and affirmed by Christians (almost the same distinctions that Gogarten makes are employed). To the establishment of systems, the fixing of boundaries, the static authorities, which the reactionaries are again bringing to bear everywhere, this group opposes a metaphor of resurrection. The incarnation of the Son is interpreted as an archetype of the apotheosis of man. How can this be said and communicated to the man of our time? Preaching as such, no matter how it may be modernized, is feckless. For the Word is no longer effectual. In a certain sense we are deluding ourselves if we think it was any different in the past. It is forgotten that incarnation, becoming a human being, is a collective, communicative process, and this is true on a far broader front in the age of emancipation and maturity than it was in earlier times. For then one could still feel secure in a sacral community or retreat into the remnants of it. Even if one broke away from the existing order in search of new, as yet hardly surmised orders, one was at least a part of an active minority sustained by hope—and to one's own surprise one always found a certain continuity. So it was, for example, in the Benedictine monasteries and the Brethren of the Common Life. This circumstance still allowed one to trust that the speech which was common to all and even a certain bold experimentation with words would be understood with a considerable degree of unambiguousness and effect. Today, however, in the process of what Bouman has called the 'revolution of the solitary,' communication by means of words has been almost completely undermined. It does not follow that one should proceed to act without a pre-understanding. Naturally, the ultimate concern is action; but first we must search for an equivalent of words and the effect which was formerly inherent in words, even though these words were used and understood by minorities. It must not be forgotten, however, that becoming a man (*Menschwerdung*) is an unconscious process, but that words as vehicles of expression have been overshadowed, gnawed away, and almost devaluated by overemphasis upon verbal communication and the conscious mind. And here the qualities of the body offer themselves as forms of expression of a deeper, more direct, more unreserved, and genuine fellow humanity.

There is no reason whatsoever to suspect that there is something heathenish in this. The real concern here is with the biblical Christian message! But this message must be transmitted in a whole way, addressing the whole man. And today this is impossible without contact with the springs of the unconscious. Education is a process that goes on in the hidden levels of personality. The strongest dam against the climate of the technological age, against the tendencies and effects of movies and advertising, against 'the spiritual powers in the air' (Eph. 2 : 2), is the group, whose members find mutual understanding in dancing, in mimic presentations which express something held in common. This includes amateur plays, 'sociodrama,' and pantomime. In the group the individual recovers his wholeness and regains control of his lost mental and spiritual powers. Then speech too is gradually delivered from being merely a functional drill. The imagination is awakened and ordinary, everyday things are perceived as they speak the language of myth, and symbols, which have faded into allegory, again become representations. Man acquires ears that are open to the silent mystery which surrounds only the Word. What Karl Rahner says is true: 'To be able to be a Christian one must . . . have the capacity to hear and to understand the primal words of the heart, the words that reach not only the technical rationality of man and his disinterested pseudo-objectivity, that are not merely signals of an assertion of biological existence and the promptings of the herd instinct, but that are rather, as it were, *sacral*, indeed, *sacramental*, and thus convey and creatively implant in the primal centre of man what they signify.'[13]

We have spoken of these three groups and we have conveyed no more than a summary impression of the attempts which are being made to proceed apostolically into the strange land. Martin Buber said in a 'Reminiscence' written on the occasion of his eightieth birthday: 'In language as in all areas of human life today nothing can be asserted to have continuance, unless it be through sacrifice.'[14] But is it necessary, desirable, or even possible, not merely to perform a service of rigorous restraint, simplification, and renewal in the realm of speech, but to sacrifice the realm of speech itself? This seems to me impossible. No estrangement or antagonism, however overwhelming it may actually be, can furnish a norm and, as it were, force a sanctioning of this alienation. And nothing normative can be established if the human phenomena do not point to an ontic structure. It is true that the conditions of human existence are all determined by sin which is factually and potentially a depleting factor, but they cannot be thought of, even experimentally, as having been changed or even abolished in their structure. This is not to deny that in this realm the *nihil* can assert itself so powerfully that we yield to the temptation to regard this disorder in man as an independent structure and to adjust all his communication to its behaviour.

Existence, presence, wholeness—these find their crown, their efflorescence, their justification, their illumination, their real goodness in the Word and only in the Word. The constant witness to this among us in this very age is the emphasis upon 'dialogue.' 'Experimental poetry' has arisen in revolt against the excess of 'talk,' against the myriad ways in which it has been emptied of meaning. It is true that in this art of

[13] 'Das Wort der Dichtung und der Christ,' *Schriften zur Theologie*, IV (1960), p. 445.
[14] 'Erinnerung,' *Die Neue Rundschau* (1957), p. 576.

327

'experimental poetry'—as well as in the earlier Expressionism—one can judge how great has been the pressure of the tyranny of the techno- logical age, but one can also see in it the hope that many have only temporarily repressed the child within them. It is in sonship that poetry is authentically preserved and secured. The challenge of art continues. The nameless powers can be named and exorcised by words. 'If the world, the glorification of which has given to art its structure, has now been shattered, the question is where the creative artist can discover the authentic being which, though now latent, can only be brought to efflorescence through him.'[15] The speechless dark is a challenge. If, because of the devaluation of human speech, we do not answer the challenge with the appropriate medium, namely, human words, then we who are committed to the biblical Word will, quite contrary to our intention, be again confronted with the mask of being from whose gorgon-stare it was precisely the Word that freed Israel and us. Today, when the silence of the gods is passing over into an imperialism of dumb facticity, the world is waiting—consciously or unconsciously— for the prophetic ministry to make its onslaught. To choose resignation, positivism, the disregard of the Word, means, in our opinion, that we do not understand the need of the hour and will fail to give the appro- priate answer. The tendency toward monological thinking and living, which seems to be inherent in the West, will be immensely intensified in our social deviations, in the context of the 'lonely crowd,' if the Word is not addressed to man, the Word that makes him an individual again, that frees him to say 'thou' and to live as 'we' with his fellow man, and that shows him a future. In this situation we dare not be ashamed—precisely because all the effort expended to bear witness in a way that will speak to our time seems to put us to shame—to be confident that we have a new and really relevant ministry of the Word today and to say with Siegfried von der Trenck (even though the tone of his statement is somewhat pretentious, and the jingling sound of it may strike us as awkward):

Wir sind die Grübler der nordischen Welt,
wir brauchen die Sonne unmittelbar,
wir brauchen das Wort, schlicht, einfach und klar,
wie es sich einst vor uns hingestellt.

[15] Karl Jaspers, *Man in the Modern Age*, tr. Eden and Cedar Paul (New York: Double- day Anchor Books, 1957), p. 141. [Translation altered.—Tr.]

Und mag denn der Stein zum Eckstein werden
und mögen da Völker untergehn,
das Wort bleibt immer und ewig stehn—
das Wort überdauert Sonnen und Erden,

das Wort, vor dem es nicht Weise, nur Narren gibt,
nicht Frommen, nur Sünder,—ganz feindlich wir alle,
das Wort, das kündet mit lautem Schalle:
Also hat Gott die Welt geliebt.

(We are the brooders of the northern world,
we need the sun directly,
we need the Word, plain, simple, and clear,
as once it stood before us.

And though the stone become a cornerstone
and though the nations perish,
the Word remains eternally and forever,
standing—the Word outlasts the suns and earths,

the Word, in the presence of which there are no wise men, only fools,
no holy men, only sinners—enemies are we all,
the Word, that proclaims in mighty tones:
God so loved the world).

Sing it, O you who are perplexed, sing it as you wait for the morning,
sing it softly into the ears of this sad world! Sing it upon your knees,
sing it as under a veil, but out in the open, sing it as women sing in
hope and as soldiers before a battle! Let it also be like a song one sings
at his work, a song that surrounds our journey into the strange land
with expectation far beyond all expectation! Our preaching should
sometimes be pervaded with the note of the hymnic speech.

We shall also have to recognize afresh and bring to light not only the
distinction but also the connection between this Word and 'speech in
general,' its connection with the wordlike quality (*Worthaftigkeit*) of
human existence, the fact that human existence is based upon words
and speech. When we say with Luther, 'The Word they still shall let
remain,' then in the threatening situation we face now when the use
of words is met with extreme antagonism, this applies also to the word
of man, to human speech. Word and love belong together. The 'de-

valuation' of speech goes hand in hand with the dying of love. Love has always been the field of the most widely propagated dilettantism. Now it appears to be close to radical impotence. Coldness preserves dying life. The last stages of the outgoing of the Word appear to be without any authority. But even to think such a thing is impossible if we know what this divine undertaking means. The Word 'outlasts suns and earths,' it creates and guides whole cultures, it visits and blesses individuals in their despair. The ministry of the Word of love dare not be allowed to remain void because of the isolation, the rebellion, and the hardening of the modern mind. 'God so loved the world'—with his heart, his act, his Word. There the Word becomes song, and as Rilke said, 'song is existence.'

PROPHECY TODAY

Thus our previous experience with preaching, with our mission, impresses upon us the necessity of seeking a new kind of prophetic proclamation. The extent to which it can or should be really new is uncertain. We shall attempt here merely to recall the equipment that we shall need today.

The aim of preaching and instruction will not be to understand the word of Scripture as a contribution to the enrichment of man's religious or quasi-religious experience. It may be that this enrichment of experience may come as a more or less generous extra gift, but to make this the real goal would be to distort the primary event toward which the prayer that the Word may be opened is directed. The purpose of it is that there may be a meeting of prophecy and history in this present hour. This applies, of course, primarily to personal life. There is no collective history, but there is a history of the church which is woven together by the life histories of its members. Here primarily is where the superreligious encounter which we seek takes place. Where the literal and historical is heard 'mythically,' where it proves its supertemporal meaning in a new time, or where the letter becomes prophecy, there we find a point of intersection with history. A new kind of listening is personal listening. And listening to the prophecy as a person is anything but merely listening as an individual; it means rather to be silent in the presence of the superpersonal, objective re-presentation of the Name and to be drawn out of the exile of godlessness into the exodus of a long journey with our Pioneer and Covenant Lord.

'In a rationalistic age, in the midst of a frenzy of textual and historical investigation, after four centuries of default of heirs . . . someone was again found who no longer considered the Bible as merely an arsenal but rather a treasure, not as something to utilize but rather as something to eat . . . someone was found . . . to take God at his word, to surrender himself *wholly and artlessly to the Word* of God as it is delivered to us by the church, to love it, to repeat it as it is, and, following the instruction given by the angel to the man of Patmos, to devour it, to allow it to pass entire into his entrails through the medium of teeth, tongue, and taste. The Word of God! Again there was someone to listen to it directly, to *prefer it just as it was to the fantasies of personal devotion.* There was found a new heart that embraced the holy enthusiasm which dictated the sublime Psalm CXVIII [=119].'[16]

This is how the church is built and preserved. In the midst of its ever latent decay there is ultimately no power that can save and preserve it except the Scripture, the Word, the Name so understood. In the last resort, the church becomes a peculiar fellowship solely through this hearing of the Word; provided that the church clearly sees what has become perfectly clear, namely, that the authority and outgoing of the Word through prophecy (preaching) frees the Scripture from the self-estrangement which it suffered by having been treated as a book. Precisely when the book is removed from the mountain of tradition under which it is buried, from abstract speculation, from liturgical formalization, precisely when the book again becomes the independent, rude, verdant, symphonic thing that it is (not a catalogue of proof texts for dogmatics, not a daily calendar for pietists, and not a target for bourgeois critics and know-it-alls), precisely then does the power of the Word rise up from the rediscovered Book like a phoenix, the divine bird, the winged sun. 'This is why, along with the pelican in her piety and the roaring lion of Judah, the phoenix appears on the pediments of the cathedrals as a symbol of Christ' (Schmidt Degener). But it is even more a symbol of the constancy of the Scripture which had languished and died in its own nest. The living church is where the

[16] Paul Claudel, *Introduction au 'Livre de Ruth.'* [In the original this quotation is given in French.—Tr.]

Scriptures, which have been wrongly relegated to the status of a book, rise to life and become speech, song, and poetry in which the Word takes wings and celebrates its triumph. Every time this occurs, there the church exists, there it is being built.

There is no conflict between this worship in the church and the fact that the peoples are to be fed and guided, that cultures are subjected by the Word to the true judgment and the right guidance. Indeed, the point is that these two things, the 'integral' devotion of the church and the wavering of the people who are to be integrated, must be kept together and constantly viewed together. Prophetic proclamation causes the individual to subject his private devotion to the passion of listening to the Word, but it also causes the church and the people to transform their distracted and only half-serious attention into a devoted worship in the cult which always has its eye upon the fact that we have been sent out into the world. The conclusion (the *ite missa est* of the Anthroposophists' service) is the *Menschenweihehandlung*, the service of the dedication of man. This way of putting it is a fair description of a good transition from cult to culture, from prophecy to politics in the broadest sense of the term.

Cult and prophecy. The sermon is an integrating, if not the central, element in the synagogal as well as the Christian cult; though from a historical point of view one must probably say that it is the central element. For people are moved and persuaded and their lives are formed essentially through preaching, namely, through preaching which regards itself and offers itself as that which confirms the fulfilment of the promise and which therefore establishes the basis for the 'courage to be' (Tillich) and the strength to work. The countermovements, the reactions, heretical and corrective, are also a part of this dominant,[17] which stimulates and modifies history, but which is always something more than merely the source of such effects. That is to say, it is the representation of the *eschaton*, which fills the heart of the individual and the church with adoration and expectation in the face of the world, the world in which they have been placed precisely in order to set an example of this kind of listening to God's Word.

'The cultic act is itself an element of the *Heilsgeschichte*.'[18] The

---

[17] I use the word 'dominant' here in the sense of Reinke's biological theory of dominants.

[18] Rudolf Bultmann, 'Kirche und Lehre im Neuen Testament,' in *Zwischen den*

hieratic constant creates a bed for the stream of power that flows from the emergent, contingent action of preaching. There is more correlation of meaning and function here than we can go into at this point. Preaching itself, even prophetic-reformatory or chiliastic-apocalyptic preaching, still retains the marks of an act of worship; it is cultic, and of all the cultic acts it impinges most strongly upon the history of man. We mean this in a purely formal sense here; for heresy, revolutionary movements, and the visions of fanatical enthusiasts are also determinative of history, and through history in many unseen ways, of our personal intellectual life. They are necessary countermovements, and more often they bear Israelitic rather than gnostic features. And when this is true they are well adapted to break through the smug proprietorship and the closed mind of the church which has become terribly secure and confident. An example of this is the neglect of the Old Testament in the Middle Ages and its consequence, the still widespread tendency among intellectuals in Roman Catholic countries either to regard the Old Testament Scriptures as a collection of Semitic stories or to deal with them in a very recondite way—covered, of course, by the highest authority in the church, which admonishes the faithful not to scorn allegorization. One could in large part explain the development of Rome by the fatality of an Old Testament which has either been radically ignored or completely denatured. It would appear that in modern intellectual life there are individuals who have some misgivings about how little the teaching in which they were reared squares with the structures of the Old Testament, and then—from a historical point of view, partially correctly, but in principle ultimately untenably—they discover that the liturgy is the norm of the proclamation. Among many others, Leon Bloy might be mentioned as an illustration. 'He who teaches the Scriptures will take care not to neglect the allegorical or analogical sense attached to certain words by the holy fathers, especially when this meaning springs naturally from the literal sense and is supported by a large number of authorities. Indeed, the church received from the Apostles this mode of inter-

---

Zeiten (1929), p. 19. Cf. Gerhard Friedrich's article 'kerysso,' TWNT, III, pp. 659ff., esp. 702f., where he points out that the act of proclamation itself is a realization of the salvation for which the prophets of the Old Testament were waiting, namely, YHWH's 'seizure of power.' This, however, is perhaps overstated, and at most one may identify the Word which the Messiah himself speaks with the event which is attested therein.

pretation and has approved it by its example, in the same way as this is apparent in the liturgy. Not that the fathers meant to prove the dogmas of faith by this method alone, but rather because in their own experience they found that this method was good for the nourishing of virtue and piety.'[19] A statement like this is the fruit of a sowing which has played a part in forming the face of the earth in Roman Catholic countries. On the other hand, the result of regular intercourse, through the medium of preaching, with a literally interpreted Old Testament in Calvinistic, particularly Anglo-Saxon, countries is clearly apparent even in political structure and the attitude of the people toward life. In this connection something should be said concerning the historical place and influence of the Dutch Reformed, the Remonstrants, and the Mennonites. These cannot be understood if one does not see the characteristic differences and agreements in their attitude toward the Old Testament. In these movements prophetism asserted itself— blazingly, smoulderingly, or quietly; hence their reserve with regard to the sacral, their refusal to have anything to do with the profane world, their acceptance of a theocratic order of life, the veiled Messianism of the direction of their life, their matter-of-course laicism which carried with it something of the priestly ministry, hence their high ethical standards and their sober combativeness, and hence also their respect for the potentialities of the ordinary man.[20] We merely allude to these things in order to remind every interpreter of what a glorious and responsible task instruction on the basis of the Old Testament must be.[21] The question 'What do you think of the Christ?' and the question 'How do you read the Old Testament?' are closely related to each other. But just as Christ can be preached under a veil where we

[19] Cf. the encyclical *Providentissimus Deus* of Leo XIII (not in Denzinger); also *Enchiridion symbolorum*, No. 1941ff.

[20] Cf. D. Heinemann in *Wending* (1951); Père Sertillanges, *Wending* (1952); Eugen Rosenstock, *Die europäischen Revolutionen* (1931), passim.

[21] John A. Mackay, *Heritage and Destiny*, p. 101f; 'The Book opened up to him [Robinson Crusoe] a strange, new world which transformed his life. The Bible, which has been traditionally unknown by the classes and masses of the Hispanic world, has been the supreme spiritual inwardness which, according to the heads of two Argentine universities, Ricardo Rojas and Juan B. Téran, and the greatest Spanish man of letters, Miguel de Unamuno, has been entirely lacking in the religious life of Hispanic American lands. . . . In their view, the greatest single need of culture, of politics, and of religion in those great southern lands is a firsthand knowledge of the Book of books.'

do not see it, so the power of the Old Testament witness communicates itself in words which appear to be very much uncircumcised. Be that as it may, history goes on revolving about the event of prophecy, and as long as it remains history (for when the apparatus of economic causality holds its autonomous sway or the consciously guiding hand of man does not operate, we can really no longer speak of 'history' at all), it is intellectually determined by what happens or does not happen on the margin of our 'post-Christian' world, namely, in the church. History—yes, it is determined by the Name, the Word, the testimony even where the stream of intellectual life turns away from this hidden bed to seek its own channel and even where events turn with over-whelming force against the salvation and the mysteries confessed and reverenced in the past. Ernst Jünger is doubtless correct when he says that Europe is a conspicuous example of the ingratitude of human nature. Even the deepest impulse of science operates only in a world from which (fortunately) the gods have been banished, a world in which the Logos sets out to serve and to govern—for the welfare of God-protected humanity. And yet this science is capable of emancipating itself to a large extent from this purpose and meaning in order finally to allow the salutary demythologization of the world to turn into an atheistic myth, the *mythos atheos* (Ziegler). This science is capable of again unleashing the powers which had been bound; it can take time, which was humanized through the Revelation, and again empty it of meaning by reducing it to a formal concept, which on top of this is loaded with the severest antinomies. Not everyone can see that it is actually the 'church' from which they are dissociating themselves, even in this extreme alienation from it ('church' as a code word for the claim to be a surviving representation of the authority of God). One could, for example, take Mauthner's *History of Atheism in the West* or Ziegler's *The Changing Form of the Gods* and pursue the question whether there has ever been a movement, an idea, a world view, a theory which has stood on its own feet completely unrelated and in-different to the salvation which once went out over the earth mediated through the testimony, binding the 'powers' and dethroning the 'gods.' If we were to do this, we would hardly find a single such movement, idea, world view, or theory. (The only place where we would find such a thing would be where all such ultimate questions have been barred, as in neopositivism and in dialectical materialism, where it should be remembered that only in the technical-national sense are these questions declared to be not worth discussing.) We cannot go into this, even though it is very definitely relevant to the theme of 'prophecy and history.' Precisely in this epoch we see an involuntary corroboration of the objective importance which proclamation and instruction, prophecy and witness have even in a dechurched society. In a city of empty churches, in a civilization that threatens to congeal in its aberrations because it has grown hard in its betrayal of its origin, we find such reminders of the presence of the Word. *Christus regnat in medio inimicorum* ('Christ reigns in the midst of his enemies'); he is always exalted, even where he is rejected. The one covenant, fulfilled in him, always remains, even where the ancient enmity of chaos flaunts its pride. And the Word remains nomadic, unfathomable in its ways as it walks the road of exodus, and compassionately near—so much so that the 'history of atheism' can become one of the partial, contrasting elements in the history of the Name of God on earth.

The Spoken Word

We need here to call attention to a point which appears to lie apart, namely, that even in this theme of 'prophecy and history' we must keep in mind the fact that the first of these elements, prophecy, is operative primarily through the spoken word and its written expression. It is remarkable that, not only in times when men were quite naturally (and also because of the illiteracy of the great majority) dependent upon the spoken word, but also in modern times, the spoken word (and its literary expression, which presents itself vocatively, pragmatically, existentially, not speculatively, theoretically, noncommittally) has proved to be the power that awakens, binds, and activates community. This applies to the French Revolution just as surely as it does to the Krishnamurti movement, to Bolshevism and Fascism as well as to—evangelism. This confronts us with a very important factor, important also for the question of what the interpreter and witness has to do in our time on a level above that of mere presence. Our inundation with an ever increasing mass of printed matter cannot proceed at this rate without evoking an enormous reaction, which will result partly in irresponsible experiments and partly in a renewed receptivity to the spoken word. This will mean not only the gaining of a formal acceptance and a new stillness, but will also diminish an essential danger that confronts the church and the synagogue, the danger of the 'literaturizing' of the message, the danger of turning it into literature. The Scriptures are not and never were intended to be a book for reading, but always a book to be read aloud to others and orally applied. We shall never be able fully to repair the damage which was done by the art of printing (despite its advantages) to the decisive importance of speech in its function as address, as encounter. It is perhaps not impertinent here to discuss this point in somewhat greater detail.

In order to characterize more sharply what is meant, we quote a few lines of the philosopher Louis Lavelle, which indicate a completely opposite tendency, as cannot be otherwise with such a consistent spiritualist. 'Scripture is a word which, instead of slipping away into time, remains *fixed in duration*. . . . Silence puts us in rapport with God as the word does with other men. . . . If the place where ideas abide is an immobile and inaccessible eternity which intervenes only in some sudden encounters, the property of the Scripture is to attach them to an object which renders them available and permits us to rediscover them. . . . It is the property of Scripture to *capture the eternal in the temporal*, that is to say, to oblige us to bring ourselves into time beyond time.' But Lavelle also says: 'The most serious danger of Scripture is that while it encloses the Word in the letter it may put the letter in the place of the Word.'[22]

In the spoken word, in oral teaching, which overcomes the harmfulness of 'writing,' the danger of 'literature,' the solitude of 'reading,'[23] man meets the 'power' of speech. In the midst of an explosive or a calm situation (though the latter too can have world-historical consequences) the Holy Scriptures are again being recognized as being speech which is actually and originally not a written word but rather essentially a spoken word. This characteristic is altogether clear in the Old Testa-

[22] Louis Lavelle, *La parole et l'écriture* (1947), pp. 159, 168, 171, 182. [In the original this quotation is given in French. The term 'spiritualist' applied to Lavelle is, of course, used in its philosophical sense.—Tr.]
[23] Reading, speaking, preaching is everywhere—in the form of the 'quibbling' of the Talmud, the dialectics of scholasticism, and the lecture business of the modern university, but above all in the form of the Sunday sermon, the Bible hour, the spoken homily or meditation—'the salvation of man by reason of the simple fact that it is *oral*' (Rosenzweig).

ment; there the accent of recitation is heard, there the 'gestural' rhythm and the 'colometric' form of the phrases leap to the eye.

What we have here is the simplest combination of speech and writing, the missive or letter. Here speech becomes something sent, something present; its aim is to 'make present'—more than this, it is a sign of a very particular presence. This is address, not poetry, this is prose that irrupts into the 'prosaic' world. This is another mystery, the inner side of the intellectual decisions of history (in so far as we still live in history), namely, that there is no other writing which is by its very nature word, *dabar*, speech from mouth to mouth, face to face, heart to heart.[24]

The habit of regarding 'Bible reading' as the really serious and fruitful thing and 'hearing' as a merely decorative addition has introduced a deterioration in our service of worship and threatens to kill the history-creating power of the spoken word. In the cultic act of preaching the Word is freed from the bonds of written form, in order that, thus freed, it may enter into a congregation, a people, a world. According to the Reformation insight, everything depends upon the letter rising up and becoming spirit,[25] the past event becoming a present event, the narrative becoming testimony, the testimony becoming the act of God. This rising up is actually a self-elevation. And this self-elevation appears as the mystery in even the most simple cult, and around its invisible altar the saints kneel and the aeons gather. It is—we retain the cultic simile—the self-elevation of the Name, the confirmation of the fathomless power of election: 'I will be with you as I will be with you' (Exod. 3 : 14). This needs to be spoken to a person; it is the ever-recurring springtime of the presence. The monstrance of the presence, the Word-which-is-Act—behold, God rises up above gods and cultures, for our welfare, in the moment when he is pleased

[24] Here reference should be made once more to the discoveries of the philosophy of language set forth earlier by Hamann and Herder and in our time by Jean Gebser and Eugen Rosenstock. The last-mentioned even demands of the university that for the sake of humanity it should learn to think in a different way, in the sense that scholarship and science should be pursued in communication with the neighbour and as such become an act of pastoral care (*Seelsorge*) for the neighbour and the community.

[25] 'God is present, and when he acts through messengers, these are not mere letter carriers who bring news of something that happened the day before yesterday, something which may already be outdated by events, but rather, directly in this their moment, God acts by them and speaks through them.' Franz Rosenzweig, 'Die Schrift und das Wort,' *Kleinere Schriften* (1937), p. 136.

to do so! And these moments are the junction points in the ongoing story of Immanuel. The light of that story shines through the window of our poor chamber to assure us that we are at home. The strong wind of the story blows through the inner courts of melancholy and sweeps away the hanging gloom. The depth of the story wells up and with gentle power floods our frozen brain. The movement of the story takes us with it into far regions where for a moment we find and possess eternal youth. The Name illumines the narrative; the purpose of the narrative is the amazingly new disclosure of the Name, its sublimity and its nearness. In the Name and through the Name the letter becomes spirit, the past event becomes present event, the narrative becomes testimony, the testimony becomes act, the act becomes the act of the presence.

The reader will certainly say that nothing is accomplished with these high-flown effusions, that they sound like empty vapourings. But however inadequately it may be expressed and despite the appearance of false portentousness, our purpose is not to prove a blustering assertion, but simply to state the real reason why we go to church. Anything that does not have in view this presence through the Word ultimately leads to stripping away the meaning of the service of worship as an event *sui generis*.

If it be asked whether such an expectation also applies to the Old Testament, we can only refer again to what was said earlier about the functional unity of the Testaments, about the Old Testament disclosing itself only as it is seen by itself, about the way it speaks 'for itself' precisely when it goes out and speaks to the Gentiles, about the way in which the 'expectation' participates in the 'fulfilment,' about the way in which the 'word world' of the time of expectation contains a 'surplus' over against the 'word world' of the time of remembrance.

The essential thing, however, remains the unutterable Name, which binds the Old Testament to the New, particularly by means of a very definite anthropomorphism. 'It is a matter of him who is present as God-with-us, as he wills to be present. It has to do with him whose deepest singular self is at the same time his revealed manifestation. It has to do with him who is nowhere more *Spirit* than he is in his *earthly* being, who deals with us humanly—humanly not despite his divinity but by virtue of his divinity.' (See p. 132 above.)

How wearisome and frustrating is the question 'How do we preach from the Old Testament, and when, and will it catch fire?' It will not catch fire if salvation has not kindled the hour. It will remain talk about these things, it will talk these things to pieces, it will be bourgeois or popular, religious or idealistic, it will be remote and increasingly remote from real life, if we regard preaching as being opposed to this anthropomorphic mystery. It remains, perhaps, to give some good advice, but it is difficult to find and is actually unobtainable where the testimony of the fathers and brethren given in the 'surplus' is still so grossly undervalued.

Rather than handing out advice, for example, about when in the church year it would be advisable to preach from the Old Testament, rather than stating themes which would be more timely and topical today, it would appear to me to be more important to urge that we avoid all theological speculation on the basis of the literary evidence and derive the real earnestness of the matter from the written form of the Old Testament itself. The high place and the practical, penetrative power of preaching can again become clear. Our calling as preachers is the calling of those who are subjected and dedicated to the letter, the letter which is in itself spirit—the calling of ministers of the Word, i.e., of an authority which by the grace of God helps men in their life through the expounding and interpreting of the Scriptures. If this is realized, vulgar popularity will fall away, the bourgeois mentality will be shattered, our embarrassment over the Old Testament will be put to shame, and our sense of responsibility will become a form of our election. What seems comprehensible will become obscure, and the incomprehensible in God will become light to a new comprehending reason.[26]

---

[26] Even in the realm of the profane what Heidegger says holds good: 'In the language which is spoken when one expresses oneself there lies an average intelligibility; and in accordance with this intelligibility the discourse which is communicated can be understood to a considerable extent, even if the hearer does not bring himself into such a kind of Being towards what the discourse is about as to have a primordial understanding of it. We do not so much understand the entities which are talked about; we already are listening only to what is said-in-the-talk as such. What is said-in-the-talk gets understood; but what the talk is about is understood only approximately and superficially. We have *the same thing* in view, because it is in *the same* averageness that we have a common understanding of what is said.' Martin Heidegger, *Being and Time*, tr. John Macquarrie and Edward Robinson (New York: Harper & Row, 1962) p. 212. [The words 'comprehending reason' represent the familiar, untranslatable wordplay *vernehmende Vernunft.*—Tr.]

TRANSLATION

Then it also becomes clear how in cultic use (in the broadest sense of the term) the intent of the book is carried out in translation (which in itself is a first form of exposition and even of application). The purpose of the translation of the Bible was not primarily to transport a literary work into another language; it arose spontaneously from the necessity of justifying the contemporization of the spoken word (in preaching and instruction) by the letters of the written word. The translation is also made in order to be read aloud in the assembly (in church or home). It owes its form among other things to a living awareness of the reciprocal relationship between the cult and history, and it therefore presupposes a theological decision of faith with regard to the unity of the Scriptures.[27] Where such translation of the whole is effective, we stand at a turning point in the history of the church, a turning point of appropriation and transmission. Translation means trusteeship and is obligated to be true to the lineaments of the whole of Scripture.

Not only preaching must start with this decision; translation too began with it; indeed, even the formation of the canon and the work of the redactors cannot be understood apart from it. This in no way precludes the fact that preaching must change and the translation must be revised, indeed, that the canon, measured by its intended content, may again present a margin of antilegomena. On the contrary, nowhere does objective philology have better prospects, nowhere will one be more receptive to a new interpretation of the Scriptures in a language that is freshly conformed to the modern mind, nowhere will one be readier to acknowledge the sovereign freedom of the Spirit (and consequently the openness of the canon) than where the

---

[27] Cf. the last conclusion in an article by J. L. Seeligmann, 'Problemen en Perspectieven in het moderne Septuaginta-onderzoek,' *Ex Oriente Lux*, VII (1940), pp. 359ff.: 'The origin of the Septuagint in the service of worship, its use in synagogal teaching and preaching, make it possible to describe it as Targum; its exegesis is Midrash, and the essence of all true Midrash is contemporization. The Septuagint is a document of the conviction which manifestly existed also in Alexandrian Judaism, namely, that the covenant which God made with the patriarchs he daily renews with him who devotedly immerses himself in his Word. The voice of God can be heard afresh every day.'

unity of the Scriptures, their public function in the cult and their hidden power in history (even in times when men turn away from them and are estranged from them) is understood.

Unity and Simplicity

In all the covenants one Covenant is meant and contained, in all the anthropomorphisms there is one *assumptio carnis*, in all the chastisements one expiation, in all the promises one and the same Future, in all the words one Word, in all the forms of communion one encounter, in every numinous presence one fulfilment.

Conversely, the meaning of all the multiplicity and the place of every individual, separate, historical, personal, unrepeatable word and sign is guaranteed to be genuine on the basis of the one Covenant, the one Messiah, the one Future.

In the cult we cannot content ourselves with a somewhat warmer, more religious view of things that settles down like a reconciling evening mist upon the wastelands which have been created by an emancipated intellect. The church and humanity are not helped by adding religious insights to philosophical, occult, and scientific insights.[28]

The Scripture as Word in action becomes simple, perspicuous, familiar, tender, fatherly, powerful; it is not far away, beyond the ocean of our experiences; it is not high above the stratosphere of our conceptuality; it is here, near to us, in our mouth and in our heart (cf. Deut. 30 : 11ff.).

> 't is zo eenvoudig toch wat 'k heb te zeggen
> En 't is meteen zo sterrenachtlijk groot,
> Dat ik, al vonk ik verzen tot mijn dood,
> Het niemand ooit volledig uit kan leggen.
>
> (So simple is the message which I have to
> speak, but at the same time as great as the
> starry night, that if I fashioned verses till
> I died, I could never fully expound it).[29]

[28] The intention of H. H. Rowley, *The Rediscovery of the Old Testament* (1945), namely, 'to help any reader to a fuller apprehension of the religious meaning,' will be appreciated by many, and yet in the cult, in preaching, it is not a matter of 'the religious meaning.' Cf. Martin Noth, *Geschichte und Gotteswort im Alten Testament* (1950); also in *Gesammelte Studien zum Alten Testament* (1957), pp. 230ff.
[29] Adwaita (Johan Andreas dèr Mouw), *Brahman*, I, p. 361.

This applies to the mysteries of God in a completely different way from the fundamental knowledge of the world of which this poet feels he must speak in prophetic tones; the simplicity is divine in that it carries the 'fullness' enfolded, as it were, within itself. And it is not in the power of our subjective experience to bring this about; the subjectivity of God, which cannot be replaced by anything else, has its own 'critical method' of upsetting our negations and affirmations, our calculations and judgments concerning what sounds 'simple' and what sounds 'great' to us. The church which investigates and expounds the Old Testament, which explains it in the *kairos* of each succeeding age, in new exposures and new dimensions, so that it acquires a completely new face, is the church which has become free (*in* its bondage to the unity of the Scriptures). Not only does it accompany history in its preaching, but conversely, history is also an accompaniment of its preaching.

The relation of unity with concentration upon the one central thing, of simplicity with completeness, of the new understanding of the Word with the liberation of the church has been set forth by Franz Rosenzweig in a letter from which we borrow the following: 'Everywhere created nature has become culture. Revelation has again revealed nature. It has taught us again to listen to the Word of God to us and to renounce the magical powers through which we conjure our creaturely nature into an almighty culture, a culture which is lord even over God and the gods. "I brought you up from Egypt"—this you know ... "the heaven above and earth beneath and the water under the earth"—let them not become for you graven images and likenesses; they *can* become this, you can transform them into images and likenesses ... do not do it; they are themselves created things; do not transform them, do not lose yourselves in them, do not lose yourselves at all, remain yourselves and let them be what they are, *that you may be able to hear my voice*. .... Don't you see how this restores the simple order of the world and how heaven and earth and water therefore do not cease being heaven, earth, and water, how nothing is taken from them except the worship which strips them of their character as heaven, earth, and water and idolatrizes them. Culture itself again becomes natural. Otherwise it loses nothing but its religion. Revelation has only this to do, *to make the world unreligious again*. And today too, among us. And our knowing is itself a part of this renaturalization of the world. When we know China, we do not, after all, become Chinese; whereas the Chinese, when he seeks to know Europe as we seek to know China, *becomes* a European. For he has not learned to know without worshipping. He does not know that what is *known* is not God. . . . World history travels from the Christians to the heathen. But from the heathen to the Christians there travels not world history but rather Rabindranath Tagore.'[30] Thus speaks the Jewish wise man who saw that history is the echo and accompaniment of history as perhaps none before him. What Hegel called the 'objective spirit' is decisively determined by the work of the interpreter and witness who causes us to lose our religion and bids us to affirm the mortality of the creature.

The Objective Authority

On the level of human life and its standards the assertion above would be presumptuous pride. But what can be called 'investigation' and 'exposition' and the new conclusions, results, liberations, certainties— all this is in truth the reflex of the brightness that proceeds from the Name, it is the movement of the Word itself which accompanies human life, it is generated by the truth which in actual deed breaks a path for itself in history. Again we quote Claudel: 'We must not be surprised that this dreadful virus . . . has produced reactions when it has been introduced under the skin and even into the heart of pagan society. . . . It is a question of ourselves, of a certain division within us which permits the Lord to pass by. The persecutions are nothing else but the blind convulsions of an inoculated man who snatches and howls for pieces of flesh. But ever since the world, beginning with Constantine, tried for the first time to live with Christ, the question of the Gospel has not ceased to be active. One tries in vain to bury it beneath the purple, to rebuild the sepulchre more solidly. . . .'[31] Claudel then goes on to describe how this inner conflict is carried further by missionary preaching. But then he looks at the 'frenetic controversy,' which was driven to a decision by 'the blood-stained formulas of the Credo and the unbreakable form of the anathemas', and without reserve declares: 'Rome, at the centre of all things, slowly, patiently, and potently measures, weighs, and gauges the future.' Here we discover that even a

[30] *Briefe* (1935), pp. 430f.
[31] Paul Claudel, *Pages de prose*, ed. André Blanchot (1949), pp. 394f. [Quoted in French in the original.—Tr.]

mind which can so highly exalt the Scriptures, and particularly the Old Testament, still does not recognize them as the ruling power itself. In our opinion, there is an optical illusion at work here. The Word constitutes its own authority by distinguishing itself from its ministers; and in its passage through the world it asserts itself by distinguishing itself from the history of the church. It is perfectly possible for opposition to the church to be based on the authority of the Word. And when an age or a culture passes by and ignores the existing form of the church, this can very well be an instance of the passing of the Word—its passing from here into other zones. A statement like that of Claudel shows clearly that here the authority of the Word has not been thought through and that its passage through the world, its criticism, and its passing by are not being taken completely seriously. Though all of us are subject to this error, we nevertheless are not living in a darkness in which all cats are grey. Israel and the church of the Reformation are definitely dissociated from the idea of the church and the concept of truth which are here rejected. They do not go along with such a sacralization of authority; they therefore have no need to defend the measure, the weight, and the prescience of authority against the voice of the facts.

How can one, for example, see the spiritual aridity in Byzantium and Russia caused by the anathema of the church and still remain blind to the judgment that has fallen upon the Christian peoples of Spain and Italy, of France and Poland, of Mexico and Brazil in the form of a total estrangement from the Holy Scriptures, in the 'frenetic controversy' between red and black totalitarian systems and godforsaken tyranny and terror?

'This dreadful virus' [which is Christianity], we believe, becomes ineffectual where the Old Testament cannot speak for itself—in the unity and perichoresis of the Testaments—and, we believe, it is most effectual and it makes history where the spirit of the prophets explodes the existing religion and unmasks the cryptopagans, in short, where independents and dissenters, Gueux and Camisards, diaspora groups and churches under persecution are awakened to life. It is impossible that an existing order will maintain itself when those who control it distrust the freedom of the Word and set themselves up as judges over the truth which becomes act, over the revolution that is caused by the saving power of Him who in various places causes his 'name to be remembered' (Exod. 20 : 24). In order to understand the Word of God, indeed, even to be able to perceive it, a person, a congregation dare not bring to it any preconceived knowledge of what is fundamental and what is peripheral; this knowledge must be suspended until the new encounter with the Word compels one to make new decisions.[32] Then the dissenters too will not wish to be anything more than witnesses, and they will turn away from the danger of becoming onlookers and wiseacres, partisans and founders of churches. Be that as it may, prophecy and history, preaching and national life, the Old Testament and the Messiah of the earth, the Word of the God of Israel and the salvation of the *goyim*, the theophany and the sanctification of our whole distorted life—the connection between these is patent.[33]

The gods are silent. The day of paganism, which was splendid in its way, is past. It may be that we are still using a subtle exegesis in order to explain that when we say 'God is dead' we mean no more than that we no longer meet him anywhere. Nihilism has superseded religion. If it be asked where man escapes the suction of nothingness, the answer must be; in Soviet Russia—for where men no longer suffer from the ambivalence of religion, the ambivalence of nihilism also cannot enter in.[34] Whether this means that every depth dimension of

[32] Such a suspension is the presupposition of dogmatics especially; and this explains the apparently ungrateful role it plays in the church. For dogmatics is critical reflection upon the preaching and teaching of the church which claims to be a translation of the Word of God. 'How can the church like being told that at the first, or at latest the second step, it becomes guilty of a deviation, and therefore needs to stop and reflect, and turn round from teaching to listening? How can it like hearing that it is exposed to attack and shock from the very point where it originated and that it must begin all over again at that point? The doctrinal forms . . . necessarily have a certain *stability*, which is not at all to be explained merely as the result of human sloth and self-love, but is certainly connected also with the fact that *at one time* it did listen and actually did listen to the Word of God. . . . It is not natural that men will feel free or allow themselves to be called away, and perhaps again and again, from these old to new attachments.' Karl Barth, *Church Dogmatics*, Vol. I, pt. 2, p. 805. [Translation altered.—Tr.]

[33] A number of illustrations of this connection can be found in literature, for example, in the historical novels of Marie von Ebner-Eschenbach (Rom. Cath.), Ricarda Huch, Conrad Ferdinand Meyer, A. L. G. van Bosboom-Toussaint. The book entitled *Lennacker* by Ina Seidel, in which twelve generations of typical pastors are delineated, deserves special attention.

[34] Cf. among the Communist philosophers of history Georg Lukacs, *Die Zerstörung der Vernunft* (1954), pp. 412ff.

life is completely blocked and every 'point of contact' for the Word has ceased to exist, or whether the absence of all this could rather mean a new openness, this is a question which we cannot here pursue. The answer depends above all on whether Communism itself has taken over the function of religion. We probably must be very cautious about making a judgment in this matter; meanwhile, who knows what may yet appear, for what Barth says remains true: 'When and where has man not had what is in relation to the being of the world the very "natural" capacity, quite apart from grace and miracle, to persuade himself and others of the existence of a higher and divine being? All idols spring from this capacity.'[35]

Meanwhile the church bells ring out over the dwellings of men, the Scriptures lie open, the preacher stands in his place to perform his ministry; the expectation that we may rest in the peace of God's presence still lives and timidly reaches out to receive its appointed portion. Is this a mere survival, an ideological delusion, a mutual deception, a pompous play put on by licensed Christian augurs? Prophecy and history! This distressing problem too has its place in this connection; the aridity, the perplexity, the compromise, these too are a part of the effect of the Word itself. Will we remain under this judgment? And how long shall we be fortified against being led astray and leading others astray? And when will the door at which we knock, the door of new great mysteries be opened? Are not these ultimately the last chances for church and people and state? And is not the first of these chances perhaps this, that we hear (yes, hear!) the silence of the Word in our regions and realize that it is passing us by to go to other places, to the equator perhaps? And may not the strongest reason for this silence be the fact that the Word is being smothered in untruth, that is, in 'our' Bible, in our 'academic' or 'dogmatic' fixation of what is right and correct, but as such insulated against the event of a real encounter between Word and world, preaching and existence, prophecy and history? 'The Word of God *itself is silent,* and yet it speaks even by its silence, when the church wishes to hear only the human word of prophets and apostles as such and therefore the voice of a distant historical occurrence which does not really concern it or lay any obligation upon it. The Word of God *itself* veils itself in darkness when the Bible is interpreted with violent and capricious one-sidedness

[35] *Church Dogmatics,* Vol. II, pt. 1, p. 84. [Translation altered.—Tr.]

according to the promptings of various spirits instead of under the leading of its own Holy Spirit.'[36]

The 'eclipse of God' actually signifies not only the possibility that for us the thought of God would be obscured for our understanding ('dimmed' on earth), not only the possibility that God would be purloined, alienated ('embezzled')[37] from the totality of our experience, but also the possibility that God himself causes the darkness, that he hides himself from us, that his Word of self-witness and self-disclosure is silenced. As we mentioned in the first part of this book, 'A Mirror of Our Times', this is the marginal possibility to which Martin Buber also has called attention.[38] 'The Word of God can change its human expression. In different times and circumstances it is the same and not the same. It produces the same effect in continually new forms. Therefore man's encounter and dealings with it have a history which is not the history of a solitary man standing by himself nor the history of a self-contained, self-centred church, but a history which on the side of the church and individual members in the church has the character of a response, the initiative being always with the Word of God as the first and *truly acting Subject*.'[39]

The beginning of all the misery does not lie in the incomprehensibility of the Revelation, the changing times and changing concepts; it lies in the solitariness, the very definite solitariness of the man who for his part has withdrawn from the Covenant in which he was included. The Word is not obscure for the initiate, it does not need to be obscure for the outsiders, but it is obscure for a generation and for the individuals who stand in the light and yet do not live by it, because they live in solitude. The fact that late in history there are figures who are characterized as the 'fourth' and the 'third' man is also a part of church history; the 'revolution of the solitaries' (Bouman) also had its matrix somewhere in the regions of the church. The 'lonely crowd' (Riesman) also had its origin there. 'It is no metaphor when we say that the Word of God speaks, acts, and rules; we denote thereby the characteristic and essential feature of the whole movement called church history. This is the characteristic and essential thing to which the life and deeds and opinions, all the insights and errors, the ways and

---

[36] Ibid., Vol I, pt. 2, p. 684.   [37] Cf. p. 49, n. 59.   [38] *Eclipse of God*, pp. 66f.
[39] Karl Barth, *Church Dogmatics*, Vol. I, pt. 2, p. 684.

aberrations, not only of the men who are gathered in power or weakness within the church, but the world which surrounds the church with its goodwill, hatred or indifference, necessarily have to refer and respond.'[40]

'We do not truly appreciate either the light which the church receives from the Bible, or the darkness which enshrouds it from the same source, until we recognize in both, beyond all human effort and human refusal which is *also* present, the overruling power of the Word of God itself, either to exalt or to abase.'[41]

If the lost word is lost, if the spent word is spent,
If the unheard, unspoken
Word is unspoken, unheard;
Still is the unspoken word, the Word unheard,
The Word without a word, the Word within
The world and for the world;
And the light shone in darkness and
Against the World the unstilled world still whirled
About the centre of the silent Word.

   O my people, what have I done unto thee?

Where shall the word be found, where will the word
Resound? Not here, there is not enough silence
Not on the sea or on the islands, not
On the mainland, in the desert or the rain land,
For those who walk in darkness
Both in the day time and in the night time
The right time and the right place are not here
No place of grace for those who avoid the face
No time to rejoice for those who walk among noise and deny the voice

.   .   .   .

   O my people, what have I done unto thee.[42]

The Old Testament too is familiar with the silence of God; curiously, his silence consists more in not acting than in not speaking. 'Is it not

[40] Ibid., pp. 684f.   [41] Ibid., p. 684.
[42] T. S. Eliot, 'Ash Wednesday,' in *The Complete Poems and Plays* (New York: Harcourt, Brace and Co., 1952), p. 65.

because I am silent that you do not fear me?' (Isa. 57 : 11). 'This you do and I remain silent' (Ps. 50 : 21). But 'our God will come and not be silent.' 'I will not keep silent, but will repay.' And also, 'For Zion's sake I will not keep silent . . . until her vindication goes forth as brightness and her liberation burns like a torch' (Ps. 50 : 3; Isa. 65 : 6; Isa. 62: 1). The tremendous weight of silence sets the measure from far off for the tremendous royal acts which press on toward the time of the end.

THE TREE OF LIFE

It will surprise no one that in a believing or unbelieving, conscious or unconscious experiencing of the history of man's mind, which we have discussed from the point of view of the 'authority and outgoing of the Word,' the question of results should arise: Does anything remain, and if so what is it that remains? This applies to the past, which, even though, according to Goethe, it presents itself as 'a farrago of lies and violence,' is here set down under the light of the Name. But above all we stand embarrassed in the face of our present day. For, after all, the 'revolt of the masses' (Ortega y Gasset) has been a complete success; the 'treason of the intellectuals' (Julien Benda) is hardly felt to be treason anywhere. The twenty-fourth hour has struck or is already past. The 'fourth man' crowds the streets and halls of the metropolis. And the 'third man' never stops propagating and reproducing himself. The gods are silent. And Yahweh, that brontosaurus, is quartered, like a freak fossil, among the other primeval skeletons.

This is a kind of automatic disparagement through mere talk, the favourite occupation of the intellectual masses. We must pass this by even though in a certain sense we share these odd humours of ungenuine nihilism; we must pass it by because we see the ambivalence of this matter and are concerned in a totally different way with the history of the Word, even in its tremendous silence, that is, in the sense that we know at least remotely that it was a matter of life and death and will continue to be so in the future. This spurs our earnestness, but it also relieves the strain, because the ultimate earnestness is not borne by us.

One may ask what response the work of the interpreter and witness will find in this world, and how it will react in its concern over all these godless men around us. Far more important for the world and more decisive for ourselves is that which overrides all these cares, that which humbles and exalts us after our burdensome depressions with all the weight of its gladness.

Perhaps the reader, like the author, has often been fascinated by the story of paradise and especially by the tree of life (Gen. 2 : 9; 3 : 22, 24). Is it not strange that something so mysterious, something which exegesis has never quite fully solved, should have become here and there in the Old Testament a simile for the *chokmah*, the wisdom of life, the 'truth' by which Israel lives (Prov. 3 : 18), or also a simile of the fruit, the gain, the benefits which the righteous (the faithful who keep the Covenant) find on earth (Prov. 11 : 30) ? Is it not interesting that it appears to have passed over into a proverb: 'Hope deferred makes the heart sick, but a desire fulfilled is a tree of life' (Prov. 13 : 12); that it is also applied to the utterance of healing wisdom (especially in the 'house of instruction'); the tongue, the language, the speech of the wise is a medicine, a balm and as such is to be compared with the tree of life, whereas perverseness (especially in instruction) 'breaks the spirit' (Prov. 15 : 4); and that Isa. 65 : 29 (in the Septuagint translation) says in an evocation of the coming age of salvation that what they plant they will also eat the fruit of, 'for the days of my people will be like the days of the tree of life.'? This would be the consummation of the outgoing of the Word.

Reference might also be made to the trees in Ezekiel 47 : 12, or the great tree in Ezekiel 31, and the palm trees which were engraved on the bronze sea in the temple. What is meant is a full life today and in future. A central thought in Israelitic wisdom literature is that it is not life that makes us wise but rather that wisdom brings life. When the simile of the tree of life appears in connection with wisdom, this may be a small argument on the side of the conjecture of those scholars who maintain the thesis that in an older narrative behind our paradise story the tree of knowledge and the tree of life were perhaps one and the same.

However, we cannot think of going into this question, though we would find in this tremendous domain of Genesis 2 and 3 a great deal of typical Old Testament 'surplus,' a surplus which could perhaps contribute to even greater clarity—could, that is, if it were not that right here the disagreement among the scholars seems to be almost boundless.[43]

We speak of the tree of life here not only because this ancient mythical symbol fascinates us for its own sake but also because of what has been done with it in the service of the Name. The shift of its meaning describes a curve which may be typical of the place of Israel in the midst of the religions. In our view, little is gained from playing with the simile, as is done in the later Midrash and in the Haggadic portions of the Talmud; we need rather to keep securely in mind the *tertium comparationis*, the point of comparison, namely, that knowledge of God brings life, the life, true life. *Bereshith Rabba*, ch. 15, says that the tree of life spread over all living things, that the circumference of its crown was equal to a five-hundred-years' march on foot, and that all the waters flowed from it to all the world (see also *Berachoth*, I, 1). In the *Targum of Jonathan* it is said that the height of the tree of life was equal to a foot march of five hundred years (i.e., as high as heaven; see *Chagigah*, 13a, 7). There is a curious reference in the Midrash *Tanchuma*, 27b, 33, where it is said that the soul which has been freed from *gehinnom* (hell) takes a bath every hour in the rivers of Baca and eats continually from the tree of life which is planted in the realm of the righteous and whose branches spread over the table of every righteous man; thus the soul (redeemed from *gehinnom*) lives on into eternity (cf. also *Pesikta Rabbathi*, 198a, 14).[44] Conclusive, however, is the application of the simile to the Torah and to the study of the Torah. In the Midrash to Song of Songs 6 : 8f. (123b, 37) it is said that the righteous sit under the tree of life in the Garden of Eden and study the Torah (cf. Midrash to Ps. 1 [19]: As the tree of life in the Garden of Eden extends over all who come into the world, so the Torah is spread out for

---

[43] B. D. Eerdmans, 'De betekenis van het paradijsverhaal,' *Theol. Tijdschr*, (1905), p. 489; J. C. Sikkel, *Het Boek der Geboorten* (1906), pp. 210f.; Th. C. Vriezen, *Onderzoek naar de paradijsvoorstelling bij de oude semietische volken* (1937), pp. 125f.; W. Eichrodt, *Theology of the Old Testament*, I, 178ff.; P. Humbert, 'Mythe de création et mythe paradisiaque,' *Revue Th. et Rel.* (1936), p. 453; G. W. Browning, 'The Tree of Life in Eden,' *The Expository Times* (1933–34), p. 44; P. A. H. de Boer, *De hof van Eden* (1948); H. Gunkel, *Genesis*, p. 8; B. Jacob, *Das erste Buch der Tora*, pp. 126ff.

[44] Cf. Strack-Billerbeck, *Kommentar zum Neuen Testament aus Talmud und Midrasch*, IV, pp. 1049, 1143; A. Wünsche, 'Aus Israels Lehrhallen,' *Beth Hamidrasch*, III, (1909), p. 62.

all the living in order to bring them into the life of the coming aeon).[45]

If we look back from here and ask what the tree of life signified and signifies in the religion of the nations, we are confronted with a long story. Images on cylinder seals, wall decorations, tapestries, etc., but above all the texts of Near Eastern literature, cult myths, etc., speak of a plant, a tree, a group of trees, a forest, in which the divine life is present and which grow in some inaccessible distance or are forbidden[46]—a temple tree, as well as a tree of the mountain, the garden of heaven, the fields of the gods, and also the link between heaven and earth and thus the world-tree which comprehends all life (among the Germanic peoples, Yggdrasill).

The most familiar example is the mysterious Plant of Youth (in the Epic of Gilgamesh), which the hero plucked from the primeval sea and then lost again to the foe of life, the serpent, which happened to be nearby when he laid the miraculous plant aside for a moment to bathe at a spring. We may also think of the story of Adapa, who became a victim of the false counsel of the goddess Ea, who said: If the supreme god Anu offers you the food and drink of immortality, you must refuse it—an example of the mystery of the 'divine deceiver.' There is also Egyptian material which speaks of the high sycamore on which the gods sit, of the field of food for the gods, and of the two trees between which the sun rises.[47]

If we turn then to the biblical story of paradise, we find there the tree of life, not as a timeless entity in the garden of the gods, the celestial fields, but rather as an intentionally planted tree; nor is it inaccessible and forbidden. It is rather a quiet presence, one might almost say a sacramental sign that confirms the significance of Eden, namely, that YHWH's purpose for man is altogether good. In the Israelitic saga the 'tree of life' is demythologized: the ancient mythical material is employed, so so speak, in order to say that the place of God is on earth, not in the sense of an identification of God and man but rather in the

---

[45] Also related to this are: *Lev. Rabba*, 9, 110d; 29, 127b; 35, 132c; *Nedanim*, 62a; *Arachim*, 15b; *Sifre Deut.*, 11, 12; *Josea*, 72b; *Erubim*, 54a. See Jacob Levy, *Wörterbuch über die Talmudim und Medraschim*, III (1924), s. v. 'Ets and 'Ets Chayim.

[46] Simon Landersdorfer, *Die sumerischen Parallelen*, pp. 91f.; Böhl, 'Paradijs en Zondvloed in Sumer en Akkad,' *Stemmen des Tijds* (1915–16), pp. 433f., on the personal name *Lugal-u-edina*, which may be translated 'Lord of the Holy Plant of Eden.'

[47] W. B. Kristensen, *Het leven uit de dood*, p. 51; G. van der Leeuw, *Refrigerium mnemosynes Bibl.* (1936), p. 143.

presence of YHWH among men. Life is on earth—just as later Canaan is called the land that flows with milk and honey—by virtue of the covenant which was also a covenant with the land. The signs of the presence, of the 'realization of the presence,' are on earth; in the midst of the people stands the tabernacle, the temple. The earth is not nor ever was an Elysium, but it was a garden of joy and peace, and the tree of life seals the fact that the earth is a paradise, not a garden of the gods, but a garden for men, and He will dwell with them (Rev. 21 : 3). We are manifestly confronted with a 'demythologization'; by an inner logic this had to occur, because Israel had freed itself from life in the cosmic totality, because it had decided between God and the world, between above and below, time and time, because it had experienced tensions which caused the religious life to break asunder.

This process of depriving the myth of its gods and its enchantment continued further and further, following the inner law which determined Israel's thinking with respect to the gods, until finally the whole of the mythical material concerning the cosmic tree was fused into the Torah, the teaching, the 'instruction,' and later, one may say, into the *chokmah*, Wisdom. This applies even if one were to deny that there is any relationship between the passages cited from the Book of Proverbs and the original concept of the tree of life (in my opinion there is no convincing reason for doing this). It applies because it actually represents the curve of Israel's inner development. Israel grew shy of the myth of life coming out of death, so shy that it cut off at the root all conceptions of immortality and held out no comfort or prospect except that which was contained, in almost wordless form, in the covenant of YHWH.

Indeed, the Old Testament teaches us through the image of the tree of life to affirm the limitedness of the creature; it insists that the mortality of man must be recognized—and lived. For that which is mortal still has an expectation—at the borderline of life; but the parts of the totality, the godlike entities, have no expectation as long as they possess 'eternal life.' Within the limits of time creaturely expectations harshly conflict and exclude each other; but this harshness of history also gives rise to the breadth, the balance, and the hope of humanity. Wisdom has stirred up life and filled it with contradictions, but with a gentle hand it has also warded off the temptation to overstep the bounds, to be impatient and rebellious. We have to learn what mortality is and discipline ourselves to it. Even today, within Christianity, this appears to be one of the most important tasks of preaching, in so far as the totality has been broken and in this respect too has yielded to nihilism.

Unusual light has been thrown upon this process in the earlier works of Leopold Ziegler. The same man who in the *Gestaltwandel der Götter* (1920) sketched out the outlines of the 'mysteries of the godless' summons us in *Überlieferung* (1936) to supplement the biblical revelations with the 'integral tradition' of the actual ecumenical revelation of the Gentiles. What is needed, he says, is a 'sacral re-creation.' The tree of the world will then 'flower afresh.' Mary or Eve—'are you the mother of God or the *summa mater* of all men, all beings?'[48] He regards himself as having been born into a sacral tradition, because 'my Christianity . . . begins not with the Jews but with the Greeks.'[49] Wisdom, which excels the position of the godless, appears as a tragically split but nevertheless all-embracing, gnostically conceived vitality. The freeing of human life from all limitations has its root in the conscious, modern revival of the sacral milieu. Our prodigious knowledge reveals the totality, the oneness of death and life, the absolute identity of eternal man with the changing form of the gods. All tension between 'this' and the 'other' is resolved. 'The place where the concept "God," despite its negative character, is redeemed without discount and completely fulfilled is life itself.' Hence we are challenged to turn back to the sacral tree of life.

A very astonishing specimen of this relapse into the sacral is to be found in the Jewish 'outsider,' Oskar Goldberg. He wants to convert the peoples who are capable of appreciating ritual (*ritualfähig*), in Africa, for example, to original Judaism on the basis of the tradition of the 'ritual of the Hebrews,' which, he thinks, projects into the Bible. The prophets destroyed the essence of the sacral bond, the *chokmah* is nothing more than the wisdom of the *goyim*, the Torah is saturated with it—even the testimonies concerning the patriarchs lead away from the original tradition of the Hebrews, the primitive ritual. On the basis of this religion Goldberg issues a call to missionize.[50]

---

[48] Leopold Ziegler, *Das heilige Reich der Deutschen*, II (1925), p. 419.
[49] Idem, *Selbstdarstellung* (1923), p. 12.
[50] Oskar Goldberg, *Maimonides, Kritik der jüdischen Glaubenslehre* (1935), *Die Wirklichkeit der Hebräer* (1925).

In Israel the tree of life fell into desuetude as a code word for the cosmos, as a simile for the riddle of death and the secret of overcoming it, and into the void thus created came wisdom, which stands firm against the reality of death. The Word must show the way, the Name of God must be near, the *melek*, the pioneer and companion, must go with us into the darkness of life and death. History is the field of divine and human communication. There and there alone does that life which we call 'spirit' spring up; there the spirit is made alive, there soberness in the fear of the Lord prevails. It is frightening to see what happens in the world; even among the devout there is such an exhibition of historical follies that we shudder at the confusion of the spirit in the face of the darkness, in the face of the demonic power of absurdity and the absurdity of demonic power. Nevertheless, the sound and healthy spirit, within the bounds of wisdom, remains, even in the face of this darkness, 'one who is appointed to praise' (Rilke). In the Psalms of Israel it is altogether clear that there is a close connection between this wisdom and the call to give praise.

There it becomes apparent that what is necessary is 'trust,' 'faith,' and that the great concern is the unceasing praise of God, the praise of God in life and in death, in prosperity and in adversity, in the rise and in the fall of cultures. Only he who praises, lives. But how can he praise? He who really lives, praises; the tree of life spreads its foliage over him. But who really lives? He who puts his trust in this God, this new, strange God who came from far off. And he who does this is wise. Here for the first time in history appeared what we call 'spirit' (as distinguished from emotion, soul, heart, etc.), the power to choose, the consciously taken direction, the persevering faithfulness, and the strength to live a hymnic life, a life of praise even though it be sporadic.

Thus the fusion, the reduction of the tree of life to the concept of wisdom is accompanied by a corresponding deepening of this concept which turned it into life, the true life, the life of the spirit, the life of choice and trust. It is a far cry from the mythical tree of life and the miraculous plant of immortality to the reduction and the glorification that takes place in the *chokmah*. The cosmic mystery of life is reduced to a small, special arcane discipline, namely, the *chokmah* (indeed, even God's own work in the Creation is more a working with wisdom than a flowing of Being into being—cf. Job 28; Prov. 8)—but this Wisdom alone is life, if you will, 'cosmic' life, the life of our life! And here we mean by 'cosmic' that which is applicable in all dimensions of space, because, as surely as YHWH lives, it will be valid in every age.

We said that this includes the concept of spirit with which we in the West are familiar (and which is broader than the Greek idea of *logos*, *ratio*, reason). But in the context of the Old Testament the 'spirit' remains close to the earth. It is life also in the sense of vitality, gain and abundance, joy and honour, so much so that what is said and promised (especially in many passages in the Book of Proverbs) can actually appear to be eudaemonistic. This can only confirm the fact that the salvation which the *chokmah* has in view also includes our earthly life and thus in this respect too reminds us, despite the antipagan reduction of the simile, of the 'tree of life.' Wisdom is life, wisdom brings riches, bestows abundance. Wisdom leads one into tranquillity and helps one to escape the dangers of life. It is lauded in such lofty terms that again there is an approach to myth and speculation (especially in Prov. 8).

Then finally we must note the consequence which follows from this demythologization. This tree, which encompasses life and bestows life, which preserves and seals it, is so far from being planted in some far-off inaccessible place that everyone who does not reach out for its fruit is marked with the sign of death—death in the spirit, paralysis in choosing, a hardening in unfaithfulness.

In this language we again recognize the spirit. And here we also see how 'certain potentialities of "logical" order and clarity are playfully anticipated in "prelogical" time,'[51] how in the myths the soul is reflecting itself in an ordered way, but that in Israel's history it is the spirit, in the sense in which we have understood it since that time, which is making its appearance.

Wherever choices must be made, it is the spirit which is breaking through. And wherever the spirit comes through something irrevocable occurs—so irrevocable that one cannot get rid of the dark side of the choice except at the price of revoking the whole development. In wisdom is life, namely, human life which is chosen, accepted, affirmed, and consciously pursued. Wisdom is more than a kind of religious guide or a moral guideline; wisdom is itself life, however simple, germinal, insignificant it may appear to be. One can eat it and drink it, one can feed on it and refresh oneself beneath it—and here for a moment the

[51] Edward Buess, *Die Geschichte des mythischen Erkennens* (1953), p. 84.

far-off, long-lost image of the ancient myth rises up again for a moment
—as under the Tree of Life.

But man refuses to live—this is the riddle which in the Old Testament completely superseded the riddle of religion, namely, why is it
that the gods refuse eternal life to the creature? Every feeling of
ultimate responsibility is now rooted in this view of the Old Testament
that when we face the Name and its course in the world, we are faced
with a choice—not a choice between advantage and disadvantage,
heroism and mediocrity, virtue and vice, but rather between life and
death. The tree of life spreads its branches, says the Talmud, over all
the nations in a circumference equal to a five-hundred-year march on
foot; it is wisdom to eat of it, to live by it; it is the simplest and ultimate
wisdom to understand that YHWH has nothing to do with any tree
of the gods, that he is the Other, who brings about the great revolution
in which all life is uprooted and exposed to the light of Life, namely,
the revelation of the acts of God *beqirbenu*, God in our midst. Therefore
Wisdom says (Prov. 8 : 34–36):

> Happy is the man who listens to me,
> to watch day by day at my gates,
> to guard the posts of my doors.
> For he who finds me has found life,
> and obtains favour from HIM.
> He who misses me does violence to his soul;
> all who hate me love death.

Thus everyone who asks what are the 'results' of preaching and points
to the ambiguousness of the past and the monotonous negativeness of
the present, receives the answer that the tree of life is on the road of the
Word, spreading its branches above it—and that it is the perverse
privilege of the spirit not to eat of it; for such eating (it is believed) is
neither forbidden nor commanded; either would be intolerable.

To 'love death'—is this humanly possible? We must take into
account the Old Testament idiom; to love is not primarily a feeling, it
is an act, it means to 'cleave to,' to 'remain in covenant with.' Those
who hate wisdom are in practice doing what death does. Death (again
in Old Testament language, a descent and not a paradoxical ascent)
destroys everything that by virtue of the *ruach* of YHWH withstands the
flickering, unstable existence of 'heaven and earth.' Against the background of this soberly practical conception of 'love,' it is, biblically

speaking, not necessary but also actually impossible to take nihilism
seriously when it proclaims the love of death (in this case certainly regarded as a feeling) to be something extremely desirable and declares
it to be an attitude worthy of human dignity. Raymond Poincaré once
said that the performance of the German army could only be explained
by the fact that the German people have a love for death and therefore
are capable of mustering up much more than the courage of resignation and even much more than the courage of self-sacrifice. There
have been political figures who, under the cloak of cynicism, have had
this attitude toward death.[52] Perhaps the ideal suicide, e.g., that of
Heinrich von Kleit, and the way in which the problem of suicide has
sometimes been made the centre of philosophy (e.g., Bahnsen and
Mainländer) may also point in this direction. Be that as it may,
nihilism is certainly saturated with this attitude, and where is the man
who is completely unfamiliar with it?[53] This temper of mind cannot be
refuted, because it is the reverse side of the religion of which a person
still retains a touch; in our connection one could also say, because the
nihilist has believed in the Tree of Life in the ancient mythical sense
(however he may have rationalized it). When the world is regarded
as the tree of life, then the power to say no, which has been logically
borrowed from the biblical heritage, must inevitably result in a 'limitless' negativism. But here too, says the Torah, the word 'limitless' is
ultimately an emotional, not a rational, responsible word. The ambivalence of religion as well as of nihilism becomes apparent; and the sober
realism of the *chokmah* prevails: to 'love' death is to approve the destruction which death causes, to make common cause with that which
threatens the fragile and defenceless existence of 'heaven and earth.'
Since emotion is uncertain or ambivalent, since in practice reason puts
itself at the service of death, therefore, according to the criterion of the
chokmah, even the seriousness of the nihilist is not without sophism, and
the wise man should not wear himself out arguing with sophists.
Wisdom itself sometimes cries aloud against the simpletons who play
with and further this destruction as if nothing were at stake.

[52] Thomas Mann, 'Friedrich und die Grosse Koalition,' in *Rede und Antwort* (1924).
[53] Cf. Georges Bernanos, *The Diary of a Country Priest*, tr. Pamela Morris, New York:
Image Books, p. 86. London, Fontana, p. 95: 'The sin against hope—the deadliest
sin and perhaps also the most cherished, the most indulged. It takes a long time to
become aware of it, and the sadness which precedes and heralds its advent is so delic-
ious! The richest of all the devil's elixirs, his ambrosia.'

High wisdom shrills in the street;
in the square she raises her voice;
at the head of the noisy street she cries out;
at the entrance of the city gates she utters her speech:
'How long, O simple ones, will you love being simple?
How long will the insolent delight in their insolence
and fools hate knowledge?'
Turn away from my reproof!
      (Prov. 1 : 20–23; tr. of Buber's version)

Nevertheless, the Word never gives up. Karl Jaspers, who in his way is a steward of the biblical heritage, says that we should have nothing to do with the sophists because this is not only a waste of time but a waste of oneself.[54] This is a human and inescapable reaction. But wisdom, which is life and bestows life, does not give in. And at the end of the Scriptures in the Apocalypse of John, the 'tree of life' appears once more in the vision of the new earth: 'Then he showed me the river of the water of life, bright as crystal . . . also on either side of the river the trees of life . . . yielding their fruit each month; and the leaves of the tree were for the healing of the nations' (Rev. 22 : 1–2; cf. *Shemoth Rabba*, 15).

The discontinuity between the ancient mythology and the mythic speech of the Scriptures seems to be resolved for a moment in order to make room for a cosmic expansion; the development in which the myth went through a process of diminishment and disenchantment and then was stabilized in the realm of the spirit and spiritual decision here issues in a development which has the dimensions of the originally

---

[54] 'Under the guise of devotion to everybody's interest, he wants only to exist, incapable of genuine enmity, which comes out of a high degree of resemblance to others on the same level in the questioning struggle of existence. . . . He puts on the pathos when it costs him nothing, he becomes sentimental when his will is thwarted. . . . Instead of facing the possibility of Nothingness, he believes in Nothingness. . . . Therefore, though he knows everything, he is a stranger to reverence, shame, and loyalty. . . . He adopts ways of thinking, categories, and methods indiscriminately, but only as forms of speech, not as a meaningful exercise of cognition. . . . He lacks the independence of unconditioned being, but he retains the noncommitted attitude of non-being and along with it the arbitrary assertiveness that shifts its ground at will from one moment to the next. . . . His usual attitude is that of unexistential irony. . . . To allow oneself to be drawn into discussion with him is a waste of oneself.' Karl Jaspers, *Die geistige Situation der Zeit* (1931), pp. 152ff. [Cf. another translation in the English version of this book, *Man in the Modern Age*, tr. Eden and Cedar Paul (Garden City: Doubleday Anchor Books, 1957), pp. 182ff.—Tr.]

intended, never revoked covenant. The exclusiveness of the Name leads to the universal fellowship; the particularistic authority is consummated in a universal fulfilment which heals what was broken; and in this End the outgoing of the Word comes to an end at that End where the Lamb is the lamp of the city. There the gates will never be shut and the nations shall bring their glory into it, and the tent of YHWH will be with men (Rev. 21 : 22–26).[55]

We may sum up what we have said as follows:

1. The 'demythologization' of the tree of life attests and affirms that there is no elixir of life in the cosmos and that life is to be found only in the nearness of YHWH, who makes paradise a paradise and who created him of whom it is said, 'The living, only the living gives praise to thee' (Isa. 38 : 19).

2. The seal with which the totality of existence (represented by the 'tree of life') is sealed is broken by the biblical saga. The authority to cut the ground from under this notion of eternal life is understood as a sign of God's judgment and faithfulness: man needs to die; it would be a 'religious' error for man to think that he could use the presence of God to satisfy his hunger for life and to overcome that fear of death which is born of the presumptuous, overweening soul that seeks to reach beyond itself. In terms of religion, the tree of life must become the tree of death; but in man's predestination to finitude, faith always finds, at the ultimate confines, the divine life which is given to it as a new, irreducible gift.

3. Where the remembrance of the religious complex of ideas no longer plays a part, the 'tree of life' figures as a simile for the *chokmah*. This makes it very clear how far removed the knowledge of God is from any kind of intellectualism; wisdom is practical, it is nothing else but living according to the direction of the Torah. But this is sufficient to produce a dividing of minds, a difference of opinion.

4. This demythologization of the 'tree of life,' in which it is reduced to a symbol and even less than a symbol, a mere simile, means on the other hand that all feeling about 'life,' all capacity for living, and all joy in living is brought into relationship with the Word. In this way our practical, everyday life becomes a secretly inspired life; thus there comes into being something like a restrained ecstasy over that which

[55] Cf. E. Lohmeyer, 'Der eschatologische Begriff des Zeltes,' *Zeitschrift für neutestamentliche Wissenschaft* (1922), pp. 191ff.

is given, and this is the chosen life, life in the spirit. This is where the 'autonomy' of faith enacts itself.

5. By the power of this inspiration it is realized that to reject the Torah is the ultimate threat to life. And the 'father,' the teacher, in the Book of Proverbs conceives of his undertaking as an endeavour to preserve many from spiritual death.

6. The refusal to live in this life, however puzzling and insuperable it may appear to be, must never make the interpreter and witness so weary that he gives up and writes off a person, an age, a generation. Here YHWH himself is the exemplar of untiring perseverance; 'every day he is up early in order to teach us' (Jer. 7 : 13; cf. 25 : 3f.; 35 : 14). If it is possible anywhere to speak of an 'imitation of God,' it is here— to imitate God in his *'emeth*, his steadfastness and faithfulness in communicating with rebellious man.

7. The ultimate prospect is that participation in the life of God will itself make unnecessary any mediation by word and sign. Despite a world full of sin and death, full of the madness of life and the yearning for death, in the New Jerusalem (we may dare to say) we live as the 'heathen' dreamed of living, in immediacy, in ultimate fulfilment, near the 'tree of life.'

KNOWLEDGE AND LIFE

There is no religion which does not involve knowledge—all the way from primitive magic to high speculation. In this knowledge man is linked with the cosmos, with the totality of death and life in their cyclic rotation. In the Word the original source and the rotation, into which religious knowledge initiates one, becomes ambiguous. That is to say, what is the original in actual life is not the original in truth. The command of God cuts its furrows in the totality of death and life. For Wisdom, Being is no longer sacral; it no longer presents itself to view; it no longer coincides with space. The 'given' immediacy of life and knowledge in which both together were directed toward Being has been broken by the unfolding of time. At first faith appears to be, and actually is, poor in knowledge; it lives on fragments and flashes of light; in the Old Testament 'heaven and earth' become a background that fitfully appears and disappears. One may even say that the store of knowledge diminishes, and even the flight of ecstasy is repressed by a peculiar matter-of-factness that goes in hand with the hearing of the Word. No longer can anyone mystically take shelter in 'fate.' No genuinely Israelitic thinking can take refuge in a philosophy of history like that of Hegel, which is the most sublime rationalization of Providence, wherein all reality is made to appear (not only charged with power but also) rational. We have been thrown into time, into the course of history, and—because we have forsaken religion and have had to set out under the Word on a road of pure uncertainty, given nothing but the knowledge of faith concerning the authority and outgoing of the Name, of YHWH—we are the children of time and will remain so until the end of time.

So it is that our atheism, when it does emerge, does not become really serious until it becomes, so to speak, a twofold atheism, namely, an emancipation from religion and an abandonment of faith. When this occurs, there is not only a separation between faith and knowledge (in so far as knowledge still desires to be a religious knowledge) but the knowledge gained also becomes an enemy of life (precisely in so far as knowledge is still aware that it had its origin in this lost faith). For the fact is that the Name of God has brought about a crisis of religion, which also threatens all knowledge, in so far as it has its roots in religious concepts, but which also casts a shadow upon the knowledge of faith as soon as the prophecy is received with suspicion and finally rejected. The 'Christian religion' again turns the 'Tree of life,' and this time radically, into the 'Tree of death'. In order to defend life, knowledge must be undermined—or conversely, for the sake of a remnant of insight, the last remnant of a 'natural' joy of living must also be sacrificed. Nietzsche—who can mention his name without respect and without sorrowful love?—passed through and suffered this ultimate tension of the tragedy of knowledge, for the sake of life, at the cost of life.

According to Nietzsche and other initiators of nihilism, there is a tension between life and knowledge, between joy and insight, which in the long run is fatal to both. Nietzsche regarded Christianity itself as a 'nihilistic' religion in the sense that a statement like 'God is Spirit,' once spoken, 'cannot be easily undone again,' that is, one cannot repair the alienation from life which this presupposes by making an affirmation of life. In another passage he says that the categories 'purpose,' 'unity,' 'being' are worthless, and he declares that reason is the cause of nihilism.[56] When the 'Christian religion' falls, philosophy falls with it, and along with philosophy, science also falls. What is left is life, but now robbed of its meaning and purpose; madness makes men sad; inability to arrive at joy through thought makes the life of thought a continual death. On ordinary levels the truth can only be boring or disappointing, but when it comes to the ultimate things it leads to despair.

It is true that in speech on the basis of the Old Testament it repeatedly becomes apparent that reason is alien to life if it is not integrated in the *chokmah*—but also that the *chokmah* itself embraces a 'whole' attitude toward life and sets itself against any attempt to blink the fact of death; it refuses to give death any power over our thoughts.[57] And to do this it does not need the myth of communion with the totality of death and life. Nowhere is death spoken of more frankly and realistically than in the Old Testament—and this not by virtue of a secret flight into the Beyond and even less because of a hidden loathing of life. The courage to live grows out of the strength of knowing, which is essentially identical with the ability to know oneself as one who is known, to accept oneself as one who is forever accepted, to affirm oneself as one who is affirmed by God, to limit oneself as one who is limited by God. This is the way in which and this is the reason why all the abundance of the tree of life lies in the knowledge of YHWH.

But the counterpart is there too, namely, that from the point of view of the ambivalence of religion, nihilism has 'nihilated' life through knowledge, only to discover later that knowledge has 'nihilated' itself. Analytical reason which unveils and unmasks things pays for its triumph by discovering that 'given' life loses its lustre and that precisely because it presents itself to us as 'given,' it suddenly appears to us to be 'absurd.' But even this is not enough; this sacrifice which 'honesty' presents is not accepted, in the sense that when the 'given' has lost its splendour, the author of the nihilification would have won out and could be sufficient unto himself; even science itself, the categorical determination of our spirit, turns out to be fatally arbitrary.

---

[56] *The Will to Power*, I.
[57] Thomas Mann, *The Magic Mountain*, tr. H. T. Lowe-Porter (New York: Modern Library, 1932), pp. 265f.

So it is not surprising that we should find in Nietzsche the very opposite of the peace of the *chokmah*, the peace resting in self-limitation (in the faithfulness of the Name and the promise of the Covenant), namely, the experience of all the presentiments of a man obsessed with suicide, reproduced in an appallingly lucid description of reality suffused with the livid colour of death. Only later, much later did 'Dionysus' present himself to initiate him into the art of enduring such an attitude toward life. As Ludwig Klages has correctly observed, Dionysus is the opposite of YHWH.[58] The flames of a meaningless lust for life, the wild colours of exultation in the *nihil* leap up against a background of dark despair; perhaps nowhere in the literature of the world—not in Lenau, not even in Dostoievski—is the world so compellingly seen and described in the reflected light of the storm clouds of the doom of death as it is by that great knower of the human heart, Nietzsche.

Here is one passage: 'A wintry day lies upon us, and we are living on a high mountain range, in danger and indigence. Brief is every joy and pale every gleam of sunlight that filters down to us on the white mountain. There is the sound of music, an old man grinds away at a barrel organ and the dancers are turning. The traveller is appalled to see this—so wild, so sullen, so taciturn, so colourless, so hopeless is everything, and in the midst of it the sound of joy, loud, mindless joy! But already the mist of early evening is creeping in, the music is dying away, the traveller's steps creak in the snow; as far as he can see he sees nothing but the bleak and cruel countenance of nature.'[59]

And even the crowning achievement of his thought, the doctrine of eternal recurrence, is full of anticipated despair: 'And this slow spider, which crawls in the moonlight, and this moonlight itself, and I and you in the gateway, whispering together, whispering of eternal things —must not all of us have been there before? And return and walk in that other lane, out there, before us, this long dreadful lane—must we not eternally return? This I spoke, more and more softly; for I was afraid of my own thoughts and the thoughts behind my thoughts. Then suddenly I heard a dog howl nearby.'[60]

[58] *Die psychologischen Errungenschaften Nietzsches* (1925), pp. 153, 210f.
[59] Thus as early as 1873 in *Unzeitgemässe Betrachtungen* (*Untimely Meditations*).
[60] *Thus Spoke Zarathustra*, in *The Portable Nietzsche*, ed. Walter Kaufmann (New York: The Viking Press, 1954), p. 270.

This is what the opposite view of the simultaneousness of knowledge and joy looks like. Thus the ashen light of eternal damnation falls upon Eden, upon the tree of life, upon the knowledge of the world, this world which has quite rightly lost its gods but has not entered into a new relationship with the Name and the history of the Word, this world which is our world.

Therefore Wisdom says:

> He who misses me does violence to his soul;
> all who hate me love death. (Prov. 8 : 36)

Thanks be to God that for him there are ultimately no godless men, that nihilism is just as ambivalent as religion, in order that the salvation in which there is no ambivalence at all may rest in him alone.

Foretokens of Joy

'. . . And behold, it was very good' (Gen. 1 : 36). Nobody else can say this. The powers and the gods stand like sentries of hell at the gates of the paradise of 'immediacy.' Therefore in the Old Testament there is also no immediate praise of life. But so much the louder rings out the praise of God—a thousand voices, all in one strain. And the one reason for this praise is this: He is good. And the world is good. It is good for its purpose, good for what God intended it to be, namely, to reveal the goodness of God. Knowledge and life, both together, are justified.

And from this there springs, quite incongruously, here and there in this world, joy—a joy that is the foretoken of the Joy to come. Even in the midst of the silence of the gods there was still joy for many; even in the sterile vortex of nihilism there are still some foretokens of joy. For YHWH is good, and 'there is no unrighteousness in him' (Ps. 92 : 16). Even when he is unrecognized and misunderstood, he remains faithful.

Often our lost sense of joy (as the essence of existence) has been reawakened by the symmetry and balance of a work of art. Art 'is the most gracious reflection of the archaic spiritual powers in exile, even in the diaspora of modern life. Every time we are touched by that difficult to communicate rapture that comes with the experience of a work of art the splintered spiritual powers of the *golden age* are for a moment gathered together again within us. . . . Every genuine poem has the power to evoke in a capable recipient a long-lost state of singular delight.'[61] Fine—but there is one thing in this statement that is at odds with the Old Testament witness, and that is that joy is thought of as a reminiscence of the golden age, a shining prehistoric past. In biblical thought, the experience here described is understood not as an afterglow of something past but rather as a foretoken of the future. The goodness of the world is sealed under the secret of the coming, the future Day. In the interpretation of the joy which beauty gives us, there is again a difference of opinion. One cannot say without danger of misunderstanding that it makes little difference how one interprets this. This may be true if one regards only the delight of the moment, the gift of rapture. It is imparted without respect of persons; and this too is a part of the meaning of life. Nevertheless, if we take into account the suggestion that this experience is an afterglow of prehistory, then we see how much sadness is necessarily bound up with the experience of beauty, the receiving of joy.

In the spirit of the Old Testament we must say that all joy is only anticipated joy and all beauty is an intimation of the ultimate secret of salvation: 'Behold, I create new heavens and a new earth' (Isa. 65 : 17). Beauty is a reflection and a pledge of hope, and the work of art is a *futurum*. To this extent all art is 'futuristic' art. If we were to take up another central idea, that of gratitude, we should have to point out that in the Old Testament gratitude is essentially thankfulness for the fact that there is something to hope for. 'We bid you to hope!' We are the heirs of the future, because—as listening to the Torah shows—we are the children of freedom; in God's commandment the road to the future lies open. And what touches, moves, and grips us in a work of art is the proleptic impartation of the reward of freedom. And the reward of freedom is the ultimate freedom: the Sabbath of the world. And this reward is imparted to us in the authority and the outgoing of the Word of God, in the course of the great narrative in which everything is comprehended, an inconceivable beginning and an unimaginable end—in which everything is comprehended from the centre of the ages.

'On that day the Lord will be one and his Name one; for the Lord will become king over all the earth.' 'And on that day it will happen

---

[61] Franz Werfel, *Zwischen oben und unten* (1946), p. 176 [Eng., *Between Heaven and Earth*, tr. Maxim Newmark (New York: Philosophical Library, 1944); the tr. above is mine.—Tr.]

that there will be no precious light and thick darkness, but continual light which is known to the Lord; it will be neither day nor night; and it will happen that at evening time it will be light' (Zech. 14 : 6f.).

'And YHWH Sabaoth will prepare on this mountain a feast of fat things for all peoples. . . . And on this mountain he will remove the covering with which all peoples are covered and the veil with which all the heathen are covered. He will swallow up death in victory; and YHWH Elohim will wipe away the tears from all faces, and the reproach of his people he will take away from all the earth, for YHWH has spoken' (Isa. 25 : 6ff.).

In its quality of being a futuristic conception, an anticipation of a deepened and purified reality, art is a foretoken of this joy. And therefore no art is closer to our hearts than that which is in the fullest sense *Zukunftsmusik.*[62]

> Dit is een ochtend zonder dageraad en
> dit is een middag midden in de nacht.
>
> .   .   .   .
>
> En ik begreep dat ik op nieuwe wijze
> voor iedereen verstaanbaar wezen kon:
> Dit is de jongste dag en hij zal rijzen
> achter de koepel van 't Centraal Station!
> O Amsterdammers, komt uit uw pothuizen,
> de tijden van de woningnood zijn om—
> o vrouwen, komt te voorschijn. . . .
>
> . . . Ge zijt zo morgenblank, er is een
> momentopname van een eeuwigheid,
> waarin ge zijt genomen als de nieuwe
> bewoners van een nieuwe, aardse stad,
> waarin men duiken kan alsof men kieuwen
> en stijgen kan alsof men vleugels had;
> want welke diepte zich ook doet vermoeden
> en welke hoagte zich omhoog ontwijkt,—
> de bronnen zijn zo helder als het goede,
> al het bestaande is hemels geijkt.

[62] 'Music of the future,' a polemical term developed in the contemporary criticism of the music of Richard Wagner [Tr.].

O, stedelingen, treedt uit uw verdieping,
de grond is door een Vreemdeling begaan,
die met de stem der morgenster u riep, in
de vreugde van het paradijs te staan.

(This is a morning without a dawn and
this is a noonday in the middle of night.

. . . .

And I realized that in a new way
I can speak intelligibly for every man:
This is the Last Day, and its journey
begins behind the cupola of Central Station!
O Amsterdamers, come out of the cellars,
the times of housing shortage are past—
O women, come forth. . . .

. . . You are so morning-fresh, it is a
snapshot of eternity
in which you are pictured as the new
dwellers in a new, earthly city,
in which one can swim as if one had gills
and rise up as if one had wings;
for what depths our sight surmises
and what heights on high escape it—
The fountains are shining like goodness itself,
all that exists has the measure of heaven.
O city-dwellers, come out of your depths,
a Stranger has walked the earth,
who with the voice of the morning star has called you
to stand in the joy of paradise).[63]

It may be surprising to many that, following the outlook of the Old
Testament, we should regard the relationship between prophecy and
history as being crowned by foretokens, anticipations of an ultimate
salvation. This prospect too appears to be less conspicuous in the New
Testament taken by itself. As the time between Pentecost and the
Parousia is prolonged, the truth of the Old Testament structures

[63] Guillaume van den Graft, 'Dies illa,' in his volume of poems, *Mythologisch* (1950).

emerges more clearly, including this truth that the *eschaton* becomes a present reality in qualified history in the form of a supratemporal joy *in* time. This presence can be grasped by our consciousness only by means of that which we call 'art'—a feeble word for all the forms in which 'one who has been appointed to praise' (Rilke) expresses himself under the dominion of the great outgoing of the Word of God.

But the opposite is also true, namely, that art itself is by its very nature to be understood only as a sign of the anticipation which is a reflection of the assurance of God: 'Behold, I create new heavens and a new earth' (Isa. 65 : 17). For what the tree of life, the forest of peace was intended to be for men has not yet been realized. The *chokmah* is 'like' the tree of life, it spreads over particular men and particular regions and particular times; but still it cannot provide that life which the heathen dreamed of living, that unmediated access to the mysteries of created existence and that fulfilment of the yearning in human nature which is good in itself.

Though Wisdom eradicates the desire for death and does away with the tragic mind, it makes no secret of the fact that there is still a great chasm between the here and the beyond, between the life which has been visited and reconciled by God and the life which has been glorified. So when the prophecy again surpasses the *chokmah*, it necessarily becomes 'poetry' (as in Isa. 9 : 11 and Rev. 5 : 19 and 21). But then there is also something daring and something lonely in the tone of its voice. It cries and cries for God to confirm it.

It is the prophets, more than the wise men, who share the sorrow of the groaning creation. They are the ones who are conscious of the future, which even though it is present today in its foretokens, nevertheless, infinitely transcends the present. When the prophets speak of it, their language has in it a strange note of playfulness in the midst of all seriousness, the note of a lonely act which cannot be justified by any experience, even an experience of faith; then it too becomes— art.

THE APPEAL OF ART

It is art which, as it were, invites us beforehand to sit under the tree of life whose branches extend five-hundred-years' march over the nations and the world. It is art which has had to 'cry aloud'—as Wisdom quite rightly did in its time (Prov. 9)—against the irreligious and religious stupidity of men and which even now raises its voice, 'a voice of tremulous silence' (I Kings 19 : 12)—not so much to warn us away from death as to show us life directly. True, the *chokmah* seals life, the life of the spirit, the life of choice, direction, and faithfulness, but the spirit (in this biblical sense) is not 'all that is within me' (Ps. 103 : 1). Art, which is the story of the *eschaton*, the spoken foretoken, must be content to be relegated as 'play' to the margin of society, to the border of law, politics, suffering, anxiety, chaos, and anxiety over the hiddenness of God.

Therefore it is not surprising to us 'that the artist must appeal to the others at the point of their openness to the Ultimate in order to be able to count on a hearing and an understanding for this highly peculiar speech.'[64] Whenever prophecy becomes poetry (and conversely, whenever any poetry has a futuristic content), it will appear strange, because then in the last analysis it no longer takes seriously the present state of the world and the present existence of 'sin.'

Perhaps the aesthetic estrangement and elevation of the human heart has never been so well expressed as it is in a few lines of Wordsworth's 'Tintern Abbey':

> . . . that blessed mood,
> In which the burthen of the mystery,
> In which the heavy and the weary weight
> Of all this unintelligible world,
> Is lightened:—that serene and blessed mood,
> In which the affections gently lead us on,—
> Until, the breath of this corporeal frame

---

[64] Karl Barth, *Ethik* (lecture notes), II (1928), p. 290. Among many of the neo-Thomists the opposite is emphasized, namely, the interpretation of art on the basis of the creation, of order, of *homo faber*; cf. Jacques Maritain, *Art et Scolastique* (1927); *Frontières de la Poésie* (1929).

And even the motion of our human blood
Almost suspended, we are laid asleep
In body, and become a living soul:
While with an eye made quiet by the power
Of harmony, and the deep power of joy,
We see into the life of things.

Whether we know and admit it or not, art is justified in playing with 'reality' only on the basis of the Name. For it is through the Word of promise that art, which we have called the story of the *eschaton*, is driven, given wings, and enabled—wilfully and arbitrarily, it seems— to know reality better than does experience and to reach higher than the branches of the one tree of life, the *chokmah*. Like a wandering minstrel who follows the course of prophecy and history, ever again at evening greeting the morning with the Morning, art goes its way, defenceless and alone, making its pilgrimage to the Holy of Holies, imaging in round and dance the shimmering dawn of salvation.

Art dares to transcend human speech between 'I' and 'thou' with poetry, in which in some fabulous way language again becomes self-sufficient and hiddenly hymnic (for what it looses on earth today will be loosed in heaven in future), poetry in which language seeks to prove nothing and yet proves all things.

In painting, art dares to see the real, given world with other eyes; it is constantly occupied with the dream (with the 'delusion,' say the Philistines) of bringing out the ultimate in a tragic situation, the deepest depths of a stricken heart, and, hoping against hope, the most hidden remnant of hope. Like humour, it dares to see, beyond all the deadly dull chatter and cheating, life sparkling in the conflicting attempts of man finally to live in the full sense, for once to be himself. It dares (whether consciously or not) in drama and novel to proclaim, in hope, the justification of the sinner. It gathers together all the futile, confusing voices of the earth that drown each other out and 'transfigures' them into the eschatological potential of 'absolute' instrumental music which is essentially disjoined from the human voice and any cantabile whatsoever. When the occasion arises, it is well to point out the danger of the 'aesthetic life' (even the artist cannot *live* aesthetically!) and to remember the wise words of Goethe, 'that the Muse knows how to accompany but not to lead'—the spectator's attitude is an impossible attitude—but here what matters is the work, in which a foretoken of everlasting joy is erected within the course of history moving toward its goal.

In the work, the element of play must be taken seriously; otherwise it is not genuine play and it loses its character as a pointer to something beyond itself. Therefore, by an inner necessity those who listen to the Word are also concerned with this highly serious play, this profound play of seriousness. The youthful Barth said rather surprisingly, indeed, rather sharply, but in our opinion cogently and correctly: 'It would be a shaky interpretation which would say that art is something optional for those who happen to enjoy it. The Word and commandment of God require art just as surely as it is true that we are set down under the Word which says there will be a new heaven and a new earth. A person who would wish on principle or because of laziness to evade the anticipatory creativeness of *aisthesis* would certainly not be a good person.'[65] The anticipation expressed in the tree of life, in paradise, in the new heaven and the new earth is a matter of a movement of the soul and 'all that is within me' in the direction of the time when YHWH 'will be one and his name one' (Zech. 14 : 9), toward the world in which God will 'be all in all' (I Cor. 15 : 28).

This movement of the soul repeatedly turns out to be gloriously inevitable, for 'the life was made manifest . . . and we proclaim to you the eternal life which was with the Father and was made manifest to us' (I John 1 : 2), though 'it does not yet appear what we shall be' (I John 3 : 2). On the margin of all the work of the interpreter and witness there is art—even though it be no more than a hymn tune, a classical liturgical form, or a religious play; 'but this margin is also a part of the whole, and it is altogether possible that at this margin the whole may be at stake. Fundamental exclusion of the aesthetic would mean that one refuses to have anything to do with the signs that point beyond the present, the highly impractical but equally significant signs which art erects. And this will not do, just as it will not do to wish to see in these signs anything more than *signs*.'[66] Within these limita-

[65] *Ethik*, II, pp. 292f.
[66] Ibid., p. 293. Cf. Ernst Bloch, *Geist der Utopie*, pp. 126ff. (on Anton Bruckner); Heinrich Vogel, *Die Krisis des Schönen* (concluding ch.); F. K. Schumann, 'Das Schöne als Frage des christlichen Glaubens,' in *Wort und Gestalt*, pp. 258ff.; Gerhard Nebel, *Das Ereignis des Schönen*, pp. 135ff., 160f., 173f.; Ernst Bloch, *Prinzip Hoffnung*, II, pp. 844ff.

tions and with this reservation, the words of Francis Thompson may stand:

> O world invisible, we view thee,
> O world intangible, we touch thee,
> O world unknowable, we know thee,
> Inapprehensible, we clutch thee.[67]

[67] *Collected Poems* (London: Burns, Oates & Washbourne, 1913), p. 214.

Part III: Examples of an Application

1. THE UNIVERSAL PRAISE: PSALM 100

1. The superscription prefixed to this psalm points to the fact that at least this psalm is 'a spoken rhythmic illustration of the acts of worship' (Wensinck). It refers to a more extended service of worship in which not only the sacrifice but also the praise of the individual is presented in his name to the Lord through others, through other hands and other mouths. Here a 'joyful noise', a shout of joy as in an acclamation, is demanded and expected of 'the whole earth.' The 'earth' will join in the temple service and sing as the Levites and the temple choir have sung.

(a) The 'whole earth'—this doubtless means the nations. Of 'the earth' as a creation, as the dwelling place prepared for men it is stated that it actually does shout for the Lord (Ps. 65 : 13) rather than demanding that it do so. With the nations the situation is altogether different (cf. Ps. 68 : 32, 36). They have fallen to the gods in their pantheon or pandemonium.

(b) The 'earth' is a unity only as it is seen from a given centre. To speak of a unity of mankind makes complete sense only if this unity can neither be regarded as already given nor as a task to be fulfilled but rather is seen·from a given centre, from Israel, from Zion, from the Name that dwells there.

(c) Whether the 'earth' is ripe for this, whether it will show itself willing to do this, is a question that is not asked. Here the ecstasy of faith is speaking, and it simply posits the universal, catholic substance of the Name as self-evident.

2. There are two things in this jubilation to which we are summoned which we must consider, no matter whether as participants or onlookers, two things that arouse our wonder. And yet it is only a matter of instruction; but even this instruction, just like philosophy, has to begin with wonder.

(a) The 'gods' (or the 'Godhead') in religion do not demand this jubilation or praise. The superscription of the psalm speaks of a *todah*, an offering, or more precisely, a thank offering, which has the form of an utterance of praise. *Todah* is a spiritual veneration which bestows upon the visible offerings when they are presented a certain definite, accompanying, comprehensive form. In the Psalms and elsewhere in the Old Testament *todah* became the stock expression for the liturgy, but even more than this, for life, the essential orientation of life. This jubilation is not to be expected in heathenism, not only because of the ambivalence of all religion but also because of the multiplicity of gods, their provinces and their altars. For the modern mind the 'God-head,' supposing for a moment that its existence is admitted, is any-thing but praiseworthy. One can let 'God' be something undecided, or dispute him, or accept him in an attitude of *amor fati*; but to our minds there is nothing here to call forth praise. Besides, the very idea of his being 'praiseworthy' appears to us to be too small, too anthro-pomorphic in conception. *Todah*, however, is something total, unique, and—self-evident, because YHWH is what he is.

(b) It is obviously only the Name, the nature, the character of the God who is here being exalted that calls forth this praise. Only the Name allows the conceivable to become reality, makes the possible the self-evident, lifts the limited to the universal. One may call it the eternal *a priori*.

Few changes of mental attitude have been so powerful in history and —for those who share it, even though merely by 'empathy'—so radical as the transition from doubt whether there is any place for praise at all to the certainty that there should not be a place for anything else but praise in human existence. The liturgical doxology constantly points to an ultimate fullness of life which we still have not made our own.

3. You, the whole earth, acclaim YHWH! This summons to praise reveals a mystery. We are not summoned to praise the universe, to extol nature, to exalt fate, to venerate life. On the contrary! Such praise, whether more or less forced or more or less spontaneous, would be a denial of him who is holy, other, wholly other, and who well knows that the only thing in the world before which we men are prone to 'cast ourselves down' is the glitter of glory and the power of life, and that whenever we do this, we also cast ourselves down (cf. Exod. 20 : 5). He who casts himself down prostrates himself in worship, but he who

thus casts himself down also casts himself away. This is too high an honour to pay to the silent, unspeaking world. And for man it is a dishonour, a lowering of himself. The unutterable Name, the nameless Name, however, points to a Heart that is against the gods and the powers and is known primarily in its deeds, the deeds of liberation. YHWH is our covenant ally. He has entered into a covenant with us in order to protect us against ourselves, we who in our thoughts are always ready to dally with *amor fati*, we who almost seek the tragedy and sadness of earthly existence. He must prevent us, against our inclination, from becoming covenant allies of sweet or bitter silent fate, in order that we may do exactly the opposite, namely, confess him, praise him as our covenant ally against the fate by which we think we are inescapably encompassed.

(a) It is a long way from the original meaning of *todah* to the meaning that emerges here, and yet the vestiges of the development are still contained in the act of praise: confession, acknowledgment, veneration, confession of guilt (which includes the honouring of YHWH, i.e., his rights and his law; cf. Josh. 7 : 19), bowing to his judgment, peace offering, public thanksgiving by the individual (possibly accompanied by a thank offering, in which case it remains a question whether the words of thanksgiving are primary and the offering is an accompaniment or vice versa), and finally, the praise of the congregation, liturgical doxology. The antecedent elements continue to be present in the last stage which is praise, because praise cannot separate itself from the total content of the Name. It can also be expressed in this way: to 'bow down' to the gods is, irrationally, a capitulation to power; praise is, rationally, to respond to the nature and virtues of YHWH (e.g., Exod. 34 : 6ff., Num. 14 : 18; Pss. 86 : 15, 103 : 8, 145 : 8).

(b) Praise contains within it the confession that YHWH is God in his way, that he judges in his way, and forgives in his way—and that because of this, as it were, because of his qualities, he is praiseworthy. If we ask what is the purport of this stipulation 'in his way,' the answer must be that the qualities are inferred from his concrete acts, from his saving acts in history, in accord with what was said above concerning God's being 'groundless and yet in the midst of things' (p. 180).

4. We can regard this Psalm as the brief conclusion of a series of Psalms, which are connected by many (especially Scandinavian) scholars with the rite of enthronement, in this case not of the king who

represents YHWH but of YHWH himself. The relation between the human and the divine throne would remain unfathomable if we were compelled to think in ontological and static terms. But this is rather a matter of God and the king being together and standing together in work, guidance, function, and rule. However this may be, there are two things that are excluded: (a) the identification of God and man and (b) the separation of their functions. There are two ideas that are simply incompatible with *todah*: the idea that some day YHWH will become king, and the idea that he is dependent upon the recognition of his kingship in order to be able to exercise the right and the power to rule.

5. What we find here is a third figure, namely, the leading,[1] the vicarious praise, and thus the 'exemplary existence' of Israel. As priest and liturgist, Israel leads. The 'earth' must know that the Lord is the Godhead (see the argument on pp. 119). He who says that the world must know this is himself speaking from a peculiar knowledge which has come to him as a privilege, from a knowledge which calls and qualifies him for the priestly and liturgical function. And it is in this knowledge, this certainty of salvation and knowing of the truth, that the deepest basis of the praise is to be found. Israel never thinks of praising nature or life. It praises him who 'made it his people.' This people is not autochthonous. It is called, created, shaped, and formed in history. In the time when YHWH dealt with it, it did not achieve the glory of power, it was not forged into a state after the likeness of the god-king-states of the nations. The choosing of Israel took on its own peculiar form in the midst of the power structures of the gods on earth. YHWH did not set himself up to be what he is; he did not enter into any competition. And the chosen people, at least in their praises, pursued this aristocracy. Here, by the very nature of this God, there is mildness and gentleness. It is in this quality that 'monotheism' has its root and not in the quantity of power wielded by one of the despots of the pantheon: Jahu, who worked himself up to the top![2] The manner of God's intercourse with his people is described in Psalm 100 as the leading of a

[1 There is an inimitable play on words here in the original Dutch: *voorgaan* means to 'precede,' 'go before,' 'lead' as well as to lead or officiate at a service of worship.—Tr.]

[2] T. H. Robinson, 'The God of the Psalmists,' in *The Psalmist: Essays on their Religious Experience and Teaching*, ed. D. C. Simpson (1926), pp. 25f.; O. Proksch, *Theologie des Alten Testaments*, p. 384; O. Weber, *Jahwe 'der Gott' und Jahwe 'der Götze,'* (1933).

shepherd. To be his people means to be the sheep which live on the pastures he has prepared. This pasture is never an area fixed by cadastral survey; the oriental shepherd moved from one grazing land to another. It remains one pasture, one place of blessing, because there is one flock, and it is one flock by virtue of the presence and the guidance of YHWH. Such a people, such men, must have *todah* as the crown of their cult; with all that they do not know, they do know that YHWH is *the* Godhead and that he has made them the flock that belongs to him. If Israel is exemplary in its knowledge, it also gives us an example of the praise of this pastoral leading of God.

6. But how do the *goyim*, the nations, come to give heed to this invitation: Come, the whole earth, come with us to take part in the temple service, in the liturgy that reaches its pinnacle in praise? They know perhaps that Israel knows that YHWH is the Godhead, but they still do not know it for themselves. They hear Israel's songs perhaps, but they still cannot sing them with Israel. Do they not want to do this? The fact is that they cannot do it! This is not only a matter of being initiated but also a matter of truthfulness. For them it would certainly be a 'new song' (Ps. 98 : 1), but then this would also have to come out of the experience of a new life, out of a fresh act of God! Have they seen such acts (as are presupposed in Ps. 98 : 3b)? 'All the lands which "sit still" in dull self-satisfaction and separation from God (Zech. 1 : 11) are to take up Israel's song of praise and break out into jubilation' (H. J. Kraus). How could this be possible? Israel, of all people, which was always appealing to its election, should know that it is utterly impossible. Abraham had long since turned his back on the 'universal Godhead,' i.e., nature, and the particular Godhead, i.e., YHWH, can be known only in Israel. Or is there such a thing as a praise without knowledge, a desired praise (in the same sense as a 'desired Baptism' is spoken of) and intended thanksgiving (cf. Pss. 22 : 28–32, 67, 145, 148, 149)?

(a) The simple words of the psalm seem to be quite mad; everything that is said in it is 'contrary to being' (*seinswidrig*) and thus also falls outside of historical possibility. What is being called for here is psychologically inconceivable, unless the meaning of the writer, the liturgist, and the singing people is either that, down underneath, the heathen religion is nevertheless related to the faith, that in some hidden way man knows the God whom he cannot confess, or that in a short time the heathen will be convinced and converted through our mission, our 'evangelization.'

(b) Both of these ideas, however, lie outside of the connection of this text. YHWH is the Godhead and Israel is his people. He has made us and we belong to him. We bring the *todah* to him. You, the whole earth, come to the temple gates, and praise him! Come now, without delay! In this view there is no other expectation except 'near expectation.' This is the nature of this call, this witness, this certainty of God.

7. The mystery of which the Psalm sings is the mystery of God, specifically of this God. One can also say it is the mystery of the *eschaton*—if one keeps clearly in mind that from God's point of view the eschaton is that which is real and present. Just as truly as this 'little' God is the ineffable and universal God, so truly do the nations now and everywhere belong to him. Just as surely as he is Elohim, so surely does he destine the course of the nations now and everywhere for his praise (cf. Pss. 66 : 1, 98 : 4). From Yahweh's point of view this destiny is already fulfilled.

In verse 4 the most moving thing is that the heathen are expected, without any intermediation on the part of men, to come directly to the temple to take part in the service. Without any transition or conversion, they stand in the courts, 'confessing' him and 'blessing' the Name. Exegetically, there is nothing here that would compel us to interpret verse 4 as only a call addressed to Israel; everything speaks in favour of the view that here the call that goes out *from* Israel is continued. There is no real argument for this anticipation and this eschatological presence, unless it be that which is given in the conjunction 'for': 'for the Lord is good.'

The Old Testament is concerned not only with the fact that YHWH is the Godhead but also with the fact (and this is really identical with the preceding) that God is good. Here is 'the fundamental article of revelation' (Rosenzweig): He whose eye is upon the destiny of all that exists (because for ever and ever he has affirmed it) has always been good and will always be good to his people.[3] God's action in the

[3] Cf. H. H. Rowley, *The Biblical Doctrine of Election* (London, 1950), pp. 54, 112f.; J. Blaauw, *Goden en Mensen* (1950), p. 45; F. M. Th. de Liagre-Böhl, 'Missions und Erwählungsgedanke in Alt-Israel,' in *Festschrift für Alfred Bertholet* (1950), pp. 77ff.; Th. C. Vriezen, *Die Erwählung Israels nach dem Alten Testament* (1953); G. von Rad, *Deuteronomium-Studien* (1948), p. 51.

'midst of things,' the concrete proofs of his faithfulness are the guarantee of this.

'His favour endures for ever, and his faithfulness to all generations.' This tears asunder, for the sake of love, the delusion of religion. It opens up a vista to the future and gives us a place to stand today. All by grace alone, by God alone, throughout the ages, and new in every age! Not a word about Israel's cooperation! Not a word about my correlation between God and man! The opening up of the prospect for the future and the grasping of the initiative, these are the prerogative of YHWH. Everything comes from 'beyond,' but at the same time it proves and manifests itself in deeds here and now.

Are not these words all too high-flown? They would actually be empty words, if 'his' favour and 'his' faithfulness could not be fulfilled in the history of his saving deeds, that history which has brought us forth into a new birth and preserves us to sing a new song; the Name unfolds in the humanity of YHWH in the midst of the traffic of the earth. All the words of Scripture (even though again they may be 'religious' words) find their meaning in the saving content of the reality of God, to which they emphatically and urgently point.

The heathen did come to the temple of YHWH, they did join in the *todah* and let it rise up as a thank offering. Here we are speaking of the church, of its confession and its liturgy. Nothing has been so determinative of the history of the world as the 'new song' of the nations who have entered into the ark of the church. Nothing can be so liberating for a man in his ambivalence—whether it be that of his religion or his nihilism—than finally to praise life, light, and all things, because YHWH is the Godhead and because this God is good, the God who declares that he is our shepherd and king, our covenant ally against fate, who shares our fate in the Covenant. It is to this that the church calls the 'earth,' the nations. Hopefully, it does this in the same 'religionless' way in which Israel did at that time. Without the affirmation and assurance of the words 'You men are God's,' the mission of the church is doomed to failure or to degeneration.

LITERATURE FOR NO. 1: B. D. Eerdmans, *The Hebrew Book of Psalms*; A. J. Wensinck, *Semitische Studien*, pp. 56f., and *Liturgie in het*

Oude Testament; A. R. Hulst, *Belijden en loven, opmerkingen over de betekenis van het woord 'toda' in het Oude Testament*; Karl Barth, *Church Dogmatics*, Vol. III., pt. 2, pp. 167f.; H. Gunkel and J. Begrich, *Einleitung in die Psalmen.*

2. BETRAYAL AND TERROR: EXODUS 32:25-26

1. The fact that the Name is 'groundless' and at the same time 'in the midst of things,' that the content of the Name is the nearness of YHWH, and that this nearness realizes itself in deeds, can be illustrated by many narrative parts of the Old Testament. Exodus 32–33 is probably an unusually eloquent example just because of the way in which the Name, the nearness, and deed dovetail into one another, not only in the essential purpose of what is proclaimed but also in the connecting links of the narrative. Here much will depend on how the interpreter and witness tells the story. Here the context will have to be brought in at some length.

2. The narrative (which, of course, we cannot reproduce here) contains, however, certain focal points which can be briefly presented in the form of 'theological' theses so that the whole can be kept on or lifted to the level of proclamation. The liberation is confirmed in the Covenant, the *berith*. This applies to Israel in an exemplary way, but the whole story of God's deeds on earth is characterized by the will to liberation. Life is threatened by the powers of death, by sword, plague, and famine. Men are in distress under the oppression which they suffer from their overlords and their 'sacral' power. On principle, YHWH is not on the side of the oppressors. The deliverance from Egypt is an event which as a part stands for the whole and is a prelude of all the genuine turning points of history. God creates a place to live; he sets those who are delivered over to the cosmic and Adamitic realm in the realm of his covenant. This abandonment to the cosmic, Adamitic realm is precisely the 'trouble,' the 'distress' (*tsarah*) of living under the powers (cf. I Sam. 10:19; Ps. 9:9; Jonah 2:2; Ps. 22:11; Job 5:19; Jer. 14:8: O Hope of Israel, its deliverer in time of trouble!).[1]

---

[1] Cf. the following passages in Buber's translation: Ps. 74:12: 'Yet God is my King/ from of old,/who works deliverances/in the midst of the earth'; Isa. 33:2: 'Thou, be

3. The deliverance from Egypt is a deliverance from the oppression of *she'ol*. YHWH has revealed himself as the one deliverer in the midst of a closed cosmos. He not only did so in the past; he was so, he is so. This is confirmed in the Covenant and sealed in the Torah, all of whose commandments have only one meaning and purpose: Abide with your Deliverer! In that you do this, you represent all peoples and are yourselves a sign in the midst of the earth; having been delivered from the terror of the whims of gods and powers, you will have peace in the Covenant. But here in Exodus 32 those who have been delivered and defended, the covenant people, cried out: *Make* us a God who can be a leader for us. Not another God, no, we mean YHWH, who led us out of Egypt; but in a different way, so that never again will it happen to us that our leader (Moses) will disappear in darkness and we be left without direction and 'instruction.' The Deliverer is visible, not only in his deeds, but also in those whom he sends. When they become invisible, faith is threatened. Standing or riding upon the holy animal, the invisible Godhead is near to us with its power like the roll and thunder of a storm and the upsurge of the seed of the earth, of death, and passion, and manifold primeval force, as the *goyim* understand it.

4. The Name is present in the word of speech, but speech is emphatically invisible and at times is surrounded by an emphatic silence. And he who cannot bear this may be seized by a horror vacui; he lapses into terror and abandons the one thing that would have saved him from abandonment; he grasps at the available, disposable Godhead. 'The people gathered themselves together'—but their meeting was the opposite of a 'congregation,' of the *gahel*. The terror is already upon them, though they still feel nothing but ecstasy. The golden rings from the ears of the women, the sons, and daughters! The molten image of the young bull; the liturgical adjuration, 'This is your Godhead, O Israel'; the altar erected there; the feast and the dancing before YHWH; the morning sacrifice and the exploding orgy (v. 6)—Moses

gracious to us . . . now also be our deliverance in the hour of trouble'; Ps. 88 : 1: 'Thou/God my deliverance!/by day, by night I cry out to thee'; Jonah 2 : 3ff.: 'I cried out of my distress to HIM/and he answered me/I cried out of the belly of the realm of the grave. . . . The waters raged about me/even to the soul,/the flood of the abyss compassed me about. . . . To the roots of the mountains/I sank down,/the land, its bars,/closed behind me for ever,—/then thou didst bring up my life from the slime, THOU my God.'

hastens down from the mountain—no, he is told to do so, but he does not do so at once. Then follows the dialogue between the Deliverer and his ambassador, filled with threatenings and intercessions. It teems with priceless anthropomorphisms: YHWH allows himself to be 'flattered' and softened (v. 11), the Lord allows himself to be admonished, 'Remember Abraham, Isaac, and Israel, thy servants' (v. 13). And God said, '*your* people, whom *you* brought up out of the land of Egypt' (v. 7), as if it had been an independent uprising of the horde of Israel under the leadership of a rebel chieftain, as if he were withdrawing and allowing the 'holy' history to collapse like a mad dream and become only an ordinary ancient story of the rebellion and migration of a people.

(a) This is the terror that dwarfs all terror before the powers to which we are exposed; this is the terror that goes beyond terror over the betrayal of the covenant, the covenant with the Deliverer; this is the terror of God's turning away. When he rises up in his 'wrath,' he revokes the liberation already accomplished. The Law is grace because the covenant is grace; and the covenant is grace because the liberation is the most peculiar and characteristic work of him who is called 'I will be what I will be' (Exod. 3 : 14). Life is life that is threatened. God is the 'turning toward freedom' of those who are threatened by oppression. When he turns away, the pillars of heaven are shaken and the foundations of the earth tremble. He who dwells on the cherubim turns away from the caricature of his majesty, from the religious dance in which with every step faith is more surely trampled into the ground.

What else can this turning away from those who have turned away from him mean except the revocation of the new beginning, the expunging of the seemingly conclusive beginning of liberation of those who had been seemingly elected?

5. It is part of the mystery of YHWH that he makes himself dependent upon a new beginning on earth. As a new divine history was to begin with Noah, so Israel (rejected as were the people in the Flood) would begin a new history with the 'man Moses.' For it is the nature of God to go on living in liberating; there will be a new people, the 'children of Moses,' of them 'I will make a great nation' (v. 10). And now the ambassador seems to be more faithful than the Deliverer, the servant renounces his privilege, while the Lord stands on his rights. Moses is a real mediator, and he intercedes for Israel's existence and

future. He has no desire to be the seedling of a new people; he does not want these people who are terrified by God's turning away from them to be exterminated. What he wants is just the opposite; he offers himself: 'Blot me out of thy book,' out of the purpose of election; cast me out of my determination into chaos. And the most moving touch of all —here Moses (acting in the mystery of vicariousness for Israel, but also for God) cries out to YHWH the same word that the prophets used ('turn away').[2] Repent thee, turn about, turn back, return to thyself, return to thy real deeds, the deeds of thy right hand (to use Luther's phrase). Let it repent thee! Remember thine oath!—'And YHWH repented' (v. 14). This is the great act, the primal act, groundless and yet in the midst of things. There is no fate to which the Lord is subject, there is no law of being which holds him prisoner, there is no mortal power of unchangeableness in God. He *is* the design of his own life.

6. The narrative goes on: the ambassador and mediator went down from the mountain (here the traditional text draws from another source, but the redactor regarded the spiritual value of the confluence of these sources as saving truth); and now he who had interceded for Israel (in more or less abstract terms) saw what was actually happening (concretely) on the plain below. And then—in an imitation of God prompted from within—he threw the tables of the Law to the ground and broke them in pieces. Terror! Then he heard it: 'It is not the sound of the song of triumph (might), not the sound of the cry of defeat (powerlessness, panic), but the sound of singing and dancing that I hear' (of those who are drunk; Septuagint). YHWH would destroy the people because they are too wicked to participate in the history of liberation; Moses would destroy the Torah because it is too good for a people who, though they have hardly been rescued from the *she'ol* of oppression, have already departed from the Deliverer. As so often, according to the standards of religion, the man (Moses) was nobler than God, for God is always 'more human' than man.

The man's anger blazed up, and he shattered the holy tables and

---

[2] 'Moses can do this because he speaks out of the deepest, innermost oneness with the living will and saving purpose of God and reliance upon his immovably established promise. He can do this because he relies upon the fact that God is not a rigid principle of unalterable predestination, not an unbreakable fate, but rather a living God who can change his mind, feel remorse, and alter his decisions. . . . He can do this, not because of fickleness, but on the ground of His immutability, which is at one with His freedom.' H. Frey, *Das Buch der Gegenwart Gottes unter seiner Gemeinde*, p. 106.

ground the image of God to dust under his feet (v. 20); the zeal for YHWH erupts volcanically—and what he did was human, but human by virtue of the view in which God viewed it, just as that which God did was divine, but in the framework of human 'intercourse.' Though God on high had already 'repented,' the mediator on earth is still in the trance of indignation. Aaron, who was the person responsible, is called to account: 'You have brought this people to this great sin,' and 'What did this people do to you that you have called forth this horror in which the meaning of the calling of his people has been completely nullified and the liberation is in principle revoked?' And Aaron defends himself: 'You know the people, that they are set on evil,' they demanded it, and 'there came out this calf' (vv. 23–24). It was as if some anonymous powers were driving him and the people. And in a certain sense this does indicate the dark mystery of the apostasy. The powers of nature are nameless, and under their dominion the soul loses all sense of direction.

7. Only then does the denouement come in verses 25 and 26: 'Moses saw that the people had broken loose [become unbridled], for Aaron had let them break loose, to become a hissing among their enemies' (a hissing and a malicious pleasure, a leering mockery, here and for ever and indelibly). That is what man is, even when he is elected and chosen! He would rather be either bound or unbridled than free; he would rather be under the powers in oppression or with the powers in chaos than be brought home in the covenant. Then Moses cried out—not as a threat but rather as an invitation in order to elicit a response of repentance which would answer God's repentance: 'Who is for YHWH? come over to me!' ('mi leyahweh 'elay'). This does not mean merely: whoever is agreed with 'Yahwism,' and not even whoever regards himself as belonging to the YHWH-community, but rather, whoever reaches out for YHWH to participate in his purpose. His purpose from century to century is to bring about liberation from all the oppression of the powers. Who declares that he is in solidarity with history? Who will join in the dynamic movement of resistance to the powers and of freedom from the gods? Who will screw up his courage and rouse himself out of his religious inconstancy? Who is ashamed of his debauchery? Who recognizes the pain and sorrow of this betrayed God?

8. 'Then all the sons of Levi gathered round him' (v. 26). All—this

is fine! But only one tribe came forward; this is a confirmation of the horror, a corroboration of the revolt, a persistence in betrayal. The great majority remained unmoved, inflexible in their confusion and suspicion. Was this because the leader's acts, the shattering of the holy tablets *and* the image of the God, confused them? Was it because God's judgment expressed in the 'accursed water' (v. 20; cf. Num. 5 : 17f.) aroused fear and suspicion? What can be of any avail, once the liberation has been scorned by the liberated and the elect have rejected their own election? These were desperate gestures that Moses made. And the final gesture, the cry *mi leyahweh 'elay,* which was fundamentally a new offer, a new appeal which is the result of God's repentance, is no longer heard in freedom. He stood at 'the gate of the camp,' the place which by ancient custom was the place of judgment, but instead of the judgment there sounds here an invitation to reach out for YHWH, to share his purpose, to make common cause with the history which he, the one who brings liberation and establishes the covenant, has inaugurated.

The narrative, which voiced the Name in its onward movement in judgment and grace, ends in this silence of the people, the silence which is worse than the orgies from which they have just been awakened. This silent indifference is the nadir. It shows that the elect wish to repudiate their election; and election repudiated will be the end of their liberation.

9. The Word (in this case the call: Who will belong to YHWH, because he knows that he already belongs to him) confronts men anew with decision. And after the silence, in which the decision of the heart lingers and delays in its birth like a stillborn child, the judgment breaks out upon the congregation or (what is here the same thing) the rebels. It was a ghastly judgment of the sword. The three thousand who fell were no more guilty than the others, but they were set for a sign of the rejection of those who had rejected their election. This was not a running amok nor an extreme case of church discipline. Here the narrative, with all of its various strands of motifs, also has this marginal reference which is a unique foretoken of the ultimate earnestness of God. This ultimate earnestness is the Last Judgment. Upon the world? Upon the church! Judgment begins with the household of God (I Pet. 4 : 17).

10. 'Abide with your Deliverer!'—this is the great swelling and sus-

taining pedal point of the narrative. One can rebel against all divinity, majesty, and power as such. And he who, like Israel, is 'led out' *must* at times rebel against it. This rebellion is necessarily fed by the constantly present ambivalence of natural religion. And Israel is always called upon to rebel. And yet to rebel against our Deliverer and to wrap ourselves in resentful silence when an abundant grace offers us a new opportunity to repent, to take a new step, to reach out honestly for the Lord—this must inevitably mean an irrevocable end, this is the very antipode of God's self-reversal, the naked human antithesis of his glorious 'repentance.'

But an overhasty word is still 'irrevocable.' The story goes on. And what is narrated is clearly stamped as being an 'episode.' And what we *hear* as we read on shows us that we shall never *see* the end of it. The Name is near at hand. 'I will be [with you] as I will be' (Exod. 3 : 14). And again and again will 'they put my name upon the children of Israel' (Num. 6 : 27). For the humility of God remains, as long as the days under heaven endure, the most characteristic mark of his majesty.

LITERATURE: S. R. Hirsch, *Pentateuch-Kommentar*, II; Bruno Baentsch, *Exodus*, in *Handkommentar zum Alten Testament*; M. Buber, 'Het geloof van Israel,' in *De godsdiensten der wereld*, I; H. Frey, 'Exodus,' in *Die Botschaft des Alten Testaments*; Edmond Fleg, *Moïse* (1928).

3. THE FACE OF YHWH: EXODUS 33 : 14–16

1. In 'religion' there is never any reference to election or rejection. The Godhead 'is,' and a people, a tribe, a clan simply 'is' its partner. The Godhead does not choose because it does not speak, and for the same reason there is in the given cosmic framework no rejection. And man, the partner? He 'knows no better,' he 'cannot do anything about it,' he 'remains in his place.' In the Old Testament the drama of election and rejection rages on man's part too, for nothing is constant apart from the will which 'keeps the covenant,' nothing is broken except by the will which breaks the covenant, that is, the will which refuses to will. Therefore the Old Testament does not bear the mark of an exposition of the truth, but rather has the character of narrative even in the

farthest reaches of the secret controversies between God and man. The 'Name' encompasses the one who is called, but it gives him freedom, not the *liberum arbitrium indifferentiae* ('the free will to be indifferent') but the freedom to surrender himself to creative freedom, the loving, free, sovereign power of him who has 'known' him. One may also say that freedom is obedience; obedience is hearing (*Shemaʻ Yisraʼel*), and hearing means to be put under a claim, to enter upon a prepared path of inner necessity.

All this is gambled and frittered away in the story of Exodus 32; but the story goes on and thus means that these negative attitudes are not the last word and that they cannot end in the fatality which is inherent in them. For 'punishment' is the opposite of 'fate'; 'wrath' is the opposite of the ineluctable Being of a nature god; a 'mediator' is the opposite of identity; the call 'Who is for YHWH? come over to me!' is the opposite of a coercive command or a hypnosis; it is the appeal of the faithfulness of YHWH, the latent creation of a new beginning. Thus the story goes on to reveal and unfold the 'Name.' Here the 'repetition' of the original beginning is completely a miracle.

2. Proclamation always retains the tone of narration; this remains the inalienable mark of the superreligious event to which the congregation bears witness. Conversely, the narrative itself is clear proclamation, if one pays attention to caesuras and phrasings. Now comes the call to move on, farther away from Egypt, into the desert, to the new, ancient land where the patriarchs lived with God, who had taken them under his personal guidance. Into the desert! To the land of milk and honey, the sweet food of *shalom*, the time of the end, the opposite of that *sheʼol* which was called *Mitsrayim* ('Egypt'). But there is one reservation hidden in the call to move on: *I myself* will *not* go up with you, for you are a stiff-necked people; if I were to go up among you, I would reject you on the way (v. 3). I will bring you into that land, but I will not remain in your midst; if I were to remain in your midst for a single moment (v. 5), I would have to reject you. This assurance is the response to the 'mourning' which the people finally took upon themselves by putting off all their ornaments (conjuring manipulations with amulets?). But this gesture was not born of repentance.

The King says that it is impossible for him to dwell with rebels; in their 'day of repentance' the people were again acting in another 'religious' way that separated them from God. The gestures of deprivation and regret are still not the signs of a new 'turning to' God (for repentance, turning about, is implicitly 'turning to'), they still do not demonstrate that these stiff-necked people have now repented of their rejection of God's signs. And yet it is objectively significant that the fact of God's absence weighs so heavily upon a people among whom there are still rumblings of rebellion that even the 'promised land' cannot grip their thinking. For they cannot even think of a good land without the God who has been reconciled; though still ambivalent in their turning to God, they will not accept the absence of YHWH in order to enter a perfect, but therefore an unreal, paradise. Then come the words: 'Stop your mourning, I will see what I can do for you.' Then something other than wailing and mourning comes into view, and this is the one small point of light which is the centre of the universe, the holy place where YHWH dwells.[1]

3. The tent of the presence is also the tent of meeting. The leader, Moses, pitched it 'outside the camp,' and the narrative goes on in the terse, succinct phrases of a refrain: 'And so it happened: / every one who sought Him went out to the tent of meeting, which was outside the camp. / And so it happened: / when Mosheh went out to the tent / all the people rose up; / they stood every one at his tent door / and looked after Mosheh, / until he had gone into the tent of the presence. / And so it happened: / when Mosheh entered the tent, / the pillar of cloud descended / and stood at the door of the tent, / and spoke with Mosheh. / And all the people saw / the pillar of cloud / standing at the door of the tent / and all the people rose up; / they cast themselves down, / every one at his tent door. / Thus He spoke to Mosheh / face to face, / as a man speaks to his friend.'

Outside the camp in which there is still a mingling of rebellion and repentance, where since the mourning has ceased a new respite and

---

[1] 'One point which is the centre of "heaven and earth"—what a scandalous assertion! . . . to know God, his loving, inexpressibly good and beneficent being, whose wisdom, *omnipotence* and all other attributes seem only, as it were, *instruments* of his love for men; that this preferring of men, these insects of creation, is part of the greatest depths of the divine revelation; . . . that the Holy Spirit set forth for us a book for his Word, wherein like a fool and a madman, yea, like an unholy and impure spirit, he made for our proud reason childish stories and contemptible events into the history of heaven and God'—so the 'Magus of the North,' Johann Georg Hamann (1730–88). [Tr. fr. Ronald Gregor Smith, *J. G. Hamann: A Study in Christian Existence* (New York: Harper & Row, 1960), pp. 156f.—Tr.] C. E. Jansen Schoonhoven, *Natuur en Genade bij J. G. Hamann* (1945), pp. 46f., 212ff.

tension has ensued, outside the camp stands the Tent of the Presence, which does not yet perform its function as a tent of meeting, but which, as Moses' entrance into it shows, is *intended* to be the place of meeting between the Faithful One and the unfaithful.[2] Here was the enclosed space of a dwelling place, not unlike a hundred other dwelling places of men. And there on the other side, in the camp, stood family after family or man after man at the doors of their tents, watching to see the sign of the presence also taking its place, as it were, hesitantly and watchfully, at the door of His Tent—which, after all, also signified their tent, the place where they lived, the sphere of their life.

And Moses, alone, vicariously, as a mediator, walks straight through the camp in this expectant silence to go out and do what nobody else could now dare to do—to enter that Place in order to learn what the outcome of this judgment and event would be. But—the text says anticipatorily—every one who sought Him (this was the intention and so it would be later on) would go out to this Place, which seems so fleeting and transitory and yet gives the seal of constancy to His personal life and the history of the people. Elect people who have rejected their election, people who have not yet made a response of the heart either to the absence or this new return of God, stand there watching the mediator, rising up and bowing down when *he* goes out of the camp, this time alone, in their stead. Ultimately it was not upon him that their gaze and their expectation was fixed, but rather upon the Door, the entrance to the Presence.

4. In the narrative the descent of the pillar of cloud signifies the confirmation of God's faithfulness *in* his turning away from them, a new, wholly unexpected realization of the covenant. One could almost find in this a picture of the Jewish 'doctrine of correlation';[3] for the experience of Moses it may also have been true that here the reciprocity between God and man reveals a direct proportionality in the yearning for the restoration of fellowship. The people wait just as YHWH waits. YHWH, the spurned one, shows himself to the one who waits in this image of the rejected people waiting for YHWH who had chosen them. Behold, they fall down before the Holy One, before the veiled mystery

---

[2] S. R. Hirsch (*Pentateuch-Kommentar*, II, 476ff.) believes that the tent was Moses' own dwelling place—on the basis of the chronological sequence (for there was as yet no Tabernacle).

[3] See K. H. Miskotte, *Het wezen der joodsche religie* (1932), ch. 8.

of this renewed presence. Behold, they are stirred and moved by the fact that their mediator is received into the holy place.

They know that of itself no thing, however holy and wonderful it may be, ever 'says anything,' unless God himself wishes to speak to their representative. The people confess, by their falling down to worship, that the encounter with them takes place *in* the encounter with Moses. But one could also say—in view of what is inherent in the 'Name'—that God accommodated himself to the approach of the mediator. Thus the whole of the Old Testament (though the origin of the Covenant can be called 'monopleuric' [unilateral]) is concerned with the relation between divine and human yearning and waiting, the mutual suffering and patience of God and his people. They stand over against each other and become 'as enemies,' and then again they come together and find each other. There is a divine suffering on account of men, but also a suffering *with* men, and there is a human suffering on account of God, but also a suffering *with* God.

Nowhere in the Old Testament is there a trace of an absolute, unchangeable God; nowhere is he presented as 'almighty' in the abstract sense; nowhere is there a conflict between his honour and the honour of the creature—in other words, here there is no foothold for the easy denial on the part of 'natural religion,' and negative theories about God's sovereignty are futile.[4]

5. As the first tablets contained the 'writing of God'—the record of what was established between YHWH and the mediator in the mystery of their encounter concerning the destiny of the elect and liberated people—and as the two later tablets bore a derivative human script, so the speech which the Lord and Moses engage in here in the mystery of person-to-person, face-to-face encounter is an independent, antecedent secret, a friendship, as it were, a relationship that possesses a far higher degree of immediacy than the relationship to the people. And this immediacy can hardly be called 'mystical'; it rather has the

---

[4] Cf. J. G. Hamann: 'The concept of a "supreme being" held by the worldly wise has also led to errors and prejudices which are as powerful and pernicious as the idea which the Jews had of the Messiah as a monarch. "I am a worm and no man"; these feelings of the royal psalmist seem to be the only signposts for reaching the desired idea of the *majesty of existence*. The marks of revelation should not be compared with the type of a metaphysical idol but with the great mystery of a Word become flesh.' Quoted from *Bibliothek theol. Klassiker*, ed. Franklin Arnold, I (1888), 142f. [Cf. Ronald Gregor Smith, *J. G. Hamann: A Study in Christian Existence*, p. 48n.—Tr.]

3. THE FACE OF YHWH: EXODUS 33:14–16

advantage over the mediated relationship to the people of the clarity and articulateness of living speech which is addressed to a 'thou' and to the solitary conscience. After his sojourn on the mountain, during which the people sought him in vain, Moses too could have said, 'Did you not know that I must be in the things of YHWH?' (cf. Luke 2 : 49). 'This is not a mystical silence in the twilight, not a resting in the eternal springs . . . not an immersion in the infinite. . . . Here an "I" and a "thou" face each other, separated and yet related to each other, as near, intimate, and loving as is true between friends.'[5]

6. The entire narrative which we have sketched by indicating the thematic transitions must be read first if we wish to understand and expound the testimony of the text of 33 : 12ff. How 'superhuman' all this is, and how 'subdivine'! How tremendous is this Moses who has to bear the burden of 'this horde which is thy people,' this Moses who experiences the terror of facing the cloud of the Presence, and above all this Moses who can say: Blot me out of the book of thy purposes, thy future, and show thy favour to the elect who have lost themselves—but who can also rise up and boldly accuse YHWH of dealing equivocally with his servant (vv. 12f.)! For Moses insists upon being certain whether he will be alone or whether an *angel* will accompany the march of the people; this he would regard as a withdrawal of his favour.

'Must my face go with you in order to satisfy you?' And Moses answered (in amazement and delight with such great understanding), 'If thy face will not go with us, let us not go up from here. In that case let us go back to *Mitsrayim* or let us perish in this unblessed land.' The leader must know (*yada‘*) who will go with this particular people through the menacing world. He even wants to know the way (in order that he may 'agree' with him), and he wants to know God; and the essence of this knowing of God appears to be that he may know that he *is* known (cf. v. 13 with v. 16). And finally, he wants to know how it will be possible for others, for the *goyim*, to recognize and know that a special favour rests upon this stiff-necked and fickle mob, which, along with him, Moses, is distinct from all other people on the face of the earth (v. 16).

7. Where this knowledge is present, there grace has been found, there man (the people) has the living knowledge of having found grace. This favour which changes the direction of the past cannot be regarded

[5] Hellmut Frey, *Die Botschaft des Alten Testaments*, II, p. 128.

'religiously' as something which is given; it has no continuing existence through sacrifice, it has continuance in the soul; nor is it an inherited treasure from which income can be drawn; it is 'found and received' as a finished thing. Is it a condition? No, it is received as a gift which must be divinely new, because the repudiation of the first liberation had been demonically new; it is irreducibly mighty and in its manner and its (disorderly) order a counterpart of the creative Freedom, of the original Election. The knowledge which now bursts into bloom can be a surplus over and above the initial willingness to allow oneself to be led; it can become an intimate understanding when it has left behind a mere blind following of the guidance of the Deliverer *and* a blind refusal to follow him. *O felix culpa Adae!*—something of this daring exclamation of amazement is in the continuation of the narrative after the devastating, ruinous estrangement which had taken place.

(a) This 'understanding' is mediated through the understanding of the mediator. In him the people had found a grace which is more than a remission of punishment, a grace which is positive and contains a new fellowship. In the mediator there was also an unwillingness to proceed to the promised land on his own inspiration or under the guidance of an angel—an unwillingness that sprang from a total claim, an 'all or nothing,' an unwillingness that may appear to be cranky and presumptuous, but which is the right response to the speech of YHWH in the tent of the Presence. Like a good mediator he holds fast to the new favour *and* to the old people, to the high and holy moment and to the coming march into the future. Like a good mediator he insists upon more than an undefined restoration of the broken fellowship; he asks to see God's Face. This total claim (for himself and others) includes the miracle that God himself shall be present and accompanying the people in the camp, this camp of rebels. He insists that what was previously stated to be impossible should nevertheless be true, namely, that He should not merely direct the people but actually live and march with these rebels, personally accompanying them on this march to the promised land, which is to be the new Eden and the pledge of the new world, the Kingdom.

(b) He wants the 'Name,' which is by its nature groundless and as such in the midst of things, to take on form, to be known as a status of nearness—not merely occasionally but in the regular course of the day, involved in the acts and the lot of these undependable human beings. The Face, he insists, must 'shine,' must go with them, giving them light; it must 'rise' and stand at the zenith like the sun, in order to give *shalom* and to establish an order in which all the conditions of the future, well-being, health, and prosperity will characterize the life between God and man, man and man, and man and the earth (Num. 6 : 24ff.). The 'Face' is more than the presence as such, it is the presence recognized, not merely the factual but the existential fellowship. It is nearness experienced as nearness. Therefore it will put an end to 'blind trust,' to *islam*, mere subjection and docility. The living Face expresses the fact that now, less than ever, God will be recognized in naked fate. It is one of the dangers of religion that when it no longer ventures, as in the Indian religions, to celebrate the identity of God and man, it retreats into submission to the Superior Power, as if God were Fate or as if he were to be known at least primarily in the apportionment of fate, that is, as irreducible Power. In Israel, be it noted even in this rude mob which had been led out of slavery almost against its will, there will be an 'intercourse' with God, a knowing and a being known, and a knowing of oneself as being known. And there you have an irreducible surplus!

8. This prayer, this 'demand' of the mediator, is pitched exceedingly high. We stand aghast at the temerity with which Moses insists that the apostasies which occurred so recently shall be accepted and transformed into a knowledge of God's nearness. All our later abstract talk about 'objective revelation,' which is supposed to excel human religion because it makes 'God everything and man nothing,' is already repudiated here in this 'primitive' state as being empty and untrue when measured by the Name. No, man is a genuine companion and partner of God.

It would appear to us that something essential in the acts of God will be misunderstood if we forget that they are not a blessing to us if we cannot distinguish them as acts of God from the events around them. To say 'God is great, and we know him (or it?) not' (Job 36 : 26) is a sigh uttered in a boundary situation, in which Job's faith is tried by the hiddenness of God, precisely because Job (in consequence of the affliction to which he is being subjected) ascribes the torment of his life to God (though it comes from Satan), and thus there is nothing left for him in these regions of forsakenness but to stagger between resignation to and rebellion against the Power (which is not to be equated with the Right). What is experienced in such boundary situations can lead to a glorification of the Name, but as a rule God leads us on a middle way where faith can discern the outlines of God's providence. We are allowed, quite fully, to understand something of his purposes.

9. We can describe the fact that the Face 'goes with' the people as providence and thus preclude the false religious conceptions. Providence is a providing foresight, a wise intercession for those who are oppressed or threatened by the Powers. It is characterized by wisdom, and from it there also goes an appeal to insight and sensibility of those who have been liberated and are being led onward.[6] The 'godhead' refuses to allow itself to be comprehended, but YHWH lets his face shine in order that in one small 'segment' we may distinguish from events, in order that as that face shines he distinguishes himself *in* the world *from* the world. Here too the process of knowledge proceeds from the particular to the general. Just as there is no way that leads from 'omnipotence' to the power of salvation, no way from 'omniscience' to knowing and being known, nor any way from 'omnipresence' to the Tent of the Presence, but only the reverse order, from the power of salvation to faith in the Power which is above all things, so there is also no direct way to a concept of general providence. Knowledge of God always begins with the particular, the limited, the near, the existential. Here the Face can 'shine' and be 'lifted up' upon the path of men. The other road, that of genuine 'natural theology,' of general knowledge of God, leads sooner or later to an even 'more natural' atheism.

[6] Cf. Karl Barth, *Church Dogmatics*, Vol. II, pt. 1, p. 425 (on the patience and wisdom of God): 'Was there perhaps a shadow of suspicion that remained here too [that is, in connection with the holiness and righteousness of God]? Do we need to be afraid of the question why God is so zealous to affirm his holiness and why he is so zealous to assert his righteousness? . . . Is perhaps also the unity between his grace and holiness and his mercy and righteousness a kind of quirk or accident, a brute fact which is simply there and has to be accepted as such? . . . His holiness has nothing to do with stubbornness nor his righteousness with tyranny. And the unity of grace and holiness . . . has nothing to do with a "paradox," as has often been alleged. Rather it is the *mystery* which we encounter in all these things, the mystery of the *reason* and the *meaning* and *purpose* which God has in himself, indeed, which he himself is, the mystery of his *wisdom*. . . . As long as we think of God as the abyss of chance or caprice, as long as we regard the irrational as the essentially divine, we shall certainly not have any real confidence in God, nor is it possible to have such confidence. . . . For *freedom* comes only from the *knowledge* of reason, meaning, and order, and not from the contemplation of chaos, chance, and caprice.' [Tr. altered.—Tr.]

10. A living application of all this, however, is possible only by means of the narrative. We have therefore put the narrative first in order that contemplative truth may again immerse itself in it. For only the continuing narrative is the channel of the witness. Without the dimensions of an event, the event of freedom, of apostasy and return, the facticity of the Presence, the vivid figure of the mediator, the event of mutual intercourse, the higher outreach of the intercession before the journey into the future—without this we lose contact with the full, flowering word, and again by a roundabout way we miss the tremendous miracle that our rebellious nature is met with grace in Him, a grace so great that his Face goes with the rebel into the alien world.

4. SEEING THE GODHEAD, SEEING HIS GOODNESS: EXODUS 34: 5–8

1. It was the mediator who understood from afar off—and in this too he showed himself to be acting vicariously and proved himself to be a discoverer, a 'leader'[1]—why it was that the promised land could never be the new Eden without God and why the journey to the promised land under the guidance of an 'angel' would be a token of a land of abundance but would not bring with it the blessing of the future. Now, through his insistent intercession, he had wrung from God the concrete promise that YHWH himself, that God's Face, would go with them. We have noted what this guiding and judging presence means. And we are not surprised that the narrative as witness is full of the rapturously repeated Thou—Thou, Thou wilt do it, Thou wilt again go with the rebels and dwell with them.

And because it is not easy to set a limit to this swelling rapture, Moses breaks out in this bold plea—as if he wanted to presume upon the favour he had been shown and experience the deepest depths of the promise—'Ah, let me see thy glory (kabod),' the glory before which, according to Isaiah's vision, the seraphim veiled their faces (Isa. 6 : 2, 5)! Or had the later prophet penetrated deeper, did he have a deeper sense of the qualitative difference between God and man? Is this a more primitive text, a more childlike mentality, perhaps even a 'religious'

[1] In Dutch, *voorganger*, 'minister.' Cf. p. 378, n. 1.

survival, beyond which later Judaism advanced in its spiritual consciousness of 'transcendence'? No, it is rather a passionate faith which seeks to become more than faith, which yearns to penetrate beyond the sign. Such a yearning for immediate knowledge (says our text) is a part of faith. We must be forbidden to treat this desire with suspicion. Faith wants to know concretely and objectively.

2. The narrative goes on, the narrative in which the 'Name' acquires a face. And in the Name lies the answer which was echoed far off in the prophecy. YHWH denied his plea—but it is not the refusal which is foremost. 'I will make all my beauty, all my goodness, pass before your face, and I will proclaim the "Name" before your expectant gaze: "I will be gracious to whom I will be gracious, and will spread out my mercy on whom I will spread out my mercy".' This is the 'Name,' not merely caprice, but the purposeful course of history which advances from election to election in order through the elect to bless one people after another (Gen. 12 : 3). Caprice, even 'divine' caprice, is incompatible with the 'virtues,' the 'perfections' which are mentioned in 34 : 6f. as radiations of this beauty, this divinity. But this comes later in the course of the story. Here, after the promise that his goodness will be seen, follows the refusal: 'But you cannot see my face; for no man can see me and live' (33 : 20).

Will it therefore be only a matter of seeing his goodness? No—a new surprise, see and hear how humanly and compassionately YHWH deals with man! He goes to the utmost length to meet the yearning of faith which in its rapture has this time demanded the impossible. The *kabod* will *nevertheless* be seen, but in a state of 'passing by,' which will not blind a man with its nuclear light but which the eye can gaze upon in rapture.

3. 'And He said, / here is room / by me, / you stand upon the rock, / then it will happen: / when my glory passes by / I will put you in the cleft of the rock / and shelter you with my hand / until I have passed by.' No theories about infinity and finitude, no separation of pure from impure, no paradox of the identity of nothingness and the All, no ascent to the perfection of the Absolute, but rather God-with-men, in beauty which can be experienced from all sides, and in majesty which graciously passes by us, spares us from terror, and preserves us as creatures in the place which he has prepared for us.

(a) Before we leave this point, let us note two limiting aspects of the meaning of this theophany. First, it is no accident that immediately after this promise the redactor allows the narrative to continue with the re-establishment of the covenant and the renewing of the two tablets. The majesty of God, though it is stupendous, is never abstract in the Old Testament. It is the weight of the enduring and unconditioned Ground of the Commandment, the salutary commandment, which leads the life of the people (and the nations) out of the house of bondage of the powers and the gods.

Second, the yearning of faith to pass over into sight is carried beyond its initial limits not only through rapture, but is also driven by the thirst for certainty of salvation—a certainty of salvation, be it noted, which is knowledge of the faithfulness of this God and the pledge of hope for the world.

So it was with Moses, too, the representative and mediator at the beginning of the great Journey which was to sanctify Israel and reprove and change the world.[2]

To be certain of it even for the far distant future would mean an extraordinary knowledge of salvation which would be so far from being esoteric that one could, so to speak, sell it to everyman on the streets, nay, pass it out as bread to every passerby.

4. And then, on the holy mountain it becomes apparent that the beauty and the majesty are not separated. As Moses gazes at the splendour of the Godhead that has already passed by, the beauty is 'shown.' And when the beauty is 'shown,' it is shown by being proclaimed, spoken, sworn. And when the beauty is proclaimed, announced with power as that which is near, then the 'Face' becomes manifest —the Face of which it was previously said that though it cannot be seen directly, it would nevertheless 'go with' them in order to reassure the mediator and his people and here and now 'put them at rest' (33 : 14, Authorized Dutch translation).

[2] Cf. Thomas Mann, *Das Gesetz* (a kind of Moses novel), p. 133 [Eng. tr. *The Tables of the Law*. The following is tr. fr. the German text]: 'The eternally compact, the brief, binding, succinct moral law of God had to be secured and incised in the stone of his mountain in order that Moses might carry it down to the wavering rabble of people in the camp where they were waiting and that it might stand in their midst from generation to generation, unbreakable and also engraved upon their minds, their flesh, and their blood, the quintessence of human understanding.' pp. 157f.: 'The rock of decency, the lapidary Alpha and Omega of human conduct . . . therefore the ABC's are his, and his speech, though it is directed to you, Israel, is quite unintentionally a speech for all men.'

In the moment when the veil was lifted, the moment (*'en 'atomō*, I Cor. 15 : 52) which is past as soon as it comes, because no present time can withstand the onslaught of the harmonies of God's decree,[3] in this moment, however, more is ultimately heard than seen. And the Proclaimer of the message (O miracle of incarnation!) is YHWH. For this moment the Face is contained in the Word. It is the Face which is turned toward us; therefore on our side our hearing is focused upon an intensification of that hearing so that it may become seeing, a seeing not of the Face but of the perfections of God, who 'found within himself the reasons' to establish the covenant for the centuries. YHWH himself is his own expositor, he expounds immediately what is spoken in the nonimmediate Face.

5. Now comes the text (34 : 5ff.) which is the crown of our narrative —the crown of a divine narrative of God which liberates us from religious prejudgments, from the philosophical apriorisms concerning Omnipotence, Omniscience, and Omnipresence.[4] In these lie the deepest cause of the ambivalence of religion and the rise of the atheistic reaction and the nihilistic rebellion of the human spirit. 'YHWH, YHWH, Godhead, merciful and gracious, slow to anger and abounding in steadfast love and faithfulness, keeping steadfast love unto the thousandth generation, forgiving (literally, 'bearing') iniquity and transgression and sin, but not allowing men to go altogether unpunished (Buber: 'But he does not free without punishment'), visiting the iniquity of the fathers upon the children and children's children, to the third and the fourth generation.' Here behold the visible mystery which can never be derived from the world! Behold, here is the beauty that conforms to our need! Behold, here is the revelation close enough to our need! Behold, here is the revelation close enough to touch, because it is intimately offered to the listening spirit.

Thus the word described the 'Name,' pointed to the Face, and wor-

---

[3] Cf. Kirilov's words in Dostoievski's *The Devils*. Asked whether he believed in a future eternal life, he replies: 'No, not in a future everlasting life, but in an everlasting life here. There are moments, you reach moments, and time comes to a sudden stop.' (tr. David Magarschack, Penguin Books [1953], p. 242). Cf. also the companion piece to this, Myshkin's words in *The Idiot* on the harmony that a man feels for one or two seconds, the everlasting harmony; but to be able to bear this overwhelming harmony any longer than this, a man would have to be physically changed.

[4] Hermann Cohen, *Religion der Vernunft, aus den Quellen des Judentums*, pp. 109ff., 473f., 494f., defines the attributes of God as the 'attributes of action.'

shipped the Majesty as the 'eternal,' i.e., the abiding, permanent, superior Ground of the covenant, of history, of the people (and the nations)—and as the Judgment upon the powers of nature, for no superiority surpasses the superiority of love, grace, and faithfulness. Here perceive the cosmic powers; here learn to hear the music of the spheres!

6. It begins on a high note: 'Let me see thy glory.' Then follows the promise: Yes, you may see my beauty, my goodness, but not my glory (the 'yes' coming first), succeeded by the passing by of the majestic glory and the displaying of his goodness in his virtues. The virtues are proclaimed, but by YHWH himself. One might think that this was merely an appeasement, a mollification. Did it leave behind a sense of disappointment? The text could hardly have intended to leave this impression: the proclamation holds the field, and the response to it is silent acclamation, the 'yes' of worship. And these two are so much one that the question whether the proclamation did not perhaps break forth from the lips of Moses cannot simply be answered in the negative. For here the encounter takes place, and in the encounter freedom is created, the freedom to confess what is proclaimed to us. For he who hears the Word of God with his being can also in that high moment repeat it from out of his being. For he has seen something of that Face, the revelation of which is 'sweeter to us than life and the hiding of which is more terrible than death' (Dordrecht Canons, V, 13). 'And Moses hastened to bow his head to the ground and cast himself down.'

7. It will not be possible in the one hour which the interpreter and witness has at his disposal to give powerful and thorough contour to the attributes of the beauty of God, the perfections of his goodness. But something must be said about this—while observing the order, the order of precedence. What is said first is actually the first in importance and must remain first. And the whole determines what is legitimately to be thought of the power, the knowledge, and the presence of God above all created life, above this life and in it. Thus we grasp something of the quintessence, thus we understand something of the grace which as such is 'almighty,' of the patience which as such is 'omnipresent,' of the righteousness which as such truly knows, judges, and orders all things.

Such understanding will be impossible, however, if the 'acts' of the

Lord, the holy history itself, is not 'brought to speech'[5]—verbalized in such a way that the reality and the effectiveness of God will be seen to be the centre and direction of everything that happens. All these words of Scripture are merely the precipitate of real encounters between this God and these men. And at the same time they are the promise that such encounters will continue to take place in time. He who holds to God's 'revealed attributes' (and eschews all speculation about abstract infinity and omnipotence) will discover (from that vantage point!) that **it** is precisely the 'human' God who is infinite and omnipotent—he will see God in his own life; he can take to heart his goodness, his beauty forevermore.

8. Is there, then, such a thing as 'seeing' God after all? We read not far from our text (and also not far away from it, in so far as the 'source' is concerned): 'And they saw the God of Israel; and there was under his feet as it were a beautiful sapphire, like the very heaven for clearness' (Exod. 24 : 10). Or in Buber's translation (beginning with v. 7): 'They said: / All that He has spoken / we will do, we hear it! /

[5] I have made an attempt to read the attributes of God from the history and build a bridge from there to the personal life in a collection of addresses to young people of all ages entitled *Uitkomst*, 2nd edn. (1948), pp. 42–53. An example, p. 45: 'God, abounding in faithfulness. God does not let his work go. When all securities fail, he himself is present as the ground on which we build for eternity. Godly action, monumental deed, which extends over our miniature life. . . . David is a fugitive in the mountains, an adventurer, in the end surrounded by all kinds of brave outcasts from society, and he is obliged to hide like an animal in its cave, though years ago Samuel had already anointed him king over all Israel. Again and again he finds ways to escape, a fortress in the mountains, an eagle's nest, a secret shelter, a cave, a date tree, a spring of clear water. Many of the Psalms which are sung in the Christian church today are nothing more than songs of spontaneous thanks for rescue in this disorderly life which David lived at that time. And they are all full of this one wonderful word: steadfastness, faithfulness, truth. And so the fact is that you can wait for the Lord. Wait bravely. The absence of God wounds the heart more than the tyranny which is hostile to us, and the common answers seem to have been devised to suppress our honest questions about God. And yet it is worth while to wait, for this waiting for God is full of promise. The whole of life is pervaded with help, which no one dares any longer to count upon. And in the long-drawn-out intervals in which we see nothing but the misery of our existence and the helpless efforts of men, we actually live by these distant springs, these hidden streams. Meanwhile, something is happening near at hand, tangible as the hand of a friend—even though it be no more than strengthening and steeling of your heart. "Wait for the Lord; be strong; and he will strengthen your heart; yea, wait for the Lord!" (Ps. 27 : 14), for he is faithful, and even in the feeling of his absence he is present, for he is always faithfully at work to make strong your innermost being.'

Then Mosheh took the blood / and sprinkled it upon the people / and said: / Here / the blood of the covenant / which He makes with you / in accordance with all these words. / Then went up / Mosheh and Aharon, Nadab and Abihu, seventy of the elders of Israel. / *They saw / the God of Israel*: under his feet / as it were a work of sapphire tiles, / like the very heaven for purity. / But he did not lay his hand on the corner-pillars of Israel, / *they beheld the Godhead* / and ate and drank.'

They saw the Godhead! But their eyes were there fixed upon a Place, a Field, a heavenly Field. And this Field, these sapphire pavements *spoke* to them of the God of *Israel*. And the burden of this speech is quite clearly a reference to the 'perfections' which appear in the theophany of Exodus 24! Undoubtedly this points to an ecstasy. Religion seeks ecstasy in order to escape the eternal cycle and to experience its own identity with God in rapture; it climbs up through all the tropics, past the satellites, and through the portals, beyond the borders, through renunciations, fastings, and mortifications. The Old Testament says: no man shall see God and live; remain in your own place; God comes down!

And yet, they saw God and (in the same breath) they ate and drank; they celebrated the holy meal, they communicated. But that this is the God of Israel is made clear in the fact that in the narrative no significance is attached to the ascent of the mount of vision; that not the individual but rather seventy elders were enabled to come and see; that it was the blood of the covenant that consecrated them; that they saw no form (though God is not timeless and formless), but rather something from heaven, and not in order to gaze up at it but rather to gaze expectantly beyond it and calmly down upon it; and finally, that the vision continues while they observe the sacral meal. It looks more like an excursion than an ascension, more like an idyllic exploration of the realm of goodness, the domain of beauty, than a breakthrough to the all-consuming Light, it looks more like a celebration of the covenant in pure joy and simplicity of heart than a vision of the *kabod*. If we insist upon speaking of 'ecstasy,' then it is rapture over the fact that they, the chosen representatives of the people, are permitted to know, 'objectively' to discover, that the God of Israel is the Godhead. For the covenant was established by him. He is not merely a bit of help and comfort, but rather as fundamental as the firmament, 'like the very heaven for clearness.'

There is only one firmament for the human heart to gaze upon; there is only one heaven given to us. That is the covenant, the faithfulness, the forgiveness, the promise, the patience. This is what gives rise to the rapture here, for the word which was spoken is as real as the blood that poured out, and the blood is truly a word, and it speaks of better things than we have ever dreamed of in our religion. 'As far as the east is from the west, so far does he remove our transgressions from us' (Ps. 103 : 12). He who hears this, sometimes hears it in such a way that he sees it. In Revelation 4 : 3ff. we hear an echo of this in the scene where we see the 'rainbow round about the throne' and the 'sea of glass like crystal,' and the presbyters singing with the cosmos and the angels, full of eyes, full of vision, full of knowledge: 'Holy, holy, holy, is the Lord God'—different, different from the gods, different in his salvation, and different too in his judgment, and with him also different is the ecstasy over what is to be seen.

5. PROPHETIC 'EXAGGERATION': ISAIAH 54: 7–10

1. The concern here is with the community, with Israel. The community, the congregation, is threatened. This gives the sermon on this text a proper delimitation. It is not the individual and his struggle for faith that is central here. This is the first delimitation. The second is that this is not concerned with a situation of political despair, but rather that God's Face is hidden from them whether they are in good circumstances or ill. The gracious action of God is no longer discernible in a particular time amidst the tumult of events.

Perhaps one cannot even call it a bitter 'experience'; men's eyes need to be opened to see it as in a vision, a vision which shows how greatly lacking are the visions and the voices and the signs that come from God. Exile is no longer felt by many to be a judgment, as an abandonment by God. It is possible to luxuriate in prosperity in exile. For the individual there are so many legitimate (or illegitimate) escapes and diversions. Micaiah the son of Imlah saw the situation long before this time: 'I saw all Israel scattered upon the mountains, as sheep that have no shepherd' (I Kings 22 : 17). The community is confused, the community is scattered, the community is lonely, the community is not living by the saving Presence of God. It is conscious that it is at the mercy of the sovereign powers of the world, it is subject to necessities which should not apply to it. In Isaiah 49 : 14 Zion says, 'YHWH has forgotten me, the Lord has forgotten me.' The impenetrable darkness oppresses them the more since less and less do they meet directly with the Word of judgment in that darkness.

So it is with the church—naturally the empirical church; so it is also in many respects with the apostolate. Darkness surrounds it. One should not preach on a text like this if one immediately responds to the prophetic message with a pastoral consolation. It would be better not to preach on a passage like this, which is meant to be a message of salvation, if one is still thinking in terms of the individual or even if one is thinking of the troubles of the church, but thinking of them as being ultimately caused by sociological and cultural factors.

2. 'For a brief moment I forsook you' (v. 7). The very first thing that is said here makes it clear that this situation actually cannot be understood on the two-dimensional level of experience and its interpretation. It is a real abandonment. And those who did not recognize and understand it as an actual abandonment by God are now compelled to hear it proclaimed as God's own word. It was an actual abandonment by God. Without this proclamation of the (partially recognized and partially unrecognized) abandonment by God, the prophetic word is not in the full sense the word of God. He scattered the people, he hid his Face from them. The fact is that we have actually lived under the condition of this act; but it is only the Word that reveals to us that it is an act of God, and this at the same time reveals that this word is a saving word—by reason of the fact that the event is now past and is no longer the ultimate truth about our condition.

(a) Therefore the church must be all the more aware of the reverse side of this truth, namely, that grace, which is the annulment of judgment, confirms and corroborates the judgment as God's judgment. In the multidimensional realm of his Freedom, God does not arbitrarily pass from one to the other, from no to yes, from rejection to acceptance. He resists the resistance. He breaks the rebellion by breaking his own heart.

The image of the rebel is caught and fixated in the light that comes from his saving word, and what is more, it is revealed to the rebel as one who has been chosen that the Lord considers it worth his while to bear and to make known to him the pain of his displeasure. What is it that causes him to pour out his wrath? What is it that brings pain to the heart of God? It is this—that the community thought and still thinks that it 'possesses' grace, that it is safe and secure; the exile is not a rejection, but rather God's resistance to the resistance of his own people, who think that now they are *eo ipso* his, God's resistance to this people who again and again show that they simply do not understand a statement like that made by John the Baptist: 'Do not presume to say to yourselves, "We have Abraham as our father"; for I tell you, God is able from these stones to raise up children to Abraham' (Matt. 3 : 9).

3. 'For a brief moment!' Long years of banishment, long in terms of experience, long especially for the awakened. But long not only according to man's measure; for Isaiah 42 : 14 says, 'For a long time (*me-'olam*, 'from time immemorial until now') I have restrained myself.' It may be bold but we cannot avoid saying that YHWH himself suffered because of the exile. 'In all their affliction he was afflicted' (Isa. 63 : 9).

The tension and suspense is like that expressed in II Peter 3 : 8, 'With the Lord one day is as a thousand years, and a thousand years as one day.' If this is taken as a metaphor of a timeless eternity, the whole concept of the 'eternal' acts of God in time is reduced to confusion. Nor can it be that it was long for men but short for God. No, the time lasts only a day so far as God's patience is concerned, but one day is an aeon so far as God's readiness to act now is concerned (cf. Isa. 42 : 14b, 'Now I will cry out like a woman in travail').

According to God's fixed Decree the *eschaton* is present, according to his Forbearance it is not yet fulfilled (because he desires that all should come to repentance). But this still does not get at the core of salvation in the saving word. A miracle occurs. In God's Word the past does not remain the past; it is given a new quality by the Compassion of the present hour. It shrinks and contracts at the sound of the fixed Decree, the testimony of the change that has taken place; it is given the quality of brevity by YHWH, but thus also changed in its relations. The *praesentia Dei* comes in this sound, this utterance of the testimony, and fills the present, not disqualifying but rather qualifying the past as small, short, as something that can be overlooked, something that has passed away and become new. In connection with the parallel passage, Psalm 30 : 5, Luther speaks of God's *opus proprium* ('proper work') which overarches his *opus alienum* ('strange work'). This is the answer which none but God can give to the threatened faith of the church. The time of abandonment was also God's time, but this can only be seen from the vantage point of the time of visitation, the time of the Presence.

(a) In the ninth verse the change in the covenant relationship is compared with God's oath 'that the waters of Noah should no more go over the earth' (cf. Gen. 9 : 11). The point of comparison lies in the irrevocability of the Noachic covenant and the act-character of God's Faithfulness. Just as the waters do not of themselves refrain from working chaos, but are held back by God's act, so it is with his 'everlasting,' ever-valid and ever-effectual Compassion: it is not a *status*, but an *actus purus*. Therefore the Lord is here also called *go'el* ('Redeemer'); the connection of the turning point in time with such a juridical term as *go'el* is striking and very bold. Just as the *go'el* is obligated by covenant law to redeem an impoverished fellow citizen, so the Lord (and this is said in all reverence) is legally bound. A new time has dawned. YHWH acknowledges that he is its founder, its initiator, its guarantor, its perfecter.

4. Then the opposite of the 'brief moment' comes to the fore and is set in relief: 'With everlasting kindness I will have compassion on you.' 'Everlasting'—as was the oath sworn with regard to the earth, therefore *in saecula saeculorum*. Everlasting—in constant intervention for those who are in peril. Everlastingly qualifying the past as past and gone: never, never again a Flood, i.e., never, never again an exile in which temptation overwhelms a whole people and the waters of despair overflow the peak of expectation. Mountains may depart, flooded and undermined by the primeval waters (cf. Pss. 46 : 2f.; cf. 89 : 9f. with vv. 33ff.; Prov. 8 : 28f.; Ps. 93 : 2f.; Hab. 3 : 6), but God's steadfast love and the covenant of peace are not touched by this flood. The welfare and the well-being which endure spring incessantly from this creative grace (cf. Jer. 31 : 35f.; Ezek. 36 : 26).

5. A church which is in distress and 'temptation' is not always a church calling out for help, but it is therefore all the more certainly a church that is in need of help. That help is in the first instance the reminder which comes from God that it is living in an irrevocably new time, in the 'last days' (Acts 2 : 17; Heb. 1 : 2). Is Isaiah 54 : 7ff. true? Anybody who reads the Old Testament as an isolated book

would have to say no. He would have to resort to talking about the lyrical exaggeration of the prophet on behalf of Israel or the timelessness of the idea of God's faithfulness. In the first case, we would be remaining in history, but the word as God's Word would no longer concern us. In the second case, we would be abandoning the enduring validity and power of the covenant in history. But that 'exaggeration' is truth in Jesus Christ! The history is fulfilled in the oath which is taken for ever in the epiphany of Christ. The church reads from there to here and from here to there, forwards and backwards in the one, twofold Testament; the church, in deputyship for the world, holds fast in confident despair to the faith that we are living in a new unshakable order, in a time of which men sang in the past, a time in which the praise of God's good grace can never be exaggerated. It is true that the feeling of guilt, as far as we are concerned, can never be exaggerated either. But from God's point of view this self-accusation—distended by the pressure of the 'fatalities'—is driven away and drowned in the peace of well-being. That's the way it is with prophetic 'exaggeration'!

6. It is never well for preaching, theology, and instruction if neither friend nor foe gets this impression of 'exaggeration.' We may all have due respect for soberness, responsibility, discretion, poise, and even ecstasy, fervent testimony, speculation, and an exciting voyage upon the high seas. But 'exaggeration' is quite another thing, something more offensive. The exaggeration lies in the fact that sober realism and ecstasy go together and alternate with each other, but that the covenant of God, which goes beyond all this and surpasses all subjective attitudes and moods, manifests itself from day to day as the world of the acts of YHWH, who put an end to the exile, the world of his acts in which the life of God and the life of all men is already finished and consummated. Have we really considered what we are saying when we call Jesus the Son of God? We are saying that in Jesus the self-realization of man as well as that of God is unqualifiedly and undividedly consummated. To call Jesus 'God's Son' is the 'exaggeration' beyond all exaggerations, it is to say that the life of all human beings is contemporaneous with the life of Jesus, because and in so far as this life of Jesus is at the same time the life of God itself, in the everlasting, active actuality of the Name. It is the task of theology to approach this exaggeration in terms of thought (and perhaps something is always lost in this process)—but it is above

all the concern of preaching to see to it that a tendency toward this exaggeration (which alone gives joy unimpaired and unfading) is by no means lacking.

LITERATURE: Karl Marti, in *Kurzer Hand-Kommentar*; article on *Berith* by G. Quell in *Theologisches Wörterbuch zum Neuen Testament*, II, pp. 109f.; Ludwig Kohler, *Old Testament Theology*, pp. 60ff.

6. A NEW COVENANT : JEREMIAH 31 : 31–34

1. A new covenant! Was not the first covenant 'everlasting,' valid for ever and ever? The prophet says that the first covenant was broken long ago. But is it not the very nature of YHWH to be faithful in spite of all the unfaithfulness of his own people? Is it the meaning of the text that the first covenant became old because more and more it lacked reciprocity and that the new element in the new covenant would consist in its being a covenant of grace in which love would come from one side because it must of necessity come from one, namely, God's side? But surely the first was a covenant of grace too, and the intent of the new covenant which is now proclaimed is precisely a new, living reciprocity: 'They shall all know me' (v. 34).

What is at stake is a new knowledge, a new subjective appropriation. And this requires an act of God, an event in the Spirit, in which the relationship of reciprocity is re-established. The 'monopleuric' [uni- lateral] character of the covenant must be preponderant; it will show more clearly and decisively that the covenant to which all covenants, including that of Sinai, point has more the character of a dispensation, a testament, a promise, than of an agreement, a contract, a partnership. The creative element in the Name, the verification of the oneness of the Name in the vicissitudes of history will come to light. One can also say that the ambivalence of religion will be placed under the judgment of the Word. We religious people cannot get it into our heads that it is solely the objective act of salvation that can guarantee its subjective appropriation. The Lord will create a new man, a new people. What can be the point of this 'new' thing?

2. The nineteenth century revealed its tendency (grounded in its idealism) to set up false antitheses in the way in which it interpreted

this prophetic passage. A whole era of church history reveals itself very typically (as an aberration) in the liberal exegesis of precisely this pericope. The 'new' element was interpreted as being an inner attitude over against an external following of the Law and bondage to the letter—as if Israel had never heard of this 'new' thing before, as if the *shema' Yisra'el* (Deut. 6 : 5) had never spoken of loving, clinging to, and following the Lord 'with all your heart, and with all your soul, and with all your might.' Or this liberal exegesis spoke of the 'better,' the 'higher' in man, the spontaneous, and above all the 'simple,' and also of 'autonomy' in contrast with the categories of law and command-ment; it was a matter of 'the obscure impulse of the man who is conscious of the right way, the soul's sensitiveness to its task, the "ought" which has taken form in "being".'[1] Both of these assertions are irreconcilable with the context of this passage which states ex-pressly that man is neither willing nor capable of setting out to fulfil the will of God. 'Can the Ethopian change his skin or the leopard his spots? Then also you can do good who are accustomed to do evil' (Jer. 13 : 23). The religious man does not understand that in his religion and through it he can become blind to the creativity of God, to the end, the purpose which is set for all his ambiguous strivings by God's holy purpose.

3. What is it, he will say (or think), that shows that I have broken the covenant, or indeed, destroyed it? He will reflect deeply and per-haps also concretely upon this, just as Israel or a part of Israel would have reflected upon Jeremiah's saying. Wherein lies the breaking of the covenant? In the fact that we are not so good and devout as the holy patriarchs? Or in the fact that we have not sacrificed enough or have failed to sacrifice properly? Or in that we have not adopted the simple way of life of the Rechabites? Or in that we have entered into defensive alliances with this or that world power? Or in that we have not been consistent in our opposition to the heathen and the Samaritans? Or, to put it in modern terms, was Rousseau right? Have we denied the theocracy? Should we go the way of Tolstoi? Should we be defenceless in this world? Ah, this bewilders us; if that is what is meant, then we, the church, are lacking in many things. But after all, there is nothing else we can do! We dare not turn the clock back; circumstances change,

[1]Friedrich Niebergall, *Praktische Auslegung des Alten Testaments*, II, p. 204.

and surely all this too does not lie 'outside the plan of God.' What is really expected of us? After all, we are only human beings! This is the kind of profound talk we indulge in.

Curiously and irritatingly, Jeremiah gives no indication whatsoever of what he ultimately means by this breaking, this destruction of the covenant. He regards it as obvious. The reproach does not refer to this or that particular act in their conduct, although all kinds of ethical criticism could be directed against it. The reproach is made concrete in a hidden way: 'When I took them by the hand . . .' and 'though I was their master' (or 'though I was betrothed to them'). Sin is by its very nature always a scorning of love, a rebellion against grace, a feeling of annoyance and irritation, and therefore an estrangement in thought, an interior and external destruction of the fellowship and order of life which are assumed in the giving of the treasures of the covenant.

4. This would turn the 'everlasting' into something old, if the Name of God, with its own continuity, did not watch over the unfaithful and intervene with a new contingent act. The covenant was 'nullified' by the fact that Israel, *qua* religious man, did not 'know' God. Therefore the new covenant which is to come will be the fulfilment of the promise: 'They shall know me, they shall all know me; I will write my *Torah* in their hearts; and they will no longer say to each other "Know YHWH" ' (i.e., participate in his life, walk the way of his purpose, remain in alliance with him, dwell with your Deliverer)[2]—there will be no point in admonishing one another to know God, since all, young and old, masters and servants, initiates and simple people, 'they shall all know me!' No longer will there be an *ecclesia docens* ('teaching church') as distinguished from an *ecclesia discens* ('learning church'); no longer will there be any men who stand out as religious men. Why? Because they will all have become religious? Or because all religiosity will no longer count?

5. To 'know' the Lord in the Old Testament (as well as the New) is never an intellectual process, although the 'knowledge' of God has

[2] Martin Buber in his book *Two Types of Faith* (New York: Harper Torchbook, 1961) sees (in our opinion unjustly) an antithesis between faith as trust and devotion in the Old Testament and the Synoptic gospels on the one hand and belief in the facts of salvation, expecially in Paul, on the other hand. Israel too knew YHWH not without the faith that he had led the people out of Egypt; and conversely, in Paul faith in Christ is at the same time a mystical union.

within it a cognitive element.[3] Nor is knowing a moral achievement, and it is not a religious possession. To know is to experience the having of a friend, a beloved (*yodea'*). In Hosea the knowledge of God (*da'ath 'elohim*) is above all to know that one is loved and thus to know the blessed lot of being chosen for fellowship with God. It is strange that outsiders regard this realm of experience as being quite alien to Reformed spiritual life, whereas the fact of the matter is quite different. It was precisely among our fathers that the *kennisse Gods*[4] (the term itself has a nuptial ring) was understood as an element of the 'inner life,' especially in the so-called *Nadere Reformatie*.[5] It is of great importance frequently to make room in our preaching and instruction for all that this term implies. In the 'knowledge of God' lies life, in it we meet love, in it we find the 'hidden communion,' in it too will be the sighs we utter in temptation, trial, and suffering.[6]

6. But perhaps even this does not catch the secret of this text. The strange thing is that the substantiating clauses in the text provoke us to ask once more what is really new in this covenant which brings and imparts this knowledge of God. The descriptions of what is new contain nothing that was not commonly known in Israel from ancient times: 'I will write my law upon their hearts' and (this includes) 'I will be their God, and they shall be my people' (they shall all know me!), 'for I will forgive their iniquity, and I will remember their sin no more.' And then this statement, which is religiously and logically self-evident, is surrounded with the most tremendous asseverations, with the massive solemnity of the references to the sun, the stars, the sea, the heavens, and the foundations of the earth—as surely as this cosmic order will not fall, so surely will YHWH preserve the seed of Israel, the holy descendants, as his people all the days into the far future. And most strangely of all, the firmness of the new covenant is demonstrated by the subjective (in-)ability of man to fathom the ground, the existence, and

---

[3] H. W. Wolff, 'Wissen um Gott bei Hosea als Urform der Theologie,' *Evangelische Theologie* (1952–53), pp. 533ff., and Walther Zimmerli, *Erkenntnis Gottes nach dem Buche Ezechiel* (1954), rightly emphasize that knowledge of God is also cognitive, but in my opinion they underestimate the value of the cognitive as an independent element.

[4 Old Dutch term meaning 'knowledge of God.'—Tr.]

[5 Early Pietistic movement in the seventeenth and eighteenth centuries, see *Religion in Geschichte und Gegenwart*, 3rd. edn., col. 1463.—Tr.]

[6] Cf. Abraham Kuyper, *Uit het Woord*, 6th series.

6. A NEW COVENANT: JEREMIAH 31:31-34

the order of the Creation. All this is adduced to substantiate a truth and a promise which were accepted as valid from time immemorial, which were implicit in every fundamental affirmation of the Old Testament, things which were truly self-evident.

Here we have opportunity to see what is really the content and purport of eschatological language. Here the religious man must surely become completely confused. For here the assertion is made that even the 'self-evident' is so far from being self-evident that it must remain sealed under the promise of the divine future.

What is theoretically more self-evident than the statement (which for many is all too facilely self-evident) that 'in every covenant there are two parties' (Dutch liturgy for baptism), that two partners have found each other and are answerable to each other, that the covenant rests upon reciprocity? For even though it remains true that in its origin the covenant is monopleuric, unilateral, in the carrying out and realization of the covenant it is the people, it is man, who is the other party who responds in the actions of his life. But here the very thing which Judaism finds so self-evident is, according to Jeremiah, a tremendous miracle—that Israel will really and actually respond, be obedient, and be a servant, a son, a child of God in accord with his calling. When this occurs there will be a fulfilment of that which the whole Jewish doctrine of relationship and correlation has played with in words—with a seriousness which, compared with the earnestness of YHWH, is only a Potemkin joke, a sham and a presumption. What is new here? The beginning of a new earnestness, which one finds within oneself, which one manifests by beginning to practise it even before one really knows it.

The new covenant is new in that it finally becomes in simple truth a covenant. And in order to bring this about God will have to create this covenant too from nothing. He will have to establish it. The Covenant will have to come from both sides. But what will make it possible for this to happen is the fact that again it will come wholly from one side. So dreadful is the estrangement, so irreparable is the apostasy! Creating, establishing, disposing, God will have to call into being what is self-evident, so that Israel will finally be Israel in its own place, in time.[7]

[7] Martin Noth, *Die Gesetze im Pentateuch* (1940), now in *Gesammelte Studien zum Alten Testament* (1957), pp. 127f.

7. The Torah will be written upon their hearts! And this too is something new; it is a new beginning, a new creation! 'I will write the Torah upon your hearts.' Seldom or never has a promise been so humiliating! Seldom or never has religion, even the 'revealed religion,' been so pilloried! After all these many centuries I will teach you the ABC. I, the one who has been betrayed and forsaken, I will 'rise up early' (Jer. 7 : 13, 25 : 3, 35 : 14) to instruct the rebellious children and at the same time to show my love.

One could illustrate this by means of the revealing and bewildering questions which constantly recur in the discussion of the *tertius usus legis* ('third use of the law') in which it becomes clear that not only do believers still need the *usus politicus* ('political use of the law') but that unbelievers are equally called to observe the *tertius usus*. Then one always touches upon the thought that the ultimate purpose of the law is the performance of the next thing at hand, and that God himself intervenes to humble religious men and turn them into decent men who live in accord with God's covenant. The new covenant is new in that it really becomes an objective as well as an inward covenant. Would it not be a naïve failure to see the unity of the Scriptures to say, as one commentator does, 'The *fact* that God wants to do this—therein lies the gracious promise of the new covenant. But *how* he will do it Jeremiah does not say. Nothing is said about a covenant mediator or of "the blood of the covenant" (Exod. 24 : 8; Zech. 9 : 11), and the Messiah is not mentioned?' Yes, of course! And yet there may be here an approximate understanding of what Jesus could have meant by the word *kaine diatheke* ('New Testament') at the last supper and what is meant by Paul's doctrine of *'eleutheria* ('freedom'). There the 'God with us' is answered by 'we with God.' And the suffering of the God disavowed in his Son casts a reflection of his suffering in our hearts, namely, the suffering of shame in our spirit as we begin to know him as he is. And so it is that knowledge grows out of forgiveness. And forgiveness remains the incredible miracle that wipes out time, establishes time, and illuminates time. If it is as sure as the endurance of heaven and earth, we can be liberated men and we can confidently trust that 'God, without any merit of mine, of mere grace, grants and imputes to me the perfect satisfaction, righteousness and holiness of Christ, as if I had never committed, nor had any sin, and had myself accomplished all the obedience which Christ has fulfilled for me, if only I accept such benefit with a believing heart' (Heidelberg Catechism, Question 60).

What must not happen on God's side before the Torah is engraved upon the hearts of 'many,' before the deep meaning of that haggadic wordplay on *charuth* and *cheruth*[8] is appropriated by men!

Forgiveness, the ground and content of the knowledge of God, is at its height the all-embracing and at its depth the enduring and sustaining element. Freedom, i.e., obedience which flows from an inner necessity, is the all-embracing element; the new innocence is the enduring element. Endued and armed with this, the little flock stands in a world whose meaning appears to be trampled and destroyed by the powers, which have always been favoured by men because men have had so little will to get away from their guilty past that they could not break away from it. This demonic preference will be unmasked only by this existence of the heart in this new freedom.

LITERATURE: Wilhelm Rudolph, 'Jeremia,' in *Handbuch zum Alten Testament*, I: 12 (1947), pp. 170f.; Matthaeus Hoepers, *Der Neue Bund bei den Propheten* (1933), pp. 92f.

7. A NEW WORLD: ISAIAH 65: 17-19

1. The 'Third Isaiah,' who lived in the postexilic period or at the end of the exile (Budde dates him c. 538, Sellin 519, Duhm and Meinhold c. 450) and therefore was a contemporary of Zechariah or Malachi, reflects something of the disappointment which the pioneers of a new Israel, some of whom had returned to Palestine, were obliged to experience. The rebuilding of the temple was not yet completed or not even begun. The Samaritans had their temple and were putting forward their claims. A great mass of issues making for conflict had accumulated between the individual groups in Israel. The liberation, which had come, *nota bene*, by God's own hand, had been welcomed with delirious joy, but it left behind the dregs of an invincible weariness. Socially and politically nothing was essentially changed. A new godlessness emerged and flaunted itself (vv. 11f.).

[8] Midrash on Exod. 32 : 16: *charuth*=engraved; *cheruth*=freedom; '*charuth* is what is written, but what is meant is *cheruth*.'

Nothing would have been more natural for the best people in Israel than now finally to go over to the spiritualization of Israel's expectation, though the preaching of the ancient promises of God would still —even in this situation—include the creative renewal of the hope of Israel out of nothing, over against the spirit of the times and the apostasy of the masses. Those who do not take refuge in 'heaven' retreat to the 'church,' the 'remnant,' the small core group. It would seem inevitable that Trito-Isaiah (how close he is to us in this frustration and the painful way in which he struggles with it!) would abandon the 'world,' or at least give up hope for the 'state.' It appears that he is willing to leave to 'Gad' and 'Meni' (Fortune and Destiny, v. 11) the restoration of earthly prosperity (even though he assails their servants and worshippers) and retreat in future to his place in the 'synagogue' to sit apart as a pious disillusioned man.

2. The reverse is the case, however, and this is clearly evident. It is precisely this prophetic voice that passionately points to the ancient promises: 'What God has spoken through the mouth of his prophets cannot be a lie. If all the glory has not yet appeared, then it will appear very soon' (Balla). Does he have some new revelation? Or is he just running his head against a stone wall? What is the meaning of this stubbornness?

The originality of this prophetic voice has been questioned, and in most cases it has been denied, and then Trito-Isaiah is pictured as an epigonus of Deutero-Isaiah (Duhm), or as the writer of a kind of homily who is no longer an inspired spokesman in public life (Elliger), or as the compiler of a 'prophetic liturgy' (Balla).

But the prophet, like the apostle, does not strive for personal originality in thought or expression. And yet such a radical restoration and renewal is asserted here that we probably must speak of an individual, original spiritual power, a power that comes from the original Source. The eschatology of Trito-Isaiah is altogether new in that it places the ancient expectation completely in God's creative hand, without any restrictions and without looking about for any intermediate courts of appeal, and in that it is wholly concerned with earthly fulfilment. Even the Messiah recedes into the background. And the kind of inner change of which Jeremiah 31, for example, speaks, is not demanded; at least it is not expressly given its due weight. So if we think back briefly to the situation after the liberation, as it is described above in

416

7. A NEW WORLD: ISAIAH 65:17-19

section one, we have every reason for amazement. Where there is no amazement, there is no inspiration for the sermon. Here there can be abundant amazement, for nowhere in the Old Testament is the *eschaton* spoken of more profoundly, more comprehensively, and more positively.

3. 'Behold, I create new heavens and a new earth.' We catch from far off a shimmering glimpse of the sovereign power of him who here raises his voice as the Creator, this 'I' that expresses his absolute majesty. Not always is it necessary to lay much stress on the word 'behold' in exegesis, but here we must do so. It is an invitation to perceive through hearing what must come, if YHWH is God. This invitation is an assurance, and this assurance is a promise, an oath, a vow. Here the word 'behold' comes close to meaning 'truly, truly, I say to you' and 'As the Lord lives.'

If YHWH is the Godhead, then it is impossible to diminish anything in the ancient promises. Here it is not a matter of other 'views.' Whatever the view or conception may be, it is always a matter of the nature of YHWH being absolutely determinative for the nature of the consummation of the world. The acts of God, by reason of the fact that they occur, have revealed themselves as truth, which demands understanding and concern. Here history (that which occurs) is itself prophecy (unlike church history, in which prophecy at most only 'makes' history—see the chapter 'The Authority and the Outgoing of the Word' in part two). 'Behold, I . . .,' that is to say: as truly as he is YHWH, whose being is identical with his attributes, his virtues, whose virtues are manifested in his acts, whose acts distinguish him, on his way to the End in the world from the world. Nothing gives us the strength to hold fast to the *eschaton*, and religion has long since secretly given it up; no wonder that even the holy people do not know what to do with it. 'Amen, amen, I say to you' (cf. II Cor. 1 : 20 and Rev. 1 : 6f.). The prophet casts himself into and drenches himself in the waters of the Primeval Promise.

The fulfilment of the ancient promises will be a matter of creation as from nothing. We often allow ourselves to be unsettled by the contradictory signs, just as the postexilic vanguard allowed itself to be so easily overwhelmed by its disappointment, so that we think that instead of having come closer to the theocracy, we have got farther away from it than ever. Again and again we are misled by the stretches of gradual transition in history into cherishing expectations which are based upon the idea of growth and progress. But when there no longer appears to be any basis for this, no material on which to build, no point of contact even in the chosen people, then everything will depend upon staking all upon God's total creative design, plan, and power.

No religious idea can cope with our nihilism; God does not associate himself with any scheme or design except his own seemingly forgotten design, the design which has seemingly been made obsolete by historical development. He who utters his own No (unlike the powers, whom we blame for the delay in the coming of the Kingdom), he who separates the servants from the apostates (vv. 13f.), who brings retribution (vv. 6f.), who does not destroy all, who spares even if there is only a little 'juice in the grape' (v. 8), who brings 'gladness of heart' to the faithful and 'pain of heart' to the scoffers (v. 14)—he it is who promises that he who names his name lays hold on the truth, that he who swears by his name has gained his appointed portion of the truth, namely, participation in the real Purpose for which he was created (v. 16). In our text he gives the reason for such undreamed of certainty in the very midst of total collapse, and the reason is this: 'For behold, I create. . . .' Because that is what the future is, the man who feels that he is absolutely and perfectly secure and blessed is right; the 'great words' which he utters here and now are an echo of the *eschaton*. By so declaring himself happy and blessed, he proclaims the truth of God until he comes. Because this future is the Lord's business, no thrill of joy can be too 'idealistic,' no expectation can be pitched too high. For behold, I create—a world in which the past has finally laid aside the fatalities which for century after century have burdened you every time you have made a new start.

4. 'New heavens and a new earth.' There can be no question of a destruction of the first creation, nor of a transformation of its substance. The relationship to God will be different, and what happens will have a different character. How will they be different? In the first place in that 'the former things shall not be remembered' (v. 17b), just as it was true of the blessed life that 'the former troubles are forgotten' (v. 16f.). It is a blessing to be allowed to forget—instead of staring at it or repressing it. The Lord God remembers no more, he no longer remembers our earlier status, the status of estrangement and apostasy.

7. A NEW WORLD: ISAIAH 65:17-19

'You shall be glad and rejoice forever in what I create. For behold, I create Jerusalem to be a rejoicing and her people a delight.' Just as Jerusalem did not have to be demolished in order then to be rebuilt, so the world does not need to be destroyed in order to become 'new.' The renewal lies in the new things that happen when logic and experience show that death is already present.

It should now be perfectly clear that what is central here is joy, always joy! The really new thing over the whole wide world is joy, 'everlasting' joy in so far as by its very nature it was never meant to cease and never intended to be taken away by God. In so far, it is everlasting joy!

'And I will rejoice over Jerusalem and exult in my people.' God who imparts the joy, himself takes part in the joy! God becomes man in this joy. Though in himself he has eternal joy, he shares our life and our lot, he participates in the fulfilment of all our striving, he joins the rejoicers in this present moment of joy when time stands still. He rejoices with those who rejoice and weeps with those who weep. This renewal of the universe through the baptism of joy and his leaving behind of the 'former things' (which have 'passed away,' Rev. 21 : 4c) is enacted in time as the consummation of time, and especially in the ultimate liberation from all the disappointments of the 'liberation.'

5. He who keeps the context well in view will thus see Jerusalem and 'heaven and earth' in the same perspective;[1] any thought of a Mystical *annihilatio* and *restauratio in integrum* is foreign to the Old Testament. The person who is at first surprised or offended by this is probably the most sensitive to the element in this proclamation which puts us to shame. After all, what is required to accomplish what we consider a small thing (at least, in comparison with our cosmic dreams) is nothing less than the sovereign power of YHWH, his creative 'I.' Here the truth becomes apparent to us—because God makes it apparent: so far have we wandered from home, so insoluble are the 'problems,' so completely has our actual life become mired in individual and social life, so greatly are we still under the spell of the exile, so thoroughly are we convinced that the liberation is a delusion. Even the slightest real

---

[1]Sigmund Mowinckel, 'Das Thronbesteigungsfest Jahwäs und der Ursprung der Eschatologie,' *Psalmenstudien*, II; H.-J. Kraus, *Die Königsherrschaft Gottes im Alten Testament* (1951), pp. 50ff.

restoration of genuine humanity requires the supreme creative power of God, that is, a power which is higher than any we have conceived *via causalitatis* or *via eminentiae* or *via negationis* as 'power', 'almightiness,' or 'omnipotence.'[2] In order to bring joy to God's people, the *actus purus*, which sustains all things by his mighty word, enters in and stands to arms, for nothing else is sufficient for this except the full engagement of God's faithfulness to the original promises.[3]

6. He who has been shaken and enraptured by this prophetic message knows why, in the midst of the misery of a social order which seems to be removed as far as possible from the theocracy, he no longer feels the urge to flee from this earth to 'heaven' or from the world into the 'church.' 'Behold, I create . . . that which is new'—this qualification, this justification, and thus this joy! God himself is concerned with the earth and comes down to us; he himself loves the world, and through the church and with the church he strides down a road of blessing for the world.

As if to cut the ground from under any kind of spiritualization and all the vagueness of cosmic speculation, verse 20 continues: 'No more shall there be in it an infant that lives but a few days, and no old man who does not fill out his days . . . for like the days of a tree shall be the days of my people' (v. 22). YHWH is no heavenly spiritualist, and therefore he is the model for all the well-founded hope of the 'enthusiasts.'

The prophet teaches us to see God's faithful hand which reveals the future even in the decline of infant mortality, even in welfare, order, happiness, and life, always in life.[4] This is important, for in a new age new privileges and advantages are constantly appearing, and we tend to attribute them to 'progress.' We must not spiritualize this lauded health and vitality, but we must not literally absolutize it either.[5] Here we are simply told that there is no contradiction between 'progress' and the 'creation of new heavens and a new earth.' It is nonsense to say that evolution does it; but it is a delusion to think that we can manage with anything less than the Creator of the eternal future

---

[2] Scholastic terms for ways of arriving at a knowledge of God's perfections: 'by means of causality,' 'by means of eminence,' 'by means of negation.'—Tr.]

[3] Cf. Hugo Gressmann, *Der Messias*, pp. 160f.

[4] Georges Casalis, *Eschatology and Progress*, 'Paper of the Study Department, World Council of Churches' (July 1952).

[5] Cf. Karl Barth, *Church Dogmatics*, Vol. III, pt. 4, pp. 356ff.

for the ordinary continuing existence of God's earth and God's city and the daily apportionment of the joy of life. What Nietzsche set forth as a human principle applies to God: 'We should not say: "That's the way it is and always will be," but rather, "I am determined to structure what happens to me in such a way that, even though it be 'foolishness,' it will be a parable of goodness." '

7. Only one question remains and one which is really disquieting, and that is whether it is true, whether what is stated here so simply and unguardedly actually comes from God. And from which 'God'? How do we draw near to One in whom the word embraces the act itself? How strange it is, after all, that so many have the idea either that the Old Testament must speak for itself, or that it must not be allowed to have anything to say at all, since otherwise there would be no place for 'Jesus'! What then does the Old Testament 'say'? Its words simply remain 'religious' words if the Word has not become flesh! The meaning of the anthropomorphisms (including, for example, the 'rejoicing' of God) depends, after all, upon the truth of the 'condescendence' of God. It is just when the Old Testament is allowed to speak for itself that it speaks to us in the way that it was heard by those Jews who followed Christ, those Jews who were the true Israel, the 'preformation' of the true Israel, because they found no peace in words and rather brought their lack of peace before the face of him who is not a mediator as an intermediate being, but rather God's own heart in the midst of his creatures, struggling as a man with men for the everlasting joy. The church is the Israel which knows that there was a caesura, a break between past and present, a caesura not only in the conception of history but in the very depths of history. In the resurrection of Christ. In the kingship of him who had seen in his own past and the past of all of us all the ancient promises of God fall to the ground. 'Therefore, if any one is in Christ, he is a new creation, the old has passed away, behold, the new has come' (II Cor. 5 : 17). 'And he who sat upon the throne said, "Behold, I make all things new" ' (Rev. 21 : 5a). 'The end of the ways of God is corporeality' (Oetinger). There in 'third Isaiah' the prophetic appeal has this accent: entrust the whole renewal to God alone, and in this put your hope for all things for the earth. What Rilke said (perhaps not knowing what he was saying and speaking prophetically of something which he could not fathom) is in fact true:

Wie kann
Das Geringste geschehen, wenn nicht die Fülle der Zukunft,
Alle vollzählige Zeit, sich uns entgegenbewegt?
(How can
the least thing happen, if the fullness of the future,
if all time complete, is not moving toward us)?

8. THE FIGURE OF JONAH: JONAH 1: 2, 12

1. The book of Jonah contains—though it found a place among the 'Twelve' (minor prophets)—no prophetic discourses. It is rather a discourse which is full of condemnation of false prophecy. It presupposes a group in the Diaspora which was critical of its own people and its spiritual leaders, a group which must have had some missionary consciousness and from which there later emerged those who 'traverse sea and land to make a single proselyte' (Matt. 23 : 15). Otherwise the origin of the book is obscure, but this did not prevent a jewel from emerging from this obscurity.

The humour of the story reflects the 'irony of fate' in which the judgment of God is hidden. In this form the early, pre-existent Pharisaism is pilloried, but in such a subtle, mild, impartial, and evangelical way that again and again we are moved by the reading of it. No wonder that Luther and Kohlbrügge esteemed 'Jonah' so highly. The title is correct: the subject is Jonah and not Nineveh. It is about him, not his work; he is and he remains the ludicrous chief figure, the contrasting counterpart of an apostle or missionary.

2. Warning: if a congregation has no conception of spiritual humour, if it has no sense of irony and has quite generally failed to discover the secret of laughter, it is perhaps better to let this material lie; for here the laughter never lets up. It is the laughter of an outrageously strange judgment and an outrageously strange grace, and also a laughter over the psychological impossibilities which nevertheless dreadfully reveal the souls of the pious—in their shrewdness and in their silliness, in their conceit and in their credulity.

If we ask how the Song of Solomon could have got into the canon, it is even more strange that Jonah should have received acceptance, and yet it is quite in accord with the self-humiliation with which

Israel's shameful history is registered and recorded in the Scriptures. Tremendous! Possible only by virtue of the revealing work of the Spirit!

3. There has been a great deal said—and rightly—about the 'new paganism'; we were on our way to understanding what paganism really is, namely, the religious veneration of Nature, the primeval powers, and Life itself; and it has just dawned upon us that paganism is the innate religion of human nature, always and everywhere. And here comes 'Jonah' and discloses to us a thing or two about 'revealed religion.' That is to say, it shows us what it looks like in the realities of human life. Here comes the piercing irony of this Word of God and spells out for us what is our 'Judaism,' the 'Judaism' in the church, our self-confidence and our evasion of the mission to speak in the world, to the world, against the world, and for the world.

There is in 'church' life and in the 'church' mind a bad tendency to be impervious, a capacity for keeping things at a distance. It almost looks as if being 'Christian' is synonymous with being disloyally masked by a parade of constant protestations of Loyalty. If in our first nature we are all pagans, then in our second nature we are all 'Jews.' And where is Israel, where is *'Ebed Yahweh* ('the servant of Yahweh'), where is *Shear-yashub* ('the remnant') ? Is there no one who can extricate himself from this organization of excuses which calls itself a Christianity which is interested in, sympathetic with, and in solidarity with humanity? Ah, it costs God less trouble to turn a metropolis from public injustice than to convert such a self-satisfied little flock from its piety!

4. Just as our preachers often rip into those who are absent, just as the misuse of Augustine's saying that 'the virtues of the heathen are splendid vices' could become popular without shocking the 'church people' very much—so Jonah blustered about godless Nineveh, until he was sent there; then he preferred to go in the opposite direction. Then in his resistance he became ridiculous, pathetically or offensively ridiculous—or simply thunderously ridiculous. And God became great, pathetically or offensively great—or simply superabundant in his love; God glorified himself in the very antithesis to himself, namely the disloyal, the cowardly, the absconding church. God's faithfulness sparkles and shines in the mirror of contrast with the recalcitrant pious people. Here this gospel is proclaimed not with heavy accents but with a light touch and a laughter truly heavenly.

Here is the impartiality of the God who casts out the 'children of the kingdom' (Matt. 8 : 12) and calls 'the coastlands afar off' (Isa. 66 : 19). Almost tangible here is the large-heartedness of the God who says in Isaiah, 'I have been found by those who did not seek me; I have shown myself to those who did not ask for me' (Isa. 65 : 1; Rom. 10 : 20). He sets them down beneath the rainbow of his promise. He pours out his unmerited favour in zones which we have still left unclaimed and unopened. He departs from the lines of gradual development and suddenly stands ready among the children of men and takes them into the course of the history of salvation. But Jonah—is not this almost satanic?—Jonah is not happy over this!

5. And yet—consider the infinite generosity of God—it still appears that the 'conversion of Nineveh' was effected by Jonah. It really appears as if this absconding missionary came with a good missionary attitude, as if he rejoiced over the repentance of the metropolis; but God alone knows how malicious, spiteful, grudging, grumbling, egocentric, stupid, and ungrateful he was in the secret places of his heart. But in the eyes of the world—*O magnanimitas*, divine virtue of the Lord —it may often appear that the intentions of the hypocrites were just as good as God's. And indeed, what is hypocrisy, really? Here it must be left to the preacher to show that all the little touches in chapter one are (1) psychologically improbable, and (2) yet true, but (3) true by virtue of a higher divine judgment (which speaks and it comes to be, which commands and it stands forth [Ps. 33 : 9]). The flight (why did he not simply stay at home?)—'from the presence of the Lord' (was this really his intention?); his falling asleep (v. 5) in the midst of the storm (is this trust in God, stubbornness, or even deeper flight?); the question of the crew (v. 8) concerning his occupation, whence he came, his nationality—and his proud answer (was it a profession of faith, could it be genuine, is it genuine nevertheless; and if so, does it come from the God who sustains and keeps alive this faith in Jonah?); the enigmatic verse 12: 'Take me up and throw me into the sea; then the sea will quiet down for you' (is this self-sacrifice, is it vicarious, or is it self-punishment and despair of God's grace?); and finally (v. 16) the impossible thought that these *goyim* should suddenly offer sacrifice to YHWH (is this genuine conversion, is God 'not far from each one of us' [Acts 17 : 27], is it only a step from 'false' to 'true' religion; or do they here see in YHWH only a new and unknown god whom one can turn

to in a pinch—if it does not help, no harm is done?)—what depths! And always the improbable, the first mentioned statement, is the truth, is nevertheless the truth; though the other side of it, the human side of it, the sleepy, bemused evasion of God, the ungenuine confession of faith, the self-punishment, and all the rest of the dark things are also true—the first-mentioned is even far more true in God by virtue of his working, by virtue of his goodness, which outstrips all things, even the laws of the psychical universe.

6. In the application the laughter will disappear at the first step we take. What is really genuine in us? The church people go to sleep in the lowest cabin when the storm blows over the world. While the others pray in their own way, the devout man lies there spiritually idle because he thinks the situation is not meant for him (or at least not until the last resort). 'Can a minister too be saved?'—this should be an agonizing question for ministers and for all members of the church who know very well what the truth is. The lot is cast, and it fell upon Jonah. The Lord distinguishes between the truth and the bearer, the representative, of the truth. This is the 'finger of God' which, hidden beneath the 'lot,' beneath what we call fate, is able to point to the church as being really to blame for the storm that sweeps over the world. The mariners have their own ideas: he must have committed temple sacrilege. This is nonsense; this is the way the world in its foolishness blames the church when it is itself confused and distracted; and yet in God's judgment it is not altogether nonsense. The church which is not active in the apostolate is indeed committing temple sacrilege, embezzling the treasures, robbing for itself what is intended for the world.

7. Unfathomable is man's mind: 'deceitful is the heart, yea, more than deadly' (Jer. 17 : 9). That we are not guilty of distorting the picture when we refuse to accept without examination that Jonah's plea to be thrown into the sea was a noble sacrifice, but rather regard it as possible that it was a subjective attempt to vindicate himself, an evidence that he would rather die than undertake the task of having to preach to a hostile world—this is clearly apparent in the continuation of the story (4 : 3) when, after his rescue and after the conversion of the city, he still prays that he may die in order not to have to face the humiliation of not having his prophetic fulminations come true. And this is repeated, even more extravagantly, in 4 : 8!

8. But even this unfathomable abyss of the pious soul is not the

ultimate, though it may very well be the ultimate for our power of perception. The prayer 'from the belly of the fish' shows wonderfully and clear as noonday that even such a demoralized and warped human being is not wholly estranged from the service of the Lord, that in him there still remains a spiritual life and a stirring of faith which does not come from himself, but which is actually in him. And he does not know this himself—if he did know it, the very thing he would not do (as many fear that they will do) would be to sink even further into apathy and passivity.

When God lets us know that he is concerned with us in these depths where we are ungenuine or only half genuine, when the Word overwhelms us, then we too will share in his truthfulness by faith in the truthfulness of his work. The reintegration of our split and adulterated Christian attitude comes out of the knowledge of God's integral faithfulness, which is present in, with, and under our disintegration. The old translation of a familiar passage in Hosea (14 : 8) expresses it thus: 'On me will your fruit be found.' Buber translates: '(I am like the evergreen cypress), from me will your fruits be obtained.'

LITERATURE: C. von Orelli, *Die kleinen Propheten*, 1908; Karl Marti, *Dodekapropheten*, 1904; Martin Luther, sermons on Jonah; Hermann F. Kohlbrügge, *Der Prophet Jona*; Albert Kuyle, *Jonas*.

9. IN THE ABYSS: JONAH 2 : 4

1. Though generally in our services the sermon has the preference over the homily, it is in my opinion impossible to choose a text from the book of Jonah without being obliged to bring not only the immediate but also the broader context into the sermon. It must inevitably become a 'bible study.' Even the individual chapters (the division of the book is remarkably appropriate) can be isolated from each other only for a brief time. This means that the treatment of the powerful second chapter can be made really fruitful only in a series of sermons on Jonah. The redactor certainly made a place for this interpolated section only after mature 'theological' reflection.

2. Jonah prayed 'from the belly of the fish.' The 'fish' will be strange and miraculous only if one thinks of the whole book, not as a

sermon in the form of a novella, but as a historical chronicle of the adventures of an odd character—but even then not so miraculous that it is 'impossible.' It follows from this that it is indeed an advantage to the preaching if the preacher has also learned to put the story, the haggadah, to the service of God's Word and self-witness, but that he who has not yet learned this need not find it a disadvantage, unless it be the disadvantage that he may encumber the whole sermon with the appearance of incredibility, because to many (and not merely 'modern') listeners it is this one point that appears incredible.

3. Jonah prayed 'from the belly of the fish.' The man who is cast into the sea, into the primeval waters of chaos, is at the same time preserved—by him who casts away the power of chaos and knows very well his own way of carrying out his work, however fiercely the untameable abyss may rage. The castaway is preserved; in the abyss there is a house, a protected space. And this man, who did not pray when the pagans prayed (it is striking that the 'prophet' at no time in chapter one can bring himself to pray), now prays in this straitened prison, this humiliating strait. This man, who in his unfathomable double-mindedness (sacrifice or self-punishment) welcomed his last hour, now prays when all chance of living seems to have been taken away from him. Naturally in this hour of mortal peril he did not pray in psalm form, rhythmically, in parallel verse members, etc., but what he 'uttered' in dumb terror and wordless cries, he later recapitulated in the ordered form of a profound recollection of his experience. And yet that speechless 'utterance' was the real, immediate, existential utterance, the groaning too deep for words uttered by the creation and the believers (Rom. 8 : 22–26). The ordered speech, which is the precipitate of this groaning, is used by the Spirit as a testimony for others, for Jews, for Pharisees, for 'church people,' that they may know how man, including the pious man, stands before God (cf. Acts 9 : 11, 'For behold, he is praying . . .').

4. Thus as a rule the course of life runs through these stages, in this circle, or in this direction: (1) the little prayers we have learned as children; (2) then in shallower or deeper form the 'personal' prayers—and if a certain regularity develops, a 'prayer life'; and finally, (3) at the boundaries of our existence the prayer which is a cry, as one cries 'Mother!' (or) *Abba!* ('Father!'). But then this is not merely an 'ejaculatory prayer,' but rather the outbursting of so much that has

been lying repressed within us for years; in time of distress the ambivalence and the wavering in our life, the habit of hesitation, the irresolution which is a part of 'our Judaism,' our second nature, can come to an end. It can!—for it remains the fruit of God's refusal and rejection, of God's preservation in the raging of the elements, as it was with Jonah.

In the assertions we make as a (prophetic-apostolic) community we are living above our station—and in our prayers we are at the same time living far beneath our status. In many respects we appear to be more than we are; and yet there is one respect in which (possibly) we 'are' more than we appear to be. This 'being' comes to light in the darkness, when the power of this world draws near, the power of death, the void, chaos, annihilation. This 'being' is awakened by him who in the midst of terror keeps us in his safe-keeping, as in the bowels of a sea monster which is the very thing that is to shelter us from the monstrous sea. We sometimes think (whether rightly or not?) that the whole of Christendom needs to be cast out, swallowed, and vomited out upon some unknown shore if there is ever again to be any prayer that comes from the depths—and from this new prayer a new courage to go out into strange and distant places, obedient and open to the holy adventure.

5. The one respect in which we are more than we appear to be is the way in which we cling to the temple, to the sign of God's Revelation, the place where he caused his Name 'to be remembered' (Exod. 20 : 24) on earth. Jonah was a miserable scoundrel, and he was even capable of trying, half-heroically, to cover it up by submitting to voluntary death. God and nothingness, Christ and Satan, culture and the mob, all good and evil powers are agreed that the 'empirical' church is a miserable, craven affair. But where we walk in the ways of God's foreknowledge—O laughter in the midst of tears, O summer in the midst of the season of storms—the untruth of this truth becomes evident. The dull routine was dull routine, and yet it proves itself to be more than dull routine; that 'second nature' is nevertheless not our true nature, our true humanity before God. Piety, belief, are nothing more than piety, belief, and yet faith does break forth from piety and belief and becomes faith in action, faith which is genuine deed and real devotion. This much-maligned piety is something that happens in relationship to the temple, to the presence of God, which neverthe-

less—despite all appearances to the contrary—has been the veiled mystery of love behind our, in my respects, so barren past: we have really clung to God's Word and God's House more than we knew!

6. So Jonah, this miserable wretch, no longer asks for release from life, nor for the lengthening of his days as such, nor for deliverance from death as the extinction of life, as a radical end. No—what had he 'said' in the belly of the monster? Later he was able to sing what he had said then, said with his whole being: 'I am cast out from thy presence.' The dreadfulness of death lies, as is now apparent, in falling away from the nearness of God—and therefore he knows, in this one lucid, flashing second, that the glory of life has been his 'coming in and going out' in the light of God's presence. 'Yet I will again look upon the temple of thy holiness, thy particular presence.' Jonah was far more wicked than he knew; this is why he was capable of fleeing, capable of sleeping in the ship in distress, capable of being callous and cold-blooded in the face of death. And yet there was a tie with YHWH, stronger than he himself realized, indeed, so strong that once he was back on dry land and had recovered his senses, he remembered not only that in the depths of his terror he had yearned for the temple but also that he had found within himself a strange, unfathomable trust in the future, a confidence that he would again find, see, and experience life, the nearness of God, the temple. 'Yet I shall look again upon the holy temple.'

7. Are we to conclude, then, that this experience at the confines of life and death were not real, not serious, that the abyss and his rejection were mere phantoms? Were the 'roots of the mountains' and the 'bars of the earth' which he felt closing in upon him 'forever' merely an episode, a brief ordeal? No, on the level of our perception we are actually laid low in utter earnest, we are really lost. One can be lost only within the heritage of the covenant, as a 'Jew,' as one who is disobedient, as one who is a deserter; and thus the judgment really begins 'with the household of God' (I Pet. 4 : 17).

And yet this utter peril is nothing in comparison with the fact that God 'hears' the voice, 'my voice' (v. 3); all the 'waves and billows' are nothing in comparison with the overwhelming human nearness of God to man; the chaos and the condemnation are nothing in comparison with the command of God, his creative, directive, utterance, full of an almost playful triumph: 'And the Lord spoke to the fish, and it vomited out Jonah upon the dry land.' No, this abyss is not *the* abyss; there is life for us, reckoned to us in the midst of death. This is the sign of Jonah of which Jesus spoke (Matt. 12 : 39ff.), namely, that the Son of Man will be rejected and that this sign will at the same time be the seal of the saving Presence, even for those who, precisely as church people, would be lost for ever in the judgment.

8. Are we not familiar with that strange presentiment which is one of the essential elements of faith, that premonition that makes us say, 'This is not the end, I will not be lost, nothing can happen to me any more'? If that faith is not based merely upon a general idea of God, but rather springs from the light of the temple and grows up before the face of God like a root out of dry ground, if it comes out of commitment to the 'human' God who is bound with us by the 'bars of the earth,' then it is well with us! He who is protected by God is well protected— true, but one does not say this lightly, once one knows the belly of the monster, that cave which is part of the 'wicked' world, even though by God's grace its walls protect us *from* wickedness *in the midst* of wickedness. Henceforth we know for good and all the nothingness, the emptiness, the futility of religion (v. 8), and perhaps for the first time we really mean what we say when we say, 'I will sacrifice to thee with thanksgiving, my vows I will pay' (v. 9). And the song from the bowels of the monster concludes: 'Deliverance is Thine' (Buber).

10. MISSION IN SPITE OF THE MISSIONARY: JONAH 3

1. Finally the mission begins to move, now that the man who was sent goes to the appointed place. But Jonah's whole message consisted in the announcement of doom and overthrow. It is not clear from the text whether this was the whole of his commission. Did 'the message that I tell you' contain nothing more than this? Would he now be faithful, this man who later admitted that the deepest reason for his flight was fear that the Lord would be merciful to Nineveh? 'That is why I made haste to flee to Tarshish; for it knew that thou art a gracious God and merciful . . .' (4 : 2). However that may be, the fact is that this man who, it should be noted, had himself been saved from the abyss of rejection made his message as blunt, hard, and offensive as possible. Downfall and destruction—and no escape. Everything curt

and matter-of-fact, even to the setting of a term: forty days more—
and that's the end of it!

2. God prepared a way for this heartless message so that even so it
found entrance into men's hearts. And again the story runs out into a
surprise, a miracle, a laugh, again it exceeds all bounds. The tremendous city, 'three days' journey in breadth' (it is obvious that the
reference is to the enormous numbers of the *goyim*) was thrown into
agitation. The whole state, with all violence, terror, injustice, and
wickedness, stopped in its tracks and repented. The reaction was total
—king and people, man and beast were clothed in sackcloth. And the
root of the matter is apparent in verse 8; it is 'violence' (throughout
the Bible the extreme antithesis, the 'righteousness' of the 'meek' and
'wickedness'; Gen. 6 : 13; Ps. 37 : 14; Ps. 74 : 20). They 'believed
God,' that is, they acknowledged and accepted his judgment; even the
god-king humbled himself together with his crown domains (for everything belongs to him), and everything is drawn into the anticipation—
and the fending off of the *dies ater* ('black day'). Incredible! These
people who did not know Him are taking the message seriously—no,
they are not taking it seriously. Still forty days to go; this they believe
to be the lot which is rightfully coming to them, but they do not
believe it is a death sentence. Contrary to the terms of the proclamation,
they interpret it as an ultimatum but not as an ultimum. What is this?
The undying lust for life? The strange characteristic of man which
makes it impossible for them to imagine that there is really an end to
themselves and their history? The cunning that expects to gain an
amnesty from the Despot by way of extravagant self-abasement? All
this undoubtedly played a part, but God, who made a way for Jonah's
message and made up for its deficiencies, also made up for, filled up,
and accepted as valid their strange conversion, because they said:
Who knows? Who knows? Perhaps after all the world is not ruled by
fate, perhaps there is One who somehow would show consideration.

3. Woe to us—us the good and pious, us Jews, Jonahs! The masses
will rise up in the judgment against the musty churches, sects, and persuasions—and will condemn them, for they may perhaps be converted
from their blatant form of rebellion, while the others, the Jonahs and
their like, have not even perceived that their daily respectable life
is a secret form of rebellion against what God means human life to be.
They may—says, not Jonah, but the *book* of Jonah, speaking over

Jonah's head—turn away from their public sins, from their ingrained paganism, from the 'evil way' (3 : 8), from this whole condition of torpidity and aridity in which power is no longer regarded merely as a desperate means of upholding law and order but is rather glorified as the very force of nature and the crown of human vitality (cf. Matt. 12 : 41; Luke 11 : 32).

4. What is it that actuates these 'pagans,' these people who are religiously under the grip of Nature, who are here set up as a model for us? What motivates them is that one question, that leaven of enthralling uncertainty, of audacious expectation, which exists in the outstretched hands, the uplifted heads, and the hearts that reach out beyond all that is humanly conceivable (Rom. 8 : 19). They are driven by that one question in which a good unbelief begins to stir and a good belief begins to dawn: 'Who knows, God may yet repent and turn from his fierce anger. . . .?' (3 : 9). The rudiment of an awakened conscience is this question: 'Who knows?' But we, even after God has revealed himself, after he has rescued us, we perhaps still go on believing on a higher level in the 'immutability' of God, just as Jonah did in spite of the fact that his life had been snatched from the abyss by God's new, unexpected faithfulness. But the 'people of Nineveh,' who had grown up in the belief in astrological fate, brought up under the irrevocable decrees of a king who was god on earth—these people, when they were touched by the God of Israel, suddenly believed no longer in the unchangeability of God. Even the stirring of a slight breeze that bears the fragrance of the Lord's Word means the end of this terrible superstition which makes God the prisoner of his own order. Here too we hear, as on a higher octave, the laughter floating in the air like a new springtime, a song of liberation.

5. And God 'repented.' He renounced the consequences of his words. He refused to be the reflected image of 'Jewish' pharisaic certainty which says, 'They do not really understand anyhow, they are not really repenting'; he refused to be a (melancholy?) reflection and confirmation of the natural man's animosity and impotence. The Lord repented and he did not do it, though he had said he would. Was it then merely a pedagogical threat? Is this the way for us to 'salvage' the 'immutability' of God? What Jonah says in 4 : 2, this stupefaction, this indignation over God's saving act, sounds like persiflage, like a psychological absurdity, only because it is not square with our theories—

but unfortunately, here lie the real sombre potentialities, the half-conscious or hardly conscious religious feelings of resentment that arise when things go better with the 'godless' than they deserve, and even more when it turns out that the godless live better lives than we thought, and most of all when God 'capriciously' brings salvation to the remotest and most hostile of places. What is all perversity in comparison with this perversion of faith: I did not bear witness, I did not want to do it, because I was afraid that you, O God, would be 'slow to anger and abounding in steadfast love' and that you would really 'repent' the promised 'evil' even in the case of Moscow, of Babylon and London! A hint of this emerges here and there even in 'secular' poetry, as in A. Roland Holst:

> O laughter of children, before the world began
> and again after its end—
> of a sparkling little breeze
> telling, that one day will be sent,
> to blow over pride and pain,
> until finally Babylon and London
> are forgiven and forgotten.

6. But it is precisely this God who is 'our' God. By him we live. We live by the fact that he is qualitatively immutable, that he is faithful, abounding in steadfast love, and therefore we live precisely by the fact that in order to be faithful to himself and his eternal purpose, he changes his way and averts our fate. This God—thanks be to God—is our God! From him himself—directly in his Word and indirectly in our experience—we could have learned long ago that we cannot advance even one step without asking the glorious question: Who knows, who knows, God may yet repent and turn from his anger? So often we celebrate his perfections with dead lips, the hymnic succession that recurs like a refrain in the Scriptures (Exod. 34 : 6f.; Ps. 86 : 15; Ps. 103 : 8; Num. 14 : 18; Joel 2 : 13); in the 'temple psalm' (2 : 2–9) uttered after Jonah experienced a genuine homesickness in the belly of the monster, they are lauded as the rainbow colours of God's humanity. God's ways are higher than our ways, and his thoughts higher than our thoughts, as the heavens are higher than the earth.

How remote therefore is what we are dealing with here, what a totally different dimension! Along with this passage in Jonah read Isaiah 55 : 7f.: 'For he will abundantly pardon; for my thoughts are

433

not your thoughts . . .'; and in order to understand the true immutability by which we ourselves live day by day, read Psalm 77 : 10: 'But the right hand of the Most High changes' (here in fact contrary to expectation, but in principle, as always, beyond expectation). Do we remember, we who always know better and are hard of heart (Oh, that his generous abundance might cover and overwhelm our perverse murmuring!), that the Lord always performs the good he has promised but that he does not by any means always perform the evil, just as he allows the promised good to come to thousands but visits the evil only down to the third or fourth generation (Exod. 20 : 5b–6)? In our lot and our moral distress we are abundantly justified if, like the Ninevites, we at least remember and always hold fast to this thought: who knows? We are justified in doing this even though and precisely when we cannot understand how God's *opus alienum* changes into his *opus proprium* but are permitted to have faith that the work 'on the left' will be gathered up into God's triumphant right hand.

11. THE ULTIMATE HUMOUR: JONAH 4:4

1. After all that has happened Jonah's attitude will strike us as being psychologically incomprehensible; and quite rightly! That a prophet who has been called will not preach is strange. That he should flee and fall asleep during the storm is bad. But that he should be brought to the gates of the abyss and rescued in order that he might immediately begin his work with courage and then be shocked and horrified by the wonderful result of that work; that he, Israel's prophet, should want to reduce the revelation of God, who unlike the nature gods, is 'holy,' to the level of 'nature,' to the level of immutability—this is incomprehensible. And most shocking of all is that he should sit there and wait for Nineveh's downfall and that when this does not happen he should reproach God for granting grace to the world—as if he himself were not alive by grace, as if he himself had not been rescued by grace from the monstrous depths and final catastrophe of his life. Or is there here a suggestion of the humiliating element of truth in the experience of many people who are alienated from the Church that 'church people,' when they are bad, are worse, more divided, more undependable, ignoble, and inhuman than ordinary people? Let anybody who thinks

434

there is nothing in this read the fourth chapter of the book of Jonah from beginning to end!

2. This 'element of psychological incomprehensibility' is part of the deeper anthropology of the Scriptures. The reference here is to the sin of the 'Jews,' the sin compared with which all other 'sins' are harmless. Sin is not a moral, not even a religious, concept. Sin is always rebellion against Grace, but in very different degrees of consciousness. Sin in its deepest sense—one cannot say fully conscious sin, for it is more or less true even of the devout that 'they know not what they do' (Matt. 23 : 34)—is revealed by God's Faithfulness. Therefore the Word of God in this haggadic writing says: so 'impossible' is man—in the depths of his being, which no plummet of analysis can fathom, there slumbers a sullen resistance to the sovereign power of God and a hate-inspired distaste for people who do not think the way we do and therefore are already classified almost as criminals.

The adherence to a mistaken notion of God's 'honour' (even though it has long since been apparent that the Lord sets his highest honour in the salvation of sinners), the identification of our pious indignation with God's wrath (though it has long been apparent that 'you, the judge, are doing the very same things'; Rom. 2l, 1b), the unwillingness to go along with the turnings of God's repentings (e.g., among us the feelings of resentment, the distrust, or the reserve we have toward the Germans who have turned away from their wrong thinking and action), the wickedness in which we resign ourselves to the spiritual darkness in which the multitude lives and must live, the difficulty we have in giving up our interpretations of God's counsel and providence, especially if this puts us in a 'different' (i.e., a less favourable) light—all this stands in contradiction to faith, all this is at variance with our knowledge, with the favour and grace which we have received, and yet these two things have the closest kind of connection with each other. It is a fact: there are no greater rogues than pious rogues! How can this be comprehended?

3. So high is the place we have been given in God's covenant, in our participation in the covenant, so far have we been let in on special secrets! J. H. Gunning's saying that God rules the world through the prayers of his children was no idle word. After all, in faith we transcend the bounds of our humanity in so far as God allows us to see and to judge, to see and to judge along with him. But if even for a moment the

delusion arises that these gifts are our possessions, that we have them at our disposal, if we forget that we ourselves breathe by Grace and believe by Grace, then the mist and thick darkness rise from our 'Jewish' minds. And then we are much worse than others. And that began when we ceased being witnesses, resentfully withdrew and dropped our apostolic task, and gave up the world as lost.

Then it would appear that it is of no avail even if we are cast into the sea and miraculously rescued from its depths—then we are constantly 'inclined' (to put it as conservatively as the Heidelberg Catechism does, not only in the section on affliction, Question 5, but also in the section on redemption, Question 60) to have absurd reactions like the 'psychologically incomprehensible' reactions of Jonah. Then it really does appear that in the end a pious man descends to the level of the pathological. Impressive is the way in which the book of Jonah makes the man Jonah ridiculous and shows him up in all his ridiculousness. How tremendous that the inspired author had the courage so radically to expose the piety of man 'taken by itself'! Here he shrank from no consequences whatsoever. Why? In order to give the glory to God.

4. But more tremendous than the loud laughter is the tenderness of God, the condescending goodness which does not hesitate to become almost the goodness of the 'pure fool.' Note that God, the director of the drama of history, who rules the sea and converts the metropolis, asks this rascal in all kindliness, 'Do you do well to be angry?' And he answers the sick-minded retort of the prophet that he would rather die than learn that the world is repenting even though he had so categorically asserted that it would be destroyed—God answers the complaint, the reproach, indeed, the rebellion of this moaning whiner with a miracle—a wonderful shade tree to provide some cooling for the more than overheated pate of his envoy. From all sides comes the splash of laughter upon the bystanders, and upon the complainer falls a gentle shower of cooling shade.

There he sits in the shadow of God's own creative hand, better than any homemade shelter—the unfathomable generosity of God: '. . . that it might be a shade over his head, to save him from his chagrin!' After a man has been rescued from the abyss, God proceeds to grant him something extra to 'save' him from this disgraceful, vile 'chagrin.' What kind of a God is this who is finally obliged to listen to the suicide elegy of his servant, as if it were a world catastrophe when God does not perform the evil he has declared he will perform—and on top of this a complaint without the slightest trace of self-accusation and self-examination, without any remembrance of what he himself had said: 'I will sacrifice to thee with thanksgiving, my vows I will pay' (2 : 9)? What kind of a God is this who allows all this madness to vent itself upon his own heart, who allows all this ill-humour to be swallowed up in the silence of his faithfulness, his action, the imperturbable course of his mighty acts?

5. This God is the power of forbearance, the power that saves and preserves, the power that did not come to destroy men's lives, but to preserve them (Luke 9 : 56). He is free, but yet, moved by an inner compassion, he 'must' spare men, because he sees this city, this great aggregation of *goyim*, differently. He sees the people and the children and the beasts. God takes himself more seriously than he does, the opposition of the *goyim* and also the ill-humour of the pious.

The pious too are obviously lacking in 'that by which one really sees';[1] they do not see the people, the children, the beasts. They go searching for principles and ideologies, they seek confirmation of the world view from their little sheltered places apart from the world. They do not understand the speech of the defenceless, they do not hear the groaning of the creatures. These are the same pious people whom God placed at his side in the covenant and who now have no eye for the essential reality. If God were not different from what he is in Christendom, we would long since have perished in our affliction and the judgment.

6. God is our fate; it is not Fate that is God. That is to say, it is our happy fate that this God is truly God; and we realize this in the time of need, and we forget it in our folly. 'It is of the Lord's mercies that we [we!] are not consumed, because his compassions fail not. They are new every morning: great is thy faithfulness' (Lam. 3 : 22f., A.V.). Our fate is that we have to do with the Holy One, i.e., the Other One, with him who is other than all the powers and gods, other than all 'pagans' and all 'Jews.' It is the Lord who maintains the right of the poor and afflicted and watches over the stranger (Ps. 140 : 12, Ps. 146); this generally does not happen under the rule of fate, but when it does happen, then it comes straight from this Lord. We turn our atten-

---

[1] George Bernard Shaw, at the end of *Saint Joan*. [I have been unable to find this phrase or its equivalent in *Saint Joan*.—Tr.]

tion away from God's special acts to general events and we know that there too his right hand is at work. This God of Israel is the God of Nineveh. For he is a 'human' God, and therefore in the end even the God of Jonah, the 'Jews,' the 'church people' in the perverse resistance.

7. And Jonah himself? Did he remain in his hardness of heart, in his sulks? We hear no more about him; he no longer matters. He was the image of that Israel which does not go out to the nations; he was a sign of how the pious answer can stand in inverse proportion to being given the preference by God; he is made ridiculous by the generosity of God. Will we, instead of the 'heathen' and the 'Jews,' finally turn out to be the 'third generation'? The third generation lives by God's repentance, as the true Israel always lived by it. Therefore the present certainty of faith of the 'third generation' is still surrounded by a zone of joyous expectations, all of them childlike in nature and prophetic in vision and all of them set above that one resounding pedal point: Who knows? . . . The Lord will prepare for all peoples a splendid feast, he will destroy the veil that covers the face of all peoples, he will swallow up death and annihilate it in his victory. He will wipe away the tears from all faces. 'And it will be said on that day, "Lo, this is our God; we have waited for him, that he might save us. This is the Lord; we have waited for him; let us be glad and celebrate the day of our freedom" ' (Isa. 25 : 6ff.).

12. AGAINST DUALISM: JOB 14: 1-6

1. The book of Job is included in the *Kethubim*, the third group of writings which together with the Torah and the Prophets constitute the Old Testament canon. In these writings we are dealing with the reaction of the community to the revelation, the revelation which took place in the acts of God and was illuminated by the words of God. They are responses to the Word, indirect, subjective, and in the exact sense human. This must be borne in mind, especially where dealing with the *chokmah*. Here we do not transmit and expound the immediate Word of God, but rather the broken antiphon of the community and the individual in the community. Yet this must not be allowed to lead to an impressionistic picture, supported perhaps by terminology borrowed from the existentialistic view of man. We dare not allow ourselves to be

misled into profound utterances about 'being unto death' (Heidegger) —however pertinent and true they may appear to be. For in a text like this the antiphon is peculiarly adapted to be an indirect witness to the truth of God and is thus a contribution to the illumination of existence. It is the grace of the Holy Spirit which takes these bitter laments and hallows them in order to tell us in revealing love what human life really is. The true knowledge of ourselves and our life is also a fruit of God's special acting upon our hearts. Only so does the simple truth become holy and wholesome for our hearts.

2. Eliphaz, Bildad, and Zophar have undertaken to explain the riddle of Job's suffering. They think they are the interpreters of God's judgment, whereas they are merely speculating about a hypostatized idea of Righteousness. This a man can handle; one can take this idea and, guided by the Ariadne thread of retribution, enter the darkest labyrinths. In this way one can not only explain one's own religious philosophy to others but also confirm it for oneself. And so one climbs right past what is plainly to be seen and casts, if not a joyful, yet a clear, profound, and enthralling light upon the suffering on this earth.

From the outset Job is defenceless against this argument; after all, he himself had been nurtured in these teachings. It is true that he experiences the tremendous torment of seeing that the hand of God in his life is being misinterpreted and misunderstood. It is true that he indicates, reproachfully or aggrievedly, that he is being confronted with the Power rather than the Justice of God. But he settles into a middle zone in which he cringes before the Power of God, denies and yet does not deny the Justice of God, and declares that he hopes for a higher revelation of justice. The cut and thrust of the dialogue revolve about Job's unwillingness to submit to the Justice of God, which goes hand in hand with a kind of glorification of the 'Omnipotence' of God which is not demanded of us in this way at all, but simply becomes the pure right of the stronger.

(a) Many people live in this dualism between Power and Justice. It can hardly be avoided. And this dualism can stand its ground and be justified as a form of honesty over against all religious dishonesty. And yet it leaves us unsatisfied. At most it can be, for a time, the voice of our experience; it cannot be a confession of faith. The man himself has the half-conscious presentiment that there can be no conflict between power and justice in God and that it would be a healing liberation if his eyes were opened to pierce the fog of this dualism. This would make room for a different *chokmah*, a higher and a simpler Wisdom, simpler because it does not suppose a double source of the knowledge of God and a double purpose in God's 'being,' i.e., in his deeds as they are enacted upon earth.

3. Here and there in the speeches of Job there are flashes of this insight. Thus in chapter 14 he says what God gave him to say and what we hear: 'You are a man'—this utterly simple thing must be said to us, despite our religiousness and our irreligiousness.

'You were born of a woman'—you had a beginning, you have no roots in eternity. You drew your first breath in your mother's arms, you have no pre-existence except that of an embryo. And that means that you (including your 'soul') are 'of yesterday and know nothing' (Job 8 : 9), that is, you know nothing of the things on which God's standard of power and justice must be based. As if you knew from some other source how power and justice in life must be thought of as being in balance—or even in precise agreement and harmony!

You are 'of few days!' Your life is brief. This is not merely an external limitation which leaves your inward value untouched. It also narrows your experience, your knowledge and judgment to a minimum.

You are 'full of misery' (better than 'trouble'). What this means is described in detail in Job 7. Always struggle, always under the shadow of such a lowly beginning in the womb of a woman, always under the threat of a *reductio in nihilum* ('reduction to nothingness').

'You enter into life like a flower' (cf. Isa. 40 : 6; Ps. 90 : 5; Ps. 103 : 15), and almost immediately you are cut down. What was the use of the high point in your life when already it bore within it the inevitable descent to an irresistible decay? Like a shadow, in itself a nothing, but suffered to endure for a moment in the alternation of cloud and sunshine—that is what you are!

That is what you are! That is not merely your lot, your situation; it is the characteristic mark of your 'being,' your 'existence,' your 'nature.' *Ecce homo*! That is the way in which Christ is the truth. That is the way the truth came to light. So utterly comfortless when we ourselves say it in our scepticism after our religion has faded and withered away. So full of hidden promise when God says it to us in the fullness of time. Through the Spirit our flesh, our origin, our time has the same height and depth as the time into which Christ was sent, 'born of woman, born under the law' (Gal. 4 : 4), born 'in the flesh' (John 1 : 14; I Tim. 3 : 16), in 'the form of a slave,' 'obedient unto death' (Phil. 2 : 7f.). We are 'buried' with Christ (Rom. 6 : 4; Col. 2 : 12).

(a) How brief was the life of Jesus! How he bore his misery of existence! How little he was able to do in the face of the wisdom of the scribes! How he was straitened until it was accomplished! How fleeting was his flowering! How terribly swift his downfall! How the necessity of 'man,' of the flesh, weighed him down! How his work was shattered and ruined! If one wishes to speak of his 'sinlessness' in this connection, then it must not consist in the fact that he did not flee into a super-mundane world or into the depths of the soul in order to be something different or to feel different from a 'man, born of woman'! Indeed, does not his sinlessness shine at its brightest in the fact that he declares: 'I am a worm, and no man, though I was cast upon thee from my birth' (Ps. 27 : 6, 10), upon thee and thy unutterable Name?

4. And now comes the worst, the crying wrong, apparently the ultimate confirmation of the eternal conflict between power and justice: 'And thou dost open thy eyes upon such a one.' On the level of feeling and experience this would mean: so small, so wretched is my paltry existence, and now, on top of this, you come and concern your-self with me. Verse 6 speaks very clearly in this vein. But according to the truth God intended in what he said through the mouth of the suffering Job, the Job who is here speaking prophetically beyond his own feeling and experience, this is rather the counterbalancing—the very quiet, hardly expressed, but intensely present counterbalancing—of the tension between Power and Justice. Wherein lies the beginning of this counterbalancing?

Here we should remember Psalm 8 : 4: 'What is man that thou art mindful of him, and the son of man that thou dost care for him?' Yes, God's eyes are opened upon this nugatory being, but they do so with concern and solicitude. This wretched being is completely gathered up into his knowledge. He is gathered into his heart, in his all-knowing Presence. The light of God's purpose and determination shines upon him.

God's eyes are not wandering eyes, they are not flickering lights. Constant concern, pure understanding, unmixed judgment, burning love (love that chooses and prefers without sufficient reason)—these are in him from eternity. He who 'destroys' us, eternalizes us (Simone Weil's *Waiting for God* is full of such [quasi-]paradoxes). He who recognizes that we have no pre-existence except that of unformed clods 'intricately wrought in the depths of this earth' (Ps. 139 : 15) allows us to share in his enduring life.

5. How does a man know this? 'And thou dost . . . bring me into judgment with thee.' An address goes out, a claim is made; man, this man, is summoned to judgment; he is measured by the norm of the *mishpatim*, the statutes. Therein lies judgment and grace. Therein lies the 'dignity' of man. By this road on which man becomes nothing the door to man's essential humanity before God is found. If *ecce homo* is not understood in its radical sense, if it is not understood 'in Christ,' then the fate-burdened man's feeling of guilt remains incomprehensible, then the cry 'How can a clean thing come out of the unclean?' Remains merely the morbid self-rejection of a tormented creature who, worn down and broken by the torturer's hand, is transforming his legitimate rebellion into a contemptible submission. But what is almost unobtrusively disclosed here is rather the knowledge of God which declares that 'there is no unrighteousness in Him' (Ps. 92 : 15). The process of law may be as strange as that in Franz Kafka's *The Trial*, but it is and will remain the way in which human life in its nothingness is justified and through God's caring for it actually receives its tremendous dignity in the first place.

In the depths of God's heart there can be no conflict between power and justice; that man is so small cannot be a general anthropological insight, however simple it may seem. Just as for Job there rises up another God behind the god of whim, so there rises up another man behind the man who 'does not exist,' who cannot stand his ground. Decay is the natural end, and it is a judgment. If it were only natural, there would be no feeling of guilt; if it were only judgment, there would be no divine meaning in the end of life. The fact that we perish in this way, this is the sign of the Judgment of YHWH (cf. Isa. 6 : 5: 'Woe is me, I perish; for I am a man of unclean lips, and I dwell in the midst of a people of unclean lips'). The fact that we are mortal in this state, this is owing to the everlasting grace of creation, a determination which we cannot overstep. The fact that in this we are addressed and taken seriously, therein lies for ever the dignity which is bestowed upon us in the covenant of YHWH.

6. We have been living too long in the dualism of Power and Justice. The Word of God must free us from it. It can speak through our own mouth (as it does here and there in the *Kethubim*). It speaks of the radical limitations upon our life. It speaks of the Lord's concern with this life at its limits. Always we are within a hairbreadth of fleeing to the heights in our religiosity or into the depths of a self-abasement which is dragged out of us as under torture. Often we just miss the Presence of the eyes that see all things on earth. Nowhere except in our own place will we find the wonder of God's concern with our existence. Only in the incarnation of God-with-us do we see that the Power that overshadows us is also the Justice that illuminates us, that the Power that terrifies us is also the Justice that reassures us, that the Power that sends us into the far country is also the Justice that brings us back home.

Only in the 'other man,' who is the Messiah, do we know that it is good to be a man, limited, judged—and lifted up into the life-giving knowledge of God. And if our groaning in travail continues—ought we not sometimes perceive that the Spirit himself is interceding for us with sighs too deep for words and that he who searches our hearts is paying heed above all to that in our groans and prayers which is the mind of the Spirit (Rom. 8 : 26f.)?

LITERATURE: Commentaries by B. Duhm (1897) and K. Budde (1913); Norbert Peters, 'Das Buch Hiob,' in *Exegetisches Handbuch zum Alten Testament* (Roman Catholic), pp. 144ff.; Paul Bertie, *Le poème de Job*; A. Vilmar, *Collegium biblicum V.I.*, III; F. Baumgärtl, *Der Hiob-Dialog: Aufzug und Deutung* (1933); M. Susman, *Das Hiobproblem bei Franz Kafka* (1935); P. Volz, *Weisheit* (1911); Horace M. Kallen, *The Book of Job as a Greek Tragedy* (New York: Moffat, Yard & Co., 1918); J. Middleton Murry, *To the Unknown God*, pp. 53f., 153f.)

13. THE HIGHER TRUTHFULNESS: PSALM 34: 1-10

1. Nothing can be further from a pessimistic attitude toward life, let alone a nihilistic attitude, than are these verses. They appear in the Psalms and therefore in the *Kethubim*, ('Writings'), the third division of the Hebrew Bible. Here Job and Ecclesiastes have a place, Lamentations and Proverbs, but also the collection of Psalms, and in this

collection these serenely devout verses on the goodness of life. The Psalm is postexilic. It certainly was not originally liturgical; the 'I' that speaks here is the personal 'I,' not the congregation. The first letters of the verses constitute the Hebrew alphabet—for us such formalism means the end of lyricism, but also of religious feeling.

2. The theme is the praise of God, for only in the praise of God does the spiritual life find adequate expression. Now the praise of God, the praising of the Name, is not a contemplation and exaltation of the eternal beauty, of the eternal being. After all, this God is known as God only in his acts, through his Word. And it is therefore very understandable that 'truthfulness' can be a detriment to praise. And in fact the *Kethubim* are full of this: Job submits for a while, and then his submission passes over into complaints and accusations; the Preacher sets down alongside of his scepticism the counsel to listen to God's commandment, for after all, that is still a wise thing to do; here where a boundless discouragement has swept over life, there is not a trace of praise. We have already spoken of how striking it is that this rebellion, complaint, and scepticism, is allowed to stand in the Old Testament; of how the 'hero stories,' contrary to all religious and national tradition, set forth at length the downfall of Solomon, the sins of David; of how the 'royal chronicles' contain no glorification of the dynasty, not even of its 'God' in his form of manifestation (cf. the ignominy suffered by the ark of the covenant). So it is because of similar truthfulness that in the *Kethubim* there is a repression, a forgetting, a neglect of what for Israel should be the most important of all, namely, the praise of God (*Hallelu-Yah* ['let us praise YHWH'] is just as characteristic and all-embracing as the holy syllable *Om* or the phrase *Tat tvam asi* in India)—the praise of God, be it noted, on account of his works which can be seen, which occur in history. The 'works,' as we saw, are not identical with the 'acts' of God.

3. Psalm 34 is a reaction to these reactions; the poet contrasts this truthfulness with another truthfulness. In this very late time, this time of decline and disillusionment and continual frustration, in the midst of dull resignation and dry formalism which hold the field everywhere, he raises the banner of pure praise, of sheer exaltation, of true recognition of God. Not, be it noted, as if he were able to do this as a specialist in this matter, whereas the others were merely betraying the fact that they could not cope with life; nor is he saying that at least he can

444

do so now and that inspired by the moment he had to give lyrical expression to his praise. No, he wants to show what praise is essentially and by nature, everywhere and always—and therefore that it never ceases on earth—and that consequently it is in his mouth 'at all times' (*bekol-'eth*), in his mouth, not that of the congregation, and in his mouth, not only in his heart. He wants to say that this praise is uttered because of the earth, the harvest, daily bread, the air, the sunshine, the water; he wants to say that, though it is uttered because of the earth, the reason behind the praise is nevertheless what has been bestowed upon 'this poor man' (v. 6). For the deeper reason behind this universal praise and love of life is that 'the angel of the Lord encamps around those who fear him, and delivers them.' ('A messenger from Him encamps around his fearful ones and unlooses them.')[1]

From this there follows, from this there flowers the invitation to the others: 'Taste and see that YHWH is good' (v. 8a), and the sweeping assurance—definite as a logical conclusion, simple as a sacred formula, common as a proverbial saying—that 'happy is the man who trusts in him!' So to think and so to live—this is the higher truthfulness. For it is not truthful, it is not honest to refuse to admit that one is often, strictly speaking almost always, happy. Is there not a profound suggestion in what Dostoevski says: 'Actually men are always happy, but they seldom know it.' By the higher standard it is untruthful to act as if our indictment of life always comes from deeper levels of our being than does praise.[2]

4. But then from what depth does praise come? To all appearances it comes out of a happy experience, and as an experience this is just as ambiguous as any other human experience. But beyond this it appears to be an experience with blurred edges; exegesis will not succeed in localizing it biographically. And yet it is an experience on the basis of which others are invited to join in the praise of God: 'Oh magnify YHWH with me, and let us exalt his Name together!' (v. 3). This is very strange. Would it not be more natural to say, 'You too can have such experiences, and when you have them, you will understand why I am now praising God'? It is true that following verse 12 there is a passage of instruction which is akin to the *chokma*, the wisdom literature,

[1] Martin Buber, *Das Buch der Preisungen*.
[2] We refer the reader to Barth's anthropology and his statement concerning gratitude as the ontological structure of humanity, *Church Dogmatics*, Vol. III, pt. 2, pp. 169ff.

or more precisely, to the so-called 'optimism' of the book of Proverbs. It is true that it presupposes a congregation which knows about these things in other ways and from other times; it speaks of the 'meek' ('the afflicted,' v. 2) and the 'righteous,' of the 'saints' of YHWH (v. 10). It is true that there appears to be a group of 'the quiet in the land' who cannot and do not want to offer resistance to the cunning and violence of the self-willed world. Can it be that, after all, this is being addressed to a conventicle? It must be remembered, however, that whereas Psalm 32 : 10 was still saying, 'Many are the pangs of the wicked,' it is precisely this psalm which says that 'many are the afflictions of the righteous' (i.e., those who stand in right relationship to God)—so that happiness in the abstract, even in a 'spiritual' sense, is out of the question. And furthermore we must bear in mind how sweeping the statements are, not only in the didactic section but also in the opening section up to and including verse 10 (or v. 8). And finally, it should be remembered that this originally personal utterance was admitted into the temple liturgy. 'The single exception proves the rule' (Gunkel).

5. The mystery of the praise of YHWH is above all religion and is the pure and sufficient defence against nihilism, 'genuine' or 'ungenuine,' the nihilism of the mind, the deed, or the mood. It is God's nature to respond, it is his character to save men out of all their troubles (v. 6), it is the crown of his activity to help me, us, all men out of misery. The praise of God is awakened by the experience, but it is so little dependent upon it that the experience at the same time brings to light the extent to which it is continually present in the congregation. Again and again the praise of God is sung first by the individual, but he is only the *chazzan*, the precentor of a congregation which is already filled with this praise, and it in turn is the representative of the humanity which is constantly joining in this praise from afar off, even though unconsciously. This is a great, a peculiar mystery. Therefore the words: Magnify YHWH with me!

The compilers and the redactor of the book of Psalms were already aware of this mystery, and it received expression in the title which the book finally acquired. The subdivisions of the book close with doxologies, and the whole concludes with a Psalm 'without content,' namely, a Psalm which is exclusively a doxology, a hymn. This is not to say that there are not laments and 'Psalms of vengeance,' thanksgiving songs and didactic poems, and among them here and there a *tehillah* ('praise')—rather the whole book is called *Tehillim*. God's virtues and acts march on victoriously, they flow out of a victory which fundamentally has already been won, even before God's battle to save and to protect his fallen and threatened creation has begun. Therefore even the laments and the pondering of the enigmas are in principle a praising of God. We are permitted to complain and lament over the riddles of life before this God. We are permitted to take all these things to him. We are permitted to expect that he is willing to concern himself with them. This is precisely what is not permitted with the gods, the godhead, nature! His covenant is established for ever; therefore there is a song—shadowed and unshadowed—even in the laments and the ponderings of life as it actually is.[3]

The praise of God is wonder and amazement over his Name, which is near and present in his acts. It is praise not of the good days but of the Lord of all the days, the king of the ages.

It is very strange that Fritz Mauthner at the end of his history of atheism in the West speaks of 'peace in a mysticism without God' and cites as an example of this peace the quiet, radical piety 'that accepts everything.' According to Mauthner, simple people have always loved this kind of mysticism. In my opinion, this is to overrate and also misinterpret this quietism. In any case, for the Psalmist there is no such thing as a uniformly indifferent acceptance of fortunate and unfortunate events. He knows of himself and of others that always and everywhere YHWH hears, and that therefore the burden of life, even the burden of the devout life, is taken from him. In a universe in which someone hears, in which God hears, i.e., acts, the dominion of existence is broken and along with it the care and anxiety of emptiness and the curse of weariness. But Mauthner is right about one thing, namely, that in this knowledge light and darkness, weal and woe become relative. The road of the Name is lined with people who stand there

---

[3] The old rhymed version of the Psalms, which is still used in the churches of Holland, uses the following words in Psalm 150: *zo menig blijk van zijn heerlijk Koninkrijk* ('so many signs of his glorious kingdom'). But what is meant is the whole of his acts. Therefore the new paraphrase by Martinus Nijhoff is so genuine. We repeat it here in the original because its terseness and preciseness is inimitable: *Looft God, looft Hem overal | Looft den Koning van 't heelal | om zijn wonderbare macht, | om de heerlijkheid en kracht | van zijn naam en eeuwig wezen. | Looft de daden groot en goed, | die Hij triomferend doet; | Hem zij eer, Hij zij geprezen.*

with the light burden of their woe, rejoicing and exulting as at the proclamation, the entry of a king (cf. Pss. 24; 68 : 7f., 24f.).[4]

6. Added to this there is another important correction of our Western concept of praise. We dare not overlook the fact that the Hebrew verb really means 'to bless.' It is true that we must not conclude from this that man blesses in his way as YHWH does in his, so that there is a correlation, a mutual dependence; nevertheless the word 'to bless,' to bless God, takes on from our word something of the character of 'pure' praise. Blessed be YHWH! Here again Kohlbrügge proves his affinity to the Old Testament: 'When someone blesses, this is tantamount to his saying: Thou art the one . . . upon thee must all honour and all felicity come, thou has a right to it. All that is mine, everything, I have, I lay upon thee, thou must prosper.'[5] Blessing God is therefore the abiding background of every attitude of fervour or weariness. Praise is part of the very nature of human life which has been touched by the Name, because always and everywhere there can be in our hearts the impulse to wish good fortune, prosperity, victory, and honour for God's way in this world. It is untruthful not to want to recognize this impulse that slumbers within us and that could work out into a permanent orientation of 'all that is within me' (Ps. 103 : 1) to the praise of God.

7. Humanly speaking, there is a great deal that is negative said about life and about God because of truthfulness. It takes a higher truthfulness to impel us to go beyond this judgment and overarch it with the blessing, the praise of YHWH, who is making his way through this world—this world which has been and still is sown with blessings which for us are nothing less than signs of hope.

There is little chance of holding in check the latent nihilism within us if we religiously accustom ourselves to measure out praise according to our own experience. In the Old Testament, it is true, room is left for amazement, exasperation, doubt, and bitterness. But the truthfulness of all these reactions is not a self-contained thing; it depends in

[4] Fritz Mauthner, *Der Atheismus und seine Geschichte im Abendlande*, IV, 397, distinguishes three parties with three watchwords: *Te Deum laudamus, Te Deum accusamus, Te Deum negamus*. 'The *accusers* of their God are perhaps so *addicted to religion* that they cannot get along without a god. . . . The good souls (they say, "Whatever God does is right") . . . but they do not know that in their happy, fervent faith they are standing almost on the same ground as the most recent atheism' (p. 398). See also pp. 444ff.
[5] *Schriftauslegungen* (repr. 1925), Heft 22, p. 2.

the last analysis upon another, higher truthfulness. One man in one case experiences liberation, receives it from Him whose way is the way of the liberation of this world. And he does not keep silent about it. And this is the way it should be! So it should always be; we must not keep silent about the better side of things. In the experience of this man there is always an admixture of hope. To him it is not merely a feeling. What was bestowed upon him in that experience stands as a part for the whole, it is a pledge of the Kingdom. He does not forget it, for in all eternity the future can never bring him more than this taste of the goodness of God. He speaks of it 'at all times' also because it is possible for everyone in the congregation to know that what he experienced is intended for all to experience and to know.

Everything closes up, door after door, horizon after horizon, if existence is by nature solitary and alone. Everything opens up, door after door, vista after vista, if existence is by nature sustained, liberated, and saved. Because all this is true, it is no exaggeration to say: I will praise God at all times (*bekol-'eth*), I will praise him always (*tamid*). And therefore it would be a lie, in a tragic and culpable sense, not to be essentially a praiser.[6]

LITERATURE: H. Gunkel, *Psalmenkommentar*, 1926; *Einleitung in die Psalmen* (*Göttinger Handkommentar zum Alten Testament*), 1933, pp. 318f., 363ff.; B. D. Eerdmans, *The Hebrew Book of Psalms*, 1946; J. de. Groot, *De Psalmen*, 1942; H. Herkenne, *Das Buch der Psalmen*, 1935; J. J. Stamm, 'Ein Vierteljahrhundert Psalmenforschung,' *Theologische Rundschau*, 1955, pp. 9ff.

[6] Cf. Theodor Haecker, '*Theodizee*,' *Schöpfer und Schöpfung*, I, p. 82: 'Is it not a false modesty to keep silent about the fact that there is nothing of which we are so sure, that there is nothing that we have experienced with such certainty as the love of God? God knows that very many could give this testimony today in the depths of misery, and still do not do so. This silence concerning the highest existence is a great evil. The fraud of a man's saying that he sees things which he does not see, because they do not exist, is a mere trifle compared with the stubborn lie which a man perpetrates when he says that he does not see things which he actually does see in secret.'

14. LIGHT IS SWEET: ECCLESIASTES 11:7

1. Ecclesiastes is also included among the Writings, the third division of the Old Testament witnesses. It stands on the borderline—and yet not in the sense that one can play off its scepticism against the knowledge of God and throw its pessimism into the balance over against the messianic faith in the future. Many modern philosophers and writers, like Huxley, Sartre, Jaspers, Camus, Greshoff, and Du Perron, have expressed their affinity with Ecclesiastes. This is seldom found in the church and the synagogue, and naturally not at all in the 'fourth man.' It has, however, a very strong vitality among those who have been called the 'third man,' and this, it would appear to us, for the simple reason that he has participated, though in the weakened form of reflection, in Israel's way and struggle as it is reflected, affirmed, and continued in Christianity.

The 'third man,' after all, also began his life's journey seeing that his life is subject to the one Name that unites all heaven and earth. But on this way he was also given something extra, namely, a world view, a philosophy of life, oriented upon the Name. This above all was to serve him as a defence against the 'powers,' his armour against the gods; and this was also the metamorphosis of the Torah for Christian practice. And when all this sooner or later begins to go to pieces, then this 'third man' begins to understand something of Ecclesiastes. We should therefore not try to talk him out of his fits of pessimism and not mishandle his sclerosis and his scepticism.

For it turns out that often he is not really doubting Israel's God, but rather a general idea of the godhead and its laws. His scepticism and his pessimism also frequently find expression in commonplaces. And he must be led away from this, through preaching and instruction—into the freedom of the faith which is peculiar and by its nature indubitable, or into the scepticism which really grows out of the peculiar disillusionment and therefore the peculiar expectation which is uniquely Israel's. For this kind of scepticism need not be existentially in conflict with faith; it can even be a legitimate way in which faith exists—indeed, in a certain sense, be its crown.

2. We note first that Ecclesiastes is among the five *Megilloth*, that it is

the prescribed scroll for *Sukkoth*, the Feast of Tabernacles, or Booths. On this festival the wandering through the wilderness is remembered. The story is retold and carried beyond its conclusions. Did not Israel go back through the wilderness again after the wilderness years, but with fewer signs and wonders than occurred the first time with its pillars of cloud and fire, the manna, and the water from the rock? Is it not now a road through the desert prepared and occupied by men—judges and kings, priests and prophets? And when one pursues all this in memory, so that one's 'thoughts multiply with oneself' (Ps. 94 : 19 in the Old Dutch translation), one comes into discussion with another doubter (Ecclesiastes was probably familiar with passages from Greek pessimists). In earlier times a stronger (i.e., a more believing) generation had dared to argue with YHWH (e.g., Jer. 12 : 1f.); but now men live in an *ecumene* of scepticism, and they argue with each other. And even today men discuss and dispute among themselves and with themselves; in the newspapers and on the radio everything is talked to pieces and then glued together again. The sight of this patched-up, glued-together mess is nauseating, and what remains is a weariness, an enormous weariness.

And what creeps in, even into the world of the 'third man,' this Christian man who is still really a Christian and not yet a man who has not been bowled over and turned topsy-turvy, is emptiness, boredom, nausea. And in that mood the words of Ecclesiastes sound precisely right: 'All is vanity' (3 : 1), man and beast have the same breath and their fate is the same (3 : 19), the wise are ignored and fools are set on thrones (10 : 6), knowledge only serves to increase sorrow (1 : 18), and 'man goes to his eternal home' (the grave or the realm of the dead, 12 : 5). It would be better to quarrel and haggle with God, but there is not enough strength of faith for this. And so it all seems to run out into the dead end of cool or bitter diagnosis.

3. Nevertheless Ecclesiastes is neither a 'genuine' nor an 'ungenuine' nihilist. He believes in God, that is to say, in YHWH; he has long since ceased to believe in the godhead. He does not retire to rest in his subjectivism. He rather reckons with the existence of a Constant outside of himself and beyond his reach (hence suddenly we are confronted with the 'positive' statements and admonitions which give the expositors so much trouble). True, he had fallen into despair (2 : 20f.), but he had considered time and that everything has and must have its

time (3 : 1ff.). True, he had said that everything seemed futile to him, but he distrusts the man who wants by every conceivable means to make life worth living. And what does he have left? There is no mention at all of the cult nor really of prayer either. There is no trace of a Messiah or a Messianic figure or a 'remnant that returns.' There is not a hint of hope for the nearness of God in the future of the peoples or God's people or even today in the hearts of men.

And yet, half stubbornly and half shamefacedly, he avoids mentioning the holy Name! What does this mean? It is as among us where the 'third man' occasionally utters a tepid form of the Name of God like Lord, providence, heaven. But when he says this, he still does not mean Woden or merely the moral order. He means what still lingers in his heart or his head, but what for the sake of good manners he will not come right out and mention by name; 'naturally' he means 'the good God,' *le bon Dieu*. He has a dim notion that the development which things have taken and the hiddenness of God are somehow a part of the fate of his soul. 'I will be present as I will be present' (Exod. 3 : 14); and this means that He may also be present in the far country, in alienation from him, in the 'eclipse of God.' Thus these tepid forms of the Name of God are to be interpreted as a shamefaced mental reservation.

And just because cult, prayer, Messiah, etc. are a part of the 'Name,' one cannot speak of them if one intends quite radically to get along without them, for one cannot dissimulate as if one saw or heard something vis-à-vis the Name (as long as it still remains a vis-à-vis). But one also cannot go on to total denial, for this would stultify the fruitful purpose of the denial and the mental reservation would become sterile. So what does Ecclesiastes have left? Life! 'Never before did I love life so much,' said one as he walked home past the fragrant trees after the doctor told him he had not long to live. Onward! What is there left to go on to? 'Light is sweet, and it is pleasant for the eyes to behold the sun.' Life is precious precisely because it is so brief; it is so poignantly lovely because it seems to be vanity; but one never quite accepts this vanity of life; for if one did accept it fully, life would lose its splendour, even its vain splendour; a poet, a servant of beauty, for example, who plays the radical pessimist is at bottom a shameless hypocrite. Love of life is generally not deepened by disillusionment. It is the characteristic of the disillusionment which God brings to us that a man begins to love life ever more deeply and freely as the realm in which, hoping against hope (Rom. 4 : 18), he expects that IT will happen.

4. 'Light is sweet.' This saying will be turned into a trivial platitude if we do not (however we identify Ecclesiastes) take into account the fact that then and through the centuries it is Israel that says this: Onward! After the oppression in Egypt and after the journey through the wilderness and after the confusion in Palestine and after the failure of the princes and after the apostasy to the Baalim, after the exile—onward! And then what? A lustreless restoration and the diaspora and the pogroms. And what then? Well, there stands the 'eternal people,' saying like a child: 'Behold, the light is sweet.' As no other people Israel clings to life. For the Old Testament suicide is in no sense a problem; and the anti-Semites must play the very devil to drive a Jew to this completely un-Israelitic act of giving up his life. No one can prove that there is anything else or anything more behind this than an untamed vitality or an ordinary clinging to life. No one can prove that this joyful salutation to the light is merely a last Messianic gesture. He who has known the Name—'I will be what I will be' (Exod. 3 : 14), I am what I do in my history with you, I am present even in my absence, present in the footprints of my acts, which no one has fully understood because they are occurring in constant succession and are always going onward, and only at the end will one learn what the continuing duration of the Name means—he who has known the Name knows something of what it must mean to be oppressed and violated, to be robbed of every sign of God's nearness, without becoming satirical, and to say without any irony but also without any cupidity, without any senile clutching after the pitiful remainders of sensation: This life, which is now so incomprehensible, has me in its grip. This is not paganism (though sometimes it is deceptively like it) only because the 'grip of life' is really the way in which YHWH holds his own in expectation; for He too, in His way, holds on to this earthly life with an intensity that shows that he has something great and wonderful in store for it.

5. 'It is pleasant for the eyes to behold the sun'—therefore 'go, eat your bread with enjoyment, and drink your wine with a merry heart . . . enjoy life with the wife whom you love' (9 : 7ff.). Clothe yourself in white garments and anoint your head; let life be simple

and festive, let its simplicity itself be festive. And do this every day! For what is offered to us hour by hour and breath by breath is the 'one opportunity.'

Should we then finally stand up before God and ourselves and say that hedonism is the most profound attitude toward life? No, the 'toil under the sun' goes on, and we are even admonished to take it seriously: 'Whatever your hand finds to do, do it with your might' (9 : 10) —altogether earnestly, but not nervously, but rather with a light hand, without much pressure, and not without the light of the Sabbath running through it all. 'The world is being ruined by industriousness' (the title of a Flemish novel)—is this true? Perhaps not the world, but more likely the Western mind; but quite certainly faith and good works are being ruined—these will not tolerate such an emphasis, such a burdensome weight.[1]

6. In the end what does Ecclesiastes do? How does he fill up his time—I mean now, spiritually, as a scion and servant of Israel? For one who believes in 'eternal recurrence' this question is not urgent. But how can one manage to go on living in the long-drawn-out expectation of Israel (which one says nothing about but still holds on to) with so little to do? Well, there is the sun upon one's bread and cup, wife, home, and work—but what if this 'meagre' portion is not merely an automatic filling up of one's time but the spiritual meaning of life itself? The answer is that precisely when this meagre portion is spiritually lived, Ecclesiastes with his wisdom commends to us a life which is an anticipation of the time to come when every man 'shall sit under his vine and under his fig tree' (Micah 4 : 4) and invite his neighbour to sit there with him. This would be heavenly banality—'this-worldly eternity.' This lands us in the Elysian fields, the idyll, the peace at which all modern pagans turn up their noses and in which the nihilists would really be utterly bored. Ecclesiastes, although (as has already been said) a 'decadent' spirit, still has a sense of the 'primitive.' It would be quite alien to him to separate soul and body, spiritual and natural light, eternity and time, duration and the moment. 'Onward,' he says and crosses a boundary within the totality of existence. True, this is not much, especially as far as possible knowledge is concerned, but he sees, he accepts, he blesses the light, he abides in its beams which to him are a testimony—a testimony not so much that he should go on seeking

[1]Cf. Paul Häberlin, *Das Gute*, pp. 220f.

but rather that he should go on enjoying and precisely therein hold on to his hope.

7. 'Onward!' We do go onward, though perhaps in doing so we get farther away from home. At the Feast of Booths every Israelite sits in his garden in a wooden shelter. The roof is made of primitively constructed lattice-work with branches and leaves twined upon it. Inside are placed flowers and titbits, and in this simple banquet hall he sits with his children, his family, his friends. But at the end of the feast—as if not to cover up in any way what *galuth* ('exile'), dispersion, nomadic existence, what the time when there are no prophets and wonders, the time of God's hiddenness in the coming stage will mean —the festival scroll is opened, and what is read is—Ecclesiastes.[2] Life is vanity, and what philosophy devises when it seeks by words, words, and more words to show that the powers and gods are harmless is in vain. Nevertheless we go on—in great ignorance, knowing the travesty of the Name, in great ignorance, knowing only this portion of history in which there are no wonders, which must nevertheless be an application of the mystery in the words 'I will be with you as I will be with you' (Exod. 3 : 14), even though our basis for this is only a poor, ambiguous, almost negative experience!

Therefore at times (and perhaps they are not our worst times) we are almost genuine nihilists, who are in truth ungenuine, yet (as we found) always genuine in their humanness and honesty. Therefore something tremendous can happen in a man's heart when he wakes up some evil morning to find that he has nothing and believes nothing any more (for everything takes too long) with no affirmation and no purpose except this: ' "Light is sweet, and it is pleasant for the eyes to behold the sun." Or, "Never before did I love life so much," because

---

[2] Cf. Franz Rosenzweig, *Der Stern der Erlösung*, III, p. 73: 'The old man who, in the name of the congregation, is in charge of this transition (i.e. from the last reading of the Torah on the last day of Sukkoth [Feast of Booths] to the first reading of the festival of "Rejoicing in the Law") is not called "husband of the Torah," but through all time goes by the name of "bridegroom of the Torah." It is not without good cause that the book full of corroding doubt, Ecclesiastes, is assigned to be read at the Feast of Booths. The disenchantment which follows upon the Sabbath the moment its fragrance has been breathed for the last time and the weekday asserts itself in all its unbroken strength is, as it were, included in the festival itself through the reading of Ecclesiastes. Although the Feast of Booths celebrates redemption and rest, it is nevertheless the festival of wandering through the wilderness.' Tr. Nahum N. Glatzer, *Franz Rosenzweig: His Life and Thought* (New York: Schocken Books, 1961), p. 325.

for me, the individual, it is so bitterly brief, and also because sometimes
a sudden suspicion almost breaks through my despair and tells me that
time cannot merely be a static vacuum or an endless cycle, but must
rather be a prelude to a totally different time, whose "voice we carry
within us as a liberating, redeeming word," which one day will resolve
the dissonances of the dispersion "in thy mighty harmony." '

Can one cherish such a repressed hope? Can a man live in this way,
without disbelieving his unbelief and doubting his own doubt? Can a
man see this light without naming the God whom he does not name,
without loving the unutterable Name with sighs too deep for words?
Is it not possible to recast these signs into the language of a smile?
Is it possible so to celebrate and rejoice in the sun and the summer
without acknowledging God? Objectively, it is impossible! The nature
of man is thanksgiving, gratitude that God has 'separated the light
from darkness' (Gen. 1 : 4). The nature of man remains receptive to
this primeval act of God. He has the freedom at least to regard the
light in this sense as an 'extra value.' What does Paul Gerhardt say?

> My heart for gladness springs,
> It cannot more be said;
> For very joy it laughs and sings,
> Sees naught but sunshine glad.
> The sun that lights mine eyes
> Is Christ the Lord I love;
> I sing for joy of that which lies
> Stored up for me above.[3]

The only thing that concerns us here is that even these lofty strains do
not imply a flight from the world, that this hymn clings to the light of
the earth, that the light is to be welcomed as a messenger of the salvation which lies beyond our experience, which is an act of faith and
springs from what is 'stored' up in heaven. Ecclesiastes cannot rise to
such a salutation. But he certainly knows more of the mystery of this
'natural' light than he is able to say.

8. Should we, for the sake of achieving a rounded whole, ignore verse
8? This we shall not do, though it is never wise to light all sides of a
thing at the same time. But here we are confronted with the directly
opposite side: 'If a man lives many years and rejoices in them all,
let him [also] remember the days of darkness, for these will be many.'

---

[3] Last stanza of 'Ist Gott für mich, so trete . . .,' tr. Catherine Winkworth.—Tr.]

Does this note mean that we now fall back into the old bitterness again? No, we are not falling back, we remain in the same insecure, nomadic existence. But we will not admit that death has gained the ascendancy over life in our hearts;[4] it would not be true; in any case it would be untruthful. 'The light is sweet'—this is not retracted. In any case the man will have had many days on which he could rejoice. But he will not simply live for the present; he will be wise to remember today that there will be other days; life has and retains its dark side, its mortal boundary, and also its mental decline and the extinction of vitality.

Such a way of thinking lacks the fullness of Christ, who says that, by virtue of the presence of the Father's care, we should live for today (Matt. 6 : 34); but it is a precise reproduction of the experience of the light. So it is with light, with its sweetness, but above all so it is also with sadness. Honesty is the best policy, and he who is honest already in this world has (not the highest, but) an enduring song to sing 'as long as he lives' (Ps. 146 : 2).

9. 'All that has come is vanity.'[5] This cannot be said if for us the

[4] Cf. Franz Rosenzweig's obituary of Rabbi Nehemiah A. Nobel, 'The Thinker,' whose last sermons were on Ecclesiastes (*Kleinere Schriften*, pp. 50ff.): 'For him the puzzling questions of human freedom, the existence of God, the reality of the world remained enigmas which he repeatedly pursued but never answered in the solitude of his study, and to which answers and solutions were given to him only as he stood in the pulpit before the crowds in his synagogue. For it is the mystery of these ultimate questions that we know their solution only when we must know them, when it is demanded of us, demanded by those who have a right to demand it of us. But he was human and honest enough even in these highest moments in his—and our—life when the divine answer sprang to his lips, not to forget and not to want to forget how answerless he had been when he asked the question before. He never regarded the gift of God, which he was called upon to communicate in such a moment, as his own possession, which he would later parade as if he "had" the solution. He did not "have" it, but he was permitted to give it' (p. 51). Cf. Thomas Mann, *The Magic Mountain*, tr. H. T. Lowe-Porter (New York: Modern Library, 1932), pp. 625f., where Hans Castorp says: 'I will . . . remember that faith with death and the dead is evil, is hostile to humankind, so soon as we give it power over thought and action. . . . I will let death have no mastery over my thoughts. For therein lies the goodness and love of mankind, as in nothing else. . . .'

[5] C. Ch. Aalders in his commentary (pp. 239f.) provides a good survey of the more or less possible translations of this passage. H. W. Hertzberg relates it to 'all the future.' A. Allgeier would have it relate back to life, namely, to personal human life, 'corresponding to the fact that it [too] has come to futility.' V. Zapletal suggests that this may be a gloss. It seems best to follow Allgeier's alternative view: 'all that has come'= 'all that has happened.' And yet this could ignore the peculiar accent of the word

light is a direct reflection of the light of the Revelation of YHWH. And it also seems to retract Ecclesiastes' salutation of the light as a Messianic gesture. And the counsel to enjoy life and do whatever the hand finds to do also loses the splendour that fell upon it for a moment through this negative judgment upon the whole of the past, upon the whole of life. That the future will be dark, and dark primarily because the past will prove to have been futile—this is in direct contradiction to the truth of the Name and the truthfulness of His deeds. The prophets are against it. 'That day will be different, above the thick darkness and above the good light' (cf. Isa. 60 : 1f.; Zech. 14 : 6). But on the level of our experience this whispered word of despair uttered by Ecclesiastes can and perhaps must be uttered; just on this level we may speak of 'chance' and 'fate.' The 'days' arose and became, or grew and came—but none of this, nothing that we have undertaken or seen undertaken has ever been sufficient for fulfilment. Kohlbrügge once said that we should note that the light of the gospel shines unobscured in a particular area only for a generation; then come the days of darkness, and they last a long time.[6] How long, for example, did the message of the Reformation retain its pure sound? 'All that has come'—is this too included?—has come and gone. *Habel-habalim, hakkol habel!* This too? But is not such an assertion a cry from the depths? Is it not the reason why there is no mention of the name of God here, since it is clear that these circumstances simply do not allow it to be spoken? Does it not have in it the implicit challenge to show himself in his original life of action in history in order that in the midst of disillusionment men may experience the full joy of being shown to be wrong by a new act of God which will drive this disillusionment from the field?

We do not acquire life in the light (either 'literally' or 'spiritually'!); we shall inherit it. Our 'part in this life' is our participation in all of life. And therefore we go on living secretly in hope and say, seemingly resignedly, even a bit frivolously, but always consciously (and yet simply, as a child!): We go on; the light is sweet and it is pleasant for the eyes to see the sun. And that remains valid and effectual, and the famous last chapter (12) is linked with this.

'coming' as referring to what is done by human beings (cf. 1 : 4: 'A generation goes, and another generation comes').

[6] Cf. Fritz Horn, *Der Prediger Salomo*, p. 255.

Minneboden, machtig licht,
lieve zonnestralen,
mochte ik ooit een boodschap doen
en er dank van halen,
zoo gij, zonne, er dank van haalt,
doende mij, verrezen,
boodschap, dat het morgen, en
dag nog eens zal wezen.

Dag is uwe liefde mij,
laat den nevel nijgen,
God, en eer 't nog langer lijdt
dag en dauw bedrijgen.
Minneboden, machtig licht
Alle ellende lavend,
Boodschapt mij den goeden dag,
Nooit en zij 't meer avond.

(Messengers of love, mighty light,
lovely rays of sunshine,
may I ever proclaim the message
which is the message of thanksgiving,
as thou, O sun, dost proclaim thanks,
announcing to me
the message that morning
and day shall come again.

Day is thy love for me,
let the mist depart,
God, and before much longer
let the day and the dew shine.
Messengers of love, mighty light,
all misery assuaging,
proclaims to me that good day,
which will never see its evening).

So says Guido Gezelle,[7] and for a moment here too there is no distinction between 'spiritual' and 'material' light. If only this affirmation of life may continue as a response to the light, then even our past

[7] Flemish poet, 1830–99.

459

will one day, when it has become completely past, be good and sweet:

> totdat, o God, naar U gewend,
> mijn duisternis den dag erkent
> en ziende U met mijn oogen dicht
> ik asem hale in 't zonnelicht.
> (Until, O God, turned to thee,
> my darkness discerns thy day
> and seeing thee close by,
> I draw my breath in the light of the sun).

10. Should we quarrel further with Ecclesiastes over his negativism, or weigh his words and divide them up, saying, this is devout and that is nihilistic? True. we find ourselves here at the margin of the *Kethubim*, among the reactions to the Word of God which can hardly be called genuine. But is it not more important, especially for the interpreter and witness, to remember that these dark and sombre words are in the Bible, that this split and lonely soul is one of the speakers in the canon of the Holy Scriptures? Undoubtedly he is there because of what he says about the light (and his words are interpreted as a disguised Messianic gesture,) but also in spite of (and because of) his honesty, which he devoted to becoming a prophetic power against the high-sounding talk of religion.[8] Here a man who is poor in spirit, a beggar for the Spirit, is accepted and in a very secret way brought home to the covenant of YHWH with his disheartened creation. 'It may be that your hopelessness, you children of Ecclesiastes, you disconsolate in the midst of the soundly Christian multitude, is nothing else but a reflex of your deep faith in God. . . . It is possible that you, that you may be the very ones who are being incorporated in the lay apostolate of *certainty*.'[9] And apparently this certainty has no other basis in experience except the certainty that the light is sweet and it is pleasant for the eyes to see the sun.

What is the ending of Gustav Mahler's 'Song of the Earth'? 'Everywhere the beloved earth bursts into bloom and grows green again in the spring, and everlasting blue lights the distant skies.'

---

[8] H. J. Schoeps, 'Franz Kafka oder der Glaube in der tragischen Position,' in *Gestalten an der Zeitenwende*, pp. 61ff.

[9] K. H. Miskotte, *De vreemde Vrijspraak*, p. 55; cf. pp. 57, 321. Cf. Middleton Murry, *To the Unknown God*, pp. 78f.; Erich Auerbach, *Mimesis*, p. 294 (on Montaigne).

Epilogue

LIFE AND LIGHT: PSALM 36:9 AND JOHN 1:1A, 4

1. In what sense can one say that our undertaking to allow the Old Testament to speak for itself in the way we have here set forth is 'Christian instruction' (cf. above pp. 76ff)? To what extent is a very definite and yet somewhat different view of the abiding importance of the Old Testament here given its proper place (cf. above pp. 169ff)? We have spoken of the 'unity' of the Testaments in a sense that is different from the usual one and stated that, along with a 'deficit' there is a 'surplus.' Indeed, no secret has been made of the fact that the New Testament used in isolation needs to be corrected on the basis of the fundamental words of the Old Testament. The purpose of the entire study has been to put atheism and religion on the same level and to contrast them both with the faith of Israel, and to do this on the ground that the Word actually occurs, whereas the gods cloak themselves in the silence which is their essential nature. The action of the Word presupposes the 'Name,' and the unique character of the Name can be known and encountered only in history, in the 'holy' history which, as we saw, actualizes itself in the 'authority' and the 'outgoing' of the proclamation among the peoples (see above pp. 303ff).

At the close of this third part of our study the question again arises to what extent this deserves to be called 'Christian' instruction—the more so since we have concurred with the opinion that synagogue and church, despite their schism, together represent the one congregation of God (p. 78).

2. In order to arrive at a fundamental understanding, we venture to point to the prologue of the Gospel of John. A single clue gained from this point of view is sufficient to indicate at least the direction which our thinking must take in this matter. This is not the place to go into the questions of the provenience, the meaning, the reinterpretation, and application of the Logos concept. The view of Schlatter, Schnie-

wind, and Bultmann that verse 1 must be read in the light of verse 14 and that the word *houtos* ('this one'; 'this one was in the beginning with God') has an anticipatory sense, is one that is convincing to us. Jesus Christ, his person and his work, his priestly and kingly work, is the theme of the whole prologue.

Starting with his epiphany, the prologue looks up and looks back to his origin, the reason for his presence among us. He who 'dwelt among us' is the Word, the Address, the Speech which goes out from God and which by its nature, character, and purpose can be called divine.[1] However this may be understood in detail, we are not here being referred back to some kind of cosmological supermundane space or anteroom. Rather we find ourselves in the midst of an adoring contemplation of the mystery of God's humanity on earth—or if you will, in the contemplation of the 'significance' of the act of God in Christ. (Is this term *Logos* adequate? We need not dwell upon this question in our connection. Bultmann says that 'the idea of God is . . . determined from the outset by the idea of revelation. To speak of God means to speak of his revelation; and to speak of revelation means to speak of God. And here revelation is not meant in a general sense, but rather as the saving will of God perceivable in the Revealer made flesh.')[2] Speculations concerning the hypostatic union, even if they were legitimate and unavoidable, could only divert us from the essential point here in our reflection upon the relationship of the Old and the New Testament. Therefore we shall not deal with verse 1b. Here we are concerned with the anthropological connection between Word, life, and light (v. 4). And for the moment we shall also leave out of account the problem of the possible Semitic concept of *logos*, *rhema*, except to say that it is probable that we must look for the model of the Johannine Logos in the Targum rather than in Philo.[3]

[1] Cf. Luther's sermon on John 1:1-3 (*WA* 46, pp. 531ff., Eng. tr., *Luther's Works*, 22, 5ff.); O. Procksch and G. Kittel in *Theologisches Wörterbuch zum Neuen Testament*, IV, 89ff.; G. Sevenster, *De Christologie van het Nieuwe Testament* (1946), pp. 224ff.; E. L. Smelik, *De weg van het Woord*, pp. 18f., and esp. the theological survey on pp. 21ff.; Rudolf Bultmann, 'Der Begriff des Wortes Gottes im Neuen Testament,' in *Glauben und Verstehen*, I, pp. 268ff.

[2] Rudolf Bultmann, *Das Evangelium des Johannes*, p. 18.

[3] Adolf Schlatter, *Die Sprache und Heimat des vierten Evangelisten* (1902), p. 14: 'The interpretation of Proverbs 8 as referring to the divine Word is a settled possession of the teacher who is speaking in M. [=*Mechilta*], for whom the Torah is the Word of God identical with the divine wisdom.' See also Karl Bornhäuser, *Das Johannes-*

3. When Jesus Christ is called 'the' Word and his time is identified with God's time, with the direction of God's eternal purposes upon our time, human time, then this means that the 'Name' and the 'salvation,' the sovereign power and history have become one in him. He is the Living One as God is the Living One; that is to say, he exists 'in the manner of God, and therefore prior to all else that exists, not grounded upon any other, referred to no other existence or support.' But this also means that he exists 'in the manner of a man,' that is, 'in the freedom and power of such a being as divinely determined and limited and thus in the relative dependence of a single member in the natural and historical nexus of the created world.' The witness of this life implies that whoever and whatever else may exist previously or subsequently does so with this One 'in inviolable and indissoluble co-existence.'[4] But then this co-existence of being in which all of us are included whether we know it or not is by its nature not merely a fact, but a speaking fact, an address, a promise, a liberation. It can be transmitted through speech, it can be proclaimed, because it is already speech, purposeful speech directed to a goal, speech which creates community and clarity. The fact that God is with us—this is the mystery which is already implicit in the creation of man. The mystery expresses itself in the world, antecedent to every interpretation of it. The fact that Jesus lives (and not merely lived in the past)—this means John intends to say, that the deepest, most direct speech proceeds from him; it means that in him history and prophecy are inseparably and distinctly one. His act carries its meaning within itself, and likewise his speech carries its meaning within itself; but the act enters into the light of his speech and his speech enters into the light of his act. He is the *dabar* ('speech,' 'word,' 'fact'), the life which is a deed, which is also a deed which is a word, the event which has its own light, the light which

---

evangelium eine Missionsschrift für Israel (1928), p. 7: 'When the Israelite read the first sentence in his Greek Bible . . . he heard in it the praise of the Torah. Through it Yahweh created the universe.' Bornhäuser also refers to the Septuagint text of Ps. 119 : 43, 89, 142. Whether one can speak of a 'Toralogy,' however, seems doubtful to us; we fear that this is pushing a construction too far. To be sure, it is rather striking that the life- and light-giving aspects of the Torah are so highly extolled in a popular book like that of Ecclesiasticus (cf. however the references which already appear in Ps. 119 : 54, 105). C. H. Dodd, *The Background of the Fourth Gospel* (1935), pp. 10, 35ff.
[4] Karl Barth, *Church Dogmatics*, Vol. IV, pt. 3: 1, pp. 39f.

is a new light (and yet a light which only confirms the given event) and therefore the light which becomes an event and thus a blessing to the peoples. He bears the Name which bears within it all history. Here we should recall the comprehensive concept of 'being in act' which we set forth above in part two, especially the analysis of the basic word *ma'aseh* which we developed there (pp. 191 ff.).

Therefore when we extend the *munus duplex* and make it a *munus triplex* by adding the 'prophetic office' of Christ, so much depends upon our being open to the corrective which makes it clear that this third office is, after all, really the 'third dimension' of the life of Christ, namely, his perfect, eternal co-existence with God of which we spoke above. Otherwise the term *munus propheticum*, the prophetic office, leads us to ascribe to him a kind of abstract 'teaching office' and thus to forget that what is involved here is the self-witness of him who as the reconciliation is also the revelation, and as the revelation is also the reconciliation. Here the unutterable Name is manifest as being identical with the speech which upholds all things (Heb. 1 : 3).

4. If one wishes to speak of a prophetic office, then the distinction between it and the Old Testament prophecy should be apparent. It is clear that Christ was not called to be a prophet with a separate charge which was given to him as an addition to his existence. Further, it is significant that he also speaks to Israel and speaks to it exclusively in a formal sense, but that this is precisely the way in which he addresses all men (John 8 : 12, 9 : 5, 12 : 46; Matt. 12 : 41). None of the Old Testament prophets could speak of the finished reconciliation. True, they speak of the reality of the covenant, they fight on the side of YHWH for the covenant; but their task lies on this side of the estrangement which occurred again and again between God and his people; and there is no better way for them to point to the fulfilment of the covenant than to remind the people that the salvation and the future of Israel are fundamentally threatened and jeopardized. Nor did any of the Old Testament prophets set themselves up as mediators; on the contrary, they were obliged rather to show how sharp was the tension and the contradiction. But Jesus, by throwing himself into the breach, placed himself between the two parties and also above the two parties; and as such a mediator he found no adequate analogy to himself in the life and message of the prophets, let alone that a prophet or witness could ever have called himself 'the Word.'

464

5. 'In the Word was life, and the life was the light of men' (John 1 : 4). This too cannot be interpreted in terms of a cosmological interest. Here too the structure of the 'groundless' which enters 'into the midst of things' (cf. above pp. 180ff.) carries through. Here on the basis of the concrete life of Christ a retrospective testimony is given concerning the value, the validity, the universality of the Word which appeared in him, which, indeed, 'became flesh' in him. This testimony revolves in concentric circles around this centre (the midst of things), first around us 'who have beheld this glory' (v. 14), then around Israel 'his own people,' (v. 11), then around the nations, and then around the cosmos. In this hierarchical order (which is not given any special emphasis in the prologue) the concern is obviously with the fulfilment of the covenant, and this is consummated in the co-existence of God and man in Christ Jesus. What does this mean?

In our connection we confine ourselves to the community of the Old Testament and set forth this thesis: Just as surely as there is no analogy between the prophets and Christ, so surely is there an analogy between the history of Israel and the history of Christ. That is to say, the history is itself prophecy, the acts of the Lord occur and speak, they are the acts of his hand, they have his voice, which finds utterance in them. A certain sum total of his deeds, summed up in a definitive panorama which is a song, can even 'be' the covenant (Pss. 68, 105, 106, 107, 136).

The Old Testament is 'prophecy' in that it brings to light the word-content of the acts of God. The prophecy, the proclamation accompanies the event in order to bring home to closed ears and hardened hearts the meaning which is implicit in the event. Or in the words of the prologue of John: the life was in the Word, the imparting of this life-giving life. And the life 'was' the light; it contained within it the explanation of the meaning and purpose of this peculiar life-giving life. As the event, the fact, is word, as the history is prophecy, so the life 'is' the light of men. But that this may be seen in this way—this needs to be said to us; and thus there comes into view the proclamation in human speech, the proclamation of the Word, which in itself is *dabar*, event and meaning, action and proclamation, though this biunity is not discerned and generally not even recognized at all.

(a) This accompanying proclamation of the meaning of the event, this light-bringing reference to the light implicit in the act, has its own peculiar place of origin in history, a place where it definitely emerges. Just as it was not until the exile that everything that had happened to Israel and brought it to where it was ripened into proclamation, so that the sum total of fate and act acquired a voice and became speech, so that, expressed somewhat broadly, one can assert that the Old Testament did not emerge as testimony until the Exile—so it was not until the time of the 'forty days' after Jesus' death that the history of Jesus grew to be revelation, clarifying light for the disciples and proclamation for Israel and the nations.

(b) This life was the light, that is, this history was prophecy; this being of God, this being-with-us, in complete identification encompassed within it the meaning of all the levels of existence and the tropics of the world, but the fact that this was so, the fact that salvation was implicit in it—this had to break into our comprehension somewhere. From then on preaching has borne this enlightening character, since that time a new light has shone in it, even though the light already was in the occurrence of the acts of God; after all, the life was that life which *is* the light of men. This 'new' light dwells in the kerygma as a borrowed light; it is set apart for our sake and exerts its enlightening power within its *own* peculiar channel of light for our sake. And it is in the power of this new light (which is inherent in the proclamation) that 'life as light' is subsequently brought to light.

(c) As the gospels speak of the life and sufferings of Christ in a retrospective presentation of their meaning in order to show his 'cosmic significance,' so the texts of the Old Testament set forth the history of Israel as a paradigm of the history of the world by presenting a retrospective explanation of the meaning of Israel's history. This is seen most clearly in the composition of Genesis 1–11 where the cultic motif, the Sabbath, becomes the crowning act of the creation, a seal upon its completion and a pledge of its ultimate peace, and where in the telling of the story of the Flood the ark becomes important as the preservation of a 'holy remnant,' of which the prophets had already spoken. This translation and transposition of history is proper theology; it moves in the authentic direction which is in accord with 'telling' of history and views the original 'footsteps of the anointed' (Ps. 89 : 51) as the saving history.

Thus the saving history is reflected in world history. And when the term 'servant of the Lord,' '*Ebed Yahweh,*' is used in Isaiah, the reference certainly includes *inter alia* Israel itself, of whom the others, the *goyim*, say, 'He bore our pains' (Isa. 53 : 4). The fact that the unique is also the universal, that the exclusive is also the catholic, finds its seal and sanction in the fact that this God gave his Name to the chosen people in order that life in the Name might become light for the Gentiles (Luke 2 : 32).

6. From this, then, it may perhaps be clear why what was set forth in part two can be called 'Christian instruction,' to what extent the abiding significance of the Old Testament is there given its rightful place, and in what sense we have spoken of the 'unity of the Testaments' or—to subsume it under another title—what is our understanding of 'prophecy and fulfilment.' We are not asserting that this or that Old Testament text must be regarded as 'prophecy,' not even the co-called 'Messianic' passages. There is not a single place where we would consider an 'allegorical' interpretation to be legitimate. We are not searching for harmonies and parallels. We are not on the lookout for 'precursors.' We do not regard the 'typology' of figures and situations (in so far as it occurs in the structures and tendencies of the Old Testament) as forbidden, but we rather see in it a secondary illustration of what has already become evident in other ways. The prophecy of the history of Israel in its totality is for us, as Barth says, 'an adequate prefiguration of the prophecy of the history of Jesus Christ.'

The way in which life becomes light in the Old Testament and the way in which life is light in the New Testament are so analogous that when we believe in the Word (of which the prologue of John speaks), we avow the unity of the Testaments as a matter of course. If anybody wishes to retain and use the word *Weissagung* ('prediction'), then we would be inclined to state this thesis: the life predicts the life in that its light, by its own shining, foretells the other light, or the testimony in the Old Testament proclaims a knowledge of salvation which, in that it becomes an event, already includes within it the fulfilled salvation as its own presupposition. In the beginning was the Word, this Word (John 1 : 14), and in this Word was the life, and the life was the light of men. 'The Old Testament witnesses do not *fore*tell except in so far as they attest the foretelling prophecy of the history of Israel.'[5]

[5] Karl Barth, *Church Dogmatics*, Vol, IV, pt. 3: pp. 1, 65.

(a) It follows that even though in our view of the matter any juggling with the historical method when it is applied to the Old Testament is to be regarded as highly improper and unscientific, but that on the other hand a sympathetic (not necessarily a 'believing' or 'religious') approach to the historical content (for who would claim to be sympathetic with the proclamation?) can only be welcome to us because this allows the evidence to emerge on a broad front.

(b) This also means that when it comes to the familiar question whether the New Testament use of the Old Testament is binding or even directive, we reject the presupposition of this question, namely, that the Gospel of Matthew or the Epistle to the Hebrews are subjecting the Old Testament quotations to exegesis. When the New Testament witnesses more or less literally quote an Old Testament passage and apply it to features of the history of Christ, this is rather to be understood as being an application or illustration. We shall not always be able wholly to fathom the underlying purpose, but if we want to understand it, we must clearly see what is here being applied, what is here being illustrated. It is an application, an illustration of the unity of the history of Christ with the history of Israel attested in the whole Old Testament in which the Evangelist or Apostle has everywhere perceived the 'foretelling' (and not anywhere the 'prediction'). The Evangelist or Apostle recognizes it in the life which is in the Word, and he realizes that in itself life was and is the light of men.

On the whole one can say that this relationship of life and light in the Word, of history and proclamation, of event and testimony not only leaves room but actually drives and compels us to let the Old Testament speak for itself. Precisely when it speaks for itself, it speaks of the 'time of God,' of the life of the Word in time. When one allows the *Tenak* to speak of the Name in its own way, it speaks of the life which was and is the light of men. Then it interests us very little whether Jesus is akin to the prophets and whether his message is the crown of theirs. Then the prophets and the whole *Tenak* are not witnesses to the prophet Jesus and to the truth which he is supposed to have brought to men, but simply witnesses to the unique history of Israel. Then this history itself is in its totality an analogy, a reflection, a prefiguration of that life which is in its unique divine quality the 'light of men', the 'light of life,' the 'light of the world'—in such a way that the whole of Israel's history says, in a loud or a muffled voice, what John the

468

EPILOGUE

Baptist said: 'After me comes a man who ranks before me, for he was before me' (John 1 : 30).

A test, which we cannot go into at length here, can be made by reference to the opposite of this point of view, namely, Martin Buber's interpretation of the Old Testament and his presuppositions. It is significant that he, the greatest modern spokesman of Judaism, compresses prophecy into a mystical truth (the 'dialogical life' or the 'mysticism of the deed'). True, it is concerned with the whole of reality, but it is almost completely divorced from history, and this in the face of the fact that Judaism emphasizes the unredeemedness of the world and is open to the future. But men had a decisive influence upon the coming of the Kingdom. And yet the figure of the Messiah breaks up into many Messianic figures. It is the 'turning' which overcomes 'the inner duality' of man,[6] in that the correlation of God and man and the prospect of redemption are realized. 'History is a mysterious approach. Every spiral of its way leads us both into profounder perversion and more fundamental turning. But the event that from the side of the world is called turning is called from God's side salvation.'[7] 'For him the history of God with his people recedes into the background in comparison with the existential encounter with God here and now on the one hand and the given facts of nature set by God on the other.'[8] His concept of reality is so remote from history that he allows the heathen to participate in the 'dialogical life' without reference to the historical revelation. The heathen merely takes note of a history which is alien to him; and thus again the universal prophecy of Israel's history is lost, again the faith of Israel remains apart. Since the way to God for the heathen 'need not lead either through Judaism or Christianity,' it would appear that nothing decisive had happened for us, and the expectation is that each of the goyim must enter upon a mystical way of salvation. So even in this antithesis of our interpretation we see again how important and determinative it is to resolve, precisely in our 'Christian instruction,' to let the Old Testament speak for itself.

[6] Martin Buber, *Vom Geist des Judentums* (1916), p. 55.
[7] Martin Buber, *Dialogisches Leben* (1947), pp. 127f.; Eng., *I and Thou*, tr. Ronald Gregor Smith, 1st edn. (1937), p. 120. Altered translation taken fr. Maurice S. Freedman, *Martin Buber: The Life of Dialogue*, p. 76.
[8] Franz von Hammerstein, 'Martin Bubers messianische Hoffnung und ihr Verhältnis zu seiner Philosophie,' *Judaica*, X (1954), p. 91.

II

1. We have tried here to state, all too concisely and perhaps also too sketchily, the reason why in this book we have spoken not only of the 'deficit' and the 'surplus' in the Old Testament but also of its being—in its own way—*the* witness to God. But in doing this we have become too involved in considerations which, however honestly intended and however much of truth they contain, cannot by themselves provide a pattern for preaching and instruction, for the work of the interpreter and witness.[9] And yet this Johannine text provides not only occasion for this kind of formal account but also the opportunity to ponder once more, as in a final audit, the intention of the good news, the saving content of the witness. After all, one could conclude that in the light of the prologue of John our presuppositions, which at the same time are the source of a peculiar joy, could again be cast in doubt. After all, we have said that religion is ambivalent. We have asserted that the unsteadiness of the 'third man' is understandable and normal. We have explained the alienation of the 'fourth man' as being the result of the undermining of the general concept of God in natural theology. We have said that the pioneers, the 'individualists,' the despairing challengers, are really in a state of honest (*honnête*) human resistance to a nihilism which has already become a kind of fate. We have denounced the reversal of spiritualistic terms ('God is love,' 'God is Spirit') as a position from which the man-come-of-age must dissociate himself. We have rejected the attempt to ground the 'courage to be' in an 'absolute faith' (without object and without guaranty). And we have said all this because the structure of the Old Testament recognizes no road of experience or knowledge which leads from a general consciousness of God to a particular God. It knows no All, no cosmos, no totality, (into which man's first and properly religious act would be to shelter himself or realize that he is sheltered)—no numinous presence except in the places where he causes his 'Name to be remembered' (Exod. 20 : 24), and even then this fixation in space is soon absorbed into a contingent co-existence in the course of time, in the ongoing of history.

Does it not seem that the Johannine terms 'Word,' 'life,' and 'light'

---

[9] Now it may be understood why we have intentionally spoken of 'witness and interpretation' (in this order) and of 'interpreter and witness' (in this order).

(to restrict ourselves only to these) again suggest the 'higher' natural religion, that they again open the way to speculative thinking, that again (in contrast to the whole of the Old Testament) they regard the anthropological as secondary, as dependent upon and embedded in the concept of a general God, a general revelation, a universal primeval truth, a universal 'life' which is to be affirmed (ontically), a universal 'light' which is to be affirmed (noetically)? We come back to these questions again because in the face of the silence of the gods and at the brink of alienation from God so much depends upon our gaining and establishing a clarity which can no longer be so easily obtained by underhanded resort to murky darkness or false light. Thus we are now speaking of life and light in the material sense (*materialiter*).

Thus alongside the question of the sequence and unity of the 'Testaments' there is the question of the relative order of precedence and unity of the soteriological and cosmological, of the specifically defined salvation and the higher, broader space, the 'little' covenant and the 'great' creation.

2. As a companion text for John 1 : 1, 4, we have chosen Psalm 36 : 9: 'With thee is the fountain of life; in thy light we see light.' Both passages demand the same spiritual, essential understanding of the Name and the way of knowing that the Name requires (cf. above pp. 65ff., 119ff., 161ff., 178f.). Who is being addressed here? YHWH! Israel did not speculate about him as 'the eternal Being'; he is the peculiar, special companion of Israel upon its peculiar, special journey. He cannot be deduced from the given date of man's experience of the world; his presence is in his deeds; he entered into the midst of things and put his stamp upon a definite place in time. From the vantage ground of the midst of things, where he performs his deeds, the past becomes a genuine past and the future becomes a genuine future. It is hardly possible to speak *about* him; in the vital moments of human existence he is addressed, called upon, beseeched, worshipped. So when he is addressed in this attitude of prayer and hymnic exaltation, 'With thee is the fountain of life,' then we must carefully consider the meaning of this term 'life' and apply the same distinction that was made in connection with the Name and its presence in action. Here 'life' cannot mean a sum of cosmic forces; its intent cannot be to refer to the mysteries of vitality, the principle of life; it cannot even refer to that which is biologically and psychologically specific in human exist-

ence. Here 'life' is the salvation which is given in God's covenant in his fellowship. But this verse simply says 'life,' meaning that all life, all vitality, all earthly and cosmic life comes from this peculiar and special life, flowing from the same fountain, the same source. Just as YHWH is called the Godhead (and not vice versa), so one can say that life, this life, determines and permeates cosmic relationships. And just as a reversal of the order of this thesis (or better, this cry, this confession of faith) would turn the peculiar Presence into mere caprice, reduce it to a secondary thing, an ordinary 'name,' to 'sound and smoke,' so if we were to reverse the order and say that life is first the eternal source and then the foundation of the cosmos and finally also salvation, this would fatally undermine the power of the proclamation.[10]

'With thee is the fountain of life; in thy light do we see light.' What can be meant by 'life' here? The eternal *kabod*, the everlasting glory, the primeval light, the uncreated radiance, the *shekinah*, the radiance

[10] Naturally there are many hybrid forms between the 'prophetic' and the 'gnostic,' and especially in the case of many of the utterances of Eastern theology it is difficult for us to arrive at a conclusive judgment. I am thinking of the hymnic effusions of Simeon the New Theologian (b. 949), a literary, rhetorical document of the highest order (see Ger. tr. Kilian Kirchhoff, *Die Hymnen: Licht vom Licht* [1930]). We quote here a few fragments: 'Come, true light, eternal life. Come, thou hidden mystery. Come, nameless delight. . . . Come, Being, passing human understanding. Come, unceasing exaltation. Come, thou light that has no evening. . . . Come, thou who ever remains, immovable and yet passing wholly in the hours. . . . Come, our great God, our royal purple, O girdle, sparkling like crystal, like the shimmering play of iridescent pearls. . . . Come, thou who hast set me down alone, made me a solitary upon the earth. . . . Thanks be to thee that thou has become one spirit with me, without any clouding, without change or alteration' (from the first hymn). — 'He, the Light, left me alone in my former darkness. I could not be satisfied with those unspeakable beatitudes bestowed upon me by him. . . . When he renewed me completely, clothed me completely with immortality, completely deified me and formed me into Christ. . . . I felt torment as in the old hut of misery and sitting in the midst of the tent, enclosed as in a tiny house, a vessel; I began to weep and loudly lament and no longer dared to look out. I sought him for whom I yearned, whom I loved, the beautiful Form who smote me' (from the twenty-first hymn). — Does not this smell of heresy, like the whole theology and practice of the Mount Athos monastery? Is not this a negation of the covenant, even though there are remnants of personal associations? Does not this also evidence the ambivalence of a faith which has again slipped back into religion? That this 'uncreated light' has little to do with the 'life 'which is 'the light of men' and the light that 'enlightens every man at his coming into the world' (John 1 : 9), this we may conjecture, if not prove. On Simeon the New Theologian cf. Karl Hall, *Gesammelte Aufsätze zur Kirchengeschichte*, II, 403ff. On the concept of light in the Eastern Church cf. also L. H. Grondijs, *De iconographie van Schepping en Godsverschijningen* (1942).

472

of the presence of God? No; light, here expressly called 'thy' light, that participation of God in our life through which we are not only from him but also know that we belong to him. The light proceeds from his speech; it is that side of the *dabar* which, although it is in itself both fact and word, 'particularizes' itself in address directed to those whom he has called. It refers to the light of revelation; and this light is called in the full sense "thy" light because the revelation springs from the heart of God, from his divine concern, from his will never again to be without his elect. There is no essential light except the light of the covenant. Factually and functionally (but also, even though this may seldom or never come to the fore, ontologically) God and his Revelation are identical. And this revelation is somewhere, in some definite place hidden and inconspicuous, universally valid and yet not universally intelligible.

But then the text continues: 'In thy light do we see (the) light.' And this means that when we stand at this centre where God performs his deed, we can nevertheless see the *kabod*, the primeval light, the uncreated radiance, the *shekinah*, and that only here do we really see it (though from afar). Just as it is testified that YHWH is the Godhead (and not vice versa), so here this verse speaks and sings of a unique light which includes the universal, the cosmic, the divine, the heavenly. And if the inner sequence and order of this thesis (this cry, this confession of faith) is reverse, then the very nature and meaning of what is meant here by '*the* light' will be misinterpreted. He who stands outside of this saving order will not be able to understand why the grace, the favour, the righteousness, the faithfulness of God are so particularistic and, just because this is so, are qualitatively and fundamentally understood as being sovereign and universal: 'YHWH, thy steadfast love extends to the heavens, thy faithfulness to the highest clouds; thy righteousness is like the mountains of God, thy judgments are a great deep'—and even less will he be able to understand how the Psalmist can go on and say in the same breath: 'O YHWH, thou savest man and beast' (vv. 5f.). It is therefore not only a question of a way of knowing which leads from the particular to the general; it is also and much more a matter of knowing that the full pressure of the cosmic power is deliberately concentrated upon grace for all creatures, upon the salvation of living, helpless beings which are at the mercy of the powers and the gods. No wonder that the poet, having thus explored these regions round about him, should turn back to the place where the peculiar presence dwells: 'How precious is thy steadfast love, O God: therefore the children of men take refuge in the shadow of thy wings; they feast on the abundance of thy house; and thou givest them to drink from the river of thy delights' (vv. 7f.). And then there follows this passage: 'For with thee is the fountain of life; in thy light we see light.' This is a temple song, and this is what it remains; it resists being turned into a philosophy.

3. The inner structure of Psalm 36 : 9 (and its context) coincides perfectly with that of John I (and its context). The radiance of YHWH is somewhere, at a definite place, and from this place it is to be discerned (in his light) everywhere. The Word or the Son is somewhere, at a definite place, and from the vantage ground of this presence and by virtue of the fellowship thus given, it may be seen (through the Word) that in him was life and that this life was the life of man, always and everywhere (and much more besides, which we do not deal with here because we are limiting ourselves to this text).[11] We do *not* regard this as a roundabout way, and in this lies our one chance, not of solving all 'problems,' but of posing all problems differently, namely, in such a way that, holding fast to the Name in the midst of things, to the prophecy which is history and the history which is prophecy, we can with good reason say something joyful even about the cosmos, the 'world drama.' This something may be little, but it will have tremendous sustaining power, whereas in the accustomed immediacy of experiencing and thinking about the cosmos one can say almost everything on many grounds without ever resting in the true centre of the inexhaustible interrelationship of things.[12]

What to us, in the delusion of our alleged knowledge of God, appears

[11] Cf. H. F. Kohlbrügge, *In den beginne was het Woord* (Amsterdam, 1914).

[12] A fundamental objection to the rich and thoughtful, profound and wise, honest as well as tolerant book by Dr. G. H. van Senden, who has gone largely unrecognized (*Het werelddrama*, 2 vols., publ. by the author, 1954) is that he cannot free himself from the spell of the idea of the logical precedence of the 'general,' that despite an obvious sympathy with the mythical feeling about life and a clear affinity with phenomenology, he cannot admit that the general can just as well be regarded as an abstraction of the concrete as, conversely, the particular is to be regarded as a concretization, a form, a manifestation of the general. Logically and religiously these two sides at least exist; in faith and in existence, however, the particular has the precedence, even logically. Cf. in this connection Karl Barth, 'Hengel,' *Cahiers théologiques*, No. 38 (Neuchâtel-Paris).

to be a roundabout way evokes in the community, in Israel and in the Church, a great amazement over the directness of God's way to us, over the grace of him who is Alpha and Omega, the First and the Last, the Beginning and the End (Rev. 22 : 12). He in his perfect presence, he is the first and the last; he who enters into the midst of things and causes his Name to dwell on earth, he is the ground of all beginning and the guarantor of the end. The Word which became flesh and was swallowed up in our darkness, this is the life and the light—according to our immediate encounter with and knowledge of it, to be sure, the saving life and the saving light, but nevertheless in fact the power and the meaning of the All. 'In the beginning was the Word . . . and in the Word was life, and the life was the light of men' (John 1 : 1, 4).

III

One of the fruits of preaching and instruction must be that we are freed from dread of the All, dread of the immense and overpowering, the utterly autonomous, that which is aloof, alien, and cold, dread of the unapproachable, the menacing, which, like a god, eludes all calculation and judgment. We yearn for this liberation and we think we must begin at the beginning, plumb the depths, pierce the mask of the god, tame the primordial power, understand the order of the totality of things, conjure away the enigma, in order that we may adjust and accommodate ourselves to it until in due time we can make it serve us. The fact is that release from this dread comes from the doctrine of creation. In this book we have intentionally said very little about creation, and primarily because it is not a part of the 'surplus' of the Old Testament. But now that we are speaking of the 'unity' of the Testaments—formally in the sense of 'adequate prefiguration' and materially in the sense of the precedence of the soteriological over the cosmological—it seems proper, even from a practical point of view, to come back to the doctrine of creation. And when we do this, we come back into the orbit of 'God and the world,' and then we are likely to fall back into the old habit of thinking in terms of a triangle in which God and the world stand together over against man, lonely, solitary man. We move alongside a wall which all atheism has abandoned, a wall which all nihilists—because, as is sometimes said, they have such tidy, hygienic minds—have blasted to pieces with words, such as these, for example: 'Being and not-being are identical, meaning and non-meaning amount to the same thing' (as a Dutch essayist defines nihilism). I say, we come back into this orbit, and if this is (or appears to be) so, then the reason for it is to be found in an ingrained habit of thought which Israel broke away from. The first sentence of the Bible left far behind it this compulsive delusion. 'In the beginning God created the heavens and the earth' (Gen. 1 : 1). Because we automatically think that we can comprehend the word 'God' as a general concept, we no longer feel the shock of this liberating outlook. For what is the situation? Was there another book that preceded Genesis, a book that told what was meant by the word 'God'? Was this book, this revelation, lost? No, the priestly writer also ascribes the creation of the world to the God of Israel, the God who cannot be deduced from the world, whom we know only in another way, and he does so retrospectively, in consequence of and as an application and extension of his profession of faith. Or to put it differently, so far as our knowledge is concerned the covenant with men is prior to our knowledge of the creation, and in God it is the overarching meaning of the creation. YHWH is also he who 'calls into existence the things that do not exist' (Rom. 4 : 17). His Word is creating! Which word? None other than that which appears and is at work in the history of his people.[13] And this means that no son of this people in the wide world, however alien and inhospitable it may seem, accepts or assumes any other presence except the presence of YHWH. This is the deepest reason for Israel's 'stubbornness'; and this stubbornness emerges most bluntly when in the midst of the most appalling torture the people of God confess '*YHWH echad*' ('Yahweh is one God,' Deut. 6 : 4).

This is especially clear in the proclamation of the miracle of light. The presence of Yahweh in our midst (*YHWH beqirbenu*; cf. above pp. 210ff.) obtains in all dimensions of existence. Whether this is our experience or whether it is contradicted by our experience—this is recorded in another book, namely, the diary of our religious development or decline. Faith is well aware that the world is far greater and mightier than our minds can comprehend, but it knows even more positively that the covenant is more everlasting and mightier than the world. Faith is grateful for the earth and for the history that is enacted in it, but the light that illumines the earth and fills all space comes to us

[13] Cf. Martin Buber, *Kamf um Israel*, pp. 45ff., idem, *De Godsdiensten der weerld*, I, 220ff.

through the Word; it is a spoken light, just as the Torah is a spoken light. The light orders the chaos, natural as well as spiritual. The light sets the order of human time. The light which comes from the Word overtops the mountains of opposition, the glaciers of the cold, hostile, demonic powers, the lava of our unconquered past. 'Nature' is not 'greater' than 'the history,' and he who casts himself down before this 'greatness' has forgotten that through the Word the light is essentially, qualitatively, and manifestly at work in the life of men. Deep down in our hearts we must be cured of this tendency to fall on our knees before the 'measureless' and 'boundless.' Light is the primal act of God's sovereign power; God is light, and God essentially and existentially gives light. 'In thy light do we see light'; 'in the Word was life, and the life was the light of man.' The God of Israel does not simply stand above light and darkness in the neutrality of a super-essential, inscrutable, and unimaginable apeiron. He is the source and companion, the lord and accompaniment of light, both 'spiritual' and 'natural.'[14] Creation is and remains the realm of grace. The unity of the Testaments, like the unity of the proclamation which runs through the ages, is the bond of love, the encircling ring of perfection, the heart that binds everything together in the midst of all the disintegration, all the absurdity, and all the seemingly meaningless round of

[14] Karl Barth, *Church Dogmatics*, Vol. III, pt. 1, pp. 116f.: 'It is natural light as such which is the irresistible and irrevocable declaration of life, and therefore negatively of the conquest, separation, displacement, and banishment of the alternative reality which God neither wills nor creates. . . . After the creation of light, in spite of darkness and falsehood, that reality never is today nor will be tomorrow, *but always has been yesterday*. . . . Thus even the separation of the cosmos from chaos by light depends on the Word of God. The incursion of darkness, the dawn of a dreadful counter-day, the day of falsehood, would be quite unavoidable if light were not again and again light and victorious truth by the same power in which it *came to be*.' Cf. also the whole of sect. 42: 1, pp. 330ff., 'Creation as Benefit.' 'Whatever we may say in support of this statement [that creation is a benefit] apart from the inner and real connection between creation and covenant—the well-meant arguments of a predominantly positive attitude of the Christian subject in face of existence, or even the Nevertheless of Christian faith, or the simple assertion of the identity of God the Creator and God the Redeemer—does not suffice to give the statement more than a hypothetical certainty' (p. 333). Whether the idea of God (the *Deus Optimus Maximus*) 'can actually be filled with the concept of God's goodness is something which unfortunately cannot be determined by the creaturely mind as such. . . . After all, the godhead is in this respect too only the tremendous concave mirror in which the most various attitudes of the creaturely mind (absolutizing, disparagement, boredom, etc.) can be recognized' (p. 368). [The last two sentences have been retranslated.—Tr.]

things. Yes, existence itself lies within us and around us, less as a challenge to make something of it than as a quiet evidence that we have been made—made his people and the sheep of his pasture (Ps. 100 : 3). Above all, we do not need to elevate ourselves above the world in order to find the meaning of life. We cannot 'give' meaning to life; we cannot 'find' a ground or basis for the Name. Life itself is the light of men, and the Name itself is the magic finder, discoverer, and companion.[15] Our whole creaturehood consists in the struggle to be free for the freedom of God and not to allow ourselves to be discomfited, not even by what is (for us) absolutely meaningless. As long as we continue to speak of things being 'meaningless,' we are still upholding in freedom the standard of a meaning, even a meaning which is assumed to be self-evident. Only when we say 'Meaning and non-meaning amount to the same thing' have we come to the point where there is no longer any sense in the saying, 'In the Word is life, and the life is the light of men.' That nihilistic statement would be almost as odd as to say: 'I see by means of reason and religion that "everything" is by nature meaningful and cannot be anything else but meaningful.' But it is far more deadly to the smouldering wick of our threatened life to nourish the absurd assertion (or is it merely bragging before an audience within ourselves?) that meaning and meaninglessness 'amount to the same thing.' When the gods are silent, they are silent everywhere; when YHWH speaks, he speaks somewhere, at some definite place; and in this 'somewhere' is to be found the Word which was always the life and the light of men. Pagan being loses itself in the darkness, in 'the abyss of meaninglessness,'[16] but 'the light shines *in* the darkness, and the darkness has not overcome it' (John 1 : 5). Even

[15] Cf. Hans Urs von Balthasar, *Das Herz der Welt* (1945), pp. 16f.: 'You perceive the times—and do not perceive this heart? You feel the stream of grace that presses in upon you, warm and red—and do not feel that you are loved? You search for evidence —and you yourself are the evidence. You seek to catch him, the Unknown One, in the meshes of your knowledge—and you yourself are caught in the inescapable net of his love. You seek to grasp—but you have already been grasped. You seek to master— but you have long since been overmastered. You pretend to seek—but you have long since and from time immemorial been found. . . . You thrash about in the haste of your heart and call it religion. . . . You want to find God, even though it cost a thousand pangs: what a humiliation that it was all for nothing, since long ago he already held you in his hand. Lay your finger upon the living pulse of being. Feel the beat which in one single act of creation both demands and frees you.'
[16] Paul Tillich, *The Courage to Be*, pp. 48, 186.

the light of the Word does not remain unthreatened, for this man, Jesus, is the Word. After all, the whole prologue of the Gospel of John is not talking about the 'eternal Logos' but rather about the man, *the* Man, the single one who not only dwelt among men but 'came' to them, 'sought' them, 'turned them about,' forgave them and created them anew, and thus brought them life, *the* life, and light, *the* light, and in all this came to them as the Word-of-the-beginning which became manifest as the deepest and ultimate speech behind and about and in all things visible and invisible. This is the real *good* news.

Practically, the unity of the structure of the Old and New Testaments means in this respect liberation from the fear and protection from the delusion that when we come to the ultimate root of things, we meet the absurd.[17] There is no room here for a believing world view which is objectively and statically anchored in this liberation. The reality of the gods and powers is against this. Therefore it is to be feared that such a world view only undermines the Word, cuts off the life, darkens the light. And it cannot surprise us that ambivalence comes into play at the very outset, as soon as a self-sufficient order of being is put in the place of the presence and ongoing course of the Name. 'With thee is the fountain of life; in thy light do we see light.' 'In the Word was the life, and the life was the light of men.' For the Unity which we confess cannot be the unity of being, it is the unity of the love of this God, in whom life and light coincide. The coincidence of meaning and non-meaning could take place only in the boundlessness of the cosmos, for after all, this boundlessness turns out to be a boundless confusion. But God has nothing to do with that kind of endlessness. His love is not polyinterpretable. For his action is definite, his Word is purposive, his Face, his Presence is humanly manifest to men.

Therefore the exclusive NAME is all-embracing. Therefore we can meet the Presence here and now with songs of praise on our lips.

> So at last have I expected of thee
> In every element the Presence of God.

Therefore there is room for the laughter of faith, for the lofty humour that says:

[17] Cf. Karl Barth on Marcion and Schopenhauer, *Church Dogmatics*, Vol. III, pt. 1, pp. 334f.; on Heidegger and Sartre, pp. 334ff.; on Descartes's proof of the existence of God and the reality of an external world, pp. 350ff.

The little finger of his left hand
Is named Pan.

O Kinderlachen, vor der Welt
und wiederum nach ihrem Ende—
von einem glänzend-kleinen Wind
erzählt's, der einstmals wird bestellt,
zu gehen über Stolz und Pein,
bis Babylon und London endlich
vergeben und vergessen sind.

Index

I Scripture Passages

II Hebrew terms

III Names

IV Subjects

490

494